AMERICAN RAILROADS

American Railroads

DECLINE AND RENAISSANCE IN THE TWENTIETH CENTURY

ROBERT E. GALLAMORE

&

JOHN R. MEYER

Harvard University Press

Cambridge, Massachusetts
London, England
2014

Library of Congress Cataloging-in-Publication Data
Gallamore, Robert E.
American railroads : decline and renaissance in the twentieth
century / Robert E. Gallamore and John R. Meyer.
pages cm
Includes bibliographical references and index.
ISBN 978-0-674-72564-5
1. Railroads—United States—History—20th century.   2. Railroads and state—United
States—History—20th century.   I. Meyer, John Robert.   II. Title.
HE2751.G337   2014
385.0973'0904—dc23   2013042025

CONTENTS

PREFACE

John Robert Meyer (1927–2009) passed away on October 20, 2009, at the age of 81 in Cambridge, Massachusetts. He died of complications of Parkinson's disease, first diagnosed almost twenty years earlier. He was able to work to the end, although the disease slowed his speech and made writing difficult in his last months and years. He wanted to see this manuscript completed and published, and so did his family—Leslie, Anna, and Robert encouraged me to continue working with their father until it was finished. I knew the Parkinson's might beat us to that goal, but none of us ever doubted the enterprise would endure.

John Meyer entrusted me with drafting and editing the text in the years after my retirement from full-time work responsibilities, in 2006, but he faithfully read and commented on each chapter as it was completed. Our dear friend and colleague, Tony Gómez-Ibáñez of the John F. Kennedy School of Government at Harvard University served steadfastly as our adviser and facilitator throughout the development of the book. John knew he could count on Tony and me to ensure that the final manuscript met his standards for publication, and we were more than a little intimidated by this responsibility. I always worked with full awareness that, while carrying on the Meyer legacy and helping realize John's wishes, I was unable to reproduce all of his insights—or bring to bear on the final text those new thoughts that, given more time, he would have contributed. John drafted and/or reviewed preliminary versions of chapters 2-11, but did not have the chance to see later drafts of chapters 1, 12, 13 and the Afterword, nor, of course, the final edited manuscript and its illustrations.

Tony met with John regularly in recent years, discussing a wide world of things, including the book. They went over outlines and the status of chapters, and Tony would follow up by email or telephone. I visited John at his home in Florida or his condominium in Cambridge twice each year, and we spoke often by phone. What was going on with the economy? The Red Sox? We talked about things we had been reading. Encounters with friends or news of their passing. Grandchildren. The book.

Professor Meyer (I still want to call him that) never stopped teaching me economics, and I think he appreciated the fact that I was a perpetual student of railroads. Born in Pasco, Washington, the son of a Northern Pacific Railway clerk, John had railroading in his blood and never tired of discussing trains—their economics and management, their history, their tribulations under regulation, their technology. I had many recollections from my experience in government—John having observed the same events from a different perspective. Similarly, I knew lots of people and issues from working in the trenches at Union Pacific while (and after) John was on the board of directors and serving as vice chairman. We read many of the same books and we shared our critiques openly. He extended his circle of family and close friendships to include my wife Sue and me—beginning with the annual holiday card we were always so honored to receive from John and Lee (his late wife of more than fifty years), down to making arrangements for completion and publication of this book. A man of unfailing courtesy, consummate wisdom, and perfect good sense, John Meyer leaves the field of transportation economics without its most iconic leader—and leaves us all without a cherished friend.

This work was John's idea. He said, "There are plenty of books about railroads in the nineteenth century, but one needs to be written about the full sweep of the industry in the twentieth." This book follows his outline and supports his themes; it is in all respects part of his legacy. The strong temptation is to make its dedication to his memory but, as coauthor, he would not have wanted that. What is more, we know the pride he took in the *festschrift* prepared in his honor a decade ago, published by Brookings as *Essays in Transportation Economics and Policy: A Handbook in Honor of John R. Meyer.* We have carried on because Professor Meyer was our beloved teacher, and from this we know what he would have wanted the book's dedication to be—indeed, he hinted as much in his unforgettably poignant remarks upon receiving the Crum Award from the National Academies of Science's Transportation Research Board in 2002. After thanking those who had selected him for the prestigious award, Meyer humbly thanked his students, for they were his source of ongoing inspiration. John Meyer would have approved of this dedication: "For our students, dear friends, and families."

A Note on Railroad Terminology and Maps in American Railroads

Names.   This book uses a lot of technical terms with precise meanings in the railroad industry, and a fair amount of jargon or lingo. Railroad (railway in the United Kingdom) aficionados ("rail fans" (US) "trainspotters" (U.K.) will relish this, but general readers will occasionally wish for more definition or reference. For uncommon terms or terminology with special meaning (especially if the context is not clear), we often add a parenthetical phrase or note of explanation; these terms may also be listed in the index. There are several published lexicons of railroad terms providing further reference and sometimes etymology.

We use a convention for naming and abbreviating railroads, also called roads or companies. (We try to avoid calling them carriers—a regulatory term; sometimes we call them lines, but that can be confusing because lines can be segments of track or a full railroad firm.) Nearly all railroads are named with some variation of a concatenation of origin city, possibly a main waypoint, and an originally intended or finally realized destination city or region. We use an ampersand for *and* in both the full name and abbreviation, as in New York, New Haven & Hartford (NYNH&H) or Chicago, Rock Island & Pacific (CRI&P), and we frequently shorten the name to its common form, in these cases, New Haven or Rock Island. On maps, we often drop the ampersand to save space, so you might see NH or RI (thus ATSF, CNW, or DRGW). Conrail (for the Consolidated Rail Corporation) is a rare, almost unique, exception. A glossary of railroad names and abbreviations is included in the front of the book.

Maps.   Related to our naming convention is the matter of describing with maps the geographic coverage of subject railroads and especially their competitive relationships as the result of participation in mergers. It is difficult to understand these competitive relationships without knowledge of the participating railroads' geography and service capabilities. Of course, maps can only give a broad picture of competitive dynamics. They are not determinative of subsequent business behavior and of economic performance; they are only a summary indicator. Helpful as they are, maps are not easy to prepare, publish, interpret, and keep up-to-date in a book format. The dilemma is that complex maps call for color, but book-publishing economics demand monochrome. A particular difficulty was deciding how much detail to include. On two of the maps (10.2 and 10.3), we tried to distinguish main lines from light-density lines, but this also was subjective.

Our solution in *American Railroads* is to include reference maps with grayscale graphics. This we could not have done without the splendid courtesy of *Trains Magazine*, which made available its file of merger maps to use as the basis for the maps in Chapter 10. Then our skilled illustrator, Isabelle Lewis, was able to convert the images to monochrome and make refinements to fit the style and themes of *American Railroads*. Readers can find other useful railroad maps in the monthly pages of *Trains*, in the *Routledge Historical Atlas of the American Railroads*, in Rand McNally's *Handy Railroad Atlas of the United States*, in Railroad Information Service's *Professional Railroad Atlas of North America*, company websites, and other sources.

RAILROAD COMPANIES AND ABBREVIATIONS

AA	Ann Arbor
AT&SF	Atchison, Topeka & Santa Fe (Santa Fe)
ACL	Atlantic Coast Line
B&O	Baltimore & Ohio
BAR	Bangor & Aroostook
B&LE	Bessemer & Lake Erie (Bessemer)
B&M	Boston & Maine
BN	Burlington Northern
BNSF	Burlington Northern Santa Fe
CN	Canadian National *(CN Lines in the United States, sometimes separately designated)*
CP	Canadian Pacific *(CP Lines in the United States, sometimes separately designated)*
CLIN	Carolina, Clinchfield & Ohio
C of G	Central of Georgia
CNJ	Central of New Jersey
Cen. Pac.	Central Pacific
C&O	Chesapeake & Ohio
Alton	Chicago & Alton
C&EI	Chicago & Eastern Illinois
C&NW	Chicago & North Western
CB&Q	Chicago, Burlington & Quincy (Burlington)
CGW	Chicago Great Western
Monon	Chicago, Indianapolis & Louisville
MILW	Chicago, Milwaukee, St. Paul & Pacific (Milwaukee Road)
Omaha	Chicago, Minneapolis, St. Paul & Omaha
CRI&P	Chicago, Rock Island & Pacific (Rock Island)
CR	Conrail

CSX	CSX Transportation
D&H	Delaware & Hudson
DL&W	Delaware, Lackawanna & Western (Lackawanna)
D&RGW	Denver & Rio Grande Western (Rio Grande)
DT&I	Detroit, Toledo & Ironton (Ironton)
Missabe	Duluth, Missabe & Iron Range
EJ&E	Elgin, Joliet & Eastern
Erie	Erie
EL	Erie Lackawanna
FEC	Florida East Coast
FW&D	Fort Worth & Denver
GW	Gateway Western
G&F	Georgia & Florida
GS&F	Georgia Southern & Florida
GTW	Grand Trunk Western
GN	Great Northern
GB&W	Green Bay & Western
GM&N	Gulf, Mobile & Northern
GM&O	Gulf, Mobile & Ohio
HV	Hocking Valley
IC	Illinois Central
ICG	Illinois Central Gulf
KCS	Kansas City Southern
L&HR	Lehigh & Hudson River
L&NE	Lehigh & New England
LV	Lehigh Valley
L&A	Louisiana & Arkansas
L&N	Louisville & Nashville
MEC	Maine Central
M&StL	Minneapolis & St. Louis
MP	Missouri Pacific (MoPac), MOP
M-K-T	Missouri-Kansas-Texas (Katy)
M&O	Mobile & Ohio
NC&StL	Nashville, Chattanooga & St. Louis
NYC	New York Central

NKP	New York, Chicago & St. Louis (Nickel Plate)
NYNH&H, NH	New York, New Haven & Hartford (New Haven)
N&W	Norfolk & Western (Norfolk)
NS	Norfolk Southern
NP	Northern Pacific (Nipper)
PC	Penn Central
PRR	Pennsylvania (Pennsy)
Père-M	Père Marquette
P&LE	Pittsburgh & Lake Erie
RDG	Reading (Reading)
RF&P	Richmond, Fredericksburg & Potomac
SAL	Seaboard Air Line (Seaboard)
Soo	Soo Line
	—Duluth, South Shore & Atlantic *(DSS&A)*
	—Minneapolis, St. Paul & Sioux Ste. Marie *(MStP&SSM)*
	—Wisconsin Central *(WC)*
SOU or Sou	Southern
SP	Southern Pacific
SP&S	Spokane, Portland & Seattle
SLSW	St. Louis Southwestern (Cotton Belt)
Frisco or SL—SF	St. Louis-San Francisco (Frisco)
T&P	Texas & Pacific
TP&W	Toledo, Peoria & Western
UP	Union Pacific *(or UPRR to distinguish the railroad from the corporation (UPC) or stock symbol (UNP))*
VGN	Virginian
WAB	Wabash
WM	Western Maryland
WP	Western Pacific
W&LE	Wheeling & Lake Erie

AMERICAN RAILROADS

1

THE ENDURING AMERICAN RAILROADS

[There] was made on February 1, 1804, the combination of locomotive engine power pulling a train of cars on tracks, which is the foundation of the railroad as we know it. The power was provided by a high-pressure steam locomotive, built by Richard Trevithick. The cars were loaded with minerals for the iron works at Merthyr Tydfil, in South Wales. The track was the plate way of the Pennydarran Tramroad, newly laid with flanged rails.

—ROBERT SELPH HENRY (1942)

. . . [I]n 1829, Stephenson made the locomotive a success. The next year saw the introduction of the railway into America, and two years later there was published an article proposing a railway to the Pacific.

—HENRY KIRKE WHITE (1895)

Railroads are one of the great industrial achievements of modern civilization. It is impossible to imagine the building of our Nation's commercial and military strength without the railroads. Railroading has a proud tradition, and the industry remains an indispensable part of our economy.

—FEDERAL RAILROAD ADMINISTRATION (1978)

American Railroads is the story of a great industry that dominated US freight transportation over land at the beginning of the twentieth century, lost its leadership and much of its economic power over the next eighty years, and then, almost miraculously, was reborn in the last two decades of the century. We characterize railroads as *enduring* because as the century wore on, they *survived* more than they *dominated* their rivals. They persisted as a fundamental part of the US freight transportation system more than they succeeded financially.

At the turn of the twentieth century and for decades before and after, railroads became a frequent topic of newspaper and parlor debate. Both casual and interested observers recoiled fearfully as railroad behemoths gained power in the nineteenth century, but not long afterward, experts and enthusiasts were lamenting the industry's steady retreat. During the twentieth century, the decline and near-demise of railroads was measured in lost market share, abandoned track mileage, frequent bankruptcies, and loss of employment. In 1900, railroads employed 1,018,000 persons—one of twenty-nine US nonfarm workers. By 2000, railroads employed only 246,000 workers, one of 533.

Yet railroads remained essential contributors to the US economy. Today they handle 40 percent of intercity freight revenue ton-miles (one ton of goods earning payment for being hauled one mile), a total of over 1.5 trillion annually. They have an enviable safety record, the best of any surface carriers of mixed goods or passengers. They move each ton of goods an average of nearly 500 miles on a single gallon of diesel fuel.

And freight railroads have proved remarkably resilient to inroads by competitors, reinventing themselves time and again with regard to the mix of services they provide and the kinds of traffic they carry. For example, after railroads lost a great deal of market share to motor carriers providing expedited dock-to-dock full truckload service on the interstate highway system, railroads responded with double-stack trains of intermodal containers, which can shift between trucks and rail. This rail intermodal service has allowed railroads to recapture some of the traffic lost to motor carriers in key corridors.

Railroads do have a substantial if not fatal drawback, however: Trains can go only where tracks do, and what they carry must come to them, not the reverse. That means railroads cannot be all things to all users. They specialize with enormous efficiency, but they adapt to changing markets only slowly and imperfectly.

While railroads lack much of the flexibility of their trucking rivals, rail operators can move heavily loaded freight cars safely over hill and dale on rights of way they control with great labor and fuel efficiency. That is partly because the fundamental railroad technologies of rail are marvelously productive. "Steel wheels on steel rail" give trains low rolling resistance, and powerful locomotives have prime-movers ideally sized for thermal and mechanical efficiency on the standard track width. Despite being an old technology in a new world, the railroad industry has found ways to improve its performance with continuous technological innovation and capital investment. The result has been remarkable gains in capital and labor productivity.

Land Grants: The First Railroad Public-Private Partnerships

Railroads entered the twentieth century as one of the most fully developed and modern industries in the US economy. One reason is public subsidies: Railroad construction received significant encouragement from local governments hoping to benefit from connecting to the expanding railroad network. The federal government also used its most plentiful asset, western lands, to help railroads build pathways to the Pacific—on not just one but several transcontinental routes. This aid took the form of land grants to the railroads, typically in alternating patterns ten miles square (100 square miles—each one square mile section having 640 acres), with the ten-mile squares not granted to railroad builders reserved for other government purposes or sales to homesteaders. That approach kept the railroads in the business of promoting development of town sites and immigration from Europe, and prevented railroads from monopolizing land sales because alternatives were always nearby.

It was a brilliant strategy—with one drawback, namely, state construction charters and federal land grants created in governments a sense of entitlement to impose burdens on railroads unlike those borne by any other industry. When railroads offended local commercial interests, most states saw little downside to reining in railroads with regulations administered through special commissions. Most subsequent politicians and casual observers ignored the fact that railroads eventually repaid the land grants through discounts to the government for handling its cargo and passenger traffic.

Under encouragement from farm organizations such as the Grange, state regulatory commissions proliferated and expanded their scope, until the US Supreme Court in the famous *Wabash* case of 1886 declared that federal statutes, not state commissions, would govern interstate commerce under the US Constitution's commerce clause. Thus, railroads—partly because of their own well-documented misdeeds, but mainly because local commercial interests exploited antirailroad sentiment—became not only "the Nation's First Big Business," in a well-known phrase, but also the first to face comprehensive economic regulation of rates and services administered by an independent, quasi-judicial commission. In the Act to

Regulate Commerce (1887), and in other populist reforms of the Progressive Era, big railroads met big government. Economic regulation of railroad rates and services became a singular force shaping the industry's destiny.[1]

A Fortress Built on Sand

Yet in their search for ways to constrain monopolistic railroad rates and to cross-subsidize rural areas—while also enabling enough cash flow for railroads to survive as private businesses—regulators inevitably foundered. The dilemma is that there never was a "correct" way to determine the proper rates railroads could charge to transport goods. Former Yale president Richard Levin, a fine economist and student of railroads, explains the fundamental challenge with the pithy comment that "there is no integrated theory of oligopoly," which, if there were one, might have allowed for a more deterministic solution of supply and demand interaction in the setting of efficient rates.

To explain, basic economics teaches that society is well-served when industries are competitive enough to drive prices down to the point where the next unit sold brings enough revenue—but only enough—to cover its cost of production. These incremental costs, however, are difficult to calculate for particular movements in multiproduct firms like railroads because individual services share common costs for track infrastructure, signaling, and so forth. And calculating fully distributed costs—which take into account the large overhead costs necessary for railroad operations—requires arbitrary accounting legerdemain.

College economics textbooks rely on graphs showing how proper prices—based on the intersection of supply and demand curves—"automatically" clear markets, optimize social welfare, and yield profits, which producers can then reinvest. Although the theory is straightforward, in reality, quantifying the scale and shape of the curves is extremely difficult. Perhaps Yogi Berra said it best when he remarked, "In theory there is no difference between theory and practice. In practice there is."[2]

The regulatory agency that would try to substitute itself for market forces and come up with railroad rates maximizing social welfare and carrier efficiency has two impossible challenges. It could not use marginal cost pricing because it would have no way of isolating these from broader common and overhead costs—and then attributing a proper share of these fixed costs to service over a particular set of origin–destination geographic points. Nor would it be able to look behind the curtain of shipper demand to understand its real nature—the elasticity of that demand—whether the shipment would still move at a higher rate or whether more similar goods would move if rail charges were lower. Shippers might have some idea of such things, but they have no incentive to reveal their views to railroads or regulators.

This kind of rate-setting challenge bedevils any capital-intensive industry with economies of scale, especially if users do not consume the product equally and are located randomly. For example, regulators of electricity and telephone utilities have faced such difficulties—with the single saving grace that electrons are easier to package and switch through distribution networks than are railroad freight cars.

The Railroad Problem

The justification for rail regulation was the view—still held by most micro-economists and professors of industrial organization—that railroads are natural monopolies (see Chapter 2). Railroads actually face strong competition, however, in almost all of their lines of business and key markets. Even where shippers appear to be "captive to railroads"—such as when coal companies need to ship their product to power plants served by only one rail line—the contest is really one between bilateral oligopolists—large and powerful railroads on one side, and shippers that can stand on their own feet on the other.

Charles Francis Adams, son and grandson of American presidents and later chief executive of the Union Pacific Railroad, articulated "the railroad problem" perfectly well in the 1880s. From his Massachusetts vantage point, Adams saw that fundamental engineering and financial characteristics would enable railroads to grow more powerful; it was a superior technology. Adams recognized that rail owners would not be able to convince regulators to approve timely rate increases that would allow them to keep up with inflation, or to abandon lines fallen into desuetude. That is, if railroads charged rates that recovered incremental variable costs but not overhead, firms would either have to grow to complete market dominance (the winners) or go bankrupt (the losers).

How can railroads remain vital and worthy if their DNA makes domineering monopolistic monoliths or moribund, subsidy-dependent wards of the government? Well, that needn't happen, and this book tells why. The key insights require an understanding of the economics of transportation explained by Professor Meyer and his colleagues fifty years ago.[3]

5

Early Wanderings in the Wilderness of Regulatory Price Control

Remarkably, in the early years of the twentieth century, the system that Populists and Progressives chose to control railroad rates was not even based on presumed socially optimal incremental or marginal costs. Regulation of that type might have offered the most straightforward method of guaranteeing low rates—even if it would not have allowed operators to cover their average unit costs. Instead, regulators permitted railroads acting together through cartels—so-called rate bureaus—to set higher rates according to what demand would sustain, with final approval authority resting in the Interstate Commerce Commission (ICC).[4]

The irony was that this system, called value-of-service (VOS) rate making, depended on substantially noncompetitive markets for rail service. The VOS system used high prices from customers who were relatively insensitive to price—such as manufacturers of high-value goods—to cross-subsidize shipping rates for bulk, lower-value shipments, mainly those of farmers and small-town merchants who could not absorb higher transportation costs (or so their advocates said).

Think about it. Railroads were told to charge higher rates for a boxcar or hundred-weight of easily loaded and marshaled steel shapes from an industrial zone, for example, than one of wheat that had to be boarded up and moved from a country elevator on a lightly used branch line and was subject to spoilage. This was demand-based ratemaking, in contrast to cost-based rates. It was also a system of rate differentiation—opponents might call it rate discrimination. But it allowed the regulatory system to sustain what long-ago legislation proclaimed to be railroads' common carrier obligation: to carry all goods tendered for shipment, whether profitable or not.

The simplest example is passenger service, which regulators required railroads to continue to operate long after it became unprofitable. Some regulators and others argued that higher profits from parts of their freight traffic allowed railroads to subsidize passenger trains. The problem was that, under such circumstances, railroads' overall financial performance and market share declined.

The Populists used resentment of big, intrusive railroads to perpetuate the VOS system as long as they could, despite the rise of powerful rival modes of transport—themselves encouraged by public subsidies. It is a measure of the fundamental strength of railroad economics and technology that the insult to reason of prescriptive, less-than-adequately-remunerative VOS ratemaking in the face of subsidized competition lasted so long. VOS and demand-based rates were not bad in themselves, and, as this book will show, were necessary to allow railroad profitability overall. The problem was regulatory inflexibility in the face of deteriorating traffic, and the prohibition of differential rates based on demand elasticities.

Making a bad system worse, the so-called National Transportation Policy created under the Transportation Act of 1940 declared that the ICC should honor the "inherent advantages" of competing transport modes— reflected in their perceived total average costs. That meant that railroads had to compete with barges whose rates, when set by regulators (bulk agricultural goods were exempt from regulation altogether) ignored the public costs of building and maintaining their waterways. Railroad rates were held high as an "umbrella" protecting less efficient (but nominally lower-priced) competitor modes. Such umbrella rate making was not discouraged until passage of the Transportation Act of 1958, and it did not end until the Staggers Rail Act of 1980.

Thus, the railroads were put in triple jeopardy: Their key rivals were generally subsidized, their regulators did not reckon taxpayer subsidies as part of the cost basis for comparative modal rate making, and (final insult) railroads were forced to keep their own rates above market price levels in order to shield competitors' business—at the cost of the railroads' own traffic and revenues.

Government Takeover of Railroads in the Great War

Railroads proved essential to national mobilization efforts during the Great War (World War I), but government involvement in the industry was misunderstood. In the Great War, massive congestion occurred at the Atlantic ports of embarkation for Europe because the railroads were not built for one-way operation. Initially they had no method for prioritizing shipments, unloading railcars at the docks, and returning empty cars to Midwest origins. President Woodrow Wilson and Congress intervened, setting up the US Railroad Association (USRA) to take charge of the rail industry and expedite the transport of military personnel and materièl. In addition to establishing traffic movement priorities, the USRA also started to standardize locomotives and operational procedures to improve interoperability of the national railroad network through more efficient interchange of traffic between separate private rail carriers. Most contemporary politicians maligned the USRA and this federal control, but historians ultimately judged it to have served useful purposes.

When hostilities ended, some voices wanted to continue federal operation of railroads—it was a major plank in labor union policy platforms. Thanks to the US Constitution's protection of property rights and the nation's customary popular preference for private over government enterprise, however, US railroads narrowly dodged the nationalization that most other countries adopted in those tumultuous times.

In returning the railroads to corporate control, the Transportation Act of 1920 mandated that the ICC plan consolidation into a "limited number of systems"—competitive and balanced as to financial strength, meaning strong carriers might absorb their weak neighbors, but they could only do so if the merger was part of one of the ICC's preapproved plans. This was the peril on which planned consolidation foundered. Healthy railroads rebelled against the forced absorption of financially unsustainable lines, as well they should have. The ICC eventually saw the futility of its task and prayed to have the cross of planned consolidation lifted from it. Congress did, but not finally until 1940.

By then, the United States was beginning to mobilize for another war—this time one fought in two overseas theaters—and both troops and war materièl flowed in a more balanced manner. Coming out of the Great Depression, however, deferred maintenance of rail facilities was epidemic. Had railroad finances been stronger and wartime production controls not intervened, railroads would have been replacing steam engine fleets with newly proven diesel-electric locomotives. Instead, dieselization was delayed for a decade and was not complete until about 1960.

The war had other lasting impacts on the railroads. All those troop and cargo movements wore out railroad facilities, and little time and few resources were available for adequate maintenance. The passenger fleet, which in the 1930s was beginning to convert to sleek, lightweight designs, reverted to heavyweight equipment, and was overtaxed.

Although the railroads were exhausted by the war years, they had to adjust swiftly to the profound economic, technological, and cultural changes that World War II brought about. Not least of these was the fact the American people and much of their commerce were picking up and moving south or west. Textiles and garment manufacturers moved from the Northeast to the South in search of lower wages. Petrochemical industries moved from their old homes in the Northeast to be nearer feedstocks in Louisiana and Texas. Many manufacturers moved to California to be nearer final markets. Many chicken- and hog-feeding operations moved from the Midwest to the middle South, where a more moderate climate stimulated animal husbandry and lower wages benefitted processors, but where railroads sometimes gained longer hauls of feed and grain. Later, much of the coal-mining industry moved from Appalachia and the Illinois Basin to Wyoming and Montana, where they benefitted from strip-mining of thick coal seams and nonunion labor.

Railroads don't just pick up and move, however; operators wait while old networks gradually wear out—simultaneously adding new capacity where it is more needed. That is what happened in the decades after World War II. Southern and western railroads held their own, while those in the old Rust Belt crumbled with neglect.

The Rise of Subsidized Rival Transport Modes

A core challenge to railroads was the fact that public policy is organized by mode, and public policy invariably favors new modes of transport over old. The simplest explanation for this is similar to the infant industry defense in antitrust law—new modes create new kinds of public benefits and redress the failings of the old. The real explanation may be more parochial, however: New modes offer investment opportunities, albeit speculative, for entrepreneurs and communities or economic regions, and their political supporters want to capitalize on these opportunities before they are lost to competitors or proven to be unnecessary.

Railroads themselves benefited from this bias when they received land grants for their western transcontinental expansions in the last third of the nineteenth century. Early in the twentieth century, the "good roads" movement spawned federally funded highways owned and operated by the states, and a round of new state turnpikes and toll roads. Later these became part of the Interstate Highway System, billed as key to national defense; they were owned and constructed by the states—often in advance of demand—using gasoline taxes paid into the Highway Trust Fund. Official studies later showed these fuel excises failed to recover anywhere near the full costs of road damage attributable to large, heavy, trucks—the mode most competitive with rail freight.

Another large subsidy to rival modes was state-supported construction and operation of locks and dams for inland waterways. The first and most famous was the Erie Canal, completed in 1825 before parallel railroads were constructed, but followed by a number of other rail-competitive public waterways. Because "Congress had developed a strict policy of no user fees on inland waterways," these did not charge tolls until the federal government imposed a nominal fuel excise on barge lines in 1978 (initially 4 cents per gallon in fiscal year 1980, rising to 10 cents in 1986)[5]—far less than full cost recovery levels. Notorious examples of unneeded Army Corps of Engineers waterway improvement projects include the Kerr-McGee project to make Tulsa an inland barge port and create artificial competition to rail grain rates, and the Tennessee-Tombigbee-Warrior River project, of which it has been said that the largest cargo move was spoil from its construction and maintenance. (See Chapter 4 and Map 4.1.)

The Dilemma of Mergers

Symptomatic of the seemingly endless confusion in public policy regarding railroads were persistent challenges relating to railroad mergers. If railroads were natural monopolies, they would merge or consolidate. (There is little effective difference between the terms, but we can say most simply that mergers are the specific cases and implementing arrangements, while consolidation is the generic process and result.)

Most observers believed that railroad consolidation would bring about efficiencies through economies of scale (larger firms) and density (more traffic on the network). The historical policy confusion, however, was palpable. A few years after presidents Teddy Roosevelt and William Howard Taft had campaigned to "bust the trusts"—including big railroads, big oil, steel, and tobacco—the government was pushing unification of major railroads into a limited number of firms to end the duplication and inefficiencies made evident during World War I.

What would rule: the Sherman and Clayton antitrust acts and Supreme Court precedent, or pro-merger transportation policy? Later academic research, including studies by the authors of this book, found conclusively that—before regulatory reforms and managerial advances such as computerized railroad operating plans were available to merger managers—large, complex combinations that were anticipated to yield cost savings in fact typically did the opposite. The collapse in 1970 of the largest merger, Penn Central, was proof-positive.

This book tells in detail the story of the financial collapse of railroads in the Northeast and Midwest Region after the failure of Penn Central.

Congress responded with the Regional Rail Reorganization (3R) Act, creating a second United States Railway Association (USRA) and giving it the task of reorganizing failed railroads into the publicly owned Consolidated Rail Corporation (Conrail). The federal government incurred a cost of some $8 billion for subsidizing threatened rail services in the Northeast, reconstructing lines that had suffered long-deferred maintenance, buying out redundant employees, and compensating rail property owners for what was ruled a public "taking." Despite substantial federally funded rehabilitation, Conrail lost about $1 million a day in its first years.

Soon, the Northeast Rail Services Act of 1981 provided more direct assistance in trimming Conrail's excess employment, branch lines, and costly commuter services. With these changes, the new railroad turned profitable, although it was not returned to the private sector until a successful initial public offering (IPO)—then the largest ever—in 1987. The railroad crisis had not left other parts of the country unscathed, as widespread rail bankruptcies and threatened abandonments continued to trouble railroads in the Great Plains throughout the 1970s and early 1980s.

Conrail's miraculous turnaround showed that a near-monopoly railroad backed by federal investments and unshackled from most economic regulation could prosper even in unfriendly regional confines. But the key was deregulation. Conrail was not saved through the direct prescriptions of consolidation and renewal of main lines, abandonment or transfer of branch lines, or employee layoffs alone. Instead it was these, plus the freedom provided under the Staggers Rail Act of 1980 to adjust routes, rates, and services. A rising tide of market innovations then lifted all ships.

The Genius of Deregulation and Contract Rate Making

With the Staggers Rail Act, the old VOS system finally came to an end, replaced with rules that said any rate that did not recover variable costs could be raised to that level, and further, that railroads could charge up to the neighborhood of 180 percent of variable costs under most circumstances.[6] This was not really optimal marginal cost pricing (prices set equal to the cost of producing the next unit, in a fully competitive industry), but it meant the use of cost-based rates with markups to recover overhead costs and to sustain reinvestment. Even more important was the legalization of rate and service contracts between railroads and their customers. Populist legislation would have made these a form of rate discrimination and in violation of the doctrine of tariff publication, and thus illegal. Rate contracts were therefore never part of the traditional common carrier system.[7]

Contracts were the needed cure for the intractable "railroad problem" described by Charles Francis Adams and his followers. Rate and service contracts allowed operators to balance railroad supply with customer demand, squeezing out excess capacity. The Staggers Rail Act affected even the need for the ICC to settle contentious divisions of revenues between connecting carriers because now carrier-shipper contracts could set compensation for each railroad's participation in such interline moves. It is not an exaggeration to say that deregulated rate and service contracts brought about the renaissance of American railroads.

Probably as sensible adaptations to reality, merger patterns also changed after the Staggers Rail Act. Congress newly mandated that the ICC explicitly consider competitive consequences of railroad mergers, not just the financial and labor factors called out under the previous legislation's vague public interest standard. Proponents then proposed mergers that were in fact fundamentally more pro-competition than the earlier consolidation pattern—they were more "end-to-end" than "parallel." That is, these mergers focused on extending the market reach of proponent railroads, rather than being motivated by saving operating costs through consolidating redundant facilities (or eliminating competitors, which would not have been acknowledged aloud).

With four important restructurings in the last five years of the twentieth century further streamlining the industry, the post-Staggers period saw development of new systems that are the core of today's American railroad industry: Burlington Northern and the Santa Fe joined in BNSF; Union Pacific and Southern Pacific-Rio Grande merged (retaining the UP namesake); and Conrail was divided, 58 percent going to Norfolk Southern and 42 percent to CSX. After overcoming some birthing pains (especially Union Pacific), these four consolidations, plus two strong Canadian roads and the improved Kansas City Southern, compose American railroading's highly successful industry structure—one more competitive today than it was prior to the post-Staggers mergers.

Overall, extraordinary efforts to find new cooperative arrangements for balanced competition—which could come only from enlightened management and patient federal overseers—brought the industry into the twenty-first century. America now has the basis of a sustainable industry structure, an enduring organizational framework. Talk of future transcontinental mergers—combination of either of the two western railroads (BNSF or UP) with either eastern road (NS or CSX) to produce two rather than four US giants—persists. But talk aside, transcontinental mergers are unlikely because, quite simply, they are not needed. Today's industry structure is likely to be the one that serves our grandchildren.

"Disappearin' Railroad Blues:"
The Dismal Economics of Passenger Service

Freight and passenger trains have very different underlying economics, financial returns, industry structures, and histories. For example, the remarkable gains in output for freight railroads illustrated in Figure 1.1 largely bypassed rail passenger service. Indeed, the enduring industry in the United States is freight railroading, while passenger trains are more of an endangered species. Thus, the main focus of our book is on freight railroading, but we devote two chapters to rail passenger service.[8]

Intercity passenger rail service was, in effect, nationalized in 1970. Except in the early 1920s, during World War II, and along the densely populated Boston-to-Washington Northeast Corridor, passenger train travel faced a continual and severe loss of market share throughout the twentieth century; by the year 2000, rail passenger service held on to service in the rest of the country by only a thread (and at great cost to taxpayers).

Railroads made a last effort to modernize passenger fleets after World War II, but it was too little, too late, and too unavailing, given the challenge. People wanted to drive their own cars on new highways modeled on the autobahns that returning soldiers had seen in Europe. Or they wanted to fly in the era's new fleet of swift, modern, comfortable, and safer aircraft.

Railroad passenger service could hardly keep up with publicly supported services provided by the newer modes of travel, including provision of good roads for automobiles and motor buses and the development of aircraft, airports, and airways. Over the course of the twentieth century, aviation had been subsidized through contracts to carry airmail, by airport terminal and runway construction, and by the Federal Aviation Administration's operation of the airways system, not to mention the benefits to airlines of technology originating in military aircraft.

By 1970, passenger train deficits had become an intolerable burden on freight railroad companies; once-luxurious services had sunk to disgraceful conditions, and rail labor unions were calling for costly direct government

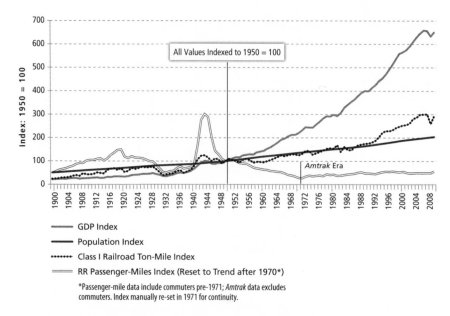

All Values Indexed to 1950 = 100

Amtrak Era

——— GDP Index
——— Population Index
••••••• Class I Railroad Ton-Mile Index
═══ RR Passenger-Miles Index (Reset to Trend after 1970*)
*Passenger-mile data include commuters pre-1971; *Amtrak* data excludes
commuters. Index manually re-set in 1971 for continuity.

Figure 1.1 Underlying Economic Relationships for Railroad Output. US Class I railroad
ton-miles are positively correlated with gross domestic product (GDP), although GDP has risen
faster, especially since midcentury. One reason is the growing importance of services relative to
mining and manufacturing in GDP. The impacts of the Great Depression and the Great
Recession of 2007–2008 are clearly evident. Rail passenger service declined sharply after peak
levels in World Wars I and II because of competition from highways and aviation, and macroeconomic factors. After Amtrak was created in 1971, intercity passenger ridership generally
matched population growth. *Sources:* GDP and population figures are readily available from the
US Department of Commerce website; for GDP, go to http://www.census.gov/statab/hist/HS-32.pdf
(for earlier years, see *Historical Statistics*) and for population, go to http://www.census.gov/statab
/hist/HS-01.pdf . For railroad data, see US Department of Commerce, *Historical Statistics*, 1960,
and various issues of the Association of American Railroads (AAR) annual booklets *Railroad Facts*,
used courtesy of the AAR.

subsidies to save jobs. The Nixon administration came up with a mildly
socialistic alternative, the National Railroad Passenger Corporation (NRPC),
marketed as Amtrak. Private railroads were induced to "join" Amtrak by
turning over their passenger rolling stock to the new national company,
paying an initial assessment based on prior years' fully distributed passenger operating deficits, and granting twenty-five-year (below full cost)
operating rights to Amtrak trains—all in return for getting out of their
common carrier obligations to operate deficit-ridden trains.

The Amtrak legislation began as an emergency alternative to an epidemic of "train-off" (technically, discontinuance) petitions to state regulatory

commissions and the ICC by carriers seeking relief for quickly mounting deficits. But then, to the astonishment of seasoned Washington observers, Congress was willing to fund Amtrak operations and improvements, and quite generously at that. When Amtrak recently celebrated its fortieth anniversary, the cumulative taxpayer investment was closing in on $40 billion (adjusted for inflation); it had established a national marketing presence and had yielded modest improvements in ridership and customer satisfaction—but it was hardly the breakeven enterprise some envisioned at its creation.

Although many observers find Amtrak a costly and dubious enterprise, most people—even if they rarely travel by train outside the Northeast Corridor—seem to love passenger trains and want to see them survive for key scenic long distance routes and promising short haul corridors. That would require significant ongoing federal efforts to improve passenger train speeds and frequencies.

Unless these trains run on separate rights of ways, however, efforts to expand intercity rail passenger services substantially would encounter opposition from the owners of the freight railroad tracks over which most (other-than-Northeast Corridor) Amtrak trains run. Quite simply, the private-sector freight railroads need existing track capacity for their own trains, and they are not fully compensated for use of their track by Amtrak. Freight railroads might rent facilities to commuter agencies for peak-period operations, but Amtrak's non-Northeast Corridor trains are another matter altogether. The freight railroads will insist that any major new commitments to passenger services include public investment in more capacity.

Adapting New Technologies

The twentieth century repeatedly showed clear synergies between large, modern, railway enterprises displaying economics of scale and the deployment of powerful new technologies and operating innovations to take advantage of growing business opportunities. The long list of technologies developed for or adapted to railroads include diesel-electric locomotives, larger and more specialized freight cars, the use of microprocessors in locomotives and signals, welded rail and use of better steel in track to reduce derailments, computerized systems to deploy assets more efficiently, advanced telecommunications for safety and productivity, automatic grade crossing warning devices, and much more. With these innovations, plus retiring the caboose, moving freight in unit trains, and double-stacking intermodal containers, the railroad industry demonstrated that its reputation of being stuck in the past was no longer true.

Railroad technology sprang from individual inventive genius marked by a dozen famous British, American, and European continental names like Trevithick, Stephenson, Bessemer, Eads, Westinghouse, Edison, and Diesel. Some important inventors hardly known except by railway historians were the Americans Stephens, Winans, Robinson, Janney, Sprague, Lamp, and Timken, and the Belgian, Walschaerts. Readers will meet some of these ingenious men as our story unfolds. They are much more important to the history of railroads than the infamous robber barons, Drew, Fisk, Gould, and Villard, or "the Associates," Huntington, Crocker, Stanford, and Hopkins, about which so much ink has been spilled.[9]

An important finding described in *American Railroads* and not fully appreciated elsewhere is that deregulation, given its impact on improved cash flows, enabled railroads to reinvest in facilities and equipment. With reinvestment came new technology because in older integrated industries, reinvestment is the main way new technology is deployed. The new facilities and technologies, in turn, made the industry much safer. In this complex way, economic deregulation—more than prescriptive safety rulemaking—was at the root of the substantial improvements in safety performance railroads achieved in the last two decades of the twentieth century, as this book explains. Turning away from and going beyond the old regulatory mind-set may even have helped foster increasing acceptance of the notion that "good safety is good business." Our book does not advocate wholesale relaxation of rail safety legislation and regulation, but it calls for more comprehensive use of safety performance standards, better education and training within a safety culture, and ongoing reinvestment in facilities and equipment that incorporate the most effective technologies.

Other technologies do not wait for the railroads, as is evident by the rise of rival modes of transportation. Still, the popular wisdom that railroads suffered from obsolete or lagging technology needs wholesale revision: The problem was old regulation, not old technology.

Deregulated Railroads in the Economy Today

Economists still debate whether railroads are natural monopolies and whether they can self-regulate to a workably competitive equilibrium, allowing normal profits for reinvestment and a fair rate structure for the industry's customer base. Few economists argue, however, for turning back the clock and reestablishing regulatory policies existed prior to the Staggers Rail Act of 1980. Yet the greatest threat to the ability of private-sector railroads to endure is new calls for old-style bureaucratic regulation. These calls come mainly from customers with few economical alternatives for moving bulk commodities over long distances.

Such reregulation is unnecessary and unwise. Loosening the regulatory grip on railroad enterprise was the key to the industry's renaissance, and deregulation must be allowed to work itself out in a lasting accommodation of national economic interests.

Although the Populists and the Progressives seemingly stumbled upon demand-based pricing at the beginning of the twentieth century, such pricing—charging what the traffic will bear—is the key to serving most customers most efficiently. Unlike VOS pricing, however, the fairest overall rate structure requires charging different rates in various market segments based on customer demand, no matter who the customers are. Modern demand-based pricing means living with the results of business negotiations between the market's largest and most powerful participants. It is folly to constrain these negotiations by adhering to artificial formulas, or even by setting rates on a case-by-case basis in court-like adversary settings conducted by the Surface Transportation Board.

A central theme of this book is that railroads, throughout their history, were so important to the US economy that politicians could not leave them alone, and when governments did intervene in transportation markets, they usually made a mess of things. Government regulation distorted consumer choices, found awkward and costly ways of subsidizing competing modes of transportation, taxed or regulated away profits needed for reinvestment and capacity expansion, and—while generally contributing to greater safety—typically fell far short of stimulating optimal safety performance for all transport modes. Much the same was true for the relationship of railroads to other public goals, such as energy efficiency, environmental protection, and consumer welfare.

The real challenge to rail freight operations and customer satisfaction today is service reliability failures, which can occur for many reasons, including derailments or washouts, insufficient locomotive availability, unrested crews, and gridlock from an unexpected surge in demand. Railroad operators can overcome some of these problems by perpetuating (or developing) excess capacity, but that can be expensive. Better strategies include individual railroads' managerial efforts to ensure that (1) data used to run their operations are accurate, timely, and complete; (2) they have adjusted their workforce and plant and equipment capacity to match expected demand; and (3) they are continuously improving employee training, operating discipline, and process controls.[10]

As long as they are not reregulated or burdened with unreasonable new public-service obligations, freight railroads can earn enough revenue to renew and expand needed capacity. This is especially true if railroads can continue to improve their reliability, as we believe they can. Given their capital intensity, however, railroads will continue to require large investments for safety and environmental upgrades. Because some major investments in railroads yield both public and business benefits (safety initiatives like derailment prevention and environmental benefits like conservation of energy come to mind), the nation should consider public–private partnerships to reach these shared goals. The final chapter of this book suggests how such policies and partnerships can work.[11]

Some observers will regard our conclusion that government should invest in railroad infrastructure but not set customer rates as contradictory. However, that is what our society does in almost every sector where public and private interests overlap, including highways, waterways, public health, higher education, medical research, national parks, military systems development, and more. As with land grants in the old days, administrative agencies will make some mistakes, and some regions will prosper more than others, but the nation as a whole will benefit in great measure.

The Railroad Bookshelf

For all the excellent books that have been written about railroads, the single most important story in their twentieth-century history—the story about deregulation and renaissance—has not been fully told. *American Railroads* seeks to fill the gap between formal histories and academic analysis, between one-issue polemics and oversimplified surveys. This book is written by authors with significant and direct experience in the industry, as well as having academic credentials. It covers ideas on which the industry's leaders and political figures have taken strong positions. As a matter of disclosure, both authors of *American Railroads* have earned livings working in the railroad industry and acting as paid consultants to it—including on some of the challenges covered in this book. So we have a viewpoint, but also a degree of what philosophers call authentic knowledge.

The most popular railroad books on the market are histories that capture driving industrial or macroeconomic forces and their broad social effects, analyses of managerial styles and accomplishments, or photo essays documenting the romance of trains in their natural settings—especially those with incisive narratives explaining to later generations why those iconic trains were so memorable. Many of these histories and specialized policy analyses are mentioned in the references. Books about mergers are abundant, but only a limited part of that genre covers consolidations at the end of the twentieth century. The books by Klein, Loving, Martin, and Saunders, especially, are well written, incisive, and accurate. *Trains Magazine* is a monthly treat. Not for sit-down reading but for valuable reference is *The Encyclopedia of North American Railroads*, which is edited by Middleton, Smerk, and Diehl.

To these we add *American Railroads*. It is the story of the fascinating railroad industry as it marked history over the full course of the American century. It is a big story, with lots of opportunities for sidetrack wanderings that could easily distract the reader. We have a destination to reach, however, and our mode of travel will take us there safely, reliably, and efficiently, if not especially quickly.

The conductor is calling "All aboard!" Let's not be left at the station.

2

THE ILLS OF GOVERNMENT REGULATION
OF RAIL RATES AND SERVICES

... [I]t has become apparent that the recognized laws of trade operate but imperfectly at best in regulating the use made of these modern thoroughfares [railroads] by those who thus both own and monopolize them. Consequently, the political governments of the various countries have been called upon for some ways to make good through legislation the deficiencies thus revealed in the working of the natural laws. This is the Railroad Problem.

—CHARLES FRANCIS ADAMS (1878)

The railroad business is very frequently spoken of as a "natural monopoly." While the term expresses a partial truth, it is apt to suggest the idea of a complete monopoly, and thus to convey a wrong meaning. . . . It is better to call railroads partial monopolies, and to apply the term complete monopolies to those businesses in which the seller has the power of dictating prices to the buyer.

—EMORY R. JOHNSON (1908)

In this chapter, *American Railroads* explores central issues of economic regulation of railroad rates and services; the next chapter then addresses regulatory oversight of the competitive organization of US railroads in the first decades of the twentieth century. The two chapters are connected in many ways, as we will make clear. The issues are jointly rooted in the fundamental economics of competitive behavior, both where it succeeds in creating functioning markets, and where it fails and must be replaced with regulatory substitutes.

The fundamental justification for public regulation of industry is always the assertion or determination that markets have failed and no longer allocate resources fairly and efficiently. Usually the failure is that some seller or sellers acting in concert have become too strong and are therefore able to restrict supply to the market, forcing prices to unreasonably high levels. To be sure, markets can fail for reasons other than too little competition, such as ruinous competition, grossly unpredictable supply, or the impossibility of disaggregating specific costs and charging users according to the benefits they receive.[1]

Still, market failure most often occurs when monopoly power allows sellers to raise prices above the point where supply and demand would intersect if the market were competitive, resulting in less than socially optimal output. Regulation's task in substituting for a failed market is to figure out how to allow the economy to produce the right amount of goods under the circumstances. This is often accomplished by allowing regulated prices to be a bit higher than dictated by average production costs at given levels of output—but only enough higher to enable sellers to earn sufficient profits to keep them producing and reinvesting.[2]

In American transportation policy and legislative history in regard to railroads, however, the distinctions among these technical terms have hardly been so precise. Assumptions about both causes and effects were broadly, almost carelessly, drawn. Political grandstanding trumped research and logic. Shibboleths ruled. Wise public policy, and sometimes railroad prosperity, paid the price. By the time reform finally arrived in the 1970s, the costs to the US economy of maladroit regulation were estimated to be several billions of dollars annually.

The Perception That Railroads are Natural Monopolies

Economists know how single sellers behave: They charge as much as they can for scarce products, and then seek to restrict total production to keep things that way. Perhaps they even set prices artificially low for a time to drive competitors out of the market or dissuade new ones from entering. English common law forbade such things, including forestalling (hindering normal trading in the market by delaying goods in transit or by persuading sellers to raise prices), regrating (buying up inventories intended for the market and reselling them at higher prices), and engrossing (cornering a market with intent to resell at higher prices).[3] The common law thus sought to protect consumers directly—as well as indirectly the reputation of markets that served them. The advance of railroads to dominance of transportation modes and modalities in the middle third of the nineteenth century brought the common law's old mercantile concerns about fair markets back to center stage in a new industrial context.

Initially, it wasn't so much the tendency of railroads to price their goods as a monopolist would that led economists to call them natural monopolies, but rather the fundamental circumstance of railroads' new dominance: the fact that they were large and getting larger by absorbing competitors. This is what needed explanation. Everyone knew railroads were costly and time-consuming to construct. The great insight of industrial economists, however, was that once built, railroads showed lower average operating costs with additional units of output they produced (say, ton-miles of cargo or number of passengers hauled). These were economies of scale. As David Besanko and Ronald Braeutigam explain in their popular microeconomics textbook, the formal defining characteristic of a natural monopoly is that, for any given level of output, the total costs incurred by a single firm producing that exact quantity of output are less than the total combined costs that would be incurred by two or more other firms if they divided production of the same amount of output. This distinguished natural monopolies from other firms that might also enjoy economies of scale, but without the characteristic that no other firms could match their unique production costs in the market.[4] (See Box 2.1 for more about natural monopoly.)

Box 2.1   Are Railroads Natural Monopolies?

The term "natural monopoly" is often used carelessly in economic discussions. To be precise, it refers to a characteristic of the production technology employed by a particular firm at a particular level of output: i.e., the output in question can be produced more cheaply by one firm than by any combination of two or more firms. When this condition pertains throughout the relevant range of output levels, the market (or industry) is said to be a natural monopoly. In such cases, it is socially wasteful for two or more firms to serve the market.

Natural monopoly technologies usually also exhibit increasing returns to scale so that average, or per unit, costs decrease with output. This makes it difficult for rivals to compete with a firm that is exploiting increasing returns to scale, because the larger firm can always underprice a smaller one and, ultimately,

---

Box 2.1 *Continued*

---

drive it from the market. The "last man standing" as an end result of this process can then exploit consumers by charging a monopoly price.

These technological and competitive facts of life give rise to the so-called natural monopoly problem: it is cost efficient for one firm to serve a natural monopoly market, but, if left unregulated, such a firm is likely to eliminate rivals and charge high prices. The natural monopoly characteristics of a firm's operations must clearly play a role in both regulatory and merger policy. It would never be socially desirable for firms to merge if there were no efficiency gains to be had. Thus the merged entity should enjoy a natural monopoly at the combined output levels of the two original firms. This is an example of an important general principle: any profit-seeking firm should be a natural monopolist with respect to the output it produces. If this were not the case, shareholders (and society) would gain by simply breaking up the firm.

The natural monopoly problem just described arises if the technology is such that cost-reducing mergers remained possible for the entire range of market output. In traditional utility industry economics, natural monopolies were usually tolerated in order for society to reap the benefits of the firms' economies of scale without duplication of distribution systems. Rates were regulated, however, so that utilities could not behave like real monopolists.

Are railroads natural monopolies? Most economists assume that they are, but the issue is a subtle one. If one closely studied the operations of any well managed railroad, one would expect to find that it was, indeed, a natural monopoly with respect to the level of output being produced. On the other hand, if it is the case that competitors (including those in other modes) can keep railroads from continuing to increase their share of the relevant market, or if a railroad's average costs level off well short of the industry's consolidation to a single firm, the larger transportation market that the railroad serves is not a natural monopoly. In that case, there is no market failure that needs regulation. This book avoids use of the term natural monopoly because it is misleading and sometimes pejorative—and too often the source of unwise or unneeded policy remedies.

With economies of scale, as developing railroads became bigger firms, they would have lower average costs and would be able to act powerfully in the marketplace. As the next chapter shows, what railroads mainly did, both in the United States and abroad, was to buy up other railroads, get larger and fewer in number, and become too important politically to be ignored. One of the big things about these big things, the railroads, was that they got bigger. It's right there in the DNA. As a result, railroads everywhere were either nationalized or regulated, or both. They endured, but not in the same form, and when bad times arrived, they only barely survived.

What would be the limits on railroad behavior if they appeared to be natural monopolies? In the United States, the limits came from three entirely different sources—three different convergences, really. The first was the end of continental expansion over newly constructed rail lines early in the twentieth century, which is addressed in the next chapter. If not constructing new lines, railroads would be less likely to add to the overcapacity that had been characteristic since the 1890s; they would be more likely to settle into respectable middle age, giving up some of their bad-boy image and the reckless "monopolizing" behavior that they had been accused of exercising. The second limitation was a decrease in railroad mergers after the Progressives began enforcing the Sherman Antitrust Act of 1890. The landmark case involving railroads was dissolution of James J. Hill's Northern Lines in 1904, also described in more detail in Chapter 3. The third was legislation for direct government intervention in regulating railroads' rates and services by means of regulatory agencies.

Of these three kinds of limits on railroads exploiting economies of scale, the third was the most enduring. Railroad rate regulation germinated in populist politics after the Civil War and came to flower in the agrarian Midwest and Great Plains, where, it seemed, politicians never met an eastern monopolist (even a natural monopolist) they liked.

The Genesis of Public Regulation of Railroads

The traditional narrative approach to rail rate regulation starts with review of the historical pressures to curb perceived pricing abuses by the railroads dominating US agricultural and community life in the 1870s and 1880s. Most noteworthy among interests aligned against the powerful railroads throughout the years of agricultural development was the Granger movement, officially, The National Grange of the Order of Patrons of Husbandry. The Grange and its political allies pushed a number of states to establish independent railroad commissions to oversee railroads' financial operations under their earlier state charters. Before long, state laws gave these commissions power to enforce restrictions on the rates that railroads could charge, and in particular, prohibitions on discrimination among persons or places.[5]

Things got confusing, though, when a rail shipment regulated by one state commission followed a route crossing a state line into a neighboring state's jurisdiction. In the seminal case, the Illinois regulatory commission contended that it could control interstate movements originating within its borders, even though the goods had crossed into another state. The Wabash Railway forced the issue, and in 1886, the US Supreme Court, citing the US Constitution's Commerce Clause, ruled that regulation of interstate commerce was fully within the purview of the federal government. To regulate most rates, the government would have to set up its own regulatory commission, for which there was ample support in Congress. Only one year later, Congress passed the Act to Regulate Commerce (1887), which established the Interstate Commerce Commission (ICC) and set the basic ground rules for economic regulation of rail rates and services.[6]

From time to time in the Progressive Era, and likely to their lasting regret, the railroads themselves supported regulation because, according to Gabriel Kolko,[7] they recognized that the ICC could legally stabilize cartel arrangements among the multiple railroads fighting for a piece of the market under otherwise chaotic and volatile rate circumstances.

The 1887 legislation had little real impact before 1900. The ICC, while capable of considerable mischief, was not regarded initially as capable of effectively regulating rail rates. There was also considerable uncertainty about the extent of the ICC's powers. The new regulatory statutes were better at listing prohibitions on rail carriers and requiring the filing of reports than in spelling out specific guidelines for the ICC to use in actual rate setting—in particular the core determination of whether or not the rates under review were "just and reasonable," which is the statutory test. If regulation were to substitute effectively for natural markets, that is what the ICC would have to do.

One of the purposes the government had in establishing the ICC as an independent regulatory agency was to resolve commercial disputes outside the stresses of congressional politics and with application of technical inputs from knowledgeable professionals. At its origin in 1887, few observers were sure what the ICC's purposes and activities might be. Predictably, there were two views that were difficult to reconcile: a producer-investor-management view and a consumer-shipper-labor view. The producer-investor-management view was associated with status quo politics and the consumer-shipper-labor view was linked with populist reforms that were the signature of the Progressive Era.

Anti-rebating legislation enacted in 1903 (the Elkins Act) was clearly in the railroads' interest, but it was not long after the turn of the century that Congress passed stronger new legislation (the Hepburn Act of 1906 and the Mann-Elkins Act of 1910) to regulate rail rates. With these enactments there could no longer be any ambiguity in the railroads' perception of their situation: It was clear to all that the ICC had become a major restraint on their behavior.[8]

Two Approaches to Rail Rate Regulation: Cost-Based and Demand-Based

A full treatment of the theories, industry practices, and ICC rulings guiding or constraining regulatory rate setting would lead us far away from the story line of *American Railroads*. The economic and legal arguments quickly become complex and subtle, and econometric evidence would be inaccessible to all but a few. For those reasons, we will limit the following presentation to a few fundamentals and an overview of the historical implications of regulation for rail industry financial health and government transport policy.

An illuminating way to launch into the topic is to go back more than eighty years, to a period when academic studies of railroad economics were *de rigueur*, to see what the experts of the day were saying. A classic text establishing the fundamentals of transportation economics is the 1924 *Principles of Railway Transportation*, by Eliot Jones, professor of economics at Stanford University.[9] Jones (following Harvard's venerated F. W. Taussig[10]) begins the theory of railroad rates with two fundamental principles: The law of *increasing returns* and the law of *joint costs*. These are key concepts that should have governed ICC rate policy over the twentieth century.

- *Increasing returns to scale*. As noted in Box 2.1, inherent in presumed natural monopoly is the idea that such firms exhibit increasing returns to scale. This means that, with increasing output, unit costs of incremental production do not increase correspondingly and natural monopolies can expand to control the entire relevant market. Economies of scale or density—decreasing average costs with additional firm size or line volume—are essentially the same thing.
- *Joint costs* means that as one product is produced (Jones uses the example of cotton fiber) a second (cottonseed) may result proportionally:

The inextricable mixing of costs for joint products means their direct unit costs cannot be ascertained; the costs for fiber and for cotton-seed can be separated only arbitrarily. What is important for rate-making, however, is that separate prices for cotton fiber and cottonseed oil or meal can be set according to demand elasticities. If they are inelastic, product prices can be raised without loss of total revenue because volumes do not fall off proportionally; if they are elastic, higher prices drive away volume and decrease overall revenues.[11]

Continuing, Jones explains the central challenge and complexity of rail-road rate making as follows:

> We may now apply this reasoning to the railway. The railway performs a vast number of heterogeneous services, some traveling long distances and some short distances, some moving in trainload lots and some in less than carload lots, some going at high speed and some at low speed, some moving in one direction and some in another, some possessing high value per pound and some low value . . . On what principle should the railroad fix the rates to be charged for these different services? Should it base its rates on the cost of performing each individual service . . . ? However desirable this basis might be if it could be realized in practice, the fact is that it can not be realized.[12]

Next, Jones describes how the cost-of-service principle—while inadequate for determining individual rates—helps establish a bound below which a group of rates should not fall. Also, because railroads are regulated as though they are natural monopolies, the regulator has a duty to establish rates that yield reasonable earnings. "And earnings are reasonable when they suffice to meet the costs of transportation, including in costs an adequate profit." Determining an adequate level of profitability is not easy, "*but the guiding principle for the future should be to establish a rate that will suffice to attract to the railroad industry sufficient capital to supply the public with the kind of service that it demands* [emphasis added]."[13] Still, what should guide the setting of individual rates? For this, Jones returned to joint costs:

> When articles are produced or services are supplied under conditions of joint cost, the price or rate is determined, *not by the cost of production or of transportation, but by the demand for*

the article or service [emphasis added]. The freight rate on each commodity must be high enough [to defray special costs incurred by its carriage]. But the proportion in which each will contribute to the joint (or general) costs depends on the intensity of the demand. To put it somewhat differently, some articles cannot stand a high freight rate; unless they are charged low rates per unit of weight they will either not be offered for transportation at all, or they will be offered in much diminished volume. . . .

The principle underlying this differentiation of charges as between commodities is that of charging what the traffic will bear (or as it is sometimes called, the value of service principle). This principle has often been criticized on the ground that it leads to extortion, yet rightly understood [as a resolution of the joint cost problem, not to maximize profits, Jones says], the principle is sound, and is in the public interest. . . .

The fixing of rates is an art, not a science. . . . It is therefore necessary for the government either to operate the railroads itself or to establish an impartial agency to hear and decide complaints alleging unreasonable or discriminatory rates. In this country we have retained private ownership, and have established an Interstate Commerce Commission to regulate the railways.[14]

Value of Service Ratemaking in Principle and Practice

Early in the twentieth century, the Progressives adopted as their model for setting and limiting railroad rates by regulatory commission (the ICC) a demand-based pricing strategy that involved classifying railroad rates according to commodities, distances moved, and other characteristics. These "classified rates" amounted to "charging what the traffic would bear"—regardless of costs or other supply-type considerations. Because it would be bad form and bad politics for a railroad to announce that it charged whatever the traffic would bear, these came to be called value-of-service (VOS) rates.

The ICC's value-of-service rate making system worked by requiring publication of giant matrices showing rates for location-to-location movement of a specific quantity of a given commodity, such as a carload of grain or hundredweight of potatoes. These classification tables evolved from railroads' own efforts to set rates roughly reflecting costs of moving goods of numerous types between different stations on the rail network under a variety of operating and competitive circumstances.

Initially rate classification tables were compromises reached by committees of railroads acting in concert, and they were published for three rate territories—the Official, Southern, and Western—but it was apparent revisions would be needed and these would have to be overseen by the ICC. Indeed, by 1897, that agency declared that the wide differences in rate tables "lead one to doubt whether present classifications are not more the result of chance than of system."[15] The IC Act of 1887 was not explicit regarding ICC's authority over rate classification, but the Commission believed it had such power, exercised it, and was not challenged by the railroads. The Mann-Elkins Act of 1910 then explicitly gave the ICC power to require the railroads to develop uniform classifications replacing those of the existing three territories.[16]

Addressing the first duty of the regulatory agency as described by Jones, the ICC built into these schedules implicit rate levels to recover a railroad's average cost—all allocable costs plus a markup to allow for overhead and return on investment. Following Jones's second principle, however, the ICC based VOS ratemaking mostly on demand within a commodity group for transport of different distances, volumes, or other characteristics.

Evaluation of VOS Ratemaking in the Progressive Era

In 1922, William Z. Ripley, professor of economics at Harvard, summarized some of the fundamentals at work in VOS rate making:

> It is indisputable that the great dynamic force in railway operation inheres in the value of service idea. The traffic manager who is always considering how much it will cost to handle business, will seldom adventure into new territory. The United States, as a rapidly growing country, is consequently the field in which charging what the traffic will bear, has been most ardently upheld as the only practicable basis for rate making.[17]

Given that disputes over railroad rate making are still raging 100 years after the Hepburn Act, it is important to emphasize that differential pricing was inherent in VOS rate making.[18] With the full sanction of the ICC, railroads were encouraged to use whatever monopoly or market power they had to charge higher markups over costs to some classes of customers than others. The 1887 Act to Regulate Commerce, however, in Sections 2 and 3 explicitly outlawed discrimination—making it illegal, directly or indirectly, to charge one person more than another for a like service under similar circumstances. That meant that the federal government based the new regulatory regime on a tough set of criteria—differential rates that were not discriminatory.[19]

The ICC took this path because it wanted railroads to have in aggregate enough surplus revenue over normal costs to haul specific kinds of traffic favored by politicians—including especially the traffic of agricultural shippers, rural communities, and government agencies—at artificially low rates. As though persistent overcapacity at the turn of the century were not enough of a crippling problem for railroads, now ICC regulation actually incorporated cross subsidies within the classified rate schedules used to implement VOS rate making! This policy subtly redistributed income from consumers and shippers of manufactured goods to investors and shippers of bulk agricultural goods. Given the antidiscrimination language of the statutes, an argument can be made that the VOS internal cross subsidies were even contrary to the law's intent, but that goes too far. As long as the preferential rates applied to an entire commodity classification and not to specific persons or places, the ICC's policy would not be seen as discriminatory.

Enter Elasticity, the Foundation for Demand-Based Pricing and VOS Rate Making

To understand regulatory rate making under the Interstate Commerce Act in its full economic context, we need to back up a step.

If a monopolist could strike a separate bargain with every consumer of a product or service, he or she would obviously want to discover and charge the price that just kept the consumer in the market. Indeed, the term *perfect pricing* is sometimes used by business economists to describe a monopolist's profit-maximizing strategy of charging the highest price a customer will pay without abandoning the purchase. In this strategy, the seller prices down the demand curve, in the process capturing all available consumer surplus. Output would remain at the same level as before because prices charged to consumers would never exceed their willingness to pay. Production costs would not change, so consumer demand and the incremental cost of the last unit produced would still cross at the same point as before.[20]

Again, under demand-based pricing, the goal was to extract as much revenue from the rate payer as possible, short of causing total abandonment of the activity. Railroads also needed to avoid situations that would leave carriers no more revenue than before any proposed rate increase if shippers sought other alternatives. In practice, this meant marking up the rates charged to different users according to what they were willing to pay. Meanwhile the rate payer was interested in finding the lowest-cost way to meet his or her shipping needs. Barring negotiations between the parties (then illegal), the system needed some means of determining willingness to pay.[21]

Economists' concept of elasticity of demand provided an elegant solution, at least in theory. Formally, price elasticity of demand is the ratio of a percentage change in quantity sold, related to the percentage change in its price. If a 10 percent price increase leads to a 20 percent drop in sales, the price elasticity of demand for that market is −2.0. In an intensely competitive market, with many suppliers of the same product, even the smallest increase in price could drive away almost all consumers. In that case, the price elasticity of demand would approach negative infinity. Conversely, if a price increase has little effect on demand, it is inelastic. In the extreme case where a price increase has absolutely no effect, the price elasticity of demand is zero. Shipments with elasticities between -1.0 and $-\infty$ are called elastic, while those between 0 and -1.0 are labeled inelastic.[22]

The elasticity of demand for a particular transport service depends not only on a theoretical elasticity of demand for the final product, but also, practically, on the share of that product's costs that the cost of transport represents. For example, utilities paying to transport coal from various, equally distant mines to an electricity-generating plant might be more sensitive to rail charges than a manufacturer that ships highly sophisticated machinery an equivalent distance. Assuming that a railroad does not face many competitors for moving the machinery, it could find it advantageous over the near- to mid-term to charge higher markups over costs to ship high-value goods than to ship coal.

From a practical and historical standpoint, these rate-making economics meant that railroads sought shippers whose products faced inelastic demand and were expensive to produce, but needed only modest amounts of transport relative to other costs. Of course, it also helped if the product did not have other ways of getting to market. Such circumstances were not unusual for railroads at the turn of the twentieth century. For the most part, the only meaningful competition came from other railroads or, occasionally (depending on the shipper's proximity to a navigable waterway) steamboats or barges. Unfortunately for railroads, however, the competitive possibilities unleashed by development of the internal combustion engine had yet to be realized.

VOS Pricing in the Real World

Ultimately, the actual practice of VOS pricing was a good deal less than ideal. Major difficulties arose because the VOS rate matrices were highly inflexible, while the real world was dynamic. The differential pricing inherent in VOS rate making might have been desirable if railroads could have easily changed the rates to reflect actual market supply and demand. VOS had the perverse effect, however, of freezing the classified rate structure and inhibiting price competition. In fact, the long-run impact of VOS was to create incentives for traffic bearing high markups to seek alternatives. In a bit of bad luck for the railroads, the new modal technologies were well suited to carrying high-value traffic (see Chapter 4). As a result, railroads found themselves hauling ever-larger shares of low-value bulk traffic, and ever-smaller shares of high-value goods. This situation thoroughly diminished their ability to finance large rail networks or any other major claim on cash flows, such as modernized passenger service. Complex rate structures also made it difficult for railroads to use pricing to eliminate excess capacity.[23]

The system encouraged—in fact depended on—collective discussion and agreement among the railroads on the structural classifications and rates in the tables published by freight rate bureaus. Railroad rate officials would gather secretly at the offices of their facilitating agency—the rate bureau for a region such as Official Territory or Pocahontas District. Individual railroads would suggest revisions in a selected rate or group of rates. After discussion, the proposal would then be put to a secret up-or-down vote by means of an electric button located under the conference table. Until reforms were made in the Railroad Revitalization and Regulatory Reform (4R) Act of 1976, anyone in the room could vote, no questions asked. (Later, voting was restricted to only railroads participating in the movement, as in the case of an interline rate.) Notes were kept but not publicly released. The rate bureau staff members would then compile and publish the revised rate in a rate table or schedule of tariffs, and it would be approved (usually) by the ICC.

This type of collusion in setting rates is what cartels do in illegal cabals. What were the secret rate bureaus doing in a rate-making system sponsored by the rather moralistic Progressives? And how could such a system be seen as truly serving the public interest? Without being too flippant, the answer is that the VOS system was serving the interests of the sitting politicians' most powerful constituents, and if they demanded rail rate regulation—reining in of railroads' "monopoly abuses"—there really wasn't any practical way to do so other than voting in rate bureaus. The secrecy, however, and the fact that railroads not participating in a movement could vote anyway, was really over the top and should not have been allowed.

Another key difficulty with this system was its aim of avoiding the appearance of discrimination by homogenizing broad categories of products and services. The classical regulatory structure has little room to accommodate subtle market and logistical differences, such as the reliability of a railroad's service, regional differences in the cost of producing goods, public subsidy of rival modes, annual maximum or minimum volume commitments (as today are routinely included in rate and service contracts between carriers and shippers), or even a railroad's provision of freight cars with custom features. The ICC effectively ruled out negotiations between shippers and carriers to charge different rates for services that appeared to be similar, as such agreements which would have seemed discriminatory to the Commission. This prohibition lasted until the fourth quarter of the twentieth century, when finally distinctions could be drawn between rate differentiation (useful) and rate discrimination (unfair). (See Box 2.2 for discussion of the key concept of Ramsey pricing, which relies on this distinction.)

Box 2.2   Ramsey Pricing: The Economist's Gold Standard.

A well-known theorem in economics holds that the losses created by deviating from marginal cost pricing are minimized if prices are differentially marked up inversely to demand elasticities for different products or groups of customers. In other words, the highest markups over marginal cost should be charged to those with little or no price elasticity of demand, while those with a high sensitivity to price (a high elasticity of demand) should be charged a low markup.

(continued)

Box 2.2 Continued

As a consequence, overhead, fixed, and other costs excluded from marginal cost would be recovered proportionally more in the prices charged to those with inelastic demands than from the prices charged to those with elastic demands. The inverse-elasticity pricing strategy just described has come to be known as Ramsey pricing after the British economist Frank P. Ramsey. Inverse-elasticity pricing met the full revenue need (assuming that it was not capped out prematurely due to unit elasticities), but at the same time it modified the efficiency objectives of marginal cost pricing and its related consumption pattern only minimally. In short, it was a differential pricing scheme that made users pay for the full costs of their indulgence, long and short term, while minimizing the welfare loss from abandonment of marginal cost pricing.

Most important, Ramsey pricing permits total costs to be recouped with minimal departure from the consumption patterns that would have occurred if prices (marginal revenues [MR]) had been uniformly set at the socially optimal level—equated with marginal costs (MC). In this manner, it minimizes the loss in social welfare created by any deviation from marginal cost pricing. It follows that output is not restricted as a pure monopolist would, and the producer does not go bankrupt as the firm might if it were restricted to charging only prices equal to marginal costs.

The built-in pricing rigidity of the classified rate tables, and the ICC's misguided desire on behalf of congressional sponsors to continue cross-subsidizing favored constituencies, meant that railroads could not readily adjust to the competitive economics forced on them by the rise of motor carriers. And before the computer age, how could the ICC, or even the regionally specialized rate bureaus charged with setting and maintaining the VOS rate classification tables, keep up with all the detail?

VOS rate making also relied on shippers to identify manufactured products under a sort of honor system, with railroads' main defense being periodic sample audits. It was rumored that some rail users were not fully honest, sometimes claiming to be shipping a lower-rated product than actually was the case.[24]

Railroads and shippers employed thousands of rate clerks to administer this system. In fact, before the IRS and the income tax, rail rate classification was probably the biggest single source of nonretail white-collar employment in the economy. Few of these clerks or their supervisors claimed that they fully understood the rate structure.[25]

Note that, in this context, VOS rate making, like the yield management practiced by airlines today, was more about revenue than costs, although they were considered together. For example, empire builder James J. Hill said in an interview with Frank L. McVey at the turn of the twentieth century "that railroad income is based on ton miles and the expense of operation on train miles. The object is to get the highest rate [operating revenue] on the ton-mile and the smallest rate [operating expense] on the train mile. In this statement is concentrated the theory of railroad management of the present day."[26] (See the Ten Principles of Transportation Economics in Box 2.3, which is the authors' more extended version of a theory of transportation economics and management such as James J. Hill had formulated.)

VOS and the Valuation Studies

Ironically, the "value" in VOS had almost nothing to do with a railroad's rate of return on the assets it had employed in delivering transportation—despite a clear statutory mandate for the ICC to establish "just and reasonable" rates, and the Supreme Court's landmark ruling in *Smyth v. Ames* (1898) that a regulated entity was entitled to earn a fair return on the value of property used in the service. Unrelated to VOS ratemaking, the ICC was required under the Valuation Act of 1913 to make detailed property valuation studies to determine if railroads were earning too much or too little income compared with the value of their assets. These valuation studies were to be a detailed accounting of all railroad property, its original cost and the cost of reproduction-new (in 1914), less depreciation. The railroads furnished maps, lists, engineers' reports, and more. Field work involved thousands of individuals over the period from 1915 to 1919, but the ICC's work continued until its final valuation report, in 1934. Besides taking twenty years and totaling 1,046 reports in all, the valuation studies were estimated to have cost hundreds of millions of then-current dollars. It was a reason to ridicule the ICC, as critics were quick to do.[27]

In the end, the valuation studies concluded that the railroads were not overcapitalized at all. As reported by Lynn Farrar in the *Encyclopedia of North American Railroads*, at the time of the ICC studies, the value of US railroads for rate-making purposes was $16.2 billion, while total railway capital in the hands of the public was $16.3 billion, a trivial difference. All of the acrimony over alleged watering of property accounts, including accusations by the ICC itself, was shown by the ICC's own studies to be misplaced. The valuation studies ended not with a bang but a whimper.[28]

Box 2.3   Ten Principles of Transportation Economics.

The relationships of underlying economic principles and historical developments to each other and to government transport policy over the course of the twentieth century may not always be intuitively obvious, so we have drawn the needed road map. We are transport economists with academic and industry backgrounds, so our views may occasionally need some clarification, starting with our Ten Principles of Transportation Economics:

1. *Transportation creates value by increasing the time and place utility of goods or personal location.* Implicitly, different geographic places have different comparative advantages (see Principle 2 below), and it follows that moving goods from one location to another associates them with the comparative value of the new location. For people (travelers, passengers), the same principle applies: If you would rather be elsewhere, going there may be costly (the price of a ticket, the time and risk of travel), but when you arrive (at some later time), you realize the advertised advantages of the new location. Time utility is important as well as place utility. There is a comparative advantage for goods or people being where they are demanded at the right time. Too early may be costly because of the time value of money; postponement of an expenditure saves cash costs in the current period, and that is why interest must be paid on borrowed money. Too late may be very costly: You may miss the train.

2. *The demand for transportation is derived.* The demand for freight transportation arises from the desire to have goods in a different location from where they were previously. Goods are transported because someone wants them more where they will be than where they were. The economic principle of comparative advantage says that a producer at one location or time may create a good, but, all other things being equal (*ceteris paribus*), someone else at another time or location may be able to do so relatively more inexpensively— that is, with less opportunity cost. Thus, Washington State is good in producing apples, and Honduras grows and exports bananas. These principles

Box 2.3   *Continued*

underlie the value of foreign or inter-regional trade and give rise to the demand for transporting goods from one place to another. Passenger travel demand is not so clear-cut because passengers may wish to travel for the pure delight of the trip. Business travel demand may be derived from the value of being at a meeting in another city; personal travel may have intrinsic value beyond getting there.

3. *Transportation is a service industry.* In general, transportation is supplied on demand and is costly or impossible to store. Goods can be moved in advance of their need, but if so, they must be kept in inventory at the new location. That requires a storage facility of some kind, protection, security, and perhaps climate control. And, of course, there is the time value of the cash flow or the holding cost to the owner of the goods while they are in storage awaiting use. For valuable goods (and busy people), these inventory holding costs can exceed the cost of transportation. Users of transportation services therefore place high value on receiving shipments on time.

   The principle of postponement says that the shipper, in order to save these inventory holding costs, should delay a request for transportation until the goods are really needed at the new location—as long as the shipper can be certain they will arrive on time. The transportation service that is reliable in this sense is valuable to the shipper and may command a premium price. Indeed, the reliability of service may be of more value to the shipper than a speedier transit time *per se.* Just-in-time is the inbound logistics strategy that relies on transportation services so precise as to have factory inputs arrive not only on time, but just before the assembly line is ready to gobble them up.

4. *In transportation, performance (output) rules input requirements.* To the shipper, the regulator, the securities investor, even the historian, outcomes are more important than inputs. We usually want to know not how many hours were expended in the making, but how precious is the product. In transportation, it is *interesting* to know what the input requirements are, but it is *important* to know how the resulting service measures up in terms of its utility (value) in the market. When we look at safety, we should not be as concerned about rules or even methods intended to improve safety, but how good was the safety performance.

5. *Transportation abides by Newtonian physics.* Once goods or people are to be moved, all the laws of physics apply: $F = M * A$. Although information

(continued)

Box 2.3   *Continued*

substitution for transportation is becoming increasingly important, we have no tele-transporters or time-machines.

Newton's first and second laws say that objects in motion tend to remain that way until acted upon by an outside force, which means that brakes or friction must be applied or there will be a "train wreck." Accelerating large masses takes energy and creates momentum. Energy efficiency and safety are critically important issues in the economics and public policy of transportation.

6. *Technology, along with capital investment and education, improves productivity.* Productivity is defined as outputs divided by inputs. Technology comes from hardware, software, and human intelligence and training, which one expert calls *wet-ware*. Capital improvements (hardware) embody technological progress over time; technology is mainly diffused or deployed over time by being incorporated in new products and thence in new capital expenditures, which is why deployment often occurs over long periods and in cycles. New equipment will not replace old unless the capital cost (less salvage) yields lower operating costs over time, discounted to reflect the time value of money (an interest rate).

   Transportation studies often focus on operating expenses such as fuel or labor costs, and capital expenditures. New technology purchased with capital spending typically presents opportunities to substitute capital for purchases of fuel or labor (making the business more capital-intensive and less fuel or labor-intensive). New technology thus may shift the nature and mix of environmental impacts and human resources required for or resulting from transportation operations. Opportunities to deploy new technology may be affected greatly by economies of scale or economies of density in the provision of transportation services.

7. Because transportation demand is derived, *economic development leads transportation investment.* Now this is not always true, so it is not really a principle but an hypothesis—and it turns out to be more true, historically, in Europe than in the Americas. Railroad development in the British Isles, for example, occurred long after cities had been built, coal had started being mined to fuel the Industrial Revolution, international trade lanes had grown up, and so on. Railroad technology, starting in Wales and England, had the benefit of established markets, but it had to prove itself in competition with well-developed systems of coastwise shipping, canals, and wagon roads. This

---

Box 2.3 Continued

---

was a straightforward competition of the new technology against the old. Was it faster, safer, more reliable, cheaper, better? In theory, there was little public benefit to subsidy of the new mode of transportation in this setting.

8. Because of the premium that Americans place on economic growth, *transportation investment leads development.* (It did not in the example given in number 7, but it might in other circumstances.) Indeed, the general historical model for the New World, in particular in Canada and the United States, was that transportation investment was used as an important engine of economic development and therefore might warrant subsidy. Roads and canals often were built with public funds to spur regional development, and tolls were collected from users to repay the initial investment. Railroads were constructed, first with sponsorship of cities and states wanting to develop their commercial hinterland or their position at the gates of national and international trade, then later with issuance of public land grants intended to develop new territories and transcontinental linkages. Public subsidy is an intervention in markets and therefore risks making the modal playing field uneven, but it may yield public benefits exceeding its cost.

9. *Transportation sometimes exhibits characteristics of a natural monopoly.* Because of favorable siting (what the real estate promoter calls location, location, location) or because of special proprietary advantages, but most notably because of economies of density and scale, transportation businesses sometimes are natural monopolies (Box 2.1). Our thinking is that the natural monopoly characterization of railroads has been overdone historically. While almost every producer has an element of natural monopoly in local markets, railroads are subject to substantial competition from each other, from competing modes, from substitute products, or from competitive geographic origins they do not serve. These conditions sharply limit the circumstances in which rate regulation would serve the public interest.

10. *Modern transportation has changed the nature of war—and peace.* Transportation vehicles have become weapons of war and terrorism, as we know only too well from the atrocities of September 11, 2001. But ever since humankind domesticated horses and elephants, they were used in warfare no less than agriculture, mining, forestry or commerce. Indeed, the modern discipline of logistics has its origins in the science of supplying war personnel and materièl to the point and at the time it was needed for the successful conduct

(continued)

Box 2.3 *Continued*

of a battle campaign. And for want of a nail, a shoe was lost, then the rider, the battle, the war, and perhaps a nation. All science, and most (but far from all) technology, is value-neutral, meaning that its advance is good in and of itself, while its use may benefit humankind or not—depending on our wisdom and goodwill. Transportation is no different than most other human inventions in this regard. The thing itself is not supreme, but rather the use we make of it.

Concluding Thoughts

It is a bit of a mystery why Populist constituencies such as farmers and small towns were so reluctant to allow railroads to earn what were later called adequate profits. These were simply returns sufficient to cover not only immediate cross subsidies, but also to maintain and improve rail facilities—that is, to keep presumably unprofitable branch lines open for the public's "convenience and necessity."

The problem with the VOS rate system developed by the Progressives was not that their system was demand-based, but that it was rigid. It could not recognize or accommodate the rise of rival modes, and it did not allow railroads the flexibility to meet local market imperatives. The classification tables might have originated from a basis of charging what the traffic would bear, but they had become ossified and so no longer reflected actual market circumstances. The Progressives wanted a system with surpluses over cost, but without differentiation, and thus without freedom to meet let alone undercut prices charged by competitors.

Cartels were at the opposite end of any possible public acceptability. Something more obscure, more democratic sounding, and less obviously pro–big business was needed. In designing the VOS system, the ICC and its acolytes were up to the challenge. Their intervention was clever but nefarious. It sounded simple but was filled with hidden complexity. Under these circumstances, value-of-service rate making could not possibly reflect the true value of rail service provided to shippers. Expert panels repeatedly pointed out that rate regulation was not sustainable in these circumstances—that it would drive traffic away from the railroads. Shippers forced to pay what seemed to them excessively high rates would eventually find alternatives. And because the ICC was still trying to prop up lines that should have been abandoned and services that should have been discontinued, railroads were being forced to dig their own graves.

No US industry was regulated more closely and for a longer period of time than railroads. Clumsy regulation, profound shifts in the composition of the US economy clearly adverse to railroads, and the remarkable rise of new modal challengers to rail dominance—were the three factors principally to blame for the decline and near-demise of railroads in the first three-quarters of the twentieth century.

3

THE POLICY DILEMMA OF COMPETITION
AND CONSOLIDATION

Where consolidation is possible, competition is impossible.

—Attributed to ROBERT STEPHENSON, ca. 1854

Curiously, deregulation is attacked as producing too much competition—"chaos" and "jungle" are words often used—and as producing, at the same time, too little competition—the shippers and the public will be "victimized" by rail monopolies . . .

—ALEXANDER L. MORTON (1975)

In every decade of the first half of the twentieth century, it seemed, something was always amiss with the capacity of the US railroad industry or the size of its constituent firms. This was the era of government intervention in the affairs of business, and politicians seemed never to be happy about the performance of railroads—still the dominant means of surface transportation in the United States. In the previous century, railroads had been constructed to within a short distance of nearly every arable acre on the continent, and over nearly every passable transcontinental route to the Pacific Ocean. Railroad technology had surpassed all rivals and seemed capable of serving all of the nation's commerce and every national emergency—assuming relationships with customers, communities, and government regulators could be made right. But politicians were unsatisfied.

Railroads were the first industry to feel the sting of government regulation aimed at the very premise of their business organizational forms and managerial prerogatives. Because they were "the nation's first big business," the railroads had been forced into a pioneering role on many public policy issues involving business and government interactions. This might be called the revenge of the Populists—payback for railroad managers' misbehavior over the previous three or four decades. As we saw in the previous chapter, Progressive Era legislation required publication of railroad tariffs in interstate commerce, nondiscriminatory application of these rates among persons and places, and control of both maximum and minimum fares or rate levels so that they were "just and reasonable," as determined by the Interstate Commerce Commission (ICC).

Only three years after passage of the Act to Regulate Commerce in 1887, Congress tried again with the Sherman Antitrust Act of 1890 to attack many of these same political concerns with a much different approach and from a much broader platform. Now the fires of reform were fed not by Granger activists protecting local movements of grain to market, but by journalists pointing out widespread abuses of the public trust by greedy "monopolists" cornering industry output or financial securities, and taking appalling shortcuts with respect to broad social concerns such as worker safety, child labor, and food purity.

The politicians' desires to accomplish two goals came together precisely at the turn of the twentieth century. These goals were (1) to regulate rates charged by the powerful railroads, and (2) to prevent further "monopolization" of markets through combinations, pooling of financial interests, or trade restraints. Until new laws strengthening rate regulation were passed in the first years of the new century (1903, 1906, and 1910), however, the ICC was not respected as a regulator of rates. Moreover, the question of whether the federal government had the right or means to intervene in rail consolidations had not been conclusively established; at the time, the only federal authority over business consolidations was via enforcement of the Sherman Antitrust Act.

This chapter of *American Railroads* focuses on three key developments in the organization of the US railroad industry and its relationship to the federal government in the first half of the twentieth century, and is divided into three parts: (I) antitrust dissolution of the Hill and Harriman empires (a lasting impact), (II) federal control of railroads during World War I (a short-lived episode with lasting lessons learned), and (III) the extraordinary but stunningly unsuccessful efforts to plan consolidation into a limited number of large and financially balanced systems under the Transportation Act of 1920 legislation mandating consolidation of the industry into a smaller number of firms. This was a naïve episode undermined by misguided efforts to preserve lines with little financial viability. The effort was eventually disbanded and railroad consolidations were returned to private initiatives under relaxed merger standards enacted in 1940.

In sum, the period of greatest federal intervention in the operation of any private American industry (with the possible exceptions of farm policy since the Great Depression, and nuclear power generation after World War II), produced very little permanent change in the industry's competitive structure. Before the end of the twentieth century, the Hill and Harriman empires were restored to forms eerily similar to those that Teddy Roosevelt and the Supreme Court had dissolved before World War I. Indeed, the surviving railroad industry was transformed by mergers into only four giant US railroads (plus two in Canada, the midsize Kansas City Southern, and numerous smaller regional and short line railroads)—all consolidated on an *ad hoc*, case-by-case basis in regulatory proceedings but without even the semblance of a federal plan and with very little national policy guidance.

This chapter is a companion to the previous chapter on rate regulation because regulatory agencies—the Interstate Commerce Commission (ICC) before 1996, and the Surface Transportation Board (STB) afterward—controlled both railroad rate making and mergers. These two regulatory powers both reflected the traditional but misleading view of railroads as natural monopolies, and both forms of control have exerted powerful influences on the economic and financial performance of the industry for the last 100 years.

Coauthor John R. Meyer captured the essence of the dilemma of competition and consolidation in railroad mergers in his testimony before the Kefauver Committee in 1962:

> Intelligent public policy formulation requires adoption of a longer run and broader perspective and consideration of objectives that normally play little role in private deliberations. In particular, deciding on an appropriate public policy with respect to transportation mergers requires that some assumptions . . . be made about the role:
> (a) That competition should play or not play as a regulator of transportation markets; and
> (b) That private enterprise is expected to perform in meeting transportation requirements.

In essence, decisions must be made about what is ultimately desired in the relationship between the transportation industry and Government and what is a desirable organization of transportation markets.[1]

Initial Government Policy Toward Rail Combinations (1900–1913): Teddy Roosevelt and the Northern Securities and Union Pacific Antitrust Cases

By the end of the nineteenth century, American free-market capitalism had erected powerful combinations of ownership and interlocking corporate directorships in railroads, meatpacking, steelmaking, tobacco, petroleum extraction, and oil refining and retail distribution. These business combinations were on a collision course with reform movements championed by Populist elected officials and the journalist/novelists muckrakers— Ida Tarbell, Upton Sinclair, and Frank Norris, among others. (See Figure 3.1. The frequent conflict of reckless tycoons and scolding cartoons was a hallmark of the Progressive era.)

At about this same time, Progressive Republicans led by President Teddy Roosevelt held somewhat contradictory goals: They were both pro-business and interested in establishing their credentials as reformers. Their chosen path of leadership for the emerging Progressive reform movement was to position themselves as champion trust busters. Then as now the central pillar of antitrust law was the prohibition in Section 1 of the act of "every contract, combination . . . or conspiracy . . . in restraint of trade," and Section 2's forbidding of "monopolization or attempts to monopolize any line of commerce."[2] Long before the Sherman Act, contracts in restraint of trade (and practices such as price fixing) had been contrary to common law, but these contracts were not legally enforceable, nor were violators subject to sanctions.[3]

As it happened, the first and best opportunity to pursue enforcement action against one of the unpopular trusts under the Sherman Act was the Northern Securities case.[4] This action was brought in 1903 against James J. Hill's scheme to pool and expand two transcontinental railroad ownerships—his fabled Great Northern (GN) railway and the parallel Northern Pacific (NP). Tracks of both GN and NP stretched from their eastern terminus at St. Paul all the way west to the Puget Sound and Portland, Oregon (see Map 3.1). Hill and his associates had been eyeing acquisition of a direct rail connection with Chicago for many years, and the property

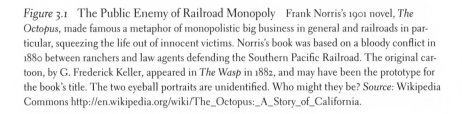

Figure 3.1 The Public Enemy of Railroad Monopoly Frank Norris's 1901 novel, *The Octopus,* made famous a metaphor of monopolistic big business in general and railroads in particular, squeezing the life out of innocent victims. Norris's book was based on a bloody conflict in 1880 between ranchers and law agents defending the Southern Pacific Railroad. The original cartoon, by G. Frederick Keller, appeared in *The Wasp* in 1882, and may have been the prototype for the book's title. The two eyeball portraits are unidentified. Who might they be? *Source:* Wikipedia Commons http://en.wikipedia.org/wiki/The_Octopus:_A_Story_of_California.

THE CURSE OF CALIFORNIA.

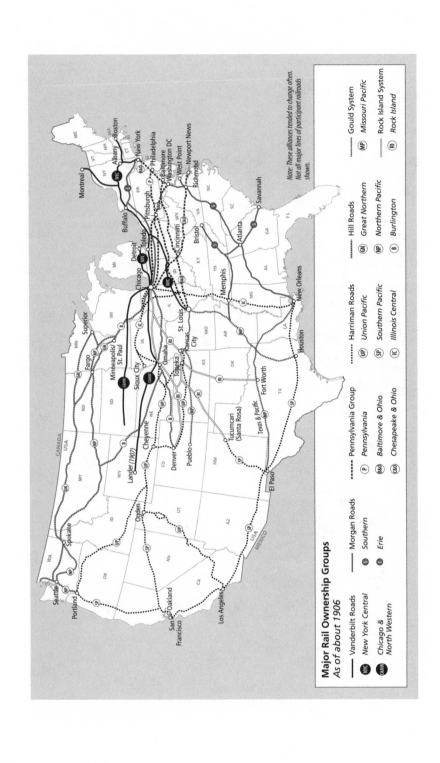

Major Rail Ownership Groups
As of about 1906

Vanderbilt Roads
— New York Central
🔘 **NYC**
Ⓒ Chicago &
Ⓝ North Western

Morgan Roads
— Southern
Ⓢ Southern
Ⓔ Erie

Pennsylvania Group
····· Pennsylvania
Ⓟ Pennsylvania
Ⓑ Baltimore & Ohio
Ⓒ Chesapeake & Ohio

Harriman Roads
······ Union Pacific
Ⓤ Union Pacific
Ⓢ Southern Pacific
Ⓘ Illinois Central

Hill Roads
——— Great Northern
Ⓖ Great Northern
Ⓝ Northern Pacific
Ⓑ Burlington

Gould System
······ Missouri Pacific
Ⓜ Missouri Pacific

Rock Island System
— Rock Island
Ⓡ Rock Island

Note: These alliances tended to change often. Not all major lines of participant railroads shown.

Map 3.1   Major Rail Ownership Groups, Early Twentieth Century   At the turn of the twentieth century, seven ownership groups controlled the nation's most important railroad networks. Of these, the James J. Hill and the E. H. Harriman "empires" were most vulnerable to political attack and to dissolution under the Sherman Antitrust Act of 1890. Hill's Northern Lines and Harriman's Union Pacific (UP) and Southern Pacific (SP) groups, dissolved in 1904 and 1912/1913, respectively, reemerged much later in the twentieth century. The alliances shown on Map 3.1 were highly changeable. For example, the Pennsylvania Railroad (PRR) gave up its ownership of Baltimore & Ohio (B&O), Chesapeake & Ohio, (C&O), and Norfolk & Western (N&W) beginning in 1906, but reacquired N&W stock in 1909. *Source:* John Stover and Routledge *Historical Atlas*, (with authors' modifications.

that made their mouths water most was the Chicago, Burlington & Quincy (CB&Q)—called the Burlington or just the Q. Burlington was a solid performer financially and provided excellent routes to Omaha, Denver, Kansas City, St. Louis, and the Ohio River as well as Chicago. James J. Hill, the clear leader of the Northern Securities group, supported by the well-known (one writer called him omnipresent) banker J. P. Morgan, began to acquire CB&Q shares.

Busting up Northern Securities gave President Roosevelt something to occupy his considerable talents, otherwise underemployed because of the relative peacefulness and sense of well-being that characterized the end of the Victorian and start of the Edwardian eras.[5]

The Back Story for Northern Securities

According to long-ago transportation authority and ICC commissioner Balthazar H. Meyer, the idea for a holding company to manage the railroad ownership interests of Hill and his associates had originated in 1901 with a small group of Great Northern railroad shareholders. Some of the GN owners lived abroad and several were becoming aged; they wanted a more permanent arrangement for coordinated operation of their railroads—one that would pass muster under US law, which was still unclear and confused a decade after passage of the Sherman Antitrust Act and two decades before the ICC was empowered to review and approve proposed transportation mergers. A small, close corporation had been suggested as a vessel in which to deposit their holdings in GN and CB&Q, but that change violated GN's shareholders equality principle, so they sought another avenue. While the Sherman Antitrust Act had pretty much ended the practice of forming trusts to hold in common ownership the stock interests of firms that otherwise would be competitors, the state legislature of New Jersey came to the aid of big business by passing a law in 1897 that legalized holding companies and did away with the need for voting trusts.[6]

Taking advantage of the serendipitous New Jersey legislation, on November 12, 1901, the Hill associates (joined by J. P. Morgan) formed a holding company with a capitalization of $400 million called the Northern Securities Co. Once Northern Securities had been created, why not allow Northern Pacific shareholders in as well? At least that is the way Hill described the origins of the holding company—it had all the earmarks of a gentleman's club of the day.

Then in the fall or early winter of 1900–1901 and to the great surprise of Hill interests came another buyer of outstanding Burlington shares, one believed to be associated with the Union Pacific. That discovery galvanized the founders of Northern Securities to quicken their efforts to prevent anyone else from gaining control of their target. It turned out that in March 1901, E. H. Harriman and Jacob H. Schiff (an investment banker with the firm of Kuhn, Loeb & Co.) acting either for themselves or on behalf of Union Pacific, asked Hill and others for a one-half interest in the final purchase of the Burlington, but their request was rebuffed. A month later, Hill's group completed their purchase of outstanding CB&Q shares for $108 million, so Burlington was now owned 50–50 by Great Northern and Northern Pacific.

Harriman and Schiff were not finished, however. Their next move was to go after ownership of Northern Pacific, controlled by Hill through his interest in the Northern Securities Co., and in this manner gain access to NP's one-half interest in the Burlington. A scramble to corner NP securities ensued. Harriman and other Union Pacific interests were able to acquire $78 million of the $155 million outstanding capital stock (50 percent) of Northern Pacific common shares in the spring of 1901.[7]

While the outside world relished this clash of titans, the contest had drawn nearly to a standstill: UP interests seemed to have enough shares to win control of NP, but before Northern Pacific's annual meeting in October 1901, its directors could change the outcome by retiring UP's preferred shares. Both common and preferred stock were listed at just over $100 in April, but common stock (which could vote to retire the preferred shares Harriman held) rose to $180 on May 8. Lured by the high prices, even Hill allies sold off some shares. Meanwhile speculators shorted NP stock, betting they could repay obligations with cheaper shares. But that did not happen. Northern Pacific stock continued to climb to over $700, and a few shares apparently traded at $1,000. "The markets of the world were convulsed, the equilibrium of the financial world shaken, and many speculative interests [were] in a critical condition."[8]

On May 9, 1901, further disaster was averted by an agreement between Schiff and the House of Morgan to settle with the "shorts" for $150 per share of Northern Pacific. A Harriman biographer says that the crisis was not caused by him, but by Hill and Morgan's counteraction—specifically the purchase of 150,000 NP shares on May 6 and 7. Harriman thought he had purchased enough shares to gain outright control of NP and to protect his preferred shares—thus also winning the battle for CB&Q—but he learned on Monday that his weekend order for additional shares to secure his position had been countermanded by Schiff. "This turned out to be a significant error: those 40,000 shares were the missing nail that cost Harriman this particular kingdom."[9]

Conciliated by events, peace was proclaimed publicly on June 1, 1901, when Hill and Harriman agreed to joint ownership of the Burlington through Northern Securities. E. H. Harriman and one other Union Pacific director joined the boards of Northern Pacific and Burlington, while composition of the remainder of the NP board was left to J. P. Morgan. "Had this battle been fought to the last ditch and the Union Pacific interests triumphed," says Balthazar H. Meyer, "the measure of injury done to the Great Northern and Northern Pacific would have been destruction . . . unless they had all gone into a single consolidation."[10]

Resolution of Harriman's bold run at control of the Northern Pacific was reached only when Hill finally granted UP access to Seattle on a paired track arrangement, one that survives to this day between the two great rivals—BNSF Railway (since 2005 the official name of the former Burlington Northern Santa Fe Railway, and the surviving descendant of GN, NP, and CB&Q) and Union Pacific. Other arrangements were made to end warfare over construction of dual routes up either side of the Deschutes River canyon to Bend, Oregon, which probably was not feasible. The two titans were in effect carving up the western rail domain into "communities of interest," a label that resonated better than "monopoly" or "trust." With the compromise, between them Hill and Harriman had secured control of the best transcontinental properties.[11]

Still, the final word on Northern Securities came from President Theodore Roosevelt and the US Supreme Court. According to Balthazar Meyer, "[It had] been persistently denied that the desire to restrain competition among the constituent companies had anything to do with the organization of the Northern Securities Company." There were plenty of grains of salt in that statement, however, and President Roosevelt wasn't buying it. The Supreme Court agreed, and in a five-to-four decision declared Northern Securities illegal on grounds it would reduce needed competition.[12] Most observers had not anticipated the progovernment decision dissolving Northern Securities and Hill's control of the three major railroads it owned, but soon the decision was widely regarded as a victory for President Theodore Roosevelt's trust-busting policies.

The Rise and Fall of the Harriman Empire

In the same battleground and bellwether year of 1901, Edward H. Harriman had thrown his small and sickly frame but enormous intelligence and energy (not to say considerable profits from the rising prices of his Northern Pacific and Burlington stocks) into acquisition for Union Pacific of the Southern Pacific Railroad (SP). Unlike Hill's Northern Securities Co., the UP+SP combination was not a pooling of separate ownerships, but instead the building of a single common ownership interest obtained through stock purchases.

E. H. Harriman originally become interested in the Illinois Central Railroad (IC) through his friend Stuyvesant Fish (son of Hamilton Fish, who was secretary of state for President U. S. Grant), and in about 1881 began to buy its stock. By 1883, the thirty-five-year-old Harriman had become a vice president for finance and gained election to Illinois Central's Board. Continuing to acquire IC stock, by 1890 he had become a dominant power in the company. After resigning his vice presidency in 1891 to pursue broader activities in the industry, Harriman remained active in the company's financial affairs through his corporate board directorship.[13]

A severe depression hit America's railroads in 1893, and one of the victims was the storied Union Pacific—already weakened by the Crédit Mobilier scandal, poor annual earnings, and indebtedness related to construction of its Oregon Railway & Navigation Company to connect the transcontinental line in Utah with the Pacific Northwest. Multiple efforts were made by the company and its bankers to restructure its debt, but Congress refused to refinance a portion of the second mortgage held by the US government. These efforts all failed, and the government ordered foreclosure of UP's mainline in November, 1897. A foreclosure sale then netted $81.5 million; the purchaser turned out to be, yes, E. H. Harriman.[14]

Harriman later acknowledged to J. P. Morgan and Jacob Schiff that—motivated by his desire to reorganize Union Pacific's finances himself—Harriman had caused some of the refinancing difficulties in 1897. Indeed, Harriman may have intended from the outset to combine his substantial ownership of Illinois Central with Union Pacific. In any event, reorganization of the new Union Pacific Company was completed by the end of 1897, and Harriman was made a director.

Union Pacific had fallen into miserable physical condition, but Harriman was a visionary and a genius in rebuilding railroad infrastructure.

Astoundingly, by May 1898 he had become chairman of UP's executive committee, and by December 1898, chairman of the board. On the basis of extensive inspection trips and incisive reports to his colleagues, Harriman had received authority to begin reconstructing key lines—which he did by following his mantra that railroads had to spend money to make money. Soon, Union Pacific was poised to reassemble nearly 6,000 miles of important lines it had lost in the reorganization. These included the Oregon Short Line, and finally in 1906, the St. Joseph & Grand Island, the line now connecting the original Platte River transcontinental route to Kansas City.[15]

Harriman had succeeded in combining his controlling interests in Union Pacific and Southern Pacific in 1901. Perhaps he had pursued the UP+SP consolidation in order to complete the grand design of the Pacific Rail Act signed by President Lincoln in 1862—namely, a continuous overland transcontinental railroad line constructed west from Omaha and east from Sacramento.[16] Even if that is so, Harriman's vision was much larger. By 1901, Southern Pacific—with its subsidiary Central Pacific (CenPac)—the original transcontinental link to Union Pacific over Ogden, Utah—had built itself south to Los Angeles and east along the so-called Sunset Route to El Paso and New Orleans.[17] Still, UP and SP (with its CenPac subsidiary) were only loosely competitive; the two systems met only at their extremes (Ogden, Portland, and Los Angeles). By contrast, Hill's Great Northern and Northern Pacific railroads served many common points and even shared a headquarters building in St. Paul.[18]

After the Supreme Court's decision in Northern Securities, it was almost inevitable that the Roosevelt and Taft administrations would go after Harriman and the UP+SP consolidation. A suit for dissolution was brought in 1907, attacking the combination as a restraint of trade forbidden by the Sherman Antitrust Act. Union Pacific defended the case on two grounds, namely, that UP and SP were only tangentially competitive, and that the acquisition was made by stock purchases, not a contract or pooling agreement. Initially the case did not go well for the attorney general, and in June 1911 the federal circuit court ruled two to one that UP and SP were just connecting roads and only "incidentally" competing.[19] Appeal was made to the US Supreme Court, but in 1912 it overruled the circuit court and dissolved the Harriman consolidations effective in 1913.[20]

The Impact of the Hill and Harriman Antitrust Cases and Teddy Roosevelt
Objectively, Northern Securities was more anti-competitive than
Harriman's Union Pacific–Southern Pacific–Illinois Central combination
because it left no competitor railway between the Dakotas and Washington
State (until the Milwaukee Road's Pacific Extension was completed in
1909—and even then Milwaukee was a weak market entry). Yet it is
remarkable how little the actual competitive circumstances of these cases
mattered in people's minds compared with the metaphor of an octopus
enveloping and victimizing the public (See Figure 3.1), a cartoon image
labeled "Railroad Monopoly" and captioned "The Curse of California,"
no doubt targeting SP.[21]

There will always be admirers and detractors of both Hill and Harriman,
their consolidation proposals, and their legacies. To this day, employees of
BNSF Railway admire Hill's strategic vision and operating and financial
discipline, while Union Pacific railroad people revere Harriman's belief in
reinvestment in track and structure improvements. With the hindsight of
100 years, we know that Teddy Roosevelt's attacks on the Hill and Harriman
empires were eventually reversed: The ICC approved the Burlington
Northern merger in 1970, and the UP+SP merger in 1996. As those transactions were moving toward approval, much was made of the historical
antecedents and how these mergers were just putting things back the way
they might have been all along.

The authors of this book have long believed that Great Northern should
have been allowed to keep its prized Burlington line, while Northern
Pacific should have been encouraged and permitted to combine instead
with the Milwaukee Road to connect along its well-engineered line from
St. Paul to Chicago, as well as to avoid construction of Milwaukee's redundant Pacific Extension. Even accepting the dissolution of Northern Securities and UP+SP, there really ought to have been found some way to allow
Union Pacific to hold on to the Central Pacific's transcontinental link
between Ogden, Utah, and Sacramento. Maybe only a few small things
tilting in the other direction would have made such results possible.[22]

Northern Securities was a classic parallel merger, before that term was
known to the literature of railroad consolidations. Its anti-competitive implications were too great to be ignored in an era of trust busting that broke up
John D. Rockefeller's Standard Oil Co.[23] Antitrust enforcement was shown

then and since, however, to be a blunt instrument of national competitive policy—both because of the impact of precedent on subsequent antitrust cases (often not with circumstances so similar in reality as perceived in the public mind) and because of alternative industry organizations that case-by-case Sherman or Clayton Act adjudications have difficulty addressing. In the case of Northern Securities, breakup of the Hill empire because of the possibility of monopolization more than the fact of it meant Harriman's system would meet the same fate, even though the government was hard-pressed to demonstrate it was an anticompetitive monopoly or that monopolization (if such it was) had serious negative consequences for society.

Had the ICC been given merger review authority comparable to its rate-making powers in the first decade of the twentieth Century, it might have found less draconian solutions than yielded by the railroad antitrust cases. With ICC review and prodding for mitigating pro-competitive adjustments, Harriman's UP+SP+IC combination would not have been seen as so threatening in consumation (nor would it appear to have been treated more favorably than Northern Lines if it the government did not force its dissolution.) Competitive facts should have made a difference. In short, the Teddy Roosevelt administration would have had ample public justification to say that railroads are regulated by the ICC and so do not need to be treated specially under antitrust rules.

Another consequence of Northern Securities and *United States v. Union Pacific*, perhaps, is that these cases may have predisposed the ICC to rule against the railroads with respect to needed general rate increases subsequent to passage of the Mann-Elkins Act of 1910. The initial contest in this series of cases was one in which the railroads were soundly "out-lawyered" by Louis Brandeis and his challenge that railroads had not shown that rate increases were warranted—and that instead, the industry should improve its efficiency by following the principles of scientific management. In fact, the ICC consistently refused to approve the railroads' requests for rate increases between 1910 and 1917, resulting in substantial revenue deficiencies and deterioration of industry hauling capacity in the critical years leading up to mobilization for US participation in World War I, the subject we turn to next.[24]

Federal Control of Railroads in World War I

Rumblings of war in Europe early in the second decade of the century bubbled over with the assassination of the Austro-Hungarian heir to the throne, Archduke Francis Ferdinand, on June 28, 1914, giving Austria an excuse to declare war on Serbia. Few countries escaped involvement in the resulting hostilities, as nation after nation was drawn into deadly conflict. It was an unnecessary war, but a bitter one. President Woodrow Wilson overcame substantial isolationist sentiment, leading the United States into the war "to make the world safe for democracy."

After declaration of war on April 6, 1917, a special committee on national defense made up of twenty-eight leading railway executives was organized with an executive group of five railroad CEOs, known as the Railroads' War Board.[25] The War Board adopted a policy of cooperation with the government in expediting rail service for the war effort, despite the railroads' complaint that America's rail carriers had been handicapped for ten years with inadequate rates and worn-out equipment, and now many of its skilled employees were being drafted into the military.

With the stimulus of domestic and foreign purchase of war materièl, traffic surged 12 percent over 1916 levels, and the Railroads' War Board found itself short of more than 140,000 cars in May 1917 due to a lack of ship capacity to receive the goods railways had rushed to the Atlantic ports. Congress gave the ICC emergency powers to suspend car service orders and direct car distribution, and together the War Board and the ICC worked the car shortage down to less than 34,000 by August. But still, traffic flows were hampered by misuse of the priority system for war materièl. Atlantic ports and port access routes became clogged, and there was no place to store cars waiting to be unloaded; sidings filled up all the way back to the Midwest. Freight congestion resulted in increasingly long delays before cars could be reloaded. The system of priority tags broke down because railway freight agents began to distribute the tags as favors to customers; ultimately four-fifths of all cars were tagged—meaning that effectively none had genuine priority.[26]

Professor Albro Martin provides a glimpse into the chaos in 1917:

> Freight cars were loaded with goods at the factories or interior grain elevators as fast as shippers could get their hands on them. . . . These cars were sent east without any promise of ocean shipping space. Boxcars loaded with goods of low priority and with no early prospect of ocean shipment blocked the piers, while high-priority goods for which ships were waiting in the harbor sat in the yards or were sidetracked miles from the coast.

In extreme cases the railroads, in desperation, brought in cranes
to sort out their cars the way a small boy impatiently lifts his toy
train from its tracks. By midwinter the port of New York was
approaching total shutdown.[27]

There was little effort put into overall planning, and if there had been,
nobody had authority to enforce implementation of a plan. "Many cases of
inane operation were witnessed."[28] Union Pacific's CEO Robert S. Lovett
was then put in charge of priority shipments, but he sought to interfere as
little as possible with normal industry operations. "It should be emphasized, therefore, that during the first nine months of the war, April to
December, 1917, the Government interfered scarcely at all with railroad
operation."[29]

Matters deteriorated further, prompting President Wilson to issue a
proclamation on December 26, 1917, under powers granted by Congress
in an act of August 29, 1916, to assume control of the transportation of
troops, materièl, and equipment through the secretary of war. Some
reporters felt that the President was misled by agitators for government
ownership, but in any event, at that point, Mr. William G. McAdoo, secretary of the treasury, became the director general of the United States
Railroad Administration (USRA), taking over operations from the Railroads' War Board.

Critics initially charged that operational snarls and railcar shortages that
plagued mobilization efforts in the months leading up to American entry
into the conflict were the result of rail carrier mismanagement. Belatedly,
however, most observers recognized that the US rail network had not
been laid out in a manner to facilitate eastbound one-way movement of
troops and war materièl to the Atlantic ports—Boston, New York/New
Jersey, Philadelphia, Baltimore, Norfolk, Charleston, Savannah. Gradually
it became clear that separate, disaggregated railroad companies could not
be reorganized quickly into more effective patterns for the war effort. Circumstance was everything. Political leaders in the Wilson administration
and in Congress were not claiming that federal operation would be inherently more efficient than private-sector management; it was simply a case
of the need for swift, nationally coordinated action to address the war
mobilization emergency.

In short, government management of railroads during World War I was
imposed without an excess of ideology or theory, but only because of the

manifest exigencies of the war—and the very real breakdowns in railroad service caused by the specific nature of the of mobilization for an overseas European war.

After the Great War (as World War I was known before Hitler and history brought about another), railroads were taken into public ownership and national scale of operations in most industrialized countries. There was considerable pressure, particularly from trade unions, to do the same in the United States—that is, to urge not just federal control, but national ownership and operation. The United States might have followed suit, but fortunately, more reasonable voices prevailed.[30]

Evaluating Federal Control and the Performance of the USRA

As to the performance of railroads under the federal government's control, there is divided opinion. The "experiment with nationalization" gave the railroads some advantages not available beforehand. Being exempt from antitrust, they could pool equipment under ICC supervision; they could get deferments from the draft for key employees; they could get their message before the President through Director General McAdoo; and they had better prospects for much-needed rate increases to support track and equipment maintenance.

Regarding policies to ensure that railroad properties would be well-maintained despite the war mobilization effort, President Wilson had said that guarantees would be put in place to ensure that railroad properties would be maintained in as good repair as when the government took over, but it turned out the mechanisms to do so were inadequate. Already the railroads had urged a substantial rate increase because of the Adamson Act's wage settlement[31] and the expenses of wartime operation, but the ICC turned a deaf ear.[32] McAdoo's USRA had the power to raise rates, and indeed the implementing contract under the Federal Control Act required the director general to "expend for maintenance such sums as would be requisite in order that the properties might be returned to companies at the end of Federal Control in substantially as good repair and substantially as complete in equipment as they were on January 1, 1918."[33]

Not surprisingly, the railroads believed that first the ICC and then USRA had squandered an opportunity to establish a more sustainable level of rates. They were joined in that opinion by none other than the chair of the Senate Committee on Interstate Commerce, Senator Albert Cummins of Iowa:

> I think the most serious complaint that can be made of the Railroad Administration lies in the fact that it did not return the railroads to their owners self-sustaining; it ought to have established rates before the railroads were returned that would make the railroads reasonably self-sustaining. . . . It was just as much the duty of the Government to return those roads with rates that would sustain them in their operation as it was its duty to return them in as good condition physically as it took them. . . . And that is a matter that has not been sufficiently understood by the people of the country. And I think when it is fully understood, that very much of the criticism that has fallen upon the railroads since that time will disappear.[34]

The USRA had some success exhorting shippers to load cars more efficiently with an intensive publicity campaign resulting in perhaps a 10 percent improvement in capacity per car. Increased demurrage (overtime fees for holding a common-use car longer than the standard use period) was also quite effective in getting receivers to unload cars faster. A "sailing day" discipline for less-than-carload shipments reduced handling costs and improved capacity utilization. The USRA also streamlined passenger train schedules and eliminated many redundant nonstop schedules that railroads previously operated for competitive reasons. In cities, ticket offices were combined. Pullman and dining cars were taken off some trains.

Overall, the experiment with nationalization was more constructive than negative, and certainly not the calamity that partisans predicted or declared in their private histories. The fundamental problems resulting in waste, delays, and congestion were mainly due to the one-way flows from West to East (not repeated in World War II, as it turned out), and inadequate port facilities along the Atlantic seaboard. The congestion and many instances of "inane operations" cited earlier occurred for the most part in the first months of US involvement in the war and were more characteristic of the period when the Railroads' Board was nominally in charge rather than later under USRA management. The railroads were fortunate that the mobilization and national operation were over quickly, as the threat of nationalization was real. It had happened in almost all other countries and—but for the strength of private property protections in the US Constitution—it could have happened here.

In fact, according to the foremost modern historian of the railroads in the war period, Austin Kerr, the Railroads' War Board greatly influenced popular notions of industry efficiency. The appearance was given that all other considerations were subordinate to the war mobilization effort, and even then, the iconic Sherman Antitrust Act policies seemed to have been rendered obsolete after only one generation of application to railroads.

Some observers marveled at the railroads' voluntary efforts toward uniting in one grand continental business system. Looking forward to postwar railroad efficiency, Senator Francis Newlands (D., Nevada) observed, "We are somewhat shattering our old views regarding antitrust laws, etc. . . . I believe that we will enter upon an evolutional condition of mind that will make a great many beneficial changes in our economic systems." Professor Kerr wrote that the prominent California state railway commissioner Max Thelen "summarized the railroad problem in one word: 'duplication,' and observed that the lack of full-scale inter-corporate coordination led to irrational administration of facilities and routing in many parts of the country. . . ."[35]

Despite Kerr's observation, others thought it regrettable that public opinion was not better informed about the period of federal control— understandings were "superficial and unfair" said the Delano Report in 1942. Such impressions were eventually countered by Walker D. Hines's *War History of American Railroads*, published in 1928; Hines was McAdoo's deputy and successor as director general in 1919. "[T]he methods and results of Federal Control of railroads do not constitute a sound argument either for or against Government ownership and operation," Hines wrote.[36] Wartime control shed "no reliable light" on the merits or demerits of Government ownership and operation in peacetime. Professor Kerr later caught the right tone: "The unification of the railroads during Federal Control and the resulting solution of the 1917 transportation crisis was impressive to many observers and participants alike."[37]

When the war was over and the railroads were returned to private ownership, however, these consolidation efficiencies were disregarded. Many interests "sought legislation allowing the carriers to take full advantage of the Railroad Administration experience. They desired a legislative program which would create an efficient railroad industry run by experts and free from internecine competition."[38] Federal control of the railroads ended with passage of the Transportation Act of 1920 and the return of operations to their private owners.[39] Enthusiasm for nationalization gradually faded during the 1920s and little more was heard about it until new economic challenges came during the Great Depression. Unfortunately, many of the operational reforms brought about under federal control were not continued; roundabout routing resumed, pooling arrangements were again illegal, locomotives went back to being built in small customized batches, and unproductive passenger service competition resumed.

One change lasted, however, and that was the determination of railroad managers never again to allow themselves to be swallowed up in government operation. When world war returned only a brief twenty years later, the railroads were better prepared and they succeeded in retaining private control.[40]

Lessons of the Period of Federal Control

It may seem illogical to include the story of federal control of railroads during World War I as one of the steps in a progression of public policies shaping railroad competitive industry structure in the twentieth century, but think about it this way: The independent actions of several hundreds of private-sector US railroads were guided by rate regulatory policy, mergers and consolidations (in a few cases, antitrust dissolution), bankruptcy reorganization, and passenger discontinuance/line abandonments. Federal control, from this perspective, was much like other ways in which the government intervened in railroad operating decisions.

Overall, the period of federal control of railroad operations in World War I showed that, contrary to Populist fears of the evils of bigness in business enterprise, consolidation of the operations of multiple railroads had enabled significant efficiencies benefiting the war effort. Taking the obverse side of the story, and despite Senator Cummins's later criticism, federal control had been good for the railroads, as USRA policies brought about some much-needed standardization of equipment and practices in the industry. Director General McAdoo and his colleagues proved better stewards of public governing responsibilities than had the Interstate Commerce Commission.

It seems odd on the surface that public policy would be insistent that the bigness of trusts was anathema, but that the bigness of federal control during war mobilization would be tolerable. That tolerance did not extend to "nationalization," however, and while this proposed remedy was suggested frequently, it was always turned aside—even as the Great Depression wiped out capital values and made active government intervention in business and social welfare policy more widespread. Railroad managers had not caused the fundamental problems, and nationalization would have been overkill. Federal control, precisely because it was both quickly implemented and not permanently imposed, was the right answer.

The authors of this book like the notion that federal control was an "experiment" in nationalization, but one that was rejected. Railroad managers were scared to death by the experience, but they were given a "free" opportunity to see what an even larger operational structure would look like and whether or not it might exhibit economies of scale. In several ways, it did. Railroads learned that they did not wish to lose control again in any future war emergency, but they might also have realized (at least subconsciously) that different and larger organizations were possible.

Maybe there was something to the presumption of economies of scale, and if so, that idea could support the industry's ongoing obsession with mergers. If the fundamental dilemma of competition versus consolidation could be worked out, the only other thing that would be needed were some key managerial innovations and development of advanced computerized information and communications systems. These would not arrive, however, until much later in the twentieth century.

Consolidation Policy in the Transportation Act of 1920

During the quarter century from passage of the Sherman Antitrust Act to the Teddy Roosevelt and Taft administrations' antitrust enforcement, to enactment of the Clayton Anti-Monopoly Act of 1914, there was no question where American policy and politicians stood on the issue of bigness in business—they were against it in every form. Firms had grown bigger not from competitive necessity or economies of scale, most believed, but because large firms could do what pools or trusts or cartels were forbidden to do—restrict output and raise prices. Bigness per se was a problem—as it also became after World War II in the Alcoa, AT&T, IBM, and other antitrust cases. And yet there was this curiosity in the Transportation Act of 1920 that all railroads were to be consolidated into a limited number of systems designed by a government agency. Why did the 1920 Act's sponsors, which included many adherents of scientific management (and who, like Brandeis, mostly took the Progressive line against bigness) find themselves advocating railroad consolidation?[41] If it was odd on the surface that the bigness of trusts was intolerable—while the bigness of federal control was necessary—wasn't it even more strange that now the bigness of consolidating the entire industry into a limited number of systems had been ordered by Congress? But after World War I, there was no waffling on the issue. Politicians of all stripes thought "grand consolidation" would be the solution to what was widely known as "the railroad problem." To congressional leaders like Senator Cummins (also an advocate of scientific management), government-led planned consolidation was the answer.

One consideration was that in returning railroads to private operation after the period of federal control, "there was fear of a 'complete breakdown' in the nation's coordinated rail network owing to the precarious financial condition in which government had placed many carriers."[42] Railroads in 1920 were worn out physically from strains imposed by the overload of wartime traffic, and because of the shifts of traffic volume from one sector to another as historical traffic patterns were disrupted by war mobilization. In this context, the first big opportunity for re-setting government policy toward railroads came with the Esch-Cummins Transportation Act of 1920, which was to be the primary transportation law of the land for the next two decades.

"Believe It or Not" Rail Consolidation Planning

The 1920 act mandated that the ICC undertake a study to determine how best to combine all of the nation's private railroads into a limited number of effective rail systems (not less than twenty and not more than thirty-five). Professor William Norris Leonard of Columbia University, the foremost scholar of the Transportation Act of 1920, summarized the ICC's task in planned consolidations as follows: "In mapping out the rail systems, the Commission was required to take into account three factors: (1) Preservation of competition as fully as possible; (2) Maintenance of existing routes and channels of trade wherever practicable; (3) Arrangement of the carriers so that, wherever possible, the systems could earn substantially the same rate of return under a uniform system of rates."[43]

The 1920 Act specified that, after preparation of a preliminary plan and hearings, the published ICC plans should create, for each system, a balance of both weak and strong firms to ensure fairness and industry financial stability. Most major markets were to be served by two or more railroads and by more than one mode—and thus maintain some competitive choice for shippers. To implement the mandate, the ICC was given the power to approve or disapprove rail mergers depending on conformance with the plan. With ICC approval, a merger was also exempt from other antitrust actions or sanctions.

The ICC entrusted Professor William Z. Ripley of Harvard with formulating the preliminary comprehensive plan. Ripley proposed the consolidation of "the nation's 185 Class I railroads [into] just 21 well-balanced systems."[44] Despite good efforts by Professor Ripley and others, no plan acceptable to all parties was found.

Professor Leonard put much of the blame for failure to realize major consolidations under the 1920 Act on its ill-advised link to the contentious valuation studies described in Chapter 2—noting that it was "a further obstacle to the adoption of a complete plan by the Commission. . . ."[45] There were two problem areas: (1) the requirement that the ICC combine railroads into systems that would earn approximately the same rate of return on property values under the same level of competitive rates, and (2) the requirement that the value of securities of consolidated properties would not be higher than the aggregate value of constituent properties.[46]

An obvious problem was that ICC regulation dictated that railroads within regional areas charge uniform rates, a legacy of the twentieth century's first decade and its value-of-service rate-making regime (see Chapter 2). Because individual railroads faced different economic and financial circumstances, it was nearly impossible for the railroads to propose and the ICC to approve uniform regional rates applying to all railroads that would raise adequate revenues to operate and maintain the system. The ICC attempted to solve the problem by imposing conditions, such as the inclusion of all or portions of smaller weak railroads in a deal, before it approved a transaction.

Indeed, it was the act's mandate to combine weak and strong railroads within each system, merging profitable lines with unprofitable to the extent possible, that proved to be the main stumbling block for success of the consolidation strategy. The railroads were against a consolidation plan; they did not want to be told which railroads they should merge, and strong railroads in particular were averse to joining with financially unhealthy carriers. Profitable railroads evidenced little interest in absorbing the less affluent, and apparently at times they expressed their displeasure at the thought rather vigorously. Following the legislative mandate, nonetheless, the commission issued a preliminary plan in 1921. After two years of hearings, Congress gave approval to the preliminary plan, requiring that the

ICC modify it into a final plan. The ICC no longer wanted the responsibility of forcing the railroads to consolidate according to a central plan, however, and beginning in 1925, repeatedly asked Congress to be relieved of the responsibility for preparing a final plan. Its request for relief unheeded, the ICC dragged its heels, waiting until 1929 to issue its final plan, just as the stock market crashed and the Great Depression began. Finally "succumbing to political pressure" to release its final plan, the ICC issued its proposal for consolidation of railroads into twenty-one systems (nineteen for domestic carriers and two Canadian-based). Frank Wilner writes that Professor Ripley "vehemently opposed the final ICC plan," and quotes him to the effect that the plan did not seem to be worked out well on the basis of either operating efficiency or financial equality.[47]

The planned consolidation mandate put on the ICC in 1920 was impossible to accomplish. The great historical irony is that, with the strongest congressional mandate for consolidation ever enacted, no comparable period in US history had less success in actual railroad consolidations than the forty-year span, 1920 to 1940, ruled by the Esch-Cummins Act.

After 1929, deterioration of industry finances generally and the Great Depression's bankruptcies greatly complicated prospects for mergers. Rail traffic declined 50 percent between 1929 and 1933, and few mergers were put forward. One astute expert on government regulation concluded, "[T]he experience of the 1920s justified a good deal of skepticism in assessing the prospects that grandiose nationwide consolidation plans would in fact be put into effect."[48] Apparently, ICC commissioners and staff members heaved a collective sigh of relief when de facto they were relieved of the mandate to develop such a scheme by the Emergency Transportation Act of 1933; the ICC was finally excused from the assignment by the Transportation Act of 1940.[49]

Perspective on the Grand Plans for Consolidation

Why did the 1920 act fail to achieve the result so many people believed was the best solution to the railroad problem? The author of the 1920 act and one of the strongest proponents of its planned consolidations was Senator Cummins of Iowa. He testified in 1925 that the prospect of railroads achieving significant cost savings under the plan was a negligible part of his thinking in putting forward the Transportation Act of 1920. This doesn't ring true, however, because if not savings, why bother? Some proponents had estimated savings at $300 to $500 million annually, a huge amount in those days; others thought the savings would be very small. Contradicting himself somewhat, Senator Cummins also said,

> The whole purpose [of the Esch-Cummins Act] was to keep the railroads of the country running at the lowest practicable rates of transportation [which would seem to require efficiencies]. It was introduced because I believe that if there be not a consolidation, there are just two alternatives—a large part of the railways of the United States must be abandoned, or the Government must take charge of the transportation system and operate it at the public cost.[50]

It should not be forgotten that the idea of a national plan to guide and channel mergers for the best interests of the general public, while naïve and probably contrary to the American ideal of private enterprise, had a strong undercurrent of "good government" or "reform" thinking. Over the entire course of the last 100 years, one hopes, mergers might have been more consistently useful in the public interest if they had been designed thoughtfully by unbiased experts, in consultation with industry operating experts and strategic leaders, rather than thrown together in an ad hoc and laissez-faire manner. (Lack of commonsense ICC constraints on big, anticompetitive mergers had resulted in Northern Securities at the turn of the twentieth century and would reemerge with the disastrous Penn Central merger in the 1960s.) Still, any planned approach to consolidation would have to be based on consensus rules of the road—and in the case of the 1920 act, such rules proved its undoing.

In any event, advocates of the 1920 act's consolidation policy undoubtedly sought a bridge too far. Instead of specifying a limited number of systems and requiring strong railroads to include weak roads in their proposals (as well as the silly requirement to require consolidation plans to facilitate rate equalization), Congress might have devised a rule encouraging voluntary mergers within a strong procompetitive and pro-efficiency mandate regardless of traditional traffic flows. This was possible, and it might have enabled much more to be accomplished.

Concluding Thoughts on Mergers
in the First Half of the Twentieth Century

It is quite remarkable how the national polity could not really make up its mind about consolidation contrasted with competition—two quite contradictory strategies for regulating railroad industry structure—over the course of the twentieth century. In fact, Americans encounter the debate between savings from consolidation and pricing or innovation benefits from competition repeatedly, and we never settle on one resolution of the contest for long. The same phenomenon occurs elsewhere in our culture all the time—as bigness versus quaintness, or standardization versus customization, or convenience versus purity. We like cities for culture and the country for charm. We like Microsoft or Apple for productivity tools and standardization, but custom software and hometown service providers for convenience and custom personal applicability to a task. We patronize the big motion picture studios for blockbusters but applaud independent filmmakers for innovative camerawork and scripts. We choose name brands for value, but prefer homemade for taste and customer service. We curse bigness more often than not, but never stray far from its advantages.

In the case of railroad mergers, there were and still are limited options—fewer today than in the days of Hill and Harriman. But too often railroads and regulators turned aside from a good solution because they were focused too much on all or nothing. As Voltaire famously put it, "the perfect is the enemy of the good."

In the post-Staggers period, the regulatory rules for evaluation of competitive losses in major markets have been applied more carefully and consistently. The ICC or STB has broadly approved some mergers that might not have passed muster earlier. But as Chapter 10 will show, the regulators have been much more careful in conditioning the merger approval on preservation of significant competitive features. Earlier mergers were often conditioned as to labor protective requirements, such as New York Dock or Washington Agreement provisions, and competing railroads might have received protection against traffic diversions such as the Ogden Gateway or Detroit, Toledo & Ironton (DT&I) conditions (see Chapter 10) that were difficult to enforce. The post-Staggers ICC/STB protections have been embedded more deeply in the fundamental operating circumstances of the industry's post-merger competitive structure, where they have been self-enforcing and successful.

The Transportation Act of 1920 (the Esch-Cummins Act) returned control of the railroads to private ownership in March of that year but, unfortunately, kept in place a continuation of the increasingly stringent prewar government regulatory regime. Indeed, the 1920 Transportation Act continued to treat railroads as if they still possessed a monopoly on inland

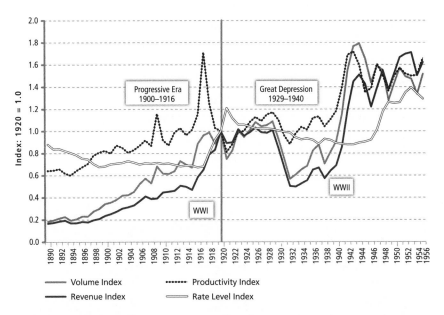

Figure 3.2 US Railroad Performance, 1890–1955 This chart shows how macroeconomic factors affected railroad performance in the first years after passage of the 1887 Act to Regulate Commerce, up to midcentury. ICC regulation appears to have held down rail rates until federal control during World War I. However, rates did not fall as quickly as traffic levels during the Great Depression. Rail productivity soared during both world wars, indicating economies of density. Economic conditions permitting railroads to use more of their capacity also allow revenue-enhancing rate increases, but the effect may be delayed (called regulatory lag), as the figure indicates. Deregulated rates do seem to fall when traffic is weak and rise when it is strong, but these real-world effects are specific to selected commodity and geographic markets. The figure uses metrics similar to those in Chapter 13 on the impact of Staggers Rail Act deregulation in 1980. Data are from the US Department of Commerce, *Historical Statistics of the United States, Colonial Times to 1957*, (Washington, DC: 1960). Productivity is ton-miles divided by a constant dollar value of total operating expenses. Rate level is constant dollar revenue per ton-mile. Revenue and expense data used in the productivity calculation are both in constant 1929 dollars, and include both freight and passenger service, but ton-miles are freight only (i.e., no conversion was made to estimate passenger-miles).

transportation, which was no longer the case. The railroads were burdened by sweeping regulations, which covered nearly all of their affairs, while the competition that they faced remained unregulated. As an article in the *Saturday Evening Post* pointed out, railroad management is "invaded at every turn by Government. Literally, the list of things a railroad president may not do without permission is longer than a list of what he may do."[51]

Constrained by governmentally imposed rates and financial regulations, railroad managers lapsed into a lethargic state. For the most part, they chose to accept the status quo and ignored signs of new external competition because these posed no immediate threat. The railroads' lethargy was not confined to freight; passenger service was affected equally, and being the weaker of the two services, suffered even more from inattention of top executives to the pervasive problems affecting the industry, as this book will show in subsequent chapters.

Box 3.1   US Railroad Economic Performance (1890-1955).

Refer to Figure 3.2 for illustration of the following points:

- The ICC held down rate levels in the Progressive Era, but the USRA under federal control allowed their recovery.
- After 1920, railroads faced increasing competition from rival modes of transport. Trucks took high-end traffic; barges and pipelines took bulk commodities. And whether diversion was actual or only threatened, it had the effect of lowering railroad rates. (The chart in this figure is corrected for general inflation, but transportation rates are highly sensitive to actual competition in specific point-to-point markets.)
- The estimated productivity spike in World War I belies the myth of poor government administration of railroads during the period of federal control. The USRA actually helped straighten out operations that had become gridlocked during the last years of private railroad operations because mobilization for war was inundating ill-prepared and poorly adapted railroad operations in support of the European war. The 1917 spike was due to the inflation index shooting up from 64 to 105, while recorded expenses increased only marginally over 1916, and with output soaring because of war mobilization traffic. The lesser spike in 1909 was also due to strong traffic and moderate expenses, but no jump in the inflation index.
- Traffic volume, revenue, and productivity fell much faster than rate levels early in the Great Depression. In the period just before and during the early years of World War II, traffic, revenue, and productivity climbed spectacularly. Real (inflation adjusted) rates fell during the war and did not catch up until after the war.
- Rate levels really do seem to fall when traffic is weak and rise when it is strong, but the effects probably would be clearer in specific commodity and

Box 3.1 *Continued*

geographic markets. This chart is for all rail traffic; thus, within the data points shown, there may be cancelling or reinforcing specifics.

- The chart data indexing was based on 1920 to help highlight any specific changes in trends attributable to policies enacted in the Transportation Act of 1920. If there are such trends—other than those clearly associated with war and depression—they do not leap from the page.
- The Transportation Act of 1920 did reestablish ICC rate making in replacement of USRA war mobilization and federal control; however, the Commission's rate and service regulation was still under the sway of value-of-service pricing principles. Both ICC reluctance to grant general rate increases and the effect of VOS rates in a period of accelerating competition from other modes seem to be reflected in the pattern of rate levels after 1921.

4

THE IMPACT OF RIVAL FREIGHT MODES
ON RAILROADS

Good roads, canals and navigable rivers, by diminishing the expense of carriage, put the remote parts of the country more nearly upon the level with those in the neighborhood of the town. They are upon that account the greatest of improvements.

—ADAM SMITH (1776)

Each mode of transport possesses individual engineering or technological characteristics, which give it an advantage or disadvantage as compared with others in certain aspects of transportation service. . . . The government has effective means to encourage or discourage, to strengthen or weaken, to preserve or destroy the several modes of transport through policies of taxation or regulation, through the bestowing of privileges or exacting restrictions on one or more special groups, or simply by allowing outmoded legislation and policies to continue.

—W. W. HAY (1961)

This chapter of *American Railroads* explores the competitive impact on railroads of the maturation of rival modes for transporting freight. The chapter focuses on competition among railroads and two other modes (waterway barges and highway motor carriers) for which traffic can switch back and forth, a definition largely excluding pipelines. These competitive modes are central to our story of the dominance, near-demise, and renaissance of the American railroad industry in the last century. While each alternative mode developed at its own pace and according to its own economic destiny, together they offered formidable challenges— often providing superior service and undercutting the level of prevailing or prospective rates as they took large shares of traffic from the railroads. Development of the competitive modes took managerial and financial resources as well as traffic from the railroads, hurrying the railroads' decline.[1]

Passenger rail also faced enormous competitive rivalry, of course, from automobiles and motor buses using the same highways, plus airlines. With the advent of jet-powered aircraft in the 1950s, airline service began to dominate long-distance, common-carrier passenger-miles, especially outside the Northeast Corridor (Boston to Washington).[2] Competition from private autos and from buses will be implicit in our story of highway development in this chapter, but we hold off discussion of aviation until Chapter 5, which focuses on the decline of rail passenger service from 1900 to the creation of Amtrak in 1970.[3]

Both Chapters 4 and 5 establish that the rival modes possessed some "inherent advantages" stemming from superior technologies, but also they were beneficiaries of favorable public policies. It will be evident, for example, that the taxpayer's huge and continuing investment in waterways, highways, and aviation has profoundly affected each mode—separately, of course, and also with respect to the division of competitive traffic among them.

The authors of this book argue that Congress never strayed far from one of its central purposes regarding transport policy: to ensure that railroads could not exploit popular constituencies Congress had taken under its wing. No mechanism was more effective in accomplishing that goal than subsidy to rival modes. If rates for movement of grain to the Gulf of Mexico for export were perceived as too high, they could be driven down by regulatory fiat—or by improving inland waterways. Barge service on these facilities would do the job—grain shippers would benefit from "water-compelled" rates. Similar factors were at work in policies toward other alternative modes. For example, from time to time, Congress authorized operation of trucks with larger dimensions and heavier weight limits on interstate highways (although these were later frozen at 1991 levels).[4]

Competitive rivalries among the several modes existed from their origins. As each new alternative appeared, it sought both natural advantages and a publicly subsidized share of available markets. Each rival mode was extended by investments and constrained by regulation, and each sought new advantages from technological developments and demand shifts within the economy. The threat of multiple kinds of government intervention in competition among the modes of transport remains an effective restraint on railroad business behavior.

The importance of this fact was never made more clearly than in the seminal work on the economics of transportation by co-author John R. Meyer, Merton J. Peck, and their colleagues more than fifty years ago:

> [T]he newer forms of transportation have displaced the railroads for substantial blocks of traffic. . . . [A]s the ICC has observed, "*Since the advent of the motor carrier and air transportation, competition is a more potent force in rate-making than ever before.*" [Emphasis added] . . . Indeed the continuing theme of this study is the existence of latent or actual inter-industry competition in transportation and the way in which relaxation of regulation will channel such competition to provide more efficient accomplishment of transportation functions in the economy.[5]

Marine (Blue-Water) Shipping and Inland (Brown-Water) Barge Operations

Ships always dominated freight and passenger transport on the seas because the fundamental technology developed centuries ago and because wind and way were free. All that was needed for commercial development were seaworthy vessels and ports.

From the Native Americans, the European explorers, French Canadian fur trappers, and from a variety of daring American adventurers, New World colonists learned about trails and waterways leading away from the oceans and into the wilderness. They became acquainted with the simple bark canoe that could negotiate shallow or rough water and that was light enough to be carried by two persons between usable waterways. These portage routes became established trails linking inland waterways into the first transportation network serving the colonial hinterland.

Early in the nineteenth century, transportation entrepreneurs began to envision substantial canals, some with mechanical lock systems to lift boats over land obstacles separating rivers and lakes. With development of railways in the second quarter of the nineteenth century in both the Old World and the Americas, great rivalries arose between traditional transport on natural waterways and the new railroads, pulled by the Iron Horse. Steam power was key to both modes, as innovations in steamboats preceded those on railways by only a few years.

Competitive Routes West Through the Alleghenies

The 363-mile Erie Canal was begun in 1817 and finished in October 1825; it was built at the then staggering cost of $8 million. The Erie Canal reduced travel time between Buffalo and New York City from 21 to eight days, however, and enabled a comparable decrease in cargo hauling rates. The Erie Canal made New York City America's greatest port—a bitter pill for the rival cities of Boston, Philadelphia, and Baltimore, but there was little they could do in response; New York had the natural advantage offered by the "water level route" of the Hudson and the Mohawk River Valleys.[6] By reaching the Great Lakes, the Erie Canal's functionality extended all the way to the new trading town of Chicago on the southwest shore of Lake Michigan, near the shortest land route to the Mississippi River. Because of its favorable location, Chicago outstripped St. Louis as the transport hub of the Midwest; it retained that distinction throughout the era of railroad building and, indeed, to current times.[7]

Maryland, meanwhile, put a great deal of effort into realizing George Washington's dream of a Chesapeake & Ohio Canal along the Potomac River, between Georgetown (Washington, D.C.) and Cumberland, Maryland, on its way over the Alleghenies to the Monongahela River and Pittsburgh.[8] Keeping up with technology trends, the enterprising fathers of Baltimore pushed the Baltimore & Ohio (B&O) Railroad's rails to the point where the C&O Canal construction ended, at Cumberland—well short of its intended terminus on tributaries of the Ohio River, but a significant penetration of the wilderness nonetheless.[9]

Now the commercial and modal rivalries westward from the Middle Atlantic port cities to the old Northwest Territories were multiple: New York City anchored the Erie Canal, the New York Central (NYC) and the Erie railroads, and subsequently the New York Thruway along the Hudson and Mohawk Valleys. In parallel fashion, Philadelphia became a hub for railroads running along the Atlantic seaboard, the Pennsylvania Inclined Railway and Canal system and the great Pennsylvania Railroad (PRR) crossing the Alleghenies, and later the Pennsylvania Turnpike. Finally, Baltimore on Chesapeake Bay and Washington on the Potomac River hosted cornerstones of the National Turnpike, the C&O Canal, and the B&O Railroad. Boston was significantly disadvantaged in this competition for western, trans-Appalachian connections.

It was the case, then, that both natural topography and human-enhanced technology foreordained the intense competitive rivalry of America's Middle Atlantic ports in reaching west by water and rail to the great mid-continent waterside entrepôts of Chicago, St. Louis, Memphis, New Orleans, Kansas City, or Omaha.[10] None of these cities was projected, initially, as a railroad terminus or even switching hub; they all had other reasons for being. But their destinies became intertwined with the trunk line railways snaking westward. Each iron road, in turn, paused at the Great Lakes, Mississippi, or Missouri River before making the long trek over the prairies—and before surmounting the Rockies, the Sierra Nevada, or the Cascade Range to reach the Pacific Coast on the other side of the continent.

The Confluence of Waterways, Trails, and Rails

It was not just happenstance that the mid-continental entrepôts were at the confluence of waterways, roads, and rails or that later they became hubs for the airlines. It was because each mode, while it had its own characteristics and economies, also served the overarching principles of transport—to add time and place utility to goods filling broader demands of the economy. Thus the transport modes of interest to us in this book were takers as well as makers of economic forces beyond their initial ken, and they became all the more important to subsequent history for having done so.

While manmade canals were important early in the nineteenth century, they generally lost out competitively to more flexible and faster railroad transport as it developed. By contrast, natural waterways provided low-cost transport alternatives throughout history, and they continued to enable effective competition to railroads wherever they existed. (The US inland waterway network made up of coastal waters, Great Lakes, improved rivers, and canals is shown in Map 4.1). An early authority on rail and waterway competition, interestingly, was Harold G. Moulton, later the first president of the Brookings Institution. Moulton wrote his dissertation for the University of Chicago on waterways versus railways.[11] A key observation from Moulton's century-old work is still relevant today:

> Competition with each other and with existing water routes, and attention to trade conditions have forced our railways to offer much lower rates on long-distance traffic than exist anywhere else in the world. On the other hand, for short hauls,

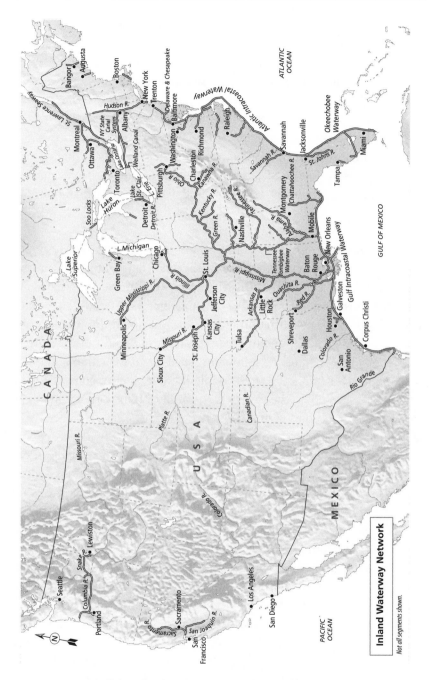

Map 4.1 Extent of the Inland Waterway Network. *Source:* Center for Climate & Energy Solutions, with authors' modifications. Used with permission.

where competition is absent [but for highways and trucks], our railway charges are unquestionably in many cases extremely high, and it is here that complaints are most often heard. . . . It is on local traffic, therefore, that we should wish to secure lower freight rates by means of water competition. But it is obviously altogether impossible for canals to reach every local point . . . Unless savings in hauling by water can be extended over a considerable distance . . . on a natural waterway rather than a canal,—the total cost of transportation, including charges on the investment in the waterway itself, will be greater than that by rail.[12]

In keeping with long precedent in transport history, the existing mode helped build the new. In the case of the first transcontinental railroad, steamboats moved iron rail up the Missouri River from St. Joseph, Missouri (then the most westerly railhead with connections to the East), to Omaha-Council Bluffs for construction of the new rail line to Promontory, connecting to California. One hundred years later, railroads would return the favor—moving concrete and reinforcing steel for construction of the interstate highways; it was good traffic while it lasted, but, of course, it would not last, as it had not in the case of the steamboat transport of iron rail and spikes from St. Joseph to Omaha.

Inland waterways are known as the brown-water network—as opposed to deep-sea blue-water service. The brown-water network enables extensive rail-competitive transport in the eastern United States, but it is almost nonexistent west of Kansas City/Sioux City and Tulsa. The only significant exceptions are waterborne services in the Bay Area of California, and barge operations on the Columbia and Snake Rivers, extending as far upriver as Lewiston, Idaho.

Water carriers known as lakers move coal, iron ore, grain, steel, petroleum products, and other bulk commodities on the five Great Lakes. Shippers using these lakes have access to international ports via the St. Lawrence Seaway, and to the Mississippi River system via the Illinois and Michigan Canal. Ocean barges and container ships provide service between Lower-48 ports and various Caribbean islands, Hawaii, and Alaska.

In the east, coal rather than grain is dominant on the Ohio, Kanawha, Cumberland, Tennessee, and connecting waterways. By far the largest inland riverine waterway system is the Mississippi River (including connections to the Gulf of Mexico by way of the Mississippi River Gulf Outlet (MR GO)—of which much was heard during Hurricane Katrina—and the Atchafalaya River shortcut west of New Orleans, much criticized for negative environmental impacts far outweighing any commercial benefits. The Mississippi River system carries highly rail-competitive (and often export-bound) coal, grain, fertilizer, petroleum products, and bulk chemicals, plus local sand and gravel.

In general, barges on the inland waterways provide low-cost bulk transport at rates close to marginal operating costs. The major disadvantages are that the waterways do not reach all traffic origins, and portions of the brown-water network freeze in winter or are prone to closings during floods or drought, when water levels are too high or too low.

Waterway User Fees and a Suggested Reform

Barge interests promoted the notion that America's waterways should be forever free, and they succeeded in keeping that objective intact until 1980. At midcentury, railroads had become vocal opponents of new, highly subsidized US Army Corps of Engineers waterway construction projects, notably the Arkansas River Project, making Tulsa a seaport; the Tennessee-Tombigbee project, creating a shortcut from the Tennessee River to the Gulf of Mexico;[13] and the Upper Mississippi River project, with its controversial Lock and Dam 26, near Alton, Illinois. Railroads worked for imposition of system-wide waterway user fees, arguing that total absence of cost-recovery user fees was a privilege no other mode received; "level the playing field," railway interests urged. A 1981 AAR report calculated that "the value of federal aid to barge operators exceeds by 17 times, the value of federal aid received by freight railroads," and noted that federal subsidies to barge operators . . . [at that time exceeded] . . . 42 percent of all barge revenues."[14]

Despite annual expenditures by the Army Corps of Engineers on inland waterways (costs that totaled more than $2 billion annually throughout much of the latter portion of the twentieth century), there were no tolls or other fees levied on users—that is, not until Congress, seemingly recognizing that this modal favoritism was unsustainable in a modern transport policy, enacted a levy on fuel in 1978, effective two years later. The excise was initially set at four cents per gallon, rising to over 24 cents by 1997; in that year it generated $108 million in revenue earmarked for the Inland Waterways Trust Fund. Under a compromise struck between the industry and the Corps of Engineers and ratified by Congress, waterway operators are to pay from the trust fund one-half of the construction and rehabilitation costs of waterway improvements, with the federal government to pay the other half, plus all waterway operating and maintenance costs. The small per-gallon excise rate, with consequent limited waterway trust fund receipts, means annual expenditures from the fund are not great, and projects the industry says are needed face long delays.[15]

The fuel tax was not a well-designed user fee. In its favor, the per-gallon excise does discourage waste of fuel (and speeding, which has negative impacts in the form of washing away unprotected river-bank soil—the source of the so-called brown water). But the fuel taxes are disconnected from the actual annual or capital construction expenditures (other than fuel use)—such as dredging and lock and dam operating expenses—that barge operators incur or impose. Also, fuel use per ton-mile of cargo moved in a tow is substantially higher going upstream than downstream, of course, or using a fast-flowing river like the Kanawha, compared with the slow-flowing Lower Mississippi.

A far better alternative suggests itself, namely, basing waterway user fees on cargo tonnage moving between pairs of locations (segments) of the waterway system. These segment charges would be set to reflect, for example, different dredging costs for various segments, or higher lock maintenance costs at one location compared with others. Where locks and dams are close together, segments would be shorter and average charges per mile might be higher, reflecting greater lock-and-dam operational costs. Fee structures might even reflect anticipated expenditures for major investments such as a replacement lock or dam; in this sense, the segment toll might function like collections for a typical capital improvement sinking fund. The recommended segment toll structure could be collected using global positioning devices, RF transponders and automatic electronic billing/payment systems.

Agriculture interests traditionally were the strongest proponents of inland waterway improvements and freedom from user fees. These were strategies for keeping the cost of shipping bulk commodities such as grain, coal, ore, and fertilizers at low levels. The well-known circumstance of "water compelled" railroad rates traces in large part to these forms of subsidy to rival brown-water transportation.[16] Ambitious efforts to improve the

Mississippi River locks and dams north of St. Louis and facilities on the Ohio/Kanawha system north and east of Cairo, Illinois, are still on the drafting boards.

Divided Highways and Unified Motor Carriers

Public roads provide ubiquitous access to markets in competition with railroads. Improved highways—paved and maintained by public authorities—connect limited access superhighways to local roads reaching "every Middlesex village and town." This vast network of public roads ensured universal access, usually at only marginal operating cost, to almost every size, style, and purpose of motor vehicle operation—private or common carriers, exempt or regulated firms, general- or special-purpose haulers, liquid bulk or dry van truckers, auto haul-away or packaged goods express operators, and household goods movers. Of all "alternative" modes, and throughout all of the twentieth century but the first decade, highway transport provided the most comprehensive and effective substitute for railroads, both freight and passenger. Even today, with few exceptions (like long-haul unit trains of coal and trainload movement of containers away from congested ports), highway transportation could substitute for railroads in almost every market, but the cost—in terms of final delivered prices, fuel use, emissions, and safety—often would be prohibitive.

The oldest inland transport rivalry is between horseback or animal-drayed conveyances on land, and coastal or river shipping powered by wind, paddle, or downstream flow of waters. For overland freight, the intermodal competition evolved to a spirited rivalry between horse-drawn wagon freight and canal construction in the eighteenth-century British Isles, particularly England.[17] The author of a fascinating book on the subject of land freighting before railroads concludes:

> The potential for improvement [in wagons, horses, and road-ways] was not exhausted by the time of the railways. In 1924 the work of a heavy horse was reckoned as about 240 ton-miles a week. . . . If either iron rails or steam locomotives had been adopted separately and applied to ordinary roads, as was frequently suggested, either might have been seen as a step in the development of carrying, and steam power would have released road transport from its dependence on the horse and enabled significant increases in speed. Only the accident of the two

innovations [iron rail and steam locomotion] being put into use together as a steam railway makes pre-railway road carrying appear a technological dead end.[18]

What a marvelous synthesis of the technology and intermodal competitive themes. From the year of their birth, railroads faced vigorous competition from road vehicles. Only the peculiar adaptability of steam locomotion to rails allowed railroads to eclipse road freighting and coach travel, and to hold that advantage for 100 years. But there would come another era and another contest railways did not win. This was one marked by competition of steam railroads with internal combustion engines—and privately built rail lines with government aided highways.

Modern Highways and Vehicles to Use Them

Limited access highways were among the twentieth century's greatest contributions to the development of modern transport. Huge locomotives on tightly engineered railways could manage long and heavy consists, but for movement over roads without guideways, vehicles needed to be light and steerable—more like horseback or a harness coach on a country lane than a large ship out of water. That would require a breakthrough in prime movers.

Once again, transport advancement took a form featuring new development of compatible technology systems to accomplish the objective of adding time and place utility to goods. The solution came from Nicolaus August Otto, whose Germanic last name seems almost implausibly felicitous to the target application, the automobile. Otto's invention was a four-stroke internal combustion engine.[19] His initial 1876 model was a small, reliable, but stationary engine fueled by coal gas. Soon, however, a mobile, gasoline-fueled version became the engine of choice for automobiles and motorcycles developed by Gottlieb Daimler and Karl Friedrich Benz in Germany, Armand Peugeot in France, Henry Ford in America, and many others. Ford, in particular, offered mass assembly of standardized components for relatively inexpensive owner-operated vehicles. And the Good Roads Movement lobbied for paved streets and country roads—"to get farmers out of the mud." Private autos and small farm tractors and trucks of the day were sufficient for local service, and they made a huge contribution to social welfare in the first half of the twentieth century, but these were not an alternative to railroads; they were more complementary than competitive.

The first entry of the US government into policy for building of general-use highways came in the Federal-Aid Road Act of 1916. It established fundamental elements of the federal–state partnership, which, although frequently amended, continues to this day. These elements include the requirement for establishment of state highway departments; the principle that construction, ownership, and maintenance of the system were state responsibilities; the matching ratio of 50:50, which led to state excise taxation funding their portion of the cost; and a formula for apportionment of funds to states based on area, population, and road mileage.

In the interwar years, for the first time in history, American passenger rail service began to face serious competitive threats, primarily from the private automobile.[20] Throughout the 1920s, motor vehicle registrations had skyrocketed, climbing from just over 8.1 million in 1920 to 23.1 million by 1929.[21] While the financial prosperity of the decade was partly responsible for this history-making increase in automobiles, the government also played an important role. As the public embraced the automobile, demand increased for new and better roads. Both state and federal agencies responded by implementing sophisticated programs.[22] From 1922 to 1930, approximately 90,250 miles of federally-aided highways were constructed or rebuilt, at a cost of nearly $1.8 billion. By 1930, total federal-aid highway mileage in the nation measured over 193,000 miles,[23] or more route mileage than Class I railroads operated in passenger service[24]

Initially, automobiles were primarily used for short distance, discretionary travel. The flexibility of the car made it more convenient than rigidly scheduled passenger trains for short trips. By 1926, automobile travel constituted the majority of total intercity passenger miles. These changes began to detract significantly from rail travel, in particular that of coach class.[25] The rapid improvement of roads also aided the growth of the bus industry, which was nascent at the time.[26]

Even in the direst years of the Great Depression, Americans continued to expand travel by automobile. Throughout the early 1930s, highway construction continued and automobile ownership remained relatively high.[27] The fact that almost all other competition remained unregulated made it virtually impossible for the railroads to keep their rates competitive.[28] Bus service also expanded steadily, partly due to the industry's offering of slightly lower fares than those charged by the railways. In 1932, the ICC estimated that losses of rail passenger volume to buses up to that time amounted to between 20 and 30 percent.[29] Throughout the 1930s, the bus industry continued to expand, primarily by capturing economy class inter-city traffic from the railroads.[30]

As the United States settled into civilian life after World War II, the nation resumed its love affair with the automobile. In the 1950s, America rapidly transported itself from the railway age to the automotive era. Motor vehicles became larger, more comfortable, and more reliable. Paved roads had been extended to nearly every town of significant size in the land. Service stations and repair shops were everywhere. It seemed they needed to be because gas mileage was low and mechanical reliability left much to be desired. Gasoline-powered trucks had become effective users of the local and regional road infrastructure; motor trucks gradually made the conversion from gasoline engines (light and inexpensive) to diesel (more powerful and fuel efficient).

The railroads, struggling to rebuild from the war, could not recover as quickly as Detroit could produce new cars. Vehicle registrations bounded from 25.8 million in 1945 to over 40 million by 1950.[31] Like the railroads, bus traffic enjoyed huge increases during the war, but in the following years, buses were able to retain their gains and continued to draw a large volume of coach class traffic away from the rails.[32]

Legislation for the Interstate Highway System

During the interwar years, Germany had developed a significant new transportation marvel, the autobahn. These high-speed, limited-access highways eventually extended almost 7,500 miles[33] and were the topic of much conversation among returning American servicemen at the end of the war. While the autobahns became a model for our National System of Interstate and Defense Highways (also known as the Eisenhower Interstate Highway System or IHS), it is not well known that the United States had already begun its own planning for a controlled-access modern highway network before the end of World War II. The Federal-Aid Highway Act of 1938 had requested preparation of a report to Congress on the topic. When finished in 1939, the report, *Toll Roads and Free Roads*, advocated "a comprehensive system of free highways with strict controls on the access to the right-of-way"—a system of 26,700 miles. A follow-up report under 1943 legislation, titled *Interregional Highways*, proposed a larger network of about 39,000 miles. The following year, legislation officially authorized an interstate highway system of 40,000 miles, and it was officially designated in 1947.[34]

In the 1950s, Congress continued to appropriate funds for federal-aid highways. Then in 1954, General Dwight D. Eisenhower become president of the United States and appointed a president's advisory committee on highways chaired by General Lucius D. Clay. The Clay Committee issued its report in January 1955, and it had a transformational role in developing the Eisenhower administration's proposals for funding and constructing the subsequent interstate highway system (IHS). Preliminary estimates showed the program might cost $101 billion over ten years. The committee explicitly rejected toll financing and only implied, but did not explicitly propose, a highway trust fund. Instead it relied on bonded indebtedness, which subsequently was dead on arrival at Senator Harry Bird's (D-Va.) Finance Committee. No legislation resulted in 1955, but the case had been made for an interstate system, and the stage was set for an historic compromise on funding.

After a conference to iron out differences between House and Senate bills, Congress authorized an interstate and defense highway system, and the program was signed into law in June 1956. "Ike's Interstates" were to be funded on a pay-as-you-go basis from a new highway trust fund (HTF) enacted at the same time and supported with dedicated collections from federal motor fuel (three cents/gallon for both gasoline and diesel fuel) and related excises. By compromise in the enabling legislation, the federal matching share was increased to 90 percent for new construction and 50 percent for maintenance; a state could tack on its own levies to cover the matching share requirements and its own supplemental highway programs. The funding formula helped large, rural states complete their parts of the national network earlier than they could have with literally applied, pay-as-you-go rules. States retained full ownership of and operating responsibility for the new interstate highways within their borders.

From the outset, the interstate system duplicated most of the routes and functions of the American railway network. Often the new divided highways were within sight distance of transcontinental rail lines built almost a century earlier. Topography and demography made it so. Some routes followed the trails, roads, and railways of the great Westward Expansion — natural pathways such as the Great Platte River route; passages over or through the mountains at Sherman Hill, Weber Canyon, Raton Pass,

Donner Summit, Lookout Pass in the Bitterroots, and the Blue Mountains of Oregon; routes along the Arkansas, Colorado, and Humboldt Rivers; and through the Columbia Gorge. But the interstate highway system was also designed to link cities of 50,000 population and the capitals of the states.

Alternative Strategies for Funding New Highways before the IHS
Necessity is the mother of invention and also the construction of transport infrastructure. If a state couldn't do it any other way (that is, if there were no federal program for limited access highway construction), it could build a tollway. The costs of a particular productive activity can only be interpreted in relation to competitive alternatives and the surrounding economic milieu. The early and mid-1950s were years of intense public policy debate about who should pay for badly needed upgrades and expansion of intercity highway capacity. The railroads favored the "Eastern" model of toll roads—financed, in most instances, by special issues of state and local tax-exempt bonds backed by toll collections; the railroads figured that, with toll roads, a better match would be achieved between user payments and their actual cost responsibility for road construction, maintenance, and policing, not to say negative externalities such as air pollution, accidents, and congestion. Without full cost recovery user fees, truckers and bus operators would enjoy implicit or explicit government subsidies.[35]

Almost all other interested parties favored the "Western" model of financing limited-access highways—paid for exclusively or largely from current excise taxes on fuel sold at the filling station pump. In the prototype, just before and after World War II, California built high-performance facilities in and around both Los Angeles and San Francisco and had plans for constructing a statewide system. Some significance resided, therefore, in Westerners describing multilane, limited access, highways as freeways while Easterners called them turnpikes.

The issue was largely resolved in favor of the freeway point of view with passage of the National Interstate and Defense Highways Act of 1956. This legislation ratified the building of approximately 41,000 miles of high-performance highways, with 90 percent of the cost to be financed by federal gas taxes; the remaining 10 percent was to come from state funds. Existing toll roads were largely incorporated into the new system, even though they did not directly benefit from the new federal aid. As a consequence of these policy choices, trucks probably did receive some subsidy, mainly from other highway users. Conversely, even though automobiles were the major sources of any truck subsidy via highway construction, private autos were little handicapped by the fuel excises in their competition with rail for intercity passenger travel.

Initially, there was no animus or disapprobation attached to assigning tolls to major bridges and tunnels, as there later was for increases in general excise taxes to fund roads; for example, tolls were and are the primary funding source for massive expenditures of the Port Authority of New York and New Jersey. In the midcentury decades—before the 1956 IHS legislation—the states of Massachusetts, Connecticut, New York, New Jersey, Pennsylvania, Ohio, Indiana, Illinois, West Virginia, and Kansas all used the tollway method to build limited-access turnpikes. Later, unfortunately, efforts were frequently made in Congress to prevent or eliminate any tolls on facilities built and designated as part of the IHS.[36]

Not long after the interstates and toll roads were built, *post hoc ergo propter hoc*, rail passenger service dwindled. Likewise motor carriers on the highways succeeded in drawing away a preponderance of high-value merchandise freight. The ubiquitous boxcars of the 1950s—with railroad names and rolling geography lessons (slogans like "Everywhere West" or "Southern Serves the South" painted on their sides)—were gradually replaced with eighteen-wheel semitrailers—these with a family name on the truck's tractor and an owner-operator at the wheel. Reliable family automobiles on smooth flowing highways, and later cars equipped with air conditioning, made long-distance trips feasible. The new divided highways were much safer than their predecessors—narrow, two-lane, winding, stop-and-go roads. Together with jet aircraft for longer journeys, the IHS effectively replaced passenger trains in almost all city-pairs except in the Northeast Corridor.

The Highway Trust Fund and Pay-As-You-Go Construction

The IHS as we know it, more than anything else, was the product of an unprecedented piece of national public financing legislation designed to support construction and maintenance of the new highways.[37] The key was a nationwide excise tax levied per gallon of gasoline or diesel fuel pumped at the point of sale—supplemented with new direct sales taxes on automobiles, tires, and inner tubes. Revenues from the excise taxes were to be dedicated to construction and maintenance of highways laid out under coordinated state-by-state plans that fit together to form the national IHS network.

The HTF was created in the same 1956 legislation as the interstate highways; it had the primary purpose of ensuring full funding for the new system. The HTF also supports construction and maintenance of non-interstate federal-aid highways and certain other related purposes. At the 1974 rate, federal highway expenditures totaled almost $5 billion annually.[38] Interstates carry between 20 and 25 percent of all highway vehicle-miles.[39]

Pay-as-you-go financing (construction at the same pace as collections came in from the new excise levies) contrasted with a competing policy proposal advanced within the Eisenhower administration, namely, using bond revenues to "front" interstate construction. Pay-as-you-go slowed construction, but perhaps not so much as one would think—because (in any event) a great deal of planning, land acquisition, and engineering design work had to be accomplished before actual construction could begin, and excise collections were already accumulating. In the West, where expenditures on the preliminaries outpaced collections from the new excises, federal officials allowed construction to proceed in advance of revenue collections from individual states but not for the IHS as a whole.[40]

The Most Potent Competition

Casual observation of the size and number of trucks operating on any segment of the interstate highways or toll roads is a reminder that big trucks are big business and are big competitors to the freight railroads. Major changes within the trucking industry greatly affected the nature and extent of truck–rail competition. Many of these would warrant a chapter of their own, but in summary fashion, the four most important factors were the rise of owner-operator trucking, trucking deregulation, larger allowable truck sizes and weights, and the optimization of supply chains.

THE RISE OF OWNER-OPERATOR TRUCKING

For about $100,000 in capital commitments, a truck driver/entrepreneur could acquire, by purchase or lease, a big rig with a sleeper cab. Husband–wife teams frequently did so to pool expenses and lengthen average hauls. For years the going rate for a truckload of freight was close to $1/mile, at 6 miles/gallon of diesel fuel. When diesel fuel costs spiked, the owner-operator might be able to force a fuel surcharge, but in a recession, that might not work, and the owner-operator would have to exit the business. Today, however, owner-operation of motor carriers is not the predominant fact of intercity freight logistics that it was twenty years ago. Four underlying causal and explanatory factors are: high fuel prices, highway congestion, the trend to employee drivers, and the competitive success of domestic rail intermodal service.

TRUCKING DEREGULATION

Public economic regulation of trucking entry, routes, and rates by the Interstate Commerce Commission (ICC) was established in 1935 and ended in 1978. Trucking regulation was a child of the Great Depression and was intended to moderate ruinous price competition by limiting entry and only allowing motor carriers to provide service over routes for which they had certificates of public convenience and necessity (PC&N). As the motor carrier industry evolved, firms tended to specialize in services like less than truckload (LTL) delivery, full truckload (TL) service, bulk (liquid) transport, haul of agricultural goods exempt from regulation (including refrigerated or reefer transport, typically by owner-operators), contract carriage (also outside normal regulatory restrictions), automobile haul-away (typically unionized), and household goods carriers (highly regulated as to routes, rates, and services).

In the 1970s, truckload and LTL services divided quite sharply between, on the one hand, regulated and unionized LTL operators (such as Roadway, Yellow, and UPS) with networks of sort terminals, and on the other hand, nonunion TL firms (like J.B. Hunt, Schneider, and Warner) specializing in nonstop, door-to-door delivery. Eventually the TL firms (which were most competitive with rail boxcar service) became as large and well-known as the longer-established certificated LTL operators. (TL firms also needed ICC authority, even after trucking deregulation, but that authority was routinely granted on a national or regional basis, not route-by-route.) There were exceptions to each class of operators, of course, but these distinctions generally held.

Motor carrier deregulation was tough on LTL operators because their certificates of operating authority awarded by the ICC or purchased in the market had come to have stand-alone franchise value. This was nonsensical, of course, because the certificates were an artifact of the peculiar style of ICC regulation that tried to make motor carrier operations conform to territories and specific highway route restrictions (in a manner somewhat analogous to railroads). Under deregulation, the certificates had no function and consequently they immediately lost their cash value.

LARGER ALLOWABLE TRUCK SIZES AND WEIGHTS

Meanwhile, some motor carriers increased their typical operating weight and length dimensions (up to 96,000 lbs. gross vehicle weight, with standard trailer lengths of 53 feet in eighteen-wheel configurations). TL firms also increased their range, service reliability, and miles-per-gallon fuel efficiency. Congress had been asked to increase allowable truck weights and lengths, permitting double-trailers on western interstates and eastern turnpikes. These threatened even more diversion of merchandise traffic from rail. Triple bottoms—a tractor pulling three 27-foot trailers—were being used by LTL and package express haulers like FedEx and UPS in these same lanes; they were not much of a competitive factor to traditional rail business, although they may have slowed the conversion of some full truckload business (such as consolidated loads between major sort facilities) from over-the-road trucking to rail intermodal service.

At the same time, public opinion surveys showed that motorists disliked long triple trailer combinations more than they objected to heavy semitrailers of normal length. Long, heavy, double-bottom truck rigs were anathema to both motorists and competing railroads, and to some state highway/transportation department officials: Motorists perceived dangers from swerving trailers and difficulties overtaking long rigs, railroads saw larger trucks as unfair competition, and some highway officials believed heavy trucks caused excessive damage to roads.

Railroads reacted from their gut instincts; they and their enlisted rail industry suppliers fought truck size and weight increases wherever the venue presented itself. Trucking lobbyists, however, were often successful in getting bellwether states to approve higher limits on truck sizes and weights (TSWs), then going to Congress to seek productivity benefits from doing on a national scale what many states had already allowed. When national TSW dimensions were effectively standardized at the higher levels, it was back to the bellwether states to up the ante once again.

Truckers favoring larger TSW limits argued, rather speciously, that bigger trucks represented fuel savings, productivity, and safety benefits for the public; these contentions depended on a static view of intermodal competition—namely, that possibly better operating performance from larger trucks could be claimed as public benefits without taking into account the dynamic view, namely, that larger trucks would divert tonnage from the generally safer and more fuel-efficient railroads. A proper analysis required looking at the system effects, not just single larger trucks individually. Indeed, it is this secondary network effect, generally ignored in public discussions by trucking advocates, that has caused significant increases in highway congestion in recent years. But again, railroads had to be careful in making their case because often their trucking competitors had become customers of their emerging intermodal service offerings.

TRUCKS HELP SHIPPERS OPTIMIZE SUPPLY CHAINS

Deregulation of motor carriers facilitated their maturation into modern logistics providers for manufacturers and retailers. Trucks operate the essential links between factories or port of entry facilities, distribution centers (DCs), and retail stores or home delivery services. Under recognized logistics principles, shipper decisions typically are based on on-time reliability and inventory minimization factors; these are more important than necessarily trying to find the lowest possible absolute level of transportation rates, and they are service qualities for which trucks have competitive advantages over railroads.

Combined air cargo and motor carrier small and express package services completely replaced the Railway Express Agency and railroads' less than carload (LCL) traffic by about 1960.

Advanced Truckload Firms Compete with Rails in Many Markets

In the last third of the twentieth century, rivalry between railroads and large trucks became both extensive and intensive. The competition became so important (and in some ways so difficult to understand) that the Association of American Railroads formed a special group investigating all aspects of truckload motor carrier economics. The group coined the term *advanced truckload firms (ATLFs)* to distinguish the most rail-competitive trucking companies from generic services provided by local, specialized, LTL carriers and other motor carriers. The AAR group described ATLFs as achieving "remarkable efficiency gains" from applying new approaches and increasing use of nonunion company drivers. ATLFs emphasized

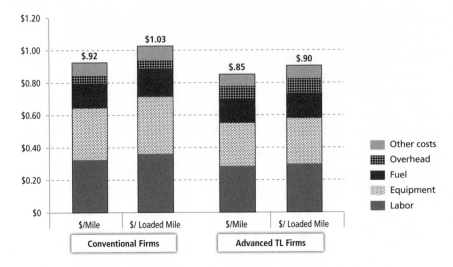

Figure 4.1 Motor Carrier Competition to Railroads. Competition to railroads from dereg-ulated truckload carriers for long hauls and a wide range of commodities became tougher after completion of much of the interstate highway system and approval of larger truck sizes and weights. This analysis by the AAR in 1987 showed how advanced truckload firms achieved oper-ating costs about 10 percent lower than those of traditional truckload firms, which may not have changed much from the older regulated trucking model.

close integration of operations and marketing—with careful actions to select and tailor services to satisfy these markets.

The AAR group documented how advanced truckload firms, by "sharply cutting almost every category of costs" and using their cost advantages to expand rapidly, dramatically changed the level and composition of TL sector productivity. ATLF firms were able then to exploit their economic advantages to "capture important blocks of railroad traffic."[41] Figure 4.1 reproduces the AAR's calculations of rail-competitive costs per ton-mile for typical truck rigs and for ATLFs, in 1986 dollars. The difference in ton-mile costs for firms in the two categories favors ATLFs by about 10 percent. Notice that these conventional TL truck costs work out to be very close to the $1/mile rule of thumb for truckload revenues, as shippers had come to expect.

The AAR group laboriously collected unpublished data and fed it to a cus-tomized computer model to narrow their focus and sharpen conclusions. The model results established that rail competitive traffic covered nonbulk, mixed manufactured traffic in almost every mileage range from 300 to 3,000 miles. There were exceptions, of course, but these were the main parameters. If distances were shorter, railroads could not compete at all; if they were longer hauls, railroads usually could mount competitive service because a single driver would have to rest overnight en route. For bulk goods, trucks could compete in some time-windows—such as trucking grain long distances after seasonal workers engaged in the harvest became available to work as long haul truck drivers. If manufactured goods were of unwieldy size or bulk—harvesters, earth-moving machinery, military impedimenta, pipe for new pipeline construction (again the older mode facilitating the newer)—railroads might have a good shot at winning the business.

Gradually, and in some respects surprisingly, ATLFs like J.B. Hunt and Schneider National also became major customers of rail intermodal services—particularly after becoming convinced enough of the advantages of using the rail intermodal option to invest in domestic containers and use them in the most dense and long-haul lanes. Railroads touted the savings in fuel, labor, and highway congestion delays that their new customers (the ATLFs) could realize. More broadly, railroads became better at telling their "green" story and enlisting allies of every stripe. CSX ran national television ads bragging that their tons get an average of 436 miles per gallon (later raised to 500 miles per gallon). High fuel prices have had a tendency to drive some freight to rail, as railroads are over three times more fuel efficient than TL service.

We do not know what course future energy prices will take, but railroads have substantial potential to benefit from further fuel-efficiency improvements in the future. Also, highway congestion will be more of a competitive factor in the future, in part because funding and right-of-way constraints are likely to make it difficult for states to keep pace with highway capacity and maintenance requirements. Indeed, several states are actively encouraging partnerships with railroads to enable improvements to rail services paralleling heavily used truck lanes.

The Contentious Problems of Highway Cost Allocation

The most difficult policy issue affecting rivalry between freight railroads and motor carriers continues to be the allocation of road construction and maintenance costs to various classes of highway users and the related issue of whether large trucks pay their way. The challenge of proper cost

Table 4.1 Modal Comparative Advantages by Market

Shipment Value/Weight	Intercity Trip Distance, in Miles				
	0–250	250–500	500–1,000	1,000–2,000	2,000 and over
Retail goods (light)	Truck	Truck	Truck Rail Intermodal	Truck Rail Intermodal	Truck Rail Intermodal
Consumer durables, other manufactured goods (moderate)	Truck Rail	Truck Rail Intermodal	Truck Rail Intermodal	Truck Rail Intermodal	Truck Rail Intermodal
Bulk goods (heavy)	Truck Rail Water	Rail Water Truck	Rail Water	Rail Water	Rail Water

The comparative advantages of several transport modes in handling high- and moderate-value manufactured goods are shown. Rail/highway intermodal service has penetrated a broad range of distances. Water competition, where available, usually sets a floor under rail rates.

Source: U.S. DOT, Bureau of Transportation Statistics, *Pocket Guide*, 2010, p. 20.

allocation has existed since the genesis of the Highway Trust Fund in the 1956 Highway Act.

Periodic highway cost allocation studies have generally shown that the largest and heaviest classes of trucks fall far short of paying their fair share of highway use.[42] This contention was supported by a 1969 cost allocation study performed by the Federal Highway Administration (FHWA) and reconfirmed in similar reports published by FHWA in subsequent years. Table 4.1 shows results from the 1997 study, which concluded: "The overall equity of combination vehicles has improved since the 1982 Federal [Highway Cost Allocation] Study, but as a group, combinations still pay only 90 percent of their cost responsibility and the heaviest combinations may pay only 60 percent of their highway costs. . . . Five axle tractor semitrailers have the largest total underpayment of any vehicle class. . . ."[43]

The Other Side of the Story: The Trust Fund and Fuel Taxes

The HTF is now going broke, and there are at least four reasons why. First, high fuel prices and under-performance of the US economy have discouraged driving somewhat, meaning lower fuel-excise collections. Second, allowable uses of the HTF have been broadened, originally to support mass transit and, more recently, various system enhancements such as

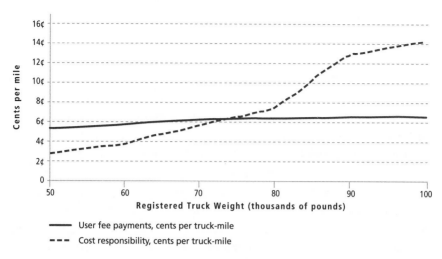

Figure 4.2 Big Trucks Do Not Pay Their Way. Federal motor vehicle excise taxes (user fee payments) do not cover the actual public costs (mainly from damage to highways) of the largest five-axle tractor-trailer combination vehicles. Clearly, heavier trucks are the problem, and for these, the cross-subsidy from lighter, less damaging vehicles is greatest. The analysis on which Figure 4.2 is based was prepared by the Federal Highway Administration (FHWA) in 1997; it confirms results from many similar studies by FHWA over the years.

bike paths. Third, revenue collections have declined relative to total highway traffic growth, again for two main reasons—motor vehicles are becoming more fuel efficient (meaning relatively less fuel consumption to tax at the same rate per gallon), and also ethanol added to gasoline domestic farmers in the name of cleaner air. Fourth, various highway construction and maintenance costs have increased, notably those linked to fuel prices (like asphalt and Portland cement), and the costs of reconstruction and maintenance of roads under traffic. Many observers complain that the cost of environmental reviews (with associated delays) and public participation in road improvement planning have also escalated unreasonably.

Broadening of the HTF probably helps restore a measure of modal equity because if rail-competitive trucks receive an implicit cross subsidy from other highway users, drawing down the HTF to benefit transit and ethanol production somewhat diminishes the effect. Railroads don't gain directly, but they don't mind the highway authorities having less money to spend on projects that aid their competitors. Also, if the HTF runs low on funds, there is more likelihood that highway fuel excises will be increased, and that would help restore modal equity vis-à-vis railroads. It is really quite astonishing that motor fuel excises have not been raised in recent years to keep pace with inflation.

The more general and economically compelling point in today's world is that highway users don't have to pay the full social costs of their decision to drive. Noise, congestion, and air pollution spillovers are pushed to neighbors. Gasoline is relatively cheap in the United States partly because all taxpayers subsidize oil companies through the percentage depletion allowance, intangible drilling cost write-offs, and foreign tax credits, not to say national defense expenditures.

An underlying issue is that the per-gallon basis of highway levies is flawed, and the rate of fuel taxation is too low. As mentioned, when fuel efficiency improves, less revenue comes in; this might be a good thing for the environment because higher effective fuel prices discourage fuel consumption per mile, if not miles driven. But the real goal should be emissions-adjusted social welfare, not more miles per gallon per se. In short, the whole basis of highway fee collection needs to be reconsidered and reset, probably on the basis of vehicle-miles travelled by vehicle classes, and calibrated to account for route-specific emissions and time-of-day-variable congestion factors—as well as road damage from heavier vehicles. This would be good economics and would restore some measure of fairness to intermodal subsidy policy.

Unless and until truckers pay their full fair share into the trust fund, they should have no complaint about diversion of HTF funds to broader transport purposes. If highway spending is truly inadequate, there is ample inelasticity in motor fuel excises and tolls to support raising excise tax rates for underwriting legitimate expenditures. It is not necessary to squeeze transit and bike path funding for this purpose. Funding for high speed rail projects from motor vehicle fuel excises is a different matter, but should not be dismissed out of hand.

Bottom Line on the Social and Competitive Impacts of Highways

Three things should be noted about highway advocates' ongoing dedication to preserving the interstate and defense highways concept.

First, emphasis on construction of inner-city freeways drained both potential supporters and public funding resources from rapid transit and modernization of commuter railroads. With notable exceptions, like Metro-North in New York and Connecticut, Metra in Chicago, NJDOT in New Jersey, and SEPTA in Pennsylvania, highway programs squeezed out much transit and commuter rail development. These trends did not hurt freight rail-roads and in some minor ways may have helped them cover certain common urban infrastructure costs, but inner-city freeways represented a huge negative impact on transit.

Second, the push to make interstate highways also serve as intra-metropolitan roadways had a substantial impact on location of industrial activity, and thus probably made rail-served locations less competitive vis-à-vis truck-served locations.

Third, railroads saw the enormous power of highway construction, auto-motive, and motor carrier advocates in developing an entire set of modal institutions and infrastructure generally adverse to rail interests. To take only one example, when railroads were hit with a special deficit reduction tax of 4.3 cents per gallon on diesel fuel in the 1990s, the proceeds went to the federal budget's General Fund (from which railroads gained no clear value); the practice continued from 1990 to 2004, at a cost to railroads approaching $200 million annually. Barges also paid the deficit reduction tax after 1993, but motor carriers and airlines were able to have their collections dedicated to infrastructure trust funds where, unlike the rail and barge taxes, they were closely aligned with their modal interests.[44]

The main argument Congress used in repealing the tax was not that the need for deficit reduction had passed, but that this particular levy was unfair to barges and railroads, which it clearly was.

Tom Lewis, in the final paragraphs of *Divided Highways* recalls Walt Whitman's line, "O public road, You express me better than I can express myself." So it was that Americans expressed themselves at midcentury, as Lewis says, "in all their glory, all of their virtues, and not a few of their vices."[45] The highways show our grace and our vision, but they also reveal, at times, our impetuousness and our shortsightedness. They represent the height of American technology. They suggest our dreams for what the United States might become—one nation, indivisible, bound for all time by concrete and asphalt strands . . . and we learned that the very roads we thought would unite us have sometimes actually divided us. Over the decades the interstates have reflected our shifting attitudes about technology, landscape, community, race relations, and the quality of our lives.[46]

In the 1991 Intermodal Surface Transportation Act (ISTEA), Congress mandated a more integrated approach to intermodal transportation improvements, "from bicycles to airplanes. No longer would America seek to meet its desire for mobility only with highways," Lewis wrote.[47]

It remains to be seen how this updated vision will work out over the decades, but it does seem to be the case that transport policy has become less rigid ideologically or more adaptable to circumstances such as higher energy prices and the cost-effectiveness of rail intermodal competition. Along the way, railroads have become considerably greener and more sustainable. For example, after the advent of containerization and double-stack trains in the last two decades of the twentieth century, railroads found far greater success in competing against motor carriers for high-value manufactured goods traffic than they had been able to achieve with mixed carload service in manifest trains.

Indeed, the rail–truck competitive picture has changed quite remarkably in the early years of the twenty-first century. Responding to historically unprecedented motor fuel costs, relatively high labor (driver) costs, and substantial congestion on key parts of the highway network, a number of large motor carriers have increased their use of rail intermodal transport, especially in unbalanced lanes. This trend, entirely in keeping with the principles of logistics management, means that traditional rail-truck competition has, in some respects, morphed into rail-truck cooperation. This is a story that is not complete.

With respect to highway competition with rail passenger service, the effect of the IHS was much like that of the development of jet aviation, which is discussed in the next chapter. Intercity auto travel on the IHS was entirely predictable once automobiles became reliable enough not to break down during a long trip away from home. Families typically owned at least one car for local use; to take it on an intercity trip was simply exploiting a characteristic similar to what Alfred Kahn had famously said about aircraft—that they were "marginal costs with wings."[48] By extension, automobiles were "marginal costs with tires." Nominal gasoline prices were only 10 percent of the level they reached by the turn of the millennium, and autos had become both comfortable and flexible for family trips. The choice to drive rather than go by train was almost a foregone conclusion. The impact on railroad passenger travel demand was huge.

Concluding Thoughts on Two Rival Modes

To an observer from another continent, it would seem that the remarkable coverage, low cost, and enviable efficiency of the American transport system is characterized by the richness of the different modes.[49] And in fact, as we have observed elsewhere in this book, American transport policy places great stock in intermodal rivalries to reinforce regulation of rates and services by independent commission. In effect, we have three different forms of restraint on transport businesses (not everywhere, of course, but in a wide array): (1) independent regulation, (2) the market within each mode, and (3) the competition from rival modes. In support of the alternative modes, American taxpayers have been willing to supplement their user-based funding quite generously. That is, to expand, repair, and nourish this intermodal competition, we offer quite extensive subsidies, direct and hidden, to firms engaging in such functions. It really should be no surprise that the overall transport system looks so robust and contributes so strongly to the national economy.

We know that appearance is not everything, however. We know that the HTF is close to bankrupt, its highways and bridges are suffering from deferred maintenance, and it cannot keep up with projected traffic growth unless higher fuel prices discourage motor vehicle freight and travel, and user fee increases and congestion tolls are enacted. We know that the inland waterways are far less efficient than they could be with a better toll system to pay for needed system improvements in locks and dams. We know that the next generation of air traffic control must be developed to a much higher standard than today's, and that it will take many years and billions of dollars to build the new system. Almost no one is satisfied with today's system of aviation security screening. Improvements to rail passenger services in promising corridors seem excessively costly and are maddeningly slow to come about.

Soberingly, we know that major transportation accidents involving large losses of lives and property, and many painful injuries, are only a headline away.

So America has "the best transport system in the world," but we are often dissatisfied with it. In this chapter we have suggested a few commonsense reforms; others will follow in remaining chapters. The authors hope more reforms will be inspired by this book.

5

THE DECLINE OF RAILWAY
PASSENGER SERVICE, 1900–1970

Competition in the passenger service is less keen than in the
freight service, and of a different nature. . . . The gross revenue
derived by the railroads of the United States from their freight
business is two and one-third times the receipts from the passenger traffic, and if it were possible to ascertain the net profits
attributable to each branch of the service, it would be found
that the profits assignable to freight transportation are more
than two and one-third times the net profits secured from carrying passengers. . . . Most persons travel for business purposes,
and the cost of the railroad ticket has but little weight with
them. There is, however, a large and growing amount of traveling for pleasure, and that is capable of stimulation by reduction in rates.

—EMORY R. JOHNSON (1908)

Who shot the passenger train? . . . It would be simpler if the
train were just a means of moving people. But the train is also
photogenic and nostalgic and fun, a source of employment and
taxes, the pride of every Chamber of Commerce, and something on which you hang mail and express cars at one end and
a business car at the other. And because trains stir up so much
emotion, they are susceptible to the magnificent myth, if not
the big lie.

—DAVID P. MORGAN, *Trains Magazine*, April 1959

At the turn of the twentieth century, railroads held a virtual monopoly
over intercity domestic passenger travel. Only an occasional riverboat
or coastal steamer would provide competition, and if it did, at costs roughly
equal to rail and at elapsed times usually three or four times as great. The
rail share of intercity travel by common carrier in 1900 was almost certainly at the 90 percent level or greater, and the rail share of service by all

modes was probably not much lower (as the mass market automobile had yet to appear in large numbers). The economic and political forces propelling the development of internal combustion engine technologies using highways and airways were just beginning to be visualized, and no one had yet taken off in a heavier-than-air flying machine. By 1970, however, the rail share of common carrier traffic was heading below 10 percent, and the rail share of all transport modes was about 1 percent or a bit below.

Transportation has been a key component in the development of the modern world. The railroad, serving as the first form of reliable, relatively fast overland travel, has been integral in the remarkable growth of the American industrial system for nearly 200 years. In particular, the railroad passenger business has played an important role in the general development and unification of the nation. While the rail service of today remains an important agent in the transport of freight, the relevance of the once profitable intercity passenger business is now negligible except in the Northeast Corridor between Boston and Washington, DC.

This chapter of *American Railroads* focuses on a part of the railroad industry that, more than the rest, survived but only barely, and certainly did not prosper. Nor has passenger service, unlike the freight business it had always accompanied in the past, realized any sort of genuine renaissance in recent years. To be sure, the persistent downward trend in passenger train service cannot be described as a continual slide. In fact, at some points during the long decline, it appeared as if the passenger industry would regain its footing, but this did not last.

The chapter will explore the economic forces causing the decline and eventual marginalization of this formerly important mode of travel. Like the soap opera David P. Morgan had in mind, we want to know who shot the passenger train?—and why?—because passenger train service is romantic and nostalgic and environmentally benign, and maybe worth re-energizing for the future. Was the fall and near-extinction of the railroad passenger business inevitable? Or could this much-loved mode of transport have been preserved and refreshed, and perhaps be raised to a higher level of service and speed, as has occurred in Japan, China, and Western Europe?

Boom Goes Bust: From the Roaring Twenties to the Onset of World War II

The roots of the decline of passenger trains lay in the years following World War I, when the railroad passenger service began a downward trend in business, which (again, except for the Northeast Corridor from Boston to Washington, DC) ultimately ended in the competitive irrelevance and virtual extinction of the service—as it remains today. Little understood by most observers is the importance of the interwar period from 1920 to 1940, during which many of the events that determined the industry's ultimate fate had their genesis. Mistakes made during that time left rail carrier passenger service with damage from which it would never completely recover.

In the first years of the twentieth century, wealthier patrons were enjoying rail travel by Pullman parlor and sleeper-cars, trans-Atlantic luxury steamships, and new-fangled automobiles; they were aware of the Montgolfier Brothers' lighter-than-air balloon flights 100 years earlier, and the Wright Brothers' recent successes at Kitty Hawk. Then in the Roaring Twenties, all the talk was about barnstorming flyers and, in the late 1920s and the 1930s, the German Zeppelins. These were even featured in a marvelous, now much-coveted commemorative issue of US postage stamps, but the Zeppelin craze ended with the Hindenburg's fiery crash in Lakehurst, New Jersey, on May 6, 1937, killing thirty-six. And then there was the outbreak of World War II.

After suffering through the Great Depression, America's fascination with aviation, not least its pride in the amazing military aircraft of World War II, became an easy acceptance of flight on commercial airlines in the 1950s. Similarly, the fondness for Model T's, Tin Lizzies, and Stutz Bearcats in the 1920s became in the 1950s an infatuation with station wagons, convertibles, and tailfins. The new Interstate Highways were powerful instruments of commercial development and personal mobility, but there were unanticipated consequences for railroads, as we saw in the previous chapter.

The decade of the 1920s witnessed the first consistent decline in railroad passenger traffic. With the exception of 1923, the total number of passengers carried decreased steadily every year. By 1929, when the nation was on the threshold of financial crisis, the number of passengers had declined to about 62 percent of the 1920 amount. The passenger losses that occurred over that span of years were indeed staggering. At the beginning, in 1920, over 1.2 billion people traveled on railroads in the United States, still the all-time record. By 1940, the annual total had dropped to just over 456 million.[1] This decline, when considered in light of the general surge in transportation demand throughout that era, makes the drift away from rail passenger travel all the more noteworthy.

Despite the steady decline in travel, railroad managers remained surprisingly complacent during the years preceding the Great Depression. In the face of setbacks in passenger numbers, the industry saw little reason for concern because most of the ridership losses had been on the relatively short-distance runs. These losses were absorbed with little regret for the short hauls, were generally regarded as unprofitable, and railroads still possessed undeniable control of long-distance travel.[2] Even with the curtailment of many local passenger trains, the surviving long-distance runs remained profitable enough to keep total operations in the black. The long-distance passenger service, then, as Hilton points out, "was expected to survive indefinitely."[3] In the late 1920s, railroads still had good reason to feel they possessed a firm foothold in the passenger market.

"Brother, Can You Spare a Dime?"

The onset of the Great Depression in 1929 rapidly changed railroad fortunes for the worse. The volume of traffic fell with the decline in business activity, costing the railways much of their remaining passenger business; these losses were centered in first class and the commuter services (a function of employment contraction, no doubt), as well as long-distance tourism (a luxury). Between 1929 and 1933, passenger miles plunged by nearly one half, from just over 31 billion to 16.3 billion.[4] Significantly, first-class parlor and sleeping car traffic suffered bigger losses than coach travel (indicating their income elasticity). Both coach and sleeping car travel expanded from 1933 to 1941 as the economy climbed out of depression but, interestingly, the less income-elastic coach travel again did better than sleeping car services, more than doubling, while sleeping and parlor car traffic was up by about 80 percent. Overall, coach travel in 1941 was more than 35 percent higher than in 1929, while sleeping and parlor car travel was down by almost 30 percent over the same period.

Starting in 1930, passenger service became unprofitable, a trend that continued for the rest of the decade.[5] As the Great Depression wore on, the industry plunged into ever-deepening financial crisis. For Class I roads, the overall rate of return on total property investment plunged from 4.9 percent in 1929 to a dismal low of 1.24 percent by 1932.[6]

As costs shot up, the impecunious railways were forced to cut capital expenditures for equipment and roadway drastically.[7] To respond, the federal government offered some temporary financial assistance primarily in the form of loans issued by the Reconstruction Finance Corporation and

Railroad Credit Corporation.[8] Later, prompted by the realization that the Great Depression would not end as expeditiously as anticipated, Congress passed the Emergency Railroad Transportation Act of 1933. The legislation provided additional loans to the railroads, but the funds were issued with greater discretion than before. Financial assistance was limited to railways that were solvent and not in need of reorganization.[9] Although these finances provided some relief in the dark days of the Great Depression, a fundamental turn in the fate of the passenger business was soon to come from within the industry itself.

With their backs against the wall financially, a few innovative railroaders began to search for ways to salvage what remained of passenger travel. Early in the Great Depression, the Interstate Commerce Commission (ICC) allowed the railroads to cut fares regionally, along with introducing incentives such as discounts on round-trip and tourism tickets. The changes aided some railroads more than others, and they did help to reverse the trend of declining traffic, especially that of coach travel.[10] At the same time, innovations that should have been added earlier were belatedly implemented. Beginning around 1930, efforts were undertaken to improve passenger travel amenities. Air conditioning was installed in many of the upscale cars. This, in turn, allowed for cleaner, more comfortable travel. Brighter interiors soon followed, as drab, dark colors were no longer needed to hide dirt.[11]

Streamliners Debut

In 1934, a new era began with the introduction of an all coach, higher speed train. Introduced by the Chicago, Burlington & Quincy (CB&Q) railroad, the Zephyr could attain speeds in excess of 100 miles an hour. Burlington's Zephyr was the first passenger application to feature diesel power, which was much cleaner and more efficient than the steam engines they replaced. The trains incorporated other innovations, including stainless steel construction, streamlined aerodynamics, and articulated cars.[12] The train's lightweight design enabled it to attain high speeds, and the Burlington made every effort to market this fact. Completed in April 1934, the train was taken on a publicity campaign that culminated in a record-breaking dawn-to-dusk run from Denver to Chicago. The train was also featured in a movie before it was put into regular service that November.[13] This new and innovative style of promotion marked an abrupt change of strategy for the railroads. As one commentator pointed out, "the most important and pertinent fact in this is . . . merchandising. What has kept the railroads static for almost twenty years has been the lack of this kind of thinking."[14]

Later in 1934, Union Pacific also inaugurated a "streamliner" into its service, the gas-distillate powered M-10000, with an aluminum alloy body. Most of the lightweight CB&Q and UP trains were placed on short, daytime runs between important cities, where their speed could be used to regain lost highway traffic. The streamliners were less costly to operate than their predecessors, and they were wildly popular with the public. A combination of public enthusiasm and a general improvement in the business cycle yielded positive results for the railways. In its first year of the Zephyr's service, *Business Week* reported that the train had been responsible for a 50 percent increase in traffic on its route of operation, much of which was claimed to have been captured from the highways. At the same time, the Zephyr's operating costs were approximately one half of the heavy steam-powered trains that it replaced.[15] The trend held for the railroad industry as a whole. The *Yearbook of Railroad Information* enthusiastically noted that 1934 saw the first annual improvements in the number of passengers and passenger mileage carried since 1923.[16]

The railways made efforts to follow up on these initial successes. To facilitate the higher speeds, track was upgraded and better signaling devices were installed. Rapid technological improvements of the mid-1930s soon allowed for the construction of full-sized locomotives with diesel propulsion. In 1936, the railroad industry outfitted heavier, long-haul trains with streamlined construction.[17] These larger, second-generation streamliners provided more comfortable high-speed travel over longer distances than the initial small diesel-powered and gas-distillate-powered lightweight streamliners.

Before long, these efforts began to pay off. A 1940 report issued by the Association of American Railroads (AAR) noted that the railroads attained record total operating efficiency that year, and average train speed remained at its highest level ever.[18] The improvements did not solve the fiscal predicament of the railroads, however. Throughout the late 1930s, the passenger business continued to lose money.[19] A 1939 study noted that "in no period in railroad history has the degree of financial distress been as serious."[20] Many of the nation's railroad companies faced bankruptcy and by 1938, nearly one-third of the nation's railroad mileage lay in receivership.[21]

One reason the passenger service continued to struggle at a time when the overall economy was beginning to recover was the lower rates charged by the railways. The effect that discounted fares had upon gross revenues is illustrated in Gregory Thompson's analysis of the Southern Pacific. He found that, although passenger traffic rose rapidly, total revenues increased at a slackened pace due to the heavily cut fares. Ironically, "the passenger deficit worsened as the economy improved."[22] This applied to most other railroad companies as well, but particularly in the South and West, where the greatest fare reductions had occurred.[23] At the same time, expenditures for modernization had been costly and had cut into operating margins significantly.

An Awakening

In September 1938, President Franklin D. Roosevelt appointed a committee comprised of three railroad managers and three labor leaders and chaired by M. W. Clement, president of the Pennsylvania Railroad, to investigate the railroad problem. The findings of the group, sometimes referred to as the Committee of Six,[24] issued that December, addressed the two major handicaps facing the industry: continued economic depression, and nearly unrestrained competition. They noted that the artificial depression of rail rates, which were at their lowest level in years, could be attributed to efforts to meet the competition. While acknowledging that an improvement in the business cycle would partially mitigate the situation, it would not provide a complete remedy. Noting the "gross inequality" that existed between regulation of the rails and their competing modes of transport, the Committee of Six concluded that a solution would come only by putting a moratorium on artificially depressed rail rates. Their report urged that legislation be enacted that would ensure uniform governmental regulation for all types of transportation.[25]

With the passage of the Transportation Act of 1940, it seemed as if the recommendations of the committee had been followed. The act ostensibly was intended by Congress to promote a fair and impartial policy of regulation, and it gave the ICC control over all significant modes of transport apart from aviation.[26] The act only served to increase the authority of the ICC, however, and overarching regulation of the railroads continued unabated.

From the depth of the Great Depression in 1933 to the advent of US entry into World War II in 1941, nevertheless, total intercity rail passenger travel more than doubled. Much but probably not all of the improvement was due to economic recovery. For example, commuter activity (which normally reflected employment) was down slightly from 1933 to 1941—almost certainly reflecting expanding ownership of private autos.

Some would argue that the relatively robust growth of intercity rail passenger service during these years reflected strong efforts by the railroads to improve both the quality and marketing of their rail passenger services. And not only was this an era of streamliners and air conditioning, but also exceptional media attention for rail travel. Among other developments just before the beginning of US involvement in World War II, Cecil B. DeMille's Union Pacific drew large crowds at the box office in 1939.[27] Only a few years later, Judy Garland's rendition of Johnny Mercer's hit "On the Atchison, Topeka and the Santa Fe" from The Harvey Girls (1945), won the Oscar for best song. UP's luxury ski resort at Sun Valley, Idaho, with a newfangled ski lift invented in the railroad's Omaha shops, was serenaded widely. Dining car meals reached new culinary heights. Sleeping car bedrooms became more spacious and comfortable. Schedule time or speed also became a competitive factor; for example, the Milwaukee Road had steam locomotives that pulled its Hiawathas at close to 110 miles per hour across parts of Wisconsin en route from Chicago to Minneapolis–St. Paul, while the Burlington roughly matched the schedule using Zephyrs.[28] For rail passenger service personnel and aficionados, those years had to be very nearly the "best of times."

Record Traffic in the War Years

America's entry into World War II in 1941 heralded unprecedented increases in business and offered new hope to the ailing railroad industry. While sorrowful in all other respects, the war seemed to be the stimulus to demand that the railroads had long sought, causing passenger traffic to surge. At the same time, shortages of gasoline, tires, and replacement parts, along with restrictions on road construction, led to the virtual curtailment of non-war-related automobile travel. Left with no alternative, civilian travelers flocked back to the railroads. Also, the armed forces relied on the railroads for massive troop movements and other war-related transport.[29] Although the annual number of passengers never reached the level of the early 1920s, the total number of passenger miles traveled during the war topped all previous records. For 1944, annual passenger mileage peaked at

95.7 billion, just over twice the 1920 level of 47.4 billion, and more than three and one-half times prewar levels.[30]

The boom from war-related travel made the passenger business profitable once more. Indeed, for the first time since the 1920s, railroads even made a profit after absorbing a "proportionate share" of general overhead. Beginning in 1942, revenues exceeded expenses for the first time since 1929, and in the peak volume year of 1944, annual passenger revenues exceeded what the ICC called the "solely related costs" of passenger services by over $1 billion, for both the first and last time. These trends would continue until the end of hostilities in 1945.[31] The railroads were largely unable to capitalize on this newfound prosperity, however, as much of their profit went toward the payment of the enormous debt that the railways had accrued during the 1930s. All this happened in spite of a government public relations campaign to reduce wartime travel that repeatedly asked: "Is this trip necessary?"

During the war, construction of new passenger rolling stock was halted as factories retooled for military production. Railroads were forced to absorb the overwhelming load of new passengers with an insufficient fleet of cars, and the existing railroad passenger cars were taxed to the limit.[32] With the lack of both funds and equipment, many necessary repairs were neglected or overlooked. As J. H. Parmalee, director of the AAR's Bureau of Railway Economics, commented in 1943, "[T]he railroads should have done more improvement work, and would have done more, had it not been for restrictions upon materials and other handicaps imposed on them by the war."[33] Because of this neglect, the railroads were in poor physical condition by the war's conclusion. Much of the equipment was simply worn out. Railroad managers planned to invest a large amount of capital in repairs and improvements, which would take time to implement.[34] Following the war, this put the railroads at a disadvantage compared with other modes of transportation, which had not borne the brunt of heavy travel.

Up Against the Postwar Competitive Reality

All in all, in 1945, rail passenger services seemed positioned for a comfortable if not overly exciting future. Railroad managers were sanguine that they could retain a profitable niche in the passenger business in the postwar era. The visionary Edward G. Budd, architect of the Burlington Zephyrs, shared this outlook. He postulated railroad streamliners becoming the "prime movers" of passengers for cities separated by a few hundred miles.[35] Postwar plans were to replace much of the worn-out passenger fleet, and additional cars were ordered to meet the anticipated demand. *Business Week* reported that railway equipment manufacturers anticipated postwar orders of approximately 3,000 cars per year.[36]

Just as predicted, much capital was poured into passenger upgrades following V-J Day. From September 1, 1945, to December 31, 1948, the railroads installed 2,700 new passenger cars. Freight might be the real source of rail economic sustenance, but rightly or wrongly, managements widely believed that railroads sold more freight services if they provided a good passenger experience for business travelers. In the circumstances, there were even some innovations; for example, "vista domes" became standard for luxury trains operating in scenic corridors. Reequipping the passenger fleet and other necessary improvements, however, were extremely costly. In 1948 alone, total expenditures exceeded $1 billion.[37]

Sadly for those millions of Americans who loved rail passenger trains and travel, the postwar results quickly dashed any hopes of a successful revival of peacetime passenger service. After 1945, passenger mileage decreased significantly every year.[38] As could be expected, passenger service also began to lose money once more and became increasingly unprofitable in the following years.[39] These deficits, coupled with increasing internal demands from railroad labor, caused railways to raise fares.[40] Higher rates made it even more difficult for the railways to cope with competition, which continued to intensify through the late 1940s.

By 1955, only a decade after the wartime highs of 1944, rail's share of total intercity travel by all modes had shrunk from almost 35 percent to under 5 percent (refer to Figure 5.2 later in the chapter). Even worse, rail passenger service by 1955 seemed unprofitable by almost any measure. Revenues no longer seemed to cover even what the ICC called solely related costs, let alone fully cover their assigned portion of overhead and fixed costs. The challenge to the railways was unstated but obvious. Despite their continued efforts to modernize, the railroads faced more grave competitive threats than ever before.

In the postwar years, government became the railroads' most debilitating competition. Throughout the 1940s and early 1950s, railroads were still subject to the same intense regulations concerning "service, rates, and fares as in the days when they indeed possessed a full traffic and travel monopoly."[41] And despite legislation intended to equalize regulation, railroad competitors still possessed an unfair advantage. For instance, the ICC mandated that the "railroads keep 258 types of records while airlines had to keep only a fifth as many."[42] During the war, a 15 percent excise tax had been imposed upon common-carrier tickets to discourage travel. Unfortunately for the railroads, this tax was retained after the war and "it succeeded all too well in its original purpose."[43]

To make matters worse, railroads, whose facilities and tracks were classified as private property, were taxed accordingly. After the war, municipalities and counties began to raise railroad property taxes significantly. In time, smaller communities began to levy special property taxes which went directly toward the support of airports. While railroads built and maintained their own facilities, their competitors utilized government-constructed property. *Transportation in America* noted that, although the railroads were taxed heavily, "other forms of transportation escape direct taxation in the degree to which they use public facilities."[44] In this way, railways were forced to make significant contributions to "the general governmental expense, including the cost of subsidies to their competitors."[45] As one writer observes, "this put the railroads in the maddening position of being able to calculate exactly how much they were being required to contribute to the welfare of their competitors."[46]

By 1950, passenger travel via railroads comprised less than 7 percent of the total volume of domestic intercity travel.[47] In the following years, the problem only worsened. Railroad leaders slashed passenger mileage in a desperate effort to economize, but continued to pour vast amounts into new passenger equipment.[48] Despite their efforts, almost nothing could have saved the passenger industry by that point. Then in 1951, airlines introduced coach class fares, which quickly captured most of the remaining rail patronage.[49] As George Hilton observes, "The experience of the early 1950s was enough to disabuse an increasing percentage of rail executives of any optimism remaining from the end of World War II."[50] The arrival of jet aircraft in the late 1950s was the final blow.

Underlying Economic Factors in Passenger Train Deficits

Turning specifically to the economics of rail passenger service, the obvious starting point is the Interstate Commerce Commission's traditional estimates of the passenger service deficit. Though theoretically and methodologically flawed, these are the most comprehensive and historically consistent estimates available. They have been subjected to almost constant review and critique by interested parties, in ICC proceedings and in court litigation as well.

Many analysts and industry people suggested over the years that the ICC's so-called fully distributed costs might understate the true costs of passenger service continuation. Instead, critics said, the ICC should tally the full amount of truly avoidable costs of continuing passenger train service—defined as those that would not be incurred if rail passenger operations were completely eliminated. Most observers believed some additional allowance was needed for other possibilities. For example, operating both freight and passenger operations over the same right of way might increase the costs of both services (diseconomies of scope) over what they would be if operated separately. Throughput on a stretch of rail main line would be greater the more tightly spaced, homogenous, and faster the operations.

For example, if all trains moved at, say, 100 miles per hour, more traffic could be moved than if all trains operated at only 50 miles per hour, all else equal. In contrast, if 50-mile-per-hour freight trains were mixed with 100-mile-per-hour passenger service, the problem becomes more complicated. Sidings must be added so that the faster trains could pull ahead of slower ones. If 100-mile-per-hour operations were added to an existing 50-mile-per-hou flow, spacing would have to be increased to allow for greater braking distances. The authorities might also require an increase in other safety margins for passenger rather than freight operations, even if everything else remained the same. Similarly, available capacity is also sensitive to the particular sequencing of slow and fast trains. In general, it was easier to schedule or dispatch a homogeneous and moderate speed freight operation than a heterogeneous mix of slow freight and high-speed passenger trains.

But that is not all. It is also much easier to design an appropriate road bed for a homogenous operation. Indeed, a fully optimal road bed design could be achieved only if the traffic were homogeneous. Slow trains don't need as much banking on curves as high-speed operations, thereby incurring less wear and tear on rail and wheel flanges for the slow trains. Heavier trains require heavier track than lighter trains. Ballast requirements are also different. The savings realized from use of concrete ties vary. The need for careful maintenance of track alignments and other physical conditions changes with the type of operation; usually, the higher the speed, the more precise the maintenance requirement. Also, the benefits from separating rail traffic from other ground-level activities increases with speed. In short, it is no accident that modern, very-high-speed rail passenger operations, such as those in Japan and Europe, generally operate on tracks exclusively for their own use and almost totally separate from other activities. By contrast, where mixed freight and passenger use has been deliberately promoted, even to the point of sometimes separating ownership and cost responsibility for road bed and operations, the results have been less than satisfactory.[51]

Avoidable Costs: A Classic Issue and Some Classic Studies

The costs of very-high-speed operations were not the issue in the United States in the 1950s, however; the focus instead was on how much of the passenger cost burden could be avoided by allowing some, or perhaps even total, abandonment of conventional rail passenger service operating over track shared with freight trains. The question had some urgency. Many senior rail executives felt that the continued imposition of passenger service obligations on the privately owned US rail system created a deficit that had to be offset by earnings from freight operations if private railroads were to remain solvent. Maintenance of this passenger "subsidy" from freight operations was becoming increasingly difficult. While few knowledgeable observers felt that the avoidable costs were less than the ICC's solely related costs, the possibility could not be fully ruled out that continuous fixed or long-term commitments embodied in those costs might render them other than immediately avoidable. The essential cost question could therefore be somewhat more narrowly defined as follows: How much cost could the railroads expect to avoid in the short to medium term if carriers were released from some or all of their passenger service obligations?

Reacting to these concerns, in 1955 the ICC's Bureau of Accounts, Cost Finding and Valuation published a "Proposed Formula for Determining the Cost of Providing Rail Passenger Train Service by Classes of Traffic and Comparing Costs with the Revenues" and invited critiques and discussion. The major conceptual step advanced in the ICC proposal was to recommend the use of "avoidable costs," as defined. The AAR responded to this initiative by, among other actions, commissioning an independent study of avoidable costs of passenger service by the nonprofit Aeronautical Research Foundation of Cambridge, Massachusetts.[52]

The most important contributions of this study were (1) to propose and illustrate the use of statistical costing when expensive experimental tests or engineering determinations are not available, (2) to formulate a procedure for better identifying and segregating so-called fixed or sunk costs that are truly invariable with output from those that were not, and (3) to outline a procedure that at least entertained the possibility that costs of passenger operations might be greater than the costs directly identifiable with such operations (e.g., the likely additional costs of freight operations if mixed with passenger service as outlined above). In general, rail passenger costs and deficits probably never received as much attention as they did in the late 1950s, reflecting a widespread belief that the industry could not survive under private ownership unless these issues were resolved.

Several conclusions seem to have emerged from all this attention. First, and most important, there really was a passenger deficit. Even limiting passenger costs to a narrow so-called above the rail operating cost calculation would still yield deficit estimates. Such a narrow definition of passenger costs was logically hard to defend. Second, traditional measures of the avoidable costs of passenger service may have systematically underestimated the degree to which passenger train costs actually were fixed, both the short term (say, one year) and medium term (two to ten years). That is, the ability of managers to adapt actual operations expenditures to changes in rail passenger outputs may have been overestimated, leading, in turn, to a systematic underestimation of variable and avoidable costs.[53] Third, given a continuation of then-existing competitive trends, the passenger deficit was likely to become larger and more difficult for privately owned railroads to finance from freight revenues. Even as of the late 1950s, the full-cost US annual passenger deficit already was in the range of $500,000,000 to $1 billion, or roughly equal to net railway operating income at the time. If the public wanted to continue extensive provision of rail passenger services, new sources of funding the deficit would have to be found, including quite possibly the nationalization of all or most of the system.

These practical and definitional problems regarding rail passenger service deficits have not gone away over the years. *American Railroads* returns to these issues as they pertain to contemporary times in Chapter 11.

A New Focus on Markets and Operating Economics

An obvious question is, Why did rail passenger service incur such substantial deficits? Why was rail service "suddenly" so uncompetitive with other modes? How universal was the rail disadvantage? Were there markets where rail could continue to be available?

The answers to such questions were reasonably obvious for longer trips. The time advantage of air travel relative to surface modes was decisive. Even a trip of only 400 miles or so, such as that from Boston to Washington, DC, or San Francisco to Los Angeles, took only a little over one and one-half hours by air, even on a prop plane, but required at least six to seven hours by car, bus, or train. At such distances, the surface modes would not be chosen unless they were substantially less costly or more convenient—or used by recreational travelers who did not much value their time. In certain circumstances, of course, these conditions or some combination of them could add up to a preference for surface travel, especially by leisure and family travelers. However, the evidence suggested that such travelers were relatively few. How else could the dramatic decline in the modal share of rail passenger service in the postwar years be explained? The experience of airline marketing and scheduling people, as well as evidence from econometric studies, indicated that air tended to dominate the other public modes, train and bus, for trips greater than 200 to 300 miles, and that even the private auto lost share substantially at such trip lengths.[54]

Still, there are many intercity trips of less than 200 or 300 miles; why couldn't rail effectively compete for these? The answer seems to hinge on particular qualities of the different modes, most important, operational divisibility or adaptability. Specifically, how big an operating unit was required to achieve minimal unit operating costs and how easily could operations be adapted to serve different levels of output efficiently? Unfortunately for rail, it was and is "the least divisible" of all the major domestic passenger modes—rail, auto, bus, and air. To a rough approximation, both bus and air can operate efficiently with units as small as fifty seats. The automobile can achieve minimal operating costs with only a driver and three or four passengers. By contrast, under conventional operating conditions, efficient rail service would usually require about five or six car train sets with 400 to 500 seats.

Furthermore, if traffic volumes vary substantially along a service corridor, it is difficult to adapt train capacity to match these variations. Cutting or adding cars to a train set requires time and spare track capacity as well as special switching crews, in most cases. Turning a bus or auto or even an aircraft is relatively simple by comparison. It is therefore easier to match capacity offerings for these nonrail modes with available markets and to offer more frequent and convenient service. As a consequence of all this, "intercity rail service is almost always more costly than other modes, the only exceptions being when government subsidies to rail are subtracted from costs or when travel volumes are extraordinarily high and trip distances quite short."[55]

In essence, trains operate most efficiently in high-volume corridors (say, at least 500,000 passengers in each direction annually) where originating and terminating passengers are distributed relatively uniformly over the entire route. It also helps to have strong polar attractions (e.g., big cities or important resorts) at either end of the corridor because balanced flows in both directions avoid empty backhauls and improve the economics of any mode. Because of the time advantage of air travel, even very-high-speed rail passenger services should not expect to serve many trips longer than 300 to 500 miles or so.

Clearly, the best match with such a market in the United States is along the Northeast Corridor between Boston and Washington, DC. An express train passing over that route could be expected to make stops minimally in Philadelphia, Wilmington, and Baltimore;[56] at these stops about as many passengers might debark as enter at most hours and days, although some variation might be expected because of special commuter and weekend patterns. While Washington is a much smaller city than New York, its status as a government center may generate more traffic demand per capita than most other cities. Traffic volumes therefore should not be too unbalanced in one direction or another (and if they were, of course, pricing policies might be devised to equalize the flows). The popular song lyrics seem to need only slight modification: "If rail passenger service can't make it in New York to Washington, it can't make it anywhere!"

At least that seems true in the United States. Actually, several relatively successful introductions of high-speed train service have been made in other countries, particularly in Japan and Europe. Significantly, these have been in corridors meeting the requisite standards more closely or at least as well as New York/Washington. Given enough national income to pay for luxury transport, Tokyo/Osaka might be the best corridor in the world for efficiently implementing high-speed rail passenger service. That, in turn, might explain why Tokyo/Osaka was the first major travel corridor to receive such service.

Other urban corridors in the United States, while not as promising as New York/Washington, might also qualify. Detailed analysis and some market testing would be needed to confirm. Among the possibilities would be Los Angeles/San Diego in California; Miami/Palm Beach/Orlando/

Tampa in Florida; Chicago/Milwaukee, Chicago/St. Louis, and Chicago/ Detroit in the Midwest; Portland/Seattle/Vancouver in the Pacific Northwest; and Dallas/Austin/San Antonio/Houston in Texas. Several of these, in fact, received considerable attention and active consideration for high-speed train service during the last few decades of the twentieth century but none were ever built, apparently because revenue projections never seemed sufficient to cover costs. This deficiency, of course, need not be permanent.

The specifications for economic success in rail passenger service also suggest what is not likely to succeed. A particularly endangered species would be the 2,000-mile or so transcontinental hauls, so dear to the hearts of true rail passenger fans and so particularly characteristic of North America, Siberia, and Australia. Obviously, these forty-hour-plus train odysseys are not undertaken for the purpose of only getting from here to there when five- to six-hour jet trips are available. The transcontinentals, with their sleeping cars, low-density day-night coaches, diner and baggage cars, and all their extra attendants, are also not cheap. In a market economy, they might be expected to survive only as special tourist excursions traversing particularly scenic areas. Their role should become to transcontinental land travel as ocean cruises are to transoceanic travel.

"Leavin' on a Jet Plane"—The Loss of Rail Passengers to Aviation

Manned, guided, heavier-than-air aviation had been dreamt about since the mythical Daedalus and his son Icarus flew out of their imprisonment in a labyrinth on Crete. Against his father's instructions, however, Icarus flew too close to the sun, melting his wax-secured wings and thereupon falling into the sea and drowning. Historical aviation began with the daring lighter-than-air hot-air balloon flights of the Montgolfier brothers of Annonay, France, late in the eighteenth century,[57] but powered, heavier-than-air, controlled flight was not to be realized until more than 100 years after the Montgolfier brothers took to the skies.

Many inventors on both sides of the Atlantic tried to be first in mechanical flight, but again two brothers won the laurels. They were Orville and Wilbur Wright, bicycle shop owners from Dayton, Ohio. Wilbur, older by four years, "was the more mechanical of the two; Orville the more outgoing."[58] The Wright brothers had to battle in the courts for years, at great cost to their financial and creative resources, to secure their essential patent from other jealous claimants—especially Glenn Curtiss.[59]

Aviation as a mode of transportation was the great beneficiary of military procurements tracing to the first years of the century, as well as from technological breakthroughs stimulated by World Wars I and II. As the Wrights, Curtiss, and other flight pioneers were still tinkering with their machines, they were preparing for extensive qualifying demonstrations sponsored by the Army Signal Corps. The Wright Brothers prevailed in the first of these, conducted after meetings and discussions as early as 1904, but others were not far behind.

World War I showed an innocent America many things, one of them being the value of aviation in wartime. In 1918, the Army Air Corps placed an order with Curtiss for 10,000 aircraft, many to be used in training pilots. The US Post Office then saw an opportunity to establish air mail service using these aircraft, designated the JN-4H Jenny, and the fliers that trained in them. The Jenny trainer could achieve airspeed of ninety-three miles per hour.

Early Developments and Subsidies for Commercial Aviation

The first flight of the new air mail service, with President Wilson in attendance as a spectator and George Boyle at the controls, took off May 15, 1918, from Washington for New York City, with a planned stop in Philadelphia. Boyle called in an hour later from Waldorf, Maryland—far off course. Gathering himself, Boyle took off again, ironically this time following the tracks of the Pennsylvania Railroad north to Philadelphia.[60] It was a precedent and a metaphor. Throughout the early history of flight, pilots followed railroads through gaps in the Alleghenies, across unmarked prairies in the Midwest, and over uncharted deserts in the West.

Early efforts to provide commercial air passenger services mainly failed because aircraft lacked speed, range, and safety, and "could barely compete with ground transportation."[61] The most successful early passenger-carrying operations were between the US mainland and offshore islands, where competition was with boats, not passenger trains. The advantages of commercial aviation were easily hypothesized but not effectively demonstrated until, in July 1924, the US Post Office Aerial Mail Service launched transcontinental air mail service between New York and San Francisco. This system featured night beacons and lighted landing strips to guide its fragile aircraft across the nation. And fragile they were. Between 1920 and 1921, nineteen aviators were killed flying air mail routes for the post office, in eighty-nine crashes. Thirty-one of the first forty pilots hired by the Post

Office lost their lives flying in the air mail service.[62] If we could do the math, no doubt it was safer to be a Pony Express rider in the Wild West during the 1860s than an air mail pilot in the 1920s.

Before long, federal subsidies to the air mail service became an important overall stimulus to advancement of commercial aviation (as we have observed, subsidies are invariably made available to new, in preference to established, modes). Initially, subsidy took the form of contracts with specialty operators to carry air mail, but after a significant dustup over conflicts of interest in the contract-awarding process, in 1934 the government cancelled all air mail contracts, replacing the private operators with Army Air Corp fliers. There was a military justification of sorts for this rather extreme reaction to the scandals: The military was going to need many qualified pilots. Air mail subsidies were resumed before long and became a key financial underpinning of the commercial airline industry throughout its early years. Between 1930 and 1933, air system mileage doubled and, despite the Great Depression, airline passenger-miles grew from 84 million to 127 million. A major factor in the growth was the introduction of new aircraft; the Boeing 247 and Douglas DC-2 had aluminum skin construction, single wings, retractable landing gear, variable pitch propellers, and engine cowlings.[63]

During and after World War II, air mail subsidies were nothing to compare with benefits to aviation from the advances in aircraft design, structural materials, and engines coming out of the military. Already possessing the unquestioned advantage in terms of speed, airline service threatened to capture the preponderance of long-distance travel as the price of air fares dropped throughout the late 1940s. Airlines knew that they had the growing ability to capture long-distance travel, and they did not fail to capitalize on that fact. As an advertisement in *The Saturday Evening Post* touted: "the airlines gain you . . . time . . . time . . . time! Thanks to the airlines you can get there and back in hours instead of days."[64]

Successful jet engine technology was actually applied to a few German fighters during the war, with substantial psychological impact, but genuine commercial applications were not made until after the war. The first commercial aircraft using jet propulsion was the British de Havilland Comet, introduced in 1952. The Comet, which subsequently had a disastrous safety record,[65] was followed by the jet-propelled Boeing 707 in 1957 and the Douglas DC-8 in 1958. The Boeing 707 enabled routine transatlantic flight by the 1960s, an indication of the maturity gained by the new mode, although its rivalry with rail passenger service, obviously, was limited to domestic travel.[66] Subsequent aircraft, like the Boeing 727 and 737, and later challengers from Airbus Industries, gained wide acceptance with airlines and the public on domestic, rail passenger-competitive routes.

Airline Regulation and Deregulation

Airline regulation became a significant fact of life for the airline industry after passage of the Civil Aeronautics Act of 1938. The new statute established a five-member Civil Aeronautics Authority (later Board—CAB), with regulatory authority over certificates of public convenience and necessity (PC&N), passenger fares, and air mail and air cargo rates. At the onset of regulation, sixteen existing airlines were grandfathered with operating authority. That number dwindled to ten between 1938 and the nation's bicentennial. During those thirty-eight years, the CAB wielded much control over the industry's structure and finances—using its authority to grant certificates of PC&N in specific city-pair markets, control of rates and services, and merger approvals, but it did not add a single new trunk airline. Also, airlines could not exit a market without CAB authority, just as railroads were not allowed to discontinue passenger trains without a train-off authorization from the Interstate Commerce Commission.[67]

Under the CAB Act, air safety investigations moved over to a separate air safety board, later merged into the National Transportation Safety Board (NTSB). Airline labor negotiations, then as now, were overseen by agencies operating under the Railway Labor Act of 1926; that rather odd status, nonetheless, superseded later applicability of the Taft-Hartley Act, with the consequence that airline labor disputes, as was the case with railroads, were unlikely to wind up in a major national strike.

Airline deregulation was talked about in the Ford administration, but John Robson, then the CAB chairman, was opposed.[68] Little was done until President Carter came into office, announcing only two months after his inauguration that he would support airline deregulation. President Carter's new CAB chairman, Cornell economics professor Alfred Kahn, really got practical deregulation steps underway shortly after his arrival in the post in June 1977. Kahn, who served President Carter as "inflation czar" as well as CAB chairman (and who passed away in December 2010), was the individual most instrumental in promoting airline deregulation.

When Professor Kahn became CAB chairman, the board expanded Robson's fare experimentation ideas and began to use proposed fare reductions as a criterion for approving applicants for new routes. In certifying routes, the board no longer looked at a carrier's financial need for an infusion of revenues from the new business, nor the long-established policy of cross-subsidizing deficit short-haul operations with revenues earned on long-haul routes. In the same vein, the CAB shifted the burden of proof for a certificate of PC&N from the applicant to opponents.[69] Meyer and Oster observed, accordingly, that

> The Airline Deregulation Act of 1978, signed into law on October 24, 1978, codified the actions of the CAB under Robson and Kahn, thus largely removing the possibility of court challenges. . . . By codifying these actions, Congress also greatly reduced the possibility of any future CAB chairman reverting to a more highly regulated state. The act thus reduced the uncertainty of how far the deregulation would go and how long it would last. Indeed, by scheduling the disbanding of the CAB, Congress made quite clear its intent that the airlines remain an industry unregulated in its economic and market characteristics.[70] Following a set of influences and timelines similar to airline deregulation, the Carter administration later did the same for trucking and railroad regulatory reform.

Impact of Modern Aviation on Intercity Railroad Passenger Service
Long-distance, economical, jet aircraft operations were the largest single factor dooming profitable rail passenger service in the United States in the last four decades of the twentieth century. This was despite premium airfares. (Figure 5.1 charts passenger revenue per revenue passenger-mile for the several modes. Airfares per mile were more than double those for intercity passenger trains throughout the Amtrak era.)

Deregulation began to check the escalation of airfares, however, while Amtrak's ongoing deficits meant that its managers needed to price upward as aggressively as they could. Figure 5.2 (page 122) shows the pattern of displacement of rail passenger service by both commercial aviation and private automobile trips from Lindbergh's day to the establishment of Amtrak. The maturation of commercial aviation just happens to coincide with arrival of the interstate highways and their overwhelming impact on

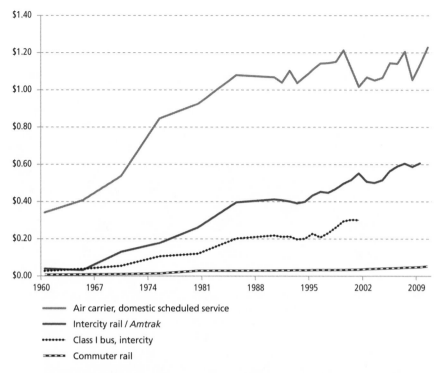

Figure 5.1   Average Fares per Passenger-Mile.   Fuel prices and macroeconomic conditions strongly affect passenger fares. For example, airfares rose sharply during OPEC I and after deregulation in the 1980s. Airfares remained more than double fares for passenger train travel until the terrorist attacks of September 11, 2001. Amtrak also began to raise fares during OPEC I and II, and again after 1995. Intercity bus fares were about half the level of rail fares throughout the period. Commuter rail fares are consistently low, reflecting efficiency, public subsidy, and competition with private autos and bus transit. *Source:* US DOT, Bureau of Transportation Statistics, online at http://www.rita.dot.gov/bts/data_and_statistics/index.html.

automotive travel, so the rapid penetration of jet aviation is somewhat muted in this display, but the effect cannot be diminished otherwise.

Nor, in all likelihood, will the parallel growth of commercial aviation and intercity travel by private auto subside in future years—this despite terrorist threats, record energy prices, and the possibility of improved Amtrak or higher-speed rail services. While there has been a great deal of interest in development of higher-speed rail passenger service alternatives since the 2008 elections, actual development has been minimal, and official projections are not yet claiming much in the way of rail inroads on highway and airline domination of intercity travel.

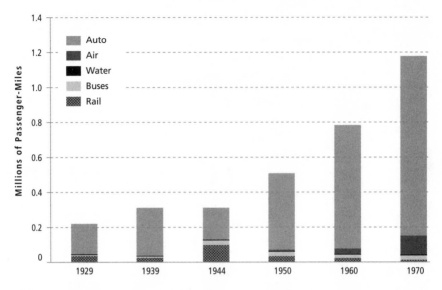

Figure 5.2   Growth and Modal Shares of Passenger Travel.   From 1930 to 1970, the automotive sector saw most of the growth in the amount and share of intercity passenger travel. Key
factors were construction of the interstate highways and development of more comfortable and reliable automobiles. Intercity rail travel declined and air travel rose after jet aircraft were introduced in
the late 1950s. Passenger train ridership peaked sharply during World War II because of troop movements and gasoline and rubber rationing, and a backlog of road construction projects due to the war.

Passenger Train Policy Options Emerge Beginning in 1958

The costs and operating fundamentals of rail passenger service thus
pointed to two central policy options in the late 1950s. One would be for
government to finance the status quo: a costly and deficit-ridden nationwide network, with declining prospects. The other would be to eliminate
federal regulation of intercity rail passenger operations and let the market
and local politics sort out what was viable—which likely would be a small
set of regional operations largely unconnected to one another and therefore without transcontinental service.

Only one of these options, the first, received much political attention in
the policy debates of the late 1950s continuing into the 1960s. This occurred
in spite of a remarkably insightful report regarding the future (or the lack
thereof) of rail passenger travel. The report was prepared by ICC staff at
the behest of the Interstate Commerce Commission and submitted to the
commission in September 1958.[71] The report came to be known as the
Hosmer Report, named after the principal author, Howard Hosmer, a

respected and experienced senior examiner on the ICC staff. The *Hosmer Report* performed a remarkably thorough and meticulous analysis of why long-distance intercity rail passenger travel was doomed in the United States. The report indicated that public policy could not do much about the demise of passenger service except at tremendous cost to taxpayers, a cost probably well in excess of any benefits.

The larger implication was that government should step aside and let the market take its course, with the probable result being that, except for a few short-haul trips on relatively high-density urban corridors of up to 600 and possibly 900 miles in length, all intercity rail passenger service would disappear. It was widely understood that the only "transcontinental" services likely to survive a market test would be scenic "cruises" intermittently organized by travel agencies.

Many reasons could be suggested as to why this good advice was ignored, but perhaps the most important was almost subliminal: Transcontinental trains had been intimately associated with nation building and it was almost unthinkable to contemplate the nation persisting without them. Not only were these trains symbols of nationhood, but they had played an important role in all three of the nation's major wars of the nineteenth and twentieth centuries: the War Between the States and World Wars I and II. If nothing else, some standby transcontinental capability seemed to be needed for national defense. Whether this was true or not under the conditions of modern warfare was not the point; it was the belief that counted and that belief had a remarkable impact.

Emotion, sentiment, and patriotism were fortified by some very practical considerations as well. It has often been observed that legislation that has a positive effect on at least 218 of the 435 congressional districts represented in Congress has a better chance of passage than legislation with a positive influence on less than 218. Continuing to run passenger trains across the country was obviously a way to amplify congressional interest and accumulate the magic number of 218. Continuity made it easier to identify beneficiaries and therefore to find political support, particularly among the rail unions and local communities affected by discontinuance of service. These are some of the considerations David Morgan was reflecting on when he wrote his famous 1959 article, "Who Shot the Passenger Train?" quoted as the keynote to this chapter.

From 1958 through 1960, passenger train discontinuances (the formal regulatory term) were above the annual levels reported for the years just before; at least some catch-up or clearing of the dockets seems to have occurred. From 1961 through 1964, on the other hand, the rate of discontinuance seems to have fallen below prior levels. This might be simply a sign that the catch-up process had run its course and that the more flagrant train-off cases had been cleared; that explanation, however, is difficult to reconcile with the surge in discontinuances that occurred in the last few years of the decade.

Transferring discontinuance authority from the states to the ICC in the Transportation Act of 1958 act did seem to make a difference but only after some delay. A typical pattern was for the ICC not to approve a train-off request on first application—if the commission could dredge up even the faintest hope for eventual profitability. This was especially true if the discontinuance faced strong community or union objections. After a year or two of growing unprofitability, however, the commission would often relent, apparently concluding (as Hosmer had) that the case was hopeless. The counterfactual question of whether the state agencies would have allowed as much service discontinuation during this period as the ICC had remains unanswered and unanswerable. By the end of the 1960s, the question was essentially irrelevant. What was important was that the railroads could not afford to continue subsidizing passenger operations out of freight earnings. The time had arrived for some sort of public policy to disentangle a failing rail passenger business from an apparently still viable, though increasingly threatened, rail freight operation.

On the Doorstep of Amtrak

In 1970, under the leadership of Secretary Volpe, the Department of Transportation did just that. The DOT proposal was to create a for-profit "mixed ownership government corporation": the National Railroad Passenger Corporation (NRPC), at the time informally called RailPax and later known as Amtrak. This corporation was to assume responsibility for providing the nation's rail passenger services over a "basic system" as initially specified by the secretary of transportation. Trackage rights, operating train crews, maintenance services, and other needed inputs that the corporation didn't control itself were to be purchased from the existing railroads at cost plus a nominal profit; the ICC was to adjudicate disagreements about the terms of these contracts.

The corporation's common stock would be owned only by the railroads exiting from passenger service. The initial capitalization of the corporation would come from $40 million in government appropriations, $100 million in government loan guarantees, and contributions made by those railroads electing to hand over their rail passenger service obligations to the corporation. These contributions were usually at a level equal to 50 percent of the fully distributed (1969) passenger service deficit for a participating railroad and were largely "paid" by the transfer of railroad passenger service equipment to the new corporation.

Under the new legislation, a railroad choosing not to participate had to operate its passenger services until January 1, 1975, before applying for any further discontinuances. Of the eighteen Class I railroads in existence at the time, only four chose not to participate and only two of these were of any importance in intercity passenger service: the Southern Railway and the Denver & Rio Grande Western (see Map 5.1.A and B). The corporation was to be governed by a board of fifteen, eight of whom were to be appointed by the president subject to Senate approval, three by the rail common stockholders, and four by preferred stockholders. The new company was to honor established arrangements for protection of employee rights and was bound by the same safety and related regulations as its predecessors. It was exempt from ICC regulation of rates, entry, and discontinuance of routes.

The legislation sailed through Congress with broad bipartisan support and was signed into law by President Nixon on October 30, 1970. Unfortunately, as Chapter 11 of this text will show, few of the new railroad's expected service economies were realized, and the goals of passenger service preservation and revitalization proved quite costly. Amtrak was more than a solution for the times; it was also to become a major public policy problem in its own right.

Concluding Thoughts

Only by considering a complex interplay of events can one adequately explain why the railroad passenger industry suffered its long decline and eventual marginalization. As Albro Martin has commented, "simplistic history is the worst possible guide for transportation policy."[72]

ICC regulation was far more stringent for the railroads than it was for any of their competitors. Suppression of railroad initiatives to decide their own policies hindered attempts to remain competitive. At the same time, government provision of right of way (or sometimes even direct subsidies) designed to nurture emerging rival forms of transport were grossly unfair

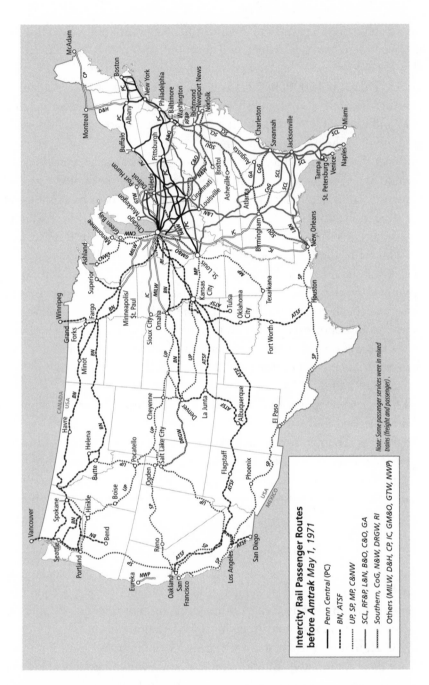

Map 5.1.A and B Intercity Rail Passenger Routes Before and After Amtrak (1971).
Map 5.1A and B displays the dramatic difference between the rail passenger networks separately operated by private freight railroads under ICC regulation before May 1, 1971 and the national system operated by Amtrak after its startup on that date. Not all eligible railroads joined the

Intercity Rail Passenger Routes before Amtrak May 1, 1971

- —— Penn Central (PC)
- •••• BN, ATSF
- ···· UP, SP, MP, C&NW
- ⁃⁃⁃ SCL, RF&P, L&N, B&O, C&O, GA
- —— Southern, CoG, N&W, DRGW, RI
- —— Others (MILW, D&H, CP, IC, GM&O, GTW, NWP)

Note: Some passenger services were in mixed trains (freight and passenger).

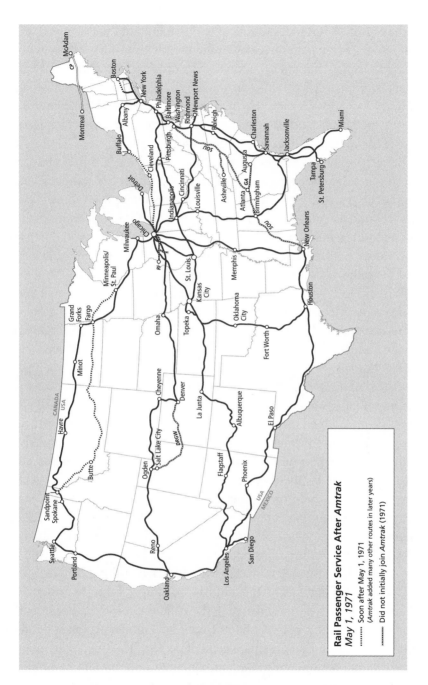

Rail Passenger Service After Amtrak
May 1, 1971
······· Soon after May 1, 1971
(*Amtrak added many other routes in later years*)
------- Did not initially join Amtrak (1971)

National Railroad Passenger Corporation, as Amtrak was officially known. Railroads continuing to provide service outside the Amtrak network until at least 1975 are indicated on the map. *Source:* Original map published in Kalmbach Pub. Co., *Classic Trains*, Summer 2011, p. 29.

to the railroads. Railroads were required to maintain their own infrastructure, paying taxes on them and their income yields (if any), without noticeable government aid after the nineteenth century land grants and before establishment of Amtrak in 1971. (Although the government did issue the railways loans to alleviate the financial strain of the Great Depression, these were largely paid back during the war, at the expense of a large portion of the railway industry's total earnings.)

Even the enormous amount of wartime traffic was a mixed blessing—causing rapid deterioration of equipment for which the railroads had to supply the necessary capital. When peace resumed, the railroads could not rebound as quickly as their competition because their entire physical plant required massive renovation. The government's dramatic increases in fiscal support following the war only served to enhance the advantages that the railway's competitors already possessed.

External forces, to be sure, were not the only reason for the collapse of passenger service. An attitude of general apathy prevailed among railroad managers during the 1920s and early 1930s. By the time railroad managers finally became aware of the serious external competition they faced, it was almost too late. While management deserves credit for their attempts at modernization in the late 1930s, the key underlying issues were largely ignored. The great popular appeal of streamlining showed railroads could innovate and helped reverse losses in some sectors of travel. Nevertheless, streamliners proved largely to be a publicity stunt, masking the underlying realities faced by the industry. More emphasis should have been placed on reevaluating the methods of pricing, overall infrastructure, and general direction of the industry during the critical years before competition became overwhelming. The boom years of World War II only concealed antiquated business practices, which continued to undermine the industry. Although costly efforts for continued modernization were enacted following the war, arguably it was too late to salvage business by that point.

Overall, the decline of the railroad passenger business was due to changing patterns of travel demand, the rapid improvement of competing technologies, and a combination of poor governmental policies and, in some but not all instances, management neglect. Had regulatory policies been altered in time, railroads possibly could have retained a profitable niche in the market. By the same token, if industry officials had been more sensitive to the changing market and restructured their business to meet those challenges, passenger service possibly would have remained more competitive with the other developing forms of transportation. Earlier reform of this sometimes efficient and generally safe form of travel would have been beneficial to the nation. The highway and air traffic congestion of the present day might not be quite so great, dependence on foreign oil imports might have been a less pressing problem, and expenditures for Amtrak subsidies (nearly $40 billion since 1970) might not have been quite so large.

6

MERGERS AT MIDCENTURY
AND THE PENN CENTRAL DEBACLE

... [W]ith ... technological changes ... tending to increase
capacity rather than reduce it; with passenger traffic continuing its dreary, long-run decline ... ; with competition
incapable of eliminating the excess capacity and with continuously low overall earnings, it is not surprising that there finally
emerged among railroad executives as well as others the conviction that drastic rationalization was essential; and the only
way to achieve it was through mergers.

—ALFRED E. KAHN, 1971

This chapter of *American Railroads* continues from Chapter 3 the story
of how consolidation of railroad firms affected performance of the
industry in the middle part of the twentieth century. It covers the period
from World War II through the Penn Central merger in 1968 and bankruptcy in 1970.

Merger (or horizontal combination) of firms was a remedy almost reflex-
ively proposed for virtually any business problem in a wide range of
American industries throughout the twentieth century. Folklore has it that
the dominant message conveyed to business school students was (and may
still be): "if in doubt, reorganize." Of course, the motive for consolidation
in many instances may not have had much to do with reducing costs or
improving product or any other general consumer benefit, but rather was
aimed at controlling markets and increasing a firm's market power.
Reflecting the long-standing ambivalence of Americans about the scope
and effectiveness of government regulation of industry, such cynicism
may have seemed misplaced for railroads because, at least before 1980 and
to a considerable degree afterward, the industry was regulated. Where was
extra revenue to be derived from having a monopoly in an industry already
regulated as a "natural monopoly"? Accordingly, shouldn't railroad mergers

have faced little opposition from public policy? Maybe so, but the railroads weren't so lucky.

Chapter 3 explained how little or no merger activity took place in the 1920s because approval required that a specific combination comport with the Interstate Commerce Commission's (ICC's) consolidation plan developed under the Transportation Act of 1920, and because railroads objected to the stipulation that merger proposals from strong railroads incorporate (and thus help preserve) lines of weaker participants in the market.

Similarly, there was almost no merger activity in the 1930s, despite the fact that the Franklin D. Roosevelt administration's powerful depression era emergency transportation czar (ICC's federal coordinator, Joseph B. Eastman) favored large-scale industry "Grand Consolidation" (his term) — and toyed with endorsing nationalization.[1] It is entirely understandable that financial conditions in the Great Depression more often led to bankruptcy receivership than consolidation, for it is a fact that industrial mergers are more likely when stock prices are rising (and future business prospects are promising) than in economic downturns.

Then during World War II, all available energies were focused on meeting war needs. Recall again from Chapter 3 that, as part of the fallout from the period of federal control during the World War I, railroad industry managers had vowed never again to find themselves in the position of having to cede operations to government authorities. Perhaps they were too busy tending to their knitting in World War II, or maybe they did not even want to go Washington to raise the question of mergers![2]

For a full decade following the Second World War, there was a de facto continuation of the wartime moratorium. Financing acquisitions takes free cash flow and/or healthy stock prices, and these still were not widely available to railroads at the time; even relatively prosperous railroads wouldn't commit much new or additional capital to the industry in the turbulence surrounding the postwar readjustment to normal traffic levels. Just after World War II, only two relatively small consolidations occurred: the Chicago & Alton (Alton) Railroad[3] was merged into the Gulf Mobile & Ohio (GM&O) in 1945, and the Père Marquette (PM) was absorbed by the Chesapeake & Ohio (C&O) in 1947. In 1955, the number of Class I roads stood at 162, down only twenty-six from 188 in 1920.[4] Thus, for all practical purposes, merger activity in the industry was frozen for three decades or more, despite major efforts by Congress in the Transportation Acts of 1920, 1933, and 1940 to encourage such activity.

Not until 1955, a decade after the end of World War II and thirty-five years after Congress had asked the ICC to draft a master plan for consolidating the industry, did mergers and restructuring once again become active tools of management and public policy. And this was in an industry experiencing considerable secular decline, substantial overcapacity, and economies of scale—all of which should have favored mergers.

Parallel Versus End-to-End Mergers

Economists and other industry analysts commonly distinguish between two types of railroad mergers: parallel and end-to-end. As the name implies, parallel merger involves consolidation of railroads that serve essentially the same markets over trackage facilities with similar endpoints and carrying capacity. With good reason, such mergers were deemed potentially anticompetitive. Parallel combinations might be justified, nonetheless, if proponents promised (and regulators anticipated) cost economies achievable by eliminating redundant facilities, by taking advantage of better grades and shorter routings, or by creating economies of density from concentrating all subject traffic flows on the trackage that remained.

In contrast, an end-to-end merger involved joining railway companies that did not serve overlapping markets, instead connected with one another at gateways where previously they had interchanged traffic; such mergers were less likely to achieve important cost economies but arguably could improve service (e.g., by eliminating time-consuming transfers from one railroad to another at gateways). Generally, end-to-end mergers were not regarded as anticompetitive; indeed, they could increase competition by strengthening the position of a secondary carrier in the relevant territory (such as by improving its finances, equipment availability and utilization, etc.). In short, the usual argument for parallel mergers was to realize substantial cost economies, albeit at some loss in intramodal competition, while the case for end-to-end mergers was based on facilitating improved service—with perhaps some modest cost economies but no substantial loss of competition.

Observers schooled in US antitrust law and practice might well assume that regulatory authorities would balk at parallel merger proposals but look favorably on competitively innocuous end-to-end consolidations. Interestingly and ironically, in the midcentury merger period, the ICC was seemingly more willing to approve parallel than end-to-end mergers—perhaps out of a political motivation to protect competitors more than a duty to preserve competition for the sake of the public welfare.

To explain, parallel mergers in this period had the advantage, from the regulators' viewpoint, of avoiding political complications because, while anticompetitive, they did not extend a carrier into new territories against the interests of incumbent connecting railroads. By contrast, end-to-end unifications usually disturbed existing and long-standing traffic divisions and other relationships among connecting carriers. The merging railroad's gains were likely to come at the expense of another line, and disadvantaged railroads were not disposed to suffer their losses quietly. No commission composed primarily of political appointees was likely to disturb those relationships if they were avoidable.

Understandably, therefore, the numerous consolidations proposed and approved in the period from 1955 to 1972 were mainly focused on cost savings rather than territorial extensions. The ICC, however, could not fully put to rest more old-fashioned worries about maintaining competition and service—not as long as there was any prospect that private market forces could deliver an industry structure as efficient as could be obtained through regulation. Even those who believed in the general efficacy of regulation still felt that it was well to rely on competition whenever you "safely" could (for example, with agricultural exemptions for barges and trucking), and it was always desirable to have a bit of competition in reserve just in case the regulators "got it wrong."[5]

Expert observers' views about the salutary or harmful effects of mergers ranged widely. Sumner H. Slichter gave one view in 1957:

> The proposal that new restrictions be placed on mergers arises from the fact that the United States in recent years has been experiencing a great wave of mergers. But recent mergers have not weakened competition. On the contrary, they have indirectly strengthened it because they have enabled managements to build more diversified and better-integrated enterprises— enterprises which are more capable of reaching all parts of the vast domestic market, of adapting themselves to market shifts and changes in technology, of riding out the ups and downs of business, and of supporting technological research and development.[6]

Those less sanguine about the abilities of regulators (and those who believed strongly in the therapeutic value of markets) viewed mergers as a threat and retention of rail-rail competition as fundamental to enhancing society's welfare. In particular, those harboring hopes that the industry might someday be "emancipated" from its regulatory yoke would want to preserve as much competition as possible. The authors of *American Railroads* were in that group.

Once conventional wisdom accepted both realistic possibilities for operating efficiencies in railroad consolidations and the new likelihood they would pass regulatory and antitrust muster, the response was strong, almost overwhelming.

Proponent railroads regarded the mergers of the postwar years up to 1968 as essential to improving railroad industry finances, but they accomplished far less than anticipated. One case, the merger of the Pennsylvania Railroad (PRR) and New York Central (NYC) into Penn Central (PC)—to that time the largest merger in US business history[7]—was disastrous; within two years the combined firm was bankrupt and subsequently ruled by the federal courts not to be reorganizable through a conventional income-based conversion of securities and debt instruments.

With the midcentury mergers significantly underperforming their anticipated benefits, and thus representing far less of a panacea for industry problems than had been advertised, the railroads were left, as one of the infamous Watergate figures said of a colleague, "to twist slowly in the wind." Reform and revitalization of the industry were still needed; it is just that they were not to be found in the parallel mergers proposed by railroads and approved by the ICC in the 1950s and 1960s. After the Northeast Rail Reorganization (see Chapter 7), a more constructive pathway was blazed by the Staggers Rail Act of 1980 and subsequent mergers of an altogether different character.

Why Does Effective Rail Competition Matter?

Competition among firms in the same industry and market is an important feature of public policy toward business in the United States. Competition, as an underlying mechanism and working premise of the private enterprise system, is protected and encouraged by the antitrust laws and numerous pieces of special legislation. Even in highly regulated industries like railroading, competition is prized as a means of controlling business abuses because it is automatic, penetrating, and persistent. Shippers and consumers generally value competition among suppliers as the best guarantor of reasonable prices and as the best means for ensuring good service, technological progress, and efficient management. Those who advocate less public regulation of quasi-public utilities like railroads—in order to give industry greater flexibility in pricing and services—place heavy reliance on the self-regulating character of competition. Without healthy and balanced competition, the public will demand more, not less, regulation.

It is well established in the economics of industrial organization that effective competition lowers prices to consumers and increases social welfare. On the other hand, with respect to industries that have some, not all, of the characteristics of public utilities, competition might be more valuable in theory than in fact. Head-to-head competition of rival firms may be useful to shippers in lowering their rates, but other, less direct forms of competition may be equally valuable over the long run. Indirect forms of competition may be sufficient to bring about improved cost performance and innovations in services. And it was almost certainly the case that, in areas of great excess trackage (as in the Granger states for most of the twentieth century), excessive competition resulted in less frequent service, poorer utilization of plant and equipment, and higher unit costs than otherwise would have been required. Historically, too much competition was one of the causes of financial instability and bankruptcy of some railroad carriers. In these cases, excessive competition was no more a friend of the shipper than inadequate competition was; plainly, competition that drives prices down to marginal cost will bankrupt railroads forced into that position.

Off to a Good Start in the 1950s

Ironically, given the emphasis on merging rich roads with poor in the search for a comprehensive national plan in the 1920s, one of the first mergers to be consummated in the late 1950s was that of the Norfolk & Western (N&W) with the Virginian (VGN), two of the most prosperous roads in the country. The only other merger of any substance to be approved in the 1950s before the N&W + VGN was that of the Louisville & Nashville (L&N) with the Nashville, Chattanooga & St. Louis Railway (NC&StL). The merger in this case was for the most part a *fait accompli* because the L&N had purchased 85 percent of the NC&StL's capital stock in 1880 and, prior to the merger, the two railroads jointly shared corporate

officers, traffic routings, and debt risks. As management put it, they "operated in harmony, not competition" and were looking forward to "eventual
unification." Their "trial marriage" must be one of the longest in recorded
human activity.

The Virginian, prior to merger with the N&W, was quite pristine in all
its relationships with other railroads. It almost had to be, given its large
number of suitors. All during the search for an acceptable national rail
consolidation plan in the 1920s, the issue with respect to the Virginian was
who would get the privilege of owning this highly profitable property.
Actually, with one exception, merger of the N&W and VGN made little
difference to any map of network coverage—as the two roads ran parallel
and quite close to one another. Both connected coal mines of the Pocahontas
District (Western Virginia, West Virginia, and Eastern Kentucky) with
tidewater at Lambert's Point (N&W) or Sewell's Point (VGN) in Norfolk to the east, as well as domestic markets for bituminous coal to the
west. The exception noted above was a bone of contention for the New
York Central, which had an important connection with VGN for receipt
of Pocahontas coal at Deepwater (VGN)/Gauley Bridge (NYC), West
Virginia.[8]

The principal businesses for both N&W and VGN were eastbound
export coal[9] traffic, which, as some put it, was just "rolling loaded coal cars
downhill to tidewater and returning empties back to the mines." Such a
simple operation suited railroads well and was highly profitable. N&W
achieved remarkably low operating ratios of 65 percent or so in the late
1950s, while the Virginian's ratio was just over 50 percent. (For perspective,
an operating ratio of 80 to 85 percent was considered reasonably satisfactory in most of the industry.[10] It was no wonder so many vied for the privilege of owning the Virginian.)

Combining the VGN and N&W further improved profitability by
enabling routing that took advantage of the differential gradients on their
parallel or paired track rights of way (loads over the more favorable grades,
empties over the steeper grades). It was not surprising, therefore, that this
merger had been proposed at least as early as the 1920s. The competitive
and network coverage characteristics of this merger were less favorable
than the financial aspects, however, and this accounted for the merger's
denial in 1926. But by 1959, with so much of the industry in financial difficulty (even if these two weren't), such compunctions no longer held and
the merger was sanctioned by the ICC. Few better signals might have

been devised to indicate that the public policy barriers were now down, or at least considerably lowered, on rail mergers. Competitive effects clearly were subordinate to financial and cost effects. It was not that the anti-competitive circumstances were completely ignored, just subordinated. The rush was on.

But Then Came the 1960s

The Interstate Commerce Commission's approval of the parallel merger of the Virginian into the Norfolk & Western in 1959 was the most dramatic illustration of its new trend in policy. Indeed, of the sixteen or so major unifications approved by the ICC in the 1960s, only two or three would be considered more end-to-end than parallel: the Soo Line (SOO) consolidation, the Norfolk & Western's acquisition of financial control over the Delaware & Hudson (D&H) and the Erie Lackawanna (EL) in 1968, and possibly the forced inclusion of the New York, New Haven & Hartford (New Haven) into Penn Central as a condition of that mega-merger. (Penn Central also reached Boston from New York City and New Jersey, but circuitously—via Albany.)

By contrast, two out of the four or so major unification procedures denied (or inordinately delayed) by the ICC during the midcentury period were largely end-to-end: These were the St. Louis–San Francisco (Frisco) proposal to establish financial control over the Central of Georgia (CoG), and the Union Pacific's proposal to acquire the northern part of the Rock Island, while Southern Pacific took its lines south and east of Kansas City. Indeed, "curiouser and curiouser," the ICC's denial of the Frisco-CoG (a perfect end-to-end combination), then later approval of the Southern-CoG (plainly parallel) cannot be explained by rational competitive policy—except for one administrative glitch: The ICC believed Frisco had exercised premature control over the Central of Georgia. Rather than an administrative remedy (a fine or stipulations affecting implementation), the ICC issued a flat denial, which had the effect of altering subsequent competitive precedents and the structure of a major region for years to come.

The midcentury period's sample of end-to-end cases is quite limited in number, however, and therefore provides little basis for generalization. It seems quite possible that idiosyncratic considerations may have heavily influenced some of these cases, particularly the Frisco's attempt to take over the Central of Georgia. And just as there were two dramatic cases of

ICC rejection of end-to-end unifications, there were also two very important denials of parallel attempts, the Southern Pacific's proposed takeover of the Western Pacific (WP) and the New York Central's attempt to merge with the C&O.

In a less convoluted case, the ICC denied application by the Atchison, Topeka, & Santa Fe (AT&SF or Santa Fe) to acquire the perpetually marginal Western Pacific, despite its innocuous end-to-end character. Presumably this was because of "optics,"—the ICC had just denied Southern Pacific's attempt to acquire Western Pacific. From a national policy perspective, however, it was no time for the ICC to parade oversimplified notions of even-handedness (i.e., treating the AT&SF the same as SP); the Commission might simply have said SP + WP would have been an anti-competitive parallel merger and gone ahead with approval of Santa Fe + WP.

Similarly, approving merger of the Monon into the L&N in 1970–1971 would be a plausible example of an end-to-end unification actually approved by the ICC, had not the ICC almost simultaneously also allowed the L&N to acquire the parallel eastern fork of the Chicago & Eastern Illinois (C&EI). Approval to merge C&EI's eastern fork into the Southern Railway would have been a more procompetitive outcome.[11]

In summary, among the most important generalizations that can be made about the great railroad merger wave of 1955 to 1970 is that, while many mergers were proposed, most of them were parallel in character and few were denied by the ICC. The emphasis on parallel unifications was quite understandable. Simply put, that was where the money appeared to be; cost savings from consolidating parallel facilities seemed more tangible and larger than the possible marketing rewards from end-to-end mergers. While apparently minor in overall impact, the indicated aberrations in ICC application of straightforward competitive evaluation of mergers in the 1960s hinted that more fundamental errors could be made.

Did Pre–Penn Central Mergers Yield Cost Savings?

After 1955, public policy shifted from a position of broad suspicion to broad approval of rail mergers. This shift was generated in large part by the growing financial difficulties of railroads. Mergers seemed to provide some badly needed cost savings to the industry, even if at the price of some reduction in direct competition between railroads. As the number of carriers shrank through mergers, the promerger policy of 1955–1970 traded off

Table 6.1   Operating Results for Midcentury Railroad Mergers

Merger Name	Date	Type	Annual Savings Anticipated by Applicants (Current $ MM)	Study Results Unadjusted	Performance Relative to Controls
L&N–NC&SL	8/31/1957	Parallel	$3.2	Excellent	Excellent
N&W–VGN	12/01/1959	Parallel	$10.3	Good	Fair
Erie–Lackawanna	10/17/1960	Parallel	$11.5	Good	Good to fair
CNW–M&StL	11/01/1960	Parallel	$3.0	Good	Poor
Soo Line	1/01/1961	Complementary	$1.2	Fair	Fair to poor
C&O–B&O	2/04/1963	Complementary	$13.4	Poor	Poor
Southern–Central of GA	6/18/1963	Complementary	$5.9	Fair	Poor
DT&I–AA	9/03/1963	End-to-end	$0.2	Good	Fair
N&W–NKP–Wabash	10/16/1964	Complementary	$27.0	Poor	Poor

This table presents summary results for mid-century railroad mergers reported in co-author Gallamore's doctoral dissertation, which was supervised by co-author Meyer. Anticipated merger savings were greatest for the large parallel and "complementary" mergers proposed late in the period, but in general, these performed poorly relative to smaller and earlier combinations covered in the analysis. The giant Penn Central merger (1968) followed, and was to prove disastrous.

Sources: Gallamore, *Dissertation*, 1968, Table IV-2, pp. 150–151, and Table II-5, pp. 65–68. Portions of the table appeared in Table III in Robert E. Gallamore, "Measurement of Cost 'Savings' of Recent Railway Mergers," *Transportation Research Forum, Papers 1968*, p. 226. Used with permission.

rail-rail competition for cost savings, with the reduction in competition to be attenuated wherever possible by grants of operating and trackage access rights.

Because cost savings drove endorsement of public policy on merger proposals, a natural question is whether the mergers delivered the projected savings. Estimates of the projected savings, wherever available, are shown in the fourth column of Table 6.1. These projections are probably subject to some puffing by advocates seeking approval for a merger. The totals were not enough to solve all railroad problems at the time, but if achieved, they would have made a significant contribution. Industry net railway operating income (NROI) in 1970 was only about $486 million.

Unfortunately for merger partners and their shareholders, however, careful contemporary studies indicated that the realization of cost economies from mergers fell far short of projections. Indeed, costs might actually have been increased in the case of some mergers, at least in the short to intermediate term.

A shortfall of actual savings relative to anticipations could happen for several reasons, as pointed out in the literature.[12] The first of two key studies was developed by venerated Yale professor of transportation, Kent T. Healy, early in the 1950s. Professor Healy's pioneering analysis indicated that standard estimates of economies of scale and density in railroading may have badly overstated the possibilities. Healy found that density economies under mid-1950s conditions were more or less fully realized at about 3 million annual freight net ton-miles per mile.[13] The second study is co-author Gallamore's doctoral dissertation supervised by co-author Meyer, and is described in Box 6.1. Table 6.1 summarizes the merger cases included in the dissertation and the conclusions it reached.

Box 6.1   A Middle-Aged View of Midcentury Mergers

Co-author Gallamore's doctoral dissertation, written under the supervision of coauthor Meyer forty-five years ago, concerned the search for merger cost savings in the context of possible competitive losses—depending on the pattern of rail lines proposed for consolidation in a merger. It argued that the basis for arriving at conclusions on details of the then-current merger wave should progress, if at all, with consideration of both competitive impacts and attainable operating cost savings. Under Professor Meyer's tutelage, the dissertation independently (and nearly simultaneously) articulated a doctrine quite similar to Professor Oliver Williamson's seminal exposition on merger economics. Williamson's Lemma (we christen it) concerned policy trade-offs between, on the one hand, cost savings justifications for mergers and, on the other hand, loss of rail-rail competition from parallel mergers.

   Gallamore's 1968 dissertation described four features of American transport policy affected by railroad mergers in the period leading up to the Penn Central merger. First, railroad regulation was costly to the economy and not (as usually assumed) inevitable. Second, parallel mergers that risked unmitigated anticompetitive consequences were doubly dangerous—they could injure competition in current markets and might have more costly downstream effects by spoiling possibilities for deregulation. Third, and this came out a bit unexpectedly as the statistical analyses of past mergers were developed, large parallel mergers also might not yield the efficiencies claimed for them. In these cases, the policy "trade-off"

Box 6.1   *Continued*

---

was really not a trade-off at all, but a double-whammy of anticompetitive consequences and managerial diseconomies.

Finally, end-to-end mergers might not yield much in the way of consolidation
savings, but they likely were benign competitively; in some cases, they might
even be a stimulus to useful rail-rail competitive rivalry. Overall, the Gallamore/
Meyer construct produced important original evidence on the cost impacts of
mergers, and it possessed the further distinction of pointing out the direct link
between merger policy and prospects for deregulation. All this was happening
about a decade before there was real progress on regulatory reform in
Washington.

Gallamore's research showed that, while simple combinations like
N&W/VGN were successful, "the larger, more recent, and more complex
mergers have produced the least favorable results."[14] The likely evidence
of extra costs—that is, diseconomies of scale and integration—was a cau-
tionary tale; additional policy scrutiny needed to be given to large mergers,
especially those with anticompetitive effects. Unstated, but as no informed
reader could mistake, the Penn Central merger (1968) was exactly the
kind that would be most likely to fail on both cost savings and anticompetitive grounds.

One source of possible overestimation of merger cost economies was
their static character. Scale and density economies were anticipated largely
on the implicit notion that nothing else except the merger would take
place. Dynamic issues were not easily incorporated into a case-by-case
consideration of individual merger proposals, and the ICC had no meaningful rules governing content or quality of merger applications put forward to it; indeed, standards like mandatory time limits on the ICC's
decision steps were among the reforms set out in the Rail Revitalization
and Regulatory Reform (4R) Act of 1976, and modified in the Staggers
Rail Act of 1980. But during the 1955–1970 merger wave, much usually
depended on what happened next—including frequent speculation about
an uncertain, even unknowable, future. Hypothetically, how might carriers C and D, now competitive with A and B, react if A and B are

permitted to merge? How will carriers E and F, who compete in a neigh-boring area, react if their traditionally important interchanges of traf-fic with A and B, respectively, are threatened by the merger of A and B (say, because B has financial control of another carrier G that competes with E or F)?

Dominoes were falling, but they had been set up in unthinking or even dangerous patterns, with consequences yet unseen. In concept, incorpo-rating these dynamic consequences likely would alter the static estimates of anticipated merger cost savings—because the impact of sensible defen-sive actions taken by others would be to offset the adverse effects on them-selves generated by competitors' merger activities.

Assuredly, too, labor unions might try to reduce or postpone some of the projected changes that might lead to cost savings, particularly those that depended on immediate and substantial cuts in employment. At a min-imum, unions would try to capture some of the projected merger savings for their membership as compensation for the dislocations and retraining that mergers might create. Indeed, the history of rail mergers includes a rich vein of trial and experimentation with labor protection issues.[15] Almost universally, such efforts by labor unions would downsize projected savings from mergers.

Governments could also be obstacles to achieving projected merger sav-ings. For example, mergers could mean that more stranded branch lines or redundant main lines might be abandoned. When faced with the reality of proposed abandonments, local political opposition could usually post-pone them for at least a while, if not in perpetuity. In essence, mergers mainly eliminated any lingering private-sector objections by offering ship-pers alternatives, but they did little to reduce critical public-sector opposi-tion. In fact, some local opposition might have increased, on the grounds that the new and larger railroad created by a merger had deeper pockets and could better afford a few inefficiencies.

Three Transitional Mergers: Seaboard Coast Line (SCL), Burlington Northern (BN), and Illinois Central Gulf (ICG)

At the end of the period we are calling the midcentury merger wave, but before the negative effects of the Penn Central had fully regis-tered, the ICC approved three mergers—all large, complex, and parallel in competitive structure. These unions did not take place until after completion of Gallamore's dissertation, and none of them, to the authors' knowledge, has been subjected to similar formal quantitative analysis by other students of the industry. It is as though Penn Central and the subsequent northeast railway crisis had mooted the need for analysis of individual mergers, shifting the public policy question to a more strategic level.

Atlantic Coast Line (ACL)–Seaboard Airline (SAL) Merger (1967)

The merger of ACL and SAL into the Seaboard Coastline (SCL) was approved by the ICC, effective July 1, 1967. These two southeastern railroads had much in common. They were of similar size and financial strength, and they competed in the same kinds of markets. Despite its parallel configuration and loss of competitive alternatives, the combination faced little opposition. The proponents focused their case on availability of huge annual cost savings from elimination of redundant routes, rationalization of maintenance facilities, and consolidation of overhead expenses. These anticipated cost-savings benefits, plus the strength of the remaining competitive presence in this region dominated by Southern Railway (which had acquired the Central of Georgia in 1963 and connected seamlessly with strong and independent Florida East Coast at Jacksonville), offset most concerns about anticompetitive effects. Both ACL and SAL were significant players in the Richmond–Florida passenger market and could argue convincingly that consolidation would improve their services; the opportunity to test that "natural experiment" was interrupted only a few years later, in 1971, by startup of Amtrak.

History will be kind to managers of the SCL after its merger. It is true that contemporary observers thought merger integration was proceeding far too slowly—as they felt had been the case with C&O–B&O earlier. It did seem that SCL managers were taking a most southern-like pace in deciding which lines to keep and use or to downgrade; SCL was extraordinarily lackadaisical in abandoning unneeded lines and pulling up reusable material. The same criticism arose again after consolidation of all of the constituent CSX lines a dozen years later. Financial interests felt they were not seeing full benefit of the anticipated integration savings as quickly as they would have liked. But sometimes things just work out. No one can argue with the success of mergers subsequent to SCL in the CSX family, and certainly the performance of those partners set a standard not always matched in later mergers.

The Burlington Northern Merger: Great Northern + Northern Pacific + Chicago, Burlington & Quincy + Spokane, Portland & Seattle (SP&S), 1970

Early in the twentieth century, railroad titan James J. Hill successfully combined ownership of the Great Northern (GN) and Northern Pacific (NP) railroads—which together controlled the Chicago, Burlington & Quincy (CB&Q)—into the Northern Securities holding company. Under prodding from the administration of President Theodore Roosevelt, the Supreme Court, in a 5 to 4 decision, declared Northern Securities to be an illegal combination under the Sherman Antitrust Act and thereupon ordered its dissolution in 1904 (see Chapter 3). GN and NP were allowed to keep joint ownership of Burlington, however, and many observers thought it only a matter of time before the Supreme Court ruling would be overturned. Meanwhile GN and NP divided their St. Paul headquarters building in two with a permanent "firewall;" CB&Q continued to run its operations out of its fine historic building in Chicago's Loop.

Late in the 1960s, and totally in keeping with the trend to larger, more complex rail mergers despite anticompetitive effects, a plan to reestablish the Northern Lines consolidation emerged from St. Paul. It proposed merger of the three strongest carriers serving the northern rail corridor from Chicago to Puget Sound, plus the SP&S short-cut to Portland, Oregon. Given the antitrust history, not to say the obvious imbalance of power between the Northern Lines and their competitors in the Northern Plains and on the transcontinental route to the Pacific Northwest, the merger should have been greeted with considerable skepticism. And yet as a consequence of the 1955–1972 merger wave, concerns about balance of financial power or better possible competitive outcomes were all pushed aside.

One modest voice of caution was raised in the US Department of Transportation/Federal Railroad Administration staff study, *Western Railroad Mergers* (January 1969)[16] This report was a last ditch effort of the Johnson administration's infant DOT—before being swept out of office by the incoming Nixon administration appointees—to deal with expected consequences of the ICC's recent approval of the Burlington Northern merger. It was apparent at the time that the Milwaukee Road (CMStP&P or MILW), with all its other underlying economic weaknesses, could not stand alone against the newly consolidated Burlington Northern (BN), but the ICC decided expressly not to require inclusion of MILW in BN.[17] *Western Railroad Mergers* concluded that, with the loss of a logical alternative merger matchup (NP + MILW),[18] about the only remaining alternative was to encourage Union Pacific (UP) to absorb the Milwaukee Road, simultaneously acquiring either the Chicago & North Western (CNW) or the northern part of the Rock Island; these options would give UP double-track or paired-track connections from Omaha to Chicago. Consolidation savings from reducing line redundancy in the upper Midwest might also help UP sustain the Milwaukee's sparse traffic base on its transcontinental link and offset some of the power concentrated by the ICC's approval of Burlington Northern.[19]

To sum up, as a consequence of the Burlington Northern merger, the chances of post-1970s restructurings in the rail industry producing a "loose oligopoly" rather than a "tight oligopoly" were greatly reduced. A public policy favoring maintenance of competition was driven back to a secondary defense, granting extensive operating and trackage rights as a condition of merger. "Second best" structural alternatives ultimately had to be created to fill in for the ICC's poorly considered decision in the second iteration of Northern Lines.

The Illinois Central—Gulf, Mobile & Ohio Consolidation into ICG (1972)

The Illinois Central (IC), America's first land-grant railroad (and at one time its longest) was an oddity—a north–south route in a region of east–west transcontinental connectors—like an odd-numbered Interstate in a region of even-numbered superhighways. IC's significantly less well-endowed merger partner Gulf, Mobile & Ohio (GM&O) was the result of a 1947 consolidation of Gulf, Mobile & Northern plus Mobile & Ohio; it ran parallel to IC throughout its length from Chicago to New Orleans. IC and GM&O even had oddly similar branches to Sioux City/Omaha (IC) and Kansas City (GM&O) in the Great Plains, and to Birmingham (IC) and Montgomery (GM&O) in the old South. Other IC branches ran to Indianapolis and to Louisville, and to Shreveport near the Texas border.

The midcentury merger wave found these far-flung, poorly focused carrier fragments just waiting to join the consolidation and rationalization bandwagon. The ICC, noting short average rail hauls in these markets and the overpowering factor of Mississippi River barge competition along the route, was all in favor of the merger. But the Department of Justice found fault; it was "unconditionally" opposed to merger because of the loss of parallel rail competition. And, in the words of Richard Saunders, other railroads in the region "made fools of themselves" fighting over pitifully small numbers of carloads that might be diverted from them as a result of the ICG merger.[20] This was, after all, the period in which Penn Central fell apart, revealing "an entire industry in deep and perhaps mortal danger," while the ICG merger seemed inconsequential by comparison.

But wouldn't consolidation of parallel carriers such as IC and GM&O yield large and much needed cost savings? Richard Saunders again hit the nail on its head:

> It was getting late in the merger game. The issue of whether or not the railroads were going to be restructured was already settled; the only question was how. Everyone knew by this time that merger studies were guesstimates. There were so many variables. The studies showed that six switching crews could be saved at St. Louis to handle the IC's daily 3,500 cars and the GM&O's daily 1,500 cars. The [rival Missouri Pacific] MoPac made detailed calculations to show that only one switch crew could be saved. Routing the GM&O's two to four freights a day between St. Louis and Jackson over the IC would require a new local train to run down the GM&O, because the GM&O's through freights used to handle the local business. Those making the studies had not thought of that. This was nickel and dime stuff. The MoPac demanded days of testimony over this. The IC had messed in the MoPac's control of the C&EI, so the MoPac messed back.[21]

Round and round the carrousel turned. Frisco, the Rock Island, and the Rio Grande all wanted IC trackage or protection against diversion of their historic shares of IC and GM&O interchange traffic. "MoPac denounced the Frisco," Saunders recorded, and some observers thought Rio Grande's claims were ludicrous. KCS fought the M-K-T's requests, probably because it wanted GM&O for itself. C&NW thought KCS claims were "nothing short of effrontery." Customers who had been asked to support the merger were put off by confusion over what really they were promised. IC kept protesting that the law required only consistency with the public interest, not promotion of it.[22] After MoPac and KCS legal ploys that delayed a decision, nonetheless, the ICC finally approved the ICG merger unanimously, and it was implemented on August 10, 1972.

Richard Saunders reports the irony that, after all of the railroad industry's insistence that only the private sector could effectively plan and execute its mergers, and after all that disgraceful bickering among the railroads' lawyers over trivial issues and impacts, ICG turned out to be a flop—"not a debacle like the Penn Central, just a flop." Income and operating statistics went the wrong direction, track condition worsened, rumors flew about (albeit quickly denied) that IC Corporation wanted to sell its railroad subsidiary.

The iconic Mainline of Mid-America could not make a success of a middling merger that looked totally straightforward on the map. It joined—not Burlington Northern as an example of the dangers of railroads inadequately constrained by competition (nor superior opportunities foreclosed by poor public policy foresight)—but instead, Seaboard Coast Line, meek and mild. Like SCL, ICG would also serve—but only by standing and waiting. We will see what the waiting meant when we return (in Chapter 10) to the topic of mergers transpiring later in the twentieth century.

The Penn Central Debacle, 1968–1970

The Pennsylvania Railroad and the New York Central Railroad merged on February 1, 1968. Historian Stephen Salsbury wrote, "The merger of the two railroads was the largest yet attempted in American business history,"[23] and it formed by far the largest transportation company in the United States.[24] The merged railroad had assets of nearly $7 billion, operated over 20,000 route miles of right of way, had more than 100,000 employees, and collected about $1.5 billion in freight revenues annually. It owned pipelines, trucking, and barge operations. It owned Manhattan real estate from 42nd to 52nd street and from Lexington to Madison Avenues—including part of the Waldorf-Astoria as well as the Biltmore, Commodore, Barclay, and Roosevelt Hotels—in all some twenty-nine acres in the heart of Manhattan. It owned shares in sports teams and a company that owned amusement parks like Six Flags Over Texas. Penn Central hauled commuters—according to the authors of *The Wreck of the Penn Central*, 175,000 trips a day in the New York City area, 75,000 in Philadelphia, and 15,000 in Boston. Another 18,000 passenger trips a day were made on Penn Central's Northeast Corridor intercity line between Washington and New York City.[25]

Only 872 days later, on June 21, 1970, Penn Central filed for protection under then Section 77 of the Bankruptcy Act in the US District Court of Philadelphia. By that time, Penn Central's three highest officers, Stuart Saunders (chairman), Alfred Perlman (president), and David Bevan (chief financial officer) had been sacked. Saunders had resolutely kept his shares of Penn Central while others were bailing out, and he lost his fortune, along with many innocents. Perlman, a knowledgeable, respected, and innovative railroad manager, escaped with his employment contract good for a few more months, but his reputation as an operating genius was shattered. Bevan, who was reported to have personally profited from insider information and questionable financial deals, was disgraced. The nation's largest railroad, serving its most populous region, was nearly out of cash and clearly out of creditors—except its banker of last resort, the US government. As legendary editor David P. Morgan of *Trains Magazine* reported one observer putting it, "the only thing left in the black on the Penn Central is its diesels."[26]

With receivables stranded and connecting service endangered, eight other Northeast and Midwest[27] railroads followed Penn Central to the courthouse: the Boston & Maine (B&M), Central of New Jersey (CNJ), Lehigh Valley (LV), Reading (RDG), Lehigh & Hudson River (L&HR), Pennsylvania Reading Seashore (PRSL), the Ann Arbor (AA), and the Erie Lackawanna (EL).[28] While Norfolk & Western Railway (principally through its earlier acquisition of the Nickel Plate and the Wabash), the C&O–B&O System (soon to be known as the Chessie System), and a few smaller railroads operating in the Northeast and Midwest remained "solvent" (i.e., not in bankruptcy reorganization), rail service east of the Allegheny Mountains and north of the Potomac River was predominantly in receivership. One observer noted, cogently, that every railroad in New Jersey was in bankruptcy reorganization. N&W's cranky CEO, John Fishwick, sought to cordon off the impact of the bankrupts on his and other solvent railroads with what he called, famously, the "firewall"—an expression now widely used in computer and Wall Street lingo.

Thus came into play a colossal conflict of market economics, constitutional principles, and regulatory policy as applied to railroads: the "great railway crisis" of the 1970s. If Penn Central and the other bankrupt railroads in the Northeast region could not be reorganized "fairly and equitably" under the bankruptcy laws and the Constitution's Fifth Amendment, two questions came to the fore: Could Penn Central and the other bankrupt railroads be reorganized and emerge from bankruptcy on their own, or would they become wards of the United States? If the bankrupts were not "re-organizable," what obligation did the federal government have to ensure continuation of "essential" rail service and to assist in structuring ongoing rail operations? (See more in Chapter 7.)

The 1970s were spent in sorting out these questions and dealing with the harsh facts that resulted. It became important to understand these antecedents, their interactions, and their impacts so that workable remedies could be fashioned across the board and with lasting effect. As an insightful commentator later put it, a final unmasking was needed of "the myth of the fabulously wealthy railroad." Under the fiction, a rich railroad could bear, without compensation, any public service obligation imposed on it by legislatures, regulators, communities, or unions. "Only a major financial 'train wreck', involving the Penn Central along with most of the other Northeastern railroads, could create the circumstances under which the myth could be seriously questioned."[29]

The Penn Central and Other Causes of the Northeast Rail Collapse

Who and what were responsible for what a popular book by Philadelphia *Bulletin* journalists Joseph Daughen and Peter Binzen called the "wreck of the Penn Central"? Overreaching labor unions? Single-minded state and local taxing jurisdictions? Passenger agencies that did not pay their full way? Greedy and shortsighted managers? The highway builders who lost perspective on "balanced" transport because of the Highway Trust Fund's largess? Economic obsolescence of a technology based on steel wheels running on steel rails? Shippers too dependent on hopelessly uneconomic markets and who were protected by the system from current economic realities, such as those served by branch lines or railcar ferries and barges in New York Harbor? Regulation of rates, services, and financial instruments by the Interstate Commerce Commission? Managerial diseconomies of scale? The answer is: all of the above, to one degree or another!

Daughen and Binzen put it as follows:

> By this time the reader may have reached some tentative conclusions to explain the Penn Central's collapse: the railroad went broke because of bad management, divided management, dishonest accounting, diversion of funds into unprofitable outside enterprises, nonfunctioning directors or a basic disinterest [sic]

in running, or even an inability to run, a railroad. Put even more bluntly, he may blame the bankruptcy on inefficiency, incompetency, gross miscalculations, practices bordering on fraud and a public-be-damned attitude.[30]

There is no dearth of analysis of the Penn Central debacle. There are so many reports and stories that the challenge for the reader is not one of reaping and shocking, but rather threshing and milling. The most comprehensive collection, and in many ways the most penetrating, was the work done for the Senate Commerce Committee, authored largely by Richard J. Barber, a former deputy assistant secretary for policy at the Department of Transportation; it was published by the Senate Commerce Committee as *The Penn Central and Other Railroads* in 1972.[31] The so-called Barber Report concluded:

> The Penn Central debacle is not an isolated idiosyncratic event solely attributable to individual misdeeds or to singular financial manipulations. The Penn Central signals the inability of present public and private institutions to provide a stable and adequate rail service for a major region of the nation in an adverse business environment. . . .
>
> The [committee's] study shows that the cause of the Penn Central bankruptcy is to be found in the complex interaction of a number of factors including questionable management policies, misdeeds of individuals, federal regulatory policies and practices, inadequate public policy toward transportation, the national economy, peculiar business conditions in the Northeastern part of the United States, flaws in the private sector's structure and response, changing demands for rail services, and successful competition from other modes of transportation.[32]

The 1972 Senate Committee report's injunction was to look for many, not a few, causes of the collapse. This same theme was taken up by the Meyer Task Force on Railroad Productivity in 1973, and, five years later (because the fundamental problems were still crippling railroad financial performance nationwide—not only in the Northeast), the Department of Transportation/ Federal Railroad Administration's landmark report, *A Prospectus for Change in the Freight Railroad Industry* (1978). Wrote the Federal Railroad Administration (FRA):

The railroad problem results from a variety of factors, not all of which are in the industry's control. If the railroads are to regain their vitality as private enterprises, it is imperative to seek improvements with respect to each of the different causes of the problem. There is no single solution that will cure all the ills of the industry; there are multiple causes, and there must be a corresponding variety of solutions. . . .

There is an urgent and unavoidable necessity for the industry to adjust, to adapt, to find new solutions to its many problems. Since government actions have been very much a part of the environment of railroading, there is an equally urgent demand for constructive changes in Government policy to be part of the solution.[33]

Drawing on all of these blue ribbon committee studies and official reports, a comprehensive catalogue can be made of the causes of the Penn Central bankruptcy. In a larger context, the list that follows provides a full spectrum of reasons for the decline in railroad fortunes and services throughout the Northeast and Midwest regions in the decade of the 1970s.

Secular Trends in the Economy.   The Northeast and Midwest regions and their railroads faced all kinds of reverses after World War II, including a deep industrial recession in the American economy in 1970 and slow recovery in 1970–1971. Perhaps most significant for Penn Central and its neighbors, Big Steel and the Big Three automobile manufacturers went into steep decline in the 1960s and 1970s.

Steel making underwent fundamental changes—converting from technology based on integrated mills (dependent on rail hauls of metallurgical coal, coke, and iron ore or taconite pellets) to decentralized minimill technology (based on truck-supplied scrap steel and taconite pellets fed into electric arc furnaces). For the integrated blast furnaces and basic oxygen steelmaking plants that remained, rail-served facilities in Pittsburgh, Eastern Pennsylvania, and Baltimore lost market share to mills on Lake Michigan in Northern Indiana. Imported steel became more cost-effective than American supplies, and when imports landed on the West Coast, railroads lost transcontinental movements of finished American steel from the Northeast to the Pacific Coast as well as the inbound materials to the traditional integrated mills in the Northeast and Midwest.

American automobile manufacturers suffered even more radical secular changes. As is well known, foreign auto making has taken leadership from traditional American models, a trend that began in the 1960s and accelerated with the first OPEC oil embargo and resulting energy crisis in the 1970s. Substitution of materials inputs and market-driven quality imperatives in auto making exacerbated the negative impact on railroad inbound services to American automotive manufacturing plants.

Railroad Operating Characteristics in the Urbanized Northeast. Penn Central received a larger share of its revenues from "manifest" carloads—mixed manufactures handled in individual carloads, as opposed to unit trains or large blocks of bulk cargo—than most other railroads. Carload traffic was assembled from industrial sidings and switched into manifest trains at terminals and classification yards—a labor-intensive and time-consuming process. Penn Central spent about 15 cents of every revenue dollar in the switching process, compared with an industry average of less than 10 cents. The terminal work in urban areas exposed PC's freight to theft, vandalism, and higher utility costs and taxes, as well as labor-intensive unionized operations. Yard congestion increased delays to shippers.[34] The irresistible pun at the time was, "The problem of the Penn Central is terminal!"

Closely related to the yard and terminal problems in PC's territory was the exceptionally low level of asset utilization achieved by the railroad. As summarized by Daughen and Binzen, authors of *The Wreck of the Penn Central*:

> The average Penn Central freight car traveled only thirty-seven miles in a day. It covered those thirty-seven miles at an average speed of seventeen miles per hour. . . . A major reason for the slow average speed was the poor condition of much of the Penn Central rails. More than 10 percent of the total trackage, 2,103 miles, was in such poor shape that "slow orders" [typically ten miles per hour] were imposed on it.[35]

These same considerations applied to expensive locomotives, of course, and Penn Central was chronically short of motive power.

Too Much Track for the Available Traffic. Penn Central's trustees in bankruptcy reported in 1971 that they believed the 20,000 route-mile system should be reduced by about 40 percent. Some 20 percent of the trackage was identified as redundant, and much of the traffic moving on light-density lines should have moved by truck or piggyback.[36] Rail line redundancy was not limited to Penn Central, as the other bankrupt lines in the region also suffered from excess capacity and loss of traditional traffic sources. A perfect example was the fate of multiple railroads built in the nineteenth century to tap rich deposits of clean-burning anthracite coal found in Northeastern Pennsylvania—notably the Lehigh Valley; Delaware, Lackawanna & Western; Central of New Jersey; and Reading railroads. Hard, low-sulfur anthracite coal was a fine residential heating fuel in its time, but it was costly and difficult to mine and handle, and thus was vulnerable to replacement by natural gas and imported heating oil after World War II. The elaborate rail trackage network used to serve anthracite coal mines was plainly obsolete by the 1970s.

Competition from Highways. The Interstate and Defense Highway System was authorized in 1956, and construction continued through the 1960s and 1970s. Once the network of non-tolled, high-capacity, limited-access Interstates was built to supplement existing toll roads and the turnpikes criss-crossing Penn Central's territory, trucks (with their superior service reliability and flexibility) were able to outcompete railroads for most manufacturing traffic. Fuel taxes to pay for the Interstates were remarkably low and have remained so for half a century. Federal highway cost recovery studies consistently show an implicit subsidy to large, long-haul, heavy trucks—those most competitive with rail freight service. (See more in Chapter 4.)

The St. Lawrence Seaway. Before the opening of the St. Lawrence Seaway in 1959, the PRR and NYC were the main links for bulk materials moving between the Great Lakes and the Atlantic Ocean. Iron ore from rich deposits in Labrador moving to steel mills in Illinois, Indiana, Michigan, Ohio, and Pennsylvania, for example, or grain from the Dakotas, Minnesota, and the Prairie Provinces of Canada that might move to Buffalo for milling and/or rail transshipment, could now move longer distances via the seaway—bypassing Northeast railroads altogether.

Forced Inclusion of the New Haven Railroad in Penn Central. Under the ruling rail merger statute, the Transportation Act of 1940 (and in keeping with the predecessor act of 1920), the Interstate Commerce Commission had authority to condition approval of a merger on protective conditions and to consider the inclusion (or failure to include) other railroads in determining whether a merger was in the public interest. Under pressure from Congress to do something about the threatened cessation of passenger service by the New Haven, the ICC foisted this sickly carrier on Penn Central. PC's president and chief operating officer Al Perlman considered this one of the key reasons for failure of the merger.

Penn Central Merger Labor Protective Conditions. Employees adversely affected by the merger were granted lifetime protection under terms of an agreement signed for the express purpose of removing labor objections to the merger. It was an extraordinarily high price to pay.[37] Not only were jobs protected, but also managers could not even move workers to where they were needed more without their assent. Labor's grip was not lessened under bankruptcy or the Regional Rail Reorganization (3R) Act and only slightly under the Rail Revitalization and Regulatory Reform (4R) Act formally establishing Conrail in 1976. It took major buyouts paid for with the Northeast Rail Services Act (NERSA) legislation of 1981 before management could come to grips with the problem of excess labor positions and cost.

Delays in Regulatory Rate Relief. In the period of Penn Central operation, the ICC held full sway over railroad rate approval. Since the 1970s were an inflationary time, the ICC's repeated delays in approving general rate increases needed to keep up with inflation were as painful as they were maddening. The ICC continued to be harshly criticized for delays in approval of general rate increases throughout the 1970s. There was no defense the ICC could make, and "regulatory lag" became a potent argument for wholesale rate deregulation as the Staggers Rail Act took shape in 1980.

Mounting Passenger Losses. Amtrak didn't come along until 1971, so Penn Central had to absorb the huge losses associated with the last days of private railroad responsibility for operating intercity passenger service. Penn Central had a larger concentration of such services than any other American railroad because it had to support Northeast Corridor trains from Washington to Boston as well as long-haul trains between the corridor and population centers like Pittsburgh, Cleveland, Columbus, Cincinnati, Indianapolis, Detroit, Chicago, and St. Louis. Nor was there yet any relief from losses due to commuter services provided in the Northeast Corridor cities of Boston, New York, Philadelphia, Baltimore, and Washington, DC. (See more in Chapter 11.)

Unprecedented Diversifications into Nonrailroad Businesses.   Most railroads worried about financial failures and the possibility of nationalization in the 1960s and 1970s, so Penn Central's constituent railroads had set up holding companies and moved marketable assets to where they could be monetized and reinvested in nonrail enterprises.[38] Penn Central pursued diversification more aggressively than most, and its portfolio of outside investments (partly listed above) came eventually to be worth more than the railroad itself.[39] While the value of the diversified outside investments surely helped Penn Central float cash instruments in its darkest days, management came under great criticism for milking the railroad and seemingly paying more attention to its portfolio than running the railroad.

Financial Shenanigans.   David Bevan, his brother, a few underlings, officers of several firms in which PRR made investments, and a few other favored insiders joined in a private investment club, called Penphil, that shadowed the investments made by the railroad and enriched its members. While reason enough to dismiss Bevan, it is unlikely that Penphil damaged Penn Central in direct financial ways, but it certainly distracted Bevan from his duties. More important, Penn Central executives backed investments in Executive Jet Aviation far too heavily and possibly in contravention of Civil Aeronautics Board and ICC policies. There was also the infamous swindle of $4 million from Penn Central by European investors using a false front company set up in Liechtenstein.[40] Given that Penn Central needed public funding support, these incidents were unfortunate.

Cultural Misfits—Red Versus Green.   Much has been made of the clash of managerial styles and loyalties of Penn Central officers who came from PRR (the Red Team) or NYC (the Green Team). Quite an effort was put into balancing powers between Red and Green, and while some conflicts must be expected in any merger, personnel dovetailing cannot be complete and can hardly satisfy every personal ambition;[41] still, Penn Central seemed extraordinarily jinxed. Not only had PRR and NYC people been brought up as direct competitors to despise and disparage each other, but also rancor was built in from day one and from the top down. Bevan was bitter that Perlman got control of his budgeting function and thought Perlman's lavish spending was irresponsible. Saunders wouldn't intercede. Backstabbing memos circulated and direct communication stopped. It was widely reported that the three top officers came to detest one another.

Operational Problems in Consummating the Merger.   Penn Central was a premonition of merger integration problems to come later in the twentieth century in many industries. Perlman thought computers would be Penn Central's salvation. He told the ICC: "Vastly improved communications and management techniques promise far greater control than ever before. In fact . . . it is my judgment . . . that the merged company will be far more susceptible to efficient management than either company alone was only a few years ago."[42]

But, said Daughen and Bitzen, the modern electronic equipment "didn't work worth a damn." In an eerily prescient passage, the two Philadelphia *Bulletin* reporters explain:

> Because the different computer systems of the Pennsylvania and Central were not made compatible in advance of February 1, 1968, they started off not talking to each other, electronically speaking. Data gathered along the old New York Central couldn't be transmitted to the PRR's—now the Penn Central's— brain center in Philadelphia. The merged railroad soon was confronted with lost waybills, missing freight cars, clogged yards, screaming shippers and a serious decline in business as freight customers . . . took their orders elsewhere.[43]

Administrative Ineptitude and Misleading Accounting.   With cash draining from Penn Central's coffers in torrents, it is remarkable how little focus and effort was put on stopping the outflow. Bevan blamed Perlman's bigspending ways and refusal to implement an "incomes budget," but this wasn't the only problem. Freight car per diem rental charges ran out of control while company-owned equipment sat unusable for lack of normal maintenance. "Creative accounting" produced a growing gap between real cash flow and reported income. Referring to official company financial reports attested to by Pete, Marwick, Mitchell & Company, Penn Central's Trustees in bankruptcy later reported to the Senate Commerce Committee, "*Without questioning the consistency of the 1969 report with*

*generally accepted accounting practices, it appears to have reflected a corpo-
rate policy at the time of putting the best conceivable face on the facts—
to the point that these facts were dubious allies of the truth* [emphasis
added]."[44]

Weather. The old railroad saying is that winter comes every year, yet
some years it comes more than others. January 1969 was one of the worst
months on record—only one day above freezing the entire month. Snow
clogged yards, switches froze, rails broke, locomotives couldn't be kept
running, and worker productivity hit rock bottom. Interestingly, the same
sequence hit Conrail exactly a decade later, when Chicago and Buffalo
railyards filled with snow in the so-called storm of the century. The January
chill of 1969 was said to have cost Penn Central some $20 million. And
then in 1972, Hurricane Agnes came storming through Maryland and
Pennsylvania, washing out many lines of the Northeastern bankrupts.

Murphy must have anticipated Penn Central when he minted his famous
law proclaiming "everything that could go wrong, did." To summarize
this catalogue of economic fundamentals converging on the unfortunate
merger of Pennsy and Central, one might return to the Senate Commerce
Committee's balanced view:

> Whatever responsibility might be assigned to the management
> of the *Penn Central* and its component companies, they were
> not the creators of the hostile market conditions that plagued
> their operations for years. The central question in evaluating
> the managements is really their response to adversity. . . . While
> there was speculation, management conflicts of interest, and
> perhaps illegal activities detrimental to the fate of the *Penn
> Central*, such activities were not on the order of the great finan-
> cial scandals that have marked the history of the rail industry
> nor were they major contributions to the collapse.[45]

We reach the strong conclusion that, poor as it was as a public policy
choice, and as poorly implemented as it was for a "bet the company" business strategy, the Penn Central merger was only the most visible of
numerous failures in the railroad industry during the 1960s and 1970s.
Getting through the Northeast rail crisis would take a decade and cost
taxpayers some $8 billion. Getting the American railroad industry as a

whole through the rest of the twentieth century would require five more pieces of major federal legislation and plenty of forbearance by shippers, employees, and investors.

Concluding Thoughts

The railroads did little better when their special status as regulated natural monopolies was recognized by Congress in 1920 than they had under American antitrust laws applicable to industry in general. From that time on, mergers in the rail industry were channeled through their "expert" regulators, the ICC; mergers were largely exempt from the general antitrust laws if the merger had been found by the ICC to be consistent with a comprehensive national plan for restructuring the industry.[46]

After World War II, a renewed interest in mergers was guided, both publicly and privately, by financial considerations such as how industry capital and operating costs could be cut the most. Given the adverse financial circumstances of so much of the industry, that was understandable, but it led to a deep neglect of the competitive maintenance goals embodied in the earlier pursuit of a comprehensive plan. No comprehensive plan was likely to be acceptable, almost everyone was sure, if its central feature was an awkward merger of two of the biggest carriers in the country at the time, the Pennsylvania Railroad and the New York Central.

Indeed, as we argued elsewhere, the Penn Central merger, long before it collapsed in bankruptcy too deep to reorganize conventionally, was the death blow to any rational restructuring of the railroad industry before the very end of the twentieth century. Thus, the negative legacy of Penn Central lasted through the government's creation of Conrail, some $8 billion in restructuring assistance, and the public offering of Conrail common shares. As told in Chapter 10, the end came only when Penn Central was effectively reversed by the division of Conrail between Norfolk Southern and CSX in 1999.

7

TWO RAILROAD REFORM AND REVITALIZATION ACTS AND THE NORTHEAST RAIL CRISIS IN THE 1970S

'The purpose you undertake is dangerous;'—Why that's certain; 't is dangerous to take a cold, to sleep, to drink: but I tell you my lord fool, out of this nettle, danger, we pluck this flower, safety.

—WILLIAM SHAKESPEARE, *Henry IV*, Act 2, Sec. 3, 1 (1597)

Decisions on the future of railroading must be made quickly as well as wisely. The costs of delay in setting a proper course are substantial, and we must get the earliest possible start on what, in any event, will be a long journey toward vitality for the industry.

—Federal Railroad Administration (1978)

As indicated by the amount and quality of work done by congressional committee staff members from 1969 to 1972, the dreadful problems of the Penn Central merger described in Chapter 6 were quite apparent to Congress. The issue soon became not whether but when and in what form legislative action would be taken. Already in 1970, Congress had enacted the Nixon administration's proposal to charter a National Railroad Passenger Corporation (see Chapters 5 and 11).

Our story in this chapter of *American Railroads* begins three decades earlier. Economic forces contrary to railroad prosperity had been gathering since before the Great Depression. These forces were held off for a time by the benefits of the twentieth century's most important railroad innovation—the diesel-electric locomotive (Chapter 12)—and by the surge of freight and passenger traffic accompanying and caused by World War II (including its restrictions on highway construction and on the use of motor fuel and, especially, rubber for tires). But the deteriorating fortunes of railroads came finally to their costly encounter with economic predestination in the Northeast railroad crisis of the 1970s. The upheaval in the Northeast in this decade changed the American railroad industry faster than at any other time since the 1880s. The crisis redrew the railroad map, but more important, brought about the conditions in which regulation by the Interstate Commerce Commission (ICC) could finally be set aside.

As in other instances, government intervention in the railroad industry was both a principal cause of the problem, and (in a very different way) the means to a solution. Overbearing regulation and the consequences of the unfortunate Penn Central (PC) merger exacerbated railroad difficulties when secular changes in the US economy hit the Northeast first and hardest. When PC declared bankruptcy only twenty-nine months later, there was no reasonable alternative but for the government to organize and fund a massive rescue operation—bringing nearly all of the bankrupt rail lines under one authority, excising the weakest lines, logically coordinating operations over newly selected and upgraded routes, and setting up a new permanent railroad called Conrail to serve the region.

With Conrail up and running, but still losing about $1 million a day, Congress allowed more accelerated abandonment of light-density lines, facilitated transfer of commuter passenger services to local authorities, and paid for severance or early retirement of thousands of redundant Conrail employees. The lesson of deregulation was not lost on the key players. Your authors invented the expression that *Staggers Rail Act deregulation could not have been enacted without its need demonstrated by Conrail, and Conrail could not have succeeded without the Staggers Rail Act reforms.* The problem, in the perspective of three decades, was not government intervention to create Conrail, but maladroit regulation that made a new start for Northeast railroads necessary. This was not a bailout as Americans have known them in recent decades, but the detritus of policies left over from the Progressive Era that could not be accommodated to postwar economic realities.

The Legal and Legislative Setting Before the Regional Rail Reorganization (3R) Act

In early 1970, Penn Central's Stuart Saunders went to Washington to meet with Transportation secretary John Volpe and his deputy James Beggs and to ask for $50 million in loans (a figure that later escalated to $200 million) to keep the company out of bankruptcy. Volpe and Beggs put together a plan for $750 million in loan guarantees for railroads and tried to arrange a $200 million package for Penn Central using Defense Production Act funds. The Nixon White House wanted nothing to do with the bailout, however, perhaps partly because it was further complicated by the closeness of several individuals in the Administration to PC's lawyers and major creditors. In December 1970, Congress did pass an Emergency Rail Services Act with $125 million in loan guarantees, but the damage was done, and creditors were furious. Saunders, his chief operating officer Al Perlman, and chief financial officer David Bevan, all were removed in June 1971, and Penn Central voluntarily sought, as it was then codified, Section 77 bankruptcy.[1]

Chief Judge John P. Fullam of the US District Court of Eastern Pennsylvania, which was to oversee the Penn Central's bankruptcy, appointed as trustees what a wire service called "W. Willard Wirtz and three other men."[2] In addition to former Secretary of Labor Wirtz, the three were George P. Baker (former dean of the Harvard Business School), Jervis Langdon, Jr. (formerly head of the Rock Island and B&O railroads), and Richard Bond (retired head of the Philadelphia merchandising firm, John Wanamaker). The trustees hired William Moore of the Southern Railway to be Penn Central's operational chief executive.[3]

In the case of most bankruptcies involving large firms in the United States, there is a presumption that, if relieved of onerous debt payments, the firm can reorganize and come back into solvency, or find another firm to purchase its assets, merge operations, and continue services. Such an "income-based reorganization" was not in the cards for the Northeast railroads, however. After PC filed for Chapter 77 protection, the trustees made an investigation as to whether such reorganization would be possible in their case. Faced with huge cash losses and unprecedented labor protection costs, the trustees reported back to Judge Fullam that Chapter 77 reorganization would be impossible without extraordinary intercession. Accordingly, the trustees' filing proposed that Congress legislate the following:[4]

- A federal grant of $600 to $800 million for one-time repair of essential facilities.
- A crew-consist concession from the United Transportation Union that would take one employee off each freight train.
- Abandonment of one-fourth of current route miles (5,000 miles out of 20,000 then operated).[5]

- Amtrak and local commuter agency underwriting of local and inter-city passenger trains that had cost Penn Central nearly $90 million in annual operating deficits.

George Baker, venerable transportation scholar, dean of the Harvard Business School, and one of the PC trustees, said in a speech, "With-out government action one way or the other, the time beyond which the Penn Central cannot continue operations constitutionally will shortly be at hand."[6]

Congress initially did nothing with the trustees' request, however, and the Nixon administration still wanted none of it, so Judge Fullam, in early March 1973, turned up the heat. He issued an opinion agreeing with the trustees that, under the Constitution's Fifth Amendment protection against seizing private property without due process of law, an estate cannot be forced over a long term to provide public services that would "erode" its value without adequate compensation. Later litigation would turn on the question of, in a public "taking," what would need to be the "Constitutional minimum" payment to the bankrupt estates to avoid erosion.

One strand of the legal debate concerned the question of whether pay-ments under a federal statute designed to compensate for erosion—the Tucker Act (legislated coincidentally in 1887, the same year as the Interstate Commerce Act)—were in fact an adequate remedy or whether, instead, Penn Central should be permitted to move immediately to liquidation.[7] With billions of dollars of Tucker Act compensation subsequently made available to the owners of the Northeast railroads in reorganization, the constitutional crisis was averted. But the tangled economic and legal issues already exposed by Penn Central's collapse gave lie to the common public perception that it was all the fault of hapless managers and a few crooked schemers—meaning that the trustees ought to be able simply to bring in new managers and set things right. That was not the case, and Judge Fullam's recognition that it was not the case became a key step toward finding real solutions.

Enactment of the Regional Rail Reorganization Act of 1973

Congressional staff studies and the trustees' report were now supplemented with appeals from a parade of railroad officials and worried Northeast-ern politicians. With the trustees' report and Judge Fullam's ruling about erosion of the Penn Central estate, the writing was on the wall. Some kind of "Amtrak Plan for Penn Central" could not be far off, as foreseen by columnist Robert Samuelson.

> The Penn Central is slowly—but probably inexorably—drifting toward nationalization. . . . Given the American genius for gimmicks, it may never be called that. Instead there may be some Amtrak-like fiction. Amtrak . . . wasn't a formal nationalization . . . [but even] if many of its present trains are eliminated, there's little prospect of Amtrak's ever weaning itself from an annual appropriation. . . . Congress, of course, isn't eager to go this route with Penn Central, but it may have little choice.[8]

Samuelson's Cassandra call would prove spot-on for almost another ten years, the passage of three more significant congressional enactments, and outlays of some 8 billion taxpayer dollars. The key to resolving the Northeast crisis was that every interest would have to give in—not a little, but a lot. Shippers wanting continued service at artificially low rates, communities wanting to preserve hopeless branch line services, solvent railroads seeking immunization from economic problems in the Northeast while not being cut off from traffic origins and destinations, labor unions wanting higher wages and job protection, rail commuters and intercity passengers demanding not only continuation but improvement of subsidized services, Penn Central owners expecting to be fairly compensated for the "taking," creditors awaiting repayment, and politicians wanting to benefit from playing the "blame game"—all would have to settle for less than 100 cents on the dollar.

After Judge Fullam's challenge, Congress's first step was to pass Senate Resolution 59 on March 26, 1973; it authorized more emergency funding and required both the Secretary of Transportation and the Interstate Commerce Commission to prepare and submit analyses and recommendations to Congress. The Department of Transportation (DOT) report was required to be made in only forty-five days, and that became its nickname.[9] The 45 Day Report was quite a tour de force. It captured the underlying economic problems inherent in the Northeast rail crisis and recommended solutions other than nationalization. It was perhaps naïve in suggesting that a private-sector solution was possible without large infusions of federal funding, but it brought attention back to the fundamental problem of ICC regulation. Unsurprisingly, the ICC volunteered a rival report, *Ex Parte*

Table 7.1   Bankruptcy and Solvency of Northeast Railroads, 1970s

Solvent Railroads	Bankrupts		
	Income Reorganizable	3R Act "Fair & Equitable"	3R Act Not "Fair & Equitable"
Bangor & Aroostook	Boston & Maine	Ann Arbor	Central of New Jersey
Chessie System	Erie Lackawanna	Reading	
Delaware & Hudson			Lehigh Valley
Detroit, Toledo & Ironton			Lehigh & Hudson River
Family Lines			
Maine Central			Penn Central
Norfolk & Western			
Southern			

Railroads in the Northeast and Midwest Region found themselves in a variety of different financial and legal situations in the early 1970s. These were determined by their owners, trustees, or federal courts under prevailing bankruptcy statutes and, after its passage in 1973, the Regional Rail Reorganization Act (the 3R Act). In the table, references to whether bankrupt estates were ruled to be reorganizable or not are divided into three categories. Traditional income-based reorganization was deemed reasonable for the Boston & Maine and Erie Lackawanna (as of 1974), and "fair and equitable" reorganization of the Ann Arbor and Reading roads was thought to be possible under the terms of the 3R Act. Courts ruled, however, that the four other estates, including the huge Penn Central, could not be reorganized on an income basis "fair and equitable" to owners and claimants.

Source: Compiled from many references cited in the text, but see especially, Harr, *The Great Railway Crisis* (Washington, DC: National Academy of Public Transportation, 1978), pp. 59–60.

No. 293, which said that the key issue was not its approval of the Penn Central merger, but how the consolidated railroad had been managed, plus the external challenge of inflation.[10]

The ICC's newly created Rail Services Planning Office (RSPO) smelled blood in DOT's policy waters and swam like Jaws toward its prey. Wrote the politically pandering and functionally unnecessary RSPO: "It can fairly be said that the DOT Report left a substantial portion of those into whose hands it came either confused or angered."[11]

Congress now had available, in addition to its staff studies and the views of the Penn Central trustees and private railroads,[12] the recommendations of the government's agencies officially charged with railroad transportation policy. Congressional committees went to work drafting a bill. As it emerged on January 2, 1974 (Public Law 93-236), the Regional Rail Reorganization (3R) Act of 1973 declared that essential rail service in the Northeast and Midwest was "threatened with cessation or significant curtailment . . ." Congress found that, while the properties were acquired for a public purpose, they had been permitted to deteriorate and now needed extensive rehabilitation and modernization. Public convenience and necessity required "adequate rail service in this region and throughout the Nation to meet the needs of commerce, the national defense, the environment, and the service requirements of [rail users and consumers]." Rail transportation offers economic and environmental advantages in terms of energy efficiency, safety, and cost per ton-mile, such that "maintenance of adequate and efficient service is in the public interest." See Table 7.1.

Provisions of the 3R Act

The purpose of the 3R Act was to establish the framework for resolution of the railroad crisis threatening businesses, employees, and the economic welfare of the entire Northeast and Midwest regions. The goals and overall legislative mandate of the 3R Act were to provide for:

- Identification of a rail service system in the region adequate for the needs of the regional and national rail system;
- Reorganization of the region's railroads into an economically viable system;
- Establishment of the United States Railway Association (USRA) [to plan the system];
- The "establishment of the Consolidated Rail Corporation [CRC, or Conrail], with enumerated powers and responsibilities;"
- Assistance to states, local, and regional authorities for continuation of local rail services threatened with cessation; and
- "[N]ecessary federal financial assistance at the lowest possible cost to the general taxpayer.

Congress then prescribed USRA's duties in detail (Section 202):

- Survey existing rail services in the region (including patterns of traffic movement, traffic densities, line costs and revenues), and plant, equipment and facilities;
- Prepare an economic and operational analysis of present and future services, including traffic movements;
- Analyze the extent to which alternative modes could move the traffic and the economic, social, and environmental costs of doing so, as well as the competitive effects on profitable railroads;

- Prepare a study of rail passenger services in the region;
- Consider the views of the ICC's Rail Services Planning Office (RSPO) created by the act and others who submit their views or testimony;
- Consider methods of achieving economies in systems operations, including with pooling or joint use of lines and abandonments consistent with meeting "needs and service requirements"; and
- Consider the effect on railroad employees of any restructuring of rail services in the region.

The injunction to consider preservation of traditional traffic flows in the region and the economic impact on communities or industries of discontinuing specific services led USRA to sponsor significant stand-alone studies—including one on the Lake Michigan car ferries and another on New York Harbor float operations. Also, Senator Russell Long of Louisiana had inserted a requirement to examine application to Conrail of his pet business remedy—an employee stock ownership plan. This provision cost USRA a lot of staff time and complicated Secretary Elizabeth Dole's privatization efforts a decade later.

A Convoluted Process for Developing the Reorganization Plans

The act was not really clear as to how these analyses and determinations were to be captured, but in Section 206 of the act, Congress described a final system plan (FSP) to be "formulated in such a way as to effectuate the following goals. . . ." There followed a long set much like that just detailed as USRA duties in Section 202. First in the list was "(1) the creation, through a process of reorganization, of a financially self-sustaining rail service system in the region. . . ." Subsequently, in Section 207 appears the requirement that "[w]ithin 420 days after the date of enactment of this Act, the executive committee of the Association shall prepare and submit a Final System Plan [which meets all of the requirements of Section 206] for the approval of the Board of Directors of the Association." The board had thirty more days to approve by majority vote and present the FSP to the ICC for a thirty-day review. Then the board could send the FSP on to both houses of Congress.

It was not until later in Section 207 of the act that there was any mention of a preliminary system plan (PSP). At enactment, the PSP seemingly was designed not so much as an early release of the FSP, but a stand-alone document to facilitate public commentary on the Northeast restructuring issues. It was due in only 300 days after the law's enactment. USRA was supposed to base the PSP on its own investigations, plus reports and other information received from the secretary, the ICC's Office (RSPO), the governor and public utilities commission of each state in the region, Congress, each bankruptcy court and the Special Court, and "interested persons," and all of this was to be accomplished in the very short period of time allowed by the law.

The PSP could have taken almost any form, but USRA wisely used it, as best it could, as a draft FSP; this meant that, rather than delaying consideration of structural options for Conrail and public release of its controversial list of excluded light-density lines, USRA went straight into the den of lions. USRA's PSP–FSP planning process outlined in the 3R Act was convoluted but politically and administratively workable because of USRA's temporary and independent status. It made for an exciting 300 days for USRA's board and staff as they tried to get all of the legislatively specified goals and required analyses accomplished in so short a time period as permitted by the law. Taking the indicated work plan (preparing the PSP as a draft FSP) signaled that USRA was serious about following all the procedural steps and considering alternative solutions on a blank slate.

As we shall see in more detail later, USRA's preferred structural system alternative for resolution of the Northeast railroad crisis work was a competitive plan based on substantial transfers of operating properties from bankrupt to solvent railroads in the region. As things turned out, the association could not make its institutionally preferred PSP/FSP designs work, but later (after the solvent railroads failed to embrace the Three-System East Plans) USRA's backup plan sailed through final approval by Congress virtually without objection. As described below, many of the USRA officers and staff members who were looking at the downstream economics of Conrail preferred the backup plan anyway (thinking it would be more financially successful over time). A strong argument can be made that the less-competitive but ultimately successful backup plan, known as Unified Conrail, would not have been as politically acceptable if it had been presented as the favored alternative in the PSP and FSP; for USRA's leadership, it was perhaps better to have loved and lost than never to have loved at all.

A final set of responsibilities detailed in the 3R Act, with similarly short deadlines, related to court review of the restructuring process. The act required each court dealing with a "railroad in reorganization" in the region to decide within 120 days whether the railroad was reorganizable on an income basis (under Section 77 of the Bankruptcy Act) within a reasonable time. If not reorganizable, the act's intention was that the railroad would come into the 3R (USRA) restructuring process.[13] The act then created a special court for the task of reviewing the final system plan when it became effective; this review was to be with respect to "matters concerning the value of the rail properties to be conveyed under the plan and the value of the consideration to be received for such properties."

The Friendly Court Ruling

Legal review of bankruptcy and financial reorganization matters for the Northeast railroads, and the 3R Act itself, were addressed with remarkable expedition in 1974. On March 1, a three-judge special court to handle railroad reorganization matters was established within the federal judiciary. Distinguished appellate judge Henry J. Friendly, who one writer calls "the greatest judge of his era," was put in charge of the special court.[14] In May, judges in various bankruptcy courts ruled that six of the eight bankrupt railroads could not be reorganized under the 3R Act. On June 25, Judge Fullam's district court in Pennsylvania, hearing the case *Connecticut General Insurance Co. v. Blanchette* (a trustee of the Penn Central), ruled that the 3R Act of 1973 was unconstitutional on two counts. USRA took immediate steps to appeal the district court's *Connecticut General* decision.[15]

Then, on September 30, Judge Friendly's special court reversed the bankruptcy and district courts, ruling that the 3R Act was "fair and equitable" to the railroad estates and agreeing with the Penn Central trustees that PC could not be reorganized through the normal bankruptcy laws. (See Figure 7.1) In the opinion of the special court, cancellation of Penn Central equity shares and outstanding debt alone would not enable an income-based reorganization. Closing out the year, on December 16, 1974, the US Supreme Court agreed with the special court, overruled the district court on *Connecticut General*, and held the 3R Act of 1973 to be constitutional.[16]

This was the way Congress addressed the issue raised by Penn Central trustees and others that a "taking" of rail property without due process (and adequate compensation) would be unconstitutional under the Fifth Amendment. USRA was to apply to the courts within thirty days for consolidation of all judicial proceedings regarding the future FSP into a single, three-judge United States district court—the special court. This was done and approved. After the legal challenges to the 3R Act's Northeast railroad restructuring process were thus resolved, the way was open for the planning process outlined in the 3R Act to be followed through to eventual certification of the FSP and the conveyance of rail lines from the bankrupt estates to form the successor railroad, Conrail.

The Importance of the USRA Board

The USRA board of directors included three federal officials: the secretaries of Transportation and the Treasury and the chairman of the ICC. The remainder of the eleven-member board was made up of representatives of the various groups that had constituent interests in the rail crisis— the rail industry, rail labor, the financial community, shippers, and state and local government. USRA's self-history[17] states that, in the final analysis, this constituent board probably helped the association achieve the critical compromises that made up its PSP and FSP. That judgment is correct, but does not go far enough. The representative nature of the board also gave voices of support to staff efforts to explore each corner of the planning process, and in the end helped Congress to accept the FSP as an honest effort to explore all options and balance political hopes with hard realities. In short, the constituent board was a fundamental part of the creation as well as the vetting of the final system plan for reorganizing the railroads of the Northeast into Conrail.

USRA, again in its own institutional history, liked to emphasize the genius of Congress in setting up a new, independent, specialized, expert, and temporary agency outside the civil service system to carry out all the studies required by the 3R Act and to develop the preliminary and final system plans. It is true that, with such a crushing timetable and the fact that railroad knowledge is more often acquired on the job than through academic study, the agency charged with developing the consolidation plans would have to be made up of experts "borrowed" from the extended rail industry.

After USRA's job was finished, the Federal Railroad Administration (FRA) experienced a rebirth of significance in the Carter administration. Many of the lessons of the Northeast collapse and restructuring fed directly into FRA policies and legislative proposals. The risk of depopulating FRA had been real in the earlier period, but in the end, it was not a crippling difficulty—as evidenced by FRA's effectiveness in handling the Midwest bankruptcies, the Northeast Corridor Improvement Project (NECIP), a number of bad hazardous-materials tank car accidents in the late 1970s, the 4R Act report and funding responsibilities, and the staff work leading up to passage of the Staggers Rail Act of 1980. Even the ICC later recovered its soul under the leadership of chairs Darius Gaskins, Heather Gradison, and Linda Morgan. It survives in the form of the Surface Transportation Board (STB), with important authority for railroad mergers and deciding the most difficult rate-making cases.

The 3R Act gave USRA an added power: For a limited period, and only in cases involving the bankrupts, USRA was to take over functions normally exercised by the Interstate Commerce Commission with respect to approval of line consolidations and abandonments, which, along with rate making, were the most potent of ICC's authorities. While the ICC had not covered itself in glory executing these responsibilities, it was extraordinary that USRA (a non-court-like administrative agency with a representative board) was given this authority. It could be argued that having pushed the ICC aside, it was also surprising that the act put the ICC back into review roles for both the PSP (through RSPO) and FSP (the whole commission). A cynic would say that these provisions were window dressing—a measure of face saving granted the ICC—but they were enshrined right there in the act. Formal consideration of the ICC's views meant a lot more work for USRA, to no real policy-making advantage.

In the drafting of the 3R Act, as often happens in legislative construction, unresolved numerous implicit debates were left hidden under the surface of contradictory statements of goals, overly specific bureaucratic process requirements, and earmarked funding authorizations. Quite apparent was the killer timetable, but the toughest challenge for USRA was reconciling all the conflicting policies and competing claimants at issue in the Northeast rail crisis. Was there a way to continue essential service; respect all the other injunctions in the 3R Act; pay to refurbish the properties conveyed to Conrail; and not soak taxpayers with any more than the constitutional, minimum required compensation for the public "taking" of bankrupt rail property? Central to meeting its statutory challenge were the decisions USRA would make on the size of Conrail and the competitive structure of Northeast railroads. Nothing like it had been attempted since General McAdoo's work in setting up the first US railroad association to take over operation of the nation's railroads in World War I.

It would be difficult to overstate the importance of USRA's strategic and structural decisions and the degree to which they turned on fundamental bankruptcy law and economic theories of industrial organization. Nothing is more remarkable about the USRA story than that there was assembled—from rusting and ill-fitting components in an artificially compressed time-table and without full cooperation of all the players named in the legislative mandate—a great and lasting civic work destined eventually to be returned to the private sector. And it was done not so much by established industry senior executives, but by aspiring apprentices of the trade, each there under a temporary assignment.

Strategic Options for USRA's System Plans: How Would the Northeast Be Restructured?

USRA was not incorporated until February 1, 1974, and hiring of staff took the rest of the spring and much of the summer.[18] To fulfill the 3R Act's analysis requirements, USRA, at the very outset of its staff work, sent out requests for proposals (RFPs) to expert consulting firms outlining most of the specialized studies and what USRA's requirements for the consultant reports would be. Issuing the RFPs, reviewing responses, selecting winners, and negotiating contracts was quite a chore; while USRA's status as an independent agency might have been able to shortcut some normal government procurement rules, its chief administrative officer had joined USRA from a similar post at DOT. He insisted on a time-consuming formal process like the federal personnel and procurement rules required—annoying to the staff members at the time, but correct in the end.

USRA's core function was to design alternative systems and route structures to meet the 3R Act goals and to prepare detailed operating plans and financial analyses for the main solution options. First, outside expert rail engineers helped analyze and rate the condition of many thousands of miles of the bankrupts' rail lines. USRA staff members' most difficult and novel work came with studying how each of the "structural options" would contribute to the financial success of Conrail and affect rail service in the region. These studies—using relatively new and untested analytical approaches and data that USRA could not have assembled were it not for the 3R Act authorizations—were needed to support the PSP and FSP strategic system design and eventual property conveyances. "Each alternative that the staff studied was examined from the viewpoint of three important considerations: the need for adequate and efficient service which would preserve, as much as possible, competition and the existing traffic flows; the proposed financial self-sufficiency of Conrail; and the effects on the financial self-sufficiency of other railroads in the region."[19]

USRA staff members well understood the need to minimize, within reason, the market value of properties intended for conveyance to Conrail—because of the implications for likely future court judgments of the value of any unconstitutional "taking." Thus, holding down the size of likely Tucker Act claims weighed on USRA's near-term thinking about what Conrail might look like on paper, intermediate political recommendations for USRA's preliminary and final system plans, and long-term structural issues affecting the future of the railroad industry. Real estate not essential for Conrail operations was set aside. Even in the case of mainlines, consideration was given to seeing if other private or nonfederal purchasers could be found.

To oversimplify and yet reveal the clash of institutional theories, USRA had to decide whether to make Conrail a unified regional monopoly with large potential leverage over freight rates in its service territory or to foster intraregional competition among smaller railroads—possibly more than one "Conrail." Next, USRA had to decide whether to keep as much rail traffic as it could on Conrail's internal properties to achieve lasting economies of traffic density over its core operation or to leave marginal properties with the bankrupt estates and set aside non-core lines for resale to other parties, both of which would help lower Tucker Act claims against the federal government.

The 3R Act seemed to charter a single nondescript, institutional-sounding Consolidated Rail Corporation (CRC), universally known as Conrail; there was no mention of the possibility of more than one "Conrail" or of any corporate form different from a traditional vertically integrated railroad.[20] But the act did not require all the bankrupt properties to be absorbed into a single "Conrail." If it had, things would have been easier for the USRA to manage. Indeed, the most straightforward way to read the 3R Act's charter for CRC was that it would be an amalgamation of the best lines and traffic sources of all the bankrupt Northeast railroads, leaving behind with the estates any nonessential lines. There would be the one Unified Conrail (USRA staff informally called it Big Conrail), and it would benefit from access to all the traffic and all the best lines and equipment of the predecessor roads.[21]

Summary of the Options That USRA Considered

While Unified Conrail was a logical and expected strategic option that could be inferred directly from the language of the 3R Act, that was not so for the other options USRA devised and analyzed. Indeed, onlookers were quite surprised by these suggestions, and some no doubt thought the association had lost its way.

It is worthwhile to describe these strategic options in some detail because their design and discussion tells a great deal about the creative dynamics among staff members, officers, and board members of the USRA; the difficulty of framing and analyzing options that offered different ways of meeting conflicting goals in the USRA charter; and, of course, how seriously USRA took its core mandate. The other options that USRA studied were two Conrails, controlled transfer, a consolidated facilities corporation (ConFac), a MARC-EL (Middle Atlantic Rail Corporation—Erie Lackawanna) plus a small Conrail, and neutral terminals.[22]

TWO CONRAILS

While somewhat oxymoronic and perhaps a stretch of the congressional mandate, formation of two Conrail-type entities was conceivable, but there was no explicit authorization in the 3R Act for a second "Consolidated Rail Corporation."

Penn Central itself provided a prototype for USRA's structural option called Unified Conrail, but there was an equally good model for the strategic alternative called Conrail North/South: essentially undoing the merger of the two major railroad companies that had formed Penn Central—New York Central (NYC) and the Pennsylvania Railroad (PRR)—supplemented with reestablishment and upgrading of their historic connections to other railroads in the region. This structural option would have preserved competition and existing traffic flows, as the 3R Act commanded. There was substantial support at USRA for the idea of splitting Penn Central back into its New York Central and Pennsylvania Railroad components, but clearly the majority view of USRA officers and staff members was that the two systems' efficiency and economic viability could not be ensured in this alternative. Alternatively, an east–west split of all the lines in Unified Conrail (perhaps along a Buffalo–Pittsburgh or a Cleveland–Columbus–Cincinnati axis), was listed in the options, but it was not seriously considered.

CONTROLLED TRANSFER

More radical still than two Conrails was the idea of transferring portions of the bankrupt northeastern railroads to other private enterprise railroads—the solvents, as they were called—allowing these firms to extend their reach into the heart of Penn Central territory. The motivation for this controlled transfer option (it was briefly called controlled liquidation until more politically correct voices were heard) was less the reestablishment of pre–Penn Central conditions than minimizing the size of Conrail per se, while also honoring the 3R Act's mandate to consider competition. In point of fact, however, meaningful implementation of a complete or final controlled transfer strategy would be out of USRA's hands, because DOT, not USRA, would own the government's Conrail shares. (See Chapter 8.)

Advocates of Unified Conrail (the majority opinion, to be sure) believed that draining good traffic away from Conrail with transfers of valuable properties to non-Conrail entities would only increase the difficulty of making the new railroad economically viable. Still, if the condemnation value of USRA-reorganized properties (the constitutional minimum compensation to the bankrupt estates) could be reduced, and the stability of operations by solvent railroads could be realized, that made for a politically attractive package.

CONSOLIDATED FACILITIES CORPORATION (CONFAC)

This strategic option would have enabled a vertically separated solution by creating a company explicitly designed to own and maintain the railway infrastructure and facilities of the bankrupt lines in the Northeast. Then a Conrail defined as a non-track-owning operating railroad (or other entities) would provide railway transport services using ConFac rights of way and trackage. That is, ConFac would not be an operating railroad but would provide physical track and structures, giving access to any qualified carrier that wanted to pay to use them. USRA staff members' expectation was that ConFac would be publicly owned and would require a large and ongoing subsidy.

The significance of the ConFac structural option does not come from any serious consideration it received in the USRA planning process (there was almost none) but from the fact that, in the last two decades, something nearly identical to it has become official policy of the European Union. Faced with economic realities of its own (nationalized railroads, overstaffed operations, massive passenger service deficits, hope for liberalized competitive operating companies), Europe decided to separate ownership and maintenance of rail rights of way from operations.[23] This was a way that passenger services could be subsidized and multiple (competitive) freight licenses could be issued within the European Union rules that generally discourage subsidized solutions.

Fans of European passenger rail services still occasionally recommend this model for portions of the North American network, but with the New World's rail freight versus passenger ratios the reverse of Europe's, adoption of the ConFac nationalization model make no more sense today than it did when the USRA board flatly rejected it for the Northeast reorganization. This conclusion has been reached and resubstantiated in nearly every credible study of the topic by railroad experts grounded in North America.

MARC-EL (MIDDLE ATLANTIC RAIL CORPORATION—ERIE LACKAWANNA) PLUS SMALL CONRAIL

This structural option was created by USRA to fit the political realities of the times. It would be made up of two "Conrails" not divided north–south or east–west as before, but as follows:

- Lackawanna routes and other non-PC bankrupts in the region (Reading, Lehigh Valley, and Central of New Jersey) grouped together and called MARC-EL.
- A smaller "Conrail" made up of the major PC lines.

Unsurprisingly, the MARC-EL Plus Small Conrail concept was advocated strongly by Governor Scranton, but it really only became feasible as a default option after Erie Lackawanna joined the planning process a month before publication of the PSP. Like USRA's Conrail north–south or east–west options, federal funding would support both restructured railroads. MARC-EL would have trackage rights and shipper access over Small Conrail lines to some gateway points, but it is still hard to see how the awkwardly located and poorly maintained combination could compete against a slimmed down and financially reorganized Small Conrail based on already (at least partially) integrated Penn Central properties.

NEUTRAL TERMINALS

The USRA staff also considered a neutral terminal option. This option would mean forming a single long-haul railroad from the bankrupt lines, with neutral terminal companies in important areas. This plan would reduce the total potential profitability of Conrail and require that many new organizations be created as the terminal companies, limiting efficiency. A variant of the neutral terminal option survived as Conrail Shared Assets territories in northern New Jersey, southern New Jersey, and the Detroit metropolitan area after the split of Conrail between Norfolk Southern and CSX in 2000.[24]

Although, in one way or another, any of the alternatives that the USRA studied could address the goals of the 3R Act with varying degrees of success, USRA had to select a preferred solution. It is a real irony that, after all the analytical work and negotiations with railroads, none of these options, exactly, became the association's PSP primary structural recommendation.

Some USRA staff work went into fleshing out such proposals, but the Two Conrails/north–south option was never a serious contender for the preliminary or final system plans. Ironically, when neither CSX nor NS could win a full merger with Conrail in 1997, the two big eastern railroads divided Conrail in a pattern reminiscent of Conrail North and South, which was true to the historical form. And then only six weeks before the PSP was to be published under the congressional timetable, the court-appointed trustees of the Erie Lackawanna announced their decision that EL could not be reorganized under Chapter 77; therefore, the trustees asked USRA to include this storied railroad in the 3R Act planning process. Not altogether unexpected, the decision nonetheless caused USRA's planners quite a scramble. New data needed to be gathered and added to the analysis model, new strategic options had to be thought through and presented to USRA's board, and special studies such as the influential PSP chapter on competition[25] had to be partly redrafted. So the young and workaholic USRA staff members put in a few more very late nights.[26]

The PSP was published February 26, 1975. To the great surprise of many observers when the plan was revealed, the USRA's board of directors had proposed two very large "controlled transfers." The board proposed to convey to the Norfolk & Western Railway the Erie Lackawanna route from Buffalo to northern New Jersey, and to convey to the Chessie System the Reading/CNJ route from near Harrisburg to New Jersey and Staten Island connections with the B&O. The remainder of Penn Central (plus the Lehigh Valley and Ann Arbor) would make up Conrail. These transactions apparently had been discussed with the "solvents" but clearly had not been reduced to contracts. Implementation of this plan, called the Three Systems East proposal, would mean "Conrail itself would then have no monopoly over any major market in the region,"[27] but success in the complex negotiations with N&W and Chessie over their acquisitions of routes from the bankrupts were far from assured. Since the Three Systems East plan was still rather conjectural, the USRA wisely decided it needed a default option and for that, USRA chose MARC-EL Plus Small Conrail.

When the PSP was announced, it encountered both bemusement and outrage—the former over the perception that the whole structural plan for resolving the Northeast rail crisis seemed to rest on wishful thinking, and the latter that so many light-density lines were slated for non-Conrail purgatory. With regard to structure, USRA's critics thought there was a huge disconnect between the chimerical perception of controlled transfer to the solvents and the frontrunner status of "Big Conrail." Shouldn't that gap have been minimized before publication of the PSP? What was USRA doing? But the more vocal criticism focused on the excluded branch lines. The question of line abandonments had been a sore subject in the best of times, and now it was multiplied in its intensity because of the unexpectedly large mileage of rail lines excluded from Conrail in the PSP.

Recall that Congress, almost as an afterthought in the 3R Act, had added the requirement for a PSP to be issued 300 days after the effective date of the legislation—for the purpose of informing public discussion of the reorganization options USRA was considering. Congress then created the Rail Services Planning Office (RSPO) as a unit of the ICC. More than Congress wanted it to, one suspects, RSPO thought of itself as a white knight committed not only to facilitating public discussion but actively fomenting criticism of USRA's analysis and proposals. USRA's history understates: "the light density line recommendations and the warning of financial problems . . . were expected to produce criticism."[28]

During the studies that had led to the PSP, USRA had analyzed the profitability of over 9,600 miles of light-density branch lines with the idea of paring off those that were a financial drain. In the PSP, USRA recommended that 6,200 miles of those lines be cut. This set off loud and sustained acrimony. Identification of so many miles of light-density lines to be excluded from Conrail gave RSPO new energy to continue its line-preservation drumbeat from a year earlier. As Eric Beshers put it in his commentary, RSPO sought to "whip up opposition to the PSP and attack it with all the vigor it could muster. Indeed, just in case the affected public failed to yell loud enough on its own, the RSPO sent staff members into the field to scout out and organize the prospectively injured so their voices could be added to the chorus of complaints."[29] USRA believed, nonetheless, that its recommendations on light-density line eliminations were economically sound and that abandonment of unprofitable lines was essential to Conrail viability.

More difficult intellectually was the widely held fear that none of the structural options (even streamlined to reduce mileage that Conrail would have to rehabilitate and maintain—plus Tucker Act claims) would result in a financially self-sustaining regional rail system. Almost everyone expected more federal money would be needed. USRA's official *Final Report* correctly observed that "[t]he Administration was alarmed by the prospect of pouring in ever greater amounts of money to implement USRA's proposed solution. It was concerned especially since the cost would far exceed the original funding specified in the 3R Act."[30] Transportation secretary William Coleman and his surrogate, deputy secretary John Barnum, voting as a USRA board member, took every appropriate opportunity to advocate tighter purse strings and the need for fundamental reforms such had been outlined in the Meyer *Productivity Task Force Report.* Indeed, Nixon and Ford administration directors campaigned vigorously for controlled transfer as an alternative to the PSP approach. At the end of the day, however, the USRA board reaffirmed its earlier position that controlled transfer would not meet the terms of the 3R Act, and, not without dissent, approved the Three Systems East structure for the PSP.

Among the many detractors of the PSP structural proposal was the Norfolk & Western Railway, which had already rejected USRA's offer to acquire some of the lines in reorganization. Instead, N&W continued to favor a proposal informally called "Fishwick's Firewall" after the N&W CEO John P. Fishwick's plan to create a "partial nationalization" made up from the terminal properties and commuter operations east of a line drawn roughly from Albany to Harrisburg. Keeping these lines separate and federally subsidized would mean they would not drag down the Region's viable rail lines.[31]

Passenger Issues Addressed in the Preliminary and Final System Plans

In tandem with the overall freight traffic, cost, and investment analyses USRA was conducting, decisions had to be made about passenger services to recommend in both the PSP and FSP. Again the dilemma was either (1) maximize political support for the plan or (2) husband resources—initially in properties that might not need to be "taken" from the estates and conveyed to Conrail, and downstream in avoided costs of passenger operations or encumbered freight capacity. As USRA leaders worked through the logic of the options, consensus formed around a basic principle not expressed in the 3R Act or in any other policy precedents that come to mind. This can and should be called the USRA Principle, though it was not so called at the time or since.

The idea is this. If a rail line is used for passenger service primarily, it should be owned, dispatched, and operated by the predominant passenger user/agency.[32] It would not be a Conrail line. If, instead, a line is predominantly used for freight and only incrementally serves passengers, it should be part of Conrail. In either case, the owner would recover a "proportionate share of all costs directly attributable to their respective operations."[33] The USRA Principle is why Amtrak now owns the Northeast Corridor (NEC) from Washington, DC, to New York City, over Hell Gate Bridge and to New Rochelle (Shell Interlocking) in New York's Westchester County. The PSP recommends specifically that "to minimize freight-passenger conflict, Conrail through-freight service should be moved, insofar as possible, to a separate right-of-way. Management and financial responsibility for the Corridor should not be vested in Conrail."[34]

The USRA Principle worked surprisingly well for all interests. Conrail did not have to carry the ownership burden of the NEC. The claims of the Penn Central estate against the government for a "taking" of their property would be no lower, but Conrail would have a better chance of self-sustainability in the private sector. Passenger agencies gained control of key properties that they were willing to support financially. Amtrak became a unifying agency for what most politicians believed was an essential national passenger operation along the heavily used NEC. Swallowing hardest were, again, the Nixon and Ford administration officials who knew owning the NEC would be costly but politically necessary as part of the overall FSP outcome. They figured that, if Amtrak owned the NEC, at least its costs would be apparent on its books, Amtrak wouldn't be blaming Conrail for inadequate track maintenance, and the government would own a hard asset to show for taxpayers' money spent on the enterprise.

Amtrak moved quickly to consolidate the benefits it received in the FSP. It now had a stronger role in the Northeast Corridor Improvement Project

(NECIP), managed and funded through the FRA. With long-needed roadway capital improvements and facility upgrades (grade crossing eliminations; concrete ties; new rail; station upgrades; drainage improvements in the PRR's Baltimore tunnel; a new power system for New York to New Haven to replace the venerable but failure-prone Cos Cob, Connecticut, power station; and improved equipment maintenance facilities at Wilmington) finally being made, Amtrak could begin planning higher-speed NEC service.

Conrail went another direction, deciding to make use of some of the alternative routes designated by USRA in the FSP to move as much traffic as possible off Amtrak's expensive NEC route and out of the way of priority passenger trains. The strategy involved three steps. First, develop an alternative freight route for traffic to northern New Jersey originating west of Harrisburg. Conrail chose the former Reading–Lehigh Valley–CNJ route from Harrisburg through Allentown, Pennsylvania, and Bound Brook, New Jersey, to Elizabeth and Newark. Second, after the Norfolk & Western–Southern merger (1982), Conrail began routing traffic for connections with Norfolk Southern (NS) via Hagerstown, Maryland, rather than Alexandria, Virginia.[35] This route avoided more of Amtrak's high NEC trackage fees, as well as freight and passenger congestion in Baltimore and Washington. Third, using these two routes and minimizing NEC train miles, Conrail could drop its electric locomotive fleets and remove catenary from the trackage used only for local freight switching in the Washington–Alexandria area, as well as its Susquehanna River freight line from Harrisburg—connecting to the NEC at Perryville, Maryland.

These new alignments continued to work well for both the eastern freight railroads and Amtrak. In the latter case, reduction of freight tonnage on the NEC has made room for growth of Amtrak's premium service, and the de facto separation of most freight and passenger service has had major implications for NEC maintenance strategies and expenses. In the short run, Amtrak lost trackage fees, but in the long run, total social costs are probably lower.[36] The USRA Principle has served all parties well over the quarter century it has had a controlling effect.

The Final System Plan

From March to June 1975, USRA staff continued work on details of the system plan, and the USRA board members met frequently to decide key issues. The 3R Act's schedule for publication of the FSP worked out to July 26, 1975, and, after a winter break following release of the PSP in late February, USRA staff worked at a frenzied pace to meet its next set of deadlines.

Solid in its commitment to a workably competitive solution without excessive taxpayer liabilities, the USRA's board in the FSP again recommended the Three Systems East structure as best for the region and the nation. Conrail, made up mainly of former Penn Central and Lehigh Valley lines, was to be the region's core railroad. The Chessie System, strengthened with the addition of the former Reading and Erie Lackawanna routes, provided balance and competition. Norfolk & Western was left pretty much as it was, but it gained access at Cincinnati to PRR's Sandusky Line in Ohio and properties in Indiana that connected other N&W lines to form through routes to Chicago and St. Louis via Toledo (Nickel Plate) and New Castle/Muncie, Indiana (Wabash). Southern Railway was offered Pennsy's Delmarva lines and the Cape Charles, Virginia, car float operation.

Realizing that, even at this late point in the planning process, participation of the solvent railroads in the Three Systems East plan was still speculative, USRA chose Unified Conrail—what it called the "next best" solution—rather than MARC-EL Plus Small Conrail as its backup recommendation for the FSP.[37] The USRA history says the board "turned down MARC-EL because that would involve the creation of two new railroads instead of one, and, however temporarily, that would be an added burden on the federal till. This was one of the factors that had killed the earlier Conrail East/West and North/South alternatives. Also, the competition that MARC-EL could . . . [provide] in the region might actually be at too great an expense to Conrail."[38]

Technically, USRA was supposed to send its FSP to the ICC for comment on June 25, 1975—in order to give Congress the benefit of ICC's input before deciding on its approval. As it happened, USRA sent the ICC an incomplete version because the board did not finish its official determinations until the meeting of July 15, 1976, and the issues decided then remained controversial to the end. Governor Scranton could not attend the July meeting but said in a statement accompanying the FSP that he would have preferred the board choosing MARC-EL as its first structure option, with a backup of Conrail defined as Penn Central + Ann Arbor.[39]

The FSP process itself was not complete until evaluated by the ICC and approved by Congress, but the 3R Act provided that if neither the House nor the Senate chose to oppose the FSP, it would become law in 120 days (November 1975). In fact, both happened: The FSP stood "approved" after 120 days, while Congress passed an omnibus authorization also approving USRA's plan.[40]

From July to November 1975, things seemed to be in order. Staff members went on vacation or started looking for other jobs. Conrail was incorporated, and (over the objections of Secretary Coleman, who believed USRA's functions should be entirely separate from Conrail's) Edward Jordan was named its CEO. USRA's legal team began preparing conveyance documents, which required close examination of real estate titles and minor technical amendments to the FSP. Over the course of many subsequent months, the technical and legal teams would remain deeply involved in supporting the US government's defense against the claims of the Penn Central and other estates for compensation because of the "taking."

To implement the FSP, an omnibus rail bill had been introduced in the House in September. The administration and Congress worked to produce a bill incorporating changes in the 3R Act's branch line provisions and Conrail financing, to comply with the FSP recommendations, as well as initial reforms in ICC regulation of the railroads This and a similar Senate bill were passed in late December as the Railroad Revitalization and Regulatory Reform (4R) Act (see below and Chapter 9), and it was signed by President Ford in February 1976.[41]

While the political compromises had been made and the legal process had been well attended to, one more FSP crisis occurred—as though to illustrate how unstable the Northeast railroad crisis still was. Only six weeks before "conveyance day"—(April 1, 1976),[42] the date FSP-designated properties were to be officially transferred from the bankrupt estates to their new owners—the Three Systems East plan cratered. Says the USRA history, "The Chessie System, after lengthy negotiations, found itself unable to get the agreements from its unions that it needed to participate in the property transfers that the plan required. USRA now had to draw up plans to implement its fallback structure, the Big Conrail alternative. Quickly, the USRA staff conducted further plant sizing and other studies, and the Association's Board approved new designations for some bankrupt lines so that the new plan could go into effect."[43]

Under the process initiated by the 3R Act and reaffirmed by the 4R Act, USRA was required to list for the special court the precise legal descriptions of properties that the bankrupts would be conveying to Conrail. It was hard work, but the dedicated USRA staff finished the chore, the special court approved the transfers, and Conrail began operations on April 1, 1976. By all accounts, the FSP property conveyances went according to plan—indeed, remarkably smoothly. As USRA's history concluded: "There was no system-wide halt in service on its lines, nor was there the chaos that had attended the Penn Central merger."[44]

The 4R Act: Conrail's Inaugural, a Start on Deregulation, and "Revitalization"

USRA's FSP was enacted into law by the 4R Act of 1976. This legislation was—with respect to its reform features and in comparison with the Staggers Rail Act four years later—only a beginning step toward regulatory reform. While a centerpiece of Ford administration policy for transportation, its regulatory change proposals were well-intentioned but not adequate, and they were easily frustrated by the ICC—at the time still firmly in the hands of traditional regulators. Rail watchers in Washington, DC, and the large cities of the Northeast were more focused on the startup of Conrail, while rail users in rural America were more concerned with branch line abandonments and the spread of bankruptcies beyond Conrail's territory. Already the Rock Island was in receivership, and that storied road extended as far west as Colorado Springs and Tucumcari, New Mexico.

It is perhaps fair to say that if Congress had not needed to enact the plan for Conrail startup, there would have been no revitalization and reform legislation in 1976. Further, if the 4R Act had not left so much room for the ICC to continue its regulatory mischief, there might have been less reason to pass the Staggers Rail Act in 1980.

For these reasons, further discussion of the 4R Act's regulatory reform provisions are deferred to Chapter 9. The remainder of the current chapter focuses on other provisions of the 4R Act related to industry structural and public funding issues assigned to the Federal Railroad Administration. Chapter 8 will then concentrate on Conrail's early years and the need for subsequent Northeast rail restructuring assistance in legislation enacted in 1981.

The 4R Act's New Funding Programs

In addition to approving USRA's plan for establishment of Conrail, the 4R Act sought, through several new financial assistance programs, to address other symptoms of failing railroad companies and lightly used rail lines in the second half of the twentieth century. These authorizations featured federal loan guarantees, preference share (quasi-equity) financing, and a federal/state continuance subsidy program for already abandoned rail lines. Despite the inherent flaws and inconsistencies of these programs, and despite strong pressures from some applicants and political figures to reach parochial decisions, the Department of Transportation and its FRA implemented the program in a highly professional manner.

The 4R Act also mandated additional studies related to the financial condition of the railroads. Of these, the most important requirement was that FRA survey and report on the amount of deferred maintenance the railroads had accumulated to that point, and what should be done about it. Observers widely assumed that the real purpose of the deferred maintenance study was to produce an estimate of how much federal rail subsidy funding should be authorized for the rest of the nation outside the Northeast, perhaps leading to a Conrail West USRA-style planning process. Also, some interests possibly sought to learn what it would cost for the government to take over ownership and repair of rail rights of way. This was a serious possibility in 1976 and 1977, with Midwest railroads collapsing and with Conrail's losses reaching about $1 million daily. While USRA's board had rejected the Consolidated Facilities Corporation proposal, the idea of nationalizing the freight rail industry's infrastructure (at least in the Northeast) had never fully gone away.

FRA's response to the 4R Act's mandate was to publish its report on deferred maintenance as a sweeping *Prospectus for Change in the Freight Rail Industry* (October 1978) under the mantle of the secretary of transportation, by then former congressman Brock Adams (D–WA). In the report, as requested, FRA calculated the industry's capital shortfall for 1976–1985 (some $13 to $16 billion). But FRA went further, cataloguing the causes of the railroad financial and service crisis and providing recommendations dealing with nearly every one of the problem areas it had identified. Over the ensuing months, the FRA and DOT staff reform proposals first outlined in the prospectus evolved into policies even more challenging to the status quo—ultimately amounting to recommendations for essentially wholesale dismantling of the ICC regulatory regime. FRA and DOT wrote those deregulation proposals into legislative language and carried their justification to Congress in official testimony and countless meetings with staff members. After many compromises, the legislation emerged as the Staggers Rail Act of 1980 (see Chapter 9).

Was There to Be a Conrail West?

With respect to the rail financial crisis in the Midwest, the Carter administration FRA believed the bankrupt Rock Island should be dismembered and pieces sold or abandoned. In the process, FRA ran into a storm of opposition from other railroads by supporting Southern Pacific's eastward extension to St. Louis over the Tucumcari route of the Rock Island (see Chapter 10). FRA also strongly supported the Milwaukee Road trustee's plan to exit its operations west of Miles City, Montana, and to reorganize as a smaller "core" railroad. Behind the scenes, FRA worked tirelessly within the guidelines of its authority under Section 401 of the 4R Act to arrange joint-use agreements coupled with line rationalizations. These were aimed at combating the manifest problem of "too much track, too little traffic" (an FRA phrase). While the yield was meager at the time, a pattern was established for successful line rationalizations a decade later.

In passenger rail affairs, FRA managed the $1.5 billion Northeast Corridor Improvement Project (NECIP), which kept Amtrak's Washington–New York corridor service functional for two more decades. FRA represented Secretary Adams on the Amtrak board and actively supported decisions such as acquisition of the Swedish AEM-7 electric locomotives to replace Metroliners on the corridor. In a 1979 report to Congress, however, FRA again made enemies on the Hill by recommending deletion of a substantial number of Amtrak's worst-performing trains, including some congressional favorites.[45]

Concluding Thoughts

USRA bent over backward to enable and facilitate the Three Systems East plan. Although this might not be as good as what resulted eventually with division of the property between NS and CSX, that major restructuring event was a long time coming and very expensive for NS and CSX shareholders. Also, in 1976, there was no guarantee that a Staggers Rail Act or Northeast Rail Service Act (NERSA) would be passed, or that managers as skillful as a Stanley Crane would be hired as Conrail's CEO. Big

Conrail was a big risk on all accounts—managerial diseconomies of scale, reversion to internecine Red Team/Green Team warfare, attraction and retention of skilled employees, insurmountable criticism of its "monopoly pricing," poor customer service, and politicians tiring of its ongoing tax-payer subsidy.

History must be harsh to N&W management. John P. (Jack) Fishwick overly personalized the situation and lacked vision. N&W was willing to let Dereco[46] (for which it had accepted responsibility in order to win approval of the N&W/NKP/Wabash merger) twist in the wind. Subsequent N&W and NS managers have coped with ownership of the New York's southern tier railroads and its connections to Guilford[47] under the less-than-benevolent eye of Empire State politicians, so "firewalling" those properties was not the only answer. NS constituent Southern Railway wanted control of the Delmarva lines (with their service to DuPont's Seaford, Delaware, nylon plant, a coal-fired utility plant, and grain or feed for its numerous poultry growers and processors), but Southern did not want to have to subsidize the Hampton Roads car-float operation. Modern NS took the Delmarva lines and services, sans car-float, and provided access via Wilmington, Delaware (PRR)—all to the good.

History's judgment of Chessie System managers is a bit more mixed. It may be true that organized labor deep-sixed Chessie's part of the Three Systems East plan, which mitigates criticism of management but does not exonerate Chessie. Hays Watkins was no stranger in Washington. If he had gone to Congress, told it Big Conrail would cost big bucks and bring big pain to Northeast rail shippers, he might have received no less than what NERSA gave Conrail for labor relief in 1983; or, considering the level of support that existed for controlled transfer in the Ford administration, he might have gotten even more.

And what was USRA really asking Chessie to do? Enter the northern New Jersey ports and warehousing district and its traffic-rich, presumably profitable "chemical coast" via well-engineered (if undermaintained) lines of the Reading, LV, and CNJ, thus supplementing its own B&O lines to Staten Island from Baltimore and Philadelphia. USRA would have allowed purchase of these lines for a song—everyone was sure of that. DOT then would have gone hand-in-hand with Watkins to Capitol Hill to ask for rehabilitation dollars otherwise destined for Conrail, as well as the NERSA-type provisions for labor. What a deal! But Chessie didn't bite.

Instead, American taxpayers had to absorb Conrail's huge deficits for another six years, the NERSA labor bailout was needed anyway, and the region's shippers were paying perhaps the highest rates charged by railroads anywhere in the United States. Chessie lost new connecting auto and chemical traffic it still has not been able to win away from NS; moreover, it had to make do with only marginal participation in new intermodal (double-stack) traffic to Little Ferry, New Jersey—handled by Suzie-Q (the New York, Susquehanna & Western) instead of better possible routings over Erie Lackawanna, Reading, Lehigh Valley, and Central of New Jersey. Lack of these connections must be one reason CSX sought the former New York Central properties (rather than more dense traffic origins and destinations on former PRR lines) when Conrail was divided between NS and CSX on June 1, 1999.[48]

Reflections a Generation Later

The first few years of the 1970s were spent in posturing and jostling. Big shots in New York City and Philadelphia had to reconcile themselves to the reality that the answer to the "great railway crisis" would be framed in Washington. Then Congress in the 3R Act, DOT in shaping initial responses to the crisis, and USRA had to complete difficult and unprecedented planning assignments. They were joined in the enterprise by a few labor leaders who recognized the need for employment cuts, the workers who (even if compensated) had to leave their jobs, and even shippers and elected officials in the Northeast (by keeping the pressure on for needed service continuation): All did their part to craft what must be called a workable, more than optimal solution. The rest of the Washington apparatus, and the rest of the railroad industry, mainly watched and waited.

As we will see in the next two chapters, it was not enough. Conrail staffed up in Philadelphia, with Ed Jordan as CEO, a competent staff and officer corps, and a distinguished board of directors, but the task was greater than anyone anticipated. Weather turned foul, and there were too many mouths to feed. Conrail's losses were about $1 million daily for the rest of the decade. Worse, the ICC could never learn its lessons and botched the 4R Act regulatory reforms. By 1978, DOT and FRA were back in print with a new analysis of railroads, estimating a total Class I railroad industry capital shortfall of $13 to $16 billion over the coming five years, if trends continued. These events and studies, all described in the DOT/

FRA *Prospectus for Change*,[49] made clear that Congress would have to legislate one more time, and the choice, yet again, would come down to (1) nationalization and subsidy or (2) more complete deregulation—meaning more relief from redundant lines, costly public services, and labor surpluses.

So do the 3R and 4R acts and their consequences add up to success or failure? Perhaps we should hold off on a final answer until after we have told the story of Conrail's initial years in the next chapter, and the making of the Staggers Rail Act of 1980 in the subsequent chapter. But enough of the cat is already out of the bag to leave as interim conclusions these three points:

1. The 3R Act, for all its awkward structure and failure to resolve conflicting goals, was an adequate vehicle for doing what most needed to be done—picking up the pieces from the collapse of Penn Central and other Northeast and Midwest bankrupt railroads. A good planning process was put in place for analysis of both strategic mainline options and tactical rationalization of light-density lines. The Northeast corridor was preserved intact and transferred to Amtrak. The claims of the bankrupt estates against the government for unconstitutional taking of their property were met with skilled legal and professional analyses and were ultimately settled fairly.

2. The 4R Act easily accomplished its first task: to confirm the FSP as devised by USRA. Conrail's legitimacy and scope at birth were never in question. The solvent railroads in the region were given every opportunity to buy into the solution (quite literally). No private solvent railroads were forced into the reorganization, although some properties, their shareholders, and their customers might have been better off if they had. Also, the 4R Act made a first effort at regulatory reform, but (as we shall see in Chapter 9) the statute was too vague in construction, too feeble in spirit, too easily thwarted by committed regulators of the old school. More purposeful and direct deregulatory legislation might have prevented the ICC from undermining the 4R Act right from the outset.

3. In neither the 3R Act nor the 4R Act did Congress do much of anything to level the playing field for surface transportation modes. The commerce committees of both the House and the Senate knew that their legislative proposals were hemmed in jurisdictionally. The

public works committees were left to take care of highways and waterways, and so they did. Ways and Means (in the House) or Finance (in the Senate) ruled on tax issues, and if there were any thoughts of subsidies, the two appropriations committees held the purse strings tightly.

Ever-Elusive Transportation Policy

It is no surprise at all that the United States does not have a crisp, reasoned, or more "balanced" surface transportation policy. We can't be naïve and say, yes we do: It is the protections of "inherent modal advantages" in the 1940 Transportation Act. We can't be blasé and say, we don't really need one. Nor we can be cynical and say, we can't ever have one anyway. The plain truth is that the United States does not now and is unlikely soon to have a meaningful surface transportation policy guiding efficient allocation of public and private resources, and yielding effective economic performance. While it may be true that we have "the best transportation system in the world" (at least for freight), it is more by good fortune than by good public policy or design.

The 1970s saw two OPEC energy crises, stubborn "stagflation," supply-side macroeconomic bewilderment, a clumsy transition after the Vietnam War, and the Iranian hostage crisis. It was, of course, also the time of the Watergate scandal, which taught us a thing or two about Washington, DC. Given the "good government" reforms of the post-Watergate years, it might not be unreasonable to criticize the railroad legislative enactments of the period for being, well, just too darned timid. The 3R Act gave back to the ICC some of the agency's old role, when the commission should have been sent packing, as it was later on, in 1995. That act wisely set up the USRA as an expert body to plan Conrail, but later Congress left the USRA in business as a gadfly for almost ten years after its legitimate assignments were finished. Congress unwisely allowed the other cabinet departments (Agriculture, Energy, Labor) plus the Corps of Engineers and (for a time) the Maritime Administration to cross deeply into transportation policy on behalf of their own constituencies, rather than taking a backseat to DOT in matters of transport policy. Meanwhile, the outgunned and underappreciated DOT was left to deal with multiple unresolved internal policy inconsistencies.

The stakes were high in the 1970s. There were many powerful interests who overreached and had to settle for less than they expected. Rapid adjustments were forced on thousands of railroad employees, communities large and small, and shippers of a long list of goods that were discommoded by the changes that the USRA planned and Congress allowed to go into effect. Overall, the outcomes could have been much worse. The alternatives—massive subsidy, wholesale line consolidation and abandonment, nationalization—would all have been disastrous. It seems crude and backhanded to put it this way, but it is the truth: The nation and common sense dodged a bullet in the 1970s.

8

THE BRIEF, MAINLY HAPPY LIFE
OF CONRAIL, 1976–1999

The expectations that lay behind the 3R Act have not been realized. . . . The problems of high costs and low productivity that afflicted its bankrupt predecessors still trouble Conrail. . . . Thus, the prospects for Conrail are clouded, and there is no basis for concluding that the expectations of the 3R Act will be realized any more in this decade than they were in the last.

—US Railway Association, December 1980

The opportunities available today are too great to overlook. They beckon our pursuit no less than the option of continuing subsidy repels it. We need not accept limp-along nationalization when a private sector solution is possible. Now is the time to take an entirely new direction—a clear path, true to our fundamental principles, leading directly to our goals.

—Secretary of Transportation DREW LEWIS, March 31, 1981

The rail problem of the Northeast and Midwest has been and remains complex. It is a problem pervasively and inexorably linked to the decline of manufacturing in the region—and at times it must appear hopeless. It is not. Conrail can become self-sustaining—if those with an interest in the continuation of Conrail's service are willing to make the types of contributions I have outlined—all the contributions, not just a portion.

—Conrail CEO L. STANLEY CRANE, April 1, 1981

Where you stand often depends on where you sit. In response to a Staggers Rail Act reporting requirement, the Reagan administration's new transportation secretary, Drew Lewis, and recently hired Conrail CEO, L. Stanley Crane, both gave their outlook for Conrail on its fifth birthday, April 1, 1981. The two powerful, well-placed, and well-informed men could hardly have had more dissimilar views. Stanley Crane wanted to apply more federal funding to complete Conrail's needed infrastructure rehabilitation, skate through the so-called Reagan recession, and give the Staggers Rail Act regulatory reforms time to catch on. Drew Lewis and his newly appointed federal railroad administrator, Robert Blanchette (a veteran attorney for the Penn Central trustees), wanted to dismantle Conrail and sell its strongest lines to whatever private-sector bidders might be interested. This strategy gambit, rechristened controlled transfer after DOT politicians realized its birth name (controlled liquidation) was too honest by half, made a matched bookend with Lewis's other key transport policy action—firing all the unionized federal air traffic controllers who had walked off their assignments August 1, 1981.

Not that Lewis and Blanchette were entirely wrong; Conrail needed to be pushed off the federal dole and into the awaiting world of deregulated private-sector railroading. Lewis and Blanchette even did Crane a favor by scaring the pussyfooting informal coalition of Northeastern politicians, rail labor, shipper representatives, and solvent railroad executives into a realization that wholesale change was both needed and probably inevitable. Surprisingly, of the trio of keynote quotations opening this chapter of *American Railroads,* the one that got the unfolding events of Conrail's first ten years wrong was the heretofore reliable United States Railway Association (USRA). Perhaps this was because USRA had no role in bringing about deregulation (outside Congress, that being mostly within DOT's sphere of influence). In any event, after April 1976, clearly the locus of railroad activity shifted from Buzzard's Point (USRA's aerie) back to "Massive Nassif" (DOT headquarters at 6th and D Streets, SW) both in Washington, and to 6 Penn Center (Conrail's office building) in center-city Philadelphia.

This chapter is a documentary telling of the birth, maturation, and passing of the Consolidated Rail Corporation (CRC, or most commonly Conrail). Not counting the three properties called Conrail Shared Assets, which survive to this day as important neutral switching service railroads outside metropolitan New York/Newark, Philadelphia, and Detroit, the Consolidated Rail Corporation no longer exists. The original railroad called Conrail lasted only twenty-five years, but its brief span does not diminish our theme in this book. It is true that Conrail was an instrumentality of the federal government—one created as the last refuge of Northeast freight railroads—and that it was afflicted, Job-like, by every manner of adversity in the 1970s and early 1980s. But Conrail did not collapse, it was transformed.

Conrail's remarkable turnaround—its clear commercial success wrought from the wreckage of Penn Central and other exhausted, broken railroads—is one of the most heartening stories in recent business literature. In the short period from its birth in 1976 to its $1.8 billion initial public offering (IPO) in 1987 and on to its successful division between two premier railroads in 1999, it added another $8 billion or more of value, easily quintupling its IPO market capitalization. A few high-tech firms may have done as well in a comparable timeframe, but this was a railroad, and railroads had not been darlings of Wall Street since before the Rough Rider was president.

As told in Chapter 7, Conrail's predecessors were devastated by the fundamental macroeconomic forces that eroded business for traditional bulk cargoes and heavy manufacturers in the Northeast and the midwestern Rust Belt. Both Penn Central and Conrail were further victimized by political institutions that impeded adaptation to the new economic realities of inflation, poorly located infrastructure, obsolete labor contracts, and globalization of markets. Conrail's management was forced to spend scarce resources and political capital to escape the publicly imposed burden of service to business segments it wanted to exit—most notably operation of local commuter passenger service. But in a different metaphor for railroads in twentieth-century America, Conrail rose like a phoenix from these ashes—not an enterprise that endured independently, but one that was reborn. See Map 8.1, shown split into two parts roughly at Pittsburgh.

The Enduring Issue for Conrail: Structure and Restructure

The Consolidated Rail Corporation began operations in America's bicentennial year. Its properties were conveyed from the trustees of the Penn Central and several other Northeast railroads on April 1 of that year. Conveyances of rail lines and facilities were made in accordance with designations published in the Final System Plan (FSP), which had been developed by the USRA under provisions of the Regional Railroad Reorganization (3R) Act of 1973—as ratified by Congress in the Railroad Reorganization and Regulatory Reform (4R) Act of 1976. On conveyance day, Conrail instantly became the largest US railroad as measured by employment and revenue, and the second largest measured by track mileage.

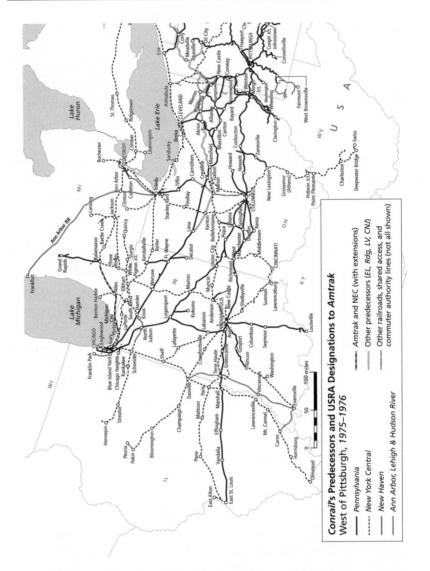

Map 8.1   Conrail Predecessors and USRA Designations to Amtrak (1975–1976)   Five years after the inauguration of Amtrak, the bankrupt estates of Penn Central and a half dozen other Northeast railroads were reorganized into the federally sponsored Consolidated Rail Corporation (Conrail). The two part map shows principal lines of Penn Central constituent railroads (Pennsylvania Railroad, New York Central, and New Haven)—as well as other key predecessor railroads (grouped here into Erie Lackawanna, Reading, Lehigh Valley, and Central of New Jersey, plus separately indicated Ann Arbor and Lehigh & Hudson River)—all brought into Conrail by the US Railway Association's Final System Plan and its affirmation in the 4R Act. USRA designated important passenger routes to Amtrak rather than Conrail, preserving trackage rights for freight and commuter service. *Source:* Original map published in Kalmbach Pub. Co.'s *Trains Magazine* January 2002, pp. 65–67, with author's modifications.

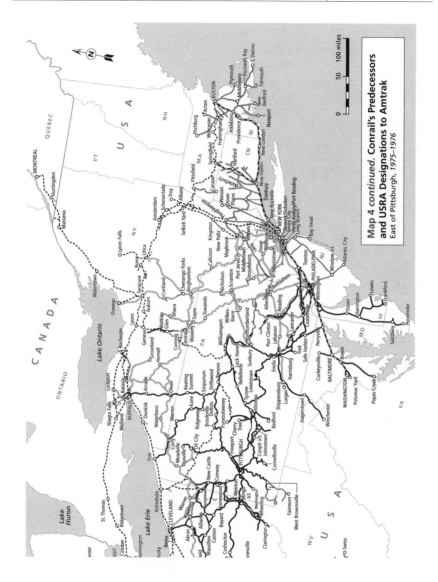

Map 4 continued. Conrail's Predecessors and USRA Designations to Amtrak
East of Pittsburgh, 1975–1976

In that bicentennial year, the US railroad industry as a whole was in pitiful shape. Conrail lost more money than was earned by the rest of the industry combined. Despite years of debate and legislation, there was as yet no real evidence of accomplishments in reform of regulation by the Interstate Commerce Commission (ICC)—the timid reforms of the 4R Act were no match for the resistance of ICC commissioners, staff, and practitioners. Most of them were dedicated to defense of traditional

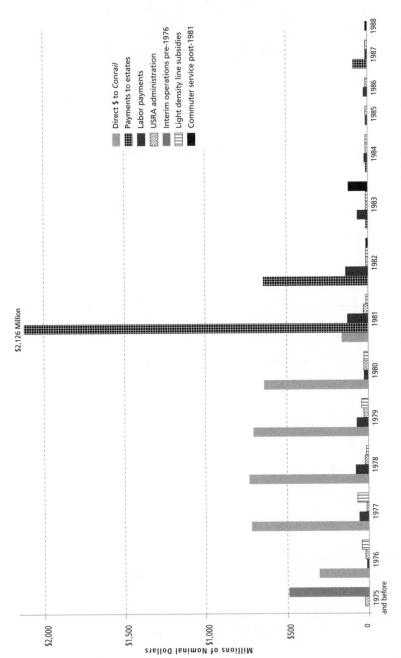

Figure 8.1 Federal Expenditures to Fix the Northeast Railroads The US government spent nearly $8 billion over a fifteen-year period to reorganize the Northeast bankrupt railroads and launch Conrail. Among the largest types of outlays were direct coverage of Conrail deficits (almost half of the total) and payments to the bankrupt estates for the "taking" of their properties to form Conrail and to acquire the Northeast Corridor for Amtrak (over $2.5 billion). *Source:* Data from Beshers, *Conrail*, 1989. Used with permission.

regulation. Amtrak was in business and providing service to over 18 million passengers annually, including over a significant portion of Conrail's freight network. In 1976, however, Amtrak's operating expenses were about $650 million, while its operating revenues were only $287 million—and the long-term outlook was that Amtrak could not be sustained without large annual subsidies from Congress. The US economy was still reeling from the spike in fuel prices caused by the first OPEC oil embargo. Already USRA's FSP financial forecast for Conrail was falling apart.[1]

Active USRA Oversight of Conrail

Few if any American for-profit enterprises have received the outside financial scrutiny and policy oversight that Conrail had to endure in its brief history. As we detailed in Chapter 8, USRA did a yeoman job drafting the preliminary and final system plans and preparing for Conrail's debut in 1976, but USRA was supposed to be a temporary agency. It is correct, as we have said (and as USRA's *Final Report* declares repeatedly), that USRA's independent status was useful during the planning process. But as the years went on, this independence was of constantly diminishing utility. Between 1976 and 1983, a lot of public money was still going into Conrail, to be sure, and the government still owned 85 percent of its equity, but the bureaucratic oversight was excessive even by Washington standards. Eric Beshers, in his useful monograph for the World Bank, points out that, of the $188 million in federal funds that USRA spent over its lifetime (1974–1986), only $26.5 million was spent during the initial planning process (up to the conveyance date); "the rest was spent in watching Conrail in operation."[2] (See Figure 8.3.) This is a little unfair because USRA did a good bit of the staff work in defending the government's case against claimants, arguing there had been an unconstitutional taking of private property.

In Chapter 7, we told the story of how USRA's staff and board struggled to come up with a recommended railroad industry structure within the Northeast ownership and operating climate of the 1970s. USRA sought a structure meeting several objectives: (1) the legal requirements of the 3R Act within the inherited body of transportation legislation and precedent; (2) the operating, service, and financial mandates imposed on USRA through the 3R Act mandate; and (3) the political predilections of its board members—as well as the Republican administrations in the White House and the democratically controlled House and Senate. Basically, the trick was to design a structure for the post–Penn Central Northeast that was workably competitive *and* self-sustaining (i.e., enduring without ongoing public subsidy). Many observers at the time thought this was impossible— at least under then-current macroeconomic and regulatory conditions. They thought the country could have (1) a publicly guaranteed and funded (nationalized) service provider, (2) an underfunded and regulated quasi-monopoly, or (3) a liquidated private-sector skeleton of all-but-abandoned rail lines operated independently of each other, but could not simultaneously have more than one of the three outcomes. The "Conrail miracle" was that the skeptical observers were proven wrong. After nearly $8 billion of public investment, the IPO of newly "privatized" Conrail securities returned (after bankers' fees) approximately $1.8 billion[3] to the US Treasury in 1987, and within a decade, the market capitalization of independent Conrail was roughly $10 billion.

Conrail Leadership

One of the essential themes we will follow through the birth of Conrail, its coming to profitability in midlife, and its spectacular endgame with division between Norfolk Southern and CSX in 1999 is the powerful contributions of Conrail's CEOs and their leadership teams. To Edward Jordan we credit the vision of how Conrail could not afford to cross-subsidize other interests and, particularly, his role in championing economic deregulation. Ed Jordan was perhaps the most effective lobbyist there was for getting the Staggers Rail Act passed, but his contribution went far beyond activities in Washington. Jordan showed his new peers in the railroad industry what could be done—indeed what had to be done— to make deregulation the foundation for revival of the industry.

Even before final passage, Jordan got things going within Conrail to ensure that his managers understood a new era was dawning with deregulation, and there would be no turning back. One of the underappreciated things Jordan did to jumpstart implementation of deregulation was to reorganize the marketing department around car types in order to get marketing and operations managers focused on customer service and asset management. Jordan and the commercial team he assembled (James Hagen, Richard Steiner, Charles Marshall, and others) made pathbreaking forward steps in implementing provisions of the Staggers Rail Act to the benefit of Conrail financial performance. Jordan had always stressed the use of hard data—making sure you had the numbers and that they were correct, for example, in preparing return on investment (ROI) justifications for capital expenditures; now marketing was to do the same for pricing and car supply decisions.

Jordan also saw the importance of leveraging the Staggers Rail Act provision that required Conrail and other parties to report by April 1, 1980, on needs for further legislation; Jordan decided his report should be a blueprint for what became the Northeast Rail Services Act in 1983 (see below), and so it was. Jordan left the chairmanship of Conrail before the report was filed, and it went out under Stanley Crane's signature, but Jordan had set the tone. L. Stanley Crane, in his autobiographical brief history of Conrail, graciously thanked Ed Jordan, "who brought order out of chaos, who provided the leadership in the massive rebuilding for Conrail, and who, more than anyone else, reversed the course of history and set the wheels of deregulation into motion."[4]

On New Year's Day of 1981, L. Stanley Crane acceded to the post of chief executive officer of the Consolidated Rail Corporation. Undeniably, Stanley Crane was the right person at the right time to administer the bitter medicine of change. Crane was a chemical engineer who had been president of Southern Railway since 1976, having matured through the ranks of legendary Southern's bullying but effective leader, D. W. Brosnan. Crane was experienced, friendly, wise, insightful, and greatly respected. In the postwar period, Southern Railway was like the Founding Fathers during the days of Independence, a collection of smart railroaders as remarkable as any ever gathered in one company: Brosnan, Graham, Claytor, Harold Hall, Robert Hamilton, Paul Banner, Stanley Crane; joined by Arnold MacKinnon, Jim Hagen, Jim McClellan, Governor Ned Bretheatt, and others.

The Importance of Enacting the Northeast Rail Services Act

The Staggers Rail Act of 1980 gave Conrail and other railroads new flexibility in rate setting and relief from certain other encumbrances unique to railroads, such as discriminatory state property taxation and interminable ICC decision procedures. However, before the Staggers Rail Act reforms had been fully engaged by railroads, including Conrail—which was an early adopter—Congress decided in the Northeast Rail Services Act (NERSA) of 1983 that additional assistance specifically targeted to Conrail's unique position would be needed.

The provision of the Staggers Rail Act that helped Jordan and Crane build the case for what became NERSA was a requirement in Section 703(C) mandating that Conrail develop plans and recommendations for three circumstances:

> Case A: No further federal funding beyond the $329 million authorized in Staggers, save as the result of new legislative proposals.
>
> Case B: Continued federal funding of Conrail "as presently structured" under current law.
>
> Case C: Future federal funding as needed "to preserve rail service in the region which can become self-sustaining." Conrail also proposed that Case C would incorporate Conrail's five-year business plan required under its funding agreement with USRA.

Conrail issued its required 703(C) report on the scheduled date, April 1, 1981, only three months after Stanley Crane had succeeded Ed Jordan as CEO. Titled *Options for Conrail,* the 703 report became Crane's keynote. The core of the report was its "Projected 1982–1986 Financial Results." It identified two types of changes that would be needed for Conrail to achieve the projected performance:

- Internal (changes Conrail could implement with its own resources)
- External (changes requiring the cooperation and/or the assistance of governmental agencies or labor organizations)

The internal changes Conrail described were strongly leveraged by its recently updated (substantially lower) traffic forecast. Conrail now had to assume more aggressive line rationalization, and a consequently lower requirement for rehabilitation funding. Conrail maintained, however, that while the 3R and 4R acts provided resources for "consolidating and rehabilitating a fragmented rail system—that emergency legislation did not lay an adequate basis for Conrail to become financially self-sustaining." These were fighting words—the Reagan administration transportation officials could not have been happy—but there was much truth to Conrail's position. The 3R and 4R acts did not reverse economic conditions in the Northeast, nor remove the burden of passenger service on Conrail, nor alter high-cost labor agreements.

Conrail acknowledged passage of the Staggers Rail Act, but it had not yet had time to chip away at long-standing discriminatory divisions and inefficient gateways harming Conrail.[5] Crane's Section 703(C) report paralleled in theme and timeline the blueprint Congress used in crafting NERSA. The new law's declared purpose was "the removal by a date certain of the Federal Government's obligation to subsidize Conrail," and in that quest it gave Conrail:

- Authority to transfer commuter operations spelled out in the FSP and 4R Act to state or regional operating agencies on December 31, 1982. At the time NERSA was enacted, Conrail was operating about 1,800 daily weekday trains and carrying some 115 million annual commuter trips.
- A special procedure to use in accelerating abandonment of uneconomic lines. Under this authority, Conrail had "the absolute right to abandon uneconomic track if no responsible buyer offered to keep the line in rail service." Conrail subsequently used this process to streamline its system by some 3,900 miles from the almost 20,000 route miles it received on conveyance day until the date of its IPO.[6] (See Figure 8.2.)
- A government-funded severance program enabling Conrail to trim its permanent workforce by about 3,700 employees. Overall, Conrail was able to reduce its payroll by some 25,000 employees between enactment of NERSA and the IPO (Figure 8.2). NERSA wage concessions ran only through June 30, 1984, but added to about $350 million in that period. Conrail also received government funding of supplemental unemployment benefits amounting to another $140 million between 1982 and 1986.[7]
- State tax exemptions amounting to over $160 million in the 1980s, before these were eliminated by the Conrail Privatization Act.[8]

Stanley Crane moved swiftly to take advantage of the NERSA benefits, and Conrail's unions saw the writing on the wall—they were now willing to discuss wage concessions. In May 1981, fifteen of sixteen unions signed a deal calling for deferral of about 12 percent of any increases until July 1, 1984. Crane cut employment by 42 percent over two years and began trimming unprofitable freight and commuter services. Conrail became the earliest and most innovative adopter of the new Staggers Rail Act rate and division reforms.

Less remarkable at the time, but of unparalleled importance within two years, were the criteria NERSA established for subsequent determinations

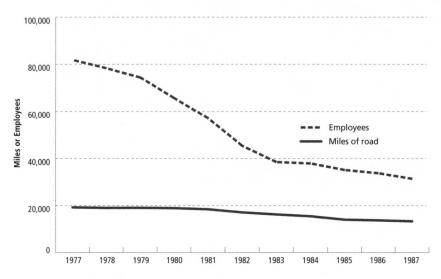

Figure 8.2 Conrail's Deep Cuts in Employees and Route Mileage Conrail cut employee headcount 60 percent and trimmed route mileage more than 30 percent, from startup (1976) to the initial public offering (1987). *Source:* Data from Beshers, *Conrail*, 1989. Used with permission.

of Conrail's ownership and organizational structure. These were to apply without regard to the success of NERSA's other provisions. In addition to providing additional financial assistance and relaxing numerous barriers to Conrail's financial and operating success, NERSA set in motion procedures for privatization of the 85 percent ownership of Conrail common stock held by the federal government.

The law also set up two periods over which Conrail's financial performance would be monitored by USRA. By June 1, 1983, USRA's board was to determine whether Conrail would become a profitable and self-sustaining carrier without further subsidy. Specifically, Conrail had to be found capable of generating revenues sufficient to meet operating and maintenance expenses and of borrowing sufficient capital in private markets to sustain needed capital investments.[9] If the first test were positive, USRA was then to evaluate whether Conrail had actually achieved profitability between June 1 and October 31, 1983. If USRA said yes again, the secretary of DOT was required to attempt to sell the railroad "as an entity," securing a competitive price for it. If Conrail failed either test, the secretary was to proceed to piecemeal sale or liquidation of Conrail assets.[10]

The tests were created as a "double win or double jeopardy" contest. If Conrail was found by USRA to pass the test on April 1, 1983, for example, DOT would be stopped from any effort to sell Conrail through piecemeal efforts like "controlled transfer." If there were to be any sale of Conrail, it would have to be as a "complete entity." If, on the other hand, Conrail failed the profitability test, DOT was authorized and mandated to turn immediately to liquidation. The politics of the matter could not be clearer: Conrail's employees, their unions, top management, Northeastern politicians, and many shippers thought dismemberment would be a calamity. But nobody knew of any buyers who were ready and able to acquire Conrail in its entirety.

Among the effective marketing actions Conrail took in the first years of deregulation was to close its least favorable interchange gateways. For example, seeking its own long haul with traffic to Norfolk Southern and CSX, Conrail successfully moved most interchange away from the Potomac (Pot) yard in Alexandria, Virginia, over to Cincinnati. Similarly, Conrail worked with Union Pacific (UP) to create an interchange route over St. Elmo, Illinois; in this case, traffic to New Jersey's "Chemical Coast," for example, that used to move over New Orleans to NS or CSX and back to Conrail at Pot yard, kept a longer haul on UP's newly acquired Missouri Pacific before interchange to Conrail in Illinois. Both Conrail and UP benefited at the expense of NS and CSX.

The Staggers and NERSA reforms, under Crane's brilliant management, paid off handsomely. Conrail announced its first quarterly profit of $39 million in January 1982. Net earnings were $172 million for all of 1982, and $313 million for 1983. Then on April 1, 1983, USRA informed DOT and Congress that Conrail had passed the first profitability test (see Figure 8.3). In December 1983, USRA officially announced compliance with the second test—Conrail was profitable and would be in the future. The USRA profitability finding meant an end to DOT piecemeal liquidation policies. USRA wrote, with an unmistakable note of triumph:

> Remarkable progress has been made since the passage of NERSA. The effect under NERSA of USRA's decision is to require that the Secretary of Transportation continue to sell Conrail as an entity. The finding does not address questions of whether Conrail can be sold, the timing of the sale, or what

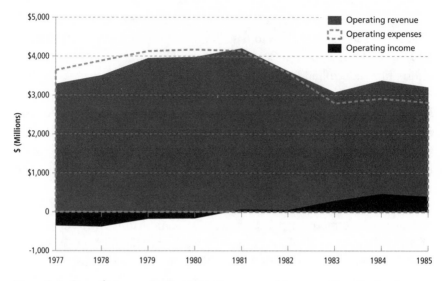

Figure 8.3   Conrail's Improving Revenue, Expense, and Income   Conrail enjoyed
increasing annual revenues over the period 1977 to 1981. While revenue fell off in subsequent
years, expenses fell further, resulting in positive operating income on a smaller revenue base.
Source: Data from Beshers, *Conrail,* 1989. Used with permission.

would constitute reasonable terms. These questions are best
answered in the marketplace through negotiations between the
Secretary's representatives and potential buyers.[11]

DOT's Effort to Sell Conrail As an Entity

At this point in the history, DOT, forestalled from pursing its longstanding
policy of dismemberment, still had several ways it could go—merger with
a solvent railroad, a leveraged buyout by an investor group (perhaps one
representing employee or management owners), or a public offering of the
government-owned equity in Conrail. But the path of least resistance and
financial risk must have seemed to new secretary of Transportation
Elizabeth Dole to be that of engineering a merger with a major Class I
railroad.

When Secretary Dole succeeded Drew Lewis, she brought in fellow
North Carolinian James Burnley as her deputy.[12] Burnley sized up the
Conrail situation and came to the belief that it would be best for the railroad to have a home in a corporation with "deep pockets." This could be
accomplished by a private sale of Conrail "as an entity" to the winner of a
publicly advertised auction. Burnley argued that his approach would put

experienced railroaders in charge and, indeed, the spectacular success of Stanley Crane's management after he came to Conrail from the Southern Railway had shown the importance of such experience. Burnley prevailed, and to implement the process, DOT put out a request for proposals with a deadline for offers of June 18, 1984.

When Conrail's leaders became aware of these proposals and Secretary Dole's handling of them, they were appalled by both her policy illogic and its counterproductive implications for railroad operations. Conrail managers, proud of their accomplishment in returning the company to profitability, thought DOT had been inattentive to prevailing circumstances and unnecessarily vindictive to them as individuals. Now management was moved to present its own alternative.

An opportunity presented itself in Harrisburg in October 1984, where Pennsylvania's senator Arlen Specter had called a special hearing. R. H. (Robert) Platt, Conrail's executive vice president of finance and administration, was the spokesperson. Crediting the reforms of the Staggers Rail Act and NERSA assistance as well as the dedication and professionalism of Conrail's employees, Platt's testimony reviewed Conrail's remarkable turnaround from a $400 million loss in 1978 to net income of $500 million in 1984. These results, Platt said, "demonstrate Conrail's ability to 'go it alone' in a marketplace which has determined that there is a need for Conrail and its service."[13]

The stage was set for Platt's "October Surprise." Conrail management declared it favored a different option, one DOT had not put on the table, that would give "the greatest assurance that Conrail will have a long-term future." That option, Platt testified, would be a financing package that includes a public offering of Conrail stock. "[S]ince $7 billion of taxpayer money was the basis for the resurrection of Conrail, it is appropriate to provide taxpayers an opportunity to invest in Conrail's future." Subsequent events filled Platt's prescription, in a way. Platt meant the comment in the conventional way of government investing in transport infrastructure for the benefit of the public, but individuals who owned Conrail shares were richly rewarded when Conrail was split in 1999.

Conrail knew Senator Specter would be receptive; in fact, he had earlier communicated the idea to Secretary Dole, saying, "A public offering would have the significant advantage of returning Conrail to private [sector] ownership while maintaining Conrail's management which has been so successful . . ." Platt's plan was for a broad ownership distribution, with no investor holding more than 5 to 10 percent of the shares. Conrail's leaders were giving a new twist to their earlier slogan, "Let Conrail Be Conrail." "Conrail management wants to be responsible for running the company under normal disciplines applicable to major companies responsible to a Corporate Board of Directors and owned by a broadly based American public."[14]

Where had the idea of an IPO of Conrail shares come from? While far from unknown, IPOs were smaller and much less common in the mid-1980s than they became later on; it is noteworthy that when Conrail went public in the spring of 1987, it was the largest IPO in US history. It turns out that before he left the top post at DOT, former Secretary Drew Lewis (a Pennsylvanian, to be sure) had brought in the investment banking house of Goldman Sachs (GS) to advise on sale options for Conrail, and GS had toyed with the idea of a public offering. Rush Loving, Jr., in his entertaining book, *The Men Who Loved Trains*, tells how Stanley Crane, shortly after the USRA determination under NERSA that Conrail must be sold as an intact entity, became concerned that Secretary Dole would choose a sale option that would injure Conrail employees, management, and shippers. Seizing on the idea of a public offering suggested to Drew Lewis earlier by Goldman Sachs, Crane gave an interview to Agis Salpukas of the *New York Times* in which he "first floated" the idea of an IPO.[15] Loving reports that Secretary Dole called Crane and "bawled him out, saying he had no right to make such statements without her permission."[16]

Neither Stanley Crane nor Robert Platt were worried about their next paychecks, so while Secretary Dole seemed to believe the government's 85 percent ownership compelled the loyalty of Conrail's leaders, Crane and Platt went on with their own plan. Ignoring DOT staff advice, Conrail hired Morgan Stanley & Co. to prepare a proposal incorporating a public offering of common stock, which Conrail released on January 4, 1985. Only a month later, however, Secretary Dole announced the selection of Norfolk Southern as DOT's "preferred buyer," for a consideration valued at $1.2 billion. In short order, that recommendation was made to Congress.

Eight or so years of marginal performance before the Staggers Rail Act reforms kicked in (and the constant threat that financially fragile Conrail could come apart at the seams) had pushed to the back burner another old issue: the lingering unease in some quarters that "Big Conrail" might have too much market power. Call it policy schizophrenia, but the simple truth is that different business and political interests worried about different things. With DOT's choice of Norfolk Southern, old populist opponents of big railroads regained their voice. The Department of Justice and the Interstate Commerce Commission both conducted staff studies, finding that there were indeed adverse competitive impacts implicit in a sale to NS.

The DOT recommendation for sale of Conrail to Norfolk Southern was hotly debated in Congress. The Senate passed an enabling bill on February 4, 1986, but in the House of Representatives, Energy and Commerce Committee chairman Dingle (D–MI) strongly opposed the proposal. The Congressional Budget Office (CBO) was asked to evaluate the contrasting proposals for sale of Conrail to the Norfolk Southern or a public sale of stock. In its August, 1986, report, CBO concluded that Conrail "appears to be a viable independent enterprise over the next decade under a broad range of conditions in both the economy in general and the railroad industry in particular."[17] Secretary Dole persuaded NS to raise its bid to $1.9 billion, but Representative Dingell declared he was opposed to the proposal "at any cost; [it is] unacceptable and my position is final."[18]

If No Sale to NS, What Could DOT Do
with the Government's Conrail Shares?

The IPO prospectus drawn up by Goldman Sachs and its cosponsors (First Boston, Merrill Lynch, Morgan Stanley, Salomon Brothers, and Shearson Lehman Brothers) and dated February 13, 1987, was a superb document. The task of the prospectus was to cast the brief but unique and complex history of Conrail in terms that were accurate and understandable to private investors. Some of Conrail's securities were unlike those commonly issued by private companies. A significant portion of the common stock shares (about 15 percent) were held by employees in an employee stock ownership plan (ESOP) that was a pet project of Senate Finance Committee chairman Russell Long. The railroad's financial future was not entirely clear. No one could say for sure how Conrail would make its way without direct government financial backing.

Conrail also had numerous legal complications, not least of which was fallout from the collision on January 4, 1987, of Amtrak's Colonial with a

Conrail way freight at Chase, Maryland, killing sixteen and injuring over 170 other persons. Ordinarily, in a collision between Amtrak and freight railroads, each absorbs its own expenses without determination of fault, but in this case Amtrak argued "reckless negligence" and, through the courts and Congress, sought to recover all costs from Conrail. Even those NERSA exemptions from state property taxation were challenged in the courts; had NERSA's constitutionality not been upheld, Conrail might have owed over $160 million in back taxes. The IPO prospectus was called on to explain each of these possible complications correctly and carefully.

Of course, there was no public market for Conrail ownership shares prior to the IPO, so valuing the 6,750,000 common stock shares offered to the public involved some guesswork. A price set too high would hurt sales and not clear the market; too low a price would give a poor return to taxpayers and a windfall to speculators if the market settled higher. Goldman and the other bankers thought the offering would be priced at between $22 and $26 per share. Your two authors, both closely engaged in the issue at the time but from very different vantage points, each thought pricing at around that level was fair and would be successful. Conrail's initial public shares went on the New York Stock Exchange March 26, 1987, at $28 per share and closed the day at $30.75. The surprise was not the initial price and return of the public offering, but how the shares performed in subsequent months and years. Those who had purchased shares near the opening price and held them for ten years would have tripled their (nominal dollar) investment.[19]

Reflections on Conrail's Privatization

At a 2007 reunion celebration of the fortieth anniversary of the establishment of the Department of Transportation, former secretary William Coleman mused that the key objective he had failed to achieve in his tenure—one later realized by Secretary Elizabeth Dole, he said—was privatization of Conrail. Coleman described how he had strongly opposed the move of USRA president Edward Jordan to the helm of Conrail in Philadelphia, dismissing Jordan's appointment as a sort of feathering of his own nest, and (incorrectly, we argue) giving Dole the credit for persevering in selling the government's ownership stake against institutionalized opposition in Congress and in Philadelphia.[20]

In retrospect, nothing could seem more logical than an IPO for the Conrail shares owned by the government. The IPO removed the government from direct ownership and participation in Conrail's governance—extracting the government from its obvious conflict of interest between the fiduciary relationship with Conrail and its broader policy responsibilities for the public interest in transportation. Secretary Dole's sale plan would have destabilized competitive relationships within the rail industry; it would have been both privatization and a major railroad merger. The IPO, on the other hand, would not favor one railroad buyer over others. The IPO was a fair and efficient way to cash out the government stake—returning over $1 billion in taxpayer funding to the Treasury. It was a way to "Let Conrail Be Conrail," to behave in the transport marketplace like other businesses; Stanley Crain could retire, and his management could carry on in the private sector without undue Washington oversight.

So why was there such reluctance by the Reagan administration to take the most direct path to privatization? Why did Secretary Dole want to sail the tricky waters of a giant "controlled transfer" to engineer a merger of Conrail into Norfolk Southern when the simple strategy of an IPO was almost certainly available? There are several possible explanations. First, throughout its first decade, Conrail's financial independence was never assured, and a public sale option was not seriously entertained until well after Conrail had established itself as a self-sustaining entity. Even in its statutorily mandated determination under NERSA on June 1, 1983, USRA could only bring itself with great difficulty to the finding that "Conrail will be a profitable carrier."

Second, recall that throughout consideration of the FSP and subsequent oversight of Conrail by the USRA, the Republican (Ford and Reagan) administrations had promoted the policy of "controlled transfer" for resolution of the remaining burden on taxpayers stemming from the Northeast railroad crisis. A key document marking this policy was the report from secretary of transportation Drew Lewis and his new federal railroad administrator, Robert Blanchette, *Recommendations for Northeast Rail Service* (March 31, 1981). It took the view that "most of Conrail's existing traffic could be handled by other railroads."[21]

Third, it is hard to escape the conclusion that Secretary Dole's greatest wish, and the threat that pushed her to the NS acquisition strategy, was that anything less, should it fail financially, would send supplicants back to the federal government for a new round of bailouts. While such a fear might have been reasonable in the case of an undercapitalized leveraged buyout (especially one sponsored by employees), in the case of a public offering of securities, the risk would be exceptionally remote. Indeed, claims subsequent to a public offering would be no more likely than those attending a merger with another large railroad.

We are left, perhaps, with a single last explanation for Secretary Dole's position—the old bureaucratic problem of NIH: "not invented here." It is entirely possible that, focused on its NS sale option, DOT strategists (being more at home with Washington legislative strategies than Wall Street investment banking alternatives), simply may not have given sufficient credence to an IPO.

Unquestionably, NERSA was a key element in the Conrail turnaround. It is impossible and (for our purposes) unnecessary to say what role was played by each of the factors (Staggers Rail Act, NERSA, new management, labor concessions under the threat of a breakup of Conrail, macroeconomic improvement, technology advances). Suffice it to say that all were important; none were meaningless. As with the failure of Penn Central and the Northeast railroad crisis overall, the causes were multiple and so the solution had to be composed of many parts. Luckily, that was the case in the 1980s. With success of the Privatization Act and STB approval of the division and sale of Conrail to NS and CSX in the final years of the twentieth century (as we shall see in Chapter 10) Conrail's most important physical assets were able to reenter the community of profit-making, privately owned enterprises. "Out of the nettle, danger, [policy] plucked the flower, safety."

Conrail on Its Own: The Final Decade Before Division

Conrail's midlife was a lot more calm that its youth or final years. In fact, there is very little to be told in this part of the narrative. Stanley Crane, after leading Conrail to profitability and a very successful public offering, was ready for retirement in early 1988. He had accomplished more after age sixty-five than most people do in a lifetime. Conrail's board chose as his successor Richard Sanborn, who had made his career at CSX. Unfortunately, Sanborn died only a year later, at age fifty-two. The board then decided to appoint Stanley E. G. Hillman to the top spot while they searched for a permanent replacement. Hillman, an international businessman with British Tobacco, had served at the Illinois Central Railroad before his appointment as trustee of the Milwaukee Road's corporate parent in bankruptcy. His contribution to Conrail was brief, but Hillman must be held in high esteem (along with his successor, former Illinois governor Richard Ogilvie) for the splendid manner in which they handled the reorganization of the Milwaukee Road.

Conrail's board next turned to James A. Hagen, a veteran of the Northeast reorganization process. Hagen worked for FRA and at USRA as its president when Ed Jordan moved to Conrail. Hagen (with a nod to Gilbert and Sullivan) was "the very model of a modern market manager" in the railroad industry. He started with Missouri Pacific and Southern Railway, to which he returned after heading USRA. Before long, he joined CSX to take over as vice president of marketing when Sanborn left for Conrail. Now he would follow Sanborn to Philadelphia as Conrail's CEO. Hagen was an inspired choice because as good as Jordan was with business policy and Crane was in operations, Hagen was with customers. And the opportunity for Conrail, Hagen knew, was to make full use of the Staggers Rail Act reforms. His belief was that the job of a marketing officer was to help the railroad's customers compete in their final markets—and with Staggers Rail Act rate flexibility, Conrail could really do that. The object was not to earn the highest margin (and certainly not the same margin) on each movement, but to extend the reach of customers more widely and share with them the resulting profits.

A manifestation of the Hagen marketing strategy was Conrail's leadership in two or three interline service management (ISM) initiatives. The first of these was a project explicitly aimed at accelerating implementation of the newly available technology for reading passive automatic equipment identification (AEI) devices affixed to freight cars and locomotives that used powered radio frequency (RF) readers placed along a railroad wayside to pick up an identification code programmed into the AEI tag.[22]

Jim Hagen eventually rotated into the chairmanship of the AAR's board of directors, where he won many friends to the cause of advancing the railroad industry's public affairs agenda, including defeating shipper proposals for reregulation. Hagen finished his term as chair of the AAR board and then, in 1995, moved up to be chairman of Conrail, leaving David LeVan as CEO.

In the Hagen years, Conrail also benefited from other fundamental industry changes that were beginning to fuel the post-Staggers "rail renaissance." In 1984, Congress moved railroad tax accounting practices out of the regulatory realm of ICC "betterment" accounting (which treated portions of some capital outlays as operating expenditures and others as replacement capital investments) and into the "normal" business world of Internal Revenue Service (IRS) accounting for depreciation. This change helped thaw old frozen assets like tunnels and bridges, enabling rapid write-down of their book values. The effect was tax savings amounting to hundreds of millions of dollars. Then, in 1989, the president's emergency board reached a landmark decision in PEB-219 to permit smaller crew consists in train service—normally two-person rather than four-person crews if a train were only performing limited switching in road service.

Also, international double-stack intermodal train service began to boom in the late 1980s because of a number of converging factors, among others:

- A general relaxation of trade barriers—especially the North American Free Trade Agreement (NAFTA);
- The strong dollar encouraging Asian imports;
- A revolution in supply-chain management—emphasizing final delivered costs and reliability of service over separately calculated manufacturing costs and transport tariff rates per se;
- Steamship lines choosing to drop containers at the US and Canadian Pacific ports for land bridging to the East rather than taking the long route through the Suez Canal or risking delays at the Panama Canal;
- Legalization of contract rate making—enabling long-term agreements between railroads and container lines; and
- The Commonwealth of Pennsylvania helping Conrail improve tunnel clearances to accommodate double-stack intermodal trains.

Conrail's effective rail monopoly in the Northeast was in no way a transport monopoly because motor carrier competition was potent and ubiquitous for the types of commodities manufactured in the Northeast. It was nonetheless a significant factor in Conrail's clear ability, after Staggers Rail Act reduction of regulation, to charge higher rates. But to some critics, Conrail, with its position of dominance in the Northeast, became the poster child of the monopolist railroad charging unreasonably high rates to customers.

Particularly galling to some electricity-generating stations was that, because they were solely served by Conrail at the receiving end of coal movements, the Conrail bottleneck was effective even if coal originated at multiple mines and had competitive rail service to one or more junctions with Conrail—where rates escalated (the shippers said) because of the bottleneck. Utility customers took their case to the ICC (later the Surface Transportation Board [STB]), arguing that whatever the through rate might be, they were clearly captive to Conrail on the bottleneck segment, and those rates should be regulated. Brilliant legal work by the lead attorney for the railroads, Arvid Roach of Covington and Burling, saved the day for Conrail and the industry because the STB ruled that Conrail's rates were permissible under the Staggers Rail Act.[23] Tragically, still a relatively young man, Roach was to survive only a short while after his triumph in the bottleneck cases.

Concluding Thoughts on Conrail

Despite management's plea—seconded by the USRA in its waning, less influential days—to "let Conrail be Conrail," the old urge in policy toward railroads was to clean up loose ends. The fact that Conrail was the third major railroad in the East (not to say its monopoly position in the Northeast)—especially now that there were only two large carriers in the West—was definitely a loose end. The initiative to fix things came first from CSX. That major railroad and its ambitious CEO, John Snow, wanted both the prestige and marketing power that would come from doing what Secretary Dole had failed to do a decade earlier with a Conrail/NS merger. Thus, Snow arranged a takeover agreement with Conrail's then-CEO, David LeVan. This would not be easy, however, as prideful and prosperous Norfolk Southern, now led by the respected David Goode, could not allow what it believed would be an unjust and further destabilizing outcome to go unchallenged.

Stanley Crane had brought an incomparable and irreplaceable operating genius to Conrail; his leadership engineered the miraculous financial turnaround. Richard Saunders says Crane "will go down as one of the great railroaders, perhaps of all time. . . ."[24] In James Hagen, Conrail found the priceless ability to comprehend market strategies—leading the entire railroad industry into the post-Staggers renaissance. Jim Hagen always left his audiences admiring his gentle effectiveness, which was critical to the realization by Conrail's old foes that, for the time being, it really should be independent of both the government and designing merger partners.

Judging LeVan's stewardship of Conrail is harder. His leadership was narrower, less inspired; his public contributions were shadowy, less heroic.

LeVan, however, proved a tough negotiator for final sale terms that almost certainly maximized his shareholders' financial interests. Within reason, that is what CEOs are supposed to do. LeVan was agile enough to shift from acquisition of Conrail by a single railroad purchaser (a strategy fraught with policy and political problems) to the brilliant, unconventional, even unprecedented solution of division between two powerful contenders. He had to give up his dream, like Snow's, of being CEO of a combined Conrail/CSX, and he made some people very angry along the way. In the end, he left with his parachute (perhaps) more gilded than it ought to have been given the sacrifices others had made for Conrail. But the "right" answer, undoing Penn Central, was finally reached.

After many twists and turns, an accommodation was reached among LeVan, Goode, and Snow. Conrail would be divided into, roughly, its pre–Penn Central parts—NYC to CSX and Pennsy to NS. There were some exceptions, of course, and the additional Northeast bankrupt properties USRA consolidated into Big Conrail needed to be accounted for. CSX paid about $4.3 billion for its 42 percent and NS put up $5.9 billion for 58 percent of Conrail. The two acquiring railroads both obtained access to independently administered Conrail Shared Assets company areas in New Jersey and Michigan.[25]

The Northeast railroad crisis and its resolution was always about two things: (1) what industry structure would enable profitable operation of private-sector railroads in the region, and (2) what structure would be workably competitive—in the sense of promoting good service to customers and avoiding any real need for intrusive economic regulation. It was a long and twisting road from the place in which northeastern railroads found themselves in the immediate postwar years to the "Great Divide" of Conrail between Norfolk Southern and CSX in 1998–1999. How appropriate that the road would end so near the close of the twentieth century.

Even more remarkably, the hard work of countless players and a large measure of good luck brought a level of success in reorganizing the railroads of the northeastern United States that could not have been imagined at midcentury. Rail passenger service was transformed from an obsolete, Balkanized, and unconscionable drain on private companies to a respectable position as a needed public service in the Northeast Corridor. The disaster that was the Penn Central merger—the idea, the approval, the concessions to labor, the forced inclusion of the New Haven, the management malfeasance, the cost to taxpayers, the delay and missteps in reaching a sensible solution—all that was now in the rearview mirror. The century-old morass of regulation by the Interstate Commerce Commission that came so close to snuffing out the economic life of railroading in the northeast and midwest was finally in retreat.

In the end, profitability returned to Conrail, and for the industry, the very real threat of reregulation was turned away by the wisdom of legislators who did not want to relive the past. The victorious final years of the century were aided in no small way by reemergence of a workably competitive structure for the industry, which was reached as a result of selling shares of Conrail to the public and then the fortuitous division of that ownership between two major competing companies. (A timeline of the key events in Conrail's brief history is provided below as Table 8.1.)

The partners in all aspects of the reorganized enterprise were very good, and the nation was indeed very lucky.

Table 8.1   Timeline for Conrail and the Northeast

Year	Event	Significance
1966	Interstate Commerce Commission approval of Penn Central merger.	Fundamentally changed application of merger rules to railroads and transport competitive dynamics in the Northeast.
1968	Penn Central merger consummated.	ICC conditions required inclusion of New Haven RR and gave labor strong job protection, making later solution far more expensive.
1970	Penn Central bankruptcy.	Forced other Northeast bankruptcies and policy acknowledgment of the rail crisis.
1970	Amtrak legislation passed (startup May 1, 1971)	Relieved private railroads of most passenger costs; set policy model for quasi-nationalization.
1973	Special Court rules Penn Central not "reorganizable."	Conventional income-based bankruptcy not possible—instead, government plan or liquidation.
1973	3R Act passed (signed 1/2/74)	Defined process for planned reorganization of Northeast bankrupts into Conrail.
1973	DOT "45 Day Report".	Nixon Administration tips hand on policy—wants private sector solution, limited public funding.
1974	U.S. Railway Association organized per 3R Act.	Specialized, representative, temporary agency charged with developing plans for Northeast under congressional goals and timetable.
1975	USRA Preliminary System Plan published February 26.	Defined core lines for retention, sought "3 System East" competitive structure, "Big Conrail" = default.
1975	USRA Final System Plan published July 26.	Road to Conrail defined. Conrail incorporated and E. Jordon elected president.
1976	4R Act passed and signed by President Ford (2/5/76)	Conrail legislatively chartered, with authorization of appropriations and limited regulatory reform.
1976	April 1 = Conveyance Date; Conrail operations start up.	Penn Central and other properties designated to Conrail in FSP officially conveyed; dollar cost TBD.
1978	FRA publishes Prospectus for Change per 4R Act mandate.	FRA documents expected multi-year capital shortfall; recommends more sweeping regulatory reform.
1979	New DOT secretary Adams intervenes to avert "Conrail West;" FRA and USRA issue report on Conrail.	Selective use of 4R Act tools and constructive work with Milwaukee Road trustee sets pattern. Joint FRA/USRA report is glum outlook for Conrail.
1980	Staggers Rail Act enacted October 14, 1980.	Conrail support helps pass fundamental reform; Conrail leads implementation of Staggers Act.
1981	"Blanchette Report" recommends Conrail dismemberment.	New Reagan Administration impatient for privatization of Conrail and end of public subsidies.
1983	Northeast Rail Services Act.	NERSA pays for Conrail employee buyouts and relief from commuter train responsibilities

Table 8.1

Year	Event	Significance
1983	Conrail reports first profitable quarter under Stanley Crane; Conrail officially "profitable."	Wide recognition that Conrail has turned corner; USRA makes statutory "profitability determination" in June 1 report, meaning Conrail no longer threatened with forced liquidation.
1983	Conrail transfers commuter services under NERSA terms.	State and local agencies assume financial responsibility for commuters, saving Conrail hundreds of millions of dollars annually.
1984	DOT Secretary Dole pushes for auction sale of government shares to highest bidder.	With overhang of losses and uncertain effects of deregulation, DOT insists on private sale but, per terms of NERSA, "as an [intact] entity."
1985	Conrail wages restored retroactive to July 1984.	Wage concessions negotiated under NERSA had served their purpose and Conrail was profitable.
1985	DOT selects Norfolk Southern as preferred purchaser of Conrail sold as an entity.	Despite Conrail management pleas to "Let Conrail Be Conrail" and urging of an IPO, DOT Secretary Dole refuses to yield.
1986	Conrail Privatization Act passed.	In reaction to Secretary Dole's ideological policy initiatives, Congress sets new rules for sale of govt. stake in Conrail. Act sunsets USRA.
1987	Conrail's worst train wreck, at Chase, MD on Amtrak's Northeast Corridor.	Engineer R. Gates ran signal, collided with Amtrak train, killing 16.
1987	Goldman Sachs leads IPO for Conrail shares.	Government's return from IPO was $1.8 billion, less bankers' fees, the largest U.S. IPO to date.
1988	Stanley Crane retires after seven years as Conrail CEO.	Richard Sanborn succeeds Crane, but unfortunately dies within a few weeks. James A. Hagen made new CEO.
1995	ICC Termination Act passed.	After over 100 years of existence, ICC passes torch to 3-member Surface Transportation Board.
1996	Battle between CSX and NS begins for acquisition of Conrail.	NS inside path to Conrail control via Secretary Dole overcome by CSX with Snow-LeVan "pact."
1997	Bidding for Conrail between NS and CSX escalates.	Congress and Justice Dept. reluctant to see all of CR merged into either NS or CSX.
1998	STB Approves Division of Conrail between NS and CSX, with "shared asset" regions in Detroit area, Northern NJ, and Southern NJ.	Competitive structure of the Northeast railroads now is the most balanced and competitive solution since well before Penn Central. It is the "Miracle of Market Street."
1999	NS 58% CR (mainly PRR-based) and CSX 42% CR (mainly NYC-based) cut-overs.	Operational problems dog NS-CR cut-over, but CSX-CR goes remarkably smoothly. Both railroads have stretched their financial resources, however, to pay the inflated cost of the buyout.

9

THE MAKING OF THE STAGGERS RAIL ACT, AND EXPERIENCE UNDER DEREGULATION

Regulation is the substitution of error for chance.

—Credited to VALÉRY GISCARD D'ESTAING

A dangerous myth created by railway economics writings of the last forty years has been that a "cost-based" charging system would have been preferable to charging what the traffic would bear. Both theory and experience disprove this assertion, however closely it may appear to match text-book notions of optimal pricing rules for public utilities.

—STEWART JOY (1973)

The current system of railroad regulation reflects a series of uncoordinated actions intended to remedy specific problems encountered during the almost 100 years since the regulatory system was first imposed. The result is a hodgepodge of inconsistent and often anachronistic regulations that no longer correspond to the economic condition of the railroads, the nature of intermodal competition, or the often-conflicting needs of shippers, consumers, and taxpayers.

—US DOT, Federal Railroad Administration (1978)

In America's bicentennial year, the railroad industry was still in complete shambles, although several important steps had been taken in public policy to recognize the problem and begin working toward solutions. The Penn Central, after its catastrophic bankruptcy in 1970, had undergone total financial and ownership reorganization through a federally sponsored planning process created by the Regional Rail Reorganization (3R) Act of 1973 (see Chapter 7). The core of the Northeast's rail system emerged from reorganization in the form of the Consolidated Rail Corporation (Conrail) on April 1, 1976, as ordained by the Rail Revitalization and

Regulatory Reform (4R) Act of 1976 see Chapter 8). That legislation also contained the first meaningful attempt to loosen the grip of Interstate Commerce Commission (ICC) regulation of the railroads.

Earlier in the turbulent 1970s, dollar deficits caused by the long decline of rail passenger services, getting ever worse, were transferred from a common carrier obligation of the individual private railroads to a more appropriate public operating and subsidy vehicle, Amtrak, by the National Railroad Passenger Corporation Act of 1970. Congress continued to support interstate highway construction and rescue of the Northeast railroads in bankruptcy, but before 1976, it put more effort into sponsorship of a blue-sky illusion, the supersonic transport (SST), than reform of railroad regulation.

President Jimmy Carter was elected in November 1976 on a platform of institutional reform and renewal—"taking government back from Washington insiders," as he put it. Nothing fit Carter's model of governance more perfectly than deregulation of transportation businesses—aviation, trucking, and railroads. By election day, the DOT's Federal Railroad Administration (FRA) had already begun work on studies commissioned by the 4R Act that would become part of the agency's remarkable analysis and policy document, A *Prospectus for Change in the Freight Railroad Industry* (1978). The FRA prospectus would detail the financial costs of the industry's deferred maintenance, document the failings of economic regulation under the ICC, and propose policy actions intended to resuscitate the railroads. It was the foundational document supporting the Carter administration's proposals for what became the most important piece of legislation in the history of the US railroad industry, the Staggers Rail Act of 1980.

The 1970s Context

It is a bit difficult for most students of US politics and business economics at the turn of the twenty-first century to comprehend the importance of the debates about regulation and regulatory reform that took place a quarter of a century earlier—unless they happen to have been involved at the time. The issues were arcane because regulation itself had become a bewildering collection of arbitrary rules piled on vague statutory language and obscure, often ill-fitting precedent. Regulatory matters were contested in quasi-judicial proceedings long dominated by lawyers making their living from the very Dickensian complexity of the "system." But a great deal was at stake. In 1976, railroads originated 23 million carloads of freight on their 200,000 route-mile network, carried 36 percent of intercity freight ton-miles, and employed 496,000 workers.

How the regulatory system worked out its decisions determined what types of freight could be handled, how much it would cost shippers, what the ownership structure of the rail industry would look like, and which companies would be winners or losers. The regulatory system in effect decided what carriers would go bankrupt and which could survive.

Unfortunately, the US system regulating interstate commerce in the two decades from 1960 to 1980 was an embarrassment to the nation. The ICC's decisions were based too often on poor information and inferior policies. The regulators may not have planned such malice aforethought, but their decisions rested on bad economic theories, faulty data analysis, biased recommendations supplied by interested parties, maladroit application of legislative mandates, a reverence for precedence at the expense of common sense, and too often the sitting commissioners' plain ignorance. Respected economists calculated the costs imposed on the economy by transportation regulation to be as high as $10 billion annually in current dollars (see Box 9.1).

Box 9.1   Regulation's Cost to the Economy

It was not easy to estimate the cost burden to the economy of excessive regulation, but economists made the attempt. One of the most widely cited studies was by Thomas Gale Moore in 1971. As reported in the *Productivity Task Force* report, Moore's estimate of the economic loss from ICC regulation of trucks, railroads, and water carriers for 1968 ranged from $3.8 billion to $8.8 billion. The medium estimate for railroad inefficient use alone (i.e., not including misallocation of traffic among the modes) was $2 billion annually. Moore explained that his tally did not identify all elements of the loss from regulation. "With many of the figures chosen on the basis of conservative assumptions, it would not be unreasonable to expect that elimination of transport regulation would result in a saving to the economy, in terms of resources, as high as $10 billion a year."[1]

Theodore E. Keeler later provided another summary of the negative economic effects of railroad regulation in 1983. Reviewing his own work and that by Meyer, et al.; Merton J. Peck, Robert W. Harbeson; Ann F. Friedlaender and

Box 9.1

Richard H. Spady; Clifford Winston; Richard C. Levin; Robert G. Harris, and other scholars, Keeler addressed regulatory inefficiencies under four headings: social welfare losses from minimum rates, from excess capacity, and from maximum rates, and miscellaneous losses in productivity from regulation of both rates and services. For rail rate inefficiencies alone, Keeler reported welfare losses estimated by Clifford Winston, and confirmed by Richard Levin, in the range of $1 billion annually for the late 1970s, (with a 1981 collection of articles edited by Kenneth D. Boyer and William G. Shepherd suggesting even higher losses to the economy). Summarizing twenty-five years of study with widely ranging results, Keeler remarks, "The only thing to remain constant is the finding that ICC policies are inefficient." Keeler concluded that "distortions in rates and the forced provision of uneconomic services cost shippers, investors, and the public as a whole at least $2 billion a year in the last half of the 1970s, and probably considerably more."[2]

1. Thomas Gale Moore, *Freight Transportation Regulation: Surface Freight and the Interstate Commerce Commission* (Washington DC: American Enterprise Institute for Public Policy Research, 1972), p. 81.

2. Theodore E. Keeler, *Railroads, Freight, and Public Policy* (Washington, DC: Brookings Institution, 1983), pp. 80–91. Quoted passages are on pp. 80-81 and 142.

And a 1960s Antecedent

It was not the case in the 1960s and 1970s that policy makers knew nothing of the postwar challenges to regulated industries. While not the political football that Populists and Progressives had made railroads in the years before World War I, nor the love affair with automobiles and interstate highways that Americans rushed into after World War II, transportation problems *did* make it onto the policy agenda of President John F. Kennedy in his tragically foreshortened administration. His Transportation Message of April 5, 1962 deserves more recognition and recollection than it receives, for it was a remarkable document, as evident in the following excerpt. It is worth quoting at length:

> A chaotic patchwork of inconsistent and often obsolete legislation and regulation has evolved from a history of specific actions

addressed to specific problems of specific industries at specific times. This patchwork does not reflect either the dramatic changes in technology of the past half century or the parallel changes in the structure of competition.

The regulatory commissions are required to make thousands of detailed decisions based on out-of-date standards. The management of the various modes of transportation is subjected to excessive, cumbersome, and time-consuming regulatory supervision that shackles and distorts managerial initiative. Some parts of the transportation industry are restrained unnecessarily; others are promoted or taxed unevenly and inconsistently.

Some carriers are required to provide, at a loss, services for which there is little demand. Some carriers are required to charge rates which are high in relation to cost in order to shelter competing carriers. Some carriers are prevented from making full use of their capacity by restrictions on freedom to solicit business or adjust rates. Restraints on cost-reducing rivalry in rate-making often cause competition to take the form of cost-increasing rivalry—such as excessive promotion and traffic solicitation, or excessive frequency of service. Some carriers are subject to rate regulation on the transportation of particular commodities while other carriers, competing for the same traffic, are exempt. Some carriers benefit from public facilities provided for their use, while others do not; and of those enjoying the use of public facilities, some bear a large part of the cost, while others bear little or none.

No simple Federal solution can end the problems of any particular company or mode of transportation. On the contrary, I am convinced that less Federal regulation and subsidization is in the long run a prime requisite of a healthy intercity transportation network.[1]

Seventeen years later, the Department of Transportation staff members who prepared the legislative vehicle that evolved into the Staggers Rail Act of 1980 proposed using the Kennedy Transportation Message and the passage quoted here as part of the Carter administration's announcement of its railroad deregulation recommendations. As these DOT staff members observed at the time: "Unfortunately, every word, every thought in that statement is still valid today [1979]. Some improvements have been made in the legislative and regulatory environment during the intervening seventeen years, but President Kennedy's indictment stands."

In earlier chapters, *American Railroads* detailed theories of regulation and the most important manifestations of prevailing regulatory policy. It related sharply contrasting interpretations of the origins and purposes of ICC regulation by economic historians such as Gabriel Kolko and Albro Martin. Subsequent chapters traced legislative developments modifying the rule of rate making and other criteria used by the ICC in managing its caseload and making its rulings. The narrative followed some of the more bizarre wild-goose chases and dead-end roads regulatory policy took. Until the mid-1970s, with the qualified exception of limited reforms made in the Transportation Act of 1958, the regulatory grip on railroads was always tightening—becoming more all-embracing, more complex and convoluted, and more deleterious in its negative economic consequences.

This chapter describes the steppingstone importance of the 4R Act of 1976 and the sweeping scope and transformational impact of the Staggers Rail Act of 1980. In summary fashion, it takes up where Chapters 2 and 3 left off with the story of regulatory intervention (including the great confusion and misdirection resulting from the Transportation Acts of 1920 and 1940) and continues through to the nadir of US railroads in the 1970s. The chapter then describes the guiding principles of the Staggers Rail Act, how its passage came about, and the impact of deregulation on railroads. The final section explores the main policy issues not entirely resolved by the Staggers Rail Act—regulatory standards and strategies that might be applied when competition is deemed "less than fully adequate" to restrain permissible maximum rail rates to "reasonable" levels.

A Good Start with the 4R Act of 1976

With publication of the US Railway Association's Final System Plan (FSP) in 1975 as mandated by the 3R Act of 1973 (see Chapter 7), official Washington turned from watching the administrative reorganization of Penn Central and the other bankrupt Northeast and Midwest railroads back to legislative policy making. The two key pieces of 1970s rail legislation (the 3R and 4R acts), because of their similar names and chronological proximity as much as their fundamental purposes, are often conflated. From a literal reading of each R in the 4R Act's title, nevertheless, it can be understood that the new legislation was focused less on industry structural arrangements in the Northeast than was the 3R Act and significantly more on changing the overall policy setting for railroads generally—so that their economic tailspin could be reversed.

The 3R Act was about regional reorganization, and the 4R Act was about revitalization and reform. Revitalization meant, to the Democratic majority in Congress, infusing public resources into a beleaguered but worthy, labor-intensive, and environmentally friendly industry. Reform meant, to the increasingly market-oriented and antifederalist Republicans on Capitol Hill and in the Ford administration, deliberate deconstruction of the commission form of economic regulation. Between these apposite but not altogether reconciled formulations lay a rough two-part consensus that the railroads could hardly endure in the current economic and policy environment but were clearly worth saving nonetheless.

4R Act Funding Initiatives

Taking first the Democratic legislators' support for federal funding assistance, the 4R Act authorized several billion dollars for a variety of measures to subsidize the financially weakest and most threatened parts of the rail industry. Conrail was the first and largest beneficiary. The new Northeast railroad was off to an administratively smooth but financially precarious start. Congress well understood that, the United States Railway Association's (USRA's) optimism and everyone's for-profit rhetoric aside, substantial additional federal assistance would be needed, just like it was for the infant Amtrak five years earlier; the 4R Act authorized an initial $2.1 billion for Conrail.[2] And since USRA'S Final System Plan (FSP) had designated to Amtrak former Penn Central lines of the Northeast Corridor (Washington–New Rochelle, New York, via the Hell Gate Bridge), the new legislation authorized $1.75 billion for the Federal Railroad Administration (FRA) to use in improving passenger operations on that important link.[3]

Beyond the Northeast, the 4R Act authorized substantial funding for reinvestment in railroads. Congress began with a requirement for the DOT secretary to develop four detailed research and policy documents intended, really, to make the case for revitalization subsidies. Summarized, these were:

(1) a catalogue and description of the system of lines of the intercity railroads in the United States (section 503);

(2) a determination of whether Federal policies towards other transportation modes have unfairly disadvantaged the railroads (section 902);

(3) an assessment for the period 1976–1985 of the capital needs of the
railroad industry and whether those needs are likely to be met by
private sources of capital, and—in the event they are not—an estimate of the amount and form of financial assistance the Federal
Government should provide to the rail industry (section 504); and

(4) an investigation of a number of other specifically identified problems of the U.S. rail system, with consideration of possible solutions
to those problems (section 901).[4]

The analysis conducted by the FRA for item (3) in this list became the
centerpiece of the secretary of transportation's report we refer to as the
FRA *Prospectus for Change* (October 1978). Based on detailed analysis of
data requested from and supplied by the private-sector railroads, FRA calculated that, over the prior decade, estimated deferred maintenance of rail
industry plant, due to inadequate earnings and reinvestment, had accumulated to about $5.4 billion. If historical trends continued, the economy
grew no more than the average annual percentage growth rate experienced in recent years, and no additional regulatory reforms were enacted,
an additional shortfall in roadway capital expenditures of some $13 billion
to $16 billion would accumulate over the ten year period from 1976 to
1985. This estimate excluded capital needs for Conrail and the Long
Island Railroad.

The FRA said that about 50 percent of the shortfall would be concentrated on marginal or bankrupt roads (together handling traffic generating
only 20 percent of rail industry revenues). Congress had in mind using the
"deferred maintenance" and "capital shortfall" study estimates for justification of subsidy authorizations, so the estimates published in the FRA
prospectus could have been half or twice these amounts with little difference in net effect; Congress would make substantial subsidy funds
available, but there is no way Executive Office budgets or even its own
congressional appropriations committees would embrace numbers of the
scale the FRA dutifully (and certainly not naïvely) had provided. FRA's
estimates (increased from $16 to $20 billion) also were to find themselves
memorialized in the introductory findings sections of additional legislative proposals.[5]

In addition to Conrail and Northeast Corridor project funds, the 4R Act had provided authorizations of $1 billion in government guarantees for below-market-rate loans to railroads; $600 million for federal purchase of FRA-approved (quasi-equity) "redeemable preference shares" issued by railroads; and $360 million for a four-year, state-administered program of subsidies to light-density lines. Strangely, only branch lines (as they were commonly called) already approved for abandonment by the ICC were made eligible for federal funding. Presumably the policy intent was to leave the burden of cross subsidy with the parent railroad as long as possible; only a hard-won ICC abandonment authority "proved" the need for federal subsidy. These branch-line subsidy programs gave rise to political rhetoric, intergovernmental bickering, and bureaucratic paperwork exceeding their practical economic effect.

The FRA followed conservative, principled (its critics would say "stubbornly uncooperative") policies for release of the 4R Act funds and continued to argue that it made no sense to invest further in lightly used, little needed lines—especially those already abandoned—when resources were so scarce and heavily used lines themselves so vulnerable. The prospectus gave FRA a platform for explaining these views and outlining more fundamental and lasting policies.

While making few friends for President Carter in the Democratic Congress, the FRA eventually prevailed on the merits. Some of the loan guarantees and preference shares were put to good purpose by FRA insistence and persistence in the project approval process—an example being rehabilitation and shared use by three railroads of the so-called C&NW/Milwaukee/Rock Island midwestern "spine line"—important for handling grain from northern Iowa and southern Minnesota to Kansas City. But with passage of the Staggers Rail Act in 1980 and arrival of the Reagan administration in 1981—and with the hardly inconsequential exception of funding for the infant Conrail—there were virtually no more calls for public grants or loan subsidies to the freight railroad industry in the remainder of the twentieth century.

A Reprise

Why did FRA prevail? Congress might simply have authorized federal appropriations to close the capital shortfall identified by the FRA, but President Carter was not of that mind. In fact, in a set of marginalia written in the president's hand on a memo relating to rail legislation and returned to DOT staff, the president made clear that his real agenda was not about funding at all, but rather about regulatory reform. And perhaps there was more to the story. Perhaps the fiscal bind our postmillennial government suffers from was already pressing on Carter administration officials.

To understand the political potency of regulatory reform and the fact that, in the last two decades of the twentieth century, it was really a bipartisan issue, we can turn to the testimony that FRA Administrator John H. Riley gave in 1985. His presentation began with praise of his predecessor once removed:

> Six years ago, the fifth Federal Railroad Administrator—Jack Sullivan—came before this Committee on the very same issue that we meet on this morning. Jack was a Democrat, of course, and I am a Republican. We represent two very different Administrations. But our position on this issue is virtually identical, and because this Committee both shared that view and took leadership in transforming it into reality, America's railroads are very different today than they were in 1979.[6]

The central point of Riley's remarks were in his conclusion:

> ... DOT strongly opposes reopening the Staggers Rail Act because the structure of that Act has worked. . . . It has delivered enormous benefits to shipper and railroad alike. It is one of the great bipartisan accomplishments of our time—proposed by a Democratic President, and defended by a Republican Administration. And I look forward to maintaining that bipartisan spirit in working with you to make certain that no railroad Administrator, Democrat or Republican, will ever again have to make the kind of arguments that Jack Sullivan made in 1979.[7]

4R Act Regulatory Reforms

The most important of the regulatory reform provisions of the 1976 4R Act were those that changed the old rule of rate making and provided additional flexibility to railroads in setting prices for their services. Under terms of the new act:

- Railroads could raise rates deemed "below costs" up to a variable cost threshold based on a "going concern value" of the enterprise—without further review.

- Railroads could reduce rates to that same going concern value level to protect their traffic moving in intermodal competition.
- The ICC could not force umbrella rate making on railroads.
- Changes involving federal preemption of intrastate rate making were made.
- Restrictions on the power of the ICC to suspend rate changes were adopted, including a 7 percent non-suspend zone for a two-year experimental basis.
- Time limits were adopted for action by the ICC on rate cases.
- A provision reversing the ICC's anti-innovation decision in the Big John jumbo hopper car case was adopted.
- Most important, the legislation took jurisdiction over rates away from the ICC in cases where railroads do not have market dominance.
- Some reforms overturning the 1948 Reed–Bulwinkle Act (passed over President Truman's veto and permitting collective rate making in rate bureaus) were enacted.
- A number of other reforms relating to divisions, exemptions, cost accounting, unit trains, rail mergers, subsidy of abandoned light-density lines, and outlawing discriminatory state taxation were included.
- As noted above, the secretary of transportation was required to prepare various reports, including one estimating the extent of Class I railroad deferred maintenance.
- The secretary of transportation was also authorized in Section 401 to call conferences of competing railroads—shielded from antitrust prosecution—for the purpose of privately negotiating efficient trackage coordination and joint use or abandonment agreements.

When Congress acted on the Ford administration's proposals for railroad revitalization and regulatory reform in 1976, the sponsors of the legislation felt that the 4R Act's changes were significant but substantially less comprehensive than they had recommended. We know this from a brief memoir written by John W. Snow and his coauthor Mark Aron, later executives with CSX.[8] Snow and Aron felt that the vagueness of language in the 4R Act was a major problem that could lead to costly litigation and that further reform depended on how the ICC administered the new law. Snow and Aron reported estimates prepared by DOT staff that the intrastate rate-making provision and the discriminatory taxation provision would save the industry approximately $100 million annually, while the ability to raise rates up to variable costs was worth between $50 million and $250 million annually to the industry. In all, DOT estimated that the benefits to railroads from the 4R Act reforms were worth some $150 million to $350 million annually. But Snow, Aron, and the DOT staff members were also aware that "the biggest gain will come from the increased ability of management to test their markets, experiment with new services, adjust prices quickly in response to cost changes and so forth."[9]

Even after passage of the 4R Act, railroads were still regulated in virtually every significant aspect of their external and financial affairs. FRA's prospectus called it "a fully regulated industry," noting

> The ICC is responsible for deciding whether a proposed rate is too high, too low, or discriminatory. The ICC may, temporarily or permanently, prohibit any rate from taking effect and may set the rate it thinks appropriate. Even intrastate rail rates are subject to some ICC control. The ICC also has authority to enforce the "common carrier obligation" that requires a railroad to provide service to anyone who seeks it and is willing to pay the charge contained in a tariff filed with the ICC.
>
> While the 4R Act gave the ICC explicit authority to exempt specific types of rail movements from regulation—subsequently important in deregulating intermodal services and even boxcar traffic—the ICC retained regulatory control over the construction and abandonment of railroad lines, mergers and acquisitions, rail accounting and costing procedures, and issuance of rail securities.[10]

The FRA prospectus, in the accompanying discussion, overstated the historical circumstances somewhat. When the Act to Regulate Commerce was enacted in 1887, said the FRA, railroads generally exercised "monopoly control over the individual markets they served." This was not the case along navigable waterways and (but for the effect of ICC-supervised rate bureaus) where multiple railroads reached communities—as was typically the case for large cities and port facilities. On the other hand, FRA correctly pointed out that the regulatory regime held on to the monopoly myth for decades longer than warranted. It was becoming better understood that economic conditions had changed radically over the course of the twentieth century, undermining the basic regulatory premise that railroads could earn sufficient profits on demand-inelastic traffic to cross-subsidize publicly popular common carrier obligations such as hauling branch-line agricultural commodities and providing passenger services to small towns below cost. "The 4R Act was the first comprehensive attempt in decades," said the FRA, "to match rail regulation with the current financial and competitive conditions of the rail industry."[11]

The DOT/FRA team that prepared the prospectus was particularly prescient in noting the difficulty of implementing partial deregulation. The 4R Act's changes opened new territory—unknown to many and unwanted by many others. As Snow and Aron had written, "we have had reasonable success in our effort to reform regulation. We must, however, await the ICC's action in implementing the various reform provisions before declaring a victory."[12]

While most of the attention in the prospectus was focused on regulatory constraints forced on the railroads, the report also took federal policy to task for specific actions preferential to other industries carried out at the expense of railroads. The FRA and DOT staff authors of the prospectus, possibly without fully realizing it at the time, were gradually inching toward the policy stance they were to take a year or two later in drafting and defending what became the Staggers Rail Act of 1980. Already they were articulating the clear theme that, to be rescued from bankruptcy and possible nationalization, railroads needed to be treated, not with favoritism, but just like other businesses operating in the private sector. As the ICC continued to drag its feet in implementation of the 4R Act—and specifically in honoring its congressional intent—FRA and DOT became bolder in recommending not just incremental reform of rail regulation, but indeed substantial dismantling of the entire regulatory apparatus. The FRA and DOT did not succeed in its quest for wholesale deregulation at the time, but in major respects, the die was cast. A measure of their final success was that, fifteen years later, the ICC itself lost its bureaucratic livelihood.

The 4R Act made limited progress toward rail rate flexibility and reforms such as not requiring railroads to carry freight at less than variable costs. Some limited federal loan guarantees, preference share qualified equity funding, and grants to states for light-density rail line continuances were made available, but these were generally too little and too late to alter the railroads' downward spiral. Other policy inequities and regulatory inefficiencies remained firmly in place, and their consequences were well known—ranging from the bankruptcy of the nation's largest railroad to apocryphal tales about details such as a "standing derailment" on a Midwest branch line—where a freight car fell off its track even though not moving at the time. Said the DOT staff team, "It is time to take a zero-based look at the system that produces such results."[13]

The regulatory reforms advanced in the 4R Act were insufficient on their face—as shown by the fact that new legislation was needed only four years later. By then the Milwaukee Road had filed for bankruptcy and the Rock Island estate had become virtually cashless. Conrail, despite billions in rehabilitation funding, was losing about a million dollars a day. What was wrong with the 4R Act's exalted deregulatory language? In short, the reforms sounded better than they were. They introduced new concepts, terms, and cost measures—but these added more to the complexity of regulatory determinations by the ICC than they yielded in rate-making flexibility or relaxed administrative restrictions on the railroads.

The Making of the Staggers Rail Act of 1980

Beyond the organizational and financial assistance to Conrail and the rather limited financial assistance to failing lines outside the Northeast, "railroad revitalization" would really depend on the other half of the 4R Act—"regulatory reform." The Carter administration economic rational-ists had largely thwarted instinctive Democratic big spending on railroads. No less ironically, Carter's liberal transportation and utility sector advisers embarked on a degree of regulatory reform that would soon put to shame the timid and feeble efforts of the Republicans in power when the 4R Act was signed into law in 1976. Strange bedfellows indeed! Just as anticom-munist icon Richard Nixon had gone to China against all odds, populist southern governor Jimmy Carter did more to demolish big government regulation of industry than any previous or subsequent occupant of the White House.

As related above, the FRA/DOT *Prospectus for Change in the Freight Railroad Industry* had several purposes and effects. It reported accumu-lated deferred plant and equipment maintenance for the US railroad industry. It analyzed the reasons for the industry's decline. It offered com-mentary on a wide range of issues such as intermodal traffic opportunities, branch-line abandonments, and structural changes (both mergers and line coordination short of merger). And it provided an extended critique of regulatory reforms begun in the 4R Act and still needing to be accomplished in new legislation. Altogether, FRA and DOT had recommended sweeping remedies that shook the prevailing regulatory, labor, and managerial institutions to their foundations. Rarely had a US cabinet agency made such fundamental recommendations for change in a privately owned industry.

Soon after finishing the prospectus, the Department of Transportation formed a task force of staff from the secretary's Office of the Chief Counsel and FRA policy officers to draft a legislative vehicle for the Carter administration's railroad deregulation initiatives—as had been done earlier with respect to regulation of aviation by the Civil Aeronautics Board (CAB) and of trucking by the ICC. The team met regularly over a period of several months (all had other responsibilities), working through the complexities of the existing regulatory structure and the likely effects of relaxing ICC control over the railroads. Starting with the analysis and recommendations found in the prospectus, the team tried at first to write legislative language that would cure the flaws evident in current statutes and ICC interpretations. As their work progressed, however, the team increasingly became convinced that the complexity of the reform provisions they were trying to draft—and the opportunity for ongoing ICC regulatory mischief—were too great. Gradually the team realized that piecemeal reform wasn't the answer; what was needed was wholesale deregulation, or the repeal of nearly all of the elaborate structure of regulatory restrictions and precedents.[14]

The team, by the hard route of informed situational case argument and legislative drafting, became convinced that substantial deregulation was both needed and workable. They had become, to a degree, radicalized. Why try to perfect language under which the ICC would fairly decide an interline rate-making case when there was every indication that the carriers and shippers involved could privately work out an arrangement satisfactory to themselves and the public interest? Given that there was ample rail–rail and intermodal competition, to ensure a reasonable outcome, the right answer was to minimize regulatory interference with market forces. Making sure private parties could contract for service packages at mutually agreeable rates was the key. The new rule of rate making would become, in effect, the notion that a fair and reasonable rate is one which carriers and shippers can reach in an arms-length bargain.

There would be cases, of course, in which the parties could not amicably agree on contract terms, and for these an alternative system of adjudication would be needed. Already the misleading term *captive shippers* had come into the language with public controversy especially over cases under the 4R Act involving long-distance transportation of coal to large power-generating stations. Among the FRA/DOT team members, there was good knowledge of the economic principles relating to bilateral oligopoly, optimal cost- and demand-based pricing, and price differentiation by techniques such as Ramsey pricing (see Box 2.2 in Chapter 2).

There was great dissatisfaction among team members with the 4R Act's arbitrary percent revenue to variable cost test of maximum rates, and even some feeling that a fair rate of return on investment standard would be superior to a revenue to variable cost ratio test. (This idea reflected common practice in public utility rate making and harkened back to the 1911 Hadley report that declared a "fair and reasonable" rate was one that permitted railroad reinvestment in the facilities enabling the movement. Fine in theory, the rate of return standard implied at least as much number crunching and arbitrary accounting allocations as the revenue to variable cost test, and the team did not pursue the idea further.

Viewing railroad inability to reinvest in physical plant and equipment as the central policy problem, the drafting team decided to put on the complaining shipper the burden of proof that a contract rate was unreasonable and let disputes go to an expert regulatory panel and/or the courts. All observers reckoned that deregulation proposals going as far as the DOT staff recommendations would be hugely controversial, and many predicted resounding defeat when the administration proposals (already toned down somewhat) were sent to Congress.

Committees in both the House and Senate held long hearings, and administration officials had to defend the core proposals against challenges from all sides. Coauthor Gallamore recalls a particularly contentious Senate committee hearing in which he appeared to present the administration's case. One senator, who had become quite agitated by shortages of grain cars needed by his constituents, questioned why we would be undermining the ICC at this time; wouldn't our proposal only result in higher railroad rates? Gallamore responded that no, with freedom to contract, railroads and shippers could agree on measures that might permit better adaptation to supply and demand conditions in the market, actually lowering costs and rates compared with the prevailing ICC schedules.[15] That subsequently turned out to be the case often, but not always.

Eventually, as almost always happens in legislative drafting, congressional staff members made many changes. They simply could not go as far as the FRA/DOT staff members had gone, and they kept in place much of the 4R Act regulatory apparatus for determination of maximum rates in cases where market dominance was established. Finally, a bill substantially lessening regulation emerged from the House and Senate, and in conference, it was agreed to name the legislation after the retiring chairman of the House Committee, Representative Harley O. Staggers of West Virginia. President Carter signed the bill into law on October 14, 1980, exactly two years after publication of the *Prospectus for Change in the Freight Railroad Industry*, which had in fact lived up to its name.

Railroad Performance Under Staggers Rail Act Deregulation

Favorable experience under the Staggers Rail Act, particularly the level and incidence of actual railroad rates, far exceeded expectations. Almost all observers were astonished by the degree, pace, and impact of deregulation. Reports of the speed with which railroads and shippers were signing and filing rate and service contracts with the ICC (a requirement of the act) began to surface (see Box 9.2). Then gradually it became known that, in general, these private and secret contracts represented substantially lower actual rates for moving freight than had been charged under previously published tariffs. The authors of the Staggers Rail Act had found a niche—a place less unpopular than taxpayer support for failing railroads or the illogical rulings of an archaic and imperious regulatory agency.

Box 9.2   The Core Reform Approved in the Staggers Act—Rate and Service Contracts

---

It took 18 months after passage of Staggers for railroads and shippers to get comfortable with the new reality of contract rate making and for the first 1,000 agreements to be signed. At that point, however, there was a rush to the ICC to get contracts filed, approved, and put into effect. The second 1,000 agreements took only another three months and, as ICC officials predicted, by the end of 1982, 3,000 would be in effect.[1] Then, by the time of Administrator Riley's testimony in 1985, he noted shippers had used contracts in more than 30,000 cases to lock in rates and services.[2]

A great deal of credit for advancing the legality and pace of contracts goes to then-ICC chairman Darius Gaskins, who, even before passage of the Staggers

Box 9.2

Rail Act of 1980, declared rail–shipper agreements (despite long ICC precedent to the contrary) to be acceptable. Gaskin set up a contract advisory service to encourage use of the device.

By September 1982, the diversity of contracting was evident. A published commodity breakdown showed the following: forest and paper (25 percent), chemicals and fertilizers (17 percent), feed and food products (12 percent), grain (7 percent), coal (6 percent), and all others (33 percent).

The trade press began covering contracts extensively. The journal *Traffic Management* published a full-page Checklist for Rail Contracts containing definitions, examples, and tips.

1. Francis J. Quinn, "Rail Contracts Finally Start to Roll," *Traffic Management*, September 1982, p. 67ff.

2. John H. Riley, Federal Railroad Administrator, before the Senate Committee on Commerce, Science, and Transportation, November 1, 1985, p. 3.

The cumulative impact of Staggers Rail Act deregulation was swift and staggering. A widely disparaged idea, launched by a rather inexperienced staff working for an unpopular administration and receiving only lukewarm assistance from the industry's leaders, was changing the century-old way railway economics worked. (See Box 9.3, which contrasts railroad managerial flexibility in the era of fulminant ICC regulation (as described by President Kennedy) with how railroads could run their business after enactment of the 4R Act of 1976 and especially after passage of the Staggers Rail Act of 1980.)

Passage of the Staggers Rail Act became not only the salvation of the railroads but also an enormous benefit to shippers in the form of substantially lower average rate levels. The Surface Transportation Board (STB), successor to the Interstate Commerce Commission since January 1, 1996,[16] concluded in a report published in 2000 that the average, inflation-adjusted rail rate had continued a multiyear decline in 1999 and that, since 1984, real rail rates had fallen 45 percent. According to the board, the study implied that, although railroads retained a degree of pricing power in some instances, nearly all productivity gains achieved by railroads since the 1980s (when railroad economic regulation was reduced) had been

Box 9.3 Contrasting Regulatory Regimes Before and After the Staggers Rail Act of 1980

Under Regulation

The ICC, in cases such as *Ingot Molds*, rigidly enforced the *"National Transportation Policy"* contained in the *Transportation Act of 1940*. The ICC's interpretation was that "inherent advantage" comparisons between modes should be based on fully distributed costs rather than out-of-pocket costs (ignoring sunk and threshold costs), and thus apparently regardless of public subsidies to waterway operators. The ICC ruled that if railroads could charge rates only covering out-of-pocket costs it would not allow the competing barge-truck operators to "assert their inherent advantage because it would compel them to go well below their own fully distributed costs to recapture the traffic." [http://supreme.justia.com/cases/federal/us/392/571/case.html, accessed 12_14_2013.]

Investors and railroads withdrew capital to more profitable ventures. Railroads were squeezed between protected and/or subsidized competitors (e.g., barges and heavy trucks) and maximum rate regulation.

Under perceived notions of equity and the statutory ban on discrimination, different rail carriers' *rates* between the same points were *equalized*. This rectilinear approach appealed to those trained in legal or accounting representations of reality, but was at odds with the curvilinear world of commerce.

Railroad rates were arrived at in secret meetings of ICC-sanctioned regional *"rate bureaus"* exempt from anti-trust prohibitions against price fixing. Voting was made on individual rates to be published by the cognizant Bureau and adhered to by all carriers serving the identified points. Votes were taken on a yes or no basis, un-weighted by market share. All railroads that were members of the Bureau (whether participating in the movement or not) could vote, which was accomplished by means of buttons installed under the meeting table so that other members could not see how each road voted on specific proposals. A secretary recorded only the yes/no outcome, and filed revised rate schedules with the ICC. At one point it was said that over a trillion rates were on file and published by the ICC.

Rail Form A (average) *costing* discouraged innovation that would have improved efficiency; minimum rate regulation used Rail Form A average costs to discourage rail marginal cost pricing by considering it predatory and counter to National Transportation Policy.

In keeping with the long haul/short haul clause of the *Transportation Act of 1920* and other statutes, railroads could not charge a lower rate to a more distant

Box 9.3

point on a given route than to an intermediate point, regardless of volumes shipped, absence of switching complexities, or generation of back-haul freight at the more distant point.

Regulatory *review of management* decisions dampened entrepreneurial spirit and favored conservative financial decisions and aversion to risk- taking. Regulatory lag slowed benefits of innovation and railroads' recovery of inflation-driven costs.

Mergers were viewed skeptically and subjected to almost interminable review. Mergers were judged with an eye to cost savings rather than market extensions: parallel mergers were more likely than end-to-end mergers to be approved, as the ICC sought protection of "competitors" more than competition. The ICC failed to develop consistent standards for measuring anticipated or *post facto* merger performance.

Regulation imposed *gateway traffic routing* protections on mergers—again protecting competitors rather than competition, and reducing economic savings from mergers.

Labor protection was appended to mergers, service discontinuances, and aban-donments; protection discouraged development and deployment of labor-saving innovations.

Railroads were held to have a *"common carrier obligation"* to provide service to all comers at published rates, and they could not—on their own volition—withhold (boycott) service to a customer or abandon rail lines connecting any points, even if all traffic evaporated or a line suffered a washout. Similarly, before establishment of *Amtrak* in 1970 (and even thereafter if a railroad had not "joined" *Amtrak*), the railroad could not discontinue published passenger trains without ICC permission, even if no customers were to use the service.

After Deregulation

Railroads and shippers could *contract* for specific services and committed vol-umes, enabling operations and investments planned around efficiency objectives. Contract summaries were filed with the ICC and made public, but sealed con-tracts were not otherwise subject to regulation or public disclosure.

Railroads *could not participate in rate discussions* with other railroads (such as in rate bureaus) unless they were involved in a specific interline movement at issue; this left other railroads with uncertainty about competitors' marketing objectives and prodded non-participants to come up with their own innovations.

(continued)

Box 9.3   Continued

Market share soon became more dependent on improved *cost performance* reflected in price reductions (and, to a somewhat lesser extent, superior service quality and equipment availability). Traffic became less a function of traditional flow patterns based on published rates and established sales relationships. Rate equalization was abandoned and rate *discrimination redefined* to a minor role.

Railroad *revenue adequacy* became a statutory concern and a threshold below which railroads had greater freedom from regulation. (Few railroads met the revenue adequacy test until recent years.)

Maximum rate regulation was changed from a vague standard of reasonableness to specific procedures for dealing with cases *where shippers proved absence of effective competition*. In these cases, the ICC and STB required that experts calculate "stand-alone" costs in a counterfactual manner to enable rate setting consistent with Ramsey pricing principles.

While higher than average rates for service to so-called "captive shippers" continued to cause controversy, overall, rail rates *declined* in nominal dollars from 1980 to the end of the 20th Century, and, in inflation adjusted dollars, *by roughly one-half!* Productivity soared, as railroads were able to haul more ton-miles with less track and fewer employees.

The ICC *exempted* a number of transactions or services from regulatory review altogether: intermodal traffic, boxcar movements, perishables, minor abandonments, trackage rights agreements, and minor line construction projects. Line sales to new railroads were exempted from labor protection.

Although petty regulatory constraints on management initiatives were lifted, a regulatory "overhang" continued to affect *entrepreneurial risk-taking* in the railroad industry throughout the 1980s. As the century closed, however, market imperatives stimulated new boldness in mergers, marketing and ownership initiatives related to Mexico rail privatization, and a variety of terminal and car supply investments to support intermodal operations, as well as huge increases in capital spending for additional line and switching capacity and locomotive purchases.

Merger review was expedited, and the focus changed to obtaining merger benefits while preserving competition through tailored *negotiated conditions*. Some strengthening of labor contract preemption was made. Most gateway routing restrictions were dropped.

Railroads touted mergers as presenting opportunity for extended single-line service and reversion of lost traffic to railroads. Larger rail firms and *rationalized route structures* enabled railroads with effective managerial organizations and technology to derive productivity and marketing benefits from mergers. One

---

Box 9.3

---

merger was denied on anticompetitive grounds and others were conditioned to require replacement competition in markets where otherwise it would be lost.

In the post-Staggers competitive environment for all forms of transportation, railroads sought relief from restrictive *labor work rules*. The Presidential Emergency Board ruling 219 (1991), at last resulted in a standard two-person crew consist for trains of Class I railroads not assigned more than limited switching *en route* from origin to destination.

---

passed on to rail customers in the form of lower rates. The board estimated that rail shippers would have paid an additional $31.7 billion for rail service in 1999 if revenue per ton-mile had remained equal to its 1984 inflation-adjusted level.[17]

In that same timeframe, the General Accountability Office (GAO) produced two reports that are models of understated objectivity on the issue. For example, in 2002, the GAO found that:

> . . . rates for coal, grain (wheat and corn), chemicals . . . and transportation equipment . . . generally fell from 1997 through 2000. . . . These decreases followed the general trend we previously reported on for the 1990–1996 period, and, as before, tended to reflect railroad cost reductions brought about by continuing productivity gains in the railroad industry that have allowed railroads to reduce rates in order to be competitive.[18]

The Association of American Railroads (AAR) also publishes and periodically updates a summary of Class I railroad annual performance since 1980 (see Figure 13.6 in Chapter 13). It shows the remarkable growth of total productivity and a corresponding pattern of declining railroad average rates since deregulation in 1980.

In 1980, only a few observers had foreseen the impact of legalizing carrier–shipper contracts and how that and other reforms could take deadweight regulatory losses out of the system for the win-win benefit of both railroads and their customers.[19]

Most of them, that is.

Persistent Perceptions About Railroad Pricing Power and Abuses of It

While the Staggers Rail Act of 1980 lessened regulation—yielding substantial cost savings, dramatic productivity improvements, unambiguously lower average rates, and improved industry profitability—it did not satisfy all claimants. In particular, the Staggers Rail Act left significant struggles over maximum rate levels to be resolved by the ICC, or its successor, the STB, and the courts.

Chief among these struggles was the manner in which shippers with highly inelastic demand, especially those served by a single rail carrier and having few good logistics alternatives, might seek relief from what they believed were unreasonably high rates. These are the so-called captive shippers, a highly vocal and politically active collection of rail users, sometimes trade associations informally organized into ad hoc groups, whose members feel they are being exploited by the major railroads. In particular, the exclusively served shippers contend that they pay supranormal rates and are being forced to cross-subsidize other rail users.[20]

The captive shipper group holds these beliefs despite the fact that rail users overall have generally realized lower average rates since the Staggers Rail Act lessened regulation. Moreover, the governing regulatory authority has found no firm evidence of a widening gap since 1984 between exclusively served and other rail shippers. In the end, political resolution of the captive shipper controversy may come down to whether a reasonable balance has been struck between the iron laws of economics driving railroads to depend on price differentiation and the howls of shippers who do not like paying higher than average rates just because their demand is relatively inelastic.

As noted in Chapter 2, this book by and large refrains from using the standard economic characterization (and term) *natural monopoly* because it has become too pejorative. To micro-economists, natural monopoly conditions are specific (having to do with declining unit costs over greater output), and related policy prescriptions are carefully nuanced. Popular use of the term, however, conjures actions illegal under the antitrust laws and never reaches the sophisticated understanding that nearly all sellers have some local and short-run market power. Providers do not give away their goods at marginal cost even when competitive alternatives appear to be abundant; doing so is unnecessary because of the dynamic structure of most transport markets and because it would be foolhardy financially.

John R. Meyer thought that the characterization of railroads as natural monopolies requiring unique, activist forms of economic regulation was overdone and had led to some rather extreme proposals for legislative and regulatory policies to help "captive shippers." Professor Meyer thought these discussions were unwarranted "diversions" (his term) from the more fundamental issue—getting railroads into shape to serve ongoing transport functions in the national economy. Meyer strongly believed railroads should be left free to act as other businesses could, which, after all, was the fundamental policy invocation of the Staggers Rail Act of 1980.[21]

American Railroads recognizes that railroads frequently have significant pricing power in selected markets. There are not many carriers between any two points on the national map; except for intermodal (trailer or container) freight and transloading (often done for commodities as diverse as coal, grain, cement, fertilizer, and even auto parts and refrigerated produce), frequently only one railroad directly serves both the origin and destination of a given shipment. Some customers finding themselves in this position claim they are "captive" to the single railroad serving that particular route and believe government intervention is necessary to protect them from rate gouging. Under the Staggers Rail Act, shippers able to prove such circumstances to the Surface Transportation Board (prior to 1996, the Interstate Commerce Commission) are entitled to rate relief.

Maximum Rate Regulation Under Rail Market Dominance and the Coal Rate Guidelines—*Ex Parte* No. 347

The Staggers Rail Act of 1980 set criteria for determination of rate reasonableness when the ICC found competition in the relevant market was "ineffective." It took some time, however, for the ICC to get comfortable with the full implications of what Congress had said and what the courts were finding in major coal rate cases. Two months after passage of Staggers, the ICC instituted a rule-making proceeding, *Ex Parte* No. 347, for the purpose of establishing nationwide coal rate guidelines. The accompanying *Notice of Proposed Guidelines* recognized the need for railroad rate flexibility and endorsed a demand-based approach, but then immediately adopted the reverse—a proposal to use a fully allocated cost ceiling based on a ton/ton-mile ratio method for allocating markups above variable costs in determining maximum reasonable rates.

The major railroads were appalled by the commission's proposed guidelines and filed strong responses in May 1981. The railroads' submission contained "the testimony of many of the most eminent economists in the country—including Nobel Prize–winner Kenneth Arrow, and Professors [William] Baumol and [Robert] Willig, [Leon] Moses and [Ronald] Braeutigam, and [William] Wecker."[22] The railroads' filings and their all-star witnesses apparently had some effect because the ICC, in its preliminary decision of December 16, 1981, acknowledged having to give up on the notion of allocating constant costs with a ratio method and conceding that the additive factor amounted to double-counting ("our thinking on this issue was flawed").[23]

The Role of Revenue Adequacy

In "rethinking" its position on maximum rate policy, the ICC realized it needed to draw a stronger link to the statutory revenue adequacy standard, and that meant giving more effect to rate making that reflects customer demand and not strictly costs.[24] But Ramsey pricing (see Chapter 2, Box 2.2)[25] as proposed by the railroads "entails a different regulatory philosophy than the one this agency has operated under since its inception." The ICC was not yet ready to settle on a specific approach but agreed that "differential pricing is an important tool in assisting the railroads to revenue adequacy," the standard Staggers had required.

It is the thinnest of lines that separate the two statutory criteria of market dominance and revenue adequacy. Public policy fears the former but embraces the latter.

In their comments for the ongoing *Ex Parte* proceeding, the Class I railroads said that the ICC's December 1981 interim decision was an "historic milestone in the long history of rate regulation under the Interstate Commerce Act." It had brought the testimony of leading economists and regulatory experts to bear on the issues, resolved a number of fundamental principles, and framed the remaining questions. We had come a long way, the railroads said, since Congress in the 4R Act found the railroad industry in financial chaos. But Congress had "decided the railroads should remain in the private sector, without subsidy."[26] To accomplish the purpose, the railroads' brief says that Congress created a new rule of rate making, Section 10704(a)(92) of the act, which provided that, in determining whether a rate exceeded a maximum reasonable level, "the Commission shall make an active and continuing effort to assist [the railroads] in attaining revenue levels prescribed under this paragraph"—that is, revenues which cover total operating expenses, plus "a reasonable and economic profit or return (or both) on capital employed in the business."[27]

The railroads' brief went on to describe how, in numerous post–4R Act cases, the commission laid out the concept of what it called "revenue need costs"—reflecting the cost of both debt and equity capital. "This principle— that in order to attract needed capital, railroads must be permitted to earn returns at least equal to their cost of capital—has since been reaffirmed on numerous occasions . . . and has since become a cornerstone of analysis in maximum rate cases." The railroads argued that development of coal rate guidelines took on more urgency with passage of the Staggers Rail Act, "in which Congress expressly found that railroad earnings were insufficient to generate or attract needed capital, and that unless major regulatory change were made, there would be a capital shortfall within the industry of $16–20 billion by 1985 . . ."[28]

Determining the level of particular rates designed to achieve overall revenue adequacy was still controversial. Given a range of competition and demand in a variety of markets for rail service, the answer necessarily was "differential pricing" because, if rates were based on fully allocated average costs, much of the traffic would not move—which would only increase the costs that would have to be covered by the remaining traffic. Better to let this competitive traffic yield whatever contribution to over- head it might, thereby lowering the burden on captive customers.

It just might be impossible to be revenue adequate without a degree of market dominance and price differentiation. That is why deregulation is not wildly popular—not in a society that invented rail regulation, then lob- bied its legislators and regulatory agencies for 100 years to refine it and apply it for local commercial advantage, and today appears to be bored of the subject.

A Duty to Be Efficient

The ICC's coal rate guidelines also focused briefly on the old issue Louis Brandeis had advanced seventy years earlier: railroad owners' duty to operate with maximum efficiency, so that manufacturing customers— while they were forced to cross-subsidize other favored customers—were not also forced to carry a burden of managerial waste. Neither Brandeis nor the post-Staggers coal shippers and receivers were technically wrong in bringing up this issue, but it was more rhetorical than economically significant. In *Ex Parte 347—Coal Rate Guidelines Nationwide,* the rail-roads took several lines of argument to counter the shipper position that managerial inefficiency was a cause of inadequate revenues:

1. First, railroad expert economic witnesses such as Baumol and Willig argued persuasively that, under their proposal, railroads would have every incentive to be efficient and none to be wasteful. By contrast, under a full cost allocation basis with a rate ceiling, there might be no incentive for efficiency; all "rate of return" regulatory schemes have this problem in that unnecessary costs hidden in the "rate base" allow higher profits.[29]
2. Next, management consultant Hugh Randall testified for the rail-roads that many factors affecting efficiency (including regulation, labor rules, and traffic sources) were largely outside management's control. Commonly used measures of management skill do not them-selves make the case.[30]
3. Third, "[e]vidence that managerial efficiency can be improved is not relevant to rate reasonableness unless the allegedly possible improve-ments would themselves ensure the railroad adequate revenues." There was little evidence that shippers would be able to argue suc-cessfully for such inquiries, or that the amounts so discovered would fill the revenue gap.[31]

Constrained Market Pricing—Rate Caps

Still remaining was the issue of any upper limit on rate reasonableness. How high is too high? The railroads repeated that any regulatory ceiling below the maximum established by demand and competitive factors would simply move the revenue adequacy goal further away. On the other hand, they claimed, the suggested approach would not result in skyrock-eting rates nor unfair treatment of customers facing market-dominant car-riers because shippers can still appeal to the ICC for an opportunity to prove that an efficient railroad specializing in serving that shipper should have lower costs and therefore could charge lower rates .

The railroads' proposal to the ICC for addressing the unresolved issues had three procedural advantages: (1) It would end irrelevant disputes over full cost allocation, (2) it would avoid monumental efforts to recon-struct in excruciating detail historical or hypothetical costs for spe-cific movements, and (3) it would streamline the ICC's case load by screening out shipper claims based on meaningless formulas rather than economic reasoning.

Proposals for Re-regulation and Rate Guidelines

Application of the Staggers Rail Act provisions to rate setting in markets where railroads have been determined to be market-dominant has continued to give rise to more outspoken angst than any other aspect of railroad deregulation. There has been a fairly steady stream of litigation and calls for new anti-rail legislation over the last quarter century. These have included, in particular, proposals for reversing the burden of proof of market dominance (putting it back on the railroads) and amending procedures for cost determination. Sometimes the "re-regulators" have wanted to give a government agency (ICC or STB) the power to force "open access" for foreign operators[32] over an incumbent railroad with market dominance in the movement of freight from or to facilities of a captive shipper. Though it may seem bizarre, this kind of compelled track access would mean that a different railroad could be licensed to offer competing service to the shipper, using the original carrier's own facilities.

Such an extreme policy, this book argues, would amount to a "taking" of private property forbidden by the US Constitution,[33] unless the original carrier were paid trackage fees based on full market value of the asset in that application; the net effect of this fair compensation standard might well be a fee, which if added to the accessing railroad's normal rate, would yield no rate relief to the shipper! But the complexity does not end there. How would the regulatory agency determine which shippers deserved competitive access and which carriers should be allowed or forced to provide it? And how would the costs of access (including those related to dispatching, operational interference, and liability for damage) be calculated? These are reasons why opponents of "open access" proposals call it re-regulation. It is a tangled web indeed.

Two Strategies for Escaping Captivity

Over the course of the post-Staggers period, captive shippers have tried to escape their bondage to railroads dominating the relevant markets by two quite different routes. Both strategies relied on artificial interventions in established markets by the regulatory authorities: one to compel new competition, and the other for the regulator to stipulate use of a specific kind of hypothetical cost estimates in setting maximum rates. Alike in their intent to cap or drive down the offending rates, these two escape routes have different legislative/regulatory underpinnings and different operational consequences. The two alternative rate mitigation strategies can be evaluated with the same economic logic, however. It turns out that while legal/legislative strategies—and railroad operational impacts—would be sharply different in the two different remedies, their net economic effects would be similar. Both escape routes depend on the regulatory agency creating and imposing artificial circumstances—either *unnatural competition* or *hypothetical costs*.

The next sections endeavor to show the problems inherent in maximum rate regulation based on artificial competition and/or fictitious costs. It explores the theoretical issues and several practical problems arising in both stand-alone cost methodologies and compelled competitive access proposals. It concludes that constrained market pricing under case-by-case ICC and STB supervision has been the correct national policy and that more radical measures such as compelled access are not warranted.

The First Escape Route: Artificial Rate Caps
with Hypothetical Cost Standards

The first escape path for captive shippers was explicitly authorized in the Staggers Rail Act, and it had been the subject of an exhaustive rule-making proceeding at the ICC referred to earlier, *Coal Rate Guidelines—Nationwide (Ex Parte 367)*. Ultimately, the rule-making docket legitimized a complex set of procedures to be used in determining maximum charges for rail tonnage moving under the rates being challenged (the so-called issue traffic). The guidelines are based on a nontraditional cost standard imagining a hypothetical new competitor to handle the issue traffic.

The hypothetical carrier would be efficiently designed, built, and operated, and its artificially constructed cost levels would serve as a benchmark estimate for capping maximum rates in the real world. This methodological tour de force is known as the stand-alone cost case (SACC), and the hypothetical carrier—one specializing in serving that shipper—is called the stand-alone railroad (SARR). Presumably the SARR would have lower costs than the defendant railroad, and the ICC and STB would lower any rates to the captive shipper exceeding the hypothetical stand-alone cost estimates to that level.[34]

Whether a fictitious SARR in an SACC was to serve the alleged captive shipper *exclusively* or just *predominantly* was not altogether clear. The ICC and STB allowed SACCs to include significant amounts of so-called cross-over traffic as base-load business for the SARR. These (coal) volumes from other customers were not part of the issue traffic, but the rules governing such inclusions in SACCs were not rigorously determined and crossover traffic remained controversial.

While casual observers may find it rather odd to have to postulate a fictitious railroad to estimate a benchmark level of costs—and then force these into a model for constrained rate ceilings for an actual railroad's charges to its customer—that is what the SACC procedure does. There is, nonetheless, some theoretical validity to the SACC because the rail routings, haul lengths, traffic volumes, equipment types, labor contract wages, and so on, used in the STCC have real-world prototypes and because even the hypothetical enterprise would have to charge rates covering all operating costs, plus markups sufficient to imply a competitive return on capital employed—without cross-subsidizing unrelated traffic. As railroad witnesses Baumol and Willig pointed out in the ICC proceeding:

> This test [the SACC] provides the direct means to limit rates in the same manner as the market. It shows what rates would be if an efficient new carrier entered the market and set rates at the level that is just adequate to cover its long-run costs . . . Since it prevents railroads from charging in excess of the efficient cost of providing service to any shipper or group of shippers, it also guarantees that no shipper or shippers are required to cross-subsidize other traffic.[35]

The motivation for all this effort is to attempt to find some way to set a ceiling on the maximum rates that a dominant railroad can charge a captive shipper—but one that does not appear to be totally arbitrary. The cases arise because advocates assume that the observed rates for the issue traffic are higher than those an efficient carrier would need to charge to yield normal profits.

The logic is much like that used by Louis Brandeis in the Progressive Era to argue against the ICC granting general rate increases to railroads— if they could not show that they were operating efficiently according the principles of scientific management. The SARR would thus have to be a sort of Candide in Voltaire's best of all possible worlds, cultivating a garden of delights to soothe bad memories of past troubles and to prove humans were not born to be idle. "Work then without disputing; it is the only way to render life supportable."[36]

The Second Escape Route: Artificial Competition

The second escape route for captive shippers would require new legislation to force incumbent railroads under their common carrier obligation to open their tracks to additional competition from rival railroads. Usually called open access, we prefer the term *compelled competitive access* because access almost certainly would not be "open" to all comers and it is inconceivable that the competitive benefits for shippers could be achieved without a substantial degree of governmental compulsion. Proponents believe such a policy would result in lower rates for the issue traffic, while railroads maintain that compelled access amounts to re-regulation.[37] It runs counter to Staggers Rail Act principles, railroads argue, and, by reducing enterprise profitability and ability to invest, would leave railroads vulnerable to the downward spiral of deferred maintenance, inadequate service, derailments, and bankruptcy, as experienced in the 1960s and 1970s.

Competitor access issues are currently at the center of the public policy debate in most network infrastructure industries. The complexity and controversy arises because, by its very nature, competitor access policy involves regulatory intervention not only in the industry's organization, but also in the internal operations of an affected firm. The greatest single flaw in proposals for competitor access is that the access more often than not would be ordered to be provided over the facilities of (and perhaps in conflict with) the existing provider; this is what makes it artificial competition. We believe that, unless owning railroads were fully compensated for the market value of forced access rights (which might negate the motivation for compelled access), the policy would run afoul of the Constitution's Fifth Amendment protections against government taking of private property without due process, meaning compensation at the market value of the property seized or condemned for the public purpose—in this case competitive access.

TYPES OF ACCESS TO RAILROAD FACILITIES PROPOSED IN CAPTIVE SHIPPER CASES

To focus the economic issues, we first list and briefly discuss the types of railroad access policies currently under discussion:

Vertical separation and competitive access. This approach to competitive access is in place in the United Kingdom and under a policy mandate elsewhere in the European Union. It requires that the owner and operator of the infrastructure be separate institutional entities from the firms that operate trains. The infrastructure owner is required to grant operating access to various train operators on nondiscriminatory terms. Nowhere, to our knowledge, is the infrastructure owner a private firm.

Operating access. Railroads remain vertically integrated, but competitors must be granted access to operate trains over portions of a railroad's infrastructure where it has been determined to dominate certain traffic types.

Shipment access. Shippers and/or competitive railroads can contract with a railroad for shipments over a portion of the railroad network at regulated rates. In some versions of shipment access proposals, shippers could choose the interchange point they want to use.

Mandated reciprocal switching. Regulatory authorities may order vertically integrated railroads to switch ("set out and pick up") freight cars at on-line industries within switching limits of a terminal that are, nonetheless, waybilled for the account of another railroad; these cars would then be delivered or returned to the competitor railroad at a nearby junction or established interchange point. In the United States, mandatory reciprocal switching may be ordered by the STB if it is in "the public interest." In Canada, interswitching access is available to shippers served by a single railroad at origins or destinations and at prescribed rates to junctions as far away as thirty kilometers.

Construction access. Regulators may encourage or prevent construction by a competitor railroad proposing new rail facilities to reach a single-served shipping or receiving point.[38]

The effects of any competitive access policy depend, obviously, on the details of the proposal. The third type, shipment access, would seem to give rise to fewer coordination problems than the other two, unless shippers were permitted to dictate interchange points. It is important to emphasize, however, that *any* policy of mandated access must be carefully evaluated because, if effective, it necessarily would interfere with the internal organization and revenue adequacy of the incumbent firm and may give rise to new transaction costs.

Also, it is manifestly the case that any of the indicated forms of competitive access amount to re-regulation; once mandated, implementation would be anything but automatic. Every aspect of the access rollout would be contested in some form: hours of operation, dispatching priority, freight tonnage and volumes, maintenance standards, basic rates and access fees, billing and reporting procedures, liability for damages, and on and on.

The Railroad Problem at the End of the Twentieth Century: Insufficient Earnings to Sustain Reinvestment

The persistent railroad problem, never fully resolved in over 100 years of regulatory history, is that, as a declining average cost industry, socially optimal levels of railroad production (volume) occur at pricing levels lower than those needed to recover total costs—meaning that the railroad firm cannot be profitable without charging differential prices to existing customers. In such cases, the railroad cannot simultaneously price at marginal cost (the socially optimal level) *and* recover their total fixed costs necessarily incurred in providing the service.[39]

The corollary is equally important for both economic theory and policy conclusions: If a railroad cannot cover average fixed and variable costs with efficient prices, it runs a deficit and cannot adequately reinvest. It consumes (old) capital to cover the deficiencies in its rates—that is, it works off excess overhead; it converts capital to operating expense as though it were having a continuing going-out-of-business sale. It subsidizes current customers with the dwindling capital reserves of current shareholders while taking from future owners and customers the promise of legitimate economic benefits. The way the reinvestment dilemma facing railroads is most often expressed in North America is that the industry or one of its major constituent firms is not "earning its cost of capital." Figure 9.1 charts these relationships over recent history.

Some observers frame the reinvestment problem slightly differently, as the current and future prospect of insufficient industry capacity, with attending problems of service reliability. In truth, these are only manifestations of the industry's economy of scale and related pricing problems come home to roost in a different part of their life cycle. Capacity shortages are the direct descendents of insufficient investment, traceable entirely to inadequate earnings (and inadequate public investment, if that is your orientation). Within reason, the fault is not unwillingness of

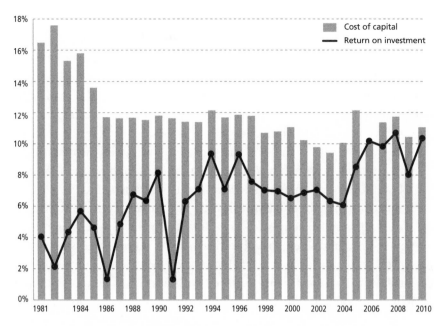

Figure 9.1   Return on Investment Versus Cost of Capital   To reinvest in plant and equipment and expand or renew their enterprises, railroads must "earn their cost of capital." Recent return on investment (ROI) has been trending toward this goal, and that is a key indicator of a genuine railroad renaissance. Funds for railroad reinvestment come largely from internal cash flow but may be supplemented with debt financing or issuance of new shareholder equities, which together establish the enterprise's total weighted cost of capital. *Source:* AAR research using data collected by the STB or predecessor ICC, as reported and interpreted in Carrier's Exhibit No. 7, before the President's Emergency Board No. 243, October 11, 2011. Used with permission.

railroad managers to make capital investments in their firms, but the insufficiency of available funds—due in turn to inadequate total revenues and prospective earnings at current output and price levels.

The railroad problem in the United States today is that there will not be private-sector railroads into the future without permitting price differentiation according to customers' willingness to pay. Any regulatory system that does not permit railroads to use some kind of differential pricing, probably with a markup strategy for customers able and willing to pay more than the marginal cost of their services, will end private-sector railroading as we know it. The choice for public policy comes down to permitting price differentiation or accepting nationalization.

Concluding Thoughts on Regulatory Rate Making

Railroads are multiproduct firms that usually enjoy economies of scale and density. The simple classical model of competitive equilibrium does not apply to most markets served by railroad operations. Railroads normally must charge prices greater than marginal costs if they are to cover their fixed costs. Various compelled access proposals would result in prices that do not cover fixed costs. In the short run, the addition of competition to the market through new access would result in lower rates to shippers, but in the long run, mandated competitive access would likely cause what has been called competitive waste—redundant service resulting in increased operating expenses, lower total revenue due to lower unit prices, reduction in capital stock, loss of traffic through diversions, disincentives to reinvest, gradual obsolescence of technology that cannot remain state of the art because it is not being replaced with advanced technologies and designs incorporated in newer investments, and greater costs to society as a whole.

American Railroads concludes that, while compelled competitive access would help some specific shippers realize lower rail rates in the short run, it is difficult to see what this radical change in US transport and regulatory policy would accomplish for the overall public interest. Are there serious deadweight losses in rail markets today being born by the economy? If so, they are not well documented, and the regulatory authorities charged with determining whether abuses exist have not been one-sidedly sympathetic to either railroads or rate protestors in captive shipper cases.

The Proper Basis for Rate Making

The long-standing legal rule embedded in US utility regulation that rates shall be "reasonable" is not very helpful on its own. Bureaucracies need guidance; they can be good at rationalizations for decisions, but they likely are clueless as to what would be a proper basis guiding a regulatory agency to an approximation of market forces. As this book pointed out in Chapter 2, two traditions have developed to fill the vacuum: demand-based rates and cost-based rates. Regulatory pricing limits, in turn, can be rate ceilings (to prevent exploitation of market power) but sometimes rate floors (to protect competitors or potential market entrants from being undercut with short-term predatory prices that will not be sustained over the long run).[40]

Demand-based rates derive from the principle that markets ultimately fix rate limits—in that no goods will change hands unless they are demanded at prevailing prices. If the supply of goods is in any way limited (i.e., if they are scarce) prices rise until consumers are no longer willing to pay more for the enjoyment of them. Competitors enter markets to supply goods at prices they believe will be profitable. Competitors need not use identical technology and production methods; as long as their products supply the demands of the market, they effectively contribute to limiting prices.

Demand-based rate making seems to be trying to do just what the doctor ordered: serve as a proxy for the market. The catch is that demand-based rates (charging what the traffic will bear),[41] may appear to be too pro-business to politicians bent on reining in powerful interests; similarly, with respect to the pricing of public goods or services, conservatives may see demand-rationing user charges as an excuse to collect more "taxes" that could support additional government spending. This is the bind that the current US political gridlock has created for itself, and it will not be overcome soon or easily.

Cost-based rates sound good in theory, but they have not proven to be very useful in establishing regulatory ceilings for railroad rates. While political authorities long favored cost-based rate making and distrusted market limits as too permissive, a cost-based rate is no more scientifically measured nor less arbitrarily determined than a demand-based rate set "by what the traffic will bear." Moreover, railroads are invariably oligopolies facing a wide range of competitive circumstances, so even the homey rule "what the traffic will bear" leads to an indeterminate result. US regulatory experience yields the irony that the apparently simple and theoretically sound idea of cost-based rate making typically foundered in implementation, while demand-based rates—seemingly fraught with theoretical complexity and political anathema—have become the more practical alternative.

The variety of means by which, historically, the regulatory rate-making apparatus might be used to determine lawful rates serves to underscore our thesis, namely, that there never was a "correct" way to determine rates under railroad regulation. Over 100 years of theorizing, lawmaking, case adjudication, litigating, arbitration, and statistical analysis have not solved what Ann Friedlaender called *The Dilemma of Freight Regulation* because there was no theoretically correct way to accomplish the task other than to rely steadfastly on markets and accept any resulting imperfections in pricing. Richard Levin was correct: "[E]conomics has no unified theory of oligopoly." That means regulation has no incontrovertible method for setting rates for specific rail movements.

Concluding Thoughts on Railroad Regulation

There are two quite different ways to think about the great divide between advocates of tighter regulation and those who support *laissez-faire* in US policy toward railroads: The first considers the debate as centered on different political preferences; the second realizes it is a struggle between economic interests. When regulation/deregulation is a broad political discussion, the debate usually comes down to this:

- One side argues the public interest of promoting railroads to win extra-market benefits of public mobility, energy-efficient transport, and mitigation of highway congestion, while
- The other side takes the case for minimal government intervention.

In another formulation of the debate over regulatory intervention, the divide between proponents of regulation and voices against government intervention exists not because of political philosophy but because of economic interests. The regulators want government intervention to counteract railroad monopoly market power and perhaps to require their sharing rights-of-way with passenger services. They may care hardly at all about railroad company profitability. The deregulators want railroads to be able to charge what the market will bear in order to be profitable overall and to reinvest in capacity for future service (see Figure 9.2); they suppose that shippers (whether captive to railroads or not) participate in the market at issue for all sorts of reasons making it a logical production location— relatively low input costs (labor, public utilities, inbound materials) and proximity to markets. Railroads ordinarily would not price their services in a manner jeopardizing their customers' livelihood.

Similarly, any plan to force new market entry (compelled competitive access) as a policy alternative to price differentiation (simulating the market's interplay of supply and demand to reach equilibrium output and rates) will have a bad result—railroads will not be able to be profitable and reinvest in capacity to handle future business, and they will exist only with large government subsidies.[42] This is why it is self-defeating for rail customers, as a group, to urge what they call open access and to rail against

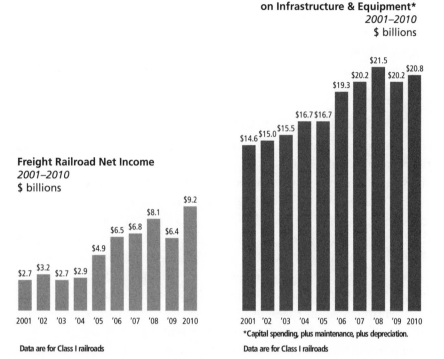

Freight Railroad Spending on Infrastructure & Equipment*
2001–2010
$ billions

Freight Railroad Net Income
2001–2010
$ billions

*Capital spending, plus maintenance, plus depreciation.

Data are for Class I railroads

Data are for Class I railroads

Figure 9.2   It Takes Earnings to Enable Reinvestment Spending   Rising net income for US freight railroads has supported historic levels of private investment in the new millennium. Remarkably, the industry continued high levels of reinvestment despite a sharp falloff of traffic during the Great Recession of 2007 to 2009. *Source:* Data courtesy of the AAR.

price differentiation. Indeed, average prices tending to low marginal cost levels exacerbate any existing supply shortages. Better for all but the truly marginal (and perhaps the most captive) customers to allow average prices to rise to a level that discourages low-value purchases consuming scarce capacity in peak periods.[43]

The authors of this book remain of the opinion that, in matters of private enterprise business negotiations, he or she who regulates least regulates best. Public utilities, chemical manufacturers, port operators, and other railroad users have reasons for locating generating stations, major production plants, or export/import facilities where they do; sizing thesefacilities to the scale they do; choosing which fuels to generate their power; managing their relationships with customers, unions, and utility rate regulators; fulfilling their obligations to appropriate tax, safety, and environmental authorities; satisfying investors; and more. They are large businesses with monopsony power at least equivalent to any monopoly power their serving railroads can exercise. Little do they need the protection of artificial, legalistic, cumbersome, expensive, error-prone, and uncertain regulation. Here we have a classic case of Galbraithian bilateral oligopoly. Let the big boys fight it out!

Final Thoughts on Regulation and Deregulation

There are several summary conclusions to be drawn. First, if economic theory cannot establish the "correct" rate, even with full information, then a bureaucratic administrative process or a quasi-courtroom adversary proceeding will not either. Second, because an economically efficient rate is impossible to find, all that can be expected is a "fair and reasonable" rate, which even regulatory rules would consider lawful. Third, regulatory process (administrative cost) could easily exceed any possible benefits from moving closer to the elusive efficient rate. Fourth, if any consumer surplus were extracted by the producer (converted into producers' surplus) it would be comforting to know that these resources likely will be used to increase producer capacity and improve service to consumers.

In this sense, Levin's conclusion that the $1 billion in deadweight losses from suboptimal pricing observed in the 1970s "was a small price to pay for keeping railroads viable in the private sector" seems prescient. We applaud his implicit assumption that private-sector ownership and operation of railroads are superior to takeover by the state (nationalization). This fourth overall conclusion prompts further discussion of the public policy setting in which railroads find themselves today—a task held for the final chapter of this book.

10

HOW RAILROADS GOT THEIR FINAL
SIZES AND SHAPES

Prior to the onset of deregulation, rail mergers typically
involved unions of systems having a great deal of parallel
trackage. Under such circumstances, hearings at the Interstate
Commerce Commission (ICC) typically focused on the traditional welfare trade-off that mergers could provide between
the cost efficiencies occasioned by consolidation and economies of scale on the one hand, and the potential for noncompetitive pricing on the other.

    In contrast, proposed mergers in the post-Staggers era have
principally been end-to-end unions, in which the proponents
have cited significant economies through the elimination of
freight transfer, the implementation of joint marketing agreements, the consolidation of tracking and maintenance systems, increased run-through operations and more efficient car
utilization.

            —BERNDT, FRIEDLAENDER, SHAW-ER
           WANG CHIANG, and VELLTURO (1993)

This chapter of *American Railroads* focuses on the nature and consequences of the wave of large railroad consolidations, often called
megamergers, initiated and approved in the last quarter of the twentieth
century.[1]

    The first part of the chapter describes the megamergers proposed in the
initial deregulatory period, from just before passage of the Staggers Rail
Act[2] until 1995. The second part of the chapter continues the narrative
with an analysis of four transactions that rounded out the twentieth century and completed the American railroad industry structure as we know
it today.

    This last group of mergers, which we call the fin-de-siècle or the final
four mergers, involved the western giants: Santa Fe, Burlington Northern,

Southern Pacific, and Union Pacific. This section also covers the division of Conrail between Norfolk Southern and CSX at the very end of the century because, like mergers, these realignments required formal proceedings before the Surface Transportation Board (STB), major financial commitments, substantial changes in operations, and corporate rebranding.

Earlier chapters of the book described how government policy under the Sherman Antitrust Act of 1890 addressed railroad consolidations after the fact and noted that federal policy did not institute prior review/approval of rail mergers until passage of the Transportation Act of 1920. The criteria for the ICC's approval or denial of a merger application were revised twenty years later in the Transportation Act of 1940. That legislation established the fundamental test that a merger must be in the public interest, and required such determinations to rest on consideration of four factors:

(1) the effect of the proposed transaction on the adequacy of transportation to the public;
(2) the effect on the public interest of including, or failing to include, other rail carriers in the area involved in the proposed transaction;
(3) the total fixed charges that result from the proposed transaction; and
(4) the impact on railroad employees affected by the proposed transaction.

Chapter 6 noted, however, that in applying the 1940 act's merger standards during the midcentury merger wave, the Interstate Commerce Commission (ICC) only infrequently approved end-to-end mergers; it seemed to favor protection of competitors at the expense of competition. This chapter of *American Railroads* tells a much different history for the remainder of the twentieth century.

In part the pattern of railroad merger types changed because the Staggers Rail Act of 1980 imposed a fifth condition for the ICC to consider in evaluating mergers: whether the proposed transaction would have an adverse effect on competition among rail carriers in the affected region. Surprisingly, this fifth criterion was the first "explicit directive to the ICC emphasizing the need to preserve competition when considering a major rail merger."[3] As a result, the ICC came to favor end-to-end over parallel mergers almost completely and began to compel merger proponents to grant trackage rights to other railroads to mitigate significant anticompetitive effects.

The law regulating mergers had caught up with commonsense notions about what regulatory oversight of mergers should be. It is amazing, perhaps miraculous, that the railroads and their regulator could shift emphasis from consolidation policies almost totally focused on achieving cost savings in one era (1955–1976) to an entirely different paradigm focused on end-to-end penetration into new markets in a subsequent period (1980–2000). This simple provision of the Staggers Rail Act (together with the poor performance of the Penn Central merger, of course), was instrumental in causing that sea change in ICC/STB policy.

It would be perfectly reasonable to consider the fundamental motivation for the group of large mergers in the period 1976–1982 as simply a resumption of the post–World War II merger wave after a Penn Central–induced hiatus, but already these mergers were of a different kind. Railroad managers had taken note of the operating disaster that was Penn Central; consequently, in this period railroads were more comfortable using consolidations to extend their market reach than to grasp at cost savings—which Penn Central had proven to be elusive.[4] By the late 1970s, even before the ICC's merger rules were changed in the Staggers Rail Act, large railroads began staking out their merger futures in the new manner of end-to-end combinations.[5]

The post–Staggers Rail Act wave of very large rail combinations both accompanied and facilitated fundamental shifts in the demand for freight transport. The economic forces controlling and characterizing these changes showed themselves in several ways, making mergers more likely to be successful: in implementation of the Clean Air Acts of 1970 and 1990, which stimulated great demand for low-sulfur coal, and with it rail transport of Powder River Basin coal to power plants as far away as Georgia; in wholesale shifts in the composition and location of domestic manufacturing; and in a boom in world trade. The corporate strategies of railroads after 1980—both their responses to Staggers Rail Act deregulation and the proposals put forward in the associated rail merger movement—turned on a dime. The post-Staggers railroad mergers were transformative but, at the same time, productive of more industry cohesion than any previous merger movement in the industry's history

Still, as pointed out by Ernst Berndt, Nan Friedlaender, and their colleagues, the story of railroad economic performance in the period after the Staggers Rail Act of 1980 is nine parts deregulation and one part merger consequences.[6] This simply means that cost savings from the post–Penn

Central combinations were not large relative to total revenues or expenses, while the impacts from deregulation of rates and services were on their way to becoming indisputably and overwhelmingly significant.

The Staggers Rail Act of 1980, and the spirit of Staggers, changed everything. Railroad managers felt they could act boldly, anticipating that their actions would not be overturned by nonsensical regulatory rulings. Operating executives were not to be so easily hamstrung by their own lawyers telling them what regulators would not allow. The lawyers had enjoyed their long venture into policy making, but now they had to respond to CEOs wanting to know how to get things done, not why they could not do them.

Taking advantage of the new commercial freedoms—as well as the larger firm size and market reach afforded by the post-Staggers mergers— American railroads changed many aspects of their operations and swiftly adapted to new market realities. Railroads learned to use unit train economies to lengthen interregional hauls of grain, coal, and intermodal containers. While preservationists could lament that trains were leaving small towns (at least in regard to passenger service and local branch-line operations), in a larger sense the new post-Staggers railroads were becoming a more important instrument of the national economy.

The Post-Staggers Mega-Mergers

Clearly the Penn Central fiasco and the subsequent Northeast railroad crisis had a chilling effect on railroad mergers for most of the 1970s. As Chapter 6 showed, not only were the purported benefits of the midcentury mergers not realized, they were swamped in red ink.[7] The ICC could not bask in the accomplishments of its largest decision, nor cite Penn Central as a useful precedent, and it was not even given the job of cleaning up the mess left by Penn Central. That went to the US Railway Association (USRA), which presided over planning for the establishment of Conrail in 1976 (see Chapter 7). Subsequently, railroads in the revitalized Northeast had to figure out how they would interchange traffic with Big Conrail in place of its erstwhile constituents—many of whose gateways had been closed or downgraded (Chapter 8).

More broadly, during the 1970s, most or all of the major railroads were trying to figure out where their futures lay and how they could best realize their preferred strategic alignments within the merger movement. This first section of Chapter 10 covers ten transactions from 1979 to 1995.

Although the Staggers Rail Act was not signed until after the first merger was approved, all the transactions fit the spirit of Staggers, as they were generally procompetitive—except the one proposal denied by the ICC.

Southern Pacific–Cotton Belt Purchase of Rock Island's Tucumcari Line (1979)

For nearly a century, Southern Pacific (SP) had needed a less circuitous line from California to St. Louis and eastern connections. To serve these routes, SP was required to rely on its Sunset Route (Los Angeles–El Paso–Houston–New Orleans) to reach the Southeast, and its St. Louis southwestern (Cotton Belt) connections from Texas to St. Louis. Then, in the mid-1970s, Southern Pacific sought to acquire the Tucumcari–Golden State Route out of the bankruptcy reorganization of the famous old Chicago, Rock Island & Pacific (CRI&P or Rock Island).[8]

The Golden State route represented a saving of about 380 miles (23 percent) for Southern Pacific compared with its conventional route from El Paso to East St. Louis, Illinois, via Corsicana, Texas.[9] The SP acquisition of the Tucumcari Line had been at least tacitly agreed between SP and UP earlier as part of the Rock Island merger proposal (1962–1974)[10] and was a logical part of the much-needed rationalization of most Granger railroads (in that long-term homes needed to be found for important lines at risk).[11] Nonetheless, this was an end-to-end transaction—and a realignment of properties to enhance marketing strategies—more than a drive for economies of density and cost reduction.

Complicating the Tucumcari Line purchase was the fact that Rock Island's trustee in bankruptcy, William Gibbons, had made many enemies during the Midwest restructuring process. Eventually, Southern Pacific did reach agreement with the trustee on a purchase price of $57 million.

Because the transaction would destabilize the competitive status quo, it stirred up enormous opposition from incumbent railroads in the region—especially Missouri Pacific (MP or MoPac), and Santa Fe (AT&SF)—plus labor representatives. According to Richard Saunders, Santa Fe "whined" that the market had spoken—the Golden State was a route that the market had weeded out. SP's angry response was that the traffic could be won back once Rock Island's management difficulties were put behind it; SP's CEO Ben Biaggini discounted Santa Fe's complaint by saying outright that it had benefitted from an undeserved windfall—that being Rock Island's demise.[12]

The Golden State Route, and its connection from Kansas City to St. Louis, was in deplorable condition. The Rock Island's Kansas City—St. Louis line, via Eldon, Missouri, had been virtually "abandoned in place" from Metropolitan St. Louis to Lee's Summit outside Kansas City. Contemplating resurrection of the line at one point, observers noted suburban encroachment and overgrown vegetation obstructing the right of way—"trees growing between the rails."

An ICC grant of rights over MP between Kansas City and St. Louis saved SP the cost of that upgrade, and SP was able to draw on Federal Railroad Administration (FRA) funding for additional rehabilitation of the Tucumcari route. These improvements made possible the rerouting of additional traffic formerly moving via the Cotton Belt. Also, SP was able to attract Chicago gateway traffic with Milwaukee and BN over Kansas City.[13] The Tucumcari Line acquisition saw further service after the UP + SP merger (1996), when Union Pacific began to build its Chicago–Los Angeles intermodal service strategy around the Golden State routing, sinking tens of millions of dollars into upgraded signaling, longer sidings, and welded rail for the line.

Burlington Northern + Frisco (1980)

In 1970, the Burlington Northern Railway had gained a clear strategic first-mover advantage over its large western rivals by reconsolidating the James J. Hill Northern Lines that Teddy Roosevelt and the US Supreme Court had foiled in 1904.[14] As discussed earlier in *American Railroads* the Burlington Northern merger made that railroad by far the largest in the United States but in so doing foreclosed other options that might have proved useful in rationalizing western rail systems in the 1970s and 1980s.

During the postwar period, the Granger Roads—Rock Island, Chicago & North Western (C&NW);[15] Milwaukee Road, Soo, Missouri-Kansas-Texas (M-K-T or Katy); and parts of the Illinois Central—and their constituents—all faced various degrees of business jeopardy. The exception was Chicago, Burlington & Quincy (CB&Q). Although Burlington did not escape all of the negative effects (it had plenty of its own redundant route-mileage), CB&Q was able to avoid the worst of the maladies suffered by the other Granger roads—deferred maintenance and murderous pricing competition. CB&Q benefited in particular by handling overhead traffic to the Pacific Northwest and western Canada in conjunction with

Great Northern and Northern Pacific, primarily via the Twin Cities and Laurel, Montana (near Billings). CB&Q also provided service to Powder River Basin deposits of low-sulfur, sub-bituminous utility coal in Wyoming and Montana, primarily after the mid 1970s (See Map 10.6).

Burlington Northern's head start in network building was extended by acquiring the St. Louis–San Francisco Railroad (Frisco or SL-SF)[16]—in the Staggers enactment year of 1980. Earlier, the Frisco had expressed interest in acquiring the Chicago & Eastern Illinois to extend its territory beyond St. Louis. Also, one imagines both Southern Railway (Sou) and Missouri Pacific kept a close eye on the regional carrier, albeit from quite different perspectives and with different merger motives. (To Sou, Frisco would extend market reach, while for MP, it was a formidable competitor on traffic over Memphis to and from the West). Frisco was put at considerable risk by deregulation because of its substantial bridge traffic and because it did not serve the Texas-Louisiana Gulf Coast. Frisco was something of a smaller but better-maintained version of the Rock Island, which went "everywhere but nowhere," and was bound to be absorbed sooner or later.

Burlington Northern's interest in Frisco may have had its genesis in the fact that CEO Louis Menk had been president of the Frisco and that he and his successor at SL-SF and BN, Richard C. Grayson, were good friends. (It was often the case that personal relationships facilitated mergers of railroads.)

BN + Frisco was a classic end-to-end merger: Frisco had few routes overlapping with the routes included in Northern Lines, but it could boast connections from CB&Q interchange points at Kansas City and St. Louis deep into the Southeast (to Pensacola, Florida, and Mobile via Memphis and Birmingham), and into the Southwest (to Dallas/Fort Worth). The ICC had little difficulty arriving at a majority opinion favoring the applicants and rejecting most appeals for conditions or indemnification.[17]

Notably, chairman Darius Gaskins appended additional comments to the majority opinion, observing that the ruling statute required consideration of "the effect on the public interest of including, or failing to include other rail carriers in the area involved in the proposed transaction." Gaskins pointed out that the record in the case was replete with studies regarding the effect on other carriers, but not "the effect on the public interest" of possible inclusions, which was the statutory test.[18] This was the point USRA had made in its preliminary system plan (PSP), namely, that the impact on competition mattered a lot more to society than the impact on competitors. End-to-end mergers might upset the status quo, but parallel mergers unambiguously reduce rail-rail competition—and that could be harmful to the public interest. Chair Gaskins's comments were a notification to his colleagues and future petitioners that a new sheriff was in town, and merger policies would change. At last, public policy toward rail mergers was becoming both clearer and more rational economically.

Frisco routes turned out to be instrumental to Burlington Northern—and to successor BNSF Railway—in subsequent years.[19] Frisco had enabled first BN and later BNSF to penetrate the Southeast, to Birmingham. From there, BN could reach Atlanta markets with over-the-road (piggyback) intermodal service, or hold BN's long haul on trains interchanged to the Southern (later Norfolk Southern) or Seaboard Coast Line (later CSX).

These merger impacts were not earth shattering either for proponents or competitors, but they clearly had both strategic and tactical benefits for BN. Also, it was a game changer in that (like the Tucumcari Line sale) it marked a shift in ICC merger policy. It gave Burlington Northern a set of top managers who guided the firm through the decade of the 1980s. Also, Frisco's plant was in relatively good shape, so it provided BN a lot of incremental ton-miles of service. Finally, BN + Frisco solidified BN's reputation as a strategic first mover.

Grand Trunk Western Acquisition of Detroit, Toledo & Ironton (1980)
Detroit, Toledo & Ironton (DT&I, or Ironton) (see Map 10.1) was a specialized railroad serving its namesake cities in Michigan and Ohio. It was purchased by Henry Ford mainly to supply his River Rouge integrated auto manufacturing plant with coal and coke for steelmaking. Ford later sold his DT&I ownership to Pennsylvania Railroad interests. Historically, the DT&I was marginally successful, perhaps more as a competitive benchmark for other railroads seeking to serve Ford Motor Company than for its own sake. In 1965, the Ironton road completed its acquisition of an end-to-end merger partner in Michigan, the Ann Arbor Railroad, which gave DT&I connections to Toledo and (via car ferry service across Lake Michigan from Frankfort, Michigan) to Manitowoc and Menominee, Wisconsin. As reported in Chapter 6, the results of the merger were unexceptional.

In the late 1970s, DT&I appeared to be headed for inclusion in a larger consolidated system. Chessie System, Norfolk & Western, and Conrail all coveted the line, but once again, an end-to-end arrangement carried the

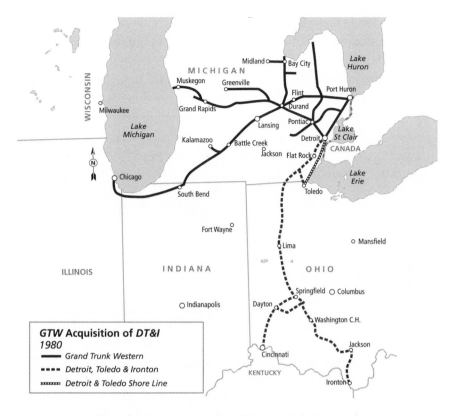

Map 10.1   Grand Trunk Western Acquisition of Detroit, Toledo & Ironton
(1980).   Passage of the Staggers Rail Act of 1980 reenergized the wave of railroad mergers that
had been interrupted by the Penn Central fiasco. Starting with ICC approval of the Grand Trunk
Western's acquisition of Detroit, Toledo & Ironton, the post-Staggers combinations were generally
of an end-to-end description, in contrast to the previous period's parallel mergers. ICC chose a
small US subsidiary of Canadian National over a joint proposal by N&W and Chessie System to
control Henry Ford's old DT&I supply line. *Source: Trains Magazine*, June 1978, p. 15.

day. Canadian National subsidiary Grand Truck Western filed merger
applications with the ICC, and quite unexpectedly won approval over the
inconsistent joint application filed by N&W and Chessie.[20]

At the time it was unclear how GTW would integrate DT&I, and Conrail's financial position was still quite shaky. To its credit, the ICC took the
risk of going with CN/GTW. This marked a major shift in ICC merger
policy. The idea of joint ownership and operation by Chessie and N&W
was actually quite innovative and might have worked well as a second best
solution; it likely would have diminished competition somewhat in the

near term and might have been regarded as the coward's way out of a tough decision. In any event, the ICC still was not ready for the idea of a joint operation.

GTW began abandoning and spinning off portions of DT&I in the 1980s. By 1997 it had sold most of its lines to the Indiana & Ohio Railway.[21]

Box 10.1   The "DT&I Conditions" Imposed by the ICC (1950–1980)

DT&I had stumbled into fifteen minutes of fame (or rather three decades of infamy) by having its name joined to the ICC's conventional policy of attaching traffic flow protective conditions to merger approvals. Having the same sort of economic effect as a job protection order, the so-called DT&I conditions sought to protect traditional patterns of traffic flow against changes initiated by the approved merger—in the process undermining the success of the very transaction it approved. To merging railroads and outside observers, this made no economic sense, but it was supported by railroads opposing the proposed transaction, shippers, labor, and adversely affected local interests.

DT&I conditions were routinely added to merger approvals from 1950 (their genesis in the ICC control case of that year consolidating DT&I) until they were finally relaxed by the ICC under the chairmanship of Darius Gaskins near the time of passage of the Staggers Rail Act in 1980. According to Gaskins, "When the conditions were first proposed to me in connection with a rail merger in a meeting with the ICC staff, I asked what their purpose was and was told that stable traffic patterns represented 'competition' and that 'we had always done it that way.' When the new Commission majority renounced the DT&I conditions, the railroads all had to amend their pending merger applications to take advantage of the new competitive alternatives, such as increasing their market share when they had the most efficient route."[1]

There could not be a sharper distinction between passive and active models of rail-rail competition: (1) on the one hand, passive stability and traditionally patterned (inside-the-box) traffic flows, and (2) on the other hand, dynamic rivalry using pricing and comparative advantage to compete (outside-the-box) for market reach and share. Another of the innumerable ironies of twentieth-century railways and government policy toward them is that the thirty-year reign of the ICC's DT&I conditions was terminated by the GTW-DT&I merger decision.

1. Darius W. Gaskins, Jr., "Regulation of Freight Railroads in the Modern Era: 1970–2010," *Review of Network Economics*, Vol. 7, Issue 4 (December, 2008), pp. 562–563.

Formation of CSX from Chessie System and Seaboard Coast Line (1980)
The fascination with transcontinental mergers had already begun, however, and as BN and Frisco were applying to the ICC to merge, Southern Pacific began acquiring shares of Seaboard Coast Line, including Louisville & Nashville—together known as the Family Lines. By the time SCL backed out of a potential transcontinental alliance in 1978, SP's ownership had reached 4.8 percent ownership of the Family Lines.[22] SP kept buying, however, its holdings reaching nearly 10 percent—until SP was restrained against further share purchases by an ICC temporary order. Chessie System also bought SCL stock, and it eventually offered to exchange Chessie shares for SP's stake in Family Lines. In January 1979, SP blasted the ICC for preventing its purchase of SCL while acquiescing in the Chessie transactions. For reasons that were never made public, SP reversed itself later that month and cast its 1.5 million shares in favor of the Chessie + Family Lines combination—the foundation of CSX (see Map 10.2).[23] The rather slow integration of the predecessor roads into Chessie System (not complete until 1987) allowed key western competitor N&W + Nickel Plate + Wabash—as well as future partners Atlantic Coast Line (ACL) + Louisville & Nashville (L&N and Seaboard Air Line (SAL)—to keep pace.

The CSX mergers raised only moderate opposition.[24] L&N had been the most aggressive in expanding its service network, adding two routes to Chicago by acquiring both the eastern half of the Chicago & Eastern Illinois (C&EI) and the Monon (which did prompt the ICC to require L&N to give Milwaukee Road replacement trackage rights from Bedford, Indiana, into Louisville). The managers of the fledgling CSX combination then rounded out their complex network by internalizing control of the Richmond, Fredericksburg & Potomac (RF&P), connecting those Virginia cities and Washington, DC, in 1991. CSX also gained full control of the Clinchfield at the time of the CSX union in 1982. Clinchfield was an important carrier of trans-Appalachian coal that had been leased since 1924 by Atlantic Coast Line (ACL) and L&N.

CSX was an underperforming railroad for many years. The L&N infrastructure was substandard, suffering some thirty-nine hazardous materials (hazmat) derailments in the 1970s, including two major ones resulting in evacuations (at Waverly, Tennessee, and Crestview, Florida); during cleanup of the Waverly derailment, a tank car breached, caught fire, and blevied (exploded), resulting in thirteen casualties and nearly wiping out the town.

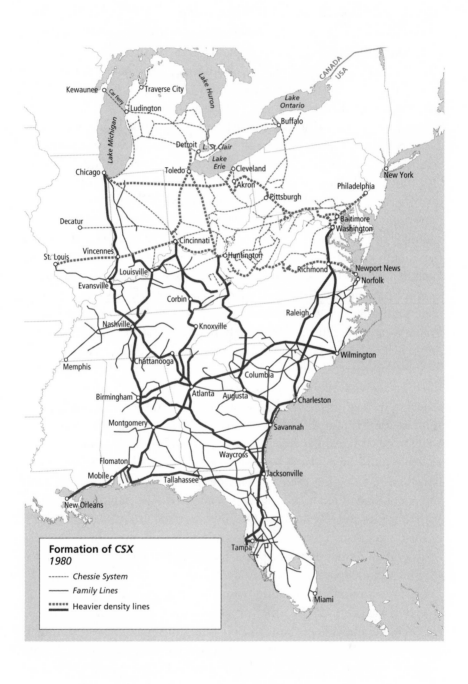

Kewaunee
Traverse City
Ludington
Car Ferry
Lake Huron
Lake Ontario
Buffalo
Detroit
L. St. Clair
Lake Erie
Cleveland
Chicago
Toledo
Akron
Pittsburgh
Philadelphia
New York
Lake Michigan
Decatur
Baltimore
Washington
St. Louis
Vincennes
Cincinnati
Huntington
Newport News
Norfolk
Louisville
Richmond
Evansville
Corbin
Raleigh
Nashville
Knoxville
Memphis
Chattanooga
Wilmington
Columbia
Birmingham
Atlanta
Augusta
Charleston
Montgomery
Savannah
Flomaton
Waycross
Mobile
Tallahassee
Jacksonville
New Orleans
Tampa
Miami
CANADA
USA

Formation of *CSX*
1980

- - - - - *Chessie System*
——— *Family Lines*
▬▬▬▬ Heavier density lines

Map 10.2 Formation of CSX (1980).   Combination of a half dozen historic railroads (some previously affiliated) into CSX formed the first of the new post-Staggers megamergers. These combinations generally added longer hauls, market "reach" into new territories, and economies of density or asset utilization. CSX presumably stands for the multiplier effects of the combination of Chessie System and the Seaboard Coast Line systems, and the crossing of constituents' main routes.

Chessie had its modern beginnings with combination of the Baltimore & Ohio (B&O) and Chesapeake & Ohio (C&O) Railroads (1962) during the midcentury merger wave. B&O's corporate name had endured since 1827; B&O gained control of Western Maryland (WM) in 1967, formally merging WM into its railroad in 1967. That same year, the ICC approved the merger of ACL/L&N and Seaboard into the Seaboard Coast Line (SCL), which soon began using the marketing moniker Family Lines.

This map (and the similar Map 10.3 for NS) shows the more important lines in bold or wide halftone, but doing so requires subjectivity. The authors have consulted with experts and studied Harry Ladd's *US Railroad Traffic Atlas*[2] to estimate which lines were more important at the time of the merger, but traffic patterns could shift or lines might be upgraded or abandoned in the intervening years. There should be no implication that the distinction between heavy and light lines is exactly comparable between CSX and NS. *Source: Trains Magazine*, February 1979, p. 3. Readers wishing to see similar merger maps in full color are referred to *Trains Magazine*, *Railroad Maps: The Best from the Pages of Trains Magazine Extra 2013* (Milwaukee, WI: Kalmbach Publishing Co., 2013). See also Harry Ladd, *US Railroad Traffic Atlas* (Orange, CA: Ladd Publications, 1995).

The FRA issued emergency orders against L&N, then began rule making to require modification of the design and operation of hazmat tank cars—the beginning of FRA's thirty-year involvement in tank car design improvements. These were conducted jointly with the railroad industry, tank car manufacturers, and chemical shippers.

Still, CSX was lucky in several respects, particularly at the ICC, where its 1982 merger was approved without major conditions. Apparently, the Gaskins dictum in DT&I had become precedent. The story is told that when Southern went to the commission to ask for compensating conditions to mitigate the impact of CSX, its officials were flatly refused and were told to "go get your own merger."[25] The rejected applications for conditions and the ICC's verbal injunction to Southern might have had something to do with the next of the post-Staggers merger proposals—joining of the N&W and Southern Railway.

Formation of Norfolk Southern (1982)

Mergers often made strange bedfellows. Of today's US final four railroads (CSX, NS, BNSF, and UP) perhaps none had fewer historical markers or anticipated synergies than NS (see Map 10.3). Richard Saunders is correct in observing himself and quoting Don Phillips as follows:

> If the creation of CSX had not been so frightening to the leadership of both the Southern and the N&W, it is not a given that they would have merged [into NS]. Both were profitable and successful railroads in peak physical condition, well managed and proud—some thought a little too proud to make good merger partners. "Many of us wondered how two such stubborn, Prussian-like outfits could carry off a merger of equals," wrote Don Phillips.[26]

Southern and Norfolk & Western shared operation of passenger trains over Bristol, Virginia / Tennessee, but otherwise were not substantial interchange partners.[27] Southern, with its controlled line Central of Georgia (CoG), was predominantly a merchandise carrier serving Mississippi River points, the deep South, and the Southeast. By contrast, Norfolk & Western (and its merger partner of 1959, the Virginian (see Chapter 6), were heavily involved in hauling coal and coke between Central Appalachia and the deep water port at Norfolk.

Culturally, Southern and N&W were also quite different. Southern "Gives a Green Light to Innovation" its slogan proclaimed, and for years

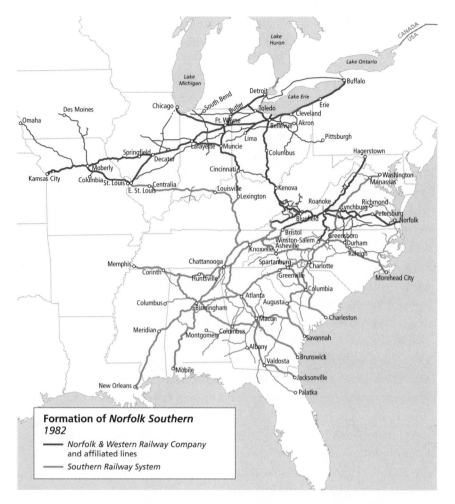

Map 10.3   Formation of Norfolk Southern (1982).   Union of prosperous Norfolk & Western and progressive Southern Railway was at least in part a competitive response to CSX. Southern was predominantly a merchandise carrier serving the Southeast. By contrast, Norfolk & Western (and its merger partner of 1959, the Virginian) were heavy haulers of coal from Central Appalachia to tidewater at Norfolk. N&W added traffic in steel, automotive, and other manufactures, as well as service to western gateways with the acquisition of Nickel Plate and Wabash in 1964. *Source: Trains Magazine,* June 1979, p. 8.

Southern was the industry leader in both technical research and development (R&D) and marketing strategies, while its headquarters location in Washington, DC, made Southern among the most savvy of railroads with respect to government policy and labor relations. Sharing Confederate roots with N&W, Southern always managed to attract the highest-caliber executives, while N&W, under Stuart Saunders and later John Fishwick, seemed parochial, hidebound, shortsighted.

Despite these contrasts, Southern and N&W managers saw the potential of an interregional merger. The two carriers could develop longer hauls (and less circuitous interchange points) between the South and Conrail in the Northeast by integrating services along N&W's route through the Shenandoah Valley to Hagerstown, Maryland, via Roanoke, as well as Southern's excellent Crescent line to Potomac Yard in Alexandria, Virginia. Southern's strong route to Cincinnati (affectionately called the Rathole because of its many tunnels) could funnel traffic over N&W's line to Kenova, West Virginia, and north to Columbus and beyond via its newly acquired Sandusky Line to Lake Erie and Toledo, where the N&W's Nickel Plate (NKP) and Wabash lines extended on to Detroit, Chicago, and Kansas City. Combined NS traffic from the Southeast or Hampton Roads could also use the route from Cincinnati to Chicago and the Midwest via New Castle and Muncie, Indiana, a portion of which N&W obtained in USRA's Final System Plan (FSP) in 1975.[28]

Norfolk & Western filed its application to the ICC to consolidate operations with Southern in a new holding company given the name of an older regional railroad called Norfolk Southern, in December 1980. The application argued that the recent consolidation of Chessie System and Family Lines railroads into CSX had created a 27,500-mile system throughout the same territory served by N&W and Southern, and establishment of single system holding competitive parity with CSX was in the public interest.[29] The applicants projected annual savings of $95 million after the third year from route rationalizations. These would generate annual savings of nearly 1.5 billion ton-miles, with fuel savings of 5 million gallons.[30] Presumably, there would also be traffic generation benefits. The ICC approved the NS consolidation in June, 1982.

The Tri-Pac Merger, UP + MP + WP

Union Pacific Railroad, pivotal historically, had continued to prosper after E. H. Harriman's conflict with the Teddy Roosevelt and Taft administrations finally ended in 1913. UP always had solid geographic coverage west of Omaha and Kansas City, the best central overland route, and a balanced distribution of commodities. UP hauled coal and soda ash from Wyoming, forest products from the Pacific Northwest, and grain gathered from originations in the Midwest—which it hauled to export terminals in the Pacific Northwest (PNW) or the ports of Los Angeles/Long Beach. UP handled food from California orchards and gardens; Idaho and Washington "spud and onion" producers; and midwestern millers, chillers, and distillers. Union Pacific had substantial shares of domestic and import automotive business from on-line points and interline connections.

As a strong traffic originator, UP had good traffic connections with interline partners, and it benefitted historically from favorable divisions of revenues with them. Yet Union Pacific's franchise was missing several key assets: its own entry to the Chicago and St. Louis gateways, good connections with growing Southeast markets over Memphis, petrochemical originations in Texas and Louisiana, Gulf port outlets at New Orleans and Houston/Galveston, and service to the Bay Area and Northern California. With these obvious gaps in its coverage, UP was highly dependent on "bridge" and interchange traffic. Union Pacific's strong originations and divisions were enviable, but UP was not always happy within its confines. E. H. Harriman had well understood these dynamics in the first decade of the twentieth century, and had tried his best to overcome their effects.

Missouri Pacific (MP), like UP, had a storied past. Its predecessor, the Pacific Railroad of Missouri, was the first to operate a train west of the Mississippi River, in St. Louis in 1852. In 1853, another predecessor, the Iron Mountain, laid track with an ambitious plan to serve Arkansas, Louisiana, Texas, Mexico, and California. After the Civil War ended in 1865, the Pacific Railroad completed its line linking St. Louis and Kansas City. Famous (or infamous) Wall Street financier Jay Gould bought control of Missouri Pacific in 1879 and added five other roads in 1880.

Serendipitously, every one of the aforementioned gaps in UP's coverage was filled in the Tri-Pac consolidation—Union Pacific + Missouri Pacific + Western Pacific (see Map 10.4).[31] Wags called it the "Mop-UP" merger, but this was more envy than grounds for antitrust challenge because there was very little overlap in the three systems—it was almost entirely an end-to-end merger. The only network connecting points were at Salt Lake City (UP with WP); and Denver, Salina (Kansas), Kansas City, Lincoln, and Omaha (on the UP and MP). As to significant competitive flows, only Kansas City–Denver qualified, and both the Burlington Northern and the Santa Fe (AT&SF)—even Rock Island minimally until the late 1970s—also served this relatively short and light-traffic corridor. UP + MP + WP

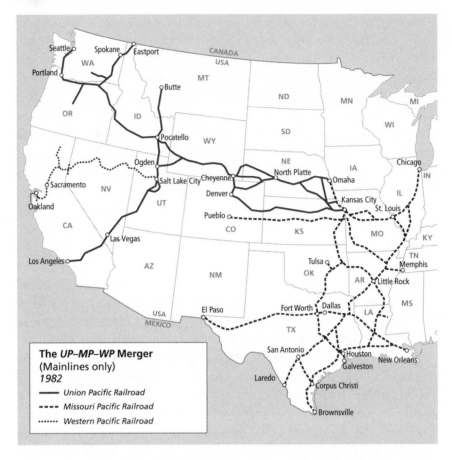

Map 10.4   The UP + MP + WP Merger (1982).   The two eastern megamergers paved the way for a classic end-to-end combination that filled gaps in Union Pacific's storied franchise and developed longer hauls for Missouri Pacific's growing chemicals and international traffic. Unit trains of grain from Nebraska, for example, had new direct outlets at ports or gateways in Oakland, St. Louis, New Orleans, and Galveston and at the Mexican border, as well as domestic mills and feed lots located in MoPac territory. *Source: Trains Magazine*, December 1982, p. 4.

was a classically synergistic merger by geographic coverage, and it moved its partners to the top rank of railroad performers in reality and in Wall Street's reckoning.

After collapse in 1974 of the UP and SP proposals to conquer and divide Rock Island, UP had undertaken studies of various other combinations of western railroads. In 1976, UP president John Kenefick and UP Corporation chairman Frank Barnett had even met with Southern Pacific's chairman Ben Biaggini at Palm Springs to discuss a possible merger. UP was SP's first choice for a merger partner, but the UP executives thought SP's markets were "waning" and put an end to the discussions.[32] (Several years later, Southern Pacific still felt a need for a merger partner, and so it turned to Seaboard Coast Line and subsequently acquired the Tucumcari Line from Rock Island's trustee—see above.)

The BN + Frisco merger was now a reality, and it was much more of a real challenge to UP than the earlier rumblings of a Southern-Frisco combination had been. Also, because of the SP's Tucumcari Line purchase for the Golden State route, the Ogden Gateway interchange with SP was now unmistakably vulnerable. AT&SF was a potential wild card. Most worrisome in Omaha, however, was a hot new rumor that Southern Railway and Missouri Pacific were planning a merger. Big Yellow felt surrounded and imperiled. If Southern controlled Missouri Pacific and were then to link with AT&SF, all southeast–southwest traffic over Memphis or Kansas City (i.e., whether bridged by MP or Frisco) would be vulnerable to diversion by UP's competitors. Also, UP's Kansas City–Texas traffic would be left twisting in the winds of independent KCS and marginal Rock Island and M-K-T.

When later interviewed by the UP employee magazine for a 1993 retrospective on the Tri-Pac merger, John Kenefick said:

> We decided to go for the Missouri Pacific and Western Pacific. We knew we couldn't afford to wait. It wasn't a matter of expanding [for its own sake]; we had to do this or lose our strategic position in the West.
>
> I called Bill Cook, who was President of the UP Corporation, and told him we couldn't go on any longer. I said, "If we don't do this, we're going to be left as a small railroad." [Cook invited Kenefick to New York to discuss the matter, but at that point Kenefick suggested also buying the Western Pacific, and Cook asked how much that would cost. Kenefick said about $15 million, and then Cook said,] "Oh hell, we can take that out of petty cash." I told him I'd talk to Mike Flannery, who was Western Pacific president.[33]

In the INFOmagazine article (see more in Box 10.2), John Kenefick goes on to tell the rest of the story as it related to Southern Pacific and SP's CEO Ben Biaggini: After the MoPac papers were signed, Kenefick called his friend Ben (they were in fact friends) to tell him he had a little surprise, that UP was going to merge with Missouri Pacific. Biaggini said, "I don't know why you are doing that. You could have bought the Southern Pacific for less money." Kenefick said, "Ben, we didn't want to buy the Southern Pacific." Then a few weeks later the Western Pacific deal was completed and Kenefick again called Biaggini, saying he had another little surprise: UP was bringing Big Yellow right into Oakland, to which the SP leader responded, "This is the greatest act of corporate treachery since Benedict Arnold tried to sell West Point."[34]

Box 10.2   Tri-Pac CEOs' Perspectives on the UP + MP + WP Merger

When John Kenefick, former MoPac CEO Downing Jenks, and former WP CEO Mike Flannery were interviewed by UP's employee magazine for the Tri-Pac merger retrospective, they remarked about the ease of implementation and transition. Downing Jenks acknowledged that MoPac, like UP, had felt surrounded, and had considered combinations with Southern Railway and M-K-T (Katy) because "everyone else was merging around us." Jenks noted that the "UP and MP railroads fit together very well. We each had what the other one needed." All of the top managers agreed there was no need to merge the companies physically on day one. The companies "weren't on top of each other," and the only big terminal served by both UP and MP was Kansas City (overlaps in other locations were much smaller).

Asked by the magazine writers if the UP + MP + WP merger produced the expected results, Jenks, Flannery, and Kenefick had interesting perspectives. Jenks said he expected the gains in revenue, net income, and stock price, but got a "big kick out of seeing all the improvements made in technology, equipment and tools in the last 10 years." Flannery added that UP was the strongest railroad in the country, and if it didn't remain so, there was only one place for the blame—management—because commodity mix, physical layout, and all the other ingredients for success were there. John Kenefick's response was that the merger's results were even better than he expected:

> I honestly didn't foresee the market situation that would come from deregulation. We always saw advantages to a single-line haul, such as the Burlington Northern, Southern Pacific, and Santa Fe had. You could set your own service standards. Now [after Tri-Pac], we had all that, but much more important, the capability of single-line pricing. I didn't foresee that.[1]

1. *Union Pacific INFOmagazine*, pp. 17–18.

The story of the ICC's handling of the Tri-Pac merger is well told in a Railway Age special by veteran industry reporter and commentator Gus Welty, "UP/MP/WP: A Whole Greater than the Sum of its Parts,"[35] which the authors believe is a correct characterization of the merger's economic effects. Welty and others believed that the Tri-Pac merger was the toughest for the ICC of any since the infamous twelve-year wandering in the wilderness that was the ICC's deliberation over division of Rock Island north and south between UP and SP a decade earlier. BN, AT&SF, and Southern Pacific howled their opposition. SP fought the merger in the courts on grounds that it violated Ogden Gateway provisions dating back to the Harriman era.[36] Even the Pacific Railroad Acts of 1862 and 1864 had sought to ensure that the Union Pacific and Central Pacific would operate what we would now call seamless service over the Ogden/Promontory Gateway— as though it were "one continuous line."[37]

Hedging its bets, however, SP asked the ICC for extensive trackage rights if UP + MP + WP should be approved. The ICC's decision addressed the matter directly:

> This provision will not be violated by the proposed transactions for [sic] the operating plan set forth by UP and WP does not contemplate closing the Ogden gateway to SP traffic. With SP's extensive trackage in northern California, it will maintain a strong position for interline traffic with UP even after the consolidation. Furthermore, we believe that the fundamental purpose of the "one continuous line" provision will also be satisfied by the existence of several other alternative transcontinental routes, including the SP-D&RGW route. . . .[38]

In its decision, the ICC "refused to prescribe any trackage rights compensation payments, saying it would prefer that the individual parties negotiate such agreements;"[39] failing that, the commission would step in.

BN took the same course, asking for conditions on PRB coal traffic beyond Kansas City to five power plants served by MoPac, as well as removing DT&I conditions imposed at the time of the 1970 Burlington Northern merger. BN and virtually every other Great Plains road (C&NW, KCS, D&RGW, M-K-T, ICG, Milwaukee, and Soo Line) opposed the UP's merger. SP estimated revenue losses of $100 million annually; Santa Fe put its revenue losses at $75 million; D&RGW figured revenue losses of up to $30 million; KCS and Katy thought the applicants underestimated diversions substantially.[40] Welty observed that the ICC had approved BN/ Frisco and the formation of CSX in recent month, and soon would render a decision in N&W + Southern. But the specter of Rock Island—"an auld acquaintance that should be forgot," Welty memorably said—"kept being brought to mind."

One final thing of considerable significance came out of the Tri-Pac application and the related ICC decision. This was the thoughtful and rather unexpected concurring opinion offered by vice chairman Reginald E. Gilliam:

> In sum, this merger is an affirmation of the national consensus for reduced railroad regulation and increased private sector initiative. The clear message of this decision is that the transportation industry is undergoing a fundamental change and that the era of total coordinated transportation networks has arrived.[41]

Gilliam's dictum was perhaps wishful and premature, but it was widely quoted and as such became part of the backdrop for regulatory policy toward railroads in the post–Staggers Rail Act era.

Santa Fe + Southern Pacific (Denied 1986 and again in 1987)
Shortly after the Staggers Rail Act was passed and—while the railroad industry was still abuzz with the news of Conrail's resurrection as well as fallout from the several mergers that had recently created the modern rail giants—the other two western railroads started talking. These were the Atchison, Topeka & Santa Fe (AT&SF) and the Southern Pacific (SP). Both had been involved in smaller transactions[42] and had made feeble runs on the Western Pacific a decade earlier; SP's proposal was anticompetitive, and AT&SF's harmless, but the ICC denied both. Santa Fe's acquisition of the sprawling SP, however, was a different matter altogether (see Map 10.5).

In the first place, Santa Fe + SP was not a natural continuation of long-term coordinated developments in the industry, like the Overland Transcontinental Route, the Golden State service partnership, or J. J. Hill's Northern Lines combination. It had no historical antecedents like UP and SP's alliance in building of the transcontinental railroad and affiliation under E. H. Harriman's common ownership in the first decade of the twentieth century.[43] A union of Santa Fe and Southern Pacific wasn't needed to fill any obvious gaps in each other's networks. SF + SP didn't

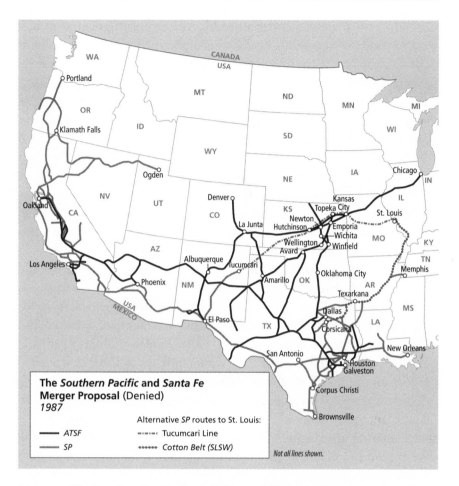

The *Southern Pacific* and *Santa Fe*
Merger Proposal (Denied)
1987

Alternative *SP* routes to St. Louis:

—— ATSF   ▪━▪━▪ Tucumcari Line
—— SP   ●●●●● Cotton Belt (SLSW)

Not all lines shown.

Map 10.5   The Southern Pacific–Santa Fe Proposal (Denied 1987).   A plainly anticompetitive proposal to merge the two strongest carriers in California and the Southwest defied post-Staggers policy trends and was denied by the ICC. Merger of Southern Pacific and Santa Fe would have substantially reduced rail-rail competition in the southern transcontinental market, from Mississippi Gateways through Texas to California and Oregon. A "smoking gun" pertaining to SP + SF managements' intended postmerger pricing strategy (found by merger opponents in legal discovery) doomed the case for proponents. *Source: Trains Magazine,* December 1983, p. 8.

feature completion of established interline traffic patterns, or (with few exceptions) even new single-line services that would be welcomed by shippers. This proposal was not at all like the others that immediately preceded it: It was not an end-to-end combination, but a monopolistic regional consolidation. It was not like CSX or NS, and certainly not like BN + Frisco or UP + MP + WP; instead, it was more like a far-flung Penn

Central—with management rivalries like the red-team/green-team animosities, and an impending financial collapse if SP should continue its downward spiral. Warning bells should have been clanging loudly in Chicago and San Francisco.

Santa Fe's acquisition of Southern Pacific first surfaced as rumors, and then a public announcement came in September 1983. The Department of Justice (DOJ) immediately and strongly opposed the combination on anticompetitive grounds.[44] But economic theory and antitrust precedent may not have been sufficient to stop SF + SP at the outset, just as they weren't in the cases of Penn Central and Burlington Northern.

Santa Fe's CEO John Schmidt misread the political situation and refused to make competitive concessions. AT&SF and SP leaders had trouble articulating good reasons for the union because the real reasons couldn't be spoken out loud—they were reserved for discussion behind closed doors. But then, and this is what really derailed the merger—a smoking gun in the files came to light in legal discovery preparatory to the ICC case; it was an embarrassing memorandum from the Santa Fe CEO to his board of directors having to do with intended postmerger pricing benefits. Now the DOJ opposition wasn't just theoretical; it was solid grounds for the ICC flatly to reject the merger proposal.

The ruling was so unexpected that some locomotives had already been painted in a new Southern Pacific–Santa Fe color scheme with "SPSF" speed lettering in red. Santa Fe quickly returned its units to the old paint scheme, but not before wags could declare that SPSF meant "shouldn't paint so fast."[45]

Union Pacific Acquisition of Missouri-Kansas-Texas (M-K-T) (1988)
UP's absorption of the small Class I M-K-T railroad, often called Katy, was mostly unremarkable, but it should be mentioned in the context of post-Staggers mergers. It is the one significant example of an ICC-approved merger in the period that was more parallel than end-to-end in its fundamental layout. The reason for this is that, over a period of about a decade (and with ICC approval), Katy and MoPac had coordinated trackage between many points in the territory bounded by Kansas City, San Antonio, and Houston, and MoPac had granted M-K-T rights on its Kansas City–St. Louis line, allowing Katy to abandon its own line.

These were a form of self-help addressing the Granger roads' old ailment of overbuilding, and they also represented classic Williamson public interest trade-offs (see Chapter 7). Katy gained far better track facilities on which to operate, while MoPac gained shorter routes and better alignments. Shippers gained improved service; the public gained safety and reduction of highway/rail intersections.[46] With the UP + M-K-T merger, on paper shippers lost an independent source of competitive pricing but gained stability and innovation. There was little change, nonetheless, in the actual real-world situation as developed by M-K-T and Missouri Pacific acting piecemeal under ICC authority.

D&RGW Acquisition of Southern Pacific–Cotton Belt (1988)

At the end of World War II, the Southern Pacific railroad had seemed well-poised to prosper with America's great migration west and south, but in truth SP was headed into sharp decline despite its great gathering and delivery network along the Pacific Coast south of Portland and throughout California, except for San Diego. SP saw a relative decline of West Coast lumber origins, automobile traffic from California plants, and loss of refrigerated produce business to rival trucks.

SP's strategic and managerial problems were no mystery to seasoned railroad observers. SP's local market coverage was unmatched, but SP wanted to focus on transcontinental, not local, origin and destination business. The tragedy of the once-mighty SP was twofold. It failed to respond adequately to changes happening all around it in its core business, and when it did try to adapt, it made some questionable strategic decisions. Contrast, for example, Missouri Pacific's successful development of its petrochemical business in Texas and Louisiana with the similar but less-well-exploited opportunities for Southern Pacific in those states. Instead SP diversified into capital-intensive title insurance (Ticor) and telecommunications (Sprint) investments that were difficult for it to sustain.

Several events in the years after passage of the Staggers Rail Act of 1980 caused traditional UP–SP (Central Pacific) Ogden Gateway traffic almost to vanish: SP's purchase of the Tucumcari Line in 1978 and UP's acquisition of Western Pacific in 1983 both drew traffic away from the traditional Ogden/Overland interchange. Then, Phillip Anschutz (a Colorado ranch owner and oil and gas billionaire) purchased Denver & Rio Grande Western (Rio Grande–D&RGW) in the late 1980s, and had Rio Grande expand from its base by acquiring Southern Pacific in 1988. With the subsequent Denver & Rio Grande Western + SP transaction and connection of these roads at Ogden, a modest reinvigoration of interchange traffic to SP's old Central Pacific line seemed likely.[47]

Southern Pacific already connected with D&RGW at Ogden, so it could really benefit from participation in an expanded system. The SP system now bridged the Rockies to Denver and Pueblo, Colorado; traversed Rio Grande rights on the MoPac to reach the Tucumcari Line via Hoisington and Herington, Kansas; and extended to Kansas City, where it enjoyed a healthy interchange with Burlington Northern. Also, SP could consolidate D&RGW traffic into its trains at Herington for forwarding to East St. Louis; later D&RGW + SP could connect at Kansas City with the Gateway Western to complete its own long-sought entry into Chicago. UP resisted SP + D&RGW's use of its lines, but the ICC was committed to reinvigorating competition in the Overland Corridor, and UP had no choice but to acquiesce. Soon, however, unprecedented flooding of the Great Salt Lake; lake-bed subsurface problems on the storied Lucin Cutoff right of way; and a massive mudslide at Thistle, Utah, conspired to plague the route once again.

Union Pacific Acquisition of Chicago & North Western (1995)

This book has already mentioned that, after both Rock Island (1975) and Milwaukee Road (1977) declared bankruptcy, public policy championed by the FRA narrowly avoided a "Conrail West" outcome for the Granger railroads. Also in the 1970s, the Chicago & North Western (C&NW) teetered but did not topple. It was partly good managers making the best of a bad economic situation, partly the strategic lay of C&NW routes over the canvas of the northern Great Plains (especially Union Pacific's need for a strong connection to Chicago and C&NW's access to the Powder River Basin), and partly good fortune.

Although a C&NW predecessor, the Galena & Chicago Union, was the first railroad in Chicago, the Chicago, Burlington, & Quincy (CB&Q) and Rock Island railroads had gotten off to considerable head starts over North Western with regard to westward expansion. Rock Island reached and bridged the Mississippi River first (in 1856), and a CB&Q predecessor was first to build to St. Joseph on the Missouri River (in 1859), via Quincy (Illinois) and Hannibal (Missouri). Rock Island served both Iowa state capitals (initially Iowa City, then Des Moines). C&NW came later with service to Cedar Rapids and reached Omaha (in 1867); also, the North Western projected crossing the Continental Divide over the South Pass (as the Oregon, California, and Mormon Trails, and the Pony Express famously had),[48] but got only as far as Lander, Wyoming. That was a line to nowhere, but it was not abandoned due to the inherent preservationism of regulation. When the two Organization of Petroleum Exporting Countries (OPEC) oil shocks came in the 1970s, C&NW's Lander line, with its proximity to the southern Powder River Basin, became more valuable as a bargaining chip than it ever had been as a freight-hauling route. (See Box 10-3 on Project Yellow.)

Box 10.3   Project Yellow

The great leap forward for C&NW in the 1980s was Project Yellow, which enabled C&NW to expand into the enormous Powder River Basin (PRB) coal fields (shown on Map 10.7). Historian Roger Grant calls the Coal Line Project North Western's "greatest triumph during its twilight years." Project Yellow took a decade to plan and $500 million to implement.

C&NW's cowboy line from the Missouri River via Valentine and Chadron, Nebraska, to Lander, Wyoming, ran only about seventy-five miles south of the main coal deposits, but, of course, C&NW needed ICC permission to build north into the PRB. Burlington Northern already served Montana's Fort Deposit coal fields, just north of the Powder River Basin, but in order to serve the larger PRB fields, BN also needed ICC permission—in this case, to construct a 113-mile extension connecting its Laurel, Montana, and Gillette, Wyoming, lines through the basin. BN's construction application to the ICC beat C&NW's by seven months, but North Western smartly sought to catch up by asking the ICC to consolidate the rival applications and authorize construction of a single joint BN/C&NW PRB line. BN was outraged with the prospect of competition (it believed the basin was "exclusively Burlington Northern Territory")—as well as likely delays if C&NW's joint line plan were approved.

C&NW could not rebuild its cowboy line with its own finances nor even with FRA loan assistance; it had to turn to UP, and that became (with the double-track line to Chicago) the real foundation of the UP + C&NW merger. Project Yellow turned into a clever plan to connect the PRB joint line (which the ICC was happy to approve over BN objections) east a short distance on a rehabilitated portion of the cowboy line, then from Lusk, Wyoming, over new construction south to South Morrill (Scottsbluff), Nebraska, on Union Pacific's North Platte subdivision, where the PRB coal could move east and south directly to power plants or to interline connections.

The otherwise outstanding spread in the November 2010 issue of *Trains Magazine*[49] advances the dubious proposition that BN and AT&SF got together in response to the UP + C&NW consolidation of 1995. This is doubtful, and BNSF officials probably would say so—at least because BN proposed its acquisition of Santa Fe in 1994, before the UP + C&NW deal was approved. More important, UP and C&NW had worked together for years on interchange traffic to Chicago, which UP itself reached from the West only circuitously via Missouri Pacific (St. Louis) and its former Chicago & Eastern Illinois (C&EI) trackage to Dolton, Illinois (Yard Center), and downtown Chicago (Canal Street). The UP–C&NW operating alliance became even stronger after the two railroads jointly entered the Powder River Basin coal fields and after striking a ten-year contract with American President Lines to provide double-stack intermodal service between Los Angeles/Long Beach and Chicago, via North Platte, Nebraska—both in the mid-1980s. Thus, all of the main features of UP + C&NW synergy were already in place before their actual union, and an eventual formal merger was regarded as inevitable.

In reinventing itself in the last part of the 1970s, C&NW became the most active and successful applicant for US federal loan and preference share funding authorized by the Rail Revitalization and Regulatory Reform (4R) Act of 1976. Roger Grant got the story right in his history of the C&NW:

> The willingness of the federal government to assist the North Western delighted the company and annoyed competitors. Bureaucrats in Washington wished to honor the intent of Congress, and they did. The government was hardly taking a risk with the North Western; the railroad possessed a decent record of earnings.[50]

What do we make of the UP + C&NW consolidation at this remove? As had been shown in the days of the streamliners and long-distance name trains, C&NW was the most reliable and highest capacity connection for UP between Chicago and Omaha. Proviso Yard in west Chicago was well situated for UP traffic from the West, and connections to the eastern railroads could be made through the Indiana Harbor Belt, B&O Chicago Terminal, and the Belt Railway of Chicago—all proximate to C&NW's yards (and all forming linkages with MoPac's operations south of downtown Chicago, although historically, little traffic moved between the two eventual UP roads by these routes). In recent years, frac sand, grain, coal, ethanol, and intermodal traffic (all using former C&NW facilities) have experienced considerable growth.

Working relationships between UP and C&NW were quite good. C&NW had talented executives like Jim Wolfe and Jim Zito, who knew how to get along with UPRR. C&NW had made good use of the FRA funding programs. C&NW had begun to use UP's Transportation Control System (TCS) contractually through UP's subsidiary, UP Technologies. As it turned out, the integration of computer systems (because too little had been invested in modernizing their functionality and simplifying user interfaces) was one of the stumbling blocks in merger implementation; it should not have been a problem, but it was.

The Fin de Siècle XX Mergers

As the twentieth century wound down to its prosperous end for the United States, railroads had reason to be, not smug, but satisfied with their progress in the last quarter of the century. Nationwide, in both the United States and Canada, deficit-producing passenger services had been removed from the responsibility of the freight railroads, finding new homes in Amtrak, Canada's Via Rail, and regional commuter operating authorities—each with separate funding. The benefits of Staggers Rail Act lessening of regulation had begun to take hold in the mid- to late 1980s, dramatically improving railroad efficiency and financial performance; deregulated long-term contracts and the innovation of double-stacking international containers enabled long-distance mini-land-bridge (transcontinental) unit train movements of containers to grow rapidly.

Worldwide trade liberalization and macroeconomic conditions had enabled US and Canadian railroads to export record amounts of grain, and trade with Canada and Mexico surged after signing of the North American Free Trade Agreement (NAFTA) in 1993. End-to-end mergers in the period 1980–1995 and redeployment of thousands of miles of light-density rail lines from Class I railroads to new short-line and regional railroad companies further streamlined the industry structure. Mergers helped improve rail service vis-à-vis ubiquitous competition from larger and heavier trucks as well as subsidized barge competition on the inland waterways. Restructuring initiatives helped railroads dramatically increase their labor and capital productivity, which had been quite stagnant in the 1960s and 1970s. Rail safety statistics improved remarkably as management invested improved cash flows in better facilities and rolling stock, and as the benefits of new technologies found their way into rail operations.[51] Prospects for a genuine rail renaissance improved, and Wall Street began to take greater interest in railroad stocks.[52]

As detailed above, a spate of large railroad mergers followed closely on the heels of the USRA's FSP for Conrail. With passage of the Staggers Rail Act in 1980 changing the rules for merger approvals, as well as lifting most restrictions on rate making, these megamergers raised concerns that the small number of remaining railroads would attempt to merge with one another, limiting the number of railroads providing competitive service to shippers (which could lead to price gouging or further diminishing entrepreneurial initiatives). Some observers feared mergers could create still larger networks across the nation, possibly even transcontinental lines. These concerns were not unfounded.[53]

The railroad industry structure was further streamlined by four important transactions consummated in the last five years of the twentieth century: two mergers of the traditional type for railroads (union of Burlington Northern and the Atchison, Topeka & Santa Fe into the BNSF Railway, and merger of the Southern Pacific into Union Pacific Railroad)—plus an unprecedented division of a large, independent Class I railroad (Conrail) between two others (Norfolk Southern and CSX).[54] For simplicity we call all four transactions "mergers" because, after the split of Conrail, the two large remainders were in fact merged into the other eastern Class I railroads—58 percent of Conrail into NS, and 42 percent of Conrail into CSX (see below).

Today BNSF and Union Pacific compete neck and neck for favor with shippers and Wall Street. The BNSF profile features productivity from unit train operations, especially coal and intermodal; UP's rank among railroads is first in revenue, route-mileage, and employment—as befits its balanced commodity portfolio. CSX ranks as the third largest railroad if measured by revenues or physical units, while NS takes third place if the criterion is market value.

How did these four major systems reach their final sizes and shapes, and how did the mergers that created them perform in these configurations? That is the subject of the remainder of this chapter.

The Burlington Northern–Santa Fe Merger (1995)

The first important consolidation of the fin-de-siècle merger period was a 1995 consolidation of two of the major carriers in the West: the

Burlington Northern (BN) and the Atchison, Topeka & Santa Fe (AT&SF). (See Map 10.6). In June 1994, BN made an offer of $2.76 billion to purchase the Santa Fe. That union would create the largest railroad in the country, with 33,000 route-miles—topping the nearest competitor (Union Pacific) by about 10,000 route-miles. On October 5, 1994, Union Pacific made a counteroffer of $3.4 billion to acquire Santa Fe. BN matched UP's bid on October 27, 1994, and on October 30, UP raised its bid to $3.8 billion. Santa Fe's board of directors turned down this new offer, leading almost inevitably to a proxy fight.[55]

Union Pacific went to court in January 1995 to contest the validity of the Santa Fe's antitakeover poison pill but lost the case.[56] The next day UP announced that it would not bid any higher for the AT&SF. According to UP's chair, Drew Lewis: "Although a transaction at our current price would benefit Union Pacific shareholders, for us to overpay to acquire Santa Fe would not."[57] UP had succeeded, however, in forcing the BN to pay about half again more for the Santa Fe than BN originally offered.[58]

In its ICC filings applying for approval of the merger, BNSF proposed to provide improved service to customers over new single-line service routes, economies of density enabling more frequent service, and improved asset utilization (both freight car efficiencies and more use of excess AT&SF line capacity for BN-originated traffic). Proponents suggested that the merged lines could bypass yard congestion at Kansas City and St. Louis. Reduction in transit time was possible in some corridors.[59] Then and later, BNSF could provide highly efficient long-haul unit train movements of coal, grain, and intermodal containers; in recent years, ethanol and crude petroleum could be added to the list.

In handling grain, the merger added sourcing variety throughout the Great Plains wheat belt—winter wheat in Kansas, Oklahoma, and Texas, and spring wheat in the Dakotas and Montana. The merged company could offer grain merchants efficient export outlets to the Pacific Northwest, California, or the Texas Gulf, and a larger number of origins to Mexico gateways as well as domestic receivers such as cattle-feeding operations.

Combining intermodal networks added BN's extensive piggyback routes to AT&SF's strong container train service inbound over Southern California ports, which had become the major player in transcontinental and international double-stack intermodal service. The merger application proposed a new service route from the Twin Cities to Los Angeles via a BN route over Omaha and Kansas City, and some additional service was

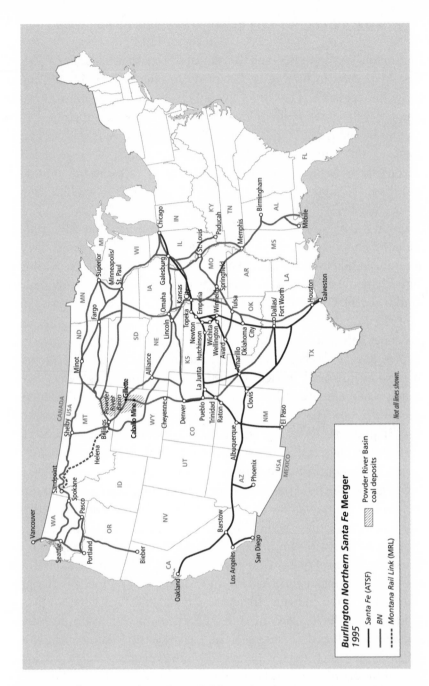

Map 10.6 Burlington Northern–Santa Fe Merger (1995). Santa Fe had been left in some disarray by the failure of the SP + SF proposal, and Burlington Northern sought first-mover advantage in the next round of merger proposals. Also, perhaps, BN was looking for an executive succession plan. Merger of the two rail networks into BNSF Railway formed the nation's largest railroad. BNSF was purchased by Warren Buffet's Berkshire Hathaway in 2009. *Source: Trains Magazine,* September 1994, p. 15.

initiated for Santa Fe destinations by way of BN's Cicero Yard in Chicago. In recent years observers have noted increased service between California and the Southeast via the Avard connection (described earlier). As a result of the BNSF merger, much of the former Santa Fe interlined double-stack traffic via Dallas has been shifted to the single-line BNSF route via Avard, Oklahoma.

In terms of technology, BN traditionally had sponsored an industry-leading research program, but unfortunately, after the merger, new management went in another direction. Regarding computerization, AT&SF had been a pioneer in applying new mainframe software and technology from IBM, and the merged BNSF was able to benefit from it after the merger.

The consolidation of BN + AT&SF also helped clarify CEO succession plans for several railroads. Santa Fe's succession plan had been interrupted by the ICC's denial of SP + SF. The BNSF merger created an opportunity to offer the top position to Robert Krebs, who was originally from Southern Pacific but became chair of Santa Fe. Krebs brought his senior operating team with him to BNSF; Mike Haverty, who was president of the Santa Fe under chair Krebs prior to the BNSF merger, did not come to BNSF but instead became president of the Kansas City Southern in 1995. Under Krebs, Matt Rose quickly moved to top management, where he continues to serve with distinction.

Overall, net annual cost savings of $453 million were anticipated by year three, nearly $350 million of which were savings in support services expenses.[60]

Once the conflict with Union Pacific was resolved, there was little other opposition to the BNSF merger. Some coal shippers opposed the merger due to fears it would limit too sharply the number of available competitive railroads, but these parties saw no likelihood of being able to block the merger proposal.

The Union Pacific–Southern Pacific Merger (1996)

Union Pacific had acquired Missouri-Kansas-Texas in 1988 and Chicago & North Western in 1995. Earlier, UP had combined with Missouri Pacific and Western Pacific (1982), and had picked up small pieces of the Milwaukee Road and Rock Island. Before the BNSF merger, Union Pacific had been the largest railroad in the United States. In 1995, it encompassed over 22,000 route-miles from Seattle, San Francisco, and Los Angeles to Chicago, Kansas City, St. Louis, Houston, and New Orleans. Of its many various merger partners, only one, Missouri Pacific, was financially strong.

After its acquisition by Denver & Rio Grande Western, Southern Pacific operated some 16,000 route-miles of railroad, from St. Louis and New Orleans, across the central Overland Corridor to the Bay Area via Denver and Salt Lake City, and along the Golden State and Sunset corridors through the southwestern states, ending at points along the West Coast between Los Angeles and Portland, Oregon. This sprawling network had been the result of several earlier restructuring initiatives, including purchase of the Tucumcari Line from Rock Island.[61]

As indicated earlier, among the great ironies of western railroads was that, until the 1980s, the fabled Union Pacific lacked its own routes from the Platte Valley and the central Overland Transcontinental line (the first transcontinental railroad, connected by the Golden Spike at Promontory, Utah)—to its natural anchors at either end—namely, the San Francisco Bay area and Chicago on Lake Michigan's shores. A merger with Southern Pacific, UP's managers knew, would fill the geographic gap that had existed since dissolution of the Harriman Trust in 1913 (see Map 10.7). A modern ICC or STB, however, would give its approval—especially since BN + AT&SF (little different from UP + SP in competitive terms and far less in need of a financial home than SP was) had already been approved. The difficulty for UP was, of course, that SP was now in financial distress; its venerable franchise was worn out—the victim of its management's twenty-year going-out-of-business sale—and losses of key customers and great amounts of traffic that could not be replaced.[62]

Two things thus made a UP + SP merger, at long last, look acceptable: (1) the routing synergies with Missouri Pacific over El Paso for eastern connections via Memphis plus restoration of the long-neglected Overland Route,[63] and (2) the fact that SP was fast failing financially and, with all its deferred maintenance, may simply have had no alternative but to close up shop. Regulators were worried, and UP had an opening.[64]

Pluses and Minuses of the UP + SP Merger

UP filed an application with the ICC to acquire the Southern Pacific on November 30; it planned to pay SP stockholders a total of $5.4 billion for the company. The new combined UP + SP system would have 31,800 route-miles, 5,500 locomotives, and 126,500 freight cars.[65] Union Pacific

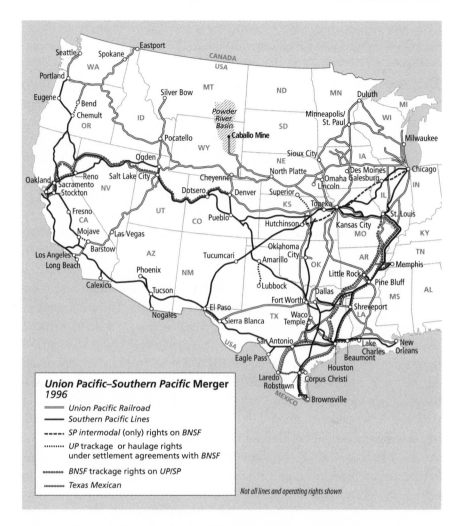

Map 10.7   Union Pacific–Southern Pacific Merger (1996).   With ICC approval of the
BNSF merger, Union Pacific again faced a strategic crisis. If it wanted to keep up with its key
competitor, there was no alternative merger partner in the West other than Southern Pacific, a
former powerhouse that had been, in effect, conducting a going-out-of-business sale for the last
quarter century. ICC successor STB would insist on mitigating competitive losses inherent in
the merger by forcing UP to grant trackage rights—not just to anyone, but to archrival BNSF.
Historically, the merger restored key portions of the Harriman consolidation dissolved by the federal government in 1912/1913, but implementation snafus proved challenging, costly, and embarrassing to UP. *Source: Trains Magazine,* October 1996, p. 22.

gave numerous justifications for a merger with SP. Cost savings and traffic benefits were estimated to be $290 million in the first year after the merger, increasing to $750 million per year until the transaction was complete. The "one-time costs of integration would total nearly $1.5 billion, [but] would cease after four years[,] while the annual savings would persist indefinitely."[66]

The proponent railroads claimed that a merged UP + SP would be a more effective competitor to the newly formed powerhouse BNSF. In anticipation of complaints about anticompetitive effects of the merger, UP and SP offered to grant BNSF trackage rights over nearly 4,000 miles of the UP + SP system, in addition to selling its main competition an interest in nearly 335 route-miles of former SP lines along the Gulf of Mexico coastal lowlands between New Orleans and Houston (plus some mileage in the Dallas area) for $150 million.[67]

Shippers, trade associations, state governments, federal agencies (most notably the DOJ), and various other groups were opposed to the merger. Opponents feared that the merged UP + SP would be able to exercise market power, particularly in geographic areas where shippers were served by few (three or even only two) railroads. UP + SP would also "dominate all the major gateways to Mexico and control access to huge petrochemical shippers along the Texas Gulf Coast."[68] The DOJ believed that the trackage agreements that the UP + SP had proposed were inadequate because they assigned BNSF "inferior" tracks and routes compared with the ones that UP + SP was keeping for itself. Finally, various groups believed that the efficiency gains that the UP and the SP planned to achieve would not materialize. Some reviewers thought that the cost savings might be significantly smaller than expected and that the size of the organization would make it more difficult to manage, leading to inefficiencies.[69]

After nearly nine months of deliberations, the STB essentially accepted most of the UP + SP justifications for the merger and voted to sanction it on July 3, 1996. UP's proactive anticipation of (and method for curing) opponents' most significant potential objections to the merger application made STB's approval substantially easier. STB wound up extending only slightly the geographic coverage of the trackage rights that Union Pacific had agreed privately to give to BNSF, but it made unprecedented expansion of the scope of the conditions—it opened up the entire mitigating trackage to all newly constructed on-line industries. STB also lowered the estimate for total benefits of the merger to $627 million annually—$534 million in operating benefits (labor savings, operations, car use, communications/computers, general and administrative) and $93 million in shipper logistics savings.[70] The transaction took effect on September 11, 1996.

Why Did the UP + SP Merger Implementation Go So Badly?

Unfortunately (and infamously), the merger ran into immediate and crippling operating failures. The full story is told in a case study published by the Kellogg School of Management and other sources.[71] Suffice it to say here that UP failed to make adequate personnel and systems preparations for the takeover, prematurely forced a quite radical new operating plan, and perhaps underestimated the challenges of improving SP properties and information systems while integrating two very different cultures. UP wound up with—among other things—too many freight cars on its system so that they could not be switched efficiently, crews dying on the hours of service law, far too many misrouted cars (the result of operating plan and computer snafus), and several serious safety incidents.

It was mainly a failure of smoothly executing postmerger integration, perhaps due to trying to achieve too much, too fast.[72] Within its first year of operation, UP + SP had at least three train crashes, and it experienced "congestion and service problems" over a wide area.[73] In October 1997, the STB launched an investigation to see if anything could be done to alleviate service problems, particularly in the Houston area. STB eventually ordered Union Pacific to allow shippers to break certain service contracts, enabling KCS and Burlington Northern to provide alternative competitive service.[74] Service problems continued, and Dow Chemical, a major Texas shipper, even sued UP + SP in March 1998 to recover $25 million of costs allegedly imposed on it by the service disruptions.

While most of the indicated problems were of UP and SP's own making, among the underlying problems hampering successful implementation of the merger were several negative consequence of the ICC/STB's long-established policy of preventing "premature effective control" by a purchasing railroad over an acquired carrier prior to final decision in a case. Union Pacific's lawyerly fear of a possible STB finding of unauthorized effective control discouraged full evaluation of the deteriorating condition of the SP property, as well as legitimate premerger planning for UP + SP postmerger operation. UP's lawyers did not want its key personnel out on the SP property before merger approval. This was unfortunate and costly, as STB could easily have structured guidance that would have advanced needed premerger planning and systems development while insulating its final ruling in the case.

The STB decision in UP + SP was also unprecedented with respect to ensuring an irreducible minimum number of competitors in a postmerger scenario; heretofore reduction of competitors in major markets from three or more down to two was considered reasonable and necessary.[75] Indeed, experience has shown that three railroads in a market, when one is crippled, is not a genuinely more competitive solution than two strong carriers—or at least it won't be for long. SP's going-out-of-business sale came to a quick end, as had those of Eire-Lackawanna, Boston & Maine, Rock Island, and Milwaukee Road a generation earlier. Real competition requires more than rate cutting—things like new investment, innovation, and service reliability, for example. Two-carrier competition, where each railroad goes everywhere the other does, is enough to promote efficiency, innovation, and service rivalry, but is unlikely to result in utterly destructive and wasteful price warfare; it is classic duopoly. One-carrier dominance by Conrail was not a good thing; neither were markets with a weak Rock Island or SP playing three's a crowd.

Nonetheless, the STB went out of its way to make the KCS the third competitor in several South Texas markets by requiring UP + SP to grant trackage rights to KCS to connect its US operations to the Texas-Mexican Railway Company over Corpus Christi and Laredo, Texas, thus accessing KCS's large Mexico operations. UP protested, but not too strongly, whether out of statesmanship or realization of its futility is not known. If statesmanship, the reward was perhaps well gained, as STB, representing the public interest, later had ample reason to excoriate UP officials after they fumbled implementation of the UP + SP consolidation—not once but repeatedly over the postmerger months. The STB was highly critical of UP management, to be sure, but it did not unwind the merger.

Union Pacific ultimately resolved its problems, but the whole situation made the STB wary of approving future unifications without first considering the possibility of similar service disruptions. Historian Richard Saunders reached a balanced and thought-provoking conclusion:

> In the years that followed, UP came back triumphant. The reopening of Roseville Yard on May 26, 1999, was a tangible sign. Roseville, near Sacramento, had been SP's northern California

pulse, and like the rest of SP, was too old and small to cope with twenty-first-century traffic. UP had it ready ($145 million later) and renamed it in honor of SP's [originally UP's] Jerry Davis. By 2002, it was BNSF that was struggling to find the capital to open up capacity, and UP was the world's premier railroad. UP's physical plant became so efficient, its costs so low, that it could underbid BNSF for key contracts, and it did so with a vengeance. But with the 1997 meltdown, the great railroad rebirth somehow lost its focus. The industry was never quite as vibrant or quite as optimistic again. A vulnerability had been exposed and an innocence lost.[76]

In a final analysis, it may be judged that STB exercised restraint in exasperating circumstances, while UP gradually replaced hubris with humility when it had no choice, thereby serving its own best long-run interests.

Reflections on the Strategic Impact of BNSF Versus UP + SP
BN and Santa Fe connected mostly end to end, with the BN operating 24,300 route-miles (much of which lay parallel to the US–Canadian border west of Lake Superior) and the AT&SF running about 11,000 route-miles[77] (mostly in the American Great Plains and Southwest, linking Chicago via Kansas City to Albuquerque, Los Angeles, San Diego, and the Bay Area). The two railroads were roughly substitutable, however, between the key points of Chicago, Kansas City, Dallas/Fort Worth, Houston, and Denver.

UP + SP's new route (Chicago–Joliet–Kansas City–Topeka–Tucumcari–El Paso–Colton, California) nearly matches BNSF's mileage and (after upgrading) service time. The route made use of rail lines that only forty years earlier had been parts of Illinois Central, Santa Fe, Rock Island, or Southern Pacific, and of which only the Kansas City–Topeka portion was "old" UPRR. Thus the extensive procompetitive realignment of western railroad routes in place in 2013 was achieved not with a great media splash, but with ICC/STB-imposed trackage rights, quiet negotiation, and piecemeal fine-tuning over a long period. In this way, the two fin-de-siècle western mergers actually increased rail-rail competition in a major market.[78]

The BNSF merger was the final consolidation that the ICC would ever approve, as the regulatory agency was terminated and replaced by the STB on December 31, 1995, under the ICC Termination Act. Most of the control that the ICC retained after 1980, such as the ability to approve mergers, was turned over to the STB, although some of the ICC's duties were transferred to the Department of Transportation (DOT). The railroad changed its name officially to BNSF Railway in 2005.

BNSF consistently established first-mover advantages over its competition (SP and UP, and to some extent CP-Soo) in the last decade of the twentieth century. BNSF constituent railroads developed regional dominance in the West with its startling 1970 New Northern Lines (GN, NP, CB&Q, SP&S) merger forming Burlington Northern Railway (BN), then adding a pattern-changing end-to-end merger (BN + Frisco) in 1980, and finally pulling off the successful blockbuster union of financial giants BN and AT&SF in 1995. BNSF roads had thus completed three game-changing consolidations in the 1970–1995 period, and each time it did so before rival Union Pacific had been able to make its corresponding strategic move. One has to admire both BNSF's bravura and UP's plucky dedication to keeping up.

Burlington Northern had been lucky in not being required by the ICC to grant major mitigating or compensatory rights to the Milwaukee Road in the 1970 merger; predictably, but for many reasons not limited to the impact of the BN merger, Milwaukee fell into bankruptcy and was truncated to a regional core operation. Of all postwar US railroad mergers, two should have been held to some substantial form of competitive mitigation, Penn Central and Burlington Northern. Failure to do so (in the wake of Penn Central) left the ICC with its troublesome Conrail bottleneck cases, and (in the case of Burlington Northern), the multiyear McCarty Farms captive shipper litigation—in addition to major job losses and other negative economic impacts in Montana and South Dakota.

The BN + AT&SF proposal (like the two BN mergers before it) caught UP off guard. UP had to play catch-up and accept a second-best outcome with its acquisition of worn-out SP, but it had no alternative. Any earlier effort by UP to merge with AT&SF (or even with D&RGW)—at the expense of a weak but strategically located Southern Pacific—would have met with the same antitrust objections raised in SF-SP, and the merger probably would not have been approved. Similarly with the situation of BN's three other postwar mergers, its attempted transcontinental lash-up with Canadian National (see below) was brilliant and bold. Only STB bravery under fire prevented BNSF from achieving a fourth coup, perhaps an unmatchable advantage, over UP.

In addition to these strategic wins, BNSF consistently realized better performance on the key operating and financial metrics than did UP + SP. UP has a wonderful franchise, but it is not as simple to manage as BNSF's; in short, bulk unit trains and double-stack container trains make an easier workweek (BNSF) than mixed manifest trains that must be assembled, classified, and spotted on customer sidings (UP + SP). As Ivaldi and McCullough say, manifest traffic can yield good profitability, but growth is slower than bulk/intermodal traffic, and excellent performance is not as "assured."

The Warren Buffett/Berkshire-Hathaway purchase of the vast majority of outstanding BNSF shares in 2011 added luster to rail stocks in general and, of course, to BNSF in particular. The Buffett purchase upstaged UP in a major way—and did so in its hometown of Omaha, where UP's headquarters are located, and near where BNSF has major operations. But we heard no Biaggini howls of "treachery" from UP. The irony is that Union Pacific Corporation (UNP) shares might have been the more Buffet-like acquisition; UP's network perhaps has the greater long-run franchise value (compared with BNSF's current commercial position—overweighted as it is with coal traffic).[79] UP's complexity in realization of franchise fundamentals is the issue. Buffett is known as a value investor, not a change-agent manager. Warren Buffett acquired BNSF securities after CEOs Robert Krebs and Matt Rose had put the systems together. UP's Mike Walsh and subsequent CEO Dick Davidson had a different and perhaps more difficult assignment; rather than maximizing current market value per se, their task was to reform the railroad's organizational structure and management incentives, and thus to prepare UP for the twentieth century's final round of western railroad mergers.

Splitting the Baby: Division of Conrail into Norfolk Southern and CSX

As noted, CSX was formed in 1980 by the merger of the Seaboard Coast Line with the Chessie System, adding Louisville & Nashville and other smaller associated carriers. Southern Railway and Norfolk & Western separately opposed the CSX consolidation and sought from the ICC conditions granting more access to coal, but they were rebuffed.[80] Returning to the ICC with their own Norfolk Southern merger proposal, the ICC granted its approval in 1982. As told in Chapter 8 of this book, Conrail had been independent since its establishment under terms of the USRA's FSP and the 4R Act in 1976.

While the BNSF and the UP + SP mergers were taking place in the West, discussions were underway for a major railroad realignment in the East. In 1994, talks began anew for NS to acquire Conrail; the two firms were close to a deal, but negotiations collapsed over the purchase price for Conrail, and once again, nothing came of the discussions. According to Frank Wilner's book, NS and CSX worked together "covertly" during the summer and fall of 1995 on development of a plan for joint purchase of Conrail.[81] Meetings went on for months in Williamsburg, Virginia, mainly on the subject of how to split Conrail between CSX and NS. When CSX announced on October 15, 1995, that it would purchase the entirety of Conrail for $8.1 billion, however, NS immediately countered with a hostile offer of $9.1 billion in cash. Norfolk Southern filed a lawsuit against CSX and Conrail, and corporate wrangling ensued for the next year. By 1997, CSX's bid had been driven up to $9.4 billion, and NS's bid stood at $10.3 billion. (This equated to $115 per Conrail share, the price finally agreed to months later.[82])

The federal government held the great majority of Consolidated Rail Corporation ownership shares from its establishment in 1976 to its initial public offering (IPO) in 1987. During her tenure as DOT secretary, Elizabeth Dole sought to privatize Conrail by selling it in its entirety to NS. Congress intervened to urge other options, and CSX made an acquisition offer favored by Conrail management. Norfolk Southern, with deep pockets, matched and raised CSX until finally a compromise was reached in which NS would acquire 58 percent of Conrail, and CSX 42 percent. (See Map 10.8) A separately managed Conrail Shared Assets subsidiary was created to facilitate access by both owners to markets in New Jersey and the Detroit metropolitan area.

In March 1997, CSX and NS decided to cooperate and divide Conrail between themselves, pretty much along the lines of the pre–Penn Central (New York Central and Pennsylvania) railroads. A workable deal needed to allow both CSX and NS to expand their service offerings in the region and strengthen their access to the Philadelphia and New York metropolitan areas. NS, fearing loss of all of Conrail to CSX, proposed the concept of "shared assets" operating units early in the negotiations, i.e. before its hostile tender offer, and while CSX was still in the catbird seat. In this manner, all of New Jersey (as well as metropolitan Detroit) came to be covered in Shared Assets territories, split into northern and southern packages roughly at Trenton, New Jersey, and all accessed equally by both NS and CSX.

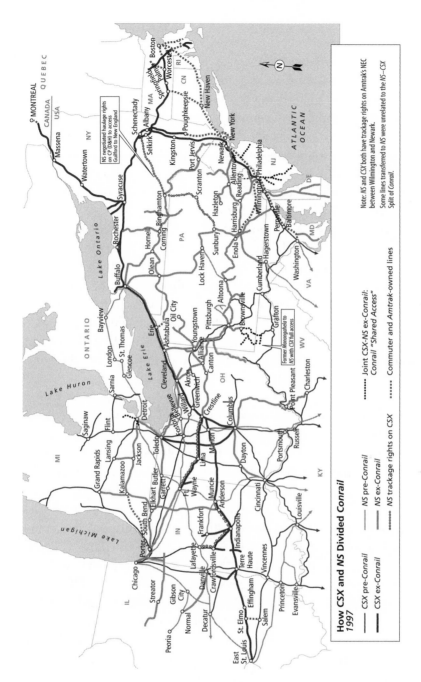

Map 10.8   How CSX and NS Divided Conrail (1997–1999).   The map shows how the 58–42 split was defined in 1997, approved in 1998, and implemented in 1999. NS was to acquire 6,000 of Conrail's approximately 10,000 route-miles for $5.9 billion, and CSX was to acquire 3,600 route-miles for $4.3 billion. In the end, Conrail's board affirmed that both NS and CSX would pay $115 per share in cash for their portion of the acquired Conrail shares. *Source:* Kalmbach Pub. Co, *Trains Magazine* June 1997, p. 26.

Before the Conrail restructuring, CSX and NS operated approximately parallel to one another. CSX was larger than NS, the former having 18,000 route-miles, and the latter 14,000, but both ran through the southeastern states and west to the Mississippi River. Since both NS and CSX had good coverage in the Great Lakes region, the two railroads really had to focus, finally, on what would happen in the East. CSX reached Buffalo over a former B&O line that had been spun off, and NS had been in Pittsburgh before selling its line there to Wheeling & Lake Erie, but both were weak routes with little access to industry.

On June 23, 1997, CSX and NS notified the STB of their intent to acquire and split Conrail. The purchase of Conrail in the proportions of about 58 percent to NS and 42 percent to CSX would leave CSX and NS at approximately the same size, with each railroad operating around 20,000 route-miles.[83] David LeVan would receive $20 million in severance.[84] In the end CSX got dominance in Boston, Montreal, and the Mohawk Valley; and NS added good routes to Pittsburgh, Harrisburg, Philadelphia, and Baltimore. Map 10.8 shows the manner in which the division was accomplished.

Pluses and Minuses in the Split of Conrail

The STB was in support of the division of Conrail because it would "create two strong competitors in the East [that would] provide improved rail service opportunities throughout the Northeast and South. Through the development of shared assets and joint access areas [in New Jersey and metropolitan Detroit, the restructuring would] bring competition back to many areas that had lost options through the creation of Conrail."[85] Numerous interest groups throughout the East supported the realignment as well. It was expected to produce "$1 billion annually in quantifiable public benefits and numerous other benefits;"[86] Similarly, the DOJ believed that the "transaction would create new competition"[87] between NS and CSX. Some shippers expressed concern that only one carrier would serve them, and so competition would not be enhanced. The arguments of these shippers were not considered very seriously, however, because they would be no worse off after the transaction than they had been before it took place. (This was the same argument made in UP + SP.)

The STB ultimately approved division of Conrail between CSX and Norfolk Southern on June 8, 1998, and the new structure was implemented in 1999. At the behest of the DOT, the STB required, as a condition for the approval of the deal, five years of oversight and the implementation of safety, environmental, and service standards. The DOT itself planned "to monitor closely the integration of Conrail into CSXT and Norfolk Southern operations in order to establish a warning system to avoid service difficulties similar to those experienced after the merger of the Union Pacific and Southern Pacific railroads."[88]

Conrail had been in existence only twenty-three years but, as we recounted in Chapter 8, it was a relatively happy life. Conrail was an all-star marketing organization under Richard Steiner, James Hagen, and Charles Marshall; it set the model for implementation of the Staggers Rail Act in the early 1980s, and took advantage of supplemental enactments to trim its employment and rail network to match available market demand. Under CEOs Stanley Crane and Jim Hagen, Conrail proved a lot about how to manage a franchise with substantial market power, but in the end it gave way to a physical restructuring far more appropriate for the nation. We all can take heart in this righting of the wrong—this undoing of the Penn Central merger after thirty years.

Postscript: The BNSF + CN Proposal

By 2000, the railroad industry looked vastly different than it had at any point in its history. Six major railroads dominated nearly all the route-miles in North America: BNSF and UP + SP controlled the western United States, NS and CSX were dominant in the East, and Canadian National (CN) and Canadian Pacific (CP) spanned Canada. These railroads interacted very differently with one another compared to their behavior earlier in their histories. In the United States, regional competitors had to cooperate with one another due to trackage rights imposed by the ICC/STB to mitigate competitive losses related to the mergers. Also, the western carriers needed to work closely with the eastern carriers to coordinate transfers of long-distance cross-regional traffic such as double-stack intermodal container trains, long-haul ethanol and chemicals movements, and Powder River Basin coal.

Also, the Canadian carriers were substantially increasing their involvement in railroading south of the US border; Canadian National, for example, bought Illinois Central and then, in 1998, entered into a long-term marketing agreement with Kansas City Southern and its partner/subsidiary in Mexico, *Transportacion Ferroviaria Mexicana (TFM)*.[89] Indeed, it was because of the involvement of the Canadian National with US railroads that several of the most recent developments in railroad merger history occurred.[90] In December 1999, CN and BNSF announced that they would merge their operations into North American Railways, Inc. The new system would be the largest on the North American continent, with 50,000 miles of track and coverage of thirty-two states and eight Canadian provinces.[91] The two railroads made their formal proposal to the STB in February 2000.

When the proposed BNSF + CN merger was announced, "[s]hippers initially reacted in horror . . ." and the four remaining railroads, "who normally have trouble agreeing on anything political, were united in full-page newspaper ads questioning the wisdom of the alliance." STB chair Linda Morgan also challenged the timing of the merger, calling hearings on "whether the alliance would automatically reduce railroading to only two giant North American railroads, and whether that would be good or bad." Indeed, the consolidation of the railroad industry into two large systems was the major concern for many interests who believed that "if the alliance [were] approved, UP would have no choice but to ally with Canadian Pacific, then choose between CSX and NS for a US merger partner. The leftover eastern road would then be forced to . . . [merge] with BNSF-CN."[92] (See Map 10.9).

Among other concerns that arose after the proposal was announced was the possibility of service disruptions. It was a priority of the STB to avoid any service disruptions similar to those that had plagued UP after its mergers, and CSX and NS after division of Conrail. Linda Morgan took careful notice of the comings and goings in her hearing room. Union Pacific had the most to lose from a BNSF + CN pairing, but was not in a position to complain. David Goode, chair and chief executive of Norfolk Southern, said what UP and perhaps others were thinking: "We need a period to concentrate on service improvements without the distraction of another major merger."[93] The two merger proponents decried this reasoning. Paul Tellier, chief executive of CN, said, "The notion that the two most efficient railroads in North America cannot combine now to improve their business because the other major railroads are having trouble running theirs . . . clearly is against the public interest."[94]

Almost immediately, opposition to the merger flared in the Canadian press; newspapers quoted government sources as saying legislation would be put forward allowing Canadian officials to "control or prevent the merger." Apparently, neither nation had the authority to set conditions for

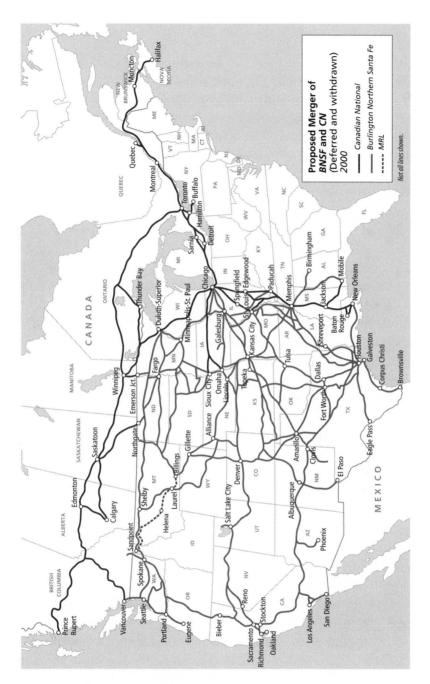

Map 10.9   Proposed Merger of BNSF and CN (Deferred and Withdrawn, 2000).
BNSF and CN withdrew their proposal after the STB formally deferred a decision in the case.
There were major issues involved in coordination of multinational transportation and regulatory
authorities, as well as strong opposition from other railroads not wanting to engage in new contests
amounting to a race to form transcontinental mergers. *Source: Trains Magazine*, March 2000, p. 17.

such a merger in the other, and so each country and each railroad would have had to agree to conditions imposed by the other.[95]

Shippers, politicians, and railroads needed to have major discussions about the future of the railroad industry before any decision was made about the BNSF + CN merger. The STB realized this, and scheduled a series of hearings for the beginning of March 2000, just after the proposal was filed. In light of the possibility that new proposals might reduce the industry to two carriers, high on STB's list was consideration of minimum standards for rail-rail competition. On March 17, 2000, the STB made the abrupt and unprecedented decision to impose a fifteen-month moratorium on Class I mergers other than those involving KCS. According to one commentator, STB's intention was to have the time to "re-examine basic tenets of merger law, such as the [informal] rule that service from two carriers is sufficient to preserve competition. . . ."[96]

While the other Class I railroads applauded the STB's decision, BNSF and CN were furious. BNSF chair Robert D. Krebs told a Senate oversight committee on March 23 that the STB decision was illegal and in clear violation of the ICC Termination Act that created the STB in 1996. CN chair Paul Tellier argued that the decision's "illegality is compounded by its blatant unfairness."[97] CN and BNSF immediately appealed the STB's decision, citing statutory language that required the STB to approve or disapprove a proposal within sixteen months of its filing date, and noting that the ICC Termination Act did not give the STB the authority simply to halt all merger activity.[98]

A federal court ruled on July 14, 2000, however, that "Congress had not specifically precluded the STB from imposing a merger moratorium. . . . [U]nder Supreme Court precedent . . . the courts must defer to the conclusion of the STB that its broad powers to regulate railroad mergers include[s] the authority to call a temporary halt to consolidation."[99] Six days later, on July 20, the CN and the BNSF called off their plans to merge. "The court's decision meant that the STB's moratorium would run its 15-month course. An appeal to the Supreme Court, the proponent railroads' only legal option, would consume roughly the same amount of time, and there [was] no guarantee that the court would take the case."[100]

During the fifteen-month moratorium, STB solicited the opinions of numerous groups that had an interest in the railroad industry, including shippers; politicians; industry representatives; and, of course, the railroads themselves. No significant consolidations and no changes in policy occurred until June 11, 2001, when the STB released its new set of guidelines to govern mergers, which it called Major Rail Consolidation Procedures. In the introduction to the guidelines, the STB defined its main purpose: "Because of the small number of remaining Class I railroads, the fact that rail mergers are no longer needed to address significant excess capacity in the rail industry, and [recognizing] the transitional service problems that have accompanied recent rail mergers, we believe that future merger applicants should bear a heavier burden to show that a major rail combination is consistent with the public interest."[101] The STB had followed Williamson's Lemma nearly to the letter, and with it the STB had perhaps shut the door on any further significant mergers among Class I railroads in the foreseeable future, with the possible exception of one involving KCS.

Concluding Thoughts on the Fin-de-Siècle Mergers

What has happened in the US railroad industry as a result of the fin-de-siècle mergers? The industry has continued its renaissance—primarily a function of Staggers Rail Act lessening of regulation, but certainly with important contributions from the final wave of twentieth-century rail mergers. Railroads have been able to adapt to changes in macroeconomic and international trade factors, including especially with long-distance unit trainload moves of coal, export grain, double-stacked containers, and an array of multicar chemicals and fuel movements. We attribute these adaptations more to deregulation than the major mergers, but they were in fact made by firms that had restructured themselves to meet new competitive realities and that had experienced increased density and longer hauls as a result of mergers. The history shows that the key success factors for modern railroads are having the right network, serving the right markets, and then running things right.

Again, to us as it was to Nan Friedlaender and her colleagues, the story of railroad competitive economics in the period after the Staggers Rail Act of 1980 is nine parts deregulation and one part merger consequences. That observation says a lot about the relative importance of different aspects of normal railroad operating performance associated with mergers—compared with marketing and pricing of services, capital investment and maintenance of facilities, safety initiatives, and (as we will argue strongly in Chapter 12) the major gains railroads made in technology deployment under deregulation.[102]

While much of the focus in merger postmortems, conventionally, is on cost economies, not to be overlooked is the impact on market reach. Throughout the post-Staggers period, railroad managers emphasized the importance of single-line service in expanding the firm's geographic coverage and the value of these extensions to shippers who were lengthening supply chains and themselves seeking to compete in new markets. Industry veteran Jim McClellan comments, "In my experience, [market reach] was far more important in CSX, NS, and the split of Conrail [i.e. the fin-de-siècle transactions] than any concern about reducing costs. The regulatory scheme favored efficiency as a measure of value, but those of us making the decisions were all into market reach."[103] Again, this was an end-to-end merger wave; had it been fundamentally about parallel mergers, the emphasis would have been on costs instead of reach, so Jim McClellan's point helps reemphasize our theme. Perhaps the regulatory body was a little slow in catching on to the shift in underlying merger motives, but its decisions were correct as to both the law and the practice of railroad mergers at the turn of the Milennium.

Have mergers been more valuable to society in realizing cost savings and service improvements than they have been costly to social welfare in terms of reduced competition? Except for the great unintended consequences of management's drive for productivity improvement (job losses and business relocation), the answer is straightforward. Because the post-Staggers period was characterized by end-to-end rather than parallel mergers—and because even for these, carefully worked-out trackage rights conditions (mandated or ratified by the ICC/STB) successfully mitigated the most serious macrocompetitive issues[104]—the post-Staggers mergers were relatively innocuous with respect to competition.

The Tri-PAC merger fundamentally changed traffic flow patterns and its subsequent financial and managerial strength made life uncomfortable for competitors who were not well positioned—even BN + Frisco that arguably had provoked the post-Staggers wave of western mergers. Union of BN and Santa Fe had analogous impacts in the fin-de-siècle period—singlehandedly toppling the twentieth century's final merger domino (UP + SP), and ushering in a period of great stability and prosperity; it was, perhaps, another unintended but ultimately welcome consequence. Division of Conrail to NS and CSX, in place of the awkward arrangements left by the FSP or even more bizarre outcomes that events threatened in the Reagan administration, turned out sweetly for the public—the icing on the cake.

Our favorable evaluation of the post-Staggers mergers, compared with the midcentury group ending with Penn Central, applies not only to the railroads involved, but also to the regulatory agency in charge. The ICC stumbled badly in the midcentury period, but recovered after 1980 (and the STB after 1995), as symbolized by the ICC's rejection of the unwise SPSF proposal, insistence upon two-carrier competition in major market corridors, and a moratorium delaying the BNSF + CN merger proposal and causing it to be withdrawn.

The great recession of 2008–2009 provided several important lessons applicable to these conclusions. One is that density is not all it is cracked up to be, or that sometimes it simply may be a function of volatile, macro-economically—driven volume, and not a permanent operating benefit. Density fell precipitously in 2008 and 2009 and seemed to take good unit cost performance with it. Still, financial returns were reasonably strong, and these had to come from somewhere. The recent experience also seems to substantiate a trend toward an increasing portion of variable, in contrast to fixed, costs in total railroad expenses. The reality of railroads becoming more of a variable cost business traces both to shedding fixed costs, and to changes in the cost mix resulting from trends such as customer-provided cars, independent short lines replacing Class I branch lines, and inter-modal drays replacing some "loose car" industry switching of manifest cars.[105] These are not unrelated to mergers, but they were more fundamental and widespread developments.

Another lesson learned is that maximizing ton-mile output is not the secret to railroad profitability because it means managers must use a variety of higher-cost strategies to reach greater throughput. For example, to maximize volume, managers must use rather than park their older, less efficient locomotives; risk congestion in yards operated above rated capacity; pay crews overtime; encourage employees to skip planned vacations; skip optimum maintenance cycles; and so on. Increasing average density is good up to a point, but Jim McClellan again correctly observes, "[D]ensity comes at a cost, and you have to watch the step functions [capacity additions, for example] very carefully." Also, not every possible capacity addition or bottleneck removal project is warranted.

To summarize railroad merger performance at the end of the twentieth century, the authors offer a final report card in the form of Table 10.1. The mergers are graded on a curve, one could say, because business performance is never absolute but rather relative to peers. In the table, the

Table 10.1 Authors' Evaluation of the Final Four Mergers

Metric Merger/Grade	BNSF (1995) A–	UP + SP (1996) B	NS + .6% CR (1999) B	CSX + .4% CR (1999) B+
Gross Margin	Decline 1998–2005, then rebound to even with merger date base by end of period.	Volatile, with deep drops in 1998 and 2004; ended period 80% above base.	Sharp rise most years to 230% over base in 2008, ending at 175% overall.	Best. After dip in 2003, a remarkable rise of over 300% by the end of the period.
Productivity (Expenses-based)	Best in class. Steady improvement postmerger to 45% increase over base; [Hours-based calculation of Productivity is even higher].	Results in middle of the pack. Rose to over 20% above base in 2003 before ending up 10%.	Rose to 20% over prime by 2005, then settled to 10% rise overall by end of the period (matched UP).	Essentially flat (no improvement) for entire period.
Density	Rose to 80% above base by 2007, declining to 60% with the great recession of 2008–2009.	Twenty-five percent improvements in the great recession of 2008–2009 before falling back to below 10% increase at end.	Lackluster results versus West. NS-CR slightly worse than CSR-CR (down 15%).	Dipped in 2002, rose to 15% above prime by 2006, then ended at 10% below base.
Average Haul	Mostly level at 15% increase over base until the great recession of 2008–2009, then increased to 25%.	Slow, steady rise to near index by end of period in 2009.	Essentially flat after 2001, ending down 5% for the period.	Steady rise to 20% improvement over base for the period.
Velocity	Sagged by 40%, then climbed back in the great recession of 2008–2009 to 25% below base.	Improved to over 15% gain by 2000, then declined.	Up almost 10% for the period.	Lackluster performance over period, ending even with base year.

Top of Class	Better than Average	Average	Below Average

The BNSF merger ranks best overall among fin-de-siècle combinations, based on key operational and financial measures. Although BNSF gross margin and average velocity were not as good as those of other mergers, it was best in the key merger-driven factors of productivity and density. CSX performed nearly as well, with results widely spread over the key metrics. NS and UP trailed the other mergers in overall performance.

Source: Authors' estimates based on analysis of data provided courtesy of the Association of American Railroads (AAR).

comparisons are not quantitative but (like most grades in school) are broadly indicative of performance relative to other cases. Also, the report card again follows our mantra that there is not a single golden metric for evaluation of railroad performance, but in fact many specialized measures calling for nuanced evaluation, and these metrics sometimes provide conflicting indications of success.

What's Next for Mergers and Industry Structure?

The proposed merger between BNSF and CN again raised the issue of what the regulatory approach to rail mergers should be. As this chapter shows, national policy regarding railroads has been highly inconsistent. If the amusement park analogy of a "roller coaster" seems exaggerated, perhaps the playground analogy of a "seesaw" fits (see Box 10.4).

Box 10.4   The Rail Merger Seesaw

With the STB Guidelines of 2000, the seesaw of US regulatory policy toward railroad mergers in the twentieth century had teetered yet again. Over the years, executive branch, congressional, and ICC/STB policy makers had seen mergers or consolidation, in turn, as:

- anathema (T. Roosevelt),
- essential to an effective war mobilization (Woodrow Wilson),
- needing a "grand plan" for a limited number of systems (1920 Transportation Act),
- impossible for the ICC to deal with in a logical master plan (1920s),
- victimized by the Great Depression (1929–1940),
- something that should be left to the railroads (1940 Transportation Act),
- irrelevant during and immediately after World War II,
- dangerous to competitors unless modified by the DT&I conditions,
- good only if proposing huge cost savings (ICC in the 1950s and 1960s),
- necessary for restructuring the Northeast and Midwest Region(1970s),
- diminished by unnecessary conventional conditions like DT&I,
- good only if end to end (1980–1995),
- benign despite great size (1995–2000), and

(continued)

Box 10.4 *Continued*

- acceptable only if procompetitive without destabilizing impacts on the industry (STB Guidelines, 2000).

Confusing? Yes. Ironic, given the original precepts of public regulation? Without a doubt. Familiar territory for *American Railroads*? Absolutely.

Few major issues in US public policy toward business have seen so many flip-flops over such an extended history; it must mean that the economic evidence—or alternatively, the ideological fundamentals, or perhaps more likely, both—are still in doubt. It is the sort of thing political scientists call muddling through. As this is written, it is hard not to reflect on another area of public policy where the United States seemingly has been unable to reach an abiding consensus—national health care.

Persistent Talk of Transcontinental Mergers

From the remove of a decade since the end of the twentieth century, it seems to us that the closing of the twentieth century has also drawn the curtain on any restructuring of railroads into so-called transcontinental mergers, such as an end-to-end combination of BNSF with NS or CSX, or UP with CSX or NS., While a move to a final twenty-first-century transcontinental merger wave cannot be ruled out, it seems more likely that the current status quo—one reached precisely at the turn of the millennium—will be the rail industry structure that greets our great-grandchildren. This is because of the improbability of transcontinental mergers under today's or most conceivable future conditions. (See Table 10.2.) It is possible, of course, that the six large Class I US and Canadian railroads could pair off into two nearly ubiquitous, transborder, and transcontinental systems, one of them picking up the final Class I (Kansas City Southern) along the way. Or, if surmounting the barriers to integration of railroads between two nations with different legal and regulatory structures is seen as too costly, there could result a pair of US transcontinental systems matching the two Canadian systems.

Table 10.2   Arguments for and Against Transcontinental (TC) Mergers

For TC Mergers	Topic	Against TC Mergers
Strong two-carrier service would remain in major lanes.	Competition	Williamson trade-off (TCs give up competitive options with few operating benefits in return); customers have few rail-rail competitive alternatives.
Single-line service from end-to-end mergers, improves transit times and velocity.	Service reliability	Not possible to give all customers interchange-free service with a competitive industry structure.
If they are to be larger, railroad mergers must be TC in scope.	Optimum scale	Current Big 6 Class I railroads approximately equal to optimal scale. Managerial diseconomies of scale still a threat from larger combinations (compare experience early in fin-de-siècle wave).
Long hauls = comparative advantage for railroad versus truck.	Regional/TC traffic flows	Few markets are genuinely TC in scope. Railroads need to focus on markets within existing structure, not "bet on the come" from mergers.
TCs might help the fact that trucks typically beat railroads across the midcontinent watershed, due to rail interchange impediments and thin flows compared with single-driver, truckload TL point-to-point movements.	Watershed traffic flows	Heavy watershed traffic flows bypassing interchange at traditional Mississippi River gateways is shorter length-of-haul than transcontinental traffic, making watershed traffic truck-intensive.
TC merger maximizes leverage from electronically controlled pneumatic ECP brakes, positive train control PTC, unit trains.	Technology	Short of TC mergers, FRA (and unions) could help by lowering artificial barriers to efficient interchange, easing transition to ECP brakes, facilitating funding for PTC, etc.
TC merger allows a railroad seeking its own long haul to postpone interchange to final delivering railroad until reaching a point near final destination; this means smaller interchange blocks at traditional gateways.	Interchange blocking/ switching	Today's industry structure still means interchange for long-haul trans-Mississippi traffic, which continues to occur mainly, but not entirely, at Mississippi River gateways. Current railroad company pattern (i.e., no TCs) allows maximum economies of density in interchange blocking and switch moves.

Proposals to encourage transcontinental mergers have surfaced often, but their benefits are speculative. Weighing the arguments in this table, the authors of *American Railroads* do not expect transcontinental mergers to be advanced and approved during the next two decades.

11

THE ENDURING PROBLEM OF RAIL PASSENGER
SERVICE IN THE AMTRAK ERA

[T]here is no profitable core here [in Amtrak's route structure].
That is a myth. That's why my position has been . . . it's a political decision, whether or not you want the long-distance trains,
and those people over there [he points toward the Capitol
dome] get paid for that. I think my job is to try to run them.
Everybody wants to set me up as the guy [who] should go in
and take off the money-losing trains. Hey, the reality of the
situation is that we barely have enough support over there to
keep anything running, and once I get involved in that kind of
debate, it's all over.

—DAVID GUNN (2002)

Amtrak as currently structured does not define markets well,
does not always assign operating, planning and funding responsibilities at the appropriate level (Federal versus state and local)
and is too insulated from market forces. In short, by trying to
do too much for too many with too little, it ends up doing a less
than optimum job for all.

—LOUIS S. THOMPSON (2003)

This chapter tackles the controversial subject of Amtrak—whether it has
been a good thing for the country, whether it could have been managed to better results, and whether it should be continued in its current or
some altered form.

The Rail Passenger Service Act of 1970 authorized establishment of a
new publicly owned entity—formally, the National Railroad Passenger
Corporation (NRPC). At the time, NRPC was informally called RailPax.
Later, its trade name and marketing moniker became Amtrak. This corporation was to assume responsibility for providing the nation's rail passenger

services over a "basic system" as initially specified by the secretary of transportation after consultation with the Interstate Commerce Commission (ICC), state public utility commissions, rail management, rail unions, and other interested parties.

As the US Railway Association (USRA) summarized in the preliminary system plan (PSP), the 1970 legislation chartering the National Railroad Passenger Corporation had three major objectives:

1. Forming a nationwide system that could achieve improved service and savings in total costs through economies of equipment utilization and restructured operations. Among the consolidation economies sponsors envisioned were reservations and ticketing, central maintenance, national advertising, and other management reforms.
2. Preserving essential rail passenger services despite dismal recent trends and wide anticipation of accelerated discontinuances.
3. Relieving the privately owned freight railroad industry of the heavy cost burden of operating passenger trains.

Said USRA four years later: "It is fair to conclude that the second and third of these goals have been substantially accomplished; progress toward the first goal has been mixed—good in some areas and fair or poor in others."[1]

Creation of Amtrak brought about a more rational organizational structure for US rail passenger operations. Instead of about two dozen railroads worrying separately about their passenger deficits and how those deficits might affect their ability to compete for freight traffic, the development and perpetuation of Amtrak meant that only one agency had that responsibility, and that was an agency directly responsible to the government for providing continued passenger service.

The idea was that by consolidating all of the useful and potentially self-sustaining passenger train services in a single entity that could offer service anywhere in the country (in contrast to separate managers within individual freight-oriented railroad companies), there could be a new focus on modernized operations—and perhaps some efficiencies could be realized through economies of scale and specialization. In fact, intercity passenger operations were continued on a significant portion of the former passenger routes, including most importantly the Northeast Corridor, New York–Chicago, and several long-haul "transcontinental" routes such as Chicago–Los Angeles and Chicago–Seattle.

Political sentiment was initially divided between direct subsidy to "essential' " passenger services operated by individual railroads or, alternatively, creating a federal corporation to oversee development of a national network of passenger service. Disagreements also arose about how much and how long any government subsidy should exist. In the end, the idea of a corporation won on the grounds that subsidies to individual roads would be more politically divisive and difficult to administer. The issues of the size and duration of subsidies were never resolved; dollar amounts for assistance to Amtrak were authorized and appropriated each budget cycle, but there was no larger consensus on the future of passenger trains.

Present at the Creation

In 1970, Department of Transportation secretary John Volpe and his assistant secretary for policy, Paul W. Cherington (on leave from the Harvard Business School) developed a comprehensive policy proposal for rail passenger service on a national scale.[2] The DOT proposal was to create a for-profit "mixed-ownership government corporation."[3] Trackage rights, operating train crews, locomotive service, and other needed inputs that the corporation itself didn't control were to be purchased from the existing railroads at cost plus a nominal profit; the Interstate Commerce Commission (ICC) was to adjudicate disagreements about the terms of these contracts, but the commission was not given a regulatory role over the fares the new government corporation could charge.[4]

The corporation's common stock would be owned only by the railroads exiting from passenger service, and preferred stock could be converted into common shares.[5] The initial capitalization of the corporation would come from $40 million in government appropriations, $100 million in government loan guarantees, and contributions made by those railroads electing to hand over their rail passenger service obligations to the corporation. These contributions were usually at a level equal to 50 percent of the fully distributed 1969 passenger service deficit for a participating railroad. They were largely "paid" by the transfer of vintage railroad passenger service equipment to the new government corporation—NRPC.

A railroad choosing not to participate in the NRPC network had to operate its passenger services until January 1, 1975, before applying for any further discontinuances. Of the twenty-seven US railroads then operating passenger trains, only four chose not to participate, and only two of these were of significant importance in intercity passenger service: the Southern

Railway and the Denver & Rio Grande Western.[6] The corporation was to be governed by a board of fifteen, eight of whom were to be appointed by the president subject to Senate approval, three by the common stock holders, and four by preferred stock holders. The new company was to honor established arrangements for protection of employee rights and was bound by the same safety and related regulations as its predecessors.

In general, the new corporation was seen as an experimental test of whether passenger train technology, emancipated from its prior management, ownership, and regulatory obligations, could survive and contribute to the creation of a better passenger transportation system. And it was clear to all that one of the principal purposes of the NRPC law was the obvious one—no less important for that reason—to alleviate the burden of passenger service deficits on the beleaguered freight railroads. They were dealing with plenty of other tribulations and needed all the help they could get.

The 1970 NRPC Act seemed to satisfy virtually all interested parties. Rail enthusiasts saw the legislation as offering an opportunity to test and implement new technologies and operating concepts that they thought would make rail passenger service more competitive with air and auto travel. The rail unions and employees saw it as slowing the process of job attrition in passenger service and possibly even reversing it if some of the new technologies actually met expectations. Rail managers viewed the legislation as a heaven-sent way to get out from under a large financial burden; they were quite content to concentrate on the freight business and forget their passenger headaches.

Fiscal conservatives liked the for-profit notion, however unrealistic its prospects were, and the implicit market tests that they saw as avoiding the budgetary open-endedness of direct government subsidy. States' rights advocates liked the reservation of the ultimate decision for discontinuances to the states at a 50 percent discount on cost reimbursement. At least some political liberals envisioned the government successfully providing a service that the private sector had badly bungled. Residents of small towns and cities in the mountains and prairies lucky enough to be located on a transcontinental train route, thereby enjoying transportation services that they could not otherwise afford, hoped for an extension of their good fortune. The general traveling public could hardly object to keeping a competitive alternative alive; as any consumer knows, the more suppliers the merrier, and rail passenger service might come in handy on a snowy day.

No wonder then that the legislation sailed through Congress with broad bipartisan support and was signed into law by President Nixon on October 30, 1970. Unfortunately, as this chapter documents, few of the new railroad's expected service economies were realized, and the goals of passenger service preservation and revitalization proved quite costly. As we mention in the chapter's conclusions, we rate the development of the NRPC concept as worthwhile—it did relieve the freight railroads of unconscionable burdens for cross-subsidizing passenger trains, and it offered passenger advocates hope for continuation of services that remained worthwhile. Still, the vehicle for these continuing operations, Amtrak, was also to become a major public policy problem in its own right. The fundamental economic problems of operating American passenger trains had not changed. Only the agency responsible for their operations and financial deficits was different.

Secretary Volpe's Route Designations

At the outset of the NRPC implementation, the secretary of transportation was to recommend the routes that the new railroad should serve, taking into account comments from the ICC, the public, and other interested parties. The secretary would designate only the endpoints of the routes, leaving Amtrak discretion to decide intermediate points to serve and the frequency of trains to operate; in some cases Amtrak could choose among alternative railroads connecting the endpoints. The secretary's initial plan, released in November 1970, called for only twenty-one routes, all but one radiating out of Chicago or New York City.[7]

The secretary's initial route plan provoked a storm of objections. One camp argued that Amtrak's comparative advantage lay in medium-distance corridors (such as New York to Buffalo) and that transcontinental service was a waste of resources. Another camp (one that included the ICC) believed that a national network was important and that the DOT plan had erred by leaving much of the West Coast, the Southwest and South, and the Upper Midwest without any significant rail passenger service. In a highly critical report, the ICC recommended that the secretary add six "essential" routes and preserve service on another five "secondary" routes. In January 1971, Transportation secretary John Volpe chose the politically wise move of accepting all of the ICC's recommendations.

Incorporation and the Initial Service Map

The NRPC legislation provided for establishment of an eight-person board of incorporators, chaired by David W. Kendall and including among others, General Frank S. Besson, Jr.; Arthur D. Lewis (later chair of USRA); former congresswoman Catherine Dean May Bedell (R–WA); and Charles Luna, president of the United Transportation Union. Forming the fifteen-member board of directors were these and other incorporators; Secretary Volpe; and Amtrak's first president, Roger Lewis. Lewis was a respected businessman from General Dynamics; he had no experience in railroads, a lacuna widely regarded at the time as more of an advantage than a handicap.[8]

In addition to administrative functions and hiring a staff, the main job of the incorporators was to determine Amtrak's route structure—putting flesh and bones on the skeleton's endpoints designated by Secretary Volpe. In March 1971, the board unveiled Amtrak's first route map, and in May the incorporators added several more "experimental" routes, some suggested by influential legislators, for a total of 27,000 miles.[9] (See Map 5.1 A and B in Chapter 5.)

James McClellan was one of the first hires, detailed to the fledgling NRPC from the Federal Railroad Administration (FRA) as director of schedules and consists. In his forthcoming memoir, McClellan describes the process for selecting routes that the incorporators would include in the initial national network. Definition of the base network was necessary before accurate estimates of equipment needs could be made and operating contracts with the railroads could be finalized.

McClellan describes how he worked with "a multitude of consultants from McKinsey" assigned to analysis of which specific routes and trains should be run. Knowing the choices would behighly controversial, the McKinsey team established basic criteria: "(1) which routes were best in terms of distance and speed, (2) which routes had the greatest existing ridership, (3) and what was the condition of the fixed plant, stations, and support facilities along the various routes."[10]

McClellan says that the most important criterion was current ridership, taking into account that one predecessor railroad might previously have downgraded service (resulting in sharp losses of ridership), while another by choice or regulatory fiat had continued service (and therefore appeared to have higher ridership potential). The overriding goal "was to save the bare bones of a national network at the lowest possible cost." In the end, there were relatively few unclear cases. Routes like New Orleans to Los Angeles were already down to one daily train. Elsewhere, in the case of Chicago–Los Angeles for example, one route logically dominated other alternatives.

Once consideration of right-of-way ownership could be set aside, McClellan and McKinsey started making efficiency adjustments to possible and likely routes. (This, of course, was a well-advertised benefit of national consolidation.) Thus, Chicago–Seattle service had previously used the Burlington Route east of the Twin Cites, but that route missed Milwaukee, a large intermediate market. Amtrak's final designated route therefore went through Milwaukee, where it remains today.[11]

Getting the Trains Running

Amtrak spent much of its first decade trying to overcome the legacy inherited from its predecessors: worn-out, obsolete, and incompatible equipment handed down from multiple railroad ancestors; a poorly trained and discouraged workforce; little or no integration of intercity trains with passenger services operated by other (local or regional) agencies; often abominably maintained stations; and so on. Roger Lewis focused on establishing a recognizable public identity for an enterprise cobbled together from twenty-seven separate railroads. He developed a national computerized reservation system, bought common uniforms for the employees, and engaged in a national advertising campaign. He spent relatively little money on replacing the aging fleet, however, perhaps because he had so little cash that he was forced almost immediately to ask Congress for another $170 million to keep the railroad running until 1973.

Lewis's request fell on receptive ears, in part because popular support for rail passenger service as an environmentally sound mode was on the rise. The environmental movement was growing rapidly in the early 1970s, and its supporters saw rail as a relatively clean alternative to the automobile. The Yom Kippur war and the Arab oil embargo of 1973–1974 had made energy security a national concern, and many activists saw passenger rail as a way to lessen US dependence on imported petroleum. But Lewis was not a believer in his own company's business, and he did not hide his feelings. Longtime industry observer and writer Frank Wilner declares that Lewis declined to support additional funding for Amtrak because he thought the money couldn't be used sensibly—prompting Senator Lowell Weicker (R–CT) to tell him, "The cause of rail passenger service in the United States would be best served by your stepping aside as president of Amtrak."[12]

A year later the Amtrak board replaced Lewis with Paul H. Reistrup. Reistrup was a career railroader, having worked his way up the ranks at the Baltimore & Ohio and Chesapeake & Ohio railroads before becoming a senior vice president at the Illinois Central. He believed that Amtrak had to offer high-quality, reliable service, which was impossible with the worn-out equipment Amtrak had inherited. Amtrak did not have enough funds to buy many new cars, so Reistrup began a massive program to rebuild Amtrak's "heritage fleet" of old passenger cars, mainly at the Beech Grove shops in Indianapolis.

The refurbishing and replacement intensified under Reistrup's successor, Alan Boyd. Boyd also had railroad experience, first in government (starting as a researcher on the Hosmer report—see Chapter 5) and rising to be the first secretary of transportation under President Lyndon B. Johnson. Attracting the senior and highly respected former secretary as Amtrak's president was a coup for the company and the Carter administration. During his tenure, Boyd managed (often deploying the strength of his personal goodwill) to purchase new cars and locomotives, renovate a few old facilities, and construct essential new ones.

Northeast Corridor (NEC) service had come into the modern post-streamliner era with development under Penn Central of the Metroliners, capable of speeds exceeding 125 miles per hour. These units gave passengers a rough ride, however, because of their heavy unsprung weight. Boyd concluded they should be replaced with locomotive-hauled trains, but Amtrak had neither proper locomotives nor coaches to deploy in the electrified NEC service. The solution was to acquire Swedish-designed (US-built) AEM-7 locomotives capable of 125-mph speeds hauling new "Amfleet" cars.

Amtrak Inherits the Northeast Corridor

In 1973, Congress created the USRA—as a temporary agency apart from but supported by the US Department of Transportation—and gave it a mandate to find solutions to the Northeast railroad crisis (see Chapter 7). The Penn Central and seven smaller Northeast railroads had been operating under bankruptcy protection during the early 1970s while the courts and the government sorted out what to do with them. Liquidation was politically unacceptable because it threatened to leave large parts of the region without rail freight or passenger service.

Among the principles developed for the reorganization, USRA sought to determine the appropriate assignment of the lines in reorganization that had historically and would prospectively have been used by surviving entities for operation of passenger services. In its designations of railroad lines, USRA followed the idea that the "dominant user" of any given line should be its custodian.

Accordingly, USRA, in its PSP and later its final system plan (FSP), proposed transfer of about 500 miles of NEC right of way and related stations to Amtrak rather than Conrail. These lines were used extensively by local transit and commuter rail operations as well as Amtrak's intercity passenger trains and numerous freight trains. Historically, considerable intercity freight moved over the Northeast Corridor, and in the transition to Conrail, much local freight switching service had to be continued. Still, it made little sense to leave these facilities permanently in the hands of Conrail, and so, over the objections of Nixon and Ford administration officials on its board, USRA designated Amtrak as their new owner. Congress appropriated $120 million to allow Amtrak to buy the right of way from the Penn Central's bankruptcy trustees and to do some immediate refurbishment.

Amtrak thus became the designee for lines along and extending the Northeast Corridor, and a Penn Central route between Kalamazoo, Michigan, and Porter, Indiana. (See Map 8.1 A and B.) USRA also addressed the issue of fair compensation to freight railroads for use of their facilities for passenger trains.[13]

Also in the Rail Revitalization and Regulatory Reform (4R) Act of 1976, Congress authorized the Northeast Corridor Improvement Project (NECIP), a major effort to rebuild the corridor's infrastructure with the goal of reducing Amtrak's travel times to 2 hours 40 minutes between Washington and New York and 3 hours 40 minutes between New York and Boston. Congress initially appropriated $1.75 billion for NECIP.[14] By 1986, when the Department of Transportation began winding the project down, the federal government had spent $2.5 billion on NECIP, and Amtrak had met the travel time goal set for Washington to New York; it was still, however, almost an hour shy of the goal for New York to Boston.

When the Reagan administration took office in 1981, nonetheless, budget director David Stockman (who was both well-informed about and ill-disposed toward Amtrak) wanted to "zero-out" its budget. FRA administrator Robert Blanchette (a former lawyer and later trustee for the Penn Central Estate) was happy to oblige. He determined that the NECIP should be trimmed, and a place to begin was terminating capital expenditures for electrification of the Northeast Corridor line north of New Haven to Boston (a decision in which Alan Boyd's successor at Amtrak, W. Graham Claytor, acquiesced). At the end of the twentieth century in the Clinton administration, long after Blanchette was out of the picture, he was reversed and funding for construction of the New Haven–Boston electrification was appropriated. The electrification meant that new Acela train sets could run from Washington or New York City straight through to Boston.[15]

Amtrak's Adolescence: Abandonments, Ambivalence, and Accountability

Even as Amtrak was improving its service and infrastructure, signs of unease with the passenger railroad's operations began to appear in Congress and the executive branch. In the Amtrak Improvement Act of 1978, Congress finally recognized that Amtrak was unlikely to become financially self-sufficient in the near future. That act amended Amtrak's corporate charter to say that it would be run *as* a for-profit corporation, but it would no longer *be* a for-profit corporation. The choice of language was significant because it implied that Congress wanted Amtrak to control its deficits even if it could not recover all costs from passengers—as contradictory, almost illusory, as that might seem.

Subsidies had ballooned (see Figure 11.2) and the 1978 act ordered the secretary of transportation to recommend a smaller and more cost-effective route network. President Jimmy Carter's Transportation secretary, Brock Adams, responded by sending Congress a report suggesting Amtrak's network should be cut from 27,000 to 16,000 miles. There was little public support for such a drastic reduction, and Congress ordered Amtrak to cut back to 23,000 miles instead, but the Carter administration service reductions were the most significant ever made to stick at any point in Amtrak's history. Other administrations talked the anti-Amtrak talk, for example, by sending budgets to Congress with no recommended funding to cover Amtrak deficits (which was a ruse for claiming budget requests were lower than, realistically, they were likely to be funded), but President Carter's team actually walked the walk on this matter.[16]

Congress demonstrated similar ambivalence in the 1979 Amtrak Reorganization Act and the 1981 Amtrak Improvement Act. The 1979 law mandated that Amtrak set performance and financial goals and submit an improvement program to Congress and the president, while at the same time increasing Amtrak's funding to a total of nearly $2.2 billion for the years 1980 to 1982. The 1981 law sought to make Amtrak more accountable by reducing the membership of Amtrak's board of directors from seventeen to nine, with four of these to be appointed by the president (with the consent of Congress). The common theme of the 1978, 1979, and 1981 laws was that Congress—following DOT's lead—began making more realistic assessments of Amtrak's capabilities and concluding that more active oversight of Amtrak was needed.

Other groups were still questioning whether there were any significant benefits to be gained from subsidizing Amtrak. These included the influential Congressional Budget Office (CBO)—a nonpartisan agency that reported to the House and the Senate. The executive branch again led the skeptics after Ronald Reagan was elected president in 1980 with a mandate to cut big government. As noted, Reagan's first budget director, David Stockman, vowed to zero-out Amtrak. Eliminating Amtrak's subsidies would save nearly $700 million per year that went to "well-heeled" passengers, Stockman believed.[17] The new budget director thought Amtrak's long-distance trains were a particular waste, explaining, "You can shut down Amtrak except in the Northeast part of the country without any great loss."[18]

Labor protection cost was a contentious area. Congress had inserted a provision in Amtrak's original 1970 statute [Section 405(c)] that eventually required the railroad to pay as much as six years' severance to any laid-off worker—a mandate that limited the achievable savings from service cutbacks in the short run. These are the so-called Amtrak conditions in railroad labor law, equivalent to "New York Dock" labor protection typically imposed in railroad merger and abandonment cases, and they remain a problem for passenger train economics in the United States. These provisions have been subsequently modified to include usually five rather than six years' severance.[19]

Graham Claytor, Self-Sufficiency, and Higher-Speed Trains

Alan Boyd resigned as Amtrak president in 1982 and was replaced by W. Graham Claytor, Jr. Claytor would serve for eleven years and come to be regarded by almost all observers as Amtrak's most important president. Like Boyd, Claytor had a strong background in both railroads and government. He had led the Southern Railway when it was regarded as one of America's five best-managed companies, and later served as secretary of the navy and acting secretary of transportation in the inter-regnum between the departure of Brock Adams and the arrival as DOT secretary of his fellow Democratic politician from the Pacific Northwest, Neil Goldschmidt.

During Claytor's tenure, Amtrak explored the possibility of providing new or improved services, the most problematic for Claytor being high-speed service. Most Amtrak trains operated with top speeds of 79 miles per hour (the fastest FRA would allow without in-cab signals), and often much less if the track had many curves or was in poor condition. An exception was between Washington and New York, where NECIP improvements and signaling allowed Amtrak's Metroliner service to operate at speeds as high as 125 miles per hour and there were few at-grade highway crossings.[20] Many state government officials and rail enthusiasts were still intrigued by the possibility of offering much higher-speed service, inspired in part by Japan's Shinkansen (or bullet train) and France's TGV (Train à Grande Vitesse) which had top speeds of 163 mph and 186 mph, respectively.[21]

The pressure for higher-speed trains posed a dilemma for Claytor. On the one hand, he had his hands full battling the Reagan administration's efforts to eliminate Amtrak's subsidies, if not altogether, then at least for its long-distance trains. In this environment, it seemed folly to commit Amtrak to developing a higher-speed rail network of its own. On the other hand, the advocates of higher-speed rail included many of Amtrak's strongest supporters, and he could not afford to offend them. Throughout the 1980s, Claytor's position was to cooperate with high-speed rail developers but to keep Amtrak's conventional and its proposed faster train networks separate.

Claytor's struggles with skeptics in the Reagan administration and Congress led to a historic commitment to eliminate Amtrak's operating deficit by 2000. Claytor had long maintained that Amtrak could be profitable if it could charge higher fares, but that couldn't be done, he thought, unless (indirect) airline subsidies were ended and gasoline prices increased. In the late 1980s, during congressional testimony on Amtrak's need for capital subsidies, Claytor went further, explaining that Amtrak's primary objective was to achieve operating self-sufficiency by 2000. This could happen, Claytor argued, only if Amtrak were guaranteed a consistent source of funding for new equipment and infrastructure (similar to airports and highways), and if it were relieved of the constraints imposed by its quasi-public status. Amtrak's 1989 annual report labeled the goal of operating self-sufficiency the Claytor commitment and outlined the mechanisms needed to achieve it.

In 1990, Claytor made a specific proposal for Amtrak funding. The federal budget was in deficit, and Congress was considering raising the federal fuel excise tax by 2.5 cents per gallon above the prevailing level as a short-term deficit reduction measure. Claytor proposed that a penny of the 2.5 cents, which he labeled the Ampenny, should be dedicated to funding for Amtrak.[22] The highway supporters had been willing to countenance the 2.5-cent increase only as a temporary measure because they thought it unfair to use taxes imposed on highway users to fund other government transportation programs. The Ampenny was intended as a long-term dedicated tax and thus aroused considerable hostility. In the end Congress approved the temporary 2.5-cent levy for deficit reduction (later increased to 4.5 cents) but rejected Ampenny.

Managerial Initiatives Under Tom Downs

In 1993, Claytor stepped down as president of Amtrak because of ill-health; he was replaced by Tom Downs. Downs had held a variety of jobs in federal and state transportation agencies, including chair of New Jersey Transit and secretary of transportation for New Jersey. Downs continued Graham Claytor's effort to get dedicated funding for Amtrak capital expenditures, and he proposed that one-half cent per gallon of the federal gas tax be dedicated to Amtrak. The Clinton administration was relatively sympathetic, but the Republican-controlled House was not. (Democrat William Clinton served as president from 1993 to 2000, but the Republicans controlled both houses of Congress after the 1994 midterm election.) Given these political disagreements, no legislation on Amtrak was passed in 1995, and Downs abandoned the effort to get dedicated taxes, at least for the time being.

Tom Downs focused instead on Claytor's overall goal of reaching operating self-sufficiency, perhaps in the hope that achieving that objective would help persuade Congress to provide an assured source of funding for Amtrak's capital expenses. Downs sought to run Amtrak more like a business by dividing the railroad into three strategic business units: the Northeast Corridor business unit operated routes between New England and Virginia, the Intercity business unit was responsible for long-haul passenger operations, and the Amtrak West unit was in charge of service along the West Coast. Each business unit was to develop proposals to increase its revenues or cut its costs and thus move toward operating self-sufficiency. These proposals were of little practical benefit. By its very nature, there was no such thing as a panacea for Amtrak; the problems were too fundamental and enduring.

Another important initiative launched under Tom Downs was to improve service on the northern half of the Northeast Corridor, from New York to Boston. The New England states complained that NECIP had focused most of its resources on the southern half of the corridor, while nothing had been done to improve speeds north of New Haven. Massachusetts led the lobbying because Connecticut and New York cared primarily about commuter services to New York City, which operated south of New Haven. Most of the money was appropriated by Congress, under pressure from the New England delegations, but some matching funds were required of the states.

Amtrak, following the FRA's notion of accelerated rail, named the new train service Acela and projected that it would cut the New York–Boston trip time to three hours and significantly increase ridership. Over the course of six years, Amtrak spent roughly $2.5 billion to electrify track and buy the Acela tilting train sets designed to negotiate the route's sharp curves at high speeds. Acela service began in 2000, a year late because of major teething problems with the new trains.

Downs's efforts to cut costs eventually cost him his job. Shortly after the passage of the Amtrak Reform and Accountability Act of 1997, Downs thought he had a mandate to toughen his stance on wage and productivity issues in labor negotiations. When negotiations reached a standstill in 1998, the Clinton administration appointed a presidential emergency board to offer nonbinding recommendations. The board recommended wage increases larger than Downs was prepared to accept, but when the unions threatened to strike, Amtrak's board of directors forced Downs to accept the emergency board's recommendations. The settlement added $260 million to operating costs in 1999, including $144 million in recurring costs and $116 million in signing bonuses and retroactive payments. Downs resigned in frustration over the board's actions.

Getting Serious: Another Round of Reform

The Amtrak Reform and Accountability Act (ARAA) of 1997 enshrined the Claytor commitment in law, although it extended the deadline by two years, to 2002. The act authorized funding for Amtrak's operating losses through 2002, but in declining amounts each year so that Amtrak would be self-sufficient by the end of 2002. The act also created an eleven-member Amtrak Reform Council (ARC) to monitor Amtrak's progress to self-sufficiency.[23] If Amtrak did not meet its goal, ARC was to inform Congress and the president and propose a plan to restructure the national passenger rail system. If Congress rejected ARC's restructuring plan, Amtrak would be liquidated.

In the same legislative session that established the ARC, Congress also passed the Taxpayer Relief Act of 1997; it authorized $2.3 billion in capital grants to Amtrak to fund the Acela program and other improvements. Then, after almost a year's delay, the Amtrak board appointed George Warrington, the head of Amtrak's Northeast Corridor business unit, as Tom Downs's replacement. In 1999, Amtrak's board approved Warrington's network growth strategy, which set a goal of increasing gross revenues by $789 million between fiscal years (FY) 1998 and 2002. Revenue growth was to come from a combination of a 21 percent increase in ridership, higher fares on the premium Acela service, and new services such as the carriage of US mail and express packages on Amtrak's passenger trains.[24] In 2000, however, the Government Accountability Office (GAO) warned Congress that Amtrak was unlikely to meet its goal of operating self-sufficiency without cutting costs more aggressively.

Generating new revenues turned out to be harder than expected, as illustrated by Amtrak's odd mail and express initiative in the late 1990s. Amtrak, and private railroads before it, had always carried US mail on its passenger trains, but the new plan called for also carrying freight in special express cars in existing passenger trains. In addition to acquiring a fleet of new express cars with scarce federal equipment guarantees—cars that had little resale value—Amtrak needed to modify fifteen passenger routes and build a hub in Chicago. Handling the freight cars in Amtrak trains meant a need for more locomotive power and delays for switching, which infuriated passengers.[25]

The Reform Council's Recommendations

In November 2001, just weeks after the terrorist attacks in New York and Washington, the ARC, composed of knowledgeable and, under the circumstances, remarkably nonpartisan folk, found in a 6 to 5 vote that Amtrak would not meet its goal of operating self-sufficiency by 2002. The dissenting votes came from Amtrak supporters, who argued that the test should be postponed in a time of national emergency, and from appointees of President George W. Bush, who wanted a delay to allow the new administration time to develop its own plan for Amtrak. But a majority of ARC members felt that it was time to acknowledge the obvious.

The finding required ARC to recommend a reorganization plan to Congress, which it did in February 2002. The proposal, though radical, was supported by nine of ARC's eleven members, with only one vote against (by the labor representative) and one abstention (by the secretary of transportation). Their proposed alternative was to dismember Amtrak into a number of regional operating subsidiaries chartered by the National Railroad Passenger Corporation.[26] It was never clear just how Amtrak's key legislated asset—the right of access to private freight railroad lines at incremental cost[27]—was going to be preserved in this reformulated tripartite arrangement.

Congress never had a chance to act on ARC's proposal. Shortly before the proposal was to be released, Amtrak announced that it needed a $1.2-billion appropriation to survive FY 2003. This request was much more than the $521 million that Amtrak had initially requested for FY 2003, but Amtrak threatened to discontinue all of its long-distance passenger trains by October 1, 2002, if it did not receive the money. Coming so soon after the upheaval of September 11, 2001, and thus faced with an entirely new and more urgent US energy security crisis—as well as a perceived alternative to at least some air travel—Congress felt it had little choice but to approve Amtrak funding. This was "Congress-think," of course; the consensus was that if air travel could be held hostage by terrorists, it certainly was no time for the United States to stop investing in rail passenger service.

By then, Congress had lost trust in George Warrington, and he stepped down as president in May. The glide-path was to a crash landing—as the whole idea of Amtrak self-sufficiency was shown to be a hollow notion under the reality of the times; Amtrak could neither control costs nor raise revenues adequately to reach overall operating self-sufficiency. Only the Northeast Corridor operations had that potential.

With respect to the ARC proposal and other suggestions for reform of Amtrak's mission and funding, good intentions alone do not yield success. As everyone has come to understand (and the authors of this book are no exception), there was no shortage of reasonable reform proposals,[28] just a shortage of political consensus and will to resolve the rail passenger service dilemma once and for all.[29]

Gunn to the Top

Warrington's successor, David Gunn, soon discovered that Amtrak's financial affairs were indeed as bad as anyone had imagined. Over the course of his career, Gunn had run the commuter rail systems for the metropolitan transportation authorities of Boston, New York, Philadelphia, and Washington, DC. He was blunt-spoken by nature and perhaps a bit more so once he had been lured out of retirement in Nova Scotia to take the Amtrak job. Gunn soon publicly confirmed what ARC suspected—that Amtrak had been misclassifying operating expenses as capital expenses to make it appear that Amtrak was on the way to improving its financial condition.[30] Partly as a result, Amtrak's physical plant was in terrible shape. In an interview with *Transportation Weekly*, Gunn said that the accounting shams and neglected investments were a logical response to the "ass backwards" incentives established by the Amtrak Reform and Accountability Act of 1997.

David Gunn's clarion call—his signature policy invocation—was that Amtrak must be "put in a state of good repair." By that he meant keeping to optimal maintenance schedules for both equipment and track where Amtrak owned its own right of way. Good repair would yield a more comfortable ride for passengers, reduce derailments, and, he hoped, keep locomotives from being unavailable for assignment or "dead in consist." Eventually, and no surprise to anyone, Gunn clashed with the second Bush administration's secretary of transportation, Norman Mineta, over its repeat of David Stockman's zero-out budget; like Tom Downs, Gunn had to make his way to the door. Not far behind him was his successor, Alexander Kummant, who spent only two years at Amtrak and left behind little of note.

The Route Profitability System: Assessing the Contributions of Specific Routes

In addition to his other contributions, Tom Downs had launched an important effort to gain better managerial understanding of costs. In this initiative, he engaged outside consultants to design a route profitability system (RPS). The system was designed to capture incremental costs on a systematic basis for all Amtrak trains—long distance *and* corridor. Where Amtrak is a tenant on properties owned by a host railroad, RPS captured the trackage fees paid to the host, as well as its own above the rail operating costs (locomotive expense, rolling stock maintenance, on-board crew costs, etc.). Where Amtrak owns the infrastructure (as in the Northeast Corridor), a separate costing system was needed to capture rail right-of-way capital and maintenance costs—which amounted to some $900 million annually in the NEC alone—so these could be allocated and added to the RPS. Sadly for ongoing analysis of Amtrak's performance and prospects, production and publication of the RPS was suspended for a number of years; development of the RPS recently resumed in a somewhat different form.

The raw RPS data for the years they are available show quite a range in financial performance. (See Figure 11.1 for more details.) The NEC Acela trains perform best, and some of the long-haul trains are clear losers.

Properly Evaluating Amtrak's Costs

The complications of costing railroad passenger service are rooted in several key issues. First is the fact that Amtrak owns the Northeast Corridor right of way, but to operate the rest of its network, it only pays trackage fees to host railroads.[31] As noted, the 1970 legislation compelled access from the private freight railroads for Amtrak's operation, and it made the cost reimbursement formula something closer to incremental cost than full economic cost coverage. While the RPS facilitated looking at Amtrak routes on a consistent basis, it was not totally definitive with respect to route economics in all cases. RPS shows that, overall, Amtrak does not cover its costs, however defined, with the possible exception of the Acela and perhaps some Northeast regional trains. Final answers depend on operating ratios developed by the RPS and on the capital sums Amtrak reinvests in its owned Northeast Corridor, its depreciation charges, and

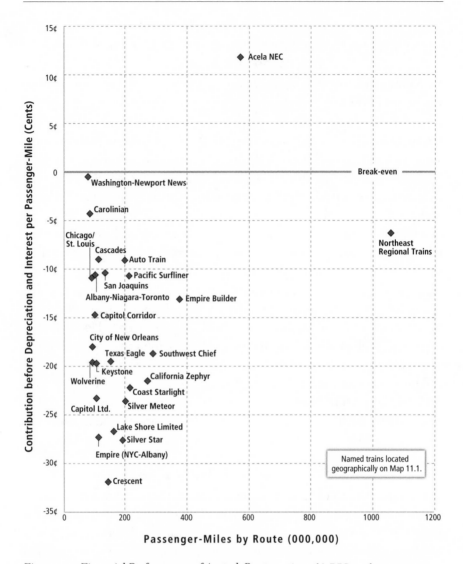

Figure 11.1 Financial Performance of Amtrak Routes. Amtrak's RPS results were suspended after 2009 and have only recently been restarted on a revised basis. As of the year ending September 2009, only Acela trains in the Northeast Corridor were profitable. Long-distance, off-corridor, named trains generally showed deficits ranging from 10 to 30 cents per passenger mile. Named train route locations are shown in Map 11.1. *Source:* Data compiled by Louis Thompson from "Amtrak Monthly Performance Summary," September 30, 2009, pp. A3.6 and C1.

how it accounts for revenues received from hosting freight and commuter trains on the Northeast Corridor.

A second matter is that incremental cost is a useful concept for analyzing the relative efficiency of alternative Amtrak services within the context of the RPS, but it is not the proper cost concept for answering the question of whether or not the fees Amtrak pays its host railroads cover the actual costs they impose. As the authors' longtime colleague Louis Thompson points out, the trackage fees Amtrak pays the host railroads are neither trivial nor overwhelming; they could be substantially increased in a different policy regime, or they could be left much as they are without bankrupting the freight roads.

That said, as a matter of fairness to the freights and to honest evaluation of Amtrak's burden, the actual cost Amtrak pays its hosts really does not equate to the true economic cost to the freight railroads of handling passenger trains. The reason is that true economic cost requires understanding and accounting for the alternatives foregone when resources are employed in one pursuit and not another. Economists call these opportunity costs, of course, and they are never the same from one time and place to another, or from one use or user to another.[32] They are as fickle as the prairie wind and almost impossible to catch in a spreadsheet.

Regarding these opportunity costs, when considering the policy implications of continuing Amtrak long-haul trains, policy makers must take into account that, by and large, Amtrak wants to use the best of the freight railroads' lines—and at the peak season no less than off peak. What is the highest and best use of that capacity—which is the same as asking, What is its opportunity cost? Does the US economy really want that scarce peak rail capacity used for travelers (who could fly or drive) as much as it wants freight railroads to attract trucks off the interstates?

The market answers opportunity cost questions silently, swiftly, and fairly, but it can only do so correctly if it is not artificially constrained by old regulatory rules and unwarranted political interventions. Almost certainly the "best" set of passenger train services is not what Congress forced Amtrak to run in its first four decades, and perhaps not what Amtrak chooses to continue to operate. Table 11.1 summarizes the complexity of costing Amtrak's network under its mixed status as owner or tenant in different route circumstances.

Table 11.1   Complexity of Costing Amtrak Routes

	Compelled Access Regime	Opportunity Cost Regime
Northeast Corridor	Amtrak owns and operates = capital + operating cost	True ownership cost: capital improvement, maintenance, and operating cost
Long-distance trains	Above rail operating cost + mandated access and trackage rental to host	Above rail operating cost + opportunity cost (freight railroads' next-best use of track capacity)

Rail passenger service in the Northeast Corridor has an entirely different cost structure compared with long-distance passenger service. The latter includes fees paid to track owners (freight and commuter railroads) for access to and maintenance of trackage used by Amtrak trains. The former reflects Amtrak's ownership and direct maintenance of Northeast Corridor properties. Different models for arriving at infrastructure costs include today's ownership or legislated access regime (center column) and the opportunity cost regime proposed in this chapter for determining trackage fees Amtrak should pay its host railroads (rightmost column).

Amtrak Funding and Policy Alternatives

The annual funding of Amtrak's ordinary operating deficit surged to over $800 million in 1980 and 1981 and then settled back to $600 million or so between 1986 and 1991, subsequently soaring to almost $800 million in 1995. From 1996 to 2000, funding for ordinary operations subsided to the $600 million range, except for 1998, when it fell to under $400 million, even though total funding in that year hit an historic high of $1.7 billion (suggesting that funds for capital purposes trickled down to alleviate pressures on the operating deficit).

These estimates assume that costs of commuter services provided by Amtrak to various communities were fully compensated. Because Amtrak supposedly provides such services at marginal costs with no allowance for use of infrastructure, it likely incurs a deficit because of them. Allowing for this possibility would only strengthen the conclusions presented here because the Amtrak subsidy would be covering some portion of the commuter operating deficits as well as its own. At the same time, the private freight railroads were probably undercompensated. Thus, it is likely that Amtrak, to some degree, was subsidizing commuter service but also being subsidized by freight railroads.

Figure 11.2 summarizes annual US government outlays on Amtrak activities (capital investments and operating subsidies) over the last three decades of the twentieth century, a total of approximately $30 billion. In addition,

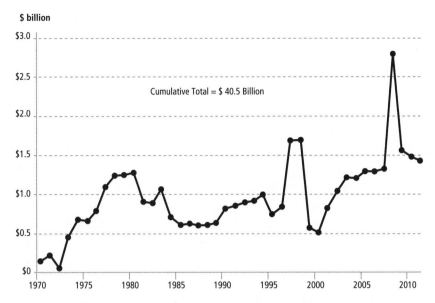

Figure 11.2   Amtrak Total Subsidy, 1971–2012.   Since its creation in 1970, Amtrak has received over $40 billion in government funding, or about $1 billion annually. The peak in 2008 was attributable in part to counter-recessionary spending proposed by the Obama administration and appropriated by Congress. *Source:* Data compilations from public information, courtesy Louis Thompson.

Amtrak was able to arrange over $4 billion in debt financing, mostly guaranteed by the federal government or against which NEC assets are pledged. State governments spent perhaps $1 billion or so more on intercity operating subsidies.

Amtrak's financial and operating record has been so mediocre that, at the end of the century, survival seemed at best an even-odds bet. As one self-styled "huge advocate" and user of rail transportation summarized the turn-of-the-century situation:

> The [Amtrak] game was played for 30 years. It's time to play a
> new game—with new players and new rules. . . . If Amtrak con-
> tinues as it is, it will be the provider of last resort. With that type
> of mentality, we'll end up with more of the same.[33]

Defining a workable alternative to Amtrak requires demystifying and reconstructing both its political and economic foundations. Should Amtrak provide service only where it can make a profit? Does the system really have to be national in scope, that is, provide some transcontinental service, even if it is unprofitable? As the CBO succinctly summarized the situation: "The chief point of contention since Amtrak's formation has been whether passenger rail should be a national system that receives federal subsidies on routes where it cannot cover its costs, or whether it should be an enterprise that offers service only where profitable"—even if that means eliminating all transcontinental service.[34]

Amtrak faced a Hobson's choice: Political survival seemed to depend on operating a collection of long-haul trains serving markets located widely throughout the United States; this wide coverage was believed to be a sine qua non for assembling a majority in Congress. On the other side of the quandary, many observers believed, economic survival might be possible only if long-haul services were discontinued. Randolph Resor[35] and other observers believed that Amtrak's focus on preservation of a national network may have distorted objective selection of the markets it should try to serve, such that maintaining the national network meant neglect of short-distance markets with greater potential. Indeed, we are back to the question of whether or not Amtrak's board and management should cling to the idea of a national network in order to try to hold together a political coalition willing to continue to fund Amtrak's ongoing deficits.

Three Options for Future Passenger Service

Financial and political realities that have dogged institutional Amtrak from its genesis continue to shape the search for a new set of alternatives from which passenger train development, retention, and subsidy policy would emanate. The most likely options are three:

1. Status quo, with catch-up funding and greater participation of the states in support of regional corridor services. Institutional bodies in motion, like inert masses in the natural world, tend to remain in motion in the direction they are headed. The status quo is likely unless a new political consensus develops for change—for example, to promote green transport policy. Such a change requires minimally a compelling voice of leadership, a message that can be trusted, and available resources for accomplishment of the consensus objectives. Lacking these, the status quo is likely to persist.

2. Deep cuts in Amtrak's route structure, based on additional efforts to determine route profitability—but otherwise regardless of their location—the goal being to take the system down to the maximum affordable set. Any policy for Amtrak that moves away from the status quo

potentially raises some major difficulties. The most serious problem created by any abrupt phasing out or downsizing of passenger train subsidies and operations is that of liability for contractual labor protection costs. Amtrak contracts with organized labor in force at the end of the century called for severance payments of up to six years' pay and benefits. The GAO estimated these claims had a potential present value of over $3 billion.

3. Breakup of Amtrak into more manageable pieces that might attract new sponsors, as proposed by the ARC and others. Passenger operators would contract with freight railroads for access to right of way or construct their own. Operators other than the NRPC (like commuter rail agencies today) would no longer be automatic beneficiaries of compelled access to freight railroad facilities.

Of the three options, (2) deep cuts would likely be least costly, while costs for (3) the breakup of Amtrak are indeterminate. Option (3) possibly would be the most thoroughgoing reform because a large number of options can be explored under contracts (see Box 11.1). Still, loss of compelled access could be the death knell for marginal passenger services on freight railroads.

Box 11.1 Contracts with Freight Railroads in an Alternative Scenario

Under the breakup scenario, operators of passenger services would occupy the same position as large shippers of freight do in the post-Staggers era. Passenger operators could bargain and contract with railroads for use of their rights of way and facilities at certain times and stipulated volumes. As with freight, potential passenger service operators would be expected to negotiate with the railroads about possible trade-offs at several margins: for example, the seasonality of the service, importance of on-time performance, need to provide locomotion, the average target speed of the operation, strength and duration of any diurnal schedule cycles, provision of on-line emergency maintenance of equipment, length of contract, and so on. The railroads would strike a bargain with the passenger service provider if they could accommodate those needs at a financial return that made the railroads better off; in particular, the bargain would not force the host railroads (due to capacity constraints) to deny service to other shippers who made larger contributions to rail overhead and profits.

(continued)

Box 11.1 *Continued*

A contractual solution also greatly reduces the chances that any resurgence in passenger travel would distort rail freight economics and operations, meaning that if there are grounds for agreement on a contract, other interests at issue (poorly understood cost consequences, conflicting operational priorities, operational difficulties, liability risks, etc.), have all been negotiated to a satisfactory conclusion.

The key issue is whether or not the NRPC would retain the right to compel passenger service, more or less on its own terms. The risk, of course, is that without federally mandated access, passenger operators might feel much like a captive shipper in the freight analogy, and that may be politically unacceptable. It is not obvious, however, that the resulting networks would look very different under these two regimes. Political markets (pursuing votes) and economic markets (pursuing dollars) are both likely to follow population density, scale, and propensity to use public (common carriage) services.

In contracts, state and local governments and their agencies could initiate or join and subsidize potential passenger service enterprises as they saw fit. New enterprises would be vested with the usual rights of eminent domain; because of the apparent advantages of running high-speed passenger services over their own exclusive rights of way, it might be expected that passenger service startups would pursue this option except in dense urban areas where land values were exceptionally high. For example, in the case of France's TGVs, high-speed trains operate on new, separated facilities over hill and dale, but return to existing (slow) rails for entry to downtown stations. Thus, access to a city and its rail terminals might be arranged more inexpensively by contracting with existing operations, either freight railroads or local transit and commuter services.

Separate Status for the Northeast Corridor

Among its accomplishments since 1970, Amtrak helped establish a strong political consensus that rail operations are essential in the Northeast Corridor and that such operations held promise for being the most important in Amtrak's network. Exactly what forms these operations should take are still in dispute, however. Alternative solution sets could be franchised private firms, contract operations under multistate public compacts (see more below), and continued quasi-public integrated ownership and operation under Amtrak, among other possibilities.

From the larger perspective of what to do with Amtrak, initially all that seems to be needed is agreement that the NEC situation is distinctively different from other passenger train issues—and is best separated from them. The authors of this book believe that the NEC should be spun out and allowed to find a politically and economically acceptable solution on its own. This is feasible because Amtrak owns the NEC from Washington, DC, to New Rochelle, New York and could secure rights to Boston in the course of creating a nine-state compact (ten if extended to Virginia) for the purpose of owning and operating the NEC service—no federally compelled access would be necessary. And formation of a separate integrated owner/operator company for the NEC is desirable, we believe, because it provides the right kind of organizational vehicle and economic incentives for improved and lasting services in the corridor.

The heart of the continuing Amtrak public policy problem, we conclude, is in the rest of the operation—away from the profitable or potentially profitable Northeast Corridor and specialized operations such as Auto-Train. It is in that "remainder," representing roughly half of the total operation, that the deep policy disagreements still reside.[36]

Future Passenger Corridors Outside the NEC

An important wild card in these policy options is the somewhat greater likelihood in the future of intercity short-haul corridor passenger services being set up outside the Northeast Corridor than was the case prior to passage of the Passenger Rail Investment and Improvement Act in 2008. The emerging model for these 200–400 mile higher-speed passenger corridors (two- to four-hour transit time) is Los Angeles to San Diego, or Chicago to St. Louis. The longer Los Angeles–San Francisco corridor has many advocates, but at nearly 500 miles via the Central Valley, it may be a project of a different kind. How might the federal government best help those regions interested in mounting regional corridor services?

One idea is to promote multistate compacts formed for the purpose of constructing and operating corridor passenger trains. For example, the government might put up capital funding for purchase of lightly used freight lines to be incorporated in networks and operating services sponsored by the compacts. Example compact initiatives might include Illinois–Wisconsin–Minnesota for Chicago–Minneapolis services; an Illinois–Indiana–Michigan compact to sponsor services in the Chicago–Detroit corridor; Virginia–North Carolina for Washington–Richmond–

Raleigh–Charlotte trains; or Oregon–Washington–British Columbia for Portland–Seattle–Vancouver, British Columbia, services. Regional compacts are rather unnatural in US governmental structure, but the promise of federal capital grants as match funding for the regional compacts might speed the process and leverage regional funding resources applied to the construction and operation of corridor facilities. Amtrak would be involved in operation of some—presumably, but perhaps not all—of these new corridors.

The issue of passenger train access to freight lines for development and operation of any new passenger service by parties other than the NRPC is far from resolved. The FRA has issued some broad guidelines for how state-based agencies should relate to the freight railroads in establishing regimes for access to existing rail lines and management of liability issues, but in most cases, actual arrangements are not likely to be finalized for some years.

Probably most passenger train advocates and their political sponsors will conclude that it simply would be too risky to go the policy route of the breakup scenario. Instead, they likely will focus all efforts on preserving the status quo, including the mandatory access authority that NRPC holds. Perhaps advocates of new services will also make more effort to find longer-term funding arrangements and more durable and flexible regional compacts.

Concluding Thoughts: Amtrak—Success or Failure?

With all this complexity and controversy, it is not easy to offer a summary judgment on whether the Amtrak experiment has been a success or a failure. Given the turmoil and confusion that have characterized Amtrak history, it would seem unequivocal that the corporation represented a failed public policy. Such a judgment might be premature, however.

A Failure?

We must say that the bar for success of Amtrak has been set rather low. Route profitability based on incremental costs would be insufficient as a standard if applied to normal private businesses, including the freight railroads.

Amtrak's supporters are quick to say in its defense that "nowhere in the world is widespread passenger service profitable" and that "America could have a viable passenger train network if we did not subsidize auto and air

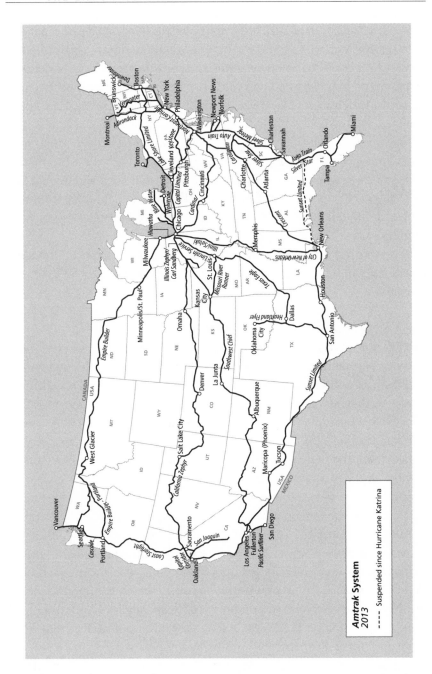

Map 11.1 Amtrak Routes as of 2013. Amtrak has always attempted to preserve a national system, often featuring service to state capitals as symbolic of that policy. This map locates key routes and named trains, which are evaluated in Figure 11.1. *Source*: Amtrak.com, where an interactive map can be used to locate detailed routes showing points served and to determine fares for specific trips.

travel." Perhaps most clearly, forty years of Amtrak passenger train service does not stack up well against its increasingly more distant cousins in the Class I freight railroad network. It is the passenger rail blues—a cost to taxpayers of roughly $1 billion annually—in contrast to Class I freight railroads, which in 2013 were worth about $200 billion in market capitalization.[37]

The United States likely does not underinvest in passenger rail, as is so often lamented. The trouble is that, because we do not allow the market and Amtrak management to make unfettered decisions about what services should be operated on what routes, the substantial public resources provided annually to Amtrak almost certainly are not spent as wisely as they could be.[38]

Passenger rail supporters can force the system to be larger than budget hawks are willing to fund. Year after year, Amtrak is caught in the same dilemma.

A Success?

Amtrak was brought into being by a remarkably broad political coalition, currying substantial support from both major political parties and a wide spectrum of political interest groups. To a considerable extent, all these groups had their interests recognized and most were catered to rather effectively. Regarding the employment and social dislocation concerns of rail trade unions, Amtrak retained a higher level of passenger service employment than otherwise was likely; even though total employment at Amtrak declined from just under 40,000 in 1971 to just over 25,000 in 2000, this was proportionally less of a decline than similar employment cuts made on the freight railroads over the same years.

Two major categories of benefits were realized by Amtrak: The agency gained control over a group of assets useful for future passenger transportation services, and intercity passenger operations were maintained on a significant portion of the pre-Amtrak network, the most important being the Northeast Corridor. In addition, and less tangibly, Amtrak helped achieve other public policy goals that probably would have been both more difficult and expensive if Amtrak had not existed.[39]

The argument that establishing Amtrak as an operating institution was superior public policy (compared with providing direct reimbursement for the passenger deficits that freight railroads incurred) could not be proven then or now. In the early 1970s there was no expectation that Amtrak would be given major ongoing subsidies, while the prospect of trying to cover railroads' losses on passenger service seemed inordinately expensive.

Today, with hindsight of the large appropriations Amtrak actually received (and the added awareness that the freight railroads were able to perform admirably once they were deregulated), the case is not so clear. Perhaps Amtrak was the cheaper alternative, and perhaps it was a more appropriate response to the crisis than traditional subsidies to the owner-operator freight railroads would have been, but perhaps not. Similarly, diverting responsibility for funding unemployment insurance and the rail retirement program from the freight railroads to the passenger sector (where they more legitimately belonged) has been seen as another corollary benefit of setting up Amtrak, but again, the bottom line is unclear. In sum, creating Amtrak may not have been the cheapest way of garnering these indirect policy benefits, but it did the job.

Some observers will be surprised by our conclusion that Amtrak appears to have done a remarkable job in holding the costs for operation of a large forty-six-state network to a politically acceptable level (perhaps partly because it adhered to the nationwide service model). While it may not have been the best service possible with budgets of between $500 million to nearly $1 billion annually, and while from time to time it was threatened with defunding by Republican administrations, Amtrak survived and kept on running its forever popular passenger trains (as judged by ridership and congressional support).

Given the sometimes awkward family relationship between freight and passenger trains, journalist Don Phillips has another perspective to offer regarding the final judgment on whether policy enabling Amtrak has been a success or a failure. Because he has followed these debates longer and more closely than just about anyone, we should let him have the last word. Phillips writes in a recent piece:

> An amazing series of things came together in just the right order to save passenger railroading, and eventually to save the freight railroad system, too. In fact, as the months progressed, the development of a government passenger corporation became more of a way to prevent nationalization of freight railroading than to save the passenger train. If the passenger train burden could be removed, perhaps the freight railroads . . . could avoid the disaster of nationalization.[40]

Phillips is right. Amtrak has been an expensive program, but it has helped preserve the higher goal, a sustainable freight railroad system in the private sector. The same or similar might have resulted from simply allowing discontinuation of all passenger trains outside the NEC— avoiding all issues of compelled access and Amtrak underpayment to host railroads—but that did not happen and probably could not have happened politically.

12

ADVANCING TECHNOLOGY
FOR AMERICAN RAILROADS

The sweeping allegation that railroads have been almost totally
resistant to change—that a great part of their current difficulties may be ascribed to a stubborn refusal to look for and to
apply technological improvements—is not supported by fact.
Science and technology are not exploited to full advantage
by the railroads, but, even if they were, they are not a panacea for all their present woes. External to the industry are the
social and political barriers that impede the effective application of research and development, and thus, in the final analysis,
these external problems are more critical than the technological ones.

—National Academy of Science, Committee on Science and
Technology in Railroads (1963)[1]

The nineteenth century brought about a splendid flowering of the
mechanical arts and the bending of machines to the labors of humankind. Among the greatest of these was the innovation of the railroad
itself—unknown before 1800 but soon to become the dominant method of
moving people and cargo almost anywhere on civilized land. Before the
end of the nineteenth century, railroads had grown to be the largest
employer in the United States and the most managerially sophisticated
business enterprises anywhere—a model for many other entrepreneurial
and governmental endeavors.[2]

In the same historical vein, however, railroads are often thought of as an
old-fashioned technology that has not kept up with space age advances in
science, engineering, materials, miniaturization, and management tools.
This chapter of *American Railroads* will demonstrate that the conventional
wisdom is manifestly untrue.

343

One of the great themes of railroading in the twentieth century—to go with government intervention, regulation and deregulation, consolidation through mergers, and the rise and fall of passenger service—is the continuing behind-the-scenes importance of technological improvement. In 1900, US railroads hauled 139,000 ton-miles per employee; in 2000, that ratio was over 8.7 million ton-miles per employee, or more than sixty-two times as much, and the main reason for the explosion of output per worker was technological progress.[3]

In the 200 years since Trevithick and Stephenson gave the industry its foundations, railroads have induced a remarkable string of technological improvements—more powerful steam locomotives, iron and then steel rail, pneumatic brakes, electric track circuits and fail-safe signaling systems, the Janney coupler, centralized traffic control, diesel-electric locomotives to replace steam engines, automated classification yards, portable two-way radio communications, applications of computerized information management systems, and initial demonstrations of positive train control (PTC). Technological innovations have helped the railroads remain young despite their old age.[4]

Technology is the force driving railroad efficiency and productivity through the decades. External events and influences such as poorly performing economies might periodically slow railroad output, and indeed, relief from government economic regulation was needed for the industry finally to prosper in recent decades, but historically railroads typically could use technology to find a way to adapt and survive in less than perfect circumstances. Technological advances made over the course of the twentieth century are the underlying reason why the American railroad enterprise endured in troubled times. Technology improvements touched every aspect of the industry and multiplied the efforts of every worker.

An Integrated Engineering System

Technologically, and following the proper definition of the term *railroads* used in this book, the industry represent what present-day engineering educators call an integrated engineering system. In this concept, railroads are composed of a number of subsystems—the most important being locomotion, track, right-of-way structures, rolling stock, communications and train control, and managerial information systems. Technological improvement in railroading usually takes the form of upgrading the performance characteristics of one or more of these subsystems. Some upgrades are powerful and ingenious innovations designed specifically for the railroad industry.

Occasionally, a subsystem upgrade can be so significant, so economically powerful, that several other subsystems find themselves reengineered to accommodate the initial technology deployment. The most important single technological change in railroading in the twentieth century, dieselization, was clearly of this type. It revolutionized virtually all of the operating, many of the maintenance, and even some of the managerial systems used in the business.

Specific railroad technologies, such as steam locomotives, iron and later steel T-rails, air brakes, fail-safe electric track circuits, and the automatic knuckle coupler, were instrumental in making railroads into one of the largest and economically most important industries of the nineteenth century. In addition to these ingenious innovations that were designed specifically for the industry, railroads had an almost uncanny ability to adapt and incorporate into their businesses new technologies arising in other sectors of the economy, for example, telegraphy and telephony, low-cost steelmaking, electric motors and lighting, and the internal combustion engine, to name the most important. Those more generic technologies could then become sources of even greater productivity when made part of the evolving integrated engineering system, which now we can fairly call modern railroads.

A Century of Progress

Technological progress, so visibly evident in the first century of railroading, continued to provide advantages to the industry in the twentieth century. Despite competition from other modes and the heavy pall of rate regulation, railroad companies and their suppliers came up with dozens of labor-saving, safety-enhancing, and productivity-boosting devices that helped the industry stay competitive and earn adequate profits for reinvestment.

When rival modes were able to leverage public subsidies and challenge railroad dominance in the first half of the twentieth century, advances in signaling systems, roller bearings, and railcar innovations gave railroads new ways to save costs and remain a useful option for shippers. When redundant labor and obsolete facilities in the Great Depression or labor and locomotive shortages in World War II threatened railroad productivity, development of diesel-electric locomotives promised an enormous store of cost savings and reliable motive power capacity. When traffic patterns changed after World War II, unit train operations helped shippers reach new, more distant markets. When service quality became an international imperative for manufacturing and distribution in the 1980s, railroad innovations in containerization and double-stack trains helped railroads hold onto or win back lost business.[5]

In that same era, when competition from heavy trucks operating on the interstate highways took market share with remarkable advances in service reliability, railroads got the message and began using technology to control operations, track shipments, and make service commitments. When fuel costs rose, railroads exploited their inherent fuel efficiency. When concerns about safety and hazardous materials handling widened, railroads found ways to drive accident rates even lower. Today, under legislative prodding, railroads are investing large sums in making preventable collisions a thing of the past.

Railroads were able to do these things because they were technological omnivores—they searched out, found, and devoured nearly every invention fertile minds could devise. They were technology-intensive. As George Westinghouse himself observed, he one of the greatest nineteenth century innovators in any field, "The more things we invent, the more we need to invent."[6] If that were so, the enormous outpouring of inventive activity in his generation was at least in part to feed the hunger of railroads for expansion, improvement, and endurance.

Technology Deployment Through Capital Investment

Still, the opinion of most experts (this book's coauthors occasionally included) is that railroads have been sluggish in adopting new technologies—especially innovations in managerial methods and occasionally in physical hardware improvements—if the costs of deployment were extraordinarily high. This conventional wisdom needs to be revisited, however, especially in light of the remarkable renaissance of railroading since passage of the Staggers Rail Act of 1980.[7]

The perception of sluggish adoption of new technology may simply be due to the exceptionally long useful lives of many common railroad components; some railroad innovations arrived almost 200 years ago and yet live on in the daily operation of US railroads. More important, perhaps, is the fact that railroads are a network industry, meaning that to realize broadly synergistic gains, the entire network must be converted to a new and compatible standard. It does little good to convert only part of the network to a new gauge, coupler design, or braking system. PTC is an example of a group of new technologies for which consensus on standards, integration, and compatibility is critical to efficient deployment.

Deployment of new technology goes hand in hand with capital expenditures. Indeed, the main path by which new technology works its way into the railroad industry is through its embodiment in new capital investments. New locomotives are equipped with the latest component technologies, new concrete ties perform better than the timber ties they replace, relay rail is made from better steel than the old rail being recycled, and so on. A remarkable fact is that railroads reinvest about 18 percent of operating revenues in capital expenditures annually. While some other industries spend more on research and development of new products, few industries must commit such a large portion of revenues to capital reinvestment.

This chapter focuses on key technologies developed or improved in the twentieth century and applied to various requirements of the industry. We arrange these under the four components that, combined, constitute railroads properly defined: locomotives, track and structures, cars and trains, and communications and control systems. (See Box 12.1.) There seems no more fitting way to organize this rich; sometimes complex; and. for us, fascinating material.

Box 12.1.   Back to the Beginnings: Railroads Defined and Described

Earlier, *American Railroads* defined a railroad as an integrated transportation engineering system that combines locomotive power to move trains of cars hauling people or goods over fixed track structures under control. Four main attributes describe railroads:

1. *Railroads Draw Motive Power from Locomotives.* The great innovation enabling railroads was to mount a steam engine on wheels that fit on and ran over track supporting the engine's considerable weight. Steam engines had been operating in stationary installations pumping water out of mine shafts for over a century when Richard Trevithick, in 1804, demonstrated the

(continued)

Box 12.1. *Continued*

feasibility of a steam locomotive that could develop traction—that is, pulling power. Railroads then held their dominance over land transportation for about 100 years because heavy steam engines were not well adapted to road vehicles—especially not before broad, hard-surfaced roads came into wide usage.

2. *Railroads Benefit from the Low Rolling Resistance of Steel Wheels on Steel Rails.* It is a cliché, but true of course, that rails and wheels (also bridges and locomotives) were fashioned initially of iron, but greater strength and lower costs came with Bessemer steel—a huge boost to railroads after 1860. Steel rails gave trains smooth paths across all kinds of terrain: along winding rivers and on bridges over broad waterways, across desert sands or muddy plains, up steep mountain grades and through long tunnels, in narrow corridors of crowded cities. What railroads gained by their fixed rails and rights of ways, however, they sometimes lost to more flexible modes that could steer their vehicles to widely dispersed markets and home again.

3. *Railroads Gain More Efficiency and Versatility by Entraining Freight or Passenger Cars.* Railroad efficiency did not end with low rolling resistance; it was extended longitudinally by the idea of a train. Coupling cars into trains behind a locomotive enabled one source of power to propel many trailing vehicles carrying goods or passengers. This is also the source of marketing flexibility for railroads because switchable cars can carry various commodities to multiple destinations. Adding another car to the end of a train means low marginal costs; running full trains of similar cars from one place to another means lower average unit costs.

4. *Railroads Build Systems to Enable Safe Control of Operations.* From their beginnings, railroads needed systems for managing the great momentum gathered in trains and allocating space and time on the track. Trains were equipped with air brakes and, like signal systems, were configured ingeniously so that if cars pulled apart, they would come to a safe stop. Other trains or vehicles crossing tracks needed to be told of their location and priority or warned of approaching danger. Malfunctioning equipment can still cause accidents, but these are decreasing in long-term trends. Rules for safe train operations are strictly enforced, with training, employee testing, and discipline for violations, but human errors remain a considerable challenge for railroads. In the future, PTC systems will intervene to prevent a collision if a train engineer misses a signal to slow or stop or becomes disabled.

> **Box 12.1.**
>
> Because they were built to stay on guiding and supporting rails, trains can efficiently use advanced technology systems to manage their normal operations and make optimal use of available capacity. Train or wayside-based systems can perform continuous health monitoring and send trains to maintenance facilities to correct incipient problems. Trains can be made to move only when and where they are commanded to, and these functions can be automated when it makes sense to do so.

Locomotives

The Arrival of Diesel-Electric Locomotives

By all accounts the most important innovation in railroading in the twentieth century was the replacement of steam engines with diesel-electric locomotives in the twenty years between 1939 and 1959. The transition from steam to diesel-electric locomotive power touched every aspect of the industry and many public institutions far afield. Historian Maury Klein summarized the impact: "The diesel locomotive revolutionized the way railroads performed their work; reconfigured the physical landscape of railroads; redefined the role of labor in this most traditional of industries; transformed the structure of labor relations; and consigned to the realm of nostalgia an entire subculture rooted in a shared passion for that dominant symbol of nineteenth-century America, the steam locomotive."[8]

Had the diesel-electric locomotive not been developed and trains thus still forced to rely on steam engines, most railroads probably could not have survived the post–World War II loss of business to highways and trucking. The pressures of the new competition from other modes (as described in Chapter 4) could not have been matched by railroads burdened by the labor intensity and poor asset utilization characteristic of steam engine operations. It is also hard to imagine how steam locomotives would have been able to operate under the mandates of the clean air legislation enacted in 1970 and 1990.

Figure 12.1 Advent of the Diesel-Electric Locomotive. The diesel-electric hybrid locomotive was, by nearly all accounts, the most important railroad invention of the twentieth century. Its key components were a prime mover (a self-igniting diesel engine of the type invented by Rudolph Diesel in 1896), married to a direct current (DC) generator, which developed power to energize DC traction motors mounted one to an axle on the locomotive. The hybrid nature of the technology meant that locomotives could pull enormous loads without wheels slipping and without gear shifting. This arrangement was first accomplished and demonstrated by a collaboration of General Electric and Ingersoll Rand in 1925. The photo shows an early example of the successful design working alongside a traditional steam engine. The image is dark and dusty, but for that reason all the more true to its actual surroundings. *Source:* Ingersoll Rand. Used with permission.

After Rudolf Diesel's efficient engine design breakthrough, it took about thirty more years to develop workable methods for marrying the internal combustion engine to an electric power generator and traction motors to power the hybrid diesel-electric locomotive.[9] The integrated technology application was the product of industrial research and design (R&D) led by General Electric's Herman Lemp, working with Ingersoll-Rand in the 1920s (see Figure 12.1). Lemp's design automatically adjusted the prime mover's generation of electricity to the draw of current for traction motors as needed for locomotive pulling power. Initial applications were limited to switching assignments, but further improvements, particularly those made by the Electro-Motive Division of General Motors in the mid- to late 1930s, yielded a streamlined, multiple unit (MU) configuration[10] of diesel-electric locomotives with ample pulling power for mainline freight and passenger operations. Railroad dieselization was delayed initially

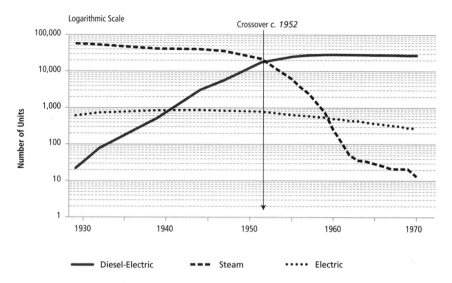

Figure 12.2   Dieselization: The Demise of Steam.   Diesel-electric locomotives were initially introduced and proven to be effective in the 1930s, but they did not fully supplant steam engines until the 1950s. Much of the delay was due to the US War Production Board restrictions during World War II that allocated diesel engine manufacturing capacity to landing craft, submarines, and other war requirements. When a railroad was able to replace substantially its steam engine roster with diesel-electric locomotives, it could retire roundhouses, specialized steam maintenance mechanics and facilities, coal chutes, water tanks, and firefighters in the engine. *Sources:* Data for 1929–1954 were published by the US Department of Commerce and include all US railroads. Data for 1955–1975 are from the AAR's *Fact Books* for 1972 and 1978, and are for Class I railroads only (the preponderance of the industry), but the two series are otherwise consistent.

(mainly because of wartime requirements for deployment of medium-speed diesel engines, notably in tanks and landing craft) and was not fully complete until about 1960.

As shown in Figure 12.2, once begun, the diesel-electric innovation quickly spread, essentially being accomplished in the first decade after World War II. Total rail output remained more or less constant during this period, suggesting that two diesel locomotives could do the work of three steam engines: 29,000 of the 35,000 or so steam locomotives in service in 1947 were replaced by an addition to the diesel fleet of approximately 19,000 units between 1947 and 1955. Steam locomotive–hauled freight trains with a caboose in those days required crews of about five persons per train; in subsequent years, trains with diesel-electric locomotives normally could manage well with a two-person crew and an end-of-train device (ETOD) instead of a caboose.[11] This would imply that (after a period of readjustment) well over 100,000 fewer operating personnel were needed industry-wide because of the substitution of diesel for steam locomotion.

The diesel's impact, however, went well beyond operating train crew requirements because maintaining diesels locomotives involved considerably less labor than maintaining steam engines. As noted, initial use of diesel-electric locomotives was limited to switching operations. Then, in 1930, General Motors (GM) decided to get into the diesel locomotive business and made the key acquisitions of the Winton Engine Co. and Electro-Motive Company (EMC). Small successes followed, including engine sales for submarines and the famous 1934 Zephyr streamliner. In 1935, GM and its subsidiary EMC (later the Electro-Motive Division of GM; now a unit of Progress Rail, a Caterpillar subsidiary), committed funds for development and demonstration of a locomotive unit suitable for line-haul operations. The result was a 3,600-horsepower double-unit for the original Santa Fe Super Chief in 1935. Freight railroads, in their usual skepticism, thought this was fine but believed they had loads too big for diesel-electrics to handle.

In response, General Motors-EMD, under legendary innovator/salesperson Richard Dilworth, developed the famed demonstrator FT-103 (see Figure 12.3), a set of four of the streamlined units (two permanently coupled pairs) totaling 5,400 horsepower. In 1939–1940, EMD sent its diesel-electric locomotive on a whirlwind 83,000-mile tour of the United States and Canada. Over all kinds of terrain and on nearly every railroad's lines, the FT-103 proved that it could develop more low-speed tractive effort than competitor steam engines, which meant smooth starts and excellent performance on long mountain grades. Dilworth's cryptic postscript was that, while demonstrating it could pull a great deal of tonnage uphill, it "pulled a lot of trains in two,"[12] meaning that the FT-103's tractive power was on occasion greater than the strength of couplers and drawbars.

The effect of Dilworth's demonstrations was much like Trevithick's 130 years earlier, and a new generation of railroad locomotive power was assured. Legend has it that Dilworth's salesmanship was augmented by threats from GM traffic managers that they would divert automobile shipments away from railroads that were slow to dieselize, but it seems that both sides had too much to gain for these considerations, even if true, to have had much effect.

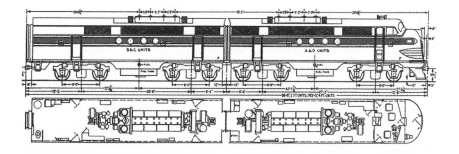

Figure 12.3 EMD's Demonstrator Diesel-Electric Locomotive. In 1939–1940, General Motors' Electro-Motive Division demonstrated the capabilities of its new FT-103 diesel-electric locomotive (shown here with an internal floor plan and trackside photo). GM/EMD took the demonstrator on a whirlwind tour of nearly every sizable North American railroad. The FT-103 proved it would develop more low-speed traction pulling power than competitor steam engines. The diagram (upper image) shows only two (B-A or C-D) of the four units in a typical consist (A-B-C-D); this arrangement was more frequently denominated A-B-B-A, with the A unit noses facing in opposite directions, as in the lower image. *Sources:* Upper image courtesy of the Burlington Route Historical Society, Thomas Whitt President, and website Burlingtonroute.com. Lower image courtesy of EMD Diesels and used with its permission.

The three-decade long process of dieselization—from first commercialization to universal application—became a textbook case in the study of the diffusion of new industrial technology. Harvard Professor Edwin Mansfield has demonstrated that the economics of dieselization were like those of stimulus and response in psychology: Railroads that could benefit the most from diesel power implemented the new technology most expeditiously. Consequently (and like jet engines later replacing piston aircraft), dieselization followed a typical logistics supply curve (slow initial acceptance in the face of skepticism and uncertainty, rapid deployment as benefits became more clearly understood, and tapering of demand as available opportunities for substitution became saturated).

A Primer on Diesel-Electric Locomotives

Locomotives are often classified into three basic types (derived from the kind of prime mover and the fuel or energy conversion system employed): steam, diesel-electric, and electric (in which the energy source is an off-board power generating station).[13] Locomotives with internal combustion or turbine prime movers are sometimes identified by the type of fuel and/or transmission apparatus; thus, we have diesel-electric, natural gas (NG) diesel-electric (NG gasified before introduction to the engine), gas-electric, turbine-electric, diesel-hydraulic, diesel-mechanical, and so on. Innovations in each generic type of locomotive gradually improved energy conversion efficiency, but inherent features of each type also limited technological improvements and ultimately (along with other capital and operating cost factors) determined success in the marketplace.

Figure 12.4 depicts conceptually the key economic and operating characteristics of the three main types of locomotives used in North America in the twentieth century. The figure asserts that steam engines have relatively low initial costs but have high all-in, life-cycle costs. Electric locomotives have the lowest operating and maintenance costs but a high initial cost, in part because they are a low-production item for manufacturers. Diesel-electrics take the middle ground: average initial and ongoing operating costs work out to the lowest total cost per unit of tractive-power output.

Comparative locomotive costs are dependent on available power sources and shifting energy prices. Thus, proximity of coal resources to rail lines affected its actual cost in steam operations; diesel fuel prices per BTU have risen substantially in recent years; how and where electricity is gener-

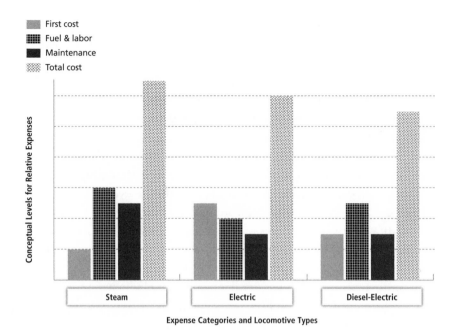

Figure 12.4 Superior Cost Performance of Diesel-Electrics. Diesel-electric locomotives have the lowest all-in costs of any of the three basic locomotive types. Steam engines had low initial costs but high operating and maintenance expenses. Electric units have low operating costs, but they represent high initial outlays. *Source:* Authors' conceptualization and estimated cost relationships.

ated affects electrification operating costs; replacement of older catenary with new is a large capital investment but lowers maintenance costs; and so on.

Diesel engine output is controlled by throttle (or notch) settings and a governor.[14] Notch settings (idle, and notches 1 through 8; notch 8" usually means full power) regulate the engine's rotational speed, and the governor limits maximum horsepower (HP) at each setting. Because HP = tractive effort (F) × velocity (V), the engine can develop either high F at low speed, or low F at high speed, or anything in between. In all settings, engine-running balances automatically to the electrical load on the generator (DC current) or alternator (AC current).

Turbochargers

Most large diesel-electric locomotives employ turbochargers, which use exhaust from the engine to spin air compressors that force additional air into the engine's cylinders. The pressurized air (along with injection of additional fuel) increases the combustion rate and thus the horsepower of the engine. This action is automatic in that the faster (harder) the engine runs, the more exhaust, the more power for compression of air, and hence the more oxygen available for combustion of additional fuel.

Turbochargers are complex machines and can be difficult and costly to maintain, but they approximately double the engine's horsepower compared with nonturbocharged diesels. Older two-stroke EMD units had roots blowers, which were devices mechanically connected to the crankshaft that were used to scavenge exhaust gas from the cylinder at the end of a power stroke and fill it with air for the next compression cycle. Figure 12.5 shows three generations of EMD diesel prime movers and points out the location of the turbocharger on the second- and third-generation engines. Other locomotive manufacturers such as General Electric have made comparable improvements to horsepower, fuel efficiency, and emissions performance of advanced diesel-electric locomotives in recent decades.

Alternating Current Diesel-Electric Locomotives

Replacement of conventional direct current (DC) traction motor diesel-electric locomotives with alternating current (AC) traction motor units beginning in the 1990s had a large and favorable impact on locomotive operating and maintenance performance. Locomotives with AC traction motors have equipment that can change the phase angle of the three-phase power supplied to the traction motors, and a device called a thyristor (a high-speed solid-state switch that can handle large ratios of controlled to controlling amperage) to adjust the frequency and amplitude of AC cycles. AC traction is particularly effective at low speed and high loads that would damage DC traction motors. Because AC motors lack the commutators (brush contacts for transfer of power to the rotating motor armature) found on DC traction motors, they can be sealed for protection from the elements, and they have lower maintenance requirements. High power at low speeds in AC units also motivated development of radial axle trucks for more efficient operation of the locomotive, further increasing adhesion by about 5 percent.[15]

Design improvements in diesel-electric locomotives continue to result in impressive gains in fuel efficiency. Revenue ton-miles per gallon of fuel have more than doubled since 1978 (see Figure 12.6). The newest

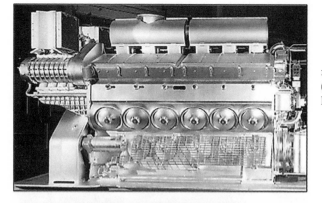

1938—First Generation—567
(cubic centimeters per cylinder)
Engine

- 12 Cylinders
- Roots Blown
- > 32,000 produced

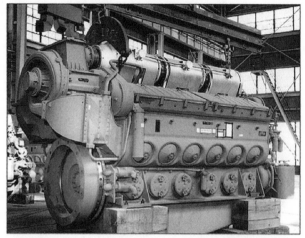

1965—Second Generation—645
(cc per cylinder) Engine

- 12 Cylinders
- Turbo-charged
- > 28,000 produced

1985—Third Generation—710
(cc per cylinder) Engine

- 16 Cylinders
- Turbo-charged
- > 10,000 produced and still
  counting
- Microprocessor controlled
- Meets Tier 3 emissions
  standards

Figure 12.5   Evolution of GM Electro-Motive Diesel Locomotive Prime Movers.   *Illustrations Courtesy of Robert Mason and EMD, a Caterpillar Company.*

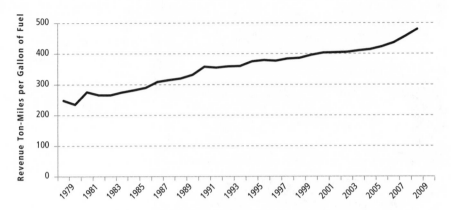

Figure 12.6 A Doubling of Fuel Efficiency Since Staggers.   Class I railroads doubled their fuel efficiency in the last thirty years and now move a ton of freight almost 500 miles on a gallon of fuel. This impressive performance is due to improvements in diesel-electric locomotives themselves; lubrication of rolling stock wheel flanges and top of rail, low-friction roller bearings, and redesigned journal seals; heavier axle loads simultaneously operated with freight car equipment having lower tare weight; and double stacking of containers on unit intermodal trains. *Source:* Data are from various annual issues of the AAR's *Fact Books* and are for Class I railroads only. Used courtesy of the AAR.

locomotives use microprocessor controls and instrumentation that compares ground speed with traction motor rotation to control tractive effort and wheel slip with great precision.

Dilworth's dramatic live demonstrations were persuasive initially in selling the industry on the advantages of diesel-electric locomotives, but more important in subsequent years was their overall operating efficiency, a story that has played itself out over three-quarters of a century. With low fuel prices prevailing in the early postwar period, the case turned on labor costs and asset utilization, but after the OPEC I and II crises of the 1970s, diesel-electric locomotive fuel efficiency became a key element in managing costs and thus retaining competitive traffic for the rails. It is only a little too hyperbolic to say that diesels and Staggers saved the industry after the nation's bicentennial.

Other Diesel-Electric Locomotives Technology Advances
The diesel revolution brought many other transformative changes to the railroad industry, with benefits ranging from environmental protection;

worker productivity, comfort, and safety; locomotive fleet flexibility; and higher asset utilization.

DELIVERY OF TRACTIVE EFFORT AND SLIP CONTROL

After the power rating of the prime mover, a second limitation to any locomotive is the tractive effort it can deliver to the unit's driving wheels without slipping on the rail. In the old days, steam locomotive engineers developed great skill at adjusting steam admission to the cylinders and sanding of the rails to minimize slipping. To start a long train, the engineer would back the locomotive into the train in order to bunch its slack and then accelerate—causing each car in succession to jerk to a roll. As EMD's Dilworth showed with the FT-103 demonstrator set, the rolling start is unnecessary with an appropriately powered diesel locomotive consist.

Modern locomotives have sensors that detect when the wheels of any powered axle are about to slip or spin; the microprocessor-based slip control then reduces energy to that traction motor until its axle can reacquire adhesion, enabling smooth application of maximum pulling traction from all powered wheels. Locomotives equipped with AC traction motors actually reallocate power from a slipping wheel set to those with greater adhesion. Traditionally, locomotives could achieve (for dry, sanded rail) an adhesion factor of about 25 percent of their weight on driving wheels, but the introduction of startup wheel-slip control in the 1990s increased the adhesion factor to about 32 percent. More recently, EMD has developed running wheel creep control technology that greatly improves usable tractive effort.

NATURAL GAS LOCOMOTIVES

The rising cost of diesel fuel and the negative spillover effects of diesel emissions in air quality nonattainment regions, coupled with recently developed abundant domestic natural gas reserves (apparently sustainable over the long term), has led to extensive experimentation with NG-powered diesel-electric locomotives for both road and switching service. Because natural gas (methane) does not compression-ignite like diesel fuel does, until recently either a spark plug or a pilot injection of diesel fuel was necessary; however, recent developments in electronic ignition technology appear to have solved that issue. As new discoveries of natural gas resources have come on line, energy experts anticipate a substantial future cost per BTU advantage for NG fuel compared with the expensive low-sulfur ("clean") diesel oil now required by air quality authorities in nonattainment regions.

The favorable economics of abundant, low-priced NG as a locomotive fuel also means that railroad fueling stations may become a logical place to liquefy pipeline natural gas. Such facilities can use the heavier hydrocarbons in pipeline gas to power the liquefaction plant, while placing pure refrigerated methane in tanks and tenders for locomotive fuel and local sale to other users such as transit agencies, agribusiness, and heavy equipment operators. Already the AAR is developing a new specification for locomotive tenders carrying liquefied natural gas (LNG), and railroads are looking for natural gas locomotives to be helpful in meeting Environmental Protection Agency (EPA) Tier 4 emissions requirements by 2015.

As a group, locomotive technologies rose to a high level of significance in twentieth-century railroading because power units routinely represent the second largest category of new capital outlays (after track investments) and because, except for labor wages and benefits, locomotive fuel is the largest operating expense railroads incur. Dieselization enabled enormous savings in labor compared with steam operations, paving the way for reforms in crew consist and streamlining locomotive support functions such as maintenance, fueling, watering, and lubrication. The savings from eliminating the multiple support functions required for steam engine operations were an important element (along with more precise management of tractive power) enabling diesel-electric locomotive economics to win out over steam technology in the postwar period.

Track and Structures

Creosoted and Concrete Ties

Hardwood timber is an excellent material for holding rails in place because it has strength in both tension and compression, is not brittle, and possesses flexibility useful in helping to distribute weight under rails and heavy trains. When properly ballasted for drainage and treated with a good wood preservative (historically, creosote was the most popular), wood ties can last twenty-five to thirty years, depending on climate and traffic density. In modern railroad practice, hardwood cross ties are fitted with tie plates to prevent tie gouging by the rails, gang nail plates are used to prevent end splitting of wood ties, and rail anchors are installed to prevent longitudinal movement of rails.

Creosoted hardwood ties served railroads well for over a century, and they still play a major role in track systems, but they have an environmental drawback: Creosote is a carcinogen and the tie plants that were used to pressure-treat ties before the risk was understood left behind some rather messy negative spillovers. Many vendors have advanced alternatives, including cross ties made of exotic hardwoods, steel, plastic resin, and concrete. Of these, steel-reinforced concrete has become most significant. The advantages of concrete cross ties are great lateral and compressive strength, durability, and stability, plus environmental mitigation benefits compared with creosoted ties. Disadvantages are higher cost and their significantly greater mass, which meant new handling machinery had to be developed. On the other hand, greater mass means less shifting and consequently lower maintenance expense for realignment and surfacing of track.

Welded Rail: No More Clickety-Clack

Today, railroads weld segments of rail into long strings rather than bolt steel rail mill standard 39-foot lengths together using joint bars in the field, as was the traditional practice. The welded strings reduce excessive wear and the likelihood of broken rail and derailments at bolted joints, and they save track maintenance labor. For these reasons, some experts place welded rail second only to dieselization in importance among twentieth-century railroad technologies.

Robert Selph Henry is one of the great chroniclers of railroads and their history, management, technology, and operations. Among the many subjects Henry addressed in his best-known book, *This Fascinating Railroad Business*, was welded rail, which has been around since the Great Depression. In 1933 the D&H Railroad risked doing away with rail joints in heavy-duty track (except where an insulated joint is needed for track circuits). At the time of Henry's writing in 1942, there were some forty stretches of welded track on a dozen US railroads, and temperature-related expansion and contraction was being watched closely.[16] Today, welded rail is found throughout the mainline railroad network, and it is a defining feature of modern, safer, heavy-haul freight railroads as well as higher–speed passenger service.

The subject of bolted versus welded rail has received media attention in the aftermath of numerous heat-kink (or sun-kink) derailments. With steel rail welded into long ribbons and secured to ties, expansion of the metal in the hottest days of summer leaves no place for the steel to go except to slither out of alignment. The advantages of welded rail (a more comfortable ride, less damage to lading, longer service lives, ability to operate heavier trains, and fewer derailments) far exceed the costs of periodically adjusting welded segment lengths to avoid sun-kinks or broken rail due to the expansion and contraction of rail from temperature extremes.

Hump Classification Yards

The first successful gravity marshaling yard was developed on a large, naturally sloping yard at Edge Hill in Liverpool, England, in about 1880.[17] Subsequently, artificial humps were constructed to gain the benefits of gravity marshaling. The Pennsylvania Railroad opened the first US hump yard at Greensburg, Pennsylvania, in 1883.[18] Modern hump yards use a locomotive to push a cut of cars up a gradual incline to the apex of the hump, where a brakeman manually uncouples one or a few cars for classification; these then roll down through a master retarder and successive group retarders to slow the cut to a computer-calculated coupling speed of 4 miles per hour, usually, based on weight, rolling resistance, distance, and even wind speed. The hump retarders are interlocked with computerized and motorized switches that direct the car or small cut of cars to the designated classification track in the bowl (so-called because it is profiled to slow and hold cars naturally, not allowing them to roll out the far end). When a classification track is filled and its cars are ready to be made up into a planned train, a yard engine pulls the string of cars out to the departure yard, doubling over as needed to fill the train with its planned complement of freight cars.

Automated hump yards are still an important feature in the operation of mixed manifest freight trains, although the percentage of cars switched through classification yards en route to final destination has declined in recent years with the growth of unit train operations and the rising popularity of rail–highway intermodal service (in which the switching of trailers or containers can take place at an intermodal terminal, widely called a ramp) equipped with gantry cranes or fork-lift-style side loaders. Alternatively, containers might be put on chassis and serially out-gated from the terminal, then delivered to their correct destinations in the course of normal operations over public streets and highways.

Premium Steel in Rail

A key factor in the observed substantial improvement of broken-rail derailments is that railroads have begun specifying a higher grade of steel in orders of new rail from rolling mills instead of accepting mill-run rail. Premium steels are obtained with alloys such as chrome-molybdenum, and with techniques for head-hardening the rail using controlled cooling. Specification of premium steel for rail means that fewer occlusions (microscopic gaps or particles of slag or other foreign matter) will be found in the rail, which lowers the chances that a flaw in the metal will morph into a crack in the rail structure or form a spall (pit) on the rail surface.

Use of premium steel in rail, improved installation practices (such as carefully controlling the temperature at which rail is laid), rail grinding to provide a proper rail-head profile and to eliminate incipient fatigue defects, and lubrication of rail in curves to minimize rolling friction and reduce rail and wheel wear have enabled railroads to operate heavier trains, with fewer derailments, and achieve much longer rail life. Main line segments with old rail that in the 1980s would be scheduled for replacement after carrying about 750 million gross ton-miles per mile now routinely last more than twice as long. Today such segments may yield as many as 1.7 billion ton-miles per mile of main-line service before being cascaded onto secondary lines or into yard trackage.[19]

Mechanized Maintenance-of-Way Machinery

Railroad maintenance-of-way (MOW) was revolutionized by application of a remarkable series of creative machines specifically designed for the railroads and touted as the ingenious Rube Goldberg contraptions that they were. (See Figure 12.8.) MOW functions take track time away from normal operations, so there is a premium on MOW equipment that can get to the work location, set up quickly, and complete the job expeditiously. So-called rapid-on, rapid-off MOW equipment that minimizes the required track-work window is particularly valuable when the railroad is running near capacity.

● Ballast cleaners and undercutters	● Spike pullers
● Ballast distribution equipment	● Tie inserters
● Ballast regulators	● Track- rail-laying equipment
● Tampers	● Spikers
● Cranes	● Rail grinders

Figure 12.7   Mechanized MOW Machinery.   Source: Brian Solomon, "Maintenance-of-Way Machinery" in Middleton, *Encyclopedia*, pp. 659–661. Solomon provides descriptions of several kinds of MOW equipment.

Box 12.2.   Testing at the Transportation Technology Center

Outside Pueblo, Colorado, on a 52-square-mile site made available by the state of Colorado, the Federal Railroad Administration (FRA) established a comprehensive railroad testing center in 1970. The Transportation Technology Center (TTC) was championed by Senator Claiborne Pell (D–RI), and its location near Pueblo by Senator Gordon Allott (R–CO). The foundational and ongoing test plan was to use computer simulations, laboratory analyses, and controlled experiments on TTC test tracks in an attempt to learn everything that could be known about forces generated by movement of rolling stock over railroad track and structures, and how these affect the wear and fatigue of both rolling stock and infrastructure components.

In the effort to understand track–train dynamics at TTC and how better to manage them, railroad researchers made lasting contributions to the economics and safety of railroads. Evaluation of improved versions of rail, cross ties, fasteners, wheels, trucks (bogies), and other devices at TTC led to the development of improved components yielding significant benefits. When the Staggers Rail Act of 1980 allowed rail earnings to increase near the turn of the twenty-first century, the railroads were prepared to invest in new railcars, locomotives, and track components that bore the benefits of this research and had in fact been tested for long-term performance at the Pueblo test center.

Box 12.2.

As an example of their successes, research and test engineers at TTC developed installation and maintenance techniques that (along with use of premium steel rail) enabled a doubling of track service life. Also, much use has been made of facilities at TTC to uncover problems in Amtrak's Acela cars, improve crashworthiness in passenger cars, and improve hazardous materials tank car designs.

TTC also serves as the RF frequency coordination agency for railroad communications channels. At the end of the twentieth century, it began installing capabilities for interoperability testing of radios and other equipment that will be used in future PTC deployments.

Train Braking Systems

Control of Air Brake Applications

Conventionally, train air brakes are engaged when the engineer sets the brakes, which sharply decreases air pressure supplied by a brake pipe to compressed air reservoirs located on each freight car in the train. The air pressure reduction signals a triple valve to switch from supplying brake-pipe air pressure to auxiliary reservoirs on each freight or passenger car, to instead applying the brakes. The system uses pneumatic pressure stored in these reservoirs for actually powering the car's brake cylinders so that, by design, they are functional even if the car is unintentionally separated from its train; that is, freight car air brakes are a fail-safe system.

This reliable system, invented by George Westinghouse, has served the industry well for over 100 years. One of its main shortcomings, however, is that air pressure signals can travel no faster than the speed of sound under the best of conditions. Although electronically controlled pneumatic (ECP) brakes were not widely implemented in the twentieth century, by the end of the century, observers could anticipate that future freight railroads likely would benefit from use of these brakes. If braking signals are communicated electronically instead of pneumatically, they can be engaged at the speed of light, and in optimal order and degree. Savings would result in brake linings, fuel use, and safety. Consider that, with conventional air brakes, an emergency application propagated from the train's head end (locomotive), because of slack action in the train, can cause rear cars to

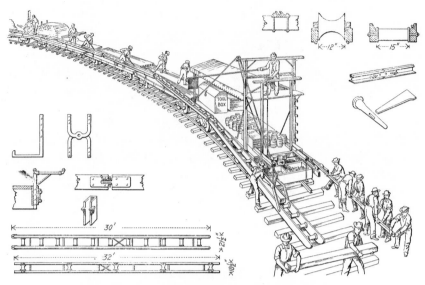

The Holman Tracklaying Machine.

Figure 12.8   Advancing Mechanization of Track Laying.   An example of improvements in track-laying technology over the twentieth century (Rube Goldberg made proud, then or now). Note the change in labor intensity, which is broadly indicative of other advances in right-of-way (ROW) construction and maintenance. *Sources:* Upper image: E. E. Russell Tratman, *Railway Track and Track Work* (New York: The Engineering News Publishing Co., 1901), p. 297. Lower Image: Courtesy of Harsco; used with permission.

pile into forward cars.[20] Also, ECP brakes (in contrast to conventional systems) allow continuous recharging of the auxiliary brake reservoirs on each car, thus avoiding the danger of running out of air pressure with repeat braking applications.

Distributed Locomotive Power

While the topic of distributed locomotive power might have fit just as well above in the consideration of locomotive technologies, it has synergies with evolving train operating and braking strategies. Distributed locomotive power (DP) in trains uses radio (RF) communications that allow multiple (slave) locomotives to be controlled from a master unit (typically the lead locomotive in a consist) without wired connections. The slave units can be placed anywhere in the train consist, although typically they are placed either halfway or two-thirds of the way back from the head-end and/or at the rear end of the train. Initially, DP units were used mostly to replace manned locomotive helper units for taking trains over steep grades, but their success in those operations led to their wider use. Among the benefits railroads found were:

- Reduced drawbar forces and break-in-twos at the head end of trains.
- Improved train handling and reduced wear and tear from slack action.
- Reduced time to charge air brakes at train initialization.
- Better performance of air brakes in cold weather due to a shorter average distance from locomotive air compressors to freight car brake cylinders.
- Improved dynamic braking performance descending steep grades.

DP systems permit operation of trains having as many as 135 cars, without pull-aparts. In 2012, Union Pacific successfully tested a train of over 400 cars using multiple sets of master and slave DP units.

It may be apparent from this discussion that the two technologies of DP and ECP brakes can be combined synergistically to yield enhanced benefits, including better train handling. If a train is wired for electronically controlled brakes, parallel circuits can be used for control of distributed locomotive power. With distributed power, air pressure for braking can be developed at multiple locations in the train continuously during the braking cycle; with ECP braking, the signal to engage or release brakes in the amount needed at each location (to bunch or stretch train slack) is instantaneous. The result is much tighter control of combined power and braking, better use of track capacity, and collateral fuel savings. Combining these with advanced new systems for monitoring and displaying dynamic forces within the train means that railroads can improve train handling to lower the risk of damage to equipment and lading, and even derailments.

Freight and Passenger Cars, and Unit Train Operations

Larger Cars and Heavier Axle Loadings

Among the most apparent changes in railroading over the course of the twentieth century is the Brobdingnagian scale of today's freight cars compared with those used 100 years earlier. The average capacity of a US freight car in 1903 was about 29 tons, less than one-third their average capacity at the millennium.[21] In parallel with increased capacity and loaded tonnage of freight cars, axle loadings (gross weight on rails [GWR]) increased substantially over the course of the years, more than doubling between 1925 and 2005, as shown in Figure 12.9.

Studies performed by major railroads at the Transportation Technology Center (TTC) showed that HAL affects nearly all cost categories for track and structures: rail; track joints; ties and fastenings; ballast; surfacing; turnouts; special track work; and, most important, bridges, particularly those already marginal at 263,000 pounds GWR.[23] These impacts increase degradation at joints and turnouts, surface spalling of rail, and the risk of derailments from cross-level misalignment of track and broken rails. Bolstered by these findings, short-line and regional railroads proposed federal and state financial assistance to help upgrade their lines to be capable of handling freight cars weighing 286,000 pounds GWR. Most experts agreed that the short-line industry could not support the ongoing requirements of HAL (needed for full and safe participation in the US railway network) without outside assistance.

Specialized Freight Cars

In 1929, there were 2.6 million freight cars in service on US railroads, and in 2000, almost exactly half that number. But railcars in 2000 averaged double the tonnage capacity of those in 1929, and they were more specialized as well, with form to fit functions. A landmark analysis prepared for the National Academy Sciences in 1963 noted that perhaps the most significant development in freight cars in the relatively short time span from World War II to that publication date was the industry's emphasis on "larger, lighter-weight, and special-purpose equipment." New features included:

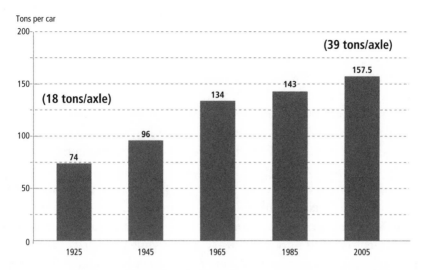

Figure 12.9 Greater Track Productivity from Heavier Axle Loads. Railroads have increased the size of freight cars so that they carry more lading per car. In the chart, the bars express average total tons per car. Thus in 1985, 143 tons gross weight on rail (GWR), translated to 286,000 pounds (the current AAR limit for standard cars). Spread over four axles, this equates to 36 tons per axle. The figure shown for 2005 reflects inclusion of some double-stack intermodal car loadings of up to 315,000 pounds GWR, or axle loads of 39 tons. While these heavy axle loadings (HALs) meant cost savings for Class I railroads and shippers, they represented a challenge for short lines and regional railroads, which operate nearly 30 percent of US rail track mileage. One short-line executive recently estimated that 45 to 60 percent of the short-line infrastructure is incapable of handling cars of 286,000 pounds GWR.[22] *Source:* Authors' estimates from AAR data.

- Insulated box cars to protect lading vulnerable to temperature extremes
- Box cars with extra-wide doors for loading with fork-lift equipment
- Plug-door cars with flush interiors to reduce cargo damage
- Mechanical reefers with substantial additional capacity tonnage
- Much larger tank cars, some with spun-wound glass filament reinforced plastic liners
- The 85-foot piggyback flat car
- Bilevel and trilevel rack cars for movement of finished automobiles, up to fifteen per carload, compared with only about three in an auto-boxcar
- Aluminum and corrosion-resistant steel coal gondolas or hoppers[24]
- Development of jumbo covered hoppers

Specialization of car types facilitated greater lading capacity per car (e.g., jumbo covered hoppers for grain instead of boarded-door boxcars), and easier loading and unloading (center-beam lumber cars). A variety of specialized tank cars was developed for different gaseous and liquid commodities; superior refrigeration technology protected perishables; and, in many cases, the lading could be handled more carefully (as in the case of auto parts and cars). Also, in the case of finished automobile rack cars, railroads have made good use of strategies like triangulation to reduce empty miles and working with customers to reload cars more quickly. With larger and more efficient specialized freight cars, and with incentives to turn cars faster, railroads have been able to carry more tonnage with a smaller fleet,[25] much more of it now owned and supplied by shippers rather than the railroads themselves. And while specialized cars might imply a higher empty-to-loaded-mile ratio, typically this factor is at least partly offset by faster unloading and cleaning or preparation of the car for its next load.

All of these examples demonstrate again that a key reason railroad enterprises have endured is that they became much more technologically proficient and better able to adapt to market requirements with innovative solutions.

Lightweight Passenger Cars and Streamlining

Forty years after the great Columbian Exposition of 1893 in Chicago, the Windy City hosted its Century of Progress Exposition. Among the exhibitors was the city's own Pullman Company and its centerpiece was an entirely new kind of sleeper-lounge car named for the company's founder George M. Pullman. These spoke for the modern art deco age sweeping through all US culture, along the way dominating railroad designs and fashions.[26] The Pullman sleeper-lounge train was sleekly designed, with a rounded roof and boat-tailed observation end. It was fashioned in "gleaming" aluminum or stainless steel, and it weighed only half as much as predecessor all-steel "heavyweight" cars. Like the contemporary industrial designs of Raymond Loewy for the Pennsylvania Railroad, Henry Dreyfuss for the New York Central, Norman Bel Geddes, and others, it was streamlined to evoke a happier future than the Great Depression's pressing reality.

Although, as Canadian writer Kevin J. Holland has noted, the aerodynamic benefits of streamlining a passenger train were marginal, new trains like the Budd Zephyrs, Union Pacific M-10000 series streamliners, and Milwaukee Road Hiawathas (all introduced from 1934 to 1936) were a marketing success.[27] Pullman-Standard followed up with its roomette designs introduced in 1937. The rush to streamlining was slowed by the industry's persistent poverty, and it was interrupted completely by wartime materials shortages. However, when "normalcy" returned after World War II, Americans had already decided to turn away from rail passenger service in favor of the speed of flying or the personal comfort of their automobiles.

Unit Freight Trains

Unit trains are dedicated trains made up (in the pure case) of only one type of freight car, such as hoppers or gondolas for carrying coal, covered hoppers for grain or minerals, tank cars for petroleum products, refrigerated cars for perishables, or intermodal flat cars for trailers or containers. The very earliest trains in the United Kingdom were often unit trains, as their only function was to haul coal from a mine in South Wales or near Newcastle-on-Tyne down to the sea. Another early reference to what today would be called a unit train was written by a general manager of the Crystal River Railroad in 1901:

> ... [We use twenty cars] to take coal from a mine ... down to
> our coke ovens, 12 miles away. At the lower end they are dumped
> in a bin, and we have dumped eight cars in 10 minutes, using
> only the train crew to dump them, and without uncoupling
> from the engine.[28]

Here are all the elements of unit train efficiencies sought by modern railways: dedicated equipment and locomotives, avoidance of intermediate switching, nonstop operation, fast loading and unloading without decoupling, and standard car consists for maintenance efficiency.

Where interline operations are necessary, unit train locomotives often run through to the destination, returning home on another train or with the unit train's empty cars. Unit train operations routinely violate the transportation officer's ingrained abhorrence of empty backhauls because there is no traffic available for a reverse haul and because the simple, efficient, unit train operation would be disrupted if delays were encountered in serving backhaul traffic.

Introduction of unit train operations were limited in the period before passage of the Staggers Rail Act of 1980 by regulatory prohibition of shipping contracts and by near-universal use of single-car rates.[29] When deregulation permitted the railroads to negotiate contracts for volume movement of coal, grain, or other commodities at rates substantially below the per-carload equivalent in traditional rate tables, replacement of single-car movements with unit trains transpired rapidly. Often this meant major adjustments in shipper logistics strategies as well as rail operations (including absorbing empty backhauls); in grain, for example, unit train operations with cuts of twenty-five, fifty, or more cars from huge grain subterminals soon replaced single-car movements from local grain elevators. An exception was the grain-gathering lines of the Burlington Northern, where the railroad initially resisted lowering rates to unit train levels, preferring to hold on to (higher) single-car rates as long as it could; on the other hand, once the Staggers Rail Act was passed, BN became a leader in rate-making innovations, including the issuance of transferrable warrants for movement of grain in multicar blocks.

Mechanical Refrigerator Cars (Reefers)

Ice-cooled railroad boxcars had existed from Civil War days, but it was meatpacker Gustavus Swift who pioneered widespread use of specialized reefers. Swift engaged Boston inventor Andrew J. Chase in 1881 to develop a system using roof hatches at both ends of a tightly sealed boxcar with specially designed ice-holding bunkers. These refrigerated cars revolutionized the logistics of meatpacking and delivery by centralizing butchering in midwestern cities and movement of dressed meat to eastern markets by rail. As early as 1890, for example, Kansas City poultry processing plants were using railroad reefers to transport 2.5 million pounds of dressed poultry to various markets annually.

In the North, natural ice was cut from ponds in the winter and stored indoors in straw for later use, but that was not possible in the deep South. Consequently, South to North use of reefers for fruits and seafood was nearly impossible before the invention of ammonia-compression artificial ice making in the 1910s.[30]

In subsequent years, movement of perishables by rail became a major sideline business. In addition to the Swift fleet of reefers, Union Pacific and Southern Pacific formed Pacific Fruit Express in 1906 to move West Coast perishables east; by the mid-1950s PFE had 39,000 reefers in service. Fruit

Growers Express was organized in 1920 to serve markets disrupted by anti-trust action against Armour Packing Co., and the Illinois Central developed a healthy business moving bananas from New Orleans to Chicago. Icing stations such as those set up along the Santa Fe by the Railway Ice Co. were instrumental in developing the business. In the 1920s, some 16 percent of Santa Fe railcars were reefers.[31] In the East, American Refrigerated Transit served the perishables industry for many years, shopping its fleet in Alexandria, Virginia.

Today, mechanically refrigerated temperature-controlled cars (including for use in moving frozen foods) are only a little over one percent of the manifest fleet, but insulated cars and intermodal reefer containers supplement railroad capacity for handling the industry's growing long-haul traffic in perishables.

Two-Way End-of-Train Devices: The Caboose (An Endangered Species)

An end-of-train device (EOTD) or flashing rear-end device (FRED) substitutes for the storied caboose on modern freight trains. EOTDs are components of a train's air brake system; their function is to measure the air pressure at the far end of the train's brake pipe and to report that pressure reading to train crews riding in the locomotive. Replacing the caboose with the EOTD yielded savings in asset purchase/ownership costs and train makeup/switching expenses for railroads. In the 1990s, labor organizations, which had fought the industry's long-time efforts to eliminate cabooses, successfully pushed for legislation to require two-way EOTDs that enable the locomotive engineer to initiate a brake application at the front and rear ends of the train simultaneously, thus shortening braking distance. The two-way radio control capability also allows an operator not on the train to make an emergency application of its brakes remotely—something that can be highly useful in the rare event (popular movies notwithstanding) of a runaway train.

Tapered Roller Bearings

Roller bearings were a great advance over their predecessor, ordinary friction bearings, which required frequent lubrication to reduce rubbing between rolling axles and car underbody trucks (or bogies) in all railroad rolling stock before the twentieth century. Roller bearings have the advantage over ball bearings in that they can carry heavier loads with fewer moving pieces, and do so at lower initial cost (albeit with somewhat greater rolling resistance). Further, roller bearings do not need to be lubricated between their remanufacturing cycles.

Roller bearings are an example of an innovation, initially patented early in the nineteenth century, that became a highly useful application for railroads in the twentieth century. In this case, the gestation period lasted over eighty years. Henry Timken, a carriage builder in St. Louis, was looking for a bearing that could withstand rugged service in carriages and wagons when he made his first drawing of a tapered roller bearing intended to be mounted *in* the wheel hub of horse-drawn vehicles. Timken and R. Heinzelman took out a patent in 1898 for their tapered roller bearing design. Timken's design realized another advantage: When set in two angles against the axle, tapered roller bearings sustain lateral forces from the railcar's taking of curves, as well as the normal vertical gravitational forces due to the weight of the car and its lading. Roller bearings gradually replaced friction bearings after midcentury, but friction bearings were not banned in interchange service until the 1990s.

Hot box derailments became quite rare, in part because of roller bearings and in part because of the innovation of infrared hotbox detectors placed about every twenty miles along mainline track rights of way. With these detectors, if the line-side equipment detects an overheated journal, it sends a warning to the supervising signal system or to the train crew by a voice announcement over the train radio so that mitigating action can be taken before the journal bearings and axle seize up.

Prolific railroad author S. Kip Farrington summarized the advantages of roller bearings as follows:

- Remove all bearing speed restrictions
- Increase hauling capacity
- Reduce starting resistance
- Allow for faster on-time schedules
- Reduce maintenance costs
- Reduce lading damage claims
- Increase life of equipment
- Reduce shop repair time
- Eliminate hot box delays
- Increase equipment availability
- Improve fuel economy

Box 12.3. **How Railroads Get 500 Miles per Gallon for a Ton of Freight**

Contemporary readers of *American Railroads* are probably familiar with the CSX television commercial touting the ability of CSX (and other railroads) to achieve what may seem to some TV viewers as a phenomenal achievement in fuel efficiency—500 ton-miles per gallon. How do they do it?

First, of course, is the fundamental efficiency of steel wheels on steel rails—the well-known concept of low rolling resistance that railroads achieve in contrast to that of motor vehicles using pneumatically inflated tires on paved surfaces. Similarly, railroads were engineered long ago to follow valleys rather than climb hills wherever they could, and to avoid sharp curves in the process. There was little new news here, but the CSX commercial made people think about other factors that might explain modern railroads' fuel efficiency.

Five contemporary technologies account for the notable progress made in fuel mileage in the last decade or two:

1. *Improvements in Locomotive Fuel Efficiency.* Newer locomotives incorporate technologies such as microprocessor controls that economize on fuel consumption per horsepower-hour and pound of tractive effort. Alternating current diesel-electric locomotives are more fuel-efficient than direct current units and have become a larger share of the fleet. Also, improvements have been made in the lubricants used in diesel engines.

2. *Lubrication of Rolling Stock Wheel Flanges and Top-of-Rail.* Spot lubrication of these heavy friction surfaces further reduces rolling resistance. Refinements in the devices for accurate application of the lubricant to the most effective locations, and again, improvement of the lubricants themselves, are noteworthy.

3. *Low Friction Bearings and Redesigned Roller-Bearing Seals.* These improvements reduced train rolling resistance, thus saving fuel and making hot boxes less frequent.

4. *Heavier Axle Loads and Lower Tare Weight.* Increasing the cargo-carrying capacity of freight cars saves fuel because greater tonnage of lading per wheel means more ton-miles can be hauled in the same train length or with the same locomotive tractive effort.

5. *Double-Stack Container Trains.* Double-stacking containers accomplishes several goals. Double-stack containers mean more cargo can be carried in a train of the same length or number of wheels, compared with trailers-on-flatcars (piggyback), for example. More important, the profile of a double-stack train, properly loaded, creates less wind resistance than a piggyback train.

- Offer no differentiation in tonnage rating for winter versus summer[32]

Telecommunications, Train Control, and Information Systems

For the most part, communications- and computer-based technologies covered in this section have roots outside the railroad industry and thus have greatly benefitted from technological developments in the broader economy. For example, use of electric lighting in signaling (a form of train control), computers for accounting and car management, two-way microwave radios for telecommunications, radio frequency (RF) and infrared technology for sensors and control systems—all came to the railroad industry from outside, often from military origins. (The authors don't want to make too much of this argument, however; railroads didn't invent diesel engines, steel for rail, or aluminum fabrication used in jumbo hoppers, either.) Using technology transferred from outside the industry is a good thing, and doing so does not diminish the efforts railroads put into adapting generic technologies for specific application to railroads—or the benefits of doing so.[33]

Communications technologies, computing applications, and the signal systems covered in this section of the chapter all use electrical circuits to do something analogous to what transportation does for commerce and industry in general: That is, these technologies (and the facilities that use and support them) increase the time and place utility of information, just as transportation services increase the time and place utility of goods. Pinpointed information—communicated at the speed of light and summarized faster than the human brain can comprehend—allows tiny energy forces to control great mass and momentum (like thyristors controlling locomotive tractive effort).

This singular concept, both simple in principle and highly complex in practical application, is the basis on which railroads of the future will be able to cure their persistent vulnerabilities to incursions by disruptive or malevolent external forces (weather, collisions, trespassers, terrorists). Indeed, pinpointed information delivery is how railroads solve lingering gaps in the reliability of their service to customers. In short, railroads have entered the information age, and they will be among its great beneficiaries. The smarter they are in developing practical applications to bend their great efficiency to the service of customers, the greater will be their productivity in the future.

Long-Distance Point-to-Point Voice and Data Communications

Railroads are information- and communications-intensive enterprises. Telegraphy had been used in train dispatching and related office communications since the mid-nineteenth century. Indeed, the history of telegraphy and telephony, from Samuel F. B. Morse through Alexander Graham Bell and Thomas Alva Edison, is inseparable from the story of the first century of railroad developments in the United States. Most of that technology blossomed before 1900 and remained dominant until well after World War II. In terms of replacement technology for long-distance communications, the twentieth century's new entrants were point-to-point microwave line-of-sight (dish) transmission (developed in World War II and widely implemented by railroads in the 1950s and 1960s) and fiber-optic cable installations (which revolutionized telecommunications in the 1980s and 1990s). In the cases of both microwave and fiber-optic technologies, railroads were first adopters of the investments made by telecom giants like AT&T, MCI, and Verizon.

In this manner, railroads were able to modernize telecommunications applications that historically were conducted over their telegraph networks (the well-known multiwire pole lines running along railway tracks) by linking into commercial microwave networks or developing their own similar installations. Railroad microwave networks were probably the most extensive outside those of government and commercial telecommunications-provider firms. One railroad microwave network, the Southern Pacific, even became the basis for what is now known as Sprint Telecommunications.

Then, when fiber-optic cable technology became practical for long-distance digital communications a decade or two later, railroads (owning just what the telecom giants needed: longitudinal rights of way between major metropolitan centers) sold or leased long-term easements for buried fiber-optic cable pathways. Financial terms for these easements typically were structured to give host railroads substantial access to low-cost, long-term telecom service capacity. These arrangements, in turn, lowered the effective cost to railroads of centralizing functions like dispatching, crew management, computer systems management, and others.

Wireless VHF Two-Way Radios

Practical two-way mobile radio was one of a number of developments that came out of military applications in World War II and were put to substantial civilian use by railroads. In the 1930s, the Federal Communications Commission (FCC) (a young agency at the time) had granted licenses to the railroads to operate radios at frequencies in the 160 MHz portion of the electromagnetic spectrum, which was formerly used for maritime operations. The FCC delegated responsibility for coordinating these frequencies (to avoid interference and monitor efficient compliance with FCC rules) to the Association of American Railroads (AAR). Development of transistors to replace vacuum tubes in the 1950s accelerated the deployment of mobile wireless phones in the industry, although they were not routinely used for communication of train movement orders until the 1970s. Conversion from analog to digital radio frequencies is underway as this is written. Digital radios can efficiently use narrower-frequency channels and are superior for data transmission, among other advantages.

Radio delivery of track warrants (or movement authorities) is a convenient and cost-saving application, but it must be accomplished in a highly formalized fashion to avoid confusion or misunderstanding. Dispatchers must keep a record of verbal authorities issued, and when a train crew receives an authority over the radio, it must be written down verbatim on a standard form and repeated to the dispatcher. Verbal authorities are used in territory without signals (dark territory) and in automatic block signal (ABS) operations. In double-track ABS territory signaled for one-way operation, for example, a crew must obtain permission to move against the current of traffic (as in a reverse move) or past a wayside signal displaying "stop." Verbal authorities are not required if trains are authorized to move forward on signal indications. Authority for maintenance forces to occupy track (as with Form B track and time authority—bidirectional within a work block) is also typically delivered verbally over the VHF radio.[34]

Conventional Train Control and Signaling Systems Technologies
Wayside and locomotive cab signaling systems are a subset of train control functions, which can be conducted with many different kinds of rules or hardware technologies. This section holds off discussion of the topical subject of positive train control (PTC) until a final subsection, but it covers the following important technologies: lighted wayside (searchlight) signals for fixed track blocks, automatic train stop (ATS) and automatic train control (ATC), cab signals, and coded track circuits.

LIGHTED WAYSIDE (SEARCHLIGHT) SIGNALS
FOR FIXED TRACK BLOCKS

In the first decade of the twentieth century, lighted color signals legible at short distances were introduced for metropolitan transit operations in the East Boston Tunnel, on the Long Island Railroad, and on approaches to both Grand Central Terminal and Pennsylvania Station in New York City. The Brooklyn Bridge was equipped with color lighted signals operated with AC track circuits in 1907. By 1913 the range of color light signals was increased to 2,500 feet in daylight, and the next year, daylight range was increased to 3,500 feet with improved light filaments and accurate optical positioning. The Hartford signal inventor, Thomas S. Hall, continued to work on improved signaling systems, and by 1920 his company came out with a searchlight signal that used a single light source of surprisingly low wattage, together with an extremely efficient parabolic reflector lens.[35]

AUTOMATIC TRAIN STOP AND AUTOMATIC TRAIN CONTROL

The very first device designed to stop a train automatically if it passed a restrictive[36] signal was demonstrated in the nineteenth century, before patents were granted for Robinson's DC track circuit or Westinghouse's air brake. The device shut off the throttle and sounded an alarm. Much as Westinghouse had implied when he said "the more we invent, the more we need to invent," deployment of air brakes made possible a better means of ATS. In a system invented by Joseph Wood and Axel Vogt of the Pennsylvania Railroad and patented in 1880, trains that might violate a restrictive signal (that is, a signal passed at danger, or a SPAD in British usage), would be stopped by the simple action of a bar coming down from the signal post and breaking a glass tube sticking up out of the locomotive cab; the glass tube was connected to the brake line so, when broken, it vented air pressure to the atmosphere, thus throwing the train into an emergency stop.[37]

According to the Union Switch & Signal history, by 1914 over 1,000 patents had been registered for ATS devices.[38] The Hepburn Act of 1906 authorized the ICC to investigate ATS, and the Transportation Act of 1920 contained a substantial section on the subject. Accordingly, in June 1922, the ICC issued its landmark Order No. 13413, which mandated that major railroads install ATS on at least one passenger division by the beginning of 1925.[39]

CAB SIGNALS: BRINGING WAYSIDE SIGNALS
INTO THE LOCOMOTIVE CAB

A variety of railroad operating circumstances (fog, dense train activity in close quarters, or high-speed operation) can make it desirable to display train control signals in the locomotive cab rather than on the wayside.[40] Additionally, the human element in train operation—the fact that fail-safe principles are difficult to enforce universally when a human is in the loop—may be mitigated to one degree or another by cab signals.

The elementary fact about cab signals, of course, is that the locomotive (or cab control car in some passenger operations) must pick up the dispatcher's instructions—from the track itself, a local wayside wireless repeater of some type, or from a more remote data radio—then repeat these instructions inside the cab with a color light or other display "right in front of [the engineer's] eyes" (to use Robert Selph Henry's phrase). Cab signals may incorporate an alerter that detects an engineer's movements and can initiate braking if no operator action is detected within a requisite (preset) time. Alerters typically require an engineer to acknowledge his or her action when passing a restricted speed signal.[41]

CODED TRACK CIRCUITS

Cab signals were an outgrowth of ATS and were utterly dependent on electric track circuits. An advance over William Robinson's direct current track circuits was the development of coded track circuits to multiply the number of possible signal aspects. (Aspects are what show on the wayside or cab signal; indications are the instructions they give the train operator.[42]) In a typical three-aspect system (red, yellow, or green), these are "stop" (in the UK, "danger"), "caution" ("proceed at reduced speed prepared to stop"), or "proceed" ("clear"). Five-aspect systems are fairly common, allowing for multiple speed indications. On the Northeast Corridor between Washington and New York City, Amtrak uses a nine-aspect speed signaling system called the Advanced Civil Speed Enforcement System (ACES).[43]

Coded track circuits were developed by US&S and installed in 1933 in electrified territory between Zoo and Arsenal interlockings[44] on the Pennsylvania Railroad (PRR) in Philadelphia. This system used an AC overlay current of 100 Hz interrupted to message three or four wayside and cab signal indications. Earlier, in 1923, PRR and US&S had tested and demonstrated a three-speed continuous train control system on the Sunbury,

Pennsylvania, line; this "was the first use of vacuum tubes outside the communications industry and the first use of a cab signal instead of wayside signals."[45]

Centralized Traffic Control

Prior to the development of centralized traffic control (CTC) in the late 1920s, moving trains over the road was a cumbersome process. Dispatchers making a train schedule wrote down instructions (called train orders); these would be telephoned or telegraphed to agents in the field, who relayed them to train crews. Usually train crews operated their own switches manually. Then a prolific inventor employed by the General Railway Signal Company, a man named Sedgwick North White, became the first to conceive a design to consolidate signal and switch controls at one site. White's CTC system was tried July 25, 1927, on the Toledo & Ohio Central with the remote central dispatching being located at Fostoria—midway along the 40-mile route. For witnesses gathered to watch the meeting of trains departing from each end of the line, the excitement was like one of Babe Ruth's record home runs that summer. A New York Central executive recalled the story twenty years later:

> We went over to the tower at Fostoria in the evening. The dispatcher was there and he was just filled up with enthusiasm on this new gadget called Centralized Traffic Control . . . [A]long about 10 o'clock he just yelled right out loud, "Here comes a non-stop meet!" Well, we all gathered around the machine and watched the lights come toward each other and pass each other without stopping. That, to me and to you, was history on American railroads, the first non-stop meet on single track [with sidings] without train orders, that we know of.[46]

CTC is defined as a combination of block signals and interlockings that provides safe train operations from a remote control location. In CTC the dispatcher can control operations from afar because turnouts are powered and interlocked with the signals. Thus, traffic can move over the remotely controlled territory on wayside or cab signal indications without interruption,[47] adding throughput capacity.

With remote control of turnouts and crossovers, dispatchers could accomplish complex moves such as permitting a faster train to overtake a slower one, but careful obedience of crews to signal indications was always essential to prevention of collisions. That is, there was fail-safe operation of the signals with gravity relays,[48] but adherence to the operating rules was a critical feature of CTC and related systems.

Active Grade-Crossing Warning Devices and Grade Separations

Railroads and their suppliers have made steady improvements in reducing the risks to highway vehicles at highway–rail intersections or grade crossings. It is astounding how successfully the toll of injuries and fatalities has been reduced during the latter part of the twentieth century and the first years of the twenty-first. In 1937, for example, 1,875 people were killed at grade crossings, while only three rail passengers were killed.[49] By comparison, in 2009, there were 248 grade-crossing fatalities, and the US population was about 2.4 times larger. More persons are now killed annually as trespassers on railroad property than are killed in grade-crossing accidents.

Grade-crossing warning devices (it is an exaggeration to call them crossing-protection installations) come in several varieties. Passive warning devices, the familiar cross bucks, do little more than mark a crossing location, especially since the imperative "Stop, Look, and Listen" wording was removed a generation ago. Cross bucks are equivalent to a "Yield" command to motorists because trains cannot stop easily and in part because the railroads were more often than not the first improved way structure at the location; that is, in most cases they were built before the conflicting highway was.

Active crossing warning devices such as flashing lights that come on when a train approaches the crossing are considerably more effective than passive markers in deterring unwise motor vehicle movements over crossings.[50] Activation of such devices results from detection of the approach of a train, typically by receiving an occupancy sensing (OS) indication from a track circuit.[51] The next higher level of active crossing warning and deterrence, automatic crossing gates, is more expensive to install but is likely to be more effective in preventing crossing fatalities. Some experimentation with active crossing barriers intended to seal off the railway physically from incursion of motor vehicles into the pathway of a train has been done, but generally with unsatisfactory results.[52] Current research efforts by highway crossing engineers are centered on strategies to dissuade or foil unwise motorist behaviors such as racing to beat a train to the crossing or driving around deployed crossing gates.

By far the most effective strategy for risk-reduction at road–rail intersections is to separate the two modes vertically. Grade-crossing separations are expensive but probably necessary where volumes of traffic and train speeds are high. The Federal Railroad Administration typically will not permit passenger trains to exceed 110 miles per hour over crossings, even if "protected" with down-gates.

The largest set of grade separations constructed in US history was, of course, those built along with the interstate highway system in the last third of the twentieth century. These separations are perhaps the greatest single reason for the decline of crossing fatalities in that period and afterward. Other factors include the effective outreach of Operation Lifesaver presentations in schools, the upgrading of warning systems at dangerous locations with Section 130 funds administered by the states on a risk-based formula, and a federal mandate to install ditch lights on locomotives to make an approaching train more visible and (because of the triangular light pattern) conceptualization of its closing speed more apparent to the motorist.

Computerized and Microprocessor-Based Information Systems

American Railroads noted earlier that the computer revolution has had a major impact on railroads, just like it has had in almost every business and social activity in the last few decades. Railroads were among the first businesses to show the public how computers could be put to work in industry, and how, by speeding accurate information to the point of a decision, better choices could be made, safety could be improved, and costs would be reduced.

Computers and computing belong to the whole of the twentieth century because just as the century was beginning, Herman Hollerith and Otto Braitmeyer collaborated to form the Tabulating Machine Company (forerunner of IBM). Hollerith and his associates improved his invention and soon were marketing card-punch and card-reading machines for keeping track of huge amounts of data such as generated by the US Census and railroads. By 1906, Hollerith cards and machines had found their way into the work of the Pennsylvania Railroad, New York Central, Southern, and other railroads. IBM showed off equipment for handling railroad waybills at the 1939 World's Fair in Flushing Meadows, New York City.[53]

Automatic Equipment Identification

Automatic identification of rolling stock (equipment) is accomplished with RF identification transponder devices that return a coded signal representing the equipment's initial and number. These automatic equipment identification (AEI) tags use for transmission energy only the radiation received when they are activated and interrogated (illuminated) by a reader device. The railroad industry equipped all of its locomotives and freight cars with AEI transponders in the mid-1990s and began to track their locations using a network of readers placed strategically around the industry, including at shops, classification yards, and mainline reporting points. In a 2005 review article, Steven Ditmeyer described AEI implementation to that date as follows:

> AEI transponders have been installed on both sides of all freight cars and locomotives in the US and Canada since 1995. The requirement was established by a railroad industry consensus standard, not by FRA regulation. AEI readers, installed along the track at yards, terminals, and junctions, interrogate the tags over UHF radio frequency (900 MHz), and the tags respond to the readers with the unique alphanumeric code identifying each car and locomotive. The readers assemble the information from all locomotives and cars on a train and then transmit the entire train consist to the railroad's operating data system over the digital data link communications network or over dedicated telephone lines.[54]
>
> Some railroads have installed substantial numbers of readers and have integrated them with their operating data systems; others have not. Installation and integration of the full network of readers [was accomplished over] the next few years. AEI readers [were] integrated with wayside equipment sensors [in numerous locations] to provide positive identification of vehicles with defects.[55]

One study in which co-author Gallamore participated involved a pilot application using AEI tags to track movement of chemical tank cars and covered hoppers from origins in Texas to a nylon plant in Delaware. Readings from the integrated AEI system's detector network were converted automatically to car location messages (CLMs) and forwarded to DuPont (the nylon manufacturer and inbound chemicals car owner) through the AAR's RAILINC subsidiary and another information vendor. The study showed average savings of many hours for the delivery of CLM data to railroad and shipper users, and much higher accuracy of the information. DuPont was able to use the upgraded information to reduce substantially the labor-intensive costs of car tracking for critical ingredients in a chemical manufacturing process.[56]

A predecessor technology to AEI, automatic car identification (ACI), used colored bar-code labels on railcars and optical scanning devices on the w ayside. It was in use from 1968 to 1978; the system was abandoned largely because of the difficulty, in the railroad operating environment, of keeping the bar-code labels clean enough for accurate readings.

Microprocessors in Locomotives, Signal Systems, and Other Railway Devices

In addition to the use of mainframe computers for car scheduling and accounting functions, railroads were early adopters of (1) minicomputers for dispatching and classification yard systems, (2) microcomputers with office productivity applications, and (3) microprocessors embedded in equipment. Among the many widespread and important uses of these devices, in addition to those described elsewhere in this section, are:

1. Precision semi-automated maintenance-of-way (MOW) machinery. Process control microprocessors ensure correct placement of ties and ballast, and alignment, cross-level, and profiling of rail.
2. Advanced signaling systems, which use vital microprocessors in place of traditional gravity drop relays to control fail-safe signal functions in wayside and cab train control equipment. In this context, "vital" means that the equipment has been designed and tested to achieve an extraordinarily high level of availability, accuracy, and predictability under extreme operating conditions. Sometimes redundant units are used to reach the required degree of performance.
3. Microprocessors are used in a variety of wireless communications systems to control channel selection, call priority, trunking (grouping and queuing of calls), error correction, and the like. Microprocessors also monitor and facilitate long-distance communications systems such as microwave and fiber-optic equipment.

Mainframe Computers Enable Freight Car Scheduling

In the Hollerith-coded IBM punch card application referred to earlier, a deck of cards represented a train's consist (one card for each freight car) and the standing order of cars (their position within the train). The cards accompanied cars as they were switched to connecting railroads at interchange points to maintain car accounting records. Improved computing machines developed for the war effort found their way to the railroads shortly after World War II. Data transfer speeds increased with development of magnetic drum, tape, and disk drives in the 1950s. The Southern Railway (SOU) led use of long-distance xerography for processing and delivering waybills over the company's microwave communications system. In 1959, Missouri Pacific (MP) initiated a computerized inventory management system.[57] System-wide real-time communication of all needed information for train operations could not be far behind.

The groundwork for the most important manifest train innovation since dieselization, freight car scheduling (FCS), was laid when the Southern Pacific Railroad (SP), Stanford University, and IBM got together in 1968 to create a total operations process system (TOPS). It was designed to communicate real-time train and car movements between SP terminals and over-the-road operations. SP set up a fee-based consultancy to share its software and know-how with other railroads, initially Burlington Northern, Union Pacific, and Missouri Pacific. Then in the mid-1970s Missouri Pacific began development of its freight car scheduling (FCS) system; the Federal Railroad Administration contributed $5.5 million to the effort in return for MP sharing source code and making documentation available to other railroads.[58]

In FCS, as soon as a freight car is made available for movement, it is assigned a trip plan, which is a series of point-to-point schedules—from origin to destination—for trains in which the car will be moved. Unlike passive timetables that tell railroad managers and customers only what trains ordinarily would move the car, FCS instructs the railroad and its operators how to handle the car. FCS subsystems generate switch lists for moving the car from sidings to yards, through intermediate classification (a hump list, for example), to outbound train makeup, on to terminal yards, and finally to a destination siding. Queries can be made against the system. Pickup and set-out instructions for blocks of cars are created automatically in the system, and crew work orders generated from these are printed out at local points. Work-order completion is conducted as part of event reporting for car location and billing purposes. Using the car's initial and number, all of these movements can be tracked by any authorized computer user, including the shipper using a car or its owner, when proper arrangements have been made.

FCS generates performance statistics, such as trip plan compliance percentages or on-time deliveries, against the initial trip plan. Cars that fall off their trip plans can be rescheduled to a new trip plan as necessary, but the trip plan compliance statistic duly notes the exception. Along the way, FCS generates and maintains a perpetual inventory of car location (PICL) (pronounced "pickle") list—part of the FCS accounting system dating to MP's original design of the system.

Computer systems such as FCS enable railroad personnel to "manage with data." The availability of real-time data and network planning tools are hugely advantageous in the modern competitive operating environment. Some advanced FCS systems allow for off-line simulation of trip plans so that the impact of changes can be assessed before they are implemented. With information available to every level of management and every function that touches the car, railroads can better plan for the resources needed to operate schedules reliably and efficiently, but, of course, keeping the data in the system "timely, accurate, and complete" is critical. Railroads have found that relying on the systems' users to maintain a high degree of data integrity is the key to success; if users take shortcuts, the discipline of data integrity can be lost and the system will fail.

Computerized Operating Information and Asset Management Systems

The 1990s saw a great flowering of computerized information applications to nearly all aspects of railroad operations. These quickly spread throughout the major railroads, and while they were reported in the trade press (and shown to visitors travelling to the large new command and control centers such as the one Union Pacific built in Omaha, BN erected in North Fort Worth, and CSX operated in Jacksonville), the public had little understanding of how these "centralized facilities" worked or what their advantages were. Among the most effective applications developed for centralized operations were the following: crew management and calling, work-order completion and event reporting, scheduling of maintenance-of-way work windows, and locomotive and car management systems.

CREW MANAGEMENT AND CALLING

When demand for car and train movements are determined and reported by the railroad's computerized control system,[59] crews must be assembled to operate designated trains. This is not an easy task because labor agreements and federal hours of service regulation set various parameters that must be honored, in addition to vagaries of employee illnesses and expectations for time off. Once eligibility for a work assignment is determined, employees can be automatically called (in proper seniority or other order) off regular crew assignment lists or, if necessary, extra boards (lists of employees eligible and available for a work assignment).

WORK-ORDER COMPLETION AND EVENT REPORTING

Instructions for spotting (setting out) or picking up (collecting) cars at customer locations are given to switching or local crews, and their responsibility is to do the work assigned (such as loading, parking the car on a repair track, or moving it to a departure yard) and then report the completion or reason for failure to complete the work order. Not too long ago, the work-order completion forms were filed with a field agent or yard office clerk who entered the data into the control system. With closing of many field agencies and consolidation of customer service functions in the late 1980s and 1990s, work-order completion was sometimes accomplished by the train conductor faxing work-order completion forms from the field to a central customer service center for entry into the computer. Most recently, systems have been developed that enable the conductor to finalize his or her work-order information from an on-board or handheld computer linked by data radio to the mainframe operating system. Event reporting (on and off duty, interchange, bad order set-outs, etc.) is accomplished in a similar manner. With near-universal implementation of automatic equipment identification technology, data entry for many event reports can be completely automated.

SCHEDULING OF MAINTENANCE-OF-WAY WORK WINDOWS

When rail traffic is robust and capacity is tight, availability of track time for scheduled maintenance-of-way work is scarce. Expert systems have been designed to help find and optimize work windows, given other requirements such as customer commitments for train service, distribution and priority of different MOW projects, and availability of track forces personnel.

LOCOMOTIVE AND CAR MANAGEMENT SYSTEMS

Railroads use data-intensive expert systems to reposition and select the right equipment for assignment to trains given current and anticipated traffic flow patterns. These systems try to optimize horsepower per trailing ton, given locomotive availability. When locomotives are in temporary surplus, the system may assign the most fuel-efficient locomotives to high horsepower assignments. They also take into account periodic inspection requirements so that these are met effectively. The systems recommend obtaining additional locomotive power when needed, or storing surplus locomotive units when traffic is down. They also keep track of locomotive-hour credits and debits with other railroads.

Car management systems are analogous. Their purpose is to get the right kind of empty equipment to customers needing it for a loaded move. Once loaded, assigned a waybill, and ready to ship, management of the car is turned over to TCS or other operating system. Car management systems keep track of foreign equipment (belonging to another railroad or its leasing company) on line. Once the car is emptied again, the system plans its movement to the next assignment, which might be a load or an empty car return to the home (owning) railroad to minimize car rental (per diem) payments.

Positive Train Control

In the future, improved railroad safety will come from a variety of sophisticated and highly integrated, proactive, train control systems. In 2008, Congress mandated installation of the best-known of these developing systems, positive train control (PTC), on most rail lines carrying passengers or hazardous materials that are toxic by inhalation (TIH)—an estimated 73,000 miles of track at this writing. Despite the importance of the mandate and the controversy it has engendered, this book can only scratch the surface of the issues because of the evolving nature of both PTC technology and national policy.

PTC uses knowledge of the precise location of trains and protected track-work blocks, issuance and communication of train movement authorities (also known as track warrants), knowledge of switch positions, and an automatic interface to train braking systems to intervene in the operation of a train if the system determines it will otherwise exceed its authorized limits. PTC components and subsystems are integrated in a robust systems architecture that provides automatic checks and balances to limit the impact and propagation of human errors.[60] PTC systems' requirements and effects are to prevent wrecks, incursions into work zones, and misrouting of trains. PTC should is to reduce greatly if not entirely eliminate the possibility of train collisions outside yards or derailments due to exceeding speed restrictions. Dissemination to maintenance crews of precise location and speed of trains determined by PTC (or other systems with similar location and communications capabilities) will improve utilization of track time and will protect roadway workers from untimely train incursions. Monitoring switch positions with PTC or other means will ensure that trains stay on the rail path for which they have movement authority.[61]

Systems such as PTC depend on the continuous availability of a highly reliable and ubiquitous digital radio communications network. Once built, the PTC communications link can be used for a variety of related applications. Indeed, continuous, accurate, real-time information on the location and speed of trains and maintenance vehicles is perhaps the key data element that GPS and the digital communications network provides to the railroad's control center and locomotive computers in a PTC system—information flows that typically are not available from conventional signal systems.

PTC and related benefits come at a large investment cost, however. It may take $5 billion for initial installation of PTC over all Class I rail lines used to haul TBI hazardous materials or passenger trains before the end of 2015, as mandated in current legislation, plus an additional $2.4 billion for commuter trains. Also there will be additional ongoing annual maintenance costs for PTC systems. Like the conversion from steam to diesel locomotive power, many of the cost-saving benefits of PTC will not be realized until whole regions can be transferred to the new technology, startup operational kinks have been worked out, and paralleling institutional and employment changes have been properly implemented.

Railroads oppose the government's unfunded mandate for PTC implementation by the end of 2015, arguing that the timetable forces suboptimal deployment strategies and, further, that many of the managerial/operational benefits attributed to PTC can be realized with less costly systems. But these are functions of the implementation strategies railroads choose to pursue for PTC and other systems. Railroads will need to make their own calculations of all-in costs for deploying PTC and determining how it will fit into future operating and technology strategies.

Concluding Thoughts on Technology

Change is doubly unwelcome in a regulated industry: Managers are ill-equipped to deal with shifting economic fundamentals, likely to be both economically and politically destabilizing. In fact, regulation can sometimes carry an aversion to change to the point of actually inhibiting technological innovation. A well-known example was the Big John case, in which Southern Railway's lower rates for handling grain in jumbo covered hopper cars were challenged as an alleged predatory practice; the resulting regulatory review delayed for two to three years introduction of low-cost rail transport of grain into southern animal feeding operations.[62]

It is understandable that where technological innovations threaten to replace labor-intensive operations, and thus jobs, union leaders may be tempted to resist introduction of new technology. This was the case with two-way radios, which some labor leaders initially argued would be a distraction to operators and thus a safety problem. The union opposition required Class I railroads to negotiate arbitraries—an additional payment to be made when union members are told to use the radios.

Historian Richard Saunders tells the story of legendary Southern Railway CEO D.W. (Bill) Brosnan's encounter with the Brotherhood of Railroad Trainmen over payment of an extra ten cents per hour arbitrary in train crew wages for use of walkie-talkies. After the pay supplement was in place, Brosnan asked the union chairman if it was still unsafe to use the radios. "Cap," he said, "the dime just made it safe."[63] Leading unionists today would take a more enlightened view. James Cumby, an official of the United Transportation Union. has said, "You cannot stop technological progress, and it is foolish to try."

The reason these fundamental principles apply to technology innovation and new technology deployment in the US railroad industry is that with passage of the Staggers Rail Act of 1980, three important transformations began to occur. First, in the spirit of deregulation, the Interstate Commerce Commission (subsequently the Surface Transportation Board) and to some extent the Federal Railroad Administration, in its safety regulatory role, began to look at the outputs of railroad service rather than focusing mainly on input requirements. As a result, service quality, profitability, and safety performance indicia became more important to the regulators, while specific rates charged for each tariff movement and detailed reports on specific financial instruments became less critical.

Second, railroad managers were better able to design service operations to meet customer expectations. These rate and service arrangements were captured in confidential rate and service contracts between carriers and shippers, which were not legal prior to deregulation. Adapting rail service supply to customer demands through business-to-business contracts—and to target specific investments and service schedules to the customer requirements identified in marketing efforts—was the critical ingredient. This was the realization of the promise of the Staggers Rail Act: allowing railroads to act like other businesses do in the American free enterprise system.

Third, Staggers Rail Act deregulation had an enormously favorable impact on railroad cash flows and bottom line profitability. This came not from rate increases in the period from 1980 to 2000, but from cost savings enabled by rate and service contracts and from the freight volume expansion that followed (with unit trains, for example). Some suppliers and railroads anticipated the changes and stepped up R&D programs to ready new technology for the less-regulated future.[64] Of course, the post-Staggers period saw other factors (like merger synergies, crew consist reforms, thawing of old frozen assets on accounting balance sheets dictated by the ICC, the explosion of both Powder River Basin coal and international double-stack container train movements, and macroeconomic forces within the US national economy), but even some of these were part of the "deregulatory spring."

The effect on cash flows was dramatic and unprecedented. Railroads now had both the cash streams and the needed confidence in the future to make long-term capital commitments to staying in the business and upgrading their facilities. With reinvestment came new capacity to handle the surge in volume, but perhaps more important, the fruits of new technology embodied in these capital improvements, for example, more reliable locomotives, larger freight cars, better rail, concrete cross ties, more efficient maintenance and track renewal machinery, safer operating facilities, better computerized management systems, more ability to control operations, and on and on. It was the germination of the seeds of deregulation, the flowering of reinvestment in the industry, and the harvest of the railroad renaissance.

Top Ten Railroad Innovations of the Twentieth Century

---

1. Diesel-Electric Locomotive (Diesel, Ingersoll Rand, GE, EMD)
   - Hybrid design enabled medium-speed diesel prime mover to power a direct current generator (later an AC inverter) developing electric power to feed traction motors on axles.
   - Load-balancing features managed generator load to traction motor requirements.
   - Adhesion improvements proved valuable in starting trains and mounting steep grades.
   - Cleaner emissions compared with steam operation.
   - Less support infrastructure (roundhouse repairs, water towers, coal chutes); lower labor costs.
2. Containerization (McLean)
   - Standard trailer-size box for lifting from truck chassis to container ship.
   - Malcolm McLean's initial demonstration moved container-loads on vessel *Ideal-X*.
   - Reducing damage, pilferage, wasted wharfage space, and labor costs associated with manual ship loading.
   - Facilitated double-stacking on unit container trains.
3. Wireless RF Applications
   - Enabled clear voice communication among train crew members, and between locomotive and wayside pickup to long-distance network.
   - Added safety and efficiency compared to earlier telegraph, written orders, hand and whistle signals.
   - Evolution to computerized digital on-board information systems is continuing.
4. Roller Bearings in Sealed Journals
   - Application of premium steel to cylindrical and later tapered rollers for heavy weight bearing and long life in locomotives and freight cars.
   - Reduced in-train rolling friction resulted in fuel and locomotive horsepower savings.
   - Eliminated frequent manual spot lubrication.
   - Provided vastly improved interval between hot-box overheated bearing journals.
5. Welded Rail and Premium Track-Work Materials
   - Railroads approximately doubled track life in the 1990s by purchasing top-grade steel for rails, welding replacement rail into strings, and grinding rail to the worn wheel profile.

(continued)

Top Ten Railroad Innovations of the Twentieth Century *Continued*

- Welded rail eliminates the clickety-clack of railcars rolling over rail track segments joined by bolted strips of metal and reduces broken-rail derailments.
- Railroads are increasingly using premium steel for construction of specialized track components such as turnouts and diamond crossings.

6. Centralized Traffic Control (CTC)
   - In the 1920s, railroads developed equipment and managerial structures enabling control of distributed track switching functions (turnouts) from regional dispatching facilities. These installations were interlocked and semi-automated for safety and efficiency.
   - CTC enabled single-track, reversible direction operation, yielding capacity equivalent to double-track block-signal systems and substantial savings in track maintenance.

7. Freight Car Scheduling
   - Foundational concept and application for managing service reliability and scheduled operations with computerized system-wide shared data and performance measures.
   - Automated car accounting and event reporting saved clerical labor and improved accuracy.

8. Microprocessor Applications in On-Board, Wayside, and Central Office Equipment
   - Computerized processing has been introduced into safety appliances and productivity tools, yielding benefits of speed, accuracy, and labor savings.
   - Microprocessor controls in locomotives yield fuel savings, emissions reductions, and antislip traction power control (rail adhesion).
   - Microprocessor applications in wayside signals improve signal system capacity and reliability. Computerized wayside monitoring devices with centralized reporting and control facilitates a new generation of safety assurance and managerial oversight.
   - Reduced clerical costs from widespread use of office productivity tools, often with centralized, communications-intensive, network functions such as dispatching, crew calling, MOW scheduling, locomotive distribution, and car management.

9. Controlled (Automated) Classification Yards, and Unit Trains
   - Automated classification yards speeded up makeup of trains, saved labor costs, and improved safety performance.

Top Ten Railroad Innovations of the Twentieth Century

- Unit trains (mainly for coal, grain, chemicals, and intermodal shipments) expedited deliveries, saved labor costs, improved car utilization, and (because shippers began to provide their own car fleets, especially for unit train moves) saved railroads capital outlays on rolling stock.
- With regard to heavy-haul, dense mainline rail operations typified by unit trains, and ultrasound and other technologies, including acoustic bearing signature detection, shows promise for in-service measurement of incipient defects before they cause a service failure. (This advantage is not limited to unit trains.)

10. Advanced Crossing Warning and Protection Devices
    - The largest source of fatalities and injuries in the railroad environment over the second half of the twentieth century was collisions between trains and motor vehicles or pedestrians at highway–rail intersections.
    - Public funding through Section 130 grants has enabled improvement of crossings objectively ranked as carrying high risk due to traffic and train volume.
    - Crossing warning devices, especially flashers and down-gates, have been developed that are more conspicuous and have greater reliability.
    - Use of locomotive ditch lights help bystanders estimate the speed of an approaching locomotive and thus better judge the safety of crossing tracks before a train arrives.
    - Upgraded crossing installations with improved sight-lines and separation of traffic lanes to prevent running around gates have been shown to be effective. Video enforcement has shown promise in reducing motorist violations in the communities that have used it.

13

DECLINE AND RENAISSANCE OF AMERICAN RAILROADS IN THE TWENTIETH CENTURY— PULLING INTO THE TERMINAL

> And if railroads are not built, how shall we get to heaven in season? But if we stay at home and mind our business, who will want railroads?
>
> —HENRY DAVID THOREAU, *Walden* (1854)

For the venerable railroads, the twentieth century brought great changes. Yet those changes did not entirely camouflage the enduring constants bequeathed to them from railroads' first century. American railroads in 2000 would be easily recognized by a visitor from Victorian times: They still operated on track with a gauge of 4 feet 8½ inches, and still used locomotives to pull freight cars or passenger coaches. The federal government, not the states, still held the fundamental authority to regulate the industry's rates and services, though regulation had greatly and repeatedly changed during the century. Similarly, labor unions had risen and fallen in membership, but they still represented nearly all nonmanagement workers employed by major railroads. US railroads remained continental in scope, but they operated only two-thirds as many miles of track at the end of the twentieth century as they had at its beginning.

Perhaps the most startling difference was that by 2000, railroads generated more than ten times as many freight ton-miles annually as in 1900, with only 16.5 percent of the employment (see Figure 13.1). A high percentage of the readers of this book had grandparents or great-grandparents who worked on the railroads, but few readers anticipate that their grandchildren will. Railroads still perform essential functions in our economy, but they no longer occupy the central position in our society that they did 100 years ago.

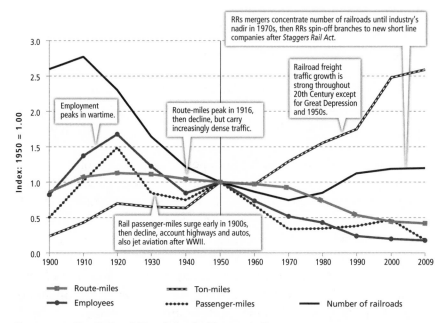

RRs mergers concentrate number of railroads until industry's nadir in 1970s, then RRs spin-off branches to new short line companies after *Staggers Rail Act.*

Railroad freight traffic growth is strong throughout 20th Century except for Great Depression and 1950s.

Employment peaks in wartime.

Route-miles peak in 1916, then decline, but carry increasingly dense traffic.

Rail passenger-miles surge early in 1900s, then decline, account highways and autos, also jet aviation after WWII.

Route-miles   Ton-miles
Employees   Passenger-miles   Number of railroads

Figure 13.1   Key Railroad Trends for the Twentieth Century   Railroads increased freight ton-miles many-fold during the twentieth century while substantially reducing employment and route-miles after World War I. Railroads dominated intercity passenger travel in the first two decades of the century, but lost share to autos and airlines, except for the World War II years. While wars, the macroeconomy, and demographic trends drove demand for US transportation, four factors determined how these would affect railroad institutions and financial performance: regulation, mergers, technology, and modal competition. *Source:* Data courtesy of the AAR.

Railroads rose to dominance in the nineteenth century; carried the nation westward; served farms, factories, mines, and mills. They framed our metropolitan areas, took us home for Christmas, and helped fight our wars. They left their imprint on logistics, law, and literature, and on music, movies, and museums. They framed recollections for nearly every soul that breathed the air of the twentieth century. As Table 13.1 shows, a variety of macro-economic, regulatory, merger, technology, and competitive issues rose and faded over the decades of the twentieth century. Yet, among the things most noticeable about railroads is that they are still, all day long or all century long, railroads. They endure.

A century ago, the popular perception was that robber barons cheated investors, abused workers, charged customers monopolistic rates, discriminated against small towns and ports, neglected new markets, and allowed rail services to deteriorate by failing to maintain facilities and equipment properly. Progressive Era trust-busters and "good government reformers," so the argument goes, were forced to set up labor protection laws and independent regulatory commissions to save the public from capitalism run amuck. One economic historian further confused the picture by arguing that the railroads themselves actively sought regulation by the government—in order to facilitate pricing cartels, which otherwise could not have been sustained.[1]

It is true that railroads were far from perfect as providers of transportation. They could run at fairly high speeds if the track were built and maintained to good standards, but they derailed frequently, suffered deadly collisions and washouts, had a fearful record of employee and bystander injuries and fatalities, darkened urban areas with coal smoke, and colluded to avoid competitive rate making.

A remarkable difference between the railroads of 1900 and those of 2000 was the nature of the competition they faced from alternative modes of transport. At the end of the nineteenth century, steamboats rivaled railroads along coastal waters, the Great Lakes, and inland rivers, but otherwise rails dominated intercity transport options, both passenger and cargo movements. "The nation's rail industry had peaked in importance in 1920," historian Keith Bryant wrote, "afterwards, other transportation industries began to diminish the significance of the rail system."[2] As everyone knows from period movies, until the development of internal combustion motor vehicles and hard-surfaced roads in the first half of the twentieth century, if there were no railroad or steamboat access to a specific location the only alternatives for travel or moving goods were animal-drawn wagons, stagecoaches, canal barges, bicycles and horseback. Much like Thomas Hobbes's description of humankind in the state of nature, travel before railroads was expensive, slow, risky, dirty, and hard.[3]

Throughout the twentieth century, the railroads' neighbors—shippers of all kinds of commodities, communities large and small, rural areas, cities, seaports, habitués of rail passenger service, labor unions, competing modes of transport, governmental taxing units, and railroads' owners and investors—all, and in various ways, sought a larger slice of the railroad pie. One hundred years after the peak of railroad track mileage, the public no longer perceived railroad owners as monopolists bent on ruining small towns, farmers, and worker organizations. Yet the old myth that railroads have vast and underutilized power to "make things right" for other sectors

Table 13.1 Forces Shaping Structure of American Railroad Industry in the Twentieth Century (Decade by Decade)*

Decade	Law and Policy	Macroeconomic Setting	Financial Factors
1900–1910	T. Roosevelt antitrust enforcement; Northern Securities declared illegal. Hepburn Act tightened ICC rate regulation.	Progressive reforms; boom and bust economy.	Overcapacity hangover from nineteenth century railroad expansion. Government orders divestiture of Hill's Northern Securities. Rise of scientific management movement.
1911–1920	Clayton Anti-Monopoly Act; Railroad Valuation Act for rate base and merger considerations.	World War I brought unified federal control of railroad operations.	Harriman empire broken up. Capital constraints as ICC disallowed rate increases.
1921–1930	Transportation Act of 1920 mandate for ICC consolidation plans; railroad antitrust exemption.	Irony: stock market boom, railroad merger bust; ICC planned consolidations policy fails.	Act of 1920 required plans for inclusion of weak railroads with strong railroads; private railroads opposed plans.
1931–1940	ICC begged release from consolidation planning. Emergency Transportation Act 1933.	The Great Depression; beginning of dieselization and streamlining.	Liquidity crisis dries up merger activity.
1941–1950	Transportation Act of 1940 = liberal "public interest" standard for mergers; repealed ICC planning role.	World War II diverted railroad investment priorities despite heavy traffic demands.	Postwar rise of competing modes; railroad future uncertain.
1951–1960	Eisenhower Interstate Highway Act = competitive shock.	Midcentury railroad merger wave begins.	ICC allows parallel mergers based on cost savings rationale.
1961–1970	Blue ribbon commissions recognize need for regulatory reform. Penn Central merger. Amtrak Act 1970.	Postwar economy and traffic mix turns against railroads; Sun Belt beckons population and industry.	Cold War has different traffic demands than World War II; Vietnam War feeds inflation. Rust Belt woes emerge.
1971–1980	Productivity task force urged end-to-end mergers, opposed parallel mergers. Environmental legislation. 3R and 4R acts.	Demise of Penn Central; Northeast and Midwest bankruptcies, reorganizations. Conrail off to a slow start.	OPEC I and II oil crises drive inflation, high interest rates; Clean Air Act of 1970 and Amendments in 1977 and 1990 encourage sourcing of coal from western low-sulfur deposits.

*White cells were decades with merger waves and the shaded decades were merger washouts.　　　*(continued)*

Table 13.1   (continued)

Decade	Law and Policy	Macroeconomic Setting	Financial Factors
1981–1990	Staggers Rail Act of 1980 adds merger criteria for impact on competition; sets timetables for ICC review. NERSA helps Conrail become profitable. Conrail IPO in 1987.	Staggers Act Era— railroad megamergers and short-line startups.	Rise of conglomerates, hostile takeovers, junk bond financing; moderate impact on railroad mergers.
1991–2000	ICC gives way to STB; policy favors curing competitive losses at key points. Threat of rate reregulation held off.	Fin-de-siècle merger wave (BNSF, UP+SP, and split of Conrail to NS and CSX)	Rail renaissance: favorable energy, clean air, NAFTA, and globalization impacts on railroads. Low interest rates lead to easy credit.

of the economy had not entirely passed away. Congress has been unwilling to level the playing field for transport modes with respect to taxes and subsidies—partly because of old myths and shibboleths, one suspects. The "myth of the miraculous railroad," in Eric Beshers's cogent phrase, has proved as durable as the railroads' actual presence in American life.[4]

There is still enormous pressure—especially from the electricity industry, chemical manufacturers, and agricultural interests—to expand government's power to control what railroads do and what they charge for their services, that is, to reregulate the industry. Even some railroad workers have hopped on this bandwagon in hopes of benefitting if policy makers take their side in wage and fringe benefit negotiations. Indeed, if railroads were to heighten their criticism of unwarranted highway and waterway policies or projects, leaders of firms and trade associations in those rival modes would join the chorus of antirail lobbying. The result would be new pressures to allow larger truck sizes and heavier weight limits for highway vehicles, or to continue to hold to artificially low levels the fees paid by other modes for the use of public infrastructure.[5]

The greatest errors in twentieth-century railroad history were not failures by railroad owners and managers to develop railroad technology and infrastructure or to exercise good corporate citizenship. Rather, those failures stemmed from a national schizophrenia on energy and transportation policy that seems always to attend railroad commercial development. Railroads made their great contributions to society despite a legacy of regulation in which adversary proceedings exaggerated and oversimplified conflicts between railroads and specific business interests or social goals. In the end, public policies regulating railroad abuses themselves needed reform; the old medicine of regulation had become worse than the ills it purported to cure.

Over the full course of the twentieth century, the American railroads endured but, except in the first years after 1900, did not dominate their rivals. The industry survived more than it prospered. Rail firms held on as private enterprises but did not excel as business powerhouses. Railroads contributed to the strength and growth of the US economy in peace and war, but for the century as a whole, they shrank in presence, power, and position among businesses and services influencing American life.

Yet in the last years of the old millennium and the first of the new—quite surprisingly, given the experience of the twentieth century—railroads had undergone something of a renaissance. They were breaking records for volume, profitability, and reinvestment, and it seemed altogether likely that the industry's renewal would endure for some considerable time into the future.

Ten Themes for Railroading in the Twentieth Century

The National Academies of Engineering (NAE) recently set out to summarize the twenty greatest engineering achievements of the twentieth century.[6] It is a reasonable list, although no one can say it is right or wrong in any objective sense. The NAE's list begins with three items integral to transportation: electrification, automobiles, and airplanes. It adds modern highways as number 11; electronics at number 5; computers at number 8; the Internet, number 13; lasers and fiber optics, number 18; and high-performance materials, number 20. The telephone (a classic nineteenth-century application) made the list at number 9, and spacecraft (small impact overshadowed by glamorous future orientation) was number 12. But wireless radio frequency technologies (so important to business and social interaction today) did not make the top twenty list!

Railroad technological advances—which exerted a huge but rather old-fashioned and pedestrian impact—are nowhere on NAE's list. Unfortunately, this is the conventional way in which Americans see railroads compared with other technologies: Railroads are pretty much out of sight and out of mind, "overflown" on a transcontinental flight, an also-ran mode, an unremarkable contributor to economic progress in our time.

One unprovable and imperfect list possibly justifies another. To summarize and conclude this book's account of railroad decline and renaissance in the twentieth century, this final chapter of *American Railroads* sorts out its ten most important themes. Like the NAE list, our summary involves some heroic assumptions and comparisons of incomparable concepts. We have no dependable scale for ordering these themes and, admittedly, it is reckless to compare in a single dimension disparate factors such as service improvements, technology advances, trends in government oversight, and the impact on railroad costs of regulatory rulings. Still, as good historians point out, some events or developments are simply more important than others and call out for recognition as such. The ten themes of our book are discussed in the following chapter sections, roughly in the order in which they were introduced in *American Railroads*.

1. The Misdemeanors of Regulation

Railroads came into the twentieth century as one of the most fully developed and modern industries in the US economy. In the phrase made famous by longtime Harvard Business School professor Alfred Chandler, they were "the Nation's First Big Business."[7] Rail track mileage actually reached its zenith in 1916, while layer upon layer of government control through economic regulation continued to be added for another sixty years, peaking in the US bicentennial year of 1976, when reform of railroad regulation at last began to change the paradigm.[8]

Because of their reach, size, complexity, and power, railroads had earned the dubious honor of becoming the vanguard of enterprises facing state and federal economic control carried out by so-called independent regulatory commissions—part legislative, part executive, and part judicial. Big railroads met big government at the dawn of the twentieth century.

The first, largest, and most powerful of the independent regulatory commissions was the Interstate Commerce Commission (ICC), established by the Act to Regulate Commerce in 1887. At first, the ICC was a placeholder agency whose most important mission may have been to preempt truly parochial and counterproductive political control of commerce at the state level. But with two pieces of legislation (the Hepburn Act of

1906 and the Mann-Elkins Act of 1910) in the new century's first decade, economic regulation became a singular force shaping the destiny of the American railroad industry. These legislative enactments legitimized and focused the powers of the ICC to make railroads a passive instrumentality of Progressive Era commercial policy. By 1910, ICC regulation extended to every aspect of the rail industry—metaphorically no different than construction and extension of railroad track into every passenger and cargo market in the nation[9]

HOW SHOULD REGULATION BE DONE?

The variety of means by which the regulatory apparatus was used, historically, to find if rates were lawful (that is, to determine if they were "just and reasonable") serves to underscore our thesis that there never was a "correct" way to determine proper levels of rates under railroad regulation. Over 100 years of theorizing, lawmaking, litigating, arbitration, and statistical analysis have not solved what Ann Friedlaender called *The Dilemma of Freight Regulation* because there was no theoretically correct way to accomplish the task, other than to rely steadfastly on markets and accept any resulting imperfections in pricing. The closest academic experts could come is what the 1920s-era textbook writers (Jones, Johnson, Daggett, Ripley, Cunningham—all cited earlier in this book) pointed out, namely, that costs could be a guide to overall rate levels perhaps, but that only demand-based rates made sense at the margin, that is, in a shipper's decision-making process at the time and point of sale.[10] The duality of opinion on the basis for railroad regulatory ratemaking was never really resolved despite multiple legislative efforts to draw a legal "rule of ratemaking" guiding the ICC in deciding rate cases. (See Figure 13.2.)

During the 1970s, double-digit inflation would become one of the most powerful forces undermining regulation as practiced by the ICC. Then, in the wake of the Staggers Rail Act of 1980, there would occur a blossoming of technology deployment tied closely to deregulation, with corresponding total productivity improvement from all sources (capital, labor, technology, knowledge, and policy). Also, federal tax and accounting rules caught up in 1981–1984, when railroads were allowed to write off a great deal of their "frozen" assets, and ICC betterment accounting (basically, specialized rules for expensing capital outlays in the current year) gave way to normal Financial Accounting Standards Board (FASB) capitalization and depreciation rules. Some railroads responded with new strategic,

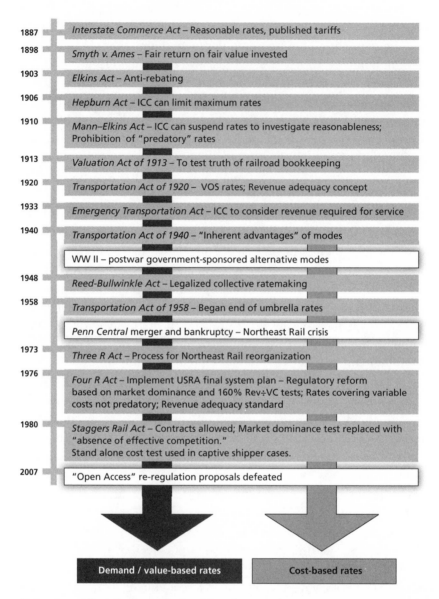

1887	*Interstate Commerce Act* – Reasonable rates, published tariffs
1898	*Smyth v. Ames* – Fair return on fair value invested
1903	*Elkins Act* – Anti-rebating
1906	*Hepburn Act* – ICC can limit maximum rates
1910	*Mann–Elkins Act* – ICC can suspend rates to investigate reasonableness; Prohibition of "predatory" rates
1913	*Valuation Act of 1913* – To test truth of railroad bookkeeping
1920	*Transportation Act of 1920* – VOS rates; Revenue adequacy concept
1933	*Emergency Transportation Act* – ICC to consider revenue required for service
1940	*Transportation Act of 1940* – "Inherent advantages" of modes
	WW II – postwar government-sponsored alternative modes
1948	*Reed-Bullwinkle Act* – Legalized collective ratemaking
1958	*Transportation Act of 1958* – Began end of umbrella rates
	Penn Central merger and bankruptcy – Northeast Rail crisis
1973	*Three R Act* – Process for Northeast Rail reorganization
1976	*Four R Act* – Implement USRA final system plan – Regulatory reform based on market dominance and 160% Rev÷VC tests; Rates covering variable costs not predatory; Revenue adequacy standard
1980	*Staggers Rail Act* – Contracts allowed; Market dominance test replaced with "absence of effective competition." Stand alone cost test used in captive shipper cases.
2007	"Open Access" re-regulation proposals defeated

Demand / value-based rates   **Cost-based rates**

Figure 13.2   A Proliferation of Railroad Legislation   A noisy variety of legislation affecting regulation and deregulation of railroads shaped the industry's economic performance throughout the twentieth century. Demand-based rate making held sway throughout the century, although after 1940 it was challenged frequently by policy-driven initiatives—some in the name of stimulating efficiency, others simply intended to reduce rail rates for affected interests. Demand-based rates were simpler and avoided arbitrary cost allocations, but some reformers believed they allowed railroads with monopoly pricing power to overcharge shippers, a controversy that continues to this day.

technology, productivity, and marketing initiatives, but not as swiftly nor thoroughly as they might have, given the urgent financial circumstances.[11]

There are several summary conclusions to be drawn. First, if economic theory cannot establish "correct" rates for rail services, even with full information, a bureaucratic administrative process or a quasi-courtroom adversary proceeding certainly will not either. Second, because economically efficient rates are impossible to find, all that can be expected are "fair and reasonable" rates that even regulatory rules would consider lawful. Third, in controversial matters, regulatory process (administrative) costs could easily exceed any possible benefits from moving closer to the elusive efficient rates. Fourth, if dominant sellers do receive supranormal profits, it would be comforting to know that these will be used to increase producer capacity and improve services for consumers.

In short, the authors of this book agree with Professor Richard Levin's implicit assumption that private-sector ownership and operation of railroads is superior to takeover by the state (nationalization), especially his conclusion that the $1 billion in deadweight losses from suboptimal pricing observed in the 1970s "was a small price to pay for keeping railroads viable in the private sector."[12]

2. Railroads Are "Imbued with the Public Interest"

From the very beginning it was understood that actions of railroads often affected other members of the body politic, for good or ill—and not just with respect to commercial relationships that are dealt with by economic regulators like the ICC or the Surface Transportation Board (STB). Railroads have normal commercial outcomes—revenues, expenses, profits or losses—but they also have impacts on society that are not captured in financial statements, impacts that economists call positive or negative spillover effects.

Negative spillovers are what people think of first. Steam engines belched smoke, startled horses, set prairie fires, and had an unfortunate propensity to explode. In fact, the very first public demonstration of a locomotive operating on George Stevenson's Liverpool & Manchester Railway at the Rainhill Trials in 1829 resulted in a fatality to an observer, and while the accident was clearly the fault of the bystander himself, a pall fell over the whole celebration; it was the first of what became millions of lives accidentally lost to mechanically powered transport in the generations that followed.[13] Railroads made old conveyances obsolete, but in accordance with the laws of momentum, they also made hazards. The impact of railroads on society cannot be weighed historically (without recalling the heavy toll of fatalities and injuries to employees and bystanders), nor today (without valuing the excellent safety record railroads have compiled over the years).

Still, it was not railroads' physical dangers to workers and neighbors that politicians sought most to control, but their economic power in local markets and with regard to commercial relationships among competing locations. Railroads were easily caricatured as unconcerned with the public consequences of their actions, too powerful vis-à-vis markets, and only too willing to quash competitors with predatory practices. Ida Tarbell, Frank Norris, and Sinclair Lewis understood these things. The Octopus cartoon we shared in Chapter 2 wrapped its tentacles around what people were thinking.

After the US Supreme Court's landmark decision in *Wabash v. Illinois* (1886) declaring the primacy of federal regulation of interstate commerce over regulation by the states—and the subsequent enactment by Congress of the Act to Regulate Commerce in 1887—there was no longer any doubt that railroad policy would be determined by the federal government. Under the Tenth Amendment to the US Constitution, states retained the power to act where Congress had not, but in this case, preemption of interstate commerce law was clear, and the states could do little more than issue local charters and require safety inspections under state policing powers. Perhaps it goes too far to call such developments the silent repeal of the Tenth Amendment, but in transport policy, the Commerce Clause reigned supreme.

Actually, the first meaningful limits on unsafe operating practices were established under the Safety Appliance Act of 1893, which took effect after a transitional period in 1900. In that law, Congress required implementation of air brakes, the automatic coupler, and grab irons on freight cars, and gave railroads only five years to install them in all equipment moving in interstate commerce. A century later, the industry would call such laws unfunded mandates, but there was no denying the effectiveness of the legislation in accomplishing what the industry had been unable to self-impose for two decades. Other federal statutory safety requirements, specifically for inspection of steam engine boilers and ash pans, followed the same pattern.

Then in 1908 the Federal Employee's Liability Act (FELA) set rules for compensation of injured railroad workers under a fault system that has resulted in generally larger compensation for injured railroad workers and their beneficiaries than have the state-run workers' compensation programs for nonrailroad industries. As with rate regulation and safety, federal preemption controlled health and welfare benefits for railroad workers, and the ground rules for collective bargaining over wages and benefits.

Independent railroad brotherhoods and the American Federation of Labor's (AFL's) Railroad Employees Department worked for passage of the 1917 Adamson Act (enshrining the eight-hour workday), as well as the Railway Labor Act of 1926 and amendments to it in 1934 (both foreshadowing the National Labor Relations Act of 1935). These were important pieces of legislation, still on the books today. The biggest health and welfare package of all was the Railroad Retirement System authorized by the Railroad Retirement Act of 1935—a clear predecessor of the Wagner Act (1935) creating the Old Age and Survivors Insurance (OASDI, or Social Security) program. In all these areas, precedents were established by Congress for application to railroad workers before similar provisions were established for all workers in interstate commerce.[14]

FEDERAL CONTROL IN THE GREAT WAR

Perhaps the clearest historical example of US railroads finding themselves under government control to further the public interest occurred during the First World War (covered in Chapter 3). President Woodrow Wilson, an activist, observed the chaos attending mobilization for war and ordered federal control of the railroads, soon ratified by Congress. Ownership of railroad assets was left in private hands, but operations of all US carriers were put under authority of the United States Railroad Administration (USRA).

American railroads came dangerously close to nationalization in this period—a step that many other countries actually took. To be sure, there is no necessary relationship of democratic institutions to private ownership of railroads. Indeed, democratic governments could and often did nationalize public utilities, including railroads; democracy and capitalism are not subsets of each other. But it was a fact that war exigencies caused dislocations on a scale that the private railroads could not at the time successfully manage.

The twenty-six-month period of federal control (1917–1920) was as remarkable for its ending as its beginning. It took more than a year of debate and political posturing, but unlike in almost every other nation of the time, US railroads (never publicly owned) were returned to private-sector control by the Esch-Cummins Transportation Act of 1920.

Under that enactment, the ICC's powers over the railroads were increased, including with a mandate from Congress to plan consolidation of the railroads into "a limited number of systems." These were to be competitive with one another and balanced as to their financial strength. The effort was stillborn because the real purpose of the 1920 law was not so much to create an efficient rail network as it was to ensure continuation of services operated by historically weak railroad lines through the mechanism of their purposeful cross-subsidization within larger, stronger systems. Said *Time* magazine in 1924: "It is a curious result of the trend of affairs, that official Washington, which ten years ago was violently opposed to railroad consolidations, is now the first to urge them upon the railroad companies."

After federal control in the Great War, a second all-out embrace of government control over railroad operations was the formation of the National Railroad Passenger Corporation in 1970, which thereafter operated under the trade name Amtrak. Its purpose was to provide a unified national passenger service network out of the dozens of preexisting, but rapidly failing, passenger services operated (typically as an adjunct to freight service) by the private-sector railroads. Amtrak was set up mainly to operate passenger services over the freight railroads' track networks on an incremental cost basis. Thus, in the first half of the twentieth century, federalization was used to make wartime freight service more efficient, while in the second half, government intervention was used to ensure continuation of important passenger trains—while relieving freight railroads of the burden of passenger service deficits. In both cases the challenge was to use what was intended to be a temporary federalized solution to fix problems in the private sector that had been created or exacerbated by maladroit government regulation.

3. Bankruptcy Reorganization and Rationalization of Surplus Lines

In 1968, the ICC permitted merger of America's largest (Pennsylvania) and by at least one measure fourth largest (New York Central) railroads to form the ill-starred Penn Central system.[15] In just over two years, Penn Central was bankrupt and ruled by the federal courts impossible to reorganize under conventional income and debt restructuring procedures. In response, Congress passed the Regional Rail Reorganization (3R) Act of 1973, creating the US Railway Association (the second USRA, with a name similar to the first USRA in World War I—see Box 13.1). The 3R Act established procedures for preparing a preliminary and a final system plan (PSP and FSP), conveying properties of Penn Central and a half dozen other bankrupt Northeast railroad estates into the Consolidated Rail Corporation, universally known as Conrail. (USRA also designated a few lines to other entities for competitive reasons, and assigned lines predominantly used for passenger service to Amtrak or commuter authorities.) An important responsibility for USRA was to determine and defend in court the minimum, constitutionally permissible level of compensation for the public "taking" of these properties to permit their continued use in rail service.

USRA's FSP had given Conrail a tightly structured rail franchise— augmented by various new authorities and funding in the subsequent

---

Box 13.1   Federalization in the Context of Railroad Problems

Separated by a half century, the tasks assigned both USRAs to manage "federalization" of railroads amounted to tiptoeing along the edge of constitutional limits on big government and teetering on the brink of railroad nationalization. From 1917 to 1920, the challenge was for a temporary government agency to provide direction in a chaotic war mobilization emergency and to avert public ownership (nationalization) afterward—that is, the task was to facilitate the war mobilization but not let federalized railroads become nationalized railroads. From 1974 to 1976, the fear was that—if the second USRA could not design a viable Conrail and marshal the case for paying the constitutional "taking" bill when it came due—there would be total collapse and permanent loss of important railroad service in the most populous part of the country.

In the earlier period, the government had to seize control and impose efficiency measures because the private railroads were acting for their own benefit rather than acting in the national interest. In the second case, the government also had to set up a replacement industry structure because the solvent railroads were hesitant or unwilling to act in their own best interests; the challenge was making an already nationalized collection of railroads look and act like a private-sector firm and then to return it to the private sector for a fair price. Not every observer could handle the head-spinning, rapid-fire developments or the subtle legal and political nuances of this grand compromise—but it was a blessing for the nation's transportation system that, as a nation, we muddled through.

Northeast Rail Services Act of 1983. The FSP's design for Conrail was the best effort of a dedicated staff constrained by time and political guidelines, but it was substantially frustrated by the unwillingness of solvent neighboring railroads in the Northeast and Midwest to step up to procompetitive actions sought by the USRA, and which history shows were pretty clearly in their own interests. The horse was led to water, but it did not drink.

Overall, the legislative changes, including the Staggers Rail Act and Conrail's management initiatives, amounted to a high-stakes, no-nonsense accommodation to railroad realities in the last quarter of the twentieth century. These helped Conrail by expediting abandonments, transferring passenger services to regional commuter authorities, and offering buyouts to employees. Then, under provisions of the Staggers Rail Act, Conrail could begin closing redundant gateways (lengthening internal hauls), earning fairer splits of interline revenue, charging more remunerative rates for its services, and trimming its operations to match available demand. Conrail and rail labor agreed to an emergency wage reduction, which was quickly restored after the railroad achieved profitability in 1982. Conrail avoided disaster and scratched its way back to "normalcy." In fact, by 1987, the franchise was fit to be sold to private investors in the largest ever (to that time) initial public offering (IPO) of securities;[16] it was at the time also the largest ever privatization of a US government-owned enterprise— a record subsequently eclipsed by re-privatizations in 2010 and 2013 of the 61 percent of General Motors stock held by the US government after its celebrated bailout of the Big 3 automakers in 2008. When these announcements were made, only a few journalists recalled the lessons learned during the Northeast regional rail crisis of the 1970s.

4. The Crisis of Granger Railroads in the 1970s

In addition to dealing with the tribulations swamping the Northeast and Midwest railroad reorganization, the US Department of Transportation (DOT) was forced by circumstances to develop policies addressing a somewhat parallel crisis of marginal midwestern (or Granger) railroads in the 1970s. The story of the rationalization of overbuilt and financially marginal Great Plains railroads (those generally stretching from Chicago, St. Louis, and Memphis west to the Rocky Mountains), however, is very different from the better-known tale of Penn Central's bankruptcy, takeover, and restructuring through the Northeast reorganization process.

The Carter administration's actions to manage otherwise almost certainly bad outcomes from the Granger rail crisis of the mid- to late 1970s—like its critical role in developing and shepherding the Staggers Rail Act through Congress (see related section below)—has escaped most historical notice. Yet these policies and implementing actions were of major significance in preventing the collapse of essential services during the transition to a less-regulated industry. Successful application of good economics and sound policy principles under difficult political pressures was nowhere better represented for twentieth-century railroads than in the story of the rationalization of the Great Plains bankrupt railroads during the 1970s.

The Rock Island Railroad had filed for Chapter 11 bankruptcy protection in 1975 and would be declared cashless in 1979. The Milwaukee Road entered bankruptcy protection in December 1977 and soon began secret discussions with other railroads (under authority of the Federal Railroad Administration) to sell off portions of its lines in the Pacific Northwest.[17]

Before long, Milwaukee had consultants preparing a core plan to shrink its system, and the trustee filed an application with the ICC for abandonment of all Milwaukee Road lines west of Miles City, Montana. Partly as a result of DOT/FRA's quick action and interaction with the bankruptcy trustees, the Midwest/Great Plains bankruptcies and near misses never reached quite the same level of economic emergency that had quickened action in the Northeast. Nor was there the same degree of government intervention because the Rock Island was soon found to be cashless and was forced into liquidation, while the Milwaukee was reduced to a small core operation by its trustee and then sold in its entirety to the Soo Line Railroad (a subsidiary of the Canadian Pacific).

In these cases, the notion of enduring railroads is strained but not broken; segments of the Milwaukee Road and Rock Island survive, but mainly as fragments subsumed into other carriers, not subsidized stand-alone operations. The two historic Granger railroads (both headquartered in Chicago, both important to Chicago commuters and midwestern small towns and farmers, and both bankrupt within two years of each other) are gone forever; their flags are fallen.

In retrospect, it is well to recall how close the railroad industry came to total collapse in the dark days of the 1970s and to remind ourselves of the role that enlightened physical restructuring played in the recovery from that low point. We are a society that lavishes fame on sometimes unworthy recipients and is stingy granting honor to those who are deserving, but the unsung heroes of this period of US history (including many railroaders who lost employment and small town neighbors who lost their economic base) may yet be acclaimed.

5. Competition from Rival Modes

The freight railroads provide their own unsubsidized rights of way and equipment; pay taxes in many forms; and offer environmentally friendly, fuel-efficient, and exceptionally safe transport at low cost to shippers. Today's railroads provide an alternative mode for much traffic that would otherwise be on congested highways. But because many believe railroads are old technology and because they are mainly out of sight and out of mind, they are no longer the employer or travel mode of first choice and they are, for the most part, taken for granted.

Few topics in transport economics and policy are as controversial as the question of the extent of public subsidies to competing modes and whether these policies are fair and balanced. In addition to the obvious point that modal rivals have economic interests at stake in winning subsidies for themselves and denying them to competitors, the debate over favoritism in public subsidies comes partly from the fact that data on the subject are incomplete, nonstandard, and chronologically disconnected—giving partisans plenty of room to interpret the numbers to their own advantage. Also, there has been little incentive for any public agency or nonprofit think tank to settle the matter definitively. In the end, getting the numbers right wouldn't change much because minds are made up and modal advocates are entrenched.

The building of railroads in the 1800s (and before them, canals) was heavily subsidized by the public, while highways, airways, and airports were the object of analogous public financial support in the century just ended. Of all the modes, however, only railroads were obligated to repay the public assistance they received; in fact, railroads were required to give 50 percent discounts on government shipments or travel by rail, and these did not end until the 1940s.

When railroads became the first industry to be comprehensively regulated by the federal government in the Act to Regulate Commerce of 1887, it was primarily because they were the dominant form of land transport and under public charters had built a nationwide network of tracks and support facilities. In those days railroads could pretty much charge what they wanted and needed to collect for their services, upkeep, and expansion. A few hundred rail firms carried out all the transport functions now distributed among motor carriers on the interstate and defense highway system; the airlines, airports, and airways; privately owned pipelines for crude oil and refined petroleum products; publicly maintained inland waterways; and commuter transit operations overseen and funded by state, local, or regional authorities.

Of course, much had changed over the course of the twentieth century. Rival modes of transportation matured and today carry a major share of high-value, time-sensitive shipments (although railroads now use containerized intermodal trains to hold on to a significant market share of expedited truckload-size shipments). Bulk liquids and natural gas move unseen in long-distance pipelines. Barges move coal, export grain, and chemicals at bargain-basement rates on waterways improved at public expense—for which they pay less than fully compensatory user fees.

As a group, the alternative modes offered a formidable rivalry to railroads. This is why rail-rail competition is only part of the story, and why American public policy toward transportation (featuring both subsidy and economic regulation) relies heavily on the combination of intramodal competition and rivalry among alternative modes of transport to moderate carrier behavior. That is, US transport policy uses both internal industry competition and intermodal rivalry to make transportation workably competitive in the service of rate reasonableness.

Commentators often miss the point that transportation policy routinely favors new modes over older ones. Historically, the states and Congress authorized early toll roads, then built canals, then gave railroads land grants, then paved designated state roads and US highways, then set up civil aviation and subsidized it with air mail contracts, then created the interstate highways (paid for with fuel excise taxes), and then made jet aviation possible as a by-product of military spending. Each time, policy makers allowed the older mode to wither away, at least relatively.

Why was this? Because the new forms of transportation were bigger, faster, and, maybe, better. Politicians loved the idea that new transport modes and vehicles made life more pleasant. We could move faster, safer, cheaper, more comfortably—and the same for the material goods we gathered around ourselves. New modes and methods of travel or shipping represented—and they have from the dawn of civilization—new opportunities for wealth creation and what was almost as good, fame and fun. Only on

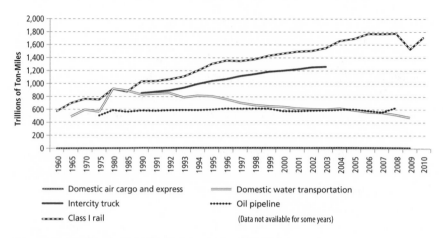

Figure 13.3   Railroads Hold Their Own in Ton-Mile Volume   Railroads have held their own over the last seventy-five years in the highly competitive freight market. Despite subsidies to inland waterways, barge ton-miles have fallen. Freight volumes for unsubsidized pipelines have held about even, while those of railroads have increased substantially. Excellent service and ubiquitous coverage notwithstanding, motor carriers have not displaced older modes for freight transport the way automobiles took over short- to medium-distance trips from rail passenger service.

reflection do we realize that some of the castaways might have been worth saving and recycling.

Amtrak may be an exception, but its popularity with politicians is at least equal parts vision and nostalgia because many in Congress and state departments of transportation want Amtrak to be a placeholder for high-speed passenger trains of the future. Indeed, most public officials pay more attention to future passenger rail service than how today's Amtrak service must coexist with the workhorse freight railroads that carry 41 percent of intercity cargo ton-miles. (See Figure 13.3.)

Box 13.2   A Level Playing Field

Back in 1944, Dr. Emory Johnson, longtime dean of the University of Pennsylvania's Wharton School of Business and a pillar of the transportation academic community, noted that the separate modes of transportation ". . . for the most part, developed independently of each other. Their relations have been mainly competitive and only secondarily co-operative. . . ."

Box 13.2

Then Professor Johnson switched his focus to say that if government ownership and operation of the railroads is to be avoided, ". . . conditions must be such
as to make possible successful private ownership and management." That in turn
depends on

> . . . a policy that requires the costs of non-railroad, as well as railroad
> transportation facilities and services, to be borne by those served; upon
> placing the rights and obligations of labor in all branches of transporta-
> tion upon a like basis; upon the levying, by the States and the Federal
> government, of taxes that are proportionate to the ability of the carriers to
> pay without being [thereby] forced into insolvency and being thus
> debarred from securing necessary capital from private sources.[1]

In short, Professor Johnson argued, government needs to guarantee a level
playing field for competition among the modes. That applies to all aspects of
the rivalry—regulation, subsidy, allocation of costs to users, taxation, labor, and
access to capital. As transportation economists, our sympathies are totally with
Emory Johnson. He wrote in a simpler time, but he understood as well as anyone
what it would take to secure American railroads in the private sector.

1. Emory R. Johnson, *The Railroads and Public Welfare: Their Problems and Policies* (New
York: Simmons-Boardman, 1944), p. 331.

6. Regulatory Reform

The nadir for railroad performance came almost precisely at the nation's
bicentennial. A plan had been made for reorganization of the Northeast
and Midwest railroads in receivership, but no one was sure it would work.
The infant Conrail was losing $1 million a day in cash it did not have. An
official government estimate of deferred maintenance for the industry (not
even including Conrail and the Long Island Railroad) was $13 to $16
billion—a sum so large that, like the national debt, politicians and railroad
managers would not even discuss how it could be met directly; as with a
promising but troubled teenager, the only answer was to outgrow the circumstance.

And then slowly a coalition came together to suggest another way—it was
time for national policy to throw off the yoke of regulation by the ICC.

Perhaps first among the emerging calls for significant regulatory reform was that of President John F. Kennedy in his Transportation Message of 1962, but the suggestion was lost in the tumult of the times. It did not emerge again with clarity until after Penn Central had gone bankrupt (1970) and stagflation occupied all things commercial in Wall Street and political in Washington. Charged with finding solutions for inflation and the feeble growth of the economy, the Council of Economic Advisers set up a productivity task force in 1973. Harvard's John R. Meyer was called to chair the task force's panel on railroads. Professor Meyer was a veteran of the team that advised President Kennedy on his Transportation Message; he assembled a bipartisan group of economists and industry experts. Their landmark report was a detailed analysis of the productivity gap and a blueprint for solutions—and its centerpiece was regulatory reform.

The railroad reform movement then matured along two paths: One was sponsored by the Ford administration, involved the US Railway Association and the relevant committee staffs in Congress, and led toward the Rail Revitalization and Regulatory Reform (4R) Act of 1976. The second was energized by the arrival in Washington of President Jimmy Carter and his institutional reform agenda. It was the Carter administration's young activists that assembled the logic and the language for what became the Staggers Rail Act of 1980. They put together a prospectus for change,[18] cleared their recommendations through Secretary Adams and the White House, and then merged efforts with the cognizant Senate and House committees that had been considering fixes and extensions of the 4R Act. The Staggers Rail Act was signed by President Jimmy Carter on October 14, 1980.

7. Mergers Post-Staggers

Between 1980 and 1995, a series of megamergers formed core portions of modern CSX, Norfolk Southern, BNSF, and Union Pacific. These followed closely on the heels of the USRA's FSP for Conrail, the Granger railroad crisis, and Staggers Rail Act deregulation. Conrail itself had effectively represented—at the time and for two generations afterward—the largest railroad merger in history.[19] By 1995, eight railroads in the lower forty-eight states and two in Canada dominated freight rail service, and both the United States and Canada had entrusted nearly all intercity rail passenger service to nationalized and heavily subsidized operators. Two railroads shared most traffic originations in the Southeast, and four major rail carriers together covered the West. In the Northeast quadrant of the United States, the Conrail "miracle" showed that a near-monopoly rail-road backed by federal investments and unshackled from most economic regulation could prosper even in the unfriendly commercial confines of that region, where congestion was greatest, hauls were shortest, labor orga-nizations were strongest, and passenger deficits were most crippling.[20]

Passage of the Staggers Rail Act in 1980 changed the rules for merger approvals and lifted most bureaucratic restrictions on rate making. Prolif-eration of these megamergers raised concerns that the small number of remaining railroads would attempt to merge with one another to create still larger networks and possibly even transcontinental lines. Shipper organizations and many economists feared that further consolidation of the industry would lead to a reduction in competition, adversely affecting shippers and the economy. Loss of adequate competitive alternatives might result in higher prices, diminished entrepreneurial initiative, slower deploy-ment of new technologies, and possibly reregulation of railroad rates and services.

THE REMARKABLE FIN-DE-SIÈCLE MERGERS

Four important restructuring transactions consummated in the last five years of the twentieth century further streamlined this already concen-trated railroad industry structure: two mergers of the traditional type for railroads (union of Burlington Northern and the Atchison, Topeka & Santa Fe into the BNSF Railway, and merger of the Southern Pacific into Union Pacific Railroad), plus an unprecedented division of one large, independent Class I railroad (Conrail) between two others (Norfolk Southern and CSX).

At the turn of the millennium, therefore, the North American railroad industry consisted of the "Final Four" US half-continental systems (BNSF, Union Pacific, CSX, and Norfolk Southern); two large Canadian trans-continental railroads with US operational units;[21] and the midsize Kansas City Southern, with its important operations in Mexico. While a move to a final twenty-first-century merger wave forming two or three truly trans-continental railroad systems cannot be ruled out, it seems more likely that the current status quo—one reached precisely at the turn of the millen-nium—will be the rail industry structure that continues to serve the nation. Figure 13.4 provides a family tree for the "Final Four" US half-continental systems, tracing their heritage through all the major rail mergers approved

Figure 13.4 "Final Four" Merger Family Trees   Mergers have characterized the railroad industry throughout its history, resulting in four major systems by the close of the twentieth century. (The two Canadian railroads and Kansas City Southern round out the list of Class I North American railroads.) Mergers were regulated by the Interstate Commerce Commission after 1920 and have been governed by the Surface Transportation Board since 1995. Rail consolidations were largely parallel in nature during the midcentury wave of mergers but began to reflect competitive considerations more directly after passage of the Staggers Rail Act of 1980. *Sources:* Based on widely reported public information, but we credit John F. Stover and the *Routledge Historical Atlas of the American Railroads* (1999) for the family tree depiction. See also the feature "Railroad Family Trees," in *TRAINS, Railroad Maps: The Best from the Pages of Trains Magazine, Extra* 2013 (Milwaukee, WI: Kalmbach Publishing Co., 2013.)

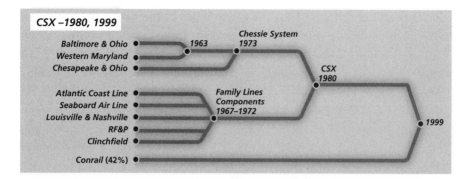

CSX –1980, 1999

Baltimore & Ohio	
Western Maryland	1963
Chesapeake & Ohio	Chessie System 1973

Atlantic Coast Line
Seaboard Air Line
Louisville & Nashville — Family Lines Components 1967–1972
RF&P
Clinchfield

Conrail (42%)

CSX 1980

1999

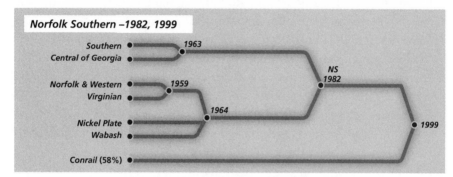

Norfolk Southern –1982, 1999

Southern — 1963
Central of Georgia

Norfolk & Western — 1959
Virginian

1964

Nickel Plate
Wabash

Conrail (58%)

NS 1982

1999

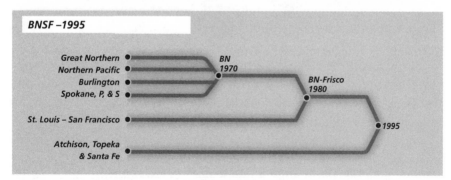

BNSF –1995

Great Northern
Northern Pacific — BN 1970
Burlington
Spokane, P, & S

St. Louis – San Francisco

BN-Frisco 1980

Atchison, Topeka & Santa Fe

1995

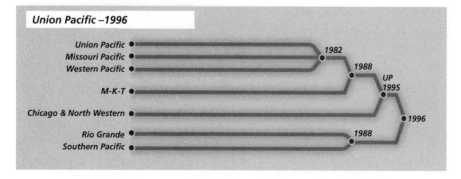

Union Pacific –1996

Union Pacific
Missouri Pacific — 1982
Western Pacific

M-K-T — 1988

Chicago & North Western

Rio Grande — 1988
Southern Pacific

UP 1995

1996

by the ICC and the STB in the second half of the twentieth century. A major conclusion is that the extraordinary efforts to find new cooperative arrangements for balanced competition—agreements that could only come with enlightened managers and a patient STB—are what brought the American railroads to their successful industry structure at the end of the twentieth century.

What could not have been imagined a half-century or even thirty years ago, is that this industry structure is not what economists malign as a second-best outcome; amazingly, it is very nearly what the best and brightest might have designed. After all the merger missteps of midcentury (and one, the Santa Fe–Southern Pacific proposed merger near the century's end), the final pattern has proven worthy of perpetuation. Despite the bankruptcies and declining share of transport markets, constant calls for reregulation, by consensus we have a railroad industry that is efficient and self-sustaining, in truth a great engine for progress of the North American industrial economies. After surviving some very close calls at several points, these railroads have become and will remain, we strongly believe, enduring enterprises for the twenty-first century.

8. Advancing Technology

Paralleling the rise (and eventual fall) of regulation in the history of railroads after 1887 was a remarkable story of developing technology; indeed, railroad technology progress characterized most of the twentieth century as it had the 1800s. Specialized railroad technologies were instrumental in making railroads into America's largest and most important industry in the nineteenth century.

In addition to those innovations designed specifically for the industry, railroads had an almost uncanny ability to adapt and incorporate new technologies arising in other sectors of the economy into their businesses— telegraphy and telephony, low cost steelmaking, electricity wired into motors and lighting, and the internal combustion engine—to name a few of the most important. Those more generic technologies could then become sources of even greater productivity when made part of the evolving integrated engineering system—which now we can fairly call modern railroads.

Railroads had moved to their dominant position at the end of the nineteenth century under the combined forces of technological superiority in the age of steel and steam, plus the new ability of railroad entrepreneurs to tap huge capital investment resources from private stockholders, bank loans, federal land grants, and community construction subsidies. The tie between advancing rail technologies of all kinds (locomotives, track, bridges, air brakes, knuckle couplers, telegraph, signaling, and more) and development of modern corporate organizations capable of financing huge investments in railroads is central to both stories.

With technology deployment and railroad reinvestment thus bound, and federal regulation of railroads substantially lessened in the last quarter of the twentieth century, the key ingredients for a railroad renaissance were finally in place. A big part of our story has been that railroads are an enduring enterprise because the industry has reinvented itself time and again—with regard to the mix of services it provides and the kinds of traffic it carries.

To keep all this in perspective, *American Railroads* offered a summary list of the most important railroad technological and operational advances of the twentieth century (see Box 12.4 in Chapter 12). The technology list facilitates a concluding observation for the book as a whole, namely, that railroads' endurance for two centuries is a function not just of the good fortune of low friction from steel wheels on steel rail, but a whole panoply of ingenious improvements to the basic nineteenth-century steam and steel railroad technologies. Technology advances have given railroads enormous competitive, safety, and productivity advantages. Their future success depends on increased funding of new investments in facilities and equipment, and the ability to continue to draw on technology improvements as they add and renew capacity.

9. Amtrak—Success or Failure?

Amtrak's passenger-miles of service in the last decade of the twentieth century ran between 5 and 6 billion per year; by contrast, Amtrak's private rail predecessors had averaged about 10 billion intercity passenger-miles per year in their last decade of full operation, the 1960s. Amtrak's share of intercity travel by all modes in 2000 was   of 1 percent; the private sector predecessors had about a 1 percent market share in their last year, 1970. Amtrak's share of common carrier passenger-miles in 2000 was 0.76 of 1 percent, while its private predecessors had 6.9 percent of that market in 1970.

Amtrak could not and did not reverse the fundamental circumstances governing passenger train economics—those attributable to its traditional technology and the sparse population of American settlement outside the Northeast, the metropolitan Chicago region, and California south of Sacramento).[22] While costly to US taxpayers, however, Amtrak was not a failure of government intervention. On the contrary, we believe government intervention in this case was surprisingly successful in achieving its initial objectives.

The private freight railroads were relieved of an immediate and costly obligation to operate deficit-producing passenger trains. Amtrak not only placed responsibility for passenger deficits where these more properly belonged (with the public sector), but the law establishing Amtrak as a separate, independent operating entity made it much easier to demarcate the scope and scale of the passenger deficit. Under the law, Amtrak was authorized to compensate the freight railroads for the incremental costs of any passenger services they continued to perform under contract. These contracts probably enabled a better estimate of elusive "indirectly related passenger costs" than any previous method.

Such a valuation would still be flawed, however, by the fact that the private freight railroads were, in effect, compelled to participate in Amtrak service operations. It was not—as normally stipulated in property value assessment cases—an arm's length bargain.[23]

Less tangibly, Amtrak may have helped realize other public policy goals that would possibly have been both more difficult and expensive if Amtrak had not existed. Heading off congressionally ordered (and labor union-sponsored) direct passenger subsidies to the private-sector railroads was, at Amtrak startup, considered to be one of the legislation's benefits. The conventional wisdom at the time was that direct public subsidies to the Class I railroads for continuation of their historic passenger trains would be more costly to taxpayers than providing general funding for Amtrak's annual operations.

Lurking in the background is the possibility that Amtrak, as a quasi-business public agency, might be less efficient in delivering passenger services than the private railroads it supplanted, but we do not believe that view to be correct. Amtrak's operation of its designated network appears to have been about as efficient as one a private firm would have managed within the same constraints.

In a larger sense, the United States likely does not underinvest in passenger rail, as is so often lamented. The trouble is that, because we do not allow the market to make unfettered decisions about what services should be operated on what routes, the substantial public resources provided annually to Amtrak almost certainly are not spent as wisely as they could be. Passenger rail supporters can force the system to be too large, and budget hawks can keep it inadequately funded. Year after year, Amtrak is caught in that same dilemma—a squeeze between unaffordable service expansion and a starvation diet. And so we are left with well-intentioned proposals for higher-speed services the nation wants but cannot afford to subsidize. We see little likelihood of these dynamics changing substantially within the lifetimes of our children and grandchildren.

10. Deregulation and Renaissance

The final part of the story of dominance, decline, and rebirth of US railroads in the twentieth century is the rail renaissance. The roots of the renaissance, we argue, are in the Staggers Rail Act of 1980, which largely deregulated railroads—most importantly by permitting rate, volume, and service commitment contracts between carriers and shippers. Deregulation overcame 100 years of enforced inefficiency built into ICC control of nearly all aspects of railroad rates, services, and financial instruments. The single notable exception to otherwise rave reviews for Staggers Rail Act regulatory reform came from so-called captive shippers, who claim that recent financial successes railroads have achieved were the result of their exploitation of monopoly power; this the organized shipper groups believe should have been checked by regulatory authorities but was not because of what they say was overzealous implementation of the 1980 act.

After 1980, railroads by and large were free to act like other responsible businesses in the American free-enterprise system. It took a few years for both railroads and their customers to learn how to accommodate each other in the new circumstances. How would long-term contracts work? Would the vestigial ICC allow railroads to adapt to the new economic circumstances on their own initiative or would managements have to continue to get ICC permission every step of the way? Could railroads downsize obsolete facilities and expand capacity where warranted? Could railroads adjust labor input requirements to match new realities? The outcome was by no means certain because so much change was needed and there was no meaningful blueprint for how to accomplish it.

But it worked. As shown in Figure 13.5, under the Staggers Rail Act of 1980, rail industry traffic volumes increased substantially and productivity soared. Shippers benefitted handsomely because railroads cut average

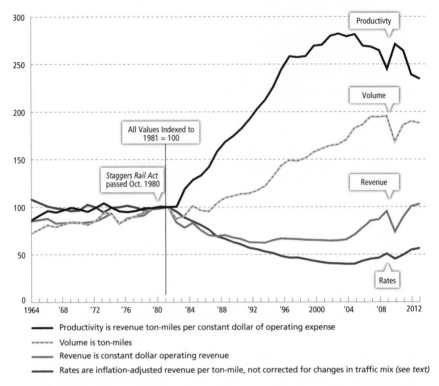

Productivity is revenue ton-miles per constant dollar of operating expense
Volume is ton-miles
Revenue is constant dollar operating revenue
Rates are inflation-adjusted revenue per ton-mile, not corrected for changes in traffic mix *(see text)*

Figure 13.5   The Miracle of Deregulation   This depiction of the impact of deregulation, first published by the authors in the late 1990s, has become the standard proof of the effectiveness of the Staggers Rail Act's regulatory reforms. Allowing railroads to respond to supply and demand increased productivity and stimulated volume and density while lowering average rates by some 50 percent. Industry revenue in constant dollars fell, then returned to 1980 levels as rates began to increase after 2000.

Inflation-adjusted revenue per ton-mile—a proxy for rates—is not corrected for changes in traffic mix, such as rising shares of coal and intermodal container traffic and declining boxcar shipments. Nor does it reflect the substantial rate discounts given shippers because they use privately owned freight cars in place of carrier equipment—an increasing trend after the Staggers Rail Act. *Source:* Data and calculations courtesy of the AAR, which frequently updates and reports current versions of the chart at www.aar.org.

revenue per ton-mile (a proxy for rate levels) in half. Lower rates had the effect of flattening revenue streams, but they helped railroads increase their share of total ton-miles, whether by winning traffic back from alternative modes or by expanding the size of the total transport market. Notable examples were expansion into and longer hauls of coal from the Powder River Basin to far-flung utility plants, and the surge of international import/export container movements in double-stack trains.

For most of the twentieth century, American railroads were in decline. They had fallen victim to a downward spiral of declining traffic, leading to loss of profit, deferred maintenance, lower service quality, more traffic erosion, discounted pricing, more losses of earnings, and disinvestment.

Now the survivors could imagine the reverse—a virtuous upward spiral of traffic growth, leading to improved pricing and profitability, reinvestment, expansion of capacity, improved service quality—all leading to expansion of markets, recapture of lost traffic, and revenue gains. This is the description of a genuine rail renaissance—the ability of railroads to earn sufficient profits to reinvest in their physical facilities and rolling stock, new technologies, and human resources. What is truly remarkable about the rail renaissance is that (unless derailed by reregulation) it shows every sign of enduring to serve its customers' requirements with improved service reliability, remarkable safety, and a shrinking environmental footprint.

Perhaps this accords with what the transcendentalist Henry David Thoreau had in mind when he wrote his mystical metaphor of railroads being needed to get us "to heaven in season. . . . We do not ride on the railroad; it rides upon us."[24]

AFTERWORD:
FUTURE POLICIES FOR US RAILROADS

> Such a public servant as the railway needs encouragement and
> sound guidance, under which it can and will work out its own
> salvation, in future as in past, and in both fair and foul eco-
> nomic weather.
>
> —JULIUS H. PARMELEE (1940)

This book has been an economic and policy history of a key American industry experienced over an entire century. We have shared policy perspectives rooted in economic theory, our reading of the events of the period, and sometimes our personal experiences from participation in these events. Until now we have, for the most part, shied away from making bold prognostications or policy prescriptions requiring congressional action.

As fun as it is to speculate about the future, it is inherently risky. The trouble with nostalgia, someone said, is that "it ain't what it used to be." In the same vein, the trouble with forecasts is that they are about the future. Still, what we have learned and told in this book about the last century of railroads has powerful implications for how railroads should be treated and what they will be able to accomplish in the future. What trends will influence the success of railroads over the next few decades? Will the rail renaissance continue? What are the main challenges that railroads will face? What will be the course of public policy? Will railroad services look the same to our great-grandchildren as they do to us?

Thirty years ago, John Naisbitt published a best-selling business book called *Megatrends*. He described ten key economic and social forces that he anticipated would have great importance for the economy and the success of various businesses—things like the emergence of a global economy, and informal networks replacing hierarchical organizations. Naisbitt's ten trends were prescient, and the idea of the book itself was powerful and memorable.

Similarly, a short list of key economic trends and public policy choices will confront railroads in the twenty-first century, greatly affecting their power to endure. And, of course, we cannot discount the impact of unexpected external events, so much a factor in the life of our times. The remainder of this afterword shares a peek into our crystal ball.

Reregulation and Reinvestment

Generally speaking, railroads prefer anonymity to notoriety. The "bad boys" of the nineteenth century were sent to regulatory jail with passage of the Act to Regulate Commerce in 1887 and increasingly tighter statutory and Interstate Commerce Commission (ICC) restrictions up through at least the Transportation Act of 1958. The regulatory burden, along with post–World War II changes in patterns of industrial and agricultural production, the rise of competing modes, and an insufficiently responsive institutional setting caused a rapid and widespread decline in railroad fortunes. Future policy toward railroads should turn from these negatives and instead be governed by five principles:

- Let markets and efficiency principles guide basic rules for rate making, congestion pricing, and intermodal rivalry.
- Allow railroads to earn sufficient returns to warrant reinvestment.
- Respect railroad private property ownership and franchise values.
- Take advantage of railroads' inherent fuel efficiency and relatively benign environmental impact.
- Encourage migration of transportation commodity and passenger flows to the safest and most efficient modes.

In view of the increasing evidence that human activities, transportation notably among them, have contributed to greenhouse gas emissions and through them, a projected rise in ocean levels, perhaps we should add a sixth fundamental policy prescription:

- Encourage migration of energy development and uses to cost-effective and environmentally sustainable alternatives that will reduce the future need for more expensive adaptations to the challenge of global climate change.

Reinvestment for the Future of Railroads

One of the unsung benefits of America's free-enterprise freight railroads is that private investors make possible the huge freight-carrying capacity of the industry, and even pay income taxes, while doing what taxpayers of most other countries have to subsidize. Railroads have invested about $500 billion in capital and maintenance expenditures over the past decade, and they are poised to invest tens of billions annually as long as demand for service warrants.[1]

Capital spending does several things. It allows the railroads to expand capacity to meet customer demands. It accelerates deployment of technological advances through their incorporation in new production equipment or facilities. It permits more reliable, safer, and environmentally friendly methods and equipment to substitute for obsolete practices and worn-out infrastructure or rolling stock. In the long run, these investments will lower operating costs and open new opportunities for railroad employees.

With the industry's new pricing power after passage of the Staggers Rail Act, and mindful of the long years wandering in a regulatory wilderness, it would be understandable if railroads simply declared victory and went on their way. Or they might have been even more aggressive in pressing their new regulatory and economic advantages—such as those falling their way with unprecedented increases in world oil prices and rising wages for truck drivers. Why should railroads compromise on principles like revenue adequacy? The so-called captive shippers are not really captive, railroads could say; under a regulatory ruling that set aside product and geographic competition as considerations in the determination of market dominance, utilities had at least as much monopoly pricing power in their customer-facing markets as railroads had in their coal supply contracts with power plants. Bilateral oligopoly characterized both markets, and modern game theory said unfettered negotiation would yield the best solution for the public at large.

Given the twin cultural and economic attitudes toward the railroads—the myth of their omnipotence, plus nearly all claimants' insatiable hunger for a larger share of their yield, it is virtually inevitable that interest groups will continue to press for public regulation of railroads. But this is a fool's errand. Because public ownership and management (as in publicly owned utilities or government services) is both unnecessary and unlikely, and because tight regulation by government authority has often been shown to be unwarranted if not unworkable, the best outcome continues to be *laissez faire*: private enterprise with antitrust and fair-trade rules, and enforcement through the courts.

Economic fundamentals will, in the end, trump nearly all artificial regulatory restrictions on business enterprise. The reason is that free enterprise unencumbered by extraordinary government interference ultimately serves the largest number of participants in society and achieves the most efficient use of resources. Regulations forcing companies to make choices a certain way, legislated subsidies favoring certain modes or regions, union contracts restricting technological deployment—these cannot comprehend the totality of markets nor make the rapid adjustments necessary to balance supply and demand. The commercial actions of individual human beings simply cannot be planned and executed as quickly, as thoroughly, nor as dispassionately as markets routinely do in a free-enterprise system. It takes a bit of faith, perhaps, to trust *laissez faire* when regulation is so popular, its premises seemingly so reasonable, and the offenders it targets apparently so unwarrantedly privileged. Yet time and again history makes the case for *laissez faire*, and no testimony in its favor is more powerful than the story of railroads in the twentieth century.

Government Funding for Selected Public-Benefit Rail Services

While private enterprise carries the base load of investment in railroad capacity, there are a few areas where public funding could leverage greater benefits from the existing rail network. The large private railroads are not begging for public funds—indeed they might need to be prodded to take them; it is the public sector that stands to gain the most from targeted investment of the following kinds:

- Continue and expand Section 130 funding for grade-crossing warning systems, which have been shown to have been highly successful in reducing casualties at highway–rail intersections.
- Support research and development (R&D) of new rail technologies, which yields high social returns on investment.
- Provide special tax credits for rail participation in public–private projects, such as a major bridge jointly used for passenger and freight service.
- Expand funding for intermodal connectors of national significance. Examples of recent high-visibility (and presumably high-return) projects

are the Alameda Corridor in greater Los Angeles and the Chicago Region Environmental and Transportation Efficiency Program (CREATE) in the Chicago area.

- Facilitate loans for upgrading necessary short lines to national axle-load and safety standards so they can become more cost-effective as part of the total rail network. Such funds help short line railroads compete against highway projects costly to local governments.
- Restructure Amtrak to improve services and make its network more robust and affordable, and provide limited funding to match or incentivize state-supported rail passenger development in selected high-use and environmentally sensitive corridors.

Sometimes, calls for more balanced transportation policy feature proposals for a railroad or transportation trust fund. These proposals typically include collection of taxes on railroad fuel, income, or property, with disbursement from the trust fund to projects benefiting both private- and public-sector interests. Because railroads own and maintain their own fixed infrastructure, however, while motor vehicles pay fuel excise taxes but operate over public roads and highways, it is obvious that the idea of a transportation trust fund of this description is logically flawed.

The only fair way to level the modal playing field in cases where public agencies provide transport infrastructure is to establish systems for automatically collecting cost-recovery tolls or user fees based on demand-management principles. Thus, barges would pay efficient waterway segment fees, and automobiles and trucks would be subject to congestion mitigation fees, with fee surpluses redirected to infrastructure capacity expansion, facility maintenance, and provision of efficient alternatives. Environmental fees such as effluent charges and cap-and-trade emissions fees are similar in structure and purpose. Efficient tolls have the great virtues of both discouraging consumption of goods that have negative social spillovers and providing a source of funding for highly beneficial public–private partnership investments in needed capacity.

Alternatively, in the near to intermediate term, if politicians cannot be persuaded to accept the logic and discipline of full cost-recovery tolls and fees designed for optimal management of public infrastructure, the fair alternative is to enact a parallel program of tax credits or deductions for qualified railroad investments in infrastructure. Ordinarily, tax expenditures are a second-best type of policy—not fundamentally efficient or optimal in themselves, but useful to redress inequities or misallocation of resources caused by other public policies. Still, compared with trust-fund spending, which inevitably is biased by the authorizing legislation (such as with site-specific preferences and restrictions), tax expenditures are relatively neutral with respect to project selection because the tax-paying entity (as opposed to a legislature or governmental agency) makes the choice of which projects will be written off against its tax liability. In contrast to public appropriations and grants, there are no "earmarks" in a well-structured tax-incentive program.

Political realities may well require that authorization of tax expenditures be limited to certain generic kinds of private investments, such as capacity expansion, research and development, environmental cleanup, and safety appurtenances. Legislators are unlikely to go along with tax credits or special deductions if they believe related cash flows will be diverted into executive salaries, wage increases, lobbying expenses, and the like.

Managing Risk and Improving Safety and Security

Trains develop great momentum and can neither stop quickly nor dodge obstacles in their path. Railroads have developed an enviable safety record, however, one that has shown continuous improvement in incidents, worker casualties, and injuries per 200,000 hours worked.

Railroad safety is regulated by the Federal Railroad Administration (FRA) under laws that have been on the books, in some cases, for over 100 years. The most important authority is the Railroad Safety Act of 1970, consolidating standards and requirements contained in dozens of enactments throughout the twentieth century. Recent safety amendments were adopted in the Rail Safety Improvement Act of 2008, which, among other things, contains the mandate for installation (in current law, by the end of 2015) of positive train control systems on rail lines carrying passengers or hazardous chemicals that are toxic by inhalation.

Most FRA safety regulations are prescriptive rules, establishing specific requirements—sometimes called command and control regulations, which railroads must follow. Thus, railroads are required to inspect major locomotive components every 92 days, brakes every 1,000 miles, and track on a "regular and routine" basis, depending on track class and train speeds.[2] An alternative regulatory paradigm would create performance standards that railroads would have to meet to avoid fines and keep operating. For example, railroads might be required to operate locomotives in a manner that results in some very low but specified level of failures interrupting service or endangering employees or bystanders for a period of, say, three months. Performance standards would permit railroads to plan optimal maintenance and inspection programs in a way that fits operating strategies, best location of facilities, and availability of inspection crews. Optimization strategies, for example, would enable railroads to make investments in preventive measures well exceeding traditional standards for an extended time period, without running afoul of FRA's time-based rules.

Federal Employee's Liability Act Reform

Railroad accidents that result in personal injuries are subject to redress under the Federal Employer's Liability Act (FELA) of 1908—a fault-based tort system dependent on court judgments to set compensation levels— typically percentages of standard payouts for loss of an arm or leg, etc., supplemented by payments for "pain and suffering." These judgments are often much larger than what an employee might have received under state-administered workers' compensation. Plaintiffs normally choose representation by an attorney specializing in FELA cases; historically these were recommended by railroad unions, a practice now frowned upon because of the appearance of conflict of interest. Overall, subjecting railroad employee injuries to FELA rules is generally thought to increase accident costs to railroads substantially, but the devil is in the details.[3]

Dealing with the Decline of Coal, the Emergence of Alternative Fuels, and Regulation of Greenhouse Gas Emissions

Virtually all the energy sources that the United States use daily are transported from somewhere else: imported petroleum by ocean tanker, natural gas by pipeline, electricity by high-tension power lines, coal by unit trains and inland waterway barges, and gasoline in product pipelines with delivery by liquid/bulk motor carriers. To this list railroads and their shippers have recently added large unit train movements of flammable ethanol and crude oil in tank cars. Transportation both moves and consumes energy prodigiously. There is no avoiding the fact that the price of fuel is a key factor in election politics in the short run and transportation policy over time.

It is a blessing for the US economy that new discoveries and drilling and field development techniques for oil and natural gas have come about in the first decade of the new millennium. The United States is still a huge net importer of oil, but suddenly we do not feel quite so dependent on sometimes-hostile foreign suppliers. For the railroads, nervous over the threatened loss of coal business, the oil and gas boom has meant at least two major new sources of traffic: (1) "frac" sand used in liberating crude oil and natural gas from tight seams or fissures in underlying geological formations, and (2) crude oil produced in locations that are not laced with gathering pipelines or well-supplied with long distance transmission capacity, and therefore must be moved to refineries by unit trains of railroad tank cars.

Railroads haul coal; for many rail companies it is their major source of traffic and the underpinning of their economic health. At the same time, coal is a major offender in greenhouse gas (GHG) emissions overall, and from electric power generation in particular. Louis Thompson gives the issue an international perspective in his paper "A Vision for the Railways in 2050:"

> Many countries have relatively weak or uncoordinated transport policies, and a few large countries have yet to establish a single focus for transport within the government. It is thus somewhat difficult to assess whether the projections [in Thompson's 2010 paper] support or contradict a clear transport policy. Even so, the freight and passenger traffic levels foreseen pose no major conflicts beyond that of capacity expansion, with one significant exception—the role of freight railways in the transport of carbon-based fuels. More than one-third of all the world's CO_2 emissions from energy production and consumption come from carbon-based fuels (principally coal) hauled by railways. By comparison, if all of the world's railway freight traffic were shifted to trucks, the world emission of CO_2 would increase by slightly more than two percent. There is thus a dilemma posed by the fact that railways' energy efficiency facilitates the transport of fuels that add to the GHG challenge.[4]

Thompson continues:

> With this in mind, if there are controls on GHG emissions in [the] future, the primary "game changer" in innovation for railways appears to be carbon capture and sequestration: without

sequestration, a major rail freight market will be threatened; with effective sequestration, rail efficiency in hauling fuels will be a continuing strength.[5]

The only real alternative to a breakthrough in carbon sequestration (saving for coal a key role in electricity generation long term) is for the economy to switch from coal to natural gas, wind, geothermal, and nuclear power—perhaps together with breakthroughs in fuel cell and battery technology to support greater use of electricity as a motor vehicle fuel.

All these alternative and unconventional fuel sources and conversion strategies may have increasing roles, but none of them is a panacea; and they bring with them other complications. (For example, a real challenge to nuclear power generation in addition to its formidable up-front capital construction costs is the problem of long term secure disposal of spent fuel rods.) There needs to be both research and development and a national consensus on energy policy vis-à-vis power plant emissions and global climate change issues, petroleum supply security (including the safety of long distance rail movement of flammable ethanol and crude oil in tank cars), fuel cell technology development, and assessment of the expected costs of distribution or mobile generation of hydrogen fuels. Could there possibly develop a national consensus on such sweeping aspects of public policy? It seems too much to hope for.

Unfortunately, while investing in the development and deployment of alternatives, the United States and the world have little choice but to continue to use coal, endanger the environment with global GHG emissions, suffer melting ice caps and sea-level rise, and wonder if these changes are affecting the frequency and severity of devastating climate and weather events—all for some time to come.

Overall, the authors of *American Railroads* hold the view that governmental intervention in the workings of the economy is not per se good or evil, but that circumstances must condition activist impulses, moderating government responses to perceived market failures or public underinvestment. Both the design and the reach of policy solutions must meet tests of comparative efficiency, cost-effectiveness, and constitutionality. The economic principles of opportunity costs (including the downside risks of doing nothing), inclusion of externalities along with direct costs and benefits, market-based allocation of resources, unbiased assessments of safety and risk, and fairness among all sectors and groups in society are the foundations of good transportation public policy.

American Railroads confronts the fundamental policy question: What is it, after all, that American society should want from its railroads? It is not an easy question. As economists we can declare the usual goals of greater efficiency, optimal pricing, and maximizing social welfare. We respect the collateral objectives of workable competition, nondiscrimination, and fairness.

Pragmatically and politically we urge the policy of keeping railroads deregulated and self-sustaining in the private sector because we think it works better than the alternatives—nationalization, subsidy, and comprehensive regulation. We recognize that, in the hardest cases, some governmental agency may need to referee boundary conditions on firm size and business behavior, but where countervailing economic power exists to help protect the public interest, policy should allow railroads to act like other businesses do in the US free-enterprise system. Laissez-faire is good policy, except in rare circumstances.

The public benefits of keeping the American railroad network safely in the private sector seem manifest but perhaps should be made explicit. Private-sector railroads have the incentives to optimize the trade-off of capital investments with operating expenses. Private firms can efficiently match their capacity to shipper demand. Sustainable private firms pay corporate income taxes rather than requiring public subsidy. Private firms employ and train workers as the economic need for labor dictates, paying wages and benefits as negotiated under public laws and collective bargaining procedures. Private railroads have a remarkably good safety record and have learned that good safety is good business. Private-sector freight railroading in the United States works and works well.

This book's authors love railroads because they have a great history, fascinating operations, intriguing technology, and untold opportunity for the future, but we also love them because no other enterprises illustrate elegant economic principles quite so well. Beyond these widely understood qualities, there is something immeasurable but noble and spirit-lifting about admirably run railroad companies, operating with well-maintained facilities and equipment, and, as Julius Parmelee wrote three-quarters of a century ago, reliably and productively contributing to public service. These are attributes we earnestly hope endure long into the future; the world and our society are far better because of them.

NOTES

1. The Enduring American Railroads

Epigraphs: Robert Selph Henry, *This Fascinating Railroad Business* (New York: Bobbs-Merrill, 1942–1943), p. 19. Henry Kirke White, *History of the Union Pacific Railway* (Chicago: University of Chicago Press, 1895), p. 2. DOT /FRA, *A Prospectus for Change in the Freight Railroad Industry*, October, 1978, p. 1.

1. The *Nation's First Big Business* was the subtitle of Alfred Chandler's popular book of business readings on railroads, which was published in 1965, but the phrase was used earlier, by (perhaps among others) John R. Meyer, Merton J. Peck, John Stenason, and Charles Zwick (Cited below as MPS&Z), *The Economics of Competition in the Transportation Industries* (Cambridge: Harvard University Press, 1959), p. 9. "The original passage of the [1887 ICC Act] represented the first attempt of the American people to deal with the problem of business bigness, that is, monopoly combined at times with destructive competition. Railroads were, simply, America's first big business." Note MPS&Z's drawing on the *Schumpeterian dialectic*, creative destruction.

2. www.brainyquote.com/quotes/quotes/y/yogiberra141506.html accessed 2/22/2012. Did he really say it? If not, it is at least characteristic of things he did say, and no one has put the familiar contrast of theory and practice more crisply. But Yogi also said, "I never said most of the things I said." (Ibid.) A good collection of Yogi quotes, which unfortunately does not include this one, is found in Appendix B of Allan Berra, *Yogi Berra, Eternal Yankee* (New York: W.W. Norton, 2009), pp. 396–399.

3. MPS&Z, *The Economics of Competition*, 1959.

4. Rates are the provider's charges for transport services—the object of regulatory zeal—often called tariffs. Rates typically cover the physical movement (but not loading and unloading) of the freight and the use of a railroad's freight car equipment for a specified period (after that period, additional storage or demurrage charges might apply). For passenger services, transport charges are usually called fares.

5. Charles V. Stern, *Inland Waterways: Recent Proposals and Issues for Congress* (Washington, DC: Congressional Research Service, May 3, Report 20137-5700 at www.crs.gov—accessed December 17, 2013), p. 4.

6. Variable costs are expense increments related to levels of output, as opposed to initial fixed (or threshold) costs incurred at startup of the firm or line of business, or overhead expenses unrelated to variation in volume of sales.

7. Coauthor Gallamore remembers a key meeting with Secretary of Transportation Brock Adams in about 1979 to obtain his approval of a staff draft of proposed Carter administration rail deregulation legislation. "What happens to the common carrier obligation?" asked the secretary, a long-time supporter of traditional ICC regulation. "It goes away," Gallamore responded, oversimplifying. Secretary Adams was not pleased and, of course the common carrier obligation was not fully lifted, only modified by contracts and new rules governing maximum and minimum rates.

8. "Disappearin' Railroad Blues" is a fragment from the lyrics to "City of New Orleans" by Steve Goodman.

9. James J. Hill and Edward H. Harriman (along with other larger-than-life characters appearing episodically in the text) represent a different cast. While some might say that their role was infamous, it really was far more constructive than that of the nineteenth-century robber barons, as *American Railroads* makes clear in Chapter 3.

10. There is little literature on the important topic of service reliability, and most of the authors' knowledge came from direct work experience in the industry. An exception is Carl D. Martland, Patrick Little, Oh Kyoung Kwon, and Rajesh Dontula, *Background on Railroad Reliability Report NO. R-803*, (Washington, DC, Association of American Railroads, March 1992), mimeo, 73 pages. See also other reports in the Massachusetts Institute of Technology sponsored series, *Studies in Railroad Operations and Economics* (Cambridge, MA: MIT Press.)

11. The Chicago Region Environmental and Transportation Efficiency (CREATE) Program is perhaps the best-known example of a contemporary rail public–private partnership; its purpose is to ease chronic delays in moving freight cars through the labyrinthine rail yards of the Chicago Hub. "Shippers complain that a load of freight can make its way from Los Angeles to Chicago in 48 hours, then take 30 hours to travel across the city. A recent trainload of sulfur took some 27 hours to pass through Chicago—an average speed of 1.13 miles per hour . . ." CREATE will replace twenty-five rail intersections with overpasses or underpasses, and "separate tracks now shared by freight and passenger trains at critical spots." John Schwartz, "Freight Train Late? Blame Chicago," *New York Times*, May 7, 2012, republished May 8, 2012, p. A15.

2. The Ills of Government Regulation of Rail Rates and Services

Epigraphs: Charles Francis Adams, *The Railroads—Their Origins and Problems* (New York: G.P. Putnam's and Son's, 1878), p. 81. Emory R. Johnson, *American Railway Transportation*, Revised Edition (New York: D. Appleton and Co. 1908), p. 270.

1. A key example of this last is pure public goods as defined in Paul A. Samuelson's "Pure Theory of Public Expenditure," namely, cases where all citizens consume the good equally and no one can diminish its availability to others—as in national defense or development of new knowledge. *The Review of Economics and Statistics*, Vol. 36, No. 4. (Nov., 1954), pp. 387–389.

2. In most market transactions, a buyer actually pays less for a product or service than she or he would be willing to pay rather than do without. This difference—the area under the demand curve and above the competitive market price—is known to economists as consumers' surplus—a sort of windfall. Because a monopolist has control over prices, he or she is able to convert some of what normally would be consumers' surplus into producers' surplus—monopoly profits.

3. http://en.wikipedia.org/wiki/Engrossing_(law), accessed July 5, 2012.

4. David Besanko and Ronald R. Braeutigam, *Microeconomics: An Integrated Approach* (New York: John Wiley & Sons, Inc., 2002), p. G-5. (Cited below as Besanko and Braeutigam, *Microeconomics.*)

5. Specifically, the Interstate Commerce Act in Section 2 declared it unlawful for a railroad to charge one person more than another for a like and contemporaneous service under substantially similar circumstances and conditions. Also, the IC Act in Section 4's *long-haul, short-haul clause* prohibited a railroad from charging more for a short haul over a given line than a long haul over the same line and in the same direction.

6. *Wabash, St. Louis and Pacific Railway Company v. Illinois.* The Supreme Court decided that state legislatures did not have the power to regulate charges for railroad transportation of freight within a state if the goods had been brought there from, or were being carried to, places outside the state (i.e. if the freight were deemed to be in interstate transportation). In the words of a classic text, the Wabash case "made necessary the enactment of federal legislation; for otherwise the railways would go uncontrolled as to their interstate commerce," which amounted to about three-fourths of their total traffic. Eliot Jones, *Principles of Railway Transportation* (New York: The MacMillan Co., 1924), p. 202.

7. Gabriel Kolko, *Railroads and Regulation 1877–1916* (New York: W. W. Norton, 1965). This is Kolko's well-known thesis that railroads were complicit in their own regulation, as though (if true) that would justify it. Kolko seems to believe that because some aspects of the regulatory regime were beneficial to railroads,

and because in later years the ICC became more solicitous of their requirements, railroads liked their situation. This was a fallacy of the undistributed
middle, and it was not true. [Regulatory clients liked a solicitous regulator; the
ICC was solicitous of client railroads; Therefore railroads liked regulation.]

8. The doctrine of rate publication was intended to facilitate nondiscrimination
among "persons, places, and things (commodities)," unless, of course, these
were inherent in the ICC-approved tariffs. But there was considerable cheating,
such as when railroads gave secret rebates on the published rates. In all likelihood, these were more often demanded by shippers seeking an advantage in
their markets than by railroads currying favor. Indeed, railroads supported the
anti-rebating legislation of 1903 because widespread rebates were hurting net
revenues.

9. Jones, *Principles* (1908), especially Part II "Rates and Rate Making," pp. 71–182.

10. http://en.wikipedia.org/wiki/Frank_William_Taussig, accessed July 7, 2012. Taussig
preceded Joseph Schumpeter (who held the same chair) and John R. Meyer at
Harvard; Taussig and Meyer are buried in Mount Auburn Cemetery, Cambridge,
Massachusetts.

11. Jones, *Principles* (1908), pp. 71, 82. See more on demand elasticities later in this
chapter. For railroads, freight and passenger service have some aspects of joint
costs, but they are not so tightly linked as in Jones' cotton example. If passenger
service is produced relatively more cheaply because of joint service using freight
facilities, there are said to be economies of scope; if freight and passenger operations get in each other's way, there are diseconomies of scope.

12. Ibid., p. 85.

13. Ibid., pp. 86–87. While brilliant and prescient, the policy prescription did not
originate with Jones, but perhaps with the Hadley Commission of 1911. *Railroad Securities Commission to the President*, 1911, Arthur Twining Hadley
(President of Yale Univ. 1899 to 1921, Chair): "A reasonable return is one under
which honest accounting and responsible management will attract the amount
of investor's money needed for the development of our national railroad
facilities."

14. Ibid., pp. 87–89.

15. Ibid., pp. 140, 141.

16. Ibid.

17. William Z. Ripley, *Railroads: Rates and Regulation* (New York: Longmans
Green, 1922), p. 177. See also M. O. Lorenz, "Cost and Value of Service in
Railroad Rate-Making," *The Quarterly Journal of Economics* (Oxford University
Press), Vol. 30, No. 2 (Feb., 1916), pp. 205–232, Stable URL: http://www.jstor.org
/stable/1884993, Accessed: 11/18/2013 06:46.

18. Technically, price *discrimination* in regulatory law was charging different rates
to "similarly situated" customers, with the effect of injuring one producer or

community in competition with others. Price *differentiation*, in addition to sounding more benign, is simply applying variable prices flexibly to match customer demand, for the purpose of covering total costs and earning a reasonable profit.

19. Section 2 of the *Act to Regulate Commerce* made it unlawful for a railroad to charge one person more than another for a "like and contemporaneous" service under "substantially similar" circumstances. Section 3 went further, creating a blanket prohibition against a railroad granting "undue or unreasonable preference" of any kind to any "person, place, or kind" of traffic. See the summary of the 1887 Act provided by Dudley F. Pegrum in *Transportation Economics and Public Policy*, Third Edition (Homewood, IL: Richard D. Irwin, 1973), pp. 276–277.

20. Indeed, this was the pricing strategy brilliantly championed by Richard Steiger and James Hagen in Conrail's renaissance after 1980—although they would not have thought of it as a monopolist's tactic, rather just good marketing practice. See Chapter 8.

21. To the objection that railroad rate making could be done in the same way utility regulation is, namely with cost-based rates overseen by regulatory authorities, it should be noted that public utilities are guaranteed a fair rate of return on their assets employed in the service provided. Railroads receive no such guarantees, and in fact when this kind of an approach was tried under the Transportation Act of 1920, it was a dismal failure. Not to be forgotten is that while large capital facilities characterize both industries, railcars are harder to switch (labor intensive with high operating expenses) than is electric current.

22. Besanko and Braeutigam, *Microeconomics*, p. 46.

23. William B. Tye and Herman B. Leonard, "On the Problems of Applying Ramsey Pricing in the Railroad Industry with Uncertain Demand Elasticities," *Transportation Research*, 17 A, November 6, 1983, pp. 439–450.

24. Remember the lyrics of the old folk song about the *"Rock Island Line*, a mighty fine road"*: The song tells how the train conductor, stopped at a junction, declared to the regulator, "I got livestock, got livestock, I got all—live - stock." Then the train pulls out of earshot, and the conductor sings, "I fooled you, I fooled you; I got pig iron, got pig iron, I got all—pig iron." The lyrics make a lot more sense a century or so later if one understands not only the play on words for barnyard animals and iron making, but what VOS commodity classification and rate making was all about, including the implicit cross subsidy of agricultural products by manufactures.

25. It was said that at one time more than a trillion rates were on file and approved by the ICC. To test the system (and deliberately embarrass the Commission), an ICC practitioner, tired of being denied authority to move lard along with meat, filed a classified rate for truck movement of (fictitious) yak fat. In those days

railroads routinely opposed all requests for class rate adjustments, and in this case, the ICC duly sustained the railroads and denied the petitioner's request for an adjustment in rates for hauling yak fat. Knowing he had great copy, the ICC practitioner went public with the story and a picture of himself posing with a yak from a Nebraska zoo. See "Duane Acklie" in *Heavy Duty Trucking*, Jan 2005, www.heavydutytrucking.com, accessed August 17, 2008.

26. Frank L. McVey, *Railway Transportation: Some Phases of its History, Operation and Regulation* (Chicago: Columbia Institute, 1921), p. 274–275. The issues of overhead expense allocation apply equally to freight and passenger rail economics. John R. Meyer was a pioneer in econometric studies of passenger service avoidable versus fully distributed cost allocations. (See Chapter 5.)

27. Richard D. Stone, *The Interstate Commerce Commission and the Railroad Industry* (New York: Praeger, 1991), p. 16.

28. William D. Middleton, George M. Smerk, and Roberta Diehl, eds., *Encyclopedia of North American Railroads* (Bloomington: Indiana University Press, 2007), pp. 1075–1076.

3. The Policy Dilemma of Competition and Consolidation

Epigraphs: Attributed to Stephenson by Edward Cleveland-Stevens, "English Railways and Their Development and Relation to the State, 1915." In *Dow's Dictionary of Railway Quotations*, Compiled and Edited by Andrew Dow (Baltimore, MD: Johns Hopkins University Press, 2006), p. 38. The meaning of the quotation is explained in the chapter discussion. Alexander L. Morton, "Is There an Alternative to Regulation for the Railroads? In James C. Miller III, ed., *Perspectives on Federal Transportation Policy* (Washington, DC: American Enterprise Institute for Public Policy Research, 1975), p. 27.

1. John R. Meyer, Statement, in *Rail Merger Legislation*, Hearings before the Subcommittee on Antitrust and Monopoly of the Committee on the Judiciary, United States Senate, 87th Congress, 2nd Session, June and July 1962 (Washington, DC: US Government Printing Office, 1962), p. 25.

2. While the Clayton Anti-Merger Act of 1914 was slightly more specific in prohibiting actions that may substantially "lessen competition" or "tend to create a monopoly," it was not until the Transportation Act of 1920 that Congress gave the Interstate Commerce Commission explicit authority to rule whether a railroad merger was in the public interest, and if so, to give it limited exemption from antitrust laws.

3. Fred S. McChesney, "Antitrust," in David R. Henderson, ed. *The Fortune Encyclopedia of Economics*, New York: Warner Books, Inc. 1993, p. 385. Again, we have no immediate resolution of the claims on one hand for consolidation savings or, on the other, competitive benefits. McChesney argues that populist muckrakers like Ida Tarbell, not economists, urged the antitrust statutes

and that economists were somewhat indifferent after balancing the pros and cons: Anticompetitive behavior might raise prices and restrict output, but even Tarbell and Teddy Roosevelt conceded the trusts might be more efficient producers.

4. *Northern Securities Co. v. United States,* 193 U.S. 197 (1904).

5. Richard Saunders, Jr., *Merging Lines: American Railroads 1900–1970* (DeKalb: Northern Illinois University Press (2001), p. 47.

6. Balthazar H. Meyer, "The Northern Securities Company," reprinted from the *Bulletin of the University of Wisconsin* (July 1906) in William Z. Ripley, *Railway Problems* (Boston: Ginn and Company, Revised Edition, 1913), Chapter XXI, p. 553.

7. At this time, Northern Securities' board of directors had six Northern Pacific (NP) representatives, four from Great Northern (GN), three from Union Pacific, and two independent. NP and GN stockholders could exchange their interests for Northern Securities shares. Lloyd J. Mercer, *E. H. Harriman: Master Railroader* (Boston: Twayne Publishers, 1985), p. 95.

8. Balthazar H. Meyer in Ripley, *Railway Problems,* pp. 559–560, quoting an unnamed observer.

   According to Albro Martin's excellent biography about Hill, *James J. Hill and the Opening of the Northwest* (New York: Oxford University Press, 1976), "Hill always claimed that he had told Harriman he was buying the Burlington Railroad," and therefore he was "surprised" to learn later that Harriman did not want Hill to have exclusive access to the CB&Q. Harriman's colleague, Jacob Schiff, said Hill flatly denied he was buying Burlington as late as March, but it soon became evident negotiations were under way. "Schiff first reproached Hill for not telling him what was going on and then made an impassioned appeal that he allow the Union Pacific a one-third interest. To this Mr. Hill replied with platitudes" (pp. 496–497).

9. Mercer, *E. H. Harriman.,* pp. 94–95.

10. B. H. Meyer in Ripley, *Railway Problems,* pp. 561–562.

11. Reconstruction and extension to Chicago of the Atchison, Topeka, & Santa Fe (AT&SF), completed by 1888, made it another player, and in later years the AT&SF became a transcontinental contender of the first rank.

12. B. H. Meyer in Ripley, *Railway Problems,* p. 563.

13. Mercer, *E. H. Harriman,* pp. 27–28.

14. Stuart Daggett, *Railroad Reorganization* (New York: Houghton, Mifflin, Cambridge,MA: The Riverside Press, 1908), p. 256.

15. Ibid., pp. 53–57.

16. SP had controlled Central Pacific (CenPac) since 1868. The government began a legal action in 1914 to require divestiture of CP from SP; the government ultimately won that point in 1922, but by then the Transportation Act of 1920 had

put the ICC in control of mergers and the Commission allowed SP to keep CenPac. The root problem, however, was that the "natural" route connecting Northern California with the rest of the US railroad network—the original two key links (Union Pacific and CenPac) in the Overland Route—had been separate from their birth. That failing was not corrected for nearly 100 years, that is, not until the "new" UP-SP merger in 1996. (See Chapter 10.)

17. From the Sunset line, branches went north from El Paso to Santa Rosa, New Mexico (near Tucumcari), and, further east, to a Texas meeting with the Cotton Belt (St. Louis Southwestern [SLSW]). (Cotton Belt was controlled by Southern Pacific after 1932 and a friendly connection before then.) The Tucumcari and Cotton Belt routes are shown on Map 10.5 in Chapter 10.

18. Don L. Hofsommer, "Southern Pacific Railroad," in William D. Middleton, George M. Smerk, and Roberta Diehl, eds., *Encyclopedia of North American Railroads* (Bloomington: Indiana University Press, 2007), p. 980. In Professor Hofsommer's major work, *The Southern Pacific: 1901–1985* (College Station: Texas A&M University Press, 1986) he tells of Harriman being his own worst enemy when called before an investigation of "Consolidation and Combination of Carriers" by the Interstate Commerce Commission. "It was not so much what he said or did not say; rather it was Harriman's bearing that stood him convicted before the public." (p. 49). Peter A. Hansen properly notes that with the perspective of 100 years, Harriman's reputation has been rehabilitated, "and he is now considered on balance to have been a positive force" in the industry. Hansen, "Harriman, E. H. (1848–1909)" in William D. Middleton, et al. *Encyclopedia* , p. 512).

19. Ripley, *Railway Problems*, p. 568.

20. Mercer, *E. H. Harriman*, p. 86. The government's case had shown in great detail that SP diverted as much traffic as it could to the Sunset Route through El Paso, where it received 100 percent of the revenue instead of only 30 percent over the Overland Route and Ogden gateway. This might show SP power in traffic originations, but it hardly proves the Harriman UP-SP combination was antisocial, as Harriman interests were the beneficiary of either routing, Sunset or Overland/Ogden.

21. Figure 3-1, and Frank Norris, *The Octopus, A Story of California*, 1901— (PROJECT GUTENBERG EBook #268, July 8, 2008).

22. In the UP+Central Pacific scenario, construction of the Western Pacific (WP) might not have been undertaken (like Milwaukee Road's Pacific extension, it was doomed to light density); if WP were built, however, Denver & Rio Grande Western (D&RGW) could merge with Western Pacific to compete with UP+CenPac on the Overland Route to the Bay Area and connect with any of multiple lines east of Denver; UP's Kansas Pacific (KP) branch might easily have gone over to Rio Grande (D&RGW) as part of that deal. These alternatives

imply a four-system West, possibly (1) Great Northern+Burlington, (2) Northern Pacific+Milwaukee Road, (3) Union Pacific+Southern Pacific, and (4) Santa Fe +Rio Grande. The other sizable carriers in the region (e.g., C&NW, Missouri Pacific, Rock Island, and Frisco) would have found logical homes in these four major systems.

23. Andrew Carnegie's U.S. Steel Corp. was indicted by the Department of Justice for monopolizing in 1911, when it had gathered together steel companies with nearly a 90 percent share of the market, but in 1920, with the company's share having falling to 50 percent in the meantime, the US Supreme Court found against the government and allowed US Steel to stand. (http://www.cbsnews .com/htdocs/microsoft/antitrust_steel.html) accessed December 21, 2013.

24. Albro Martin, *Enterprise Denied: Origins of the Decline of American Railroads, 1897–1917* (New York: Columbia University Press, 1971), p. 353. As pointed out by Stuart Bruchey in his preface to Professor Albro Martin's respected history, there was a direct causal link between the excesses of Progressive Era punitive regulation of railroad rates and the poor physical condition of the industry on the brink of the nation's greatest war emergency since the Civil War. Just as the United States was not prepared for its entry into the European conflict, so too were the railroads not ready for the challenge of mobilization. Never swaying from its preconception (prejudice would not be too strong a word), the ICC had denied railroads increases in 1910, 1913–1914, and 1915. The old rates held until, in one of the first acts taken during the period of federal control, the US Railroad Administration ordered increases in rates in an amount cumulatively reversing the ICC's three denials.

25. Members of the Railroads' War Board were Chair—Fairfax Harrison (Southern), Howard Elliott (New Haven), Julius Kruttschnitt (Southern Pacific), Hale Holden (Burlington) and Samuel Rea (Pennsylvania). K. Austin Kerr, *American Railroad Politics: 1914–1920* (Pittsburgh, PA: University of Pittsburgh Press, 1968), p. 44.

26. Kerr, *American Railroad Politics*, 1968, pp. 363–364.

27. Martin, *Enterprise Denied*, p. 337.

28. John Westwood, *Railways at War* (San Diego, CA: Howell-North Books, 1980), p. 179. Westwood cites "[P]erhaps the most stupendous of these" occurring when the Government decided to build a new seaport on swampland near Philadelphia. Before any unloading facilities were built, trainloads of construction materials began arriving, all with priority tags. Before long, sidings were blocked throughout eastern Pennsylvania." (p. 179).

29. Frank Haigh Dixon, *Railroads and Government: Their Relations in the United States 1910–1921* (New York: Charles Scribner's Sons, 1922), p. 112.

30. Switching metaphors, Canada split the baby: Canadian Pacific remained in the private sector, while Canadian National became a crown corporation.

31. The Adamson Act was passed in 1916 in an effort to avoid a national railroad strike. Effective January 1, 1917, it established an eight-hour day for railroad workers and required additional pay for overtime; it was the first federal legislation setting limits on labor hours. In a 5–4 ruling, the act was held to be constitutional by the Supreme Court in 1917. Railroads and others criticized the act and for years urged its repeal. W. Thomas White, "Labor" in Middleton, *Encyclopedia*, p. 579, and Jon R. Huibregtse, *American Railroad Labor and the Genesis of the New Deal, 1919–1935* (Gainesville: University Press of Florida, 2013) p. 23.

32. Southern Pacific's Jules Kruttschnitt, a member of the Railroads' War Board, presented some charts to the committee that had been prepared by a consultant. The charts used a concept not widely known at the time of presenting rail rates in real (or constant) dollars. Kruttschnitt showed that rail rates had consistently fallen since 1899 and that therefore shippers collectively had paid to railroads a total of almost $8 billion less than they would have if the ICC had allowed recovery of amounts equal to the decline in purchasing power of the dollar. The same trend is shown below in Figure 3.2.

33. William J. Cunningham, *American Railroads: Government Control and Reconstruction Policies* (Chicago, IL: A.W. Shaw Co., 1922), pp. 153–154.

34. Ibid., pp. 151–152.

35. Kerr, *American Railroad Politics*, p. 48.

36. *Delano Report*, p. 285. At nearly 15,000 words, the *Delano Report*'s disquisition on nationalization (surely the most extensive official published analysis) concludes with a monumental *argumentum ad consequentiam*. Renewed interest in public ownership of the railroads (in the early 1940s) "does not represent any material development of socialistic ideologies, but only a conviction that Government ownership may offer a feasible alternative to the traditional policy of regulating privately owned railroads, *since that policy has failed to accomplish rate, efficiency, and financial objectives desired by the public*" [emphasis added]. (Ibid., p. 301.)

37. Kerr, *American Railroad Politics*, p. 132

38. Ibid.

39. Probably the most bitterly fought issue in reconciliation of very different House and Senate-passed versions of the 1920 act was not consolidation or rate making, but the Senate's antistrike provision, which Representative Barkley said "would produce unrest and Bolshevism" (ibid., p. 217). In its place, agreement was reached to create a Railroad Labor Board, forerunner of the National Labor Relations Board (1934), intended to help prevent rail service interruptions.

40. Westwood, *Railways at War*, 1980, pp. 182–183.

41. Scientific management, as propounded by Frederic Taylor, was a set of ideas for running things better, not necessarily making them bigger; Frank and Lillian

Gilbreth's proselytizing for "efficiency," whether in the workplace or home (captured in their children's wildly popular play *Cheaper by the Dozen*), would seem an advertisement for economies of scale, but Justice Brandies was nothing if not a foe of size *per se* in antitrust law and practice. One reason he fought the railroads so bitterly was that they were so large—too large to be well managed, he thought.

42. Frank N. Wilner, *Railroad Mergers: History, Analysis, Insight* (Omaha, NE: Simmons-Boardman Books, 1997), p. 33, quoting the Special Study Group on National Transportation Policy for the Senate Committee on Interstate and Foreign Commerce (the Doyle Report), 1961 at p. 233.

43. National Resources and Planning Board, Frederic A. Delano, Chair, *Transportation and National Policy* (Washington, DC: US Government Printing Office, May, 1942), p. 142. (Hereafter cited as the *Delano Report*.)

44. Wilner, *Railroad Mergers*, p. 37.

45. William N. Leonard, *Railroad Consolidation Under the Transportation Act of 1920* (New York: Columbia University Press, 1946), *Railroad Consolidation*, p. 284. Leonard continues, "In establishing these valuation requirements, Congress apparently overlooked the fact that the value of properties in a consolidation is their exchange value, based on anticipated earnings rather than upon actual investment or cost of reproducing the property."

46. Leonard, *Railroad Consolidation* , p. 284. Leonard provides lists of the Tentative (Ripley–1921) and Complete (ICC - 1929) consolidation plans, as does Wilner in *Railroad Mergers*.

47. Wilner, *Railroad Mergers*, p. 57.

48. Alfred E. Kahn, *The Economics of Regulation: Principles and Institutions* (Cambridge, MA: MIT Press, Vol. 2, p. 1988), p. 282.

49. Latham, Earl, *The Politics of Railroad Coordination 1933–1936* (Cambridge, MA: Harvard University Press, 1959), p. 102. The Esch-Cummins Act's mandate on the ICC to develop a plan for rail consolidations ended, for all practical purposes, with passage of the Emergency Transportation Act of 1933 but formal repeal did not come until the Transportation Act of 1940, which also established the public interest regulatory test against which voluntary mergers could be judged.

50. *Delano Report*, p. 142. The view that consolidation was an alternative to abandonment, for which the Commission was given regulatory authority in the 1920 Act, reflects a consequence of requiring consolidation of weak with strong roads; before 1920, abondonments could only be sought through state regulatory commissions, a possible impediment to realizing cost savings.

51. Boyden Sparkes, "Passengers! The Railroads Love You," *Saturday Evening Post*, 17 October 1936, p. 17.

4. The Impact of Rival Freight Modes on Railroads

Epigraphs: Book I, *The Wealth of Nations*, quoted in Tom Lewis, *Divided Highways*, 1997, p. 279. W. W. Hay, "Engineering Characteristics and National Policy" in Robert S. Nelson and Edward M. Johnson, eds., *Technological Change and the Future of the Railways: Selected Papers from a Three Day Conference*, conducted by the Transportation Center at Northwestern University (Evanston, IL: Library of Congress Cat. #61-17929), pp. 15–16. Used with permission.

1. In some respects, rival modes may also have pushed the railroads to better performance and helped railroads escape harsher forms of regulation or government takeover, but those effects are abstract and speculative, while the direct impacts noted here are incontrovertible. See the further note below about pipelines.

2. Even in the Northeast Corridor, air travel dominates the longest trips, for example, Boston, Providence, or Hartford to Baltimore or Washington, D.C. Much depends on demand for travel to specific origins and destinations and whether these points are in suburban areas closer to airports, or the center cities where trains stop at stations and connect to mass transit.

3. Omission of oil pipelines, which diverted vast amounts of crude oil and refined product from railroads over the course of the last century, leaves a bit of a lacuna in our story. Pipeline transport covers a limited range of commodities, and they have no back hauls. The following important example illustrates that lack of ubiquitous coverage by a mode (pipelines) with otherwise inherent advantages, may open a brief niche to rivals.

   Recent developments in the exploitation of new oil and gas reserves recovered from oil sands and tight shales are of enormous importance to America's future energy security. Informed observers see a substantial opportunity for movement of crude oil by either rail unit trains of tank cars (near term), or new pipeline construction (longer term)—in particular between North Dakota's Bakken oil field and refineries having excess capacity that are located on the Middle Atlantic or Gulf Coasts. These are two markets currently underserved by the crude oil pipeline network. Railroads are playing an important transitional, but perhaps only temporary, role in those developments.

   Under John T. Gray, the AAR has produced some excellent analyses of the oil train opportunity for railroads. See "Transportation of Crude Oil by Rail" https://www.aar.org/safety/Pages/crude-by-rail-facts.aspx#.UfedR9KThyR accessed July 30. 2013.

4. http://www.aar.org/~/media/aar/Background-Papers/Keep-Fed-Truck-Size .ashx, accessed July 25, 2012.

5. John R. Meyer, Merton J. Peck, John Stenason, and Charles Zwick, *The Economics of Competition in the Transportation Industries* (Cambridge, MA: Harvard University Press, 1959) [cited as MPS&Z], pp. 238–239. The ICC

quotation (with added emphasis) is from *Western Traffic Association Agreement,* 276 ICC 183 at 214. See MPS&Z, p. 239.

6. David J. DeBoer and Lawrence H. Kaufman, *An American Transportation Story, the Obstacles, the Challenges, the Promise,* Chapter 3, "Railroads" (Greenbelt, MD: The Intermodal Association of North America, 2002), p. 26.

7. William Cronan, *Nature's Metropolis: Chicago and the Great West* (New York: W.W. Norton, 1991). This book is remarkable in relating commercial and transport developments to the history of a great city.

8. The name Chesapeake & Ohio was also taken by a railroad line that followed a more southerly route from the Atlantic seaboard to the midwestern heartland; the C&O Railroad ran from Hampton Roads and Richmond to Staunton, Virginia, then Charleston on the Kanawha River and Huntington (both now West Virginia) on the Ohio, before eventually reaching Chicago.

9. The B&O was the first major public (common carrier) railroad in the United States. Its cornerstone was laid, famously, on the fifty-second anniversary of the birth of the nation—July 4, 1828—by Charles Carroll of Carrollton, the last surviving signer of the Declaration of Independence. The cornerstone can be visited today; it is located close to the current B&O Railroad Museum on the near west side of downtown Baltimore. Charles Carroll was said to be the wealthiest man in the United States at the time.

10. James E. Vance, Jr., *The North American Railroad* (Baltimore, MD: Johns Hopkins University Press, 1960). See the maps on pages 144 and 150. Vance's is a valuable reference. Not many scholars still appreciate geography as a discipline; Vance's fine work demonstrates why they should.

11. Published by the Riverside Press of Cambridge, Massachusetts, in 1914, recently reproduced in a facsimile edition with the same title.

12. Ibid., p. 27.

13. Of the Tennessee-Tombigbee project, it was said that it moved more material in its own construction and maintenance than in subsequent commercial transport, which was probably true to a point. The Arkansas River is shallow and sandy through Arkansas and Oklahoma and could not support river barge traffic most of the year. Construction began in 1963 on a system of eighteen locks and channels along the 445 mile length of the route. The first section, running to Little Rock, opened in 1968. The first barge to reach Tulsa's Port of Catoosa arrived in early 1971. http://en.wikipedia.org/wiki/McClellan-Kerr_Arkansas _River_Navigation_System, accessed January 9, 2011.

14. Frank N. Wilner, *Competitive Equity: The Freight Railroads' Stake* (Washington, DC: Association of American Railroads, 1981). The Arkansas River Project serves as an example of how private-sector barge operations used new publicly built segments of the inland waterway network. Brown-water facilities constructed by the Corps of Engineers featured lock chambers 110 feet wide and

600 feet long, the pattern for much of the Mississippi River system. Standard barges measuring 35 by 195 feet are grouped into a tow three vessels wide and three long, with a towboat at center rear, forming a unit that can fit into a lock chamber. Larger tows may have to be broken into several sections before they are passed through a lock and rejoined on the other side.

15. http://www.marinelink.com/article/navigation/inland-waterways-industry -perspective-019 and http://www.taxfoundation.org/files/0ea7da0415c665b81754 a8b4321fefa0.pdf, both accessed January 9, 2011.

16. Examples are given in Ann F. Friedlaender, *The Dilemma of Freight Transport Regulation* (Washington, DC: The Brookings Institution, 1969). See especially Table 3.8 on page 62.

17. To take just one example of road freighting before railways, in the nineteenth century heavy Midlands horses (sixteen to seventeen hands tall) could draw about six hundredweight of mixed freight each in a flying wagon (one that stayed on the move day and night with relayed teams and teamsters) from Essex or other origins like Dorchester or Andover to London, in a trip of four and one-half days. See Dorian Gerhold, *Road Transport Before the Railways: Russell's Flying Waggons* (Cambridge, UK: Cambridge University Press, 1993), pp. 26–37, 51–62, 80–81.

18. Ibid., p. 221.

19. Rodney Castleden, *Inventions That Changed the World* (London: Chartwell Books, 2007), p. 392.

20. Herbert Spero, *Reconstruction Finance Corporation Loans to the Railroads, 1932–1937* (Boston, MA: Bankers Publishing Company, 1939), p. 10.

21. US Department of Commerce, Bureau of the Census, *Historical Statistics of the United States: Colonial Times to 1957*, Library of Congress No. A 60–9150 (Washington, DC: Government Printing Office, 1960), p. 462.

22. John F. Stover, *The Life and Decline of the American Railroad* (New York: Oxford University Press, 1970), p. 136.

23. *Historical Statistics of the United States*, p. 458. Includes estimates on federal-aid primary systems. Estimate as of end of calendar year. Yearly figures prior to 1922 are not complete.

24. The figure for 1930 is not available, but it stood at 178,000 miles in 1936, and total track mileage had declined only about 3 percent since 1930. *Historical Statistics*, p. 429.

25. James C. Nelson, *Railroad Transportation and Public Policy* (Washington, DC: Brookings Institution, 1959), p. 20.

26. Ibid., p. 21.

27. *Historical Statistics of the United States*, p. 462

28. Julius H. Parmelee, *A Review of Railway Operations in 1932* (Washington, DC: Association of American Railroads, 1933), p. 10.

29. Nelson, *Railroad Transportation and Public Policy*, p. 21.

30. Association of American Railroads, *Transportation in America* (Washington, DC, 1947), pp. 43, 46.

31. *Historical Statistics of the United States*, p. 462.

32. Nelson, *Railroad Transportation and Public Policy*, p. 21.

33. http://wiki.answers.com/Q/How_long_is_the_autobahn_in_miles, accessed January 12, 2011.

34. US Congressional Budget Office, Porter K. Wheeler (author), *Highway Assistance Programs: A Historical Perspective*, January 1978, pp. 5-6.

35. John R. Meyer and Clinton V. Oster, Jr., with John S. Strong, José Gómez-Ibáñez, Don H. Pickrell, Marni Clippinger, and Ivor P. Morgan, *Deregulation and the Future of Intercity Passenger Travel* (Cambridge, MA: MIT Press, 1987).

36. The innovation of the wireless electronic toll transponder has made several of the arguments against tollway financing obsolete but not forgotten. Electronic toll systems are so accurate and painless (and so lucrative for sponsoring highway authorities and agencies) that they are quickly displacing conventional toll booths. The prospect is that easy-pay toll systems will become the standard method by which to facilitate not only major new highway, tunnel, and bridge investments, but also congestion toll schemes designed to overcome gridlock in cities and other traffic bottlenecks.

37. Two books written in the transitional 1990s tell how the foundations of the Interstate Highway System were forged in legislation that became the National Interstate and Defense Highways Act of 1956. The first was Stephen B. Goddard's *Getting There: The Epic Struggle Between Road and Rail in the American Century* (New York: HarperCollins Basic Books, 1994). Only three years later, Tom Lewis published *Divided Highways: Building the Interstate Highways, Transforming American Life* (New York: Viking Penguin, 1997).

38. Federal Railroad Administration, *Study of Federal Aid to Rail Transportation* (Washington, DC: US Department of Transportation, January 1977), p. I-4.

39. Federal Highway Administration, 2010 *Status of the Nation's Highways' Bridges, and Transit: Conditions and Performance*, Exhibit 6-12. www.fhwa.dot.gov/policy/2010cpr/chap6.htm#3 Accessed 11_24_2013.

40. Mahlon Straszheim, a student of John R. Meyer, produced an intriguing paper on post–interstate highway planning and economics in 1966 (at a time, that is, when the interstates were scheduled to be completed in 1972.) Among other observations, Straszheim pointed out that pay as you go (the absence of bonding authority) penalized initial users of the IHS and subsidized subsequent users, who would be able to inherit windfall capacity from previous generations of users. Straszheim's study did not foresee the enormous increase in use of the interstates by long-haul, inter-urban motor carriers, however; these rail-competitive carriers (apart from any underpayment of their cost burden) may

enjoy further advantages as part of the cross subsidy from urban to interurban highway users. Straszheim did note the difficulty in estimating benefits and costs, or establishing congestion fees (in the days before electronic tolling), but he says that "is the recommended way to proceed" (p. 11). Mahlon Straszheim, "Post-72 Highway Program Planning" unpublished monograph, Harvard Department of Economics, October 1966, 44 pages.

41. L. Lee Lane, *Innovation in Trucking: Advanced Truckload Firms* (Washington, DC: Association of American Railroads, Intermodal Policy Division, February 9, 1987).

42. To make matters worse, highway pavement designs may be suboptimal. Kenneth Small, Clifford Winston and Carol Evans studied highway construction standards and concluded that important standards such as pavement thickness and entry/exit ramp radii were improperly set; if pavement is too thin and breaks up under heavy trucks, for example, the roadway may be cheaper to build initially but have higher total life cycle costs—which are likely to be overallocated to the heaviest trucks (because they break up pavements built too thin and because these vehicles have the greatest difficulty negotiating curves on entry/exit ramps). "We estimate that the pavement wear taxes and optimal investments in road durability could generate $8 billion (1982) in annual net benefits to society. . . . Congestion charges could produce additional net benefits of some $5 billion annually. . . .". Kenneth A. Small, Clifford Winston, and Carol A. Evans, *Road Work: A New Highway Pricing and Investment Policy* (Washington, DC: Brookings Institution, 1989), p. 7.

43. US DOT, FHWA, Federal Highway Cost Allocation Study Summary Report, August, 1997, pp. 14–15.

44. Andrew T. Gillies, "Railroads Throw Switch on Deficit Tax," *Forbes*, March 10, 2004, and *Congressional Record*, October 11, 2004, p. 23272.

45. Lewis, *Divided Highways*, p. 294.

46. Ibid.

47. Ibid.

48. Kahn's quip meant that ugly issues of cost allocation, productivity adjustments to published rates, and differential pricing—all so tough to resolve in railroad economics (see Chapter 3)—were, by comparison, almost trivial concerns in airline policy.

49. America's transportation system has been described as the best in the world, but certainly not because of its offerings of rail passenger service. Indeed, the virtues of our nation's freight system, personal mobility, and airline travel stand in stark contrast to the reputation of America's passenger rail system. Rail passenger service is described in Chapter 5 for the years leading up to establishment of Amtrak in 1970 and in Chapter 11 for the Amtrak era. As those two chapters will make clearer, it is in the modes alternative to railroads that answers explaining

the long slow decline of rail passenger service, and Amtrak's relatively high cost and comparative lack of success, are found.

5. The Decline of Railway Passenger Service, 1900–1970

Epigraphs: Emory R. Johnson, *American Railway Transportation* (New York: D. Appleton, Revised Edition, 1908), p. 20. David P. Morgan, quoted in Andrew Dow, ed., *Dow's Dictionary of Railway Quotations* (Baltimore, MD: Johns Hopkins University Press, 2006), p. 24. Used with permission of *Trains Magazine*.

1. U.S. Department of Commerce, Bureau of the Census, *Historical Statistics of the United States: Colonial Times to 1857*, (Washington, DC: Government Printing Office, 1961), p. 430; and *Historical Statistics of the United States*, vol. 2 (Washington, DC: Government Printing Office, 1975), p. 729.
2. Donald M. Itzkoff., *Off the Track: The Decline of the Intercity Passenger Train in the United States* (Westport, CT: Greenwood Press, 1985), p. 12.
3. George W. Hilton, *Amtrak: The National Railway Passenger Corporation* (Washington, DC: American Enterprise Institute for Public Policy Research, 1980), p. 2.
4. *Historical Statistics of the United States*, p. 729. One passenger mile represents the transportation of one passenger for the distance of one mile.
5. Association of American Railroads, *Railroad Transportation: A Statistical Record*, (Washington, DC: Author, 1960), p. 17. Estimates based on Class I railroads. From 1911 to 1955, Class I roads were classified by the ICC as those with annual revenues of $1,000,000 or more.
6. Ibid., 14.
7. Association of American Railroads, *Railroad Transportation*, p. 15.
8. Parmelee, *A Review of Railway Operations in 1932*, p. 5.
9. Spero, *Reconstruction Finance Corporation Loans to the Railroads*, pp. 136–137.
10. Gregory L. Thompson, *The Passenger Train in the Motor Age, California's Rail and Bus Industries 1910–1941* (Columbus: Ohio State University Press, 1993), pp. 115–121.
11. William Van Der Sluys, "The Lightweight Passenger Car with Special Reference to Pullman," *Railroad History* 145 (Autumn 1981), pp. 47–49.
12. Mark Reutter, "The Life of Edward Budd Part 2: Frustration and Acclaim," *Railroad History* 173 (Autumn 1995), pp. 70–71.
13. Ibid., 79–81.
14. Boyden Sparkes, "Passengers! The Railroads Love You," p. 17.
15. "New Trains Come with a Rush," *Business Week* (6 April 1935), pp. 20–21.
16. Committee on Public Relations of the Eastern Railroads, *Yearbook of Railroad Information*, 1935 ed. (New York: AAR, 1935), p. 28.

17. Reutter, "The Life of Edward Budd," pp. 85–86.

18. Julius H. Parmelee, *A Review of Railway Operations in 1940* (Washington, DC: Association of American Railroads, 1941), p. 31.

19. Association of American Railroads, *Railroad Transportation*, p. 17.

20. Cunningham, *The Present Railroad Crisis*, p. 17.

21. Ibid. pp. 17–19, 28.

22. Thompson, *The Passenger Train in the Motor Age*, p. 125.

23. Ibid., p. 117.

24. Association of American Railroads, *Transportation in America* (Washington, DC: Author, 1947), p. 298. This was a comprehensive report of twenty-two chapters, composed over a period of five years, and overseen by a committee of about sixty railroaders.

25. M. W. Clement et al., "Report of Committee . . ." (23 December 1938), pp. 7–13, 58–59.

26. Ari Hoogenboom and Olive Hoogenboom, *A History of the ICC* (New York: Norton, 1976), pp. 136–137.

27. It was one of the greatest years ever for Hollywood. The winner of the Oscar for best picture was *Gone with the Wind*. Other also-rans besides *Union Pacific* included *The Wizard of Oz*, *Stagecoach*, *Goodbye Mr. Chips*, and *Mr. Smith Goes to Washington*.

28. J. B. Hollingsworth, *The History of American Railroads* (Greenwich, CT: Bison Books, 1983).

29. Association of American Railroads, *American Railroads and the War* (Washington, DC: Author, 1943), pp. 16–19, 29.

30. *Historical Statistics of the United States*, p. 729.

31. Association of American Railroads, *Railroad Transportation*, p. 17.

32. Ibid., pp. 29–30.

33. Ibid., p. 72.

34. Julius H. Parmelee, *A Review of Railway Operations in 1945* (Washington, DC: Association of American Railroads, 1946), p. 5.

35. Mark Reutter, "The Life of Edward Budd Part 2: Frustration and Acclaim," *Railroad History* 173 (Autumn 1995), p. 93.

36. "More Streamliners," *Business Week* (25 November 1944), p. 26.

37. Julius H. Parmelee, *A Review of Railway Operations in 1948* (Washington, DC: Association of American Railroads, 1949), pp. 3, 30–31.

38. *Historical Statistics of the United States*, p. 729.

39. Association of American Railroads, *Railroad Transportation*, p. 17.

40. Ibid., pp. 13–14.

41. John F. Stover, *The Routledge Historical Atlas of the American Railroads* (New York: Routledge, 1999), p. 117.

42. Ibid.

43. Mark Reutter, "The Lost Promise of the American Railroad," *Wilson Quarterly* (Winter 1994): 25.

44. Association of American Railroads, *Transportation in America*, pp. 60–61.

45. Ibid., p. 12.

46. Reutter, "The Lost Promise of the American Railroad," p. 25.

47. Kurian, *Datapedia of the United States*, p. 262.

48. "Railroad Fares: Do the Passengers Pay Their Way?" *Time* (13 August 1956), p. 64.

49. Albro Martin, *Railroads Triumphant* (Oxford: Oxford University Press, 1992), p. 128.

50. Hilton, *Amtrak*, p. 5

51. José Gómez-Ibáñez, "An Overview of the Options," in José A. Gómez-Ibáñez and Ginés de Rus, eds., *Competition in the Railway Industry: An International Comparative Analysis* (Edward Elgar, 2006).

52. John R. Meyer and Gerald Kraft, *Avoidable Costs of Passenger Train Service* (Cambridge, MA: Aeronautical Research Foundation, 1957).

53. That is, observers thought costs were smoothly variable with changes in output, when in fact they responded sluggishly and did not go away when the service was terminated. Variable and avoidable costs were thus "higher than they should have been."

54. José Gómez-Ibáñez and Don H. Pickrell, "Toward an Equilibrium in Intercity Travel Choices" in John R. Meyer and Clinton V. Oster, Jr., with John S. Strong, José Gómez-Ibáñez, Don H. Pickrell, Marni Clippinger, and Ivor P. Morgan, *Deregulation and the Future of Intercity Passenger Travel*, (Cambridge, MA: MIT Press), 1987, pp. 183–203.

55. J. A. Gómez-Ibáñez, "Costs of the Various Intercity Modes," Appendix A in ibid., p. 247.

56. Newark, Metropark, Trenton, and BWI are other popular stops for some trains on the route.

57. The Montgolfier brothers, Joseph-Michael (born 1740) and Jacques-Étienne (born 1745), invented, built, and demonstrated the first practical lighter-than-air balloons. As described by the US Centennial of Flight Commission, "the brothers discovered that heated air from a fire directed into a paper or fabric bag made the bag rise. They demonstrated this discovery in 1782 when a balloon they made rose into the air about 3,000 feet, remained aloft some 10 minutes, and then settled to the ground more than a mile and a half from where it rose. In early June of 1783 . . . they gave a public exhibition of their discovery with a balloon made of silk and lined with paper to trap the gas. It rose to an altitude of about 6,000 feet, traveled more than a mile, and stayed aloft for 10 minutes." http://www.centennialofflight.gov/essay/Dictionary/Montgolfier/DI35.htm, accessed January 5, 2011.

58. DeBoer and Kaufman, p. 79. Wilbur contracted typhoid fever and died prematurely at age forty-five in 1912. Orville never flew again but lived to the age of seventy-six. He died in 1948 in Dayton, Ohio.

59. The patent raised difficult legal and technological issues; the Wright brothers had used "wing warping" to stabilize flight (as they had observed in an animal model—soaring vultures), but others developed aircraft with what became the more practical approach—moveable ailerons on the rear surface of the wings. French glider prototypes had used ailerons and, possibly at Alexander Graham Bell's suggestion, the Aerial Experiment Association had incorporated them in a 1904 prototype tested by the Army Air Corps. (DeBoer and Kaufman, p. 80).

60. Charles Davidson and Lincoln Diamant, *Stamping Our History: The Story of the United States Portrayed on Its Postage Stamps* (New York: Carol Publishing, 1990), p. 190. On May 14, the day before Boyle's flight, the post office issued a 24-cent red and blue air mail stamp honoring the new service and featuring the Curtiss JN-4H. A stamp collector purchased a 100-stamp sheet of the new issue, and was surprised and delighted to discover that all the blue Jennies were flying upside down! Five days later, the collector sold his prize for $15,000. A single "inverted Jenny"—to collectors the most iconic of US postage stamps—was worth over a quarter of a million dollars in 2000.

61. Ivor P. Morgan in John R. Meyer, and Clinton V. Oster, Jr., eds., *Airline Deregulation: The Early Experience* (Boston: Auburn House Publishing Co., 1981), p. 13.

62. Carl Solberg, *Conquest of the Skies: A History of Commercial Aviation in America* (Boston: Little, Brown and Co., 1979), p. 22.

63. Ibid., pp. 39–40.

64. Martin Aircraft Advertisement, *Saturday Evening Post* (24 January 1948), p. 91.

65. Robert G. Pushkar, "Comet's Tale," *Smithsonian* (June 2002), pp. 59–62.

66. Best-selling author Simon Winchester gives an illustration of the impact on rival modes of the introduction of international jet aviation in the early 1960s. "The economics of large passenger liners suddenly made no sense. BOAC and Pan American had both begun air service between Heathrow and New York's Idlewild (later JFK) airports five years before, in 1958. The first flights were obliged to make refueling stops at Gander, in Newfoundland, but then as planes became more powerful, both airlines began to cross the ocean nonstop, and scores of other carriers soon began to do the same. One by one the great passenger liners vanished from the ocean trade, and such ships as survived began to cruise instead. . . ."

67. Successful aviation entrepreneurs like Herb Kelleher of Southwest Airlines started airlines within a gap of regulatory coverage, grew their operation by exploiting economies of density in the nonregulated environment, then

flourished with acquisition of more efficient aircraft and operating strategies after deregulation.

68. Meyer and Oster, p. 48. Robson was carried over as CAB chairman in the initial weeks of the Carter administration, where he favored limited fare experimentation and a gradual approach to deregulation; he eventually became an advocate.

69. Ibid., p. 8.

70. Ibid.

71. "Rail Passenger Train Deficit: Report Proposed by Howard Hosmer, Hearing Examiner" from ICC docket 31954 in 1958. For an excellent discussion of this report and related issues, see George W. Hilton, "The Hosmer Report: a Decennial Evaluation" in the *ICC Practitioners Journal*, Vol. 39 (November 1969), pp.

72. Martin, *Enterprise Denied*, p. 364.

6. Mergers at Midcentury and the Penn Central Debacle

Epigraph: Alfred Kahn, *The Economics of Regulation: Principles and Institutions*, Vol. II (Cambridge, MA: MIT Press, 1988), p. 283. Used with permission.

1. Joseph B. Eastman (Federal Coordinator of Transportation), "Regulation of Railroads," Document No. 119, 73rd US Congress, 2nd Session, January 11, 1934. p. 21 ff.

2. An exception was the Pennsylvania Railroad's successful acquisition of financial control via lease of the storied Wabash road. Later, Wabash would move out of the PRR orbit and into the N&W-Nickel Plate-Wabash, remaining out of Penn Central and Conrail. After division of Conrail in 1998–1999, nevertheless, the Wabash would find itself back with its Pennsy cousins in Norfolk's family.

3. A glossary of US railroads with reporting marks as of 1943 appears at the end of this book. Why a list current in 1943? A full catalogue of all US railroads would be too long to reproduce, but a list drawn up at the end of the century would not include those "fallen flags" (as they are called by rail fans) involved in mergers during the midcentury period.

4. Richard Saunders, Jr., *Merging Lines: American Railroads 1900–1970* (DeKalb: Northern Illinois University Press (2001), pp. 69–71; John Sherman Porter, ed., *Moody's Transportation Manual* (New York: Moody's Investor's Service, Ltd. 1956); ICC, *Statistics of Railways in the U.S.* (Washington, DC: Government Printing Office, 1962).

5. A contrary view was published in the 1933 report rendered by the National Transportation Committee (Calvin Coolidge, chairman; Bernard M. Baruch, vice chairman; and Alfred K. Smith, Alexander Legge and Clark Howell), which concluded:

The development of regulation and new methods of transport make it unnecessary for Government further to create and foster competition with or among railroads as a defense against monopoly. That is an expensive and ineffective attempt to do indirectly what Government has shown its ability to do directly. (See Harold G. Moulton, ed., *The American Transportation Problem* [Washington, DC: Brookings Institution, 1933], p. xvi.

6. Sumner H. Slichter, "The Case for Bigness in Business," in Gerald D. Nash, ed., *Issues in American Economic History, Selected Readings,* 3rd ed. (Lexington, MA: D. C. Heath, 1980), p. 304.

7. Joseph R. Daughen and Peter Binzen, in *The Wreck of the Penn Central* (Boston: Little, Brown and Co., 1971 at p. 206) call it "the most ambitious business merger in American industry."

8. The N&W could carry its westbound coal on to Ohio for multiple competitive connections; the VGN merger into N&W allowed the merger partners to "keep their long haul" while effectively foreclosing the NYC's access to a competitive coal source. N&W was at the time controlled by New York Central's archrival— the Pennsylvania Railroad—so closing the Gauley interchange was of great concern to NYC.

9. Not all of the coal moving out of Hampton Roads (Norfolk or Newport News) was for export and not all of it was metallurgical (coking) coal. Especially after the Clean Air Act Amendments were passed in 1990, East Coast utilities took considerable amounts of relatively low-sulfur Appalachian coal by water to blend with higher-sulfur steam coal in order to meet EPA emission requirements intended to reduce acid rain. At the same time, European demand for Pocahontas metallurgical coal was leveling off due to a strong dollar and the decline of integrated (blast furnace and basic oxygen) steel making relative to mini-mill electric arc furnace technology.

10. John Sherman Porter, ed., *Moody's Transportation Manual* (1956), p. 63 (Virginian), p. 991 (N&W).

11. Missouri Pacific (MP or MoPac) was shortly afterward permitted to acquire the western fork of the C&EI south of Woodland Junction, Illinois; L&N and MoPac shared control of the C&EI north of Woodland Junction through Yard Center/Chicago Heights/Dolton to Chicago proper.

12. Robert E. Gallamore, *Railroad Mergers: Costs, Competition, and the Future Organization of the American Railroad Industry,* unpublished doctoral dissertation, Harvard University, 1968; and Kent T. Healy, "The Merger Movement in Transportation," *The American Economic Review, Proceedings,* Vol. LII, No. 2 (May 1962), p. 439ff. See also Healy's monograph, "The Effects of Scale in the Railroad Industry" (New Haven, CT: Yale University Committee on Transportation, May 1951).

13. Healy, "The Effects of Scale in the Railroad Industry," p. 3.

14. Robert E. Gallamore, "Measurement of Cost 'Savings' of Recent Railway Mergers," *Transportation Research Forum, Papers, 1968.* p. 232. These summary results were picked up in other references, including Alfred E. Kahn, *The Economics of Regulation: Principles and Institutions, Volumes I and II* (Cambridge, MA: The MIT Press, 1988), vol. II, p. 285. The suggestion of the term *complementary* mergers (coined to describe complex mergers having both parallel and end-to-end elements) did not catch on in subsequent literature.

15. Labor felt that at least some of the gains from consolidation should go to the employees whose displacement helped create those gains. Management formally accepted this principle when, as a consequence of collective bargaining, it accepted the Washington Labor Protection Agreement of 1936, which guaranteed payments of 60 percent of prior wages for five years to any worker who lost his or her job due to consolidations (later expanded to 100 percent of prior compensation for four years). See Saunders, *Merging Lines*, 2001, pp. 70–71.

16. U.S. Department of Transportation, *Western Railroad Mergers*, A staff study of the Office of the Secretary and the Federal Railroad Administration (Washington, D.C., 1969).

17. Michael Conant, *Railroad Bankruptcies and Mergers from Chicago West 1975–2001* (Amsterdam: Elsevier, 2004), p. 52.

18. A Milwaukee + Northern Pacific merger likely would have rationalized overbuilt lines in the northern transcontinental route, in keeping with economies of density first articulated by Kent Healy. Indeed, NP and Milwaukee Road sometimes used the same mountain passes through the Rockies and Cascades. NP + MILW could have joined in developing coal routes out of the Northern Powder River Basin (PRB) via Miles City, Montana, while GN + CB&Q were destined to fight with UP and C&NW over coal movements from the Southern PRB. Milwaukee Road's superbly engineered (but underutilized) line from St. Paul to Chicago would have stood up well to competition from GN + CB&Q.

19. One of the most persistent claims brought against railroads for possession of unchecked economic power is that concerning BN market dominance over movement of Montana grain—the result of the Burlington Northern merger case and demise of *Milwaukee Road* transcontinental service. The case in point was *97-1632 U.S. DC Circuit Court of Appeals, McCarty Farms, Inc., et al., Petitioners v. Surface Transportation Board* on appeal from *STB* Docket no. 37809, *McCarty Farms, Inc., et al. v. Burlington Northern, Inc.*, decided August 14, 1997.

20. Saunders, *Merging Lines*, 2001, p. 315.

21. Ibid., pp. 315–316.

22. Ibid., pp. 316–317.

23. Stephen Salsbury, *No Way to Run a Railroad: The Untold Story of the Penn Central Crisis* (New York: McGraw-Hill Book Co., 1982), p. 118.

24. John E. Harr, "The Great Railway Crisis: An Administrative History of the United States Railway Association" (Washington, DC: National Academy of Public Administration, 1978); mimeo, available on CD from the National Academy of Public Administration (NAPA), p. 52.

25. Joseph R. Daughen and Peter Binzen, *The Wreck of the Penn Central* (Boston: Little, Brown and Co., 1971), pp. 13, 139, 206, 243–246.

26. *Trains Magazine*, Vol. 30, No. 11 (September 1970), p. 3.

27. Congressional enactments referred to the "Northeast and Midwest Region" so as to convey the fact that Penn Central reached Chicago and St. Louis, and no doubt also to make clear the extent of its endangerment for purposes of building a winning political coalition.

28. Writers have some choice in saying just how many Northeast and Midwest bankrupts there were. Various sources list six or eight, not always the same. One significant bankrupt, Boston & Maine (B&M), never participated in the Northeast reorganization planning process conducted by the US Railway Association (USRA) under the Regional Rail Reorganization (3R) Act. (See Table 7.1 and more discussion in Chapter 7.)

29. Eric W. Beshers, *Conrail: Government Creation & Privatization of an American Railroad* (Washington, DC: The World Bank, Report INU 38, March 15, 1989), p. ii.

30. Daughen and Binzen, *The Wreck of the Penn Central*, 1971, p. 308.

31. Committee on Commerce, US Senate, Committee Print, *The Penn Central and Other Railroads* (Washington, DC: December, 1972), especially pp. 181–187; the section titled "The Penn Central Merger: A Study of Its Planning, Approval, and Result," pp. 313–350; and the "Financial Situation," pp. 353–430 plus Appendices.

32. Ibid., p. 181.

33. DOT/FRA, *A Prospectus for Change in the Freight Railroad Industry* (Washington, DC: Department of Transportation, October 1978), p. 39.

34. Daughen and Binzen, *The Wreck of the Penn Central*, pp. 210–211.

35. Ibid., p. 211.

36. Ibid., p. 321.

37. The PC trustees believed labor costs in 1970 were at least $120 million greater than "anything that could be considered a 'rational cost' figure" (Daughen and Binzen, *The Wreck of the Penn Central*, p. 321).

38. Speech by former Union Pacific Railroad president John C. Kenefick to the Lexington Group in Transportation History, Kansas City, 2004. Mimeo in co-author Gallamore's files.

39. Perhaps not if a condemnation value were asserted in government supervised liquidation, but certainly more than Penn Central's value as a "going concern."

40. Robert J. Samuelson, "Penn Central: The Road to Nationalization," *Washington Post*, March 11, 1973, p. B3. Salsbury, *No Way to Run a Railroad*, Chapter 15, tells the full story of Penphil, Executive Jet Aviation, and related ventures. See also Daughen and Binzen, *The Wreck of the Penn Central*, Chapter 8.

41. Daughen and Binzen, *The Wreck of the Penn Central*, see especially the pullout organization chart at pages 112–113, showing officers who came from PRR in red and those from New York Central in green.

42. Daughen and Binzen, *The Wreck of the Penn Central*, 1971, pp. 61–62.

43. Ibid., p. 62.

44. Ibid., p. 212 and following pages; p. 250.

45. Committee on Commerce, US Senate, Committee Print, *The Penn Central and Other Railroads* (Washington, DC: December 1972), p. 181.

46. Antitrust exemption is never total. Notwithstanding the exemption language of the 1920 Act, presumably, a railroad could be charged and found guilty of collusion to fix prices or harm a competitor—*per se* antitrust violations—if straying from ICC or STB oversight.

7. Two Railroad Reform and Revitalization Acts and the Northeast Rail Crisis in the 1970s

Epigraph: DOT /FRA, *A Prospectus for Change in the Freight Railroad Industry*, October 1978, p. 1.

1. Harr, John E., *The Great Railway Crisis: An Administrative History of the United States Railway Association* (Washington, DC: National Academy of Public Administration, 1978), pp. 54–57. Mimeo, available on CD from NAPA.

2. *Trains Magazine*, Vol. 30, No. 11 (September, 1970), p. 10.

3. Ibid., and Harr, *The Great Railway Crisis*, pp. 64–65.

4. Robert J. Samuelson, "Penn Central: The Road to Nationalization," *Washington Post*, March 11, 1973, p. B3.

5. USRA's Preliminary System Plan later reached a nearly identical recommendation.

6. Samuelson, "Penn Central," p. B3.

7. At the time, the only recent precedent for sizeable railroad liquidation was that of the New York, Ontario and Western, in 1957. By 1979–1980, the bankruptcies of the Rock Island and the Milwaukee Road, then in reorganization, came close to the same end, but active efforts by trustees went the way of major line sales rather than classic liquidation. These line sales brought in hundreds of millions

of dollars, enabling the owners of the estates to preserve significant remaining value. Thus the legal precedents of the Penn Central case were—quite practically—affirmed within a decade.

8. Samuelson, "Penn Central," p. B3.

9. Harr, *The Great Railway Crisis*, p. xix.

10. Ibid., p. xix

11. ICC, Rail Services Planning Office, *Evaluation of the Secretary of Transportation's Rail Services Report* (Washington, DC: US Government Printing Office, May 1974), p. 8.

12. Officials of the Union Pacific Corporation in New York City, particularly Vice President Law William McDonald, worked closely with Congressmen Brock Adams of Washington and Richard Shoup of Montana and the House Committee staff to help draft the legislation. This was quite well known publicly, and more than a few observers wondered why a Western railroad like Union Pacific would become so deeply involved in the Northeast railroad crisis. The answer is that UP was concerned about both its connecting (interline) business (which it wanted to protect) and the specter of nationalization (which it wanted very much to avoid). Even taking into account that its share (division) of interline revenues might eventually have to be reduced, *Union Pacific* had the foresight to recognize that, in the future, longer hauls would benefit both western and eastern railroads, while nationalization could jeopardize the financial yields from its railroad properties (modest as they were).

13. Only six weeks before the PSP was to be published under the congressional timetable, the trustees of the Erie Lackawanna (EL) announced their decision that this bankrupt carrier (formed from the 1960 merger of two storied actors in Northeast railroad history) could not be reorganized under Chapter 77. They therefore asked USRA to include EL in the 3R Act planning process. See Table 7.1 for the list of other railroads in the region and their status with the courts.

14. David M. Dorsen, *Henry Friendly: Greatest Judge of His Era* (Cambridge, MA: The Belknap Press of Harvard University Press, 2012), pp. 287–288.

15. Harr, *The Great Railway Crisis*, pp. xx, xxi.

16. Ibid.

17. USRA, *The Revitalization of Rail Service in the Northeast, The Final Report of the United States Railway Association* (Washington, DC: USRA, December 1986 [cited as USRA, *Final Report*]), p. ii.

18. "By mid-summer USRA had hired about half its planned contingent of staff members." USRA, *Final Report*, pp. 1–6.

19. USRA, *Final Report.*, pp. 1–7.

20. The CRC, initially (and unfortunately), was dubbed "ConRail," and spelled that way at the time. Later the use of "Conrail" (spelled that way) became

semiofficial. Lowercasing the R simply marked the transition from a shortening of the official title used as a nickname to a marketing moniker and trademark.

21. Developing a Unified Conrail, however, still required each bankruptcy court to determine within the 120-day timeframe that the railroads in receivership were not reorganizable on an income basis.

22. The final (official) version of the structure options are reported in USRA's *Preliminary System Plan*, "Appendix C Industry Structure," pp. 251–258.

23. Miriam Claes, Cheril Santini, and Jeff Vergamini, *The Liberalization of the European Railways*, unpublished student manuscript for the Kellogg School of Management at Northwestern University, no date (circa 2004), 56 pages. This analysis of the vertical separation of European railways under European Union policies in Belgium, France, Germany, Sweden, and the United Kingdom estimated value creation of 250 billion euros. "This value creation improvement arises primarily from greater efficiencies and productivity through increased competition. Additionally, functional specialization and geographic consolidation will also provide opportunities through economies of scope, scale, and density . . ." (p. 52).

24. See Fred C. Frailey, "Conrail Lives," *Trains Magazine*, October 2012, pp. 20–31.

25. Reprinted in edited form as Chapter 3, "Intermodal and Intramodal Competition" by the USRA, in Paul W. MacAvoy and John W. Snow, eds. *Railroad Revitalization and Regulatory Reform: Ford Administration Papers on Regulatory Reform* (Washington, DC: American Enterprise Institute for Public Policy Research, 1977).

26. USRA's PSP was ready by the statutory deadline, but not without several staff all-nighters. One memorable late-night meeting was spent with Ed Jordan, several vice presidents, the strategic planners, financial staff, and the system plan coordinator (charged with writing, editing, and publishing the Plan documents) putting the final touches on the PSP draft. While strategic options were updated with the most recent assessments of likely participation or not of the solvent railroads, financial analysts were reworking numbers on their calculators, and the editors were rushing revised typewriter copy to the Government Printing Office for linotype typesetting and hot lead printing. (Lotus 123, Excel, and personal computers with word processors and printers, more the pity, were still in the future.) This activity was all to be repeated six months later for the FSP.

27. USRA, *Final Report*, pp. 1–8.

28. Ibid., pp. 1–9.

29. Eric Beshers, *Conrail: Government Creation & Privatization of an American Railroad*, The World Bank, Report INU 38 (March 15, 1989), p. 5. Today, after Hurricane Katrina and Rita, we no longer seem to need to create and fund one federal agency to organize public criticism of another.

30. USRA, *Final Report*, pp. 1–9.

31. Harr, *The Great Railway Crisis*, p. 439.

32. See USRA, *Preliminary System Plan*, Chapter 13.

33. Economists know how difficult it is to separate common costs on any but an arbitrary basis. The first user wants all subsequent users to pay a percentage of initial capital fixed costs and ongoing overhead; the marginal users want only to pay direct, incremental operating costs.

34. USRA, PSP, pp. 167–168. We return to these issues in Chapter 13 of this book.

35. The Chessie System had its own alternatives to the NEC on the former B&O route to Philadelphia through the Howard Street Tunnel in Baltimore—a story well told in J. Lawrence Lee, "Baltimore's Belt," *Railroad History* (Spring–Summer, 2005), pp. 30–51.

36. Actual cost studies would be difficult because of the complexity of splitting maintenance and replacement costs when joint use is decided by compromise rather than optimization. Also, stochastic events (such as the 1987 collision between a Conrail freight and Amtrak passenger train at Chase, Maryland, that killed sixteen) are difficult to consider in cost studies.

37. USRA, *Final Report*, pp. 1–9.

38. Ibid.

39. Harr, *The Great Railway Crisis*: 1978, p. 555. Available on CD from NAPA.

40. Porter K. Wheeler, *Railroad Reorganization*, CBO Background Paper No. 2 (January 15, 1976), p. 1.

41. USRA, *Final Report*, pp. 1–10.

42. Conrail's birthday, like DOT's exactly nine years earlier, was April 1 (1976).

43. USRA, *Final Report*, p. 1–10.

44. USRA, *Final Report*, pp. 1–10, 1–11.

45. Robert Gallamore, "Federal Railroad Administration," in Middleton et al., eds., *Encyclopedia of North American Railroads* (Bloomington: Indiana University Press, 2007), pp. 443–445.

46. Dereco was the name given N&W custodianship of the Erie Lackawanna and Delaware & Hudson lines located along New York State's southern tier of counties, and connecting historically with Boston & Maine at Mechanicsburg, New York.

47. Guilford Transportation Industries (since 1998 known as Pan Am Systems) was a collection of railroads formed by Timothy Mellon in 1977 that acquired in the 1980s the former Boston & Maine, Maine Central, and Delaware & Hudson. D&H was sold to Canadian Pacific in 1991. http://en.wikipedia.org/wiki/Pan_Am_Systems. Accessed January 15, 2013.

48. Rush Loving, Jr., *The Men Who Loved Trains* (Bloomington: Indiana University Press, 2006), p. 337.

49. DOT/FRA, *A Prospectus for Change in the Freight Railroad Industry* (Washington, DC: US Government Printing Office, 1978).

8. The Brief, Mainly Happy Life of Conrail, 1976–1999

1. *Evaluation of the Financial Assumptions Contained in the USRA Final System Plan.* House Committee on Interstate and Foreign Commerce, October 1975, p. 16.

2. Eric Beshers, *Conrail: Government Creation & Privatization of an American Railroad*, mimeo (Washington, DC: The World Bank, March 15, 1989), pp. V-10–V-11.

3. Beshers, *Conrail*, p. V-11.

4. Stanley Crane, *Rise from the Wreckage: A Brief History of Conrail* (New York: The Newcomen Society of the United States, 1988), p. 14.

5. A division is the share one railroad receives of the total revenue collected from a shipper for an interline movement jointly provided by two or more connecting railroads; these meet and interchange traffic at gateways, and traditionally, shippers could specify the routing of the movement and hence which gateway would be used. Usually the rates were the same over either routing, but costs and time in transit could be quite different (and thus more or less efficient for the rail network as a whole). Under the regulatory regime, divisions were subject to ICC review under Section 15(6) of the Interstate Commerce Act, and if these were found to be unreasonable, changes could be prescribed by the commission. Resulting controversies were legendary in their scope and duration. (Brief for Appellants before the Supreme Court, October term, 1966.)

6. Goldman, Sachs & Co. et al., "52,000,000 Shares Consolidated Rail Corporation Common Stock," *Preliminary Prospectus*, February 13, 1987, pp. 22–23.

7. Ibid., p. 23.

8. Ibid.

9. Leslie K. Meyer, *Consolidated Rail Corporation—1986*, Harvard University, Kennedy School of Government Case Program (unpublished), p. 1.

10. Ibid. pp. 4–5.

11. USRA, Conrail Profitability Determination, June 1, 1983, p. 1.

12. Richard Saunders harshly criticizes Burnley for his role in Conrail's disposition and leaves an unfavorable impression, but Jim Burnley was and is a fine gentleman. Burnley succeeded Elizabeth Dole as secretary of transportation in 1980, and afterward become a highly respected Washington lawyer.

13. Testimony by R. H. Platt, mimeo, October 24, 1984, p. 3.

14. Platt Testimony, October 24, 1984, pp. 6–7.

15. Crane, *Rise from the Wreckage*, p. 37. Crane tells, autobiographically, much of the same history later reported by Rush Loving and Richard Saunders. Crane's version is more concise, more authentic, and less ornamented than the others, but Loving's is the most entertaining.

16. Rush Loving, Jr., *The Men Who Loved Trains*, 2006, p. 243.

17. Congressional Budget Office, August 1986. The CBO paper cited here is an untitled, un-paginated, and unpublished paper in the author's collection.

18. *Traffic World*, September 1, 1986. Published by Commonwealth Business Media at 33 Washington St. 13th Floor Newark, NJ. Paul Page was the editor when *Traffic World* magazine folded in Feb. 2009. Last Mailing address: 1270 National Press Building, Washington, DC 20045.

19. Richard Saunders, Jr. *Main Lines: Rebirth of the North American Railroads, 1970–2002* (DeKalb: Northern Illinois University Press, 2003), p. 240.

20. Coleman was not challenged at the time on the matter of whether Secretary Dole was willing to settle for too low a price, or that a sale to a single existing railroad purchaser (in her conception, Norfolk Southern) was really a more fair, effective, and competitive solution than the public sale actually consummated in 1987 (which DOT had done precious little to advance). It wasn't the right occasion for such a challenge, but Coleman was vulnerable on both points.

21. US DOT and FRA, *Recommendations for Northeast Rail Service* (March 31, 1981), p. I-8.

22. Peter Stiles, "The DuPont AEI Pilot," privately printed by Conrail and Union Pacific, 1994.

23. Bottleneck rate making is well-described by the Association of American Railroads at http://www.aar.org/~/media/aar/Background-Papers/Bottleneck-Policy .ashx. Accessed October 9, 2012. In the AAR's phrasing, the STB declared that "a railroad is not required to involve a second railroad in a movement that the first railroad can handle all by itself."

24. Saunders, *Main Lines*, p. 240. "Don Phillips thought railroad lore would someday include him on the same list as James J. Hill and E. H. Harriman."

25. The fascinating story of how the division of Conrail between Norfolk Southern and CSX in 1999 came about is fully told by Rush Loving, Jr. in *The Men Who Loved Trains*. Heavy with anecdotes, Loving's is nonetheless a valuable source despite the rather strange title.

9. *The Making of the Staggers Rail Act, and Experience under Deregulation*

Epigraphs: Fred J. Emery, former director of the Federal Register, having been credited with the quote, which he often used in speeches in the 1970s, recently gave this clarification to *Harvard Magazine* (November–December, 2007, Vol. 110, No. 2, p. 20): "I think I always gave credit to its true author [d'Estaing] . . . [and] I usually softened it by preceding it with 'All too often . . .' "

The Train That Ran Away (London: Ian Allan, 1973), p. 24. Used with permission.

US Department of Transportation, Federal Railroad Administration, *A Prospectus for Change in the Freight Railroad Industry* (Washington, DC: 1978), p. 114.

1. President John F. Kennedy, Transportation Message, April 5, 1962.
2. US Department of Transportation, Federal Railroad Administration (FRA), *A Prospectus for Change in the Freight Railroad Industry: A Preliminary Report by the Secretary of Transportation*. See especially the preface, pp. v–vii.
3. New Rochelle (Shell Interlocking) is where inbound commuter trains to New York City's Grand Central Station split from the Northeast Corridor (NEC). Amtrak trains north of Penn Station use the Hell Gate Bridge to reach New Rochelle and resume NEC service. Commuter train services on the Northeast Corridor north of New York City are operated by Metro North, the Connecticut DOT, and Boston's MBTA.
4. Ibid., p. vi.
5. H.R. 7235,—Report No. 96–1035. See also "Statement of Fact and Argument of Western Railroads" in *Ex Parte No. 347—Coal Rate Guidelines Nationwide*, April 13, 1982, p. 5.
6. John H. Riley, Federal Railroad Administrator, before the Senate Committee on Commerce, Science, and Transportation, November 1, 1985.
7. John Riley died tragically young, of brain cancer, in 1994. http://en.wikipedia.org/wiki/John_H._Riley. Accessed January 16, 2013.
8. Paul MacAvoy and John W. Snow, eds., *Railroad Revitalization and Regulatory Reform: Ford Administration Papers on Regulatory Reform* (Washington, DC: American Enterprise Institute, 1977).
9. Ibid., p. 184.
10. FRA *A Prospectus for Change in the Freight Railroad Industry*, p. 114.
11. Ibid.
12. Snow and Aron, *Revitalization*, p. 184. Possibly it was true that deregulation of railroad rates and services had to be taken in small steps. Academic theories were not enough; there was a need for more experimentation in the real world. But there was little to go on except for some limited steps toward deregulation that had been taken in Canada. These, especially the work of Trevor Heaver, proved popular for academic study, but the actual influence of the Canadian experience on US legislators was minimal, both in 4R Act and later Staggers Act deliberations. Trevor D. Heaver and James C. Nelson, Railway Pricing Under Commercial Freedom, The Canadian Experience (Vancouver, BC: University of British Columbia, 1977).
13. Draft message saved in the personal papers of Robert E. Gallamore. Administrator Riley was also intrigued by the "standing derailment" phenomenon; he mentioned in 1985 testimony that it had happened twice in a single year.
14. Key members of the working team were Constance Abrams, Ellen Seidman, Edward Hymson, and co- author Gallamore. FRA's Office of Policy under Steven Ditmeyer and Ronald Reimann, and Chief Counsel Raymond James provided staff support and legal advice. Gerard McCullough (now a professor of

applied econometrics) contributed valuable clarification of the issues. In later White House and congressional negotiations, FRA administrator John Sullivan, William Bonvillian, Susan Williams, Charles Swinburn, William Johnston, and Stuart Eisenstat, among others on the DOT/Carter administration team, played important roles. A group of progressive shipper representatives, including Stanton P. Sender of Sears, William K. Smith of General Mills, Clifford M. Sayre of DuPont, and William Spreitzer of General Motors were key supporters of reform. Congressional staff members like Linda Morgan, Tom Allison, Paul Cunningham, and Cliff Elkins stand out in my memory, as do several railroad Washington representatives. These names are not the entirety of those who contributed. Please forgive any egregious omissions.—REG

15. See for example, testimony of the Department of Transportation on the Railroad Deregulation Act of 1979 before the Senate Committee on Commerce, Science, and Transportation, May 22–23, 1979.

16. Under terms of the Interstate Commerce Commission Termination Act of 1995.

17. Surface Transportation Board, *Rail Rates Continue Multi-Year Decline*, Office of Economics, Environmental Analysis, and Administration (December, 2000) quoted in US General **Accountability** Office [GAO's current name], *Railroad Regulation: Changes in Railroad Rates from 1997 through 2000*, GAO-02-524 (Washington, DC: US Government Printing Office, June 2002), p. 11.

18. Ibid. p. 7. and US General **Accountability** Office, *Railroad Regulation: Changes in Railroad Rates and Service Quality Since 1990*, GAO/RCED-99-93 (Washington, DC: US Government Printing Office, April 16, 1999).

19. Here we use the term *deadweight* colloquially. In technical microeconomics, deadweight losses are the portion of consumer surpluses lost even to producers from pricing at other than the socially optimal point (the intersection of marginal revenue and marginal cost). More broadly, deadweight loss is a "reduction in net economic benefits resulting from an inefficient allocation of resources." (David Besanko and Ronald R. Braeutigam, *Microeconomics: An Integrated Approach* (New York: John Wiley & Sons, Inc., 2002), p. G-2.)

20. By one informed count, in the ten-year period between 1994, when rules for formulating railroad costing evidence were revised, and 2004, railroads had prevailed in five captive shipper cases and lost seven. In two of the seven cases in which rates were found unreasonably high, unit revenues were capped at the lowest rate the STB could prescribe under the law, 180 percent of variable costs. Information courtesy of Union Pacific Railroad, October 2004.

21. In fact, Maury Klein's recent book points out that the Carter administration's draft of the legislative proposal that became the Staggers Rail Act of 1980 had not included a maximum rate cap, but that President Carter brokered a compromise containing a ceiling on rates to captive shippers in order to secure final passage of the act before he left office. Maury Klein, *Union Pacific: The*

Reconfiguration: America's Greatest Railroad from 1969 to the Present (New York: Oxford University Press, 2011), p. 124.

22. Statement of Western Railroads, *Ex Parte No, 347 (Sub-No. 1)*, April 13, 1982, p. 6.

23. ICC, *Ex Parte 347 (Sub-No. 1), Coal Rate Guidelines—Nationwide.*

24. We saw this dilemma in Chapter 2, where the experts of the day (1900–1930) finally agreed that cost-based rates were extremely difficult to measure or to arrive at theoretically—forcing rate making back to a demand-based concept: value of service.

25. See Chapter 2. Utility economists often recommend Ramsey pricing, also known as inverse elasticity pricing, when marginal cost pricing does not permit revenues adequate to cover ongoing maintenance and reinvestment costs. (See Box 2.3 in Chapter 2.)

26. *Summary of Comments of Western Railroads*, p. 1. Specifically, what was "historic" was the notion that differential pricing might be a "useful tool" and might not founder on the long-established statutory and common law prohibitions against rate discrimination.

27. Staggers Act, Section 2, in *Summary of Comments of Western Railroads*, ibid., p. 2.

28. Ibid., pp. 2–5.

29. Verified Statement of William J. Baumol and Robert D. Willig, *Ex Parte No. 347 (Sub-No.1) Coal Rate Guidelines—Nationwide*, p. 47ff.

30. Verified Statement of Hugh L. Randall, *Ex Parte No. 347 (Sub-No.1)*, p. 11ff.

31. "Comments of Five Railroads" in *Ex Parte 347 (Sub-No.1)*, p. 49.

32. In railroad terminology, a foreign line is any connecting track or equipment owner (or in this case, an operator) not under control of the subject carrier, known as the home road.

33. Recall the similarity of this circumstance to the issue of a public taking and constitutional levels of compensation that might be made under the Tucker Act, as described in Chapter 7.

34. Besanko and Braeutigam, *Microeconomics*, p. G-7, define stand-alone cost as "[t]he cost of producing a good in a single-product firm." A related concept is economies of scope. If the summed costs of producing two comparable but different products in one firm are less than the stand-alone costs of producing the two products in separate single product firms (say one unit of product [a] in plant A, and one unit of the other product [b] in plant B), the two-product firm would be said to exhibit economies of scope. This example shows the counterintuitive possibility that variety might be more efficient than specialization. p. 331.]

35. *Comments of Five Railroads* [Chessie System, Conrail, Family Lines, N&W, and Southern] in *Ex Parte 347 (Sub-No.1)*, April 13, 1982, pp. 25–26. Baumol and

Willig elsewhere declared that "so long as no shipper or group of shippers is paying more than the true replacement cost of the services they require, . . . that railroad cannot be said to be earning adequate revenues, and assuming all shippers are being charged in accordance with their demand for service, no shipper can be paying an unreasonable amount." Verified Statement of William J. Baumol and Robert D. Willig, *Ex Parte No. 347 (Sub-No.1) Coal Rate Guidelines—Nationwide*, pp. 4–5.

36. http://www.literature.org/authors/voltaire/candide/chapter-30.html

37. Some governmental agency such as the STB would have to decide which railroad services must be open to new competition, which provider would perform the service, how the provider would be qualified, what service windows must be maintained, and how much the tenant would have to pay the owner railroad in access/maintenance fees, etc.

38. STB conditions in the UP + SP merger extended the right of tenant BNSF to serve any newly constructed industry on the UP-owned trackage opened to BNSF as mitigation for loss of SP as a competitive carrier in the subject corridor.

39. Theodore Keeler, *Railroads, Freight, and Public Policy* (Washington, DC: Brookings Institution, 1983), Chapter 3, pp. 43–61, and citations therein.

40. There would seem to be an obvious way to prevent predatory pricing—simply require that any contract price offered to current participants in the market must remain available until the contract has expired.

41. Or the environmental equivalent, effluent taxes (unfortunately seen by some as a license to pollute).

42. One needs look no further than rail public transit to see the prototype for this outcome. Private capital went into transit systems in their early days. But the economic laws of natural monopoly drove rates to extremely low and undifferentiated levels, and all profitability evaporated ages ago. To preserve service, public authorities were required to purchase and subsidize transit operations, and almost none remain in the private sector. Low transit fares may yield the socially optimum level of output (some economists even recommend free transit to maximize public benefits), but transit system deficits are endemic and virtually all capital improvements are publicly financed.

43. By this same logic, most highway users would be better off if congestion tolls were implemented to break up congestion and provide a source of funding for reducing the bottlenecks in the highway segments of interest, but doing so is politically difficult.

10. How Railroads Got Their Final Sizes and Shapes

Epigraphs: Ernst R. Berndt, Ann F. Friedlaender, Judy Shaw-ER Wang Chiang, and Christopher Vellturo, "Cost Effects of Mergers and Deregulation in the

U.S. Rail Industry," *Journal of Productivity Analysis* 4 (1993), p. 124. (Used with permission.) The "traditional welfare trade-off" referred to is usually ascribed to Professor Oliver Williamson (see Chapter 6); we call it Williamson's Lemma.

1. Special thanks to James McClellan, Dale Salzman, John Rebensdorf, and Steven Ditmeyer, who read and commented extensively on drafts of this chapter. Our debt is large, and our thanks are sincere, but all errors are mine. The title of this chapter gives a nod to the informative and entertaining book by Mark Stein, now an educational television series, *How the States Got their Shapes*, HarperCollins Publishers, 2008.—REG

2. The 4R Act of 1976 contained a Title IV on rail mergers. It encouraged the secretary of transportation to assist in coordinating operations and facilities of two or more carriers, and listed nine types of studies the secretary should carry out with respect to proposed mergers. The act set time limits for various parts of the ICC's merger procedure and reaffirmed the commission's power to approve, disapprove, or condition a merger in the public interest. As described in Chapter 9, the 4R Act contained numerous rate regulatory reforms, and with the arrival of Darius Gaskins as President Carter's appointed chair of the ICC, administrative deregulation also became significant.

3. Burlington Northern Inc. and Burlington Northern Railroad Company— Control and Merger—Santa Fe Pacific Corporation and The Atchison, Topeka & Santa Fe Railway Company, Request for Conditions and Comments submitted on behalf of Oklahoma Gas and Electric Company, Presentation of Evidence and Argument, Finance Docket 32549, 1995, p. 12.

4. The finding that cost savings might not be readily achieved was also a key result of the larger and more complex consolidations of the midcentury merger wave, as we documented in Chapter 6, but those lessons were more obscure. Penn Central could not be so easily ignored.

5. Indeed, former NS senior vice president James McClellan points out that "reaching new markets with single-line service has always been a powerful force. Why else would the New York Central and the Pennsylvania Railroad have acquired all of those lines in the Midwest?" Personal communication, November 24, 2012.

6. C. A. Vellturo, E. R. Berndt, Ann Friedlaender, et al., "Deregulation, Mergers, and Cost Savings in Class I U.S. Railroads, 1974–1986," *Journal of Economics and Management Strategy* 1, pp. 339–369.

7. It was also true that the ICC was unable, for over a decade, to reach a definitive conclusion to Union Pacific's proposal to acquire Rock Island and sell portions to the Southern Pacific. By the time the transaction was finally approved in 1974, Rock Island had seriously deteriorated, and UP had lost interest. This was a major black eye for the ICC, and, like Penn Central, had the effect of discouraging other complex merger proposals.

8. SP's subsidiary railroad, the St. Louis Southwestern (Cotton Belt), served Texas and reached St. Louis from the southwest via Corsicana, Texas (near Dallas), and Pine Bluff, Arkansas. Cotton Belt/Southern Pacific tied in with the Los Angeles–New Orleans Sunset Route at Flatonia, Texas, a point half-way between San Antonio and Houston. See Map 10.5, which was drawn for a different purpose but indicates the Tucumcari/Golden State line to St. Louis via Kansas City, and the Cotton Belt route via Corsicana and Texarkana.

9. Calculated from mileage segments shown in Rand McNally's *Handy Railroad Atlas of the United States*, 1973.

10. In the early 1960s, investor Henry Crown prompted merger talks for Rock Island with Southern Pacific, but Union Pacific "sought to diffuse or completely block this effort with a counterproposal in 1962 that the Rock Island be split between SP and UP." Bill Fahrenwald, "Chicago, Rock Island & Pacific Railroad (Rock Island)" in William D. Middleton, George M. Smerk, and Roberta Diehl, *eds.*, *Encyclopedia of North American Railroads* (Bloomington: Indiana University Press, 2007) p. 229. The ICC had great difficulty handling the complexity of the case, somewhat addressed by a proposal prepared by its administrative law judge, Nathan Klitenic, for a four-system plan dividing key Rock Island segments among Union Pacific (Chicago–Omaha), Southern Pacific (Kansas City–Tucumcari), and Santa Fe (Memphis–Amarillo), and offering D&RGW an option to purchase Denver–Kansas City). http://en.wikipedia.org/wiki/Chicago _Rock_Island_and_Pacific_Railroad#The_UP-RI_merger_case. Accessed December 28, 2012.

11. DOT's *Western Railroad Mergers* report (1969). U.S. Department of Transportation, *Western Railroad Mergers*, A staff study of the Office of the Secretary and the Federal Railroad Administration (Washington, DC: Government Printing Office, 1969), and the *Klitenic Plan* (1974). See Maury Klein, *Union Pacific: The Reconfiguration: America's Greatest Railroad from 1969 to the Present* (New York: Oxford University Press, 2011)] were two such efforts.

12. Richard Saunders Jr., *Main Lines: Rebirth of the North American Railroads, 1970–2002*, DeKalb: Northern Illinois University Press, 2003, p. 156. SP did its own share of weeding out, sending its most profitable traffic via Cotton Belt and leaving lower-profit traffic on the joint Rock Island line.

13. SP and other railroads would have liked to acquire the Milwaukee Road's line from Kansas City to Chicago, but that would have been anathema to C&NW, and the idea died.

14. Namely, combination of the Great Northern (GN), Northern Pacific (NP), and Burlington Route (CB&Q), plus Spokane, Portland & Seattle (SP&S).

15. These included the Chicago Great Western and Minneapolis & St. Louis railways.

16. Frisco's earlier history, including its transcontinental aspirations and relationship to Santa Fe predecessor Atlantic & Pacific—and its principal, future US presidential candidate John C. Fremont—is told by H. Craig Miner in *The St. Louis—San Francisco: Transcontinental Railroad* (Lawrence: University Press of Kansas, 1972). In a memorable phrase (citing Allan Nevins), Miner calls Fremont "one of those most frustrating of historical figures, the almost-great man."

17. Interstate Commerce Commission, *Burlington Northern, Inc.—Control and Merger—St. Louis–San Francisco Railway Company*, Finance Docket No. 28583 (Sub-No 1F), served April 17, 1980, p. 816.

18. Ibid., p. 962.

19. A good example of Frisco benefits to BN was the Avard connection, visible in Map 10.6. Historically, the route via Avard, Oklahoma, was the primary path for Southeast (Memphis) and St. Louis to West Coast traffic moving over Santa Fe; it provided a shortcut compromise (compared with Texas or Kansas City interchange) for trains moving east/west and to/from Southern California over the Santa Fe's L.A.–Chicago Transcon route. The Avard connection involved diversion to Frisco from AT&SF's Amarillo–Kansas City mainline at Avard, then following Frisco lines east and northeast via Tulsa before continuing to St. Louis or turning southeast at Frisco's operational headquarters city of Springfield, Missouri, to reach the Memphis gateway. This historic interchange route gained importance after BN and Santa Fe merged in 1995. Also, NS encouraged BNSF to favor Memphis over St. Louis for routing transcontinental interchange traffic to the Southeast, and that meant using the Avard connection.

20. Coauthor Gallamore testified on behalf of the Department of Transportation against the joint N&W-Chessie plan to control DT&I, arguing Ironton could survive independently as a friendly connection for Conrail and GTW.

21. George H. Drury, "Detroit, Toledo & Ironton Railroad," Middleton, *Encyclopedia*, p. 360.

22. Saunders, *Main Lines*, p. 148.

23. Ibid., pp. 148–149. The discouragement of SP's designs on Family Lines (and eventual withdrawal from the chase to acquire it) may have been a factor in SP's proposal to acquire the Tucumcari line (see above). CSX Corporation was founded as a holding company for Family Lines and Chessie System in November 1980. http://en.wikipedia.org/wiki/Seaboard_Coast_Line_Railroad. Accessed December 16, 2012. See also J. David Ingles "Merger Family Trees," *TRAINS* 59, no. 3 (March 1999), p. 68ff., and http://trn.trains.com/Railroad%20 Reference/Railroad%20History/2006/06/CSX%20merger%20family%20tree .aspx. Accessed December 16, 2012.

24. Richard Saunders observed, correctly, "Mergers seemed to go easier in the South than elsewhere, mostly as a result of good luck." Richard Saunders Jr.,

Merging Lines: American Railroads, 1900–1970 (DeKalb: Northern Illinois University Press, 2001), p. 275.

25. James W. McClellan, TRB Deen Lecture, January 2011.

26. Saunders, *Main Lines*, pp. 228–229, and quoting Phillips in *Trains Magazine*, Vol. 43, No. 1 (January 1983), p. 6.

27. The passenger operation was taken over by Amtrak in 1971 and so did not figure in the NS merger negotiations.

28. USRA's designations of routes beyond Cincinnati to NS predecessors helped even the competition vis-à-vis CSX; recall that CSX predecessor L&N had been granted approval by the ICC earlier to acquire and merge two separate routes from the Ohio River to Chicago.

29. James B. Burns, *Railroad Mergers and the Language of Unification* (Westport, CT: Quorum Books, 1998), p. 92.

30. Ibid.

31. Western Pacific was an upstart. Its lines connecting Salt Lake City to the San Francisco Bay at Oakland were begun in 1903 and not completed until 1909. It was a longer alternative to Southern Pacific and originated much less on-line traffic.

32. Union Pacific *INFOmagazine*, p. 16.

33. Ibid.

34. Ibid., p. 17. Mr. Kenefick loved to collect and point out his colleagues' malapropisms, and this imperfect historical allusion may have counted as one.

35. Gus Welty, "UP/MP/WP: A Whole Greater Than the Sum of Its Parts," *Railway Age* (April 27, 1981), pp. 20–26.

36. After the Harriman UP-SP combination was broken up for antitrust reasons, the Justice Department next went after the SP-CP combination. The decision was that SP-CP would have to be split. Because of the additional authority the Transportation Act of 1920 gave the ICC in mergers, however, the SP came up with the Ogden Gateway Agreement as a means to counter the antitrust arguments. The ICC approved the conditions in the 1920s and SP-CP was allowed to stand.

37. Union Pacific's "Brief to the ICC" featured an analysis by Richard J. Barber Associates of the single-line pricing advantages of motor carrier competition (this at a time when trucking economics were not very well understood by either railroads or the commission). "Railroads can never fully achieve the operating flexibility of motor carriers. But the present consolidations will expand the single-system control of operations, service, and pricing that has been a hallmark of motor carriers' success." *Union Pacific, Initial Brief of Primary Applicants, Vol. II—Argument and Analysis,* Before the Interstate Commerce Commission, Finance Docket 30000, March 8, 1982, p. II–56.

38. Regarding formation of the Rio Grande + SP central transcontinental route, note the importance of the ICC order that UP + MP + WP give DRG&W trackage rights on MP from Pueblo, Colorado, to Kansas City because of the loss of Missouri Pacific as an independent connection at Pueblo. *Finance Docket* No. 30000 (Sub-No. 16) St. Louis Southwestern Railway Company- Trackage Rights Over Missouri *Pacific* Railroad Company-Kansas City To St. Louis Decided November 13, 1991. (Cited below as ICC *Decision*), p. 552.

39. "The Pacrail Decision: New Ground Rules for Mergers?" *Railway Age* (November 29, 1982), p. 10.

40. Welty, "UP/MP/WP," pp. 24–25.

41. ICC *Decision*, p. 648.

42. SP with the Tucumcari Line, and AT&SF, with joint acquisition (with PRR) of the Toledo, Peoria & Western (TP&W) (1960). AT&SF later acquired the remaining share of ownership from PRR (1979). Of these, Tucumcari was far more important.

43. An exception is an early link of predecessor lines of the Santa Fe and SP at Deming, New Mexico—the second transcontinental line. This was before AT&SF completed its own route to California via Flagstaff, Arizona, and before SP completed its eastbound construction to El Paso and beyond. The connection only lasted until each of the two major railroads had completed their own lines, but it did exist.

44. Russell W. Pittman, "Railroads and Competition: The Santa Fe/Southern Pacific Merger Proposal," *Journal of Industrial Economics* XXXIX, no. 1 (September 1990), p. 25 ff.

45. Brian Solomon, *Burlington Northern Santa Fe Railway* (St. Paul, MN: MBI, 2005), p. 218. SP didnít get around to repainting its units for a number of years6- some not until after the UP merger in 1996.

46. Katy properties in Houston were recycled to build a new freeway carrying its name. Already congested, Houston's Katy Highway corridor holds some prospect of eventually supporting new commuter or higher-speed passenger rail service, as do the MoPac/M-K-T lines from Georgetown, Texas, north of Austin to San Antonio via San Marcos and New Braunfels.

47. Earlier, SP had petitioned the ICC and won trackage rights to St. Louis over MoPac's lines, which were much more adequate than the Rock Island trackage via Eldon, Missouri. These ostensibly were to mitigate negative impacts on Rock Island from the UP + MP + WP merger, rather any impacts on SP, which wasn't even in the picture until its purchase of the Tucumcari Line. It was a "make-up" call by the ICC, which belatedly realized the Rock Island line via Eldon was not a viable route in transcontinental competition. The rights were still troublesome, however, as MoPac's "River Sub" was prone to flooding, and excessive rail wear was an ongoing problem.

48. http://www.nps.gov/cali/parkmgmt/images/4TrailsFS_Newsletter_Map _030811.jpg. Accessed December 22, 2012. South Pass was a better route for wagons and horseback because drinking water was to be found along the trails. UP's original transcontinental route instead crossed Wyoming's Great Divide Basin (more than 100 miles between Rawlins and Rock Springs along the route of present-day I-80), which was possible by steam train but forbidding to people and domesticated animals on foot. Union Pacific moves huge quantities of PRB coal today because its 1990s merger partner had sought (but did not build) a westward mountain passage more than a century earlier. In such fragile and remarkable ways are geography, history, and transport economics forever linked.

49. Andy Cummings, "Mileposts Along the Iron Highway," *Trains Magazine*, Vol. 70, No. 11, p. 64.

50. H. Roger Grant, *The North Western: A History of the Chicago & North Western Railway System* (DeKalb: Northern Illinois University Press, 1996), p. 224.

51. Robert E. Gallamore, "Regulation and Innovation: Lessons from the American Railroad Industry," in José Gómez-Ibáñez et al., *Essays in Transportation Economics and Policy: A Handbook in Honor of John R. Meyer* (Washington, DC: Brookings Institution, 1999).

52. Wall Street industry analyst Anthony (Tony) Hatch has popularized this moniker. See also Christian Wolmar, *The Great Railroad Revolution* (Kindle 2012), especially Chapter 12, "Renaissance Without Passengers."

53. As of 1990, the US railroad industry consisted of seven large firms, of which three exceeded $6 billion in market capitalization. Frank N. Wilner, *Railroad Mergers: History, Analysis, Insight* (Omaha, NE: Simmons-Boardman Books, Inc., 1997), p. 224.

54. The Herfindahl index of industry concentration, calculated on the basis of revenue ton-miles for the Class I US railroads in 2009, reached about 0.28—a value indicating fairly high industry concentration.

$$H = \sum_{i=1}^{N} s_i^2$$

Herfindahl index formula: where s_i is the market share of firm i in the market, and N is the number of firms. Thus, in a market with two firms that each have a 50 percent market share, the Herfindahl index equals $0.50^2 + 0.50^2 = .5$ (in layman's language, it is half as concentrated as it might be). An alternative calculation moves the decimal point two places to the right, in our case yielding an index of 280 and suggesting the case would be investigated by the Department of Justice's Antitrust Division.

Note that the Herfindahl index is an industry-wide share calculation, not a true reflection of competitive realities in actual markets. In a city pair like Chicago–Kansas City, rail share looks quite concentrated, but overall transportation competition may be vigorous because of truck and even barge alternatives, as well as rail-rail competition. http://en.wikipedia.org/wiki /Herfindahl_index. Accessed December 7, 2013.

55. Wilner, *Railroad Mergers*, 1997, p. 298.

56. Steven Lipin and Daniel Machalaba, "Union Pacific Quits Battle for Santa Fe— Move Follows Court Ruling and Clears the Way for Burlington's Offer." *Wall Street Journal*, February 1, 1995, p. A3.

57. Steven Lipin, "Union Pacific Makes a Very '90s Decision: Company Walks Away from Santa Fe Bidding War," *Wall Street Journal*, February 6, 1995, p. A7.

58. Burns, *Railroad Mergers and the Language of Unification*, p. 164.

59. An example from the filings was the nineteen hours (43 percent) to be realized on Chicago-Tulsa traffic—admittedly a minor market.

60. Michael Conant, *Railroad Bankruptcies and Mergers from Chicago West— 1975–2001* (Amsterdam: Elsevier, 2004), p. 110.

61. Conant, *Railroad Bankruptcies and Mergers*, p. 38.

62. See Klein, *Union Pacific*, Chapters 24–28 for extensive detail on how UP + SP came together and experienced the challenge of merger integration.

63. Western Pacific, acquired quite inexpensively, made the Bay Area connection for UP, of course; it was a useful outlet for considerable auto, grain, and intermodal traffic, but it was longer and slower than SP's Donner Pass route.

64. Jim McClellan, again in a private communication, explains how NS had studied acquisition of SP several times but was frightened off by the accumulated deferred maintenance. UP knew about SP's deteriorating condition, but perhaps not the full extent of the problem nor the degree to which it could undermine postmerger startup operations. In any event, UP top executives conveniently stepped around this hazard in their desire to offset the BN + AT&SF consolidation with a merger of its own.

65. Burns, *Railroad Mergers and the Language of Unification*, pp. 109, 165.

66. John E. Kwoka Jr. and Lawrence J. White, *Manifest Destiny? The Union Pacific– Southern Pacific Merger*, October 31, 1997, p. 14. http://www.stern.nyu.edu/clb /98–012.pdf

67. Ibid., p. 7, 11.

68. Ibid., p. 6.

69. "One especially skeptical critic estimated that, after all of these adjustments were made, the applicants' claimed cost savings of $750 million per year might actually be as little as $73 million annually (Christensen, 1996)," as cited by Kwoka and White, *Manifest Destiny*, 1997.

70. Conant), *Railroad Bankruptcies and Mergers*, p. 123.

71. See the case study prepared for the Kellogg School of Management by Robert Gallamore, Patrick Lortie, and Jason Maga, *Trouble with Trains: How the Union*

Pacificó Southern Pacific Merger Went Awry, Kellogg School of Management, Northwestern University, Case 5–205–252, 2005. See also Richard Saunders, *Main Lines,* pp. 329–336, and Kwoka and White, *Manifest Destiny,* 1997, p. 14.

72. The story is told that CEO Richard Davidson wanted all of the merger benefits in twelve months, forcing the operating department to scramble and perhaps take some ill-advised shortcuts. Insiders do not blame the computer systems, however, and say that in fact implementation of UP's TCS in Texas (see Chapter 12) was one reason service was restored relatively quickly after the well-publicized service interruptions. Apparently STB took note of this development.

73. Kwoka and White, *Manifest Destiny,* p. 30.

74. http://www.unt.edu/cedr/UPReport.1998.pdf

75. Jim McClellan reminds us that the "two railroads rule" got its start in the FRA's "Orange Line" report of the early 1970s (see Chapter 14), which he views "as a seminal work in terms of defining the future shape of the railroad industry— facilitate two major systems, streamline networks, shed the rest. Ideas do matter, don't they?" Coauthor Gallamore agrees, but points to the DOT/FRA staff report *Western Railroad Mergers* (1969) as an even earlier precedent for mapping out rationalized two-carrier competitive systems. It was at least implicitly critical of the Penn Central and Burlington Northern mergers, offering alternative resolutions for other pending western merger cases.

76. Saunders, *Main Lines,* p. 336. It is perhaps noteworthy that while Roseville (now Davis) Yard was being reconstructed, earth-moving machinery struck and detonated a 500-pound bomb left over from a Vietnam War–era derailment of military ordinance that in the "clean-up of the derailment had been hastily covered; re-construction of the yard was stopped to search for other bombs; several were found and safely detonated." Speaking of metaphors, this episode epitomized what was wrong with the Southern Pacific in its pre-UP merger days— ever a "mine-field" for the acquiring UP and for the public: Whatever could go wrong, did.

77. Pamela Berkman, ed., *The History of the Atchison, Topeka & Santa Fe* (Greenwich, CT: Bonanza, 1988), p. 100.

78. The BNSF merger had in actuality raised at least as many competitive issues as UP + SP had, but these were far less widely publicized—perhaps in part because UP played the hostile acquisition card rather than fighting BNSF on anticompetitive grounds and seeking trackage rights as mitigation. SP was more successful in this pursuit, winning rights on the Chicago—Kansas City–Hutchinson, Kansas, section of AT&SF's transcontinental route.

79. Much will depend on how coal fares as a utility fuel in coming years, whether international trade over West Coast ports continues healthy expansion or not, and how domestic containerization continues to compete against truckload trucking in the future.

80. James W. McClellan, *Railroads and the New Normal: Impact of Lean and Green on Their Future*, 2011 Thomas Deen Distinguished Lecture, Annual Meeting of the Transportation Research Board, January 23, 2011. TRB Paper Number 11–0001, p. 6.

81. Wilner, *Railroad Mergers*, p. 312.

82. Burns, *Railroad Mergers and the Language of Unification*, p. 162.

83. These percentage shares were calculated after substantial amounts of Conrail service were incorporated into the three shared assets regions where NS and CSX have joint competitive access to shippers and receivers. The shared assets territories were important to the development of the financial division between CSX and NS as well as broader competitive factors. According to Jim McClellan, these difficult multibillion-dollar decisions were based on comparability of routes and projected revenues for CSX and NS, using traffic diversion models applied differently to closed and open gateways as far away as St. Louis.

84. Rush Loving, Jr., *The Men Who Loved Trains* (Bloomington: Indiana University Press, 2006), p. 322–332. Loving's may be the definitive history of the Conrail split.

85. http://www.stb.dot.gov/newsrels.nsf/5d1dee75e438b18b852565320069d8f7/8456 ee368527a3af8525661d00708300. Accessed October 12, 2012.

86. Ibid.

87. http://www.dot.gov/affairs/crbrief.htm

88. http://www.dot.gov/affairs/1998/dot13998.htm

89. Michael Blaszak, "CN, BNSF Seek to Combine; Timing Curious." *TRAINS*, Vol. 60, No. 3 (March 2000), pp. 16–18.

90. CN acquired Illinois Central in 1998; (new) Wisconsin Central in 2001; and Elgin, Joliet & Eastern in 2009. Canadian Pacific purchased Dakota, Minnesota & Eastern (DM&E) and its Iowa, Chicago & Eastern (ICE) unit in 2008. See *Trains Magazine*, Vol. 70, No. 11 (November 2010), pp. 55–57, for clarification of these "family tree" merger relationships. (Trains research by J. David Ingles, Bill Metzger, and Matt Van Hattem).

91. Anthony DePalma, "All Aboard for a Big Rail Deal? Shippers and Farmers Question Merger Plans of U.S.–Canada Lines." *New York Times*, February 22, 2000, pp. C1 and C6.

92. Don Phillips, "BNSF–CN: Is the Last Act Beginning?" *TRAINS* 60, no. 4 (April 2000), pp. 12–13.

93. Daniel Machalaba, "Big Rail Merger Plan Could Lead to More—Rivals Watch Move by Burlington, Canadian National." *Wall Street Journal*, March 7, 2000, p. A2.

94. Kevin P. Keefe, "Let's Get Some Questions Answered," *TRAINS* 60, no. 4 (April 2000), p. 6.

95. Phillips, "BNSF–CN," pp. 12–13.

96. Michael W. Blaszak, "STB Slams on the Brakes on Mergers." *TRAINS* 60, no. 6 (June 2000), pp. 16–17.

97. Ibid.

98. Michael W. Blaszak, "Stymied: *BNSF, CN* Won't Fight On." *TRAINS* 60, no 10 (October 2000), pp. 18–19.

99. Ibid.

100. Ibid.

101. STB, "Major Rail Consolidation Procedures, June 11, 2001." http://www.stb.dot .gov/boundvolumes5.nsf/b466c97893ec3be08525680b006041bd/71db6901b74c cfa385257085006d4711/$FILE/vol5-31.pdf

102. Vellturo, Berndt, Friedlaender, et al., "Deregulation, Mergers, and Cost Savings," pp. 339–369.

103. James W. McClellan, personal communication, December 28, 2010. Jim McClellan went on to say that "reach" is different for railroads than for trucks and airlines, which have more flexibility in deciding what markets to serve. "We used to say at NS that from Hagerstown you can see the lights of New York City, but there was no way of getting there." When a marketing officer noted that New York "was a great market," the CEO responded, "so is Hong Kong, but we don't go there either." The "great game," says our friend McClellan, "is to use bundled bidding as a competitive weapon—it really is all about connecting the dots."

104. Of course, service to so-called captive power plants remains an issue for maximum rate regulation. See Chapter 9.

105. Among many other developments that have had substantial impacts on operating costs: (1) track lubrication and profiling to extend rail life, (2) record fuel prices, (3) outsourcing of many clerical functions, and (4) revival in the popularity of flat or mini-grade-gravity switching yards (a substitution of operating expenses for costly development of high hump-retarder switching yards). There are related implications for the industry's ongoing effort to gain sanction for Ramsey differential pricing strategies (see Chapter 2). These, after all, are efforts to recoup overhead and common costs when marginal cost pricing (without a Ramsey markup) fails to raise adequate revenues.

11. The Enduring Problem of Rail Passenger Service in the Amtrak Era

Epigraphs: Transportation Legislative Group, *Transportation Weekly*, vol. 3, no. 43 (September 3, 2002), p. 7. Used with permission. Louis S. Thompson, "New Rail Passenger Structures in the United States: Using Experience from the E.U., Japan and Latin America" (Toulouse, France: Institut d'Economie Industrielle and Northwestern Transportation Center, November 7–8, 2003). Used with permission.

1. USRA, *Preliminary System Plan*, Volume I, February 26, 1975, p. 26. As a memory aid, Amtrak's three goals, in the USRA formulation, were: (1) savings (in total costs), (2) service (to essential markets), and (3) severance (from freight railroads' common carrier obligations).

2. Coauthor John R. Meyer, jointly with Paul Cherington, his brother Charles Cherington, and Lewis M. Schneider, conducted a popular seminar on transportation economics and policy for Harvard graduates for a number of years. The seminar fed many young scholars into the field, as did Professor Healey's transportation program at Yale. Contributing to development of the DOT proposal, among many others, were Richard J. Barber, James W. McClellan, John Williams, David DeBoer, Louis Thompson, Thomas Tidd, Arrigo Mongini, Steven Ditmeyer, James Laurie, and Robert Gallamore.

3. The ICC resisted train-offs for a number of years. Under the new legislation, the states could keep a train from being discontinued by paying 50 percent of its solely related costs, plus associated capital costs.

4. The for-profit notion may have been a convenient fiction, but it may also have had some hortatory and salutary value as a fiscal constraint.

5. The financial ownership provisions were contained in Section 304 of the act; they are a bit complex and not very meaningful today. These and other aspects of Amtrak's establishment are summarized in Frank N. Wilner, *Amtrak: Past, Present, Future* (Omaha, NE: Simmons-Boardman Books, 2012).

6. The other two railroads declining to join NRPC were the Rock Island and the Georgia Railroad. Wilner, *Amtrak*, provides further detail on railroads' motivations for joining NRPC or not.

7. See timeline and map in National Railroad Passenger Corporation, *Amtrak, An American Story* (Washington, DC: , 2011).

8. Wilner, *Amtrak*, p. 23.

9. The most notorious of the experimental routes was the Blue Ridge, a train operated between Washington, DC, and West Virginia, presumably to curry favor with two West Virginia legislators: Senator Robert Byrd, who was the majority leader, and Congressman Harley Staggers, who chaired the House Committee on Interstate Commerce. Anthony Perl, *New Departures: Rethinking Rail Passenger Policy in the Twenty-First Century* (Lexington: University Press of Kentucky, 2000), p. 106. Politics also influenced the intermediate stops of the long-distance routes. For example, "Senators from Indiana had interested themselves in transportation policy, whereas Senators and Representatives from Ohio generally had not. Indianapolis was served by three Amtrak routes, but Cleveland initially by none at all." George W. Hilton, *Amtrak: The National Railway Passenger Corporation* (Washington, DC: American Enterprise Institute for Public Policy Research, 1980), p. 19.

10. Paraphrased from James W. McClellan, draft manuscript for a forthcoming memoir. Used with author's permission.

11. Ibid.

12. Frank Wilner, *Railroad Mergers: History, Analysis, Insight* (Omaha, NE: Simmons- Boardman, 1998), p. 36.

13. ". . . USRA recommends that the approach to be used in determining the compensation rendered is for the facility to be owned/controlled by the exclusive or dominant user, bearing the full costs; the secondary user should pay an appropriate charge for the use of the facilities. . . . [This] will contribute to the improvement of both passenger and freight services in the Region . . . [and] it fixes responsibility for passenger service with authorities whose whole concern is with the passenger." USRA, *Preliminary System Plan*, Volume I, February 26, 1975, p. 26.

14. These funds were to be matched in part by state, regional, and local transportation authorities, but this initiative never amounted to much. States outside the Northeast Corridor frequently assert that federal passenger rail policy has favored the NEC; that is probably true, but it follows from realistic assessments of passenger rail economic opportunities. The American federal system does not guarantee equal treatment to states or regions with respect to public works. Some regions benefit disproportionately in national parks or fighting wildfires, others in military contracts or installations, some in farm subsidies, others in highways or mass transit, some in inland waterways, and others in flood control and coastal protection. It is *realpolitik*—US style.

15. Acela trains were designed to tilt through curves for a more comfortable ride along the winding route from New Haven to Boston; unfortunately a design flaw meant the tilt mechanism did not work satisfactorily in a portion of Connecticut DOT territory and it has been locked out there. Acelas do tilt in the run from New Haven to Westerly, Rhode Island.

16. This was the same story as deregulation. In *Contrived Competition*, business historian Richard Vietor points out that "legislative reform of regulation occurred almost exclusively during the Carter years. Congress did nothing before 1977, and passed only three deregulatory laws after 1980" (one of which contributed greatly to the savings and loan fiasco of the 1980s). Richard H. K. Vietor, *Contrived Competition: Regulation and Deregulation in America* (Cambridge, MA: Belknap Press of Harvard University Press, 1994), p. 15.

17. Neal R. Peirce, "Push to Derail Amtrak Oversimplifies the Choice," *National Journal*, May 11, 1985.

18. Donald M. Itzkoff, *Off the Track: The Decline of the Intercity Passenger Train in the United States* (Westport, CT: Greenwood Press, 1985), p. 117.

19. Amtrak's labor protective conditions history is complex. The original act establishing the NRPC required protection equivalent to that for mergers under the

Interstate Commerce Act; that act also asked the secretary of labor to certify a level of protection "fair and equitable" to affected employees, which was then set at six years' pay, or 50 percent more than freight railroad or transit workers normally received. Later, the 4R Act of 1976 explicitly linked freight (and transit) labor protection to the Amtrak level of four years' to six years' pay—as set in the ICC's ruling in *New York Dock Railway—Control—Brooklyn Eastern District*, 360 I.C.C. 60 (1979). http://dwp.bigplanet.com/johnl123 /raillaborprotectivecontitions/. Accessed August 30, 2012. See also the GAO's summary at http://www.gao.gov/assets/200/198650.pdf. (accessed July 4, 2013) with respect to the total costs of labor protective conditions in the event of liquidation of Amtrak, which concludes that labor could not settle for less than the statutorily specified four year minimum.

20. Only four at-grade crossings remain in the Northeast Corridor, all north of New York City, and all because of the insistence of local elected officials.

21. In the United States, speeds up to 125 miles per hour were sometimes possible by upgrading tracks and signals, although it was preferable to separate high-speed operations from all other service and to eliminate all grade crossings. For speeds over 125 miles per hour, new track and signal systems—straight and flat, and grade-separated—were needed. Maintenance costs for right-of-way and rolling stock, as well as operating costs, also increased nonlinearly with speed.

22. Each penny per gallon in the federal fuel tax raises over $1 billion in revenue each year. The federal fuel excise today is 18.4 cents per gallon for gasoline, and 24.4 cents for diesel fuel. The states also impose their own fuel excises taxes, which average about 30 cents per gallon, to raise additional funds for highway construction and maintenance. http://en.wikipedia.org/wiki/Fuel_taxes _in_the_United_States. Accessed January 27, 2013. For the history of the federal excise rates see: http//taxfoundation.org/article/federal-gasoline-excise-tax -rate-1932–2008 (accessed January 27, 2013); also US Congress, Congressional Budget Office, *Highway Assistance Programs: A Historical Perspective*, February 1978.

23. The ARC committee included two members appointed by the president, three by the Senate majority leader, two by the Senate minority leader, three by the speaker of the House, and one ex officio.

24. Mark Murray, "All Aboard the Profit Limited," *National Journal*, March 18, 2000. Leasing rights for fiber optic cable along the Northeast Corridor, and sale of development rights near Penn Station, New York City, are the best examples of Amtrak's successful self-help measures (actions to enhance revenues with other than passenger train services).

25. Warrington's successor, David Gunn—a no-nonsense railroader at heart—sensibly ended the flight of fantasy that was Amtrak's express operation soon after arriving on the property.

26. Emilie Feldman, *Amtrak in Crisis*, Cambridge: Kennedy School of Government, Harvard University; a case prepared for Professors Gómez-Ibáñez and Meyer, 2003. (Mimeo in files of the authors), pp. 13–15.

27. Section 402 of the National Railroad Passenger Services Act contemplated that Amtrak would contract with railroads or regional transportation agencies to use their tracks and facilities for operation of intercity passenger trains. Legislation authorizes Amtrak to pay its host railroads a fee described as incremental costs of its operations—comparable perhaps to what freight railroads pay each other when operating on a foreign line under trackage rights. The fee covers the right of access, the use of specific slot occupied, the additional maintenance costs imposed by Amtrak operations, and other miscellaneous expenses. In the event Amtrak and these entities fail to agree on fees for service, the matter may go to the ICC (now STB), which has authority to fix "just and reasonable" compensation—considering quality of service as a major factor in determining payment in excess of incremental costs. The law explicitly allows Amtrak to establish additional incentive payments for meeting established service standards and to deduct penalties from the fees it owes railroads if they do not meet the standards.

28. Perhaps an improvement on the ARC's reform proposals were the strategic reform initiatives advanced under Amtrak chair David Laney in 2005. These proposals suggested increased investment by states and private industry in passenger rail, and a "federal matching grant program comparable to those historically available for the development of highway, aviation, and transit systems." National Railroad Passenger Corporation, *Rebuilding America's Passenger Rail System* (Washington, DC: , 2005), p. iii.

29. See Louis S. Thompson, "New Rail Passenger Structures in the United States: Using Experience from the E.U., Japan and Latin America," Toulouse, France: Institut d'Economie Industrielle and Northwestern Transportation Center, November 7–8, 2003, p. 9ff. for a brief summary of comprehensive proposals for restructuring Amtrak.

30. Warrington's use of capital funds to cover operating deficits (part of his strategy for a so-called "glide-path" to financial sustainability which would gradually increase ridership and reduce public subsidies) was reminiscent of the kind of bookkeeping chicanery that got WorldCom executives indicted.

31. Again, with the exception of Kalamazoo, Michigan, to Porter, Indiana.

32. Take the matter of railroad excess capacity three decades ago—as contrasted with today's congestion delays and expenses associated with capacity expansion. The opportunity cost of hosting Amtrak on the Southern Pacific's Sunset Route in 1975 (plenty of excess capacity then) is nothing compared with what it is today, as Union Pacific struggles to handle train after train of double-stack

intermodal business, while investing heavily in double-tracking, rebuilding, and resignaling much of the line.

33. W. Bruce Allen, professor of public policy and administration and transportation, University of Pennsylvania, in an introductory message from him as the new editor-in-chief of *Transportation Quarterly* 56, no. 3 (Summer 2002), pp. 5 and 6.

34. In this context it is noteworthy that President Obama, in his State of the Union message in January 2011, called for a network of higher-speed rail corridor services accessible to 80 percent of the American people. That was perhaps the most concrete expression of a proposed national policy for passenger train development in modern times.

35. Randolph R. Resor, "Should *Amtrak* Survive as a National System," *Transportation Quarterly*, Vol. 53, No. 1 (Winter, 1999), p. 104. Resor (who unfortunately passed away as this book is being completed) says that the largest part of Amtrak ridership is on short-haul trains and that there is no "obvious and unique" transportation need for the long-distance trains making up the national network—they are the ones for which a better competitive alternative exists.

36. While the Virginia to Florida auto train operation might also be profitable, its solution will not be the same as that for the NEC because of the need for trackage rights over freight railroads; this could be accomplished independently of other Amtrak operations, however.

37. This figure includes Canadian National and Canadian Pacific.

38. A possibility of capacity limits arises because of growth in rail freight traffic (and consequent "soak-up" of available rail capacity) after deregulation, development of Powder River Basin (PRB) coal, and double-stack international intermodal service in the 1980s and 1990s. Annual ton-miles per mile of Class I track more than doubled in the United States in the first two decades after deregulation. Following seventy years or more of overcapacity in the industry, capacity bottlenecks were a possibility that was hardly discussed when Amtrak was proposed in 1970.

39. Amtrak argued, probably correctly, that it contributed more than its share of costs to the retirement system. At any rate, if Amtrak were to shut down, Amtrak employee annual contributions to the Railroad Retirement System of $400 million would cease and payments from the system to retired Amtrak employees would probably increase (because more Amtrak employees would choose early retirement).

40. Don Phillips, "The Road to Rescue," *Classic Trains* (Summer 2011), pp. 22–31. This article well describes and illustrates the story of US rail passenger service in the years prior to Amtrak's establishment and the circumstances of its creation.

12. *Advancing Technology for American Railroads*

1. National Academy of Sciences, National Research Council, Committee on Science and Technology in the Railroad Industry (Clarence H. Linder, Chair), *Science and Technology in the Railroad Industry* (Washington, DC: 1963), p. 11.

2. See Alfred D. Chandler, Jr., *The Railroads and the Beginnings of Modern Management*, in Harvard Business School Case 9-377-231 (Boston: Harvard Business School, 1977). See also Alfred D. Chandler, Jr., *The Railroads: The Nation's First Big Business* (New York: Harcourt, Brace & World, 1965), pp. 97–125, in which the venerable Harvard Business School professor provides commentary and readings.

3. A good example of technology improvement is the increasing capacity of freight cars. In the days of iron strap and wooden cars, or early steel cars, ratios of two tons of lading to one of tare weight were common. A reference in Robert Selph Henry's 1942 book cites US freight cars as having average capacity of 45 tons, with loads averaging 27 tons. [Robert Selph Henry, *This Fascinating Railroad Business*, Indianapolis: The Bobbs-Merrill Company, 1942, p. 246.]

   Assuming a train in 1900 of fifty cars, each with 16 tons of lading, the total train weight would be 800 tons, or only 7 percent of typical train tonnage a century later; it would take more than fourteen 1900 trains to carry what was hauled in one 2000 train. If the normal crew of a 1900 train consisted of five employees, and it took fourteen trains to haul the equivalent tonnage of a train in 2000 working with a two-person crew, each modern train and engine employee generated about thirty-five times the transport volume of his or her great-grandfather.

4. Paraphrased from Robert Gallamore, *Research to Enhance Rail Network Performance*, Conference Proceedings on the Web 3, Committee for Review of the Federal Railroad Administration's Research, Development, and Demonstration Programs, Transportation Research Board (Washington, DC, 2007), www.TRB .org., pp. 13–14. (Cited subsequently as Conference Proceedings on the Web 3.)

5. Containerization of freight lowered the costs of handling mixed cargoes, especially where a change in mode was involved, such as for an international shipment through a port. Expedited intermodal trains (domestic or international containers) typically have priority over mixed manifest (carload) trains, and usually avoid classification in switching yards en route. Double stacking of containers on intermodal trains means movement of more units of freight per dollar of train expense. See Marc Levinson, *The Box: How the Shipping Container Made the World Smaller and the World Economy Bigger* (Princeton, NJ: Princeton University Press, 2006).

6. Mary Brignano and Hax McCullough, *The Search for Safety: A History of Railroad Signals and the People Who Made Them* (Pittsburgh, PA: Commissioned

by Union Switch & Signal Division of American Standard Inc., Copyright by American Standard, Inc.,1981, ISBN 0-9606202-0-6), p. 94.

7. US Department of Transportation/Federal Railroad Administration, *A Prospectus for Change in the Freight Railroad Industry* (Washington, DC: October 1978), p. 39. Submitted in accordance with Sections 504 and 901 of the Rail Revitalization and Regulatory Reform Act of 1976. The prospectus gave as one reason for the decline of the railroad industry in the 1960s and 1970s the assessment that it was slow in adopting new technology. The earlier *Productivity Task Force Report* was more circumspect: "It is a widely held belief that whatever the problems and shortcomings of the railways, railroad technology is not one of them" [National Commission on Productivity and the Council of Economic Advisers, Task Force on Railroad Productivity (the Meyer Task Force), *Improving Railroad Productivity: Final Report of the Task Force on Railroad Productivity* (Washington, DC:, 1973), p. 282). Also on the same page: "It is widely felt that the pace of innovation in the 'soft' technology of railroading has been less impressive than the pace of innovation in its 'hardware.'" By the end of the twentieth century, however, the authors of this book came to a more nuanced future vision in which "the ancient efficiencies of low friction wheels on rails merge with twenty-first century 'smart' systems to create an entirely new level of transportation value added for shippers." Gallamore, "Regulation and Innovation" in José Gómez-Ibáñez, William Tye, and Clifford Winston, eds., *Essays in Transportation Economics and Policy: A Handbook in Honor of John R. Meyer* (Washington DC: Brookings Institution Press, 1999), p. 527.

8. Maury Klein, *Unfinished Business: The Railroad in American Life* (Hanover, NH: The University Press of New England, 1994), p. 144.

9. Earlier, the Prussian State Railways succeeded in pairing a diesel engine to a locomotive using direct drive. Direct drive is theoretically simple but mechanically complex and prone to breakdowns in a railroad environment. Electric traction motor drive has advantages similar to automatic transmission in an automobile{ smooth power transition without manual gear shifting.

10. MU operation is omnipresent in transit and modern heavy-haul freight practice. It relies on industry standardization around the twenty-seven-pin MU cable to transfer both electric power and control signals between locomotive units or individually powered cars in a transit or passenger rail train set. MUing locomotives (to use the gerund form common in the industry) enables right-sizing horsepower to train weight and length. The iconic A-B-A combination (with MUed A-unit locomotive noses pointed in opposite directions) became a favorite with passenger train fans in the postwar streamliner era.

11. It is noteworthy that there was about a three-decade lag from completion of dieselization to wide deployment of EOTDs and the Presidential Emergency Board (PEB) 219 findings in 1990 that permitted rationalization of freight train

crew consists. With respect to reduction of crew consists from five to two, die-selization's elimination of the need for the firefighter is clear, but that is only one of three implied redundant jobs. EOTDs meant crews weren't needed in the caboose to watch brake-pipe pressure. Also, tapered roller bearings and hot-box detectors reduced the need for crew members in the caboose to watch for burned-off journals in the train ahead. Likewise, diesel operations likely resulted in less frequent train break-in-twos, meaning there was less need for train crews to ride in a caboose at the end of a train to flag following trains and make repairs to broken couplers.

12. Franklin M. Reck, *The Dilworth Story* (New York: McGraw Hill, 1954), p. 71.

13. According to historical usage, steam locomotives were typically called engines, while individual diesel-electric locomotives are referred to as units. Electric locomotives are frequently referred to as motors, and transit system powered passenger cars are often called traction. Locomotives of all kinds displayed numbers for identification, usually following a standard classification system. Thus, the cover illustration for *American Railroads* features the Santa Fe No. 3266, a Mikado 2-8-2.

14. A governor is a commonly used mechanical device to self-regulate the max-imum speed of an engine's operation at given settings, usually employing cen-trifugal motion to adjust fuel intake.

15. Quoted by Thomas Hoback in "Unit Trains," William D. Middleton, George M. Smerk, and Roberta Diehl, eds., *Encyclopedia of North American Railroads* (Bloomington: Indiana University Press, 2007), p. 1070.

16. Robert Selph Henry, *This Fascinating Railroad Business* (New York: Bobbs-Merrill, 1942–1943), pp. 75–76.

17. Cecil J. Allen, *Modern Railways: Their Engineering, Equipment & Operation* (London: Faber and Faber, 1959), p. 221.

18. Brignano & McCullough, *The Search for Safety*, p. 179.

19. Robert Gallamore, "Regulation and Innovation: Lessons from the American Railroad Industry," in José Gómez-Ibáñez et al., eds., *Essays in Transportation Economics and Policy: A Handbook in Honor of John R. Meyer* (Washington, DC: Brookings Institution, 1999), p. 513.

20. Such an incident occurred in India in July 2011, with the loss of dozens of lives.

21. Department of Commerce, *Historical Statistics*, p. 430.

22. Reilly McCarren, *Heavy Axle Loads on Short Lines and Regional Railroads*, Presentation at the Sandhouse Gang, Northwestern University Transportation Center, February 13, 2006. See also *Ronald R. Newman, Allan M. Zarembski*, and Randolph R. Resor, "Economic Implications of *Heavy Axle Loads* on Equipment Design, Operations, and Maintenance," American Society of Mechanical Engineers, Rail Transportation Division, Volume 4, 1991. This

study was the first published on the subject, and it won the American Society of Mechanical Engineers' (ASME's) best paper award in 1991. It used data from BN, TTC and Australia, but not short lines.

23. TTC presentation on HAL to Michigan State's Railway Management Program, September 2012.

24. Hoppers unload through chutes in the car bottom; in contrast, each gondola typically has a rotating coupler enabling a paired set (two cars joined at the nonrotating end) to be turned upside down for unloading.

25. As an analogy, the US navy now has fewer warships, but far more naval power, than it did in World War I.

26. Think of the New York Central's Twentieth Century Limited, the setting of Ayn Rand's *Fountainhead* and *Atlas Shrugged*, public art and architecture of the Great Depression, symbolic monuments at the New York World's Fair of 1939, aircraft and airports of the 1930s, or Hollywood icons and roadside diners lasting to this day.

27. Kevin J. Holland, "Streamlining Arrives," in Middleton et al., *Encyclopedia*, p. 830. *American Railroads* develops the narrative of passenger train streamlining in more detail in Chapter 6. Landmark developments in Amtrak-era passenger rolling stock include Budd Co. Metroliners (1968), Budd Co. Amfleet coaches (1974), Pullman-Standard's bilevel coaches and sleepers (introduced in the late 1970s), and Bombardier-Alstom Acela train sets (2000).

28. J. Parker Lamb, "The AC Revolution," in Middleton, et al., *Encyclopedia*, pp. 379–382.

29. Paul MacAvoy and James Sloss, *Regulation of Transport Innovation, the ICC and Unit Coal Trains to the Eastern Seaboard* (New York: Random House series in industrial economics, 1967).

30. Dennis S. Nordin, "Agricultural Development," in Middleton et al., *Encyclopedia*, pp. 103–106.

31. Ibid.

32. S. Kip Farrington, *Railroading from the Head End* (Garden City, NY: Doubleday, Doran & Co. 1943), pp. 212–213.

33. While railroads were fortunate to have the continuing flow of external inventions and innovations, it would be unwise of them to assume that they would always be able to find what they need on the outside and that therefore internal industry R&D is unnecessary, which it manifestly is not. Indeed, internal R&D, while subject to uncertainty, probably has a higher internal rate of return than other physical investments. See Conference Proceedings on the Web 3.

34. Brian Solomon, *Railroad Signaling* (St. Paul, MN: MBI Publishing, 2003), pp. 111–114. Verbal movement authorities delivered by radio in the United States use formal rules spelled out in one of several governing systems, such as direct

traffic control (DTC), track warrant control (TWC), or the Form D control system (DCS). DTC is specific to defined blocks, whereas TWC is more flexible, resembling train orders for a specific train's operation.

35. Brignano & McCullough, *The Search for Safety*, pp. 139–140.

36. A restrictive signal is one that commands a train to slow (to 15 miles per hour or as specified in train orders) or to stop.

37. Brignano & McCullough, *The Search for Safety*, p. 155.

38. Ibid., p. 157.

39. All of this gives rise to a sense of déjà vu in the context of the Rail Safety and Improvement Act of 2008's mandate for PTC systems to be installed by the end of 2015 on rail lines carrying passengers or toxic by inhalation (TIH) chemicals. The legislation (which had been in the works for some time) was passed shortly after a September 12, 2008, collision between a freight train and a Metrolink commuter train in Los Angeles that killed twenty-five. Later it was found that the engineer of the Metrolink train had been texting on a cell phone when he passed a restrictive signal.

40. Solomon, *Railroad Signaling*, Chapter 7, "Train Control and Cab Signaling," pp. 136–143.

41. The first recorded effort to accomplish cab signaling was back in 1872, an incredibly fertile year for railroad invention, when the Chemin de Fer Nord arranged zigzagging parallel brass plates between the rails in a pattern giving the device the name crocodile. As of about the turn of the millennium, antique crocodiles could occasionally still be seen in European track networks. Later improvements in cab signals were of two main types, the means of picking up instructions from outside the locomotive and, a corollary, rendering cab signals continuous to reflect changing conditions ahead of the train for considerable distances. With this innovation, an engineer could resume track speed as soon as a restriction cleared, wherever the train was at the time.

42. Precise language and terminology are important to any rules-based human enterprise. In baseball, we learned during the 2013 World Series that interference is a base runner hampering a fielder's play on a batted or thrown ball, while obstruction is a fielder impeding a base runner's safe advance to the next base. The occurrence may be a once in a 100-year event, as the last out in the inning of a World Series game, but there was a rule to cover it.

43. Geoffrey Kitchenside and Alan Williams, *Two Centuries of Railway Signalling* (Somerset, UK: Oxford Publishing Co., 1998), is a comprehensive and beautifully illustrated technology history and manual of signaling practice.

44. An interlocking (plant) is a railroad junction with one (or more) crossings or turnouts where train collisions are possible but for the expedient of physically and/or electrically ensuring only one (otherwise conflicting) path over or through the junction is available at any one time.

45. Robert W. McKnight, "Union Switch & Signal Co.," in Middleton et al., *Encyclopedia*, p. 1068. Coded track circuits are based on coders supplying AC pulses to the track, typically 180 pulses per minute (ppm) for a "clear" indication, 120 ppm for an "intermediate," or 75 ppm for an "approach" indication. S. Kip Farrington, Jr., *Railroads of Today* (New York: Coward-McCann, 1949), p. 105.

46. Quoted in Brignano and McCullough, *The Search for Safety*, p. 184. The first installation of Sedgwick North Wight's CTC was on the Toledo & Ohio Central in 1927, and US&S put in a system on the Père Marquette in 1928.

47. In the early days of remote block signaling, on sparsely used lines such as the Rock Island between Omaha and Denver or the Western Pacific between Salt Lake City and Oakland, dispatchers could control wayside signals, but crews would have to stop a train to throw switches manually—hence not true CTC.

48. Gravity relays are devices for regulating electrical current flows; they are designed to fall by the force of omnipresent gravity to a safe condition if external power (such as might be holding a semaphore signal in a vertical position) should be lost.

49. Brignano and McCullough, *The Search for Safety*, p. 145.

50. The first improvements in grade-crossing warning devices beyond employment of flagmen at crossings occurred around 1870, when manually raised and lowered gates appeared. Pneumatic or electrical operation of gates followed, around the turn of the twentieth century, and about that time a lighted flashing red lamp came into use in wig-wag signals that emulated a crossing guard's back and forth motion. By the 1930s, flashing red lights, two to a mast on both sides of the roadway, were common and were standardized at 8 inches. Today's larger 12-ince roundel came into use in 1971, and high-visibility LED bulbs appeared in the last two decades. Robert W. McKnight, "Grade-Crossing Safety," in Middleton et al., *Encyclopedia*, pp. 495–499.

51. It is interesting to note in this historical survey of advancing railway technologies that no better system has been developed for detecting the approach of trains to crossings and activating their warning systems than the venerable track circuit first patented by William Robinson in 1872.

52. See Solomon, *Railroad Signaling*, Chapter 8, "Grade Crossing Signals," pp. 144–155, and the Federal Railroad Administration's *Five Year Strategic Plan for Railroad Research, Development and Demonstrations*, March 2002, Section 5.3.

53. David C. Lester in Middleton et al., *Encyclopedia*, 2007, p. 325.

54. Steven R. Ditmeyer, "Network-Centric Railway Operations Utilizing Intelligent Railway Systems," *Journal of Transportation Law, Logistics and Policy* 77, no. 3 (Third Quarter, 2010), p. 7. There are voluntary AEI tagging standards for ISO containers, and the American Trucking Association maintains voluntary

standards for truck trailer and chassis tags. These are compatible with the AAR standard for railroad vehicle AEI.

55. Ibid.

56. Peter Stiles, The DuPont AEI Pilot—an Initial Customer/Carrier Application, Advantage Design, Inc., 1993–1994.

57. David C. Lester, "Computerization" in Middleton et al., *Encyclopedia*, pp. 325–330.

58. Jim Fuller, "Car Scheduling," in ibid. pp. 206–207. Guerdon Sines of Missouri Pacific and the late Richard Shamberger of FRA deserve recognition for their efforts in development and advocacy of FCS.

59. Examples in this subsection are based on the functionality of Union Pacific's transportation control system (TCS). Other large railroads have similar systems. TCS incorporates freight car scheduling and a variety of other subsystems.

60. Testimony of the Burlington Northern Railroad Company at the Federal Railroad Administration's Special Safety Inquiry on Radio Communications, January 27, 1987.

61. Switch position monitoring prevents the type of human error that happened in Graniteville, South Carolina, in January 2005, when the crew of the local train left a mainline switch in the wrong position at the end of their shift and a later train diverted onto a siding rather than holding the main. The train then collided with freight cars parked on the siding—rupturing a tank car, releasing poisonous chlorine gas into the atmosphere, and killing eight workers in a nearby factory as well as the train engineer.

62. See Robert E. Gallamore, Chapter 15, in José Gómez-Ibáñez et al., *Essays in Honor of John R. Meyer*, especially pp. 509–511.

63. Saunders, Merging Lines, p. 296, citing Charles O. Morgret, Brosnan: *The Railroads' Messiah*, Vol. 1 (New York: Vantage Press, 1966), p. 220.

64. See, for example, "Comments of Burlington Northern Railroad at the US Department of Transportation's Transportation Policy Forum on Innovation and Human Factors," in BN Team Technical Bulletin 3, Special Report (September 11, 1989).

13. Decline and Renaissance of American Railroads in the Twentieth Century—Pulling into the Terminal

Epigraphs: Henry David Thoreau, *Walden*, 1854. In Dow, *Dictionary*, p. 106.

1. Gabriel Kolko, *Railroads and Regulation 1877–1916* (Princeton, NJ: Princeton University Press, 1965.

2. Keith L. Bryant, Jr., *Railroads in the Age of Regulation, 1900–1980, Encyclopedia of American History and Biography* (New York: Facts on File Publications, 1988), p. xxi. See more discussion of rival modes below and in Chapter 5.

3. Hobbes called life in the state of nature before civilizing social contracts "solitary, poor, nasty, brutish, and short." *Leviathan*, Part 1, Chapter 13 (1651).

4. Eric W. Beshers, *Conrail: Government Creation & Privatization of an American Railroad* (Washington, DC, The World Bank, Report INU 38, March 15, 1989), Conrail, p. I-1.

5. These are not idle worries. When railroads campaigned against larger truck sizes and weights two decades ago, some major trucking firms threatened diversion of traffic. Railroads usually refrain from criticizing motor carrier safety performance for fear of retaliation by trucking associations and their allies at the local level.

6. http://www.greatachievements.org/. Accessed August 17, 2011.

7. Chandler, Alfred D., Jr., *The Railroads: The Nation's First Big Business* (New York: Harcourt, Brace & World, 1965).

8. Most scholars would accept our view that the high water mark for economic regulatory legislation was reached with the Transportation Act of 1958, and that meaningful reform did not begin until passage of the 4R Act of 1976, which made only timid advances, but which paved the way for genuine reform in the Staggers Rail Act of 1980. By that time, much of the railroad industry was in or near bankruptcy.

9. Historian Albro Martin called it *Enterprise Denied*. His indictment in *Enterprise Denied* was ultimately reconciled with *Enterprise Triumphant*, the sequel he wrote a decade later. Albro Martin, *Enterprise Denied: Origins of the Decline of American Railroads, 1897–1917* (New York: Columbia University Press, 1971), and *Railroads Triumphant: The Growth, Rejection and Rebirth of a Vital American Force* (New York: Oxford University Press, 1992.)

10. At the margins of a trade, users compare their demand for the good—its expected value to them—to what the seller is charging for it; the real manufacturing or acquisition cost is irrelevant.

11. See Robert Gallamore, "Regulation and Innovation: Lessons from the American Railroad Industry," Chapter 15 in José A. Gómez-Ibáñez et al., eds., *Essays in Transportation Economics and Policy* (Washington, DC: Brookings Institution Press, 1999).

12. Richard C. Levin, and Daniel H. Weinberg, "Alternatives for Restructuring the Railroads: End-to-End or Parallel Mergers? *Economic Inquiry* XVII, no. 3 (July 1979), pp. 371–388.

13. The victim was William Huskisson, honorable member of Parliament for Liverpool. Christopher McGowan, *Rail, Steam, and Speed: The "Rocket" and the Birth of Steam Locomotion* (New York: Columbia University Press, 2004), tells the whole fascinating story in Chapter 11, "Triumph and Tragedy," pp. 231–261.

14. Jon R. Huibregtse, *American Railroad Labor and the Genesis of the New Deal, 1919–1935* (Gainesville: University Press of Florida, 2010), pp. 3–5.

15. For example, see John R. Meyer, Merton J. Peck, John Stenason, and Charles Zwick, *The Economics of Competition in the Transportation Industries* (Cambridge, MA: Harvard University Press, 1959), Figure B-1, p. 283, which plots railroad company gross ton-miles of freight versus total freight car-miles, as of the middle 1950s.

16. The IPO prospectus is a solid document. It offers history and data that cannot be found elsewhere. Goldman, Sachs & Co. et al. *Preliminary Prospectus Dated February 13, 1987—52,000,000 Shares Consolidated Rail Corporation Common Stock.*

17. Only days after the Milwaukee Road declared bankruptcy (still early in the Carter administration), DOT secretary Brock Adams summoned railroaders, state DOTs, and ICC practitioners back to Washington from their holiday break for a workshop on the Midwest crisis—one that was to mark a sea change in policy toward the ailing railroad industry. Secretary Adams took a strong stance against the idea (actually it was the prevailing expectation in Washington, DC) that there needed to be a "Conrail West." That is, Secretary Adams implied (and everyone in the room understood his meaning) that there should not be another government-sponsored railroad takeover and planned reorganization like the one that the USRA managed for the Northeast. Instead, Secretary Adams said that he would use existing statutory rules, along with the new 4R Act's restructuring tools, to rationalize excess capacity in the Granger states; the Secretary said he would dedicate already authorized funding programs to upgrading limited portions of the deteriorating midwestern rail network.

18. US Department of Transportation, Federal Railroad Administration, *A Prospectus for Change in the Freight Railroad Industry* (Washington, DC: Government Printing Office, 1978).

19. Conrail was not literally a merger, but, as its formal name implies, a "consolidation" of Penn Central and other bankrupt railroads in the Northeast and Midwest region of the United States. Once established under the USRA's FSP as approved by Congress in the 4R Act, Conrail effectively operated like a railroad that had merged under ICC authority.

20. Frank N. Wilner, *Railroad Mergers: History, Analysis, Insight* (Omaha, NE: Simmons-Boardman Books, Inc., 1997), p. 224.

21. Canadian National subsidiaries Illinois Central, Grand Trunk Western, and Elgin, Joliet & Eastern (EJ&E), plus Canadian Pacific's Soo Line and Dakota, Minnesota & Eastern (DM&E)/Iowa, Chicago & Eastern (IC&E).

22. Why don't the economics add up? Basically, passenger equipment is expensive to purchase initially and to maintain for cleanliness and good mechanical condition; on-board crewing is labor-intensive at relatively high wages, and the assets move slowly—i.e., they cannot be "turned" quickly like an aircraft. With respect to non–Northeast Corridor operations, sparse population and long

distances between stops ordinarily means too little aggregate demand inelastic enough to support strong pricing.

Let's compare Amtrak with Southwest Airlines (SWA), for example. SWA has estimated revenue per passenger-mile of 13.9 cents; Amtrak's comparable figure is 27.1 cents, but SWA has revenue per employee of $298,000, while Amtrak has $132,000. SWA's average salary and benefits were $100,000 per employee versus Amtrak at $86,000). SWA annually generates almost exactly one dollar in revenue per dollar of net investment, while Amtrak generates only 28 cents. (Freight railroads are notoriously capital intensive, but they generate 40.3 cents.) The numbers show the economic disadvantage Amtrak faces vis-à-vis aviation. The source of these numbers is the SWA 2011 Annual Report and the Amtrak Monthly Performance Summary, September 2009. Thanks to Louis Thompson for the example.

23. The federal government also retained arbitration powers to settle matters if the host freight railroad and Amtrak disagreed about costs and compensation, but this should have been a neutral factor.

24. Henry David Thoreau, Walden 1854. Available online at www.thoreau.server .org/default.html and quoted in Andrew Dow, *Dow's Dictionary of Railway Quotations* (Baltimore: The Johns Hopkins University Press), p. 106. Thoreau likened sleepers (crossties) to the dead, but since railroad crews had to keep tamping them down, he saw life and the possibility of resurrection in them.

Afterword: Future Policies for US Railroads

Epigraph: Julius Parmelee, *The Modern Railway* (New York: Longmans, Green and Co. 1940), p. 704. Parmelee was the director of the Bureau of Railway Economics for the industry's trade group, the Association of American Railroads (AAR).

1. Several external circumstances may already have affected the pace of these plans: (1) the Great Recession of 2007–2009, which appears to have added up to ten years to the time horizon for railroads' new capacity investments; (2) expansion of the Panama Canal, scheduled for completion in 2014, which may divert some overland container train traffic originating in Asia from US West Coast to East Coast ports of call; and (3) the surge in rail movement of crude oil from the Bakken deposits in North Dakota and elsewhere to refineries along the Atlantic and Gulf coasts.

2. Ian Savage, *The Economics of Railroad Safety* (Norwell, MA: Kluwer Academic Publishers, 1998), p. 144. See also http://www.fra.dot.gov/downloads/PubAffairs /track_standards_fact_sheet_FINAL.pdf. Accessed September 26, 2011.

3. See Government Accountability Office, *Federal Employers' Liability Act Issues Associated with Changing How Railroad Work-Related Injuries Are Compensated,*

RCED-96-199, August 15, 1996. http://www.gao.gov/products/157464. Accessed November 20, 2012.

4. Louis Thompson, "A Vision for Railways in 2050," presented at the OECD International Transport Forum 2010 *Transport and Innovation: Unleashing the Potential*, 26–28 May 2010, in Leipzig, Germany, p. 6.

5. Ibid.

ACKNOWLEDGMENTS

There are many friends to thank for teaching me about railroads, economics, and fundamental truths—and correcting errors and omissions in the manuscript. None were more enduring in their support than Steven Ditmeyer, James McClellan, and Dale Salzman. Also warranting much appreciation but no blame are José Gómez-Ibáñez, Louis Thompson, Alexander Morton, Gerard McCullough, John Panzar, John Rebensdorf, Charles Dettmann, William Wimmer, William Schafer, Victor Hand, Hugh Randall, Allan Schimmel, Porter Wheeler, Gerhard Thelen, John Rowe, Ed King, Michael McClellan, and my brother, John Gallamore.

John Gray and his staff at the Association of American Railroads made available the complete set of annual railroad analysis spreadsheets (1978–2010). Few if any industries maintain such comprehensive data on their operations and finances. Megan Davy, a student at the Kennedy School of Government at Harvard provided fine research assistance in converting these data for use in the book.

Grant Meyer's assistance with research for chapter 5 is much appreciated.

Some material in Chapter 12 (the sections titled "A Primer on Diesel-Electric Locomotives" and "Turbochargers," and Figure 12.2) was presented in different form in an earlier article by Robert Gallamore, "Locomotives," in John Zumerchik, ed., *The MacMillan Energy Encyclopedia* (New York: MacMillan, 2001), pp. 723–731.

Special thanks to the staff at Harvard University Press and the reviewers and copyeditors they arranged for insightful suggestions, to Sandra Hackman for expert editorial guidance, and to Isabelle Lewis for her skill in creating (and patience in revising) the artwork. Last and most, heartfelt appreciation to my loving wife, Suellen, for her abiding support and assistance.

INDEX

Water-compelled rates, 18, 32, 73, 76, 78, 80
Waterway user charges, 79–80, 99
Waterways: barge competition to rail, 7, 9, 10, 70, 72–74, 76, 145; Great Lakes, canals, 75–76, 153
Weather, 157, 187, 367, 376, 434
Western Pacific, 138, 273, 275–278, 281, 289, 272, 277, 279

World War I, 8, 43, 56–59, 61–64, 70–71, 116, 123, 407
World War II, 8–9, 13, 43, 59, 63, 70, 84, 101–102, 106–107, 110, 116, 122–123, 128, 131, 159, 345–346, 349, 371

Yards, classification, 152, 344, 362, 371, 384–386, 394